# Strategic Management and Organisational Dynamics

## The Challenge of Complexity

THIRD EDITION

RALPH D STACEY

FINANCIAL TIMES
Prentice Hall

*An imprint of* **Pearson Education**

Harlow, England · London · New York · Reading, Massachusetts · San Francisco
Toronto · Don Mills, Ontario · Sydney · Tokyo · Singapore · Hong Kong · Seoul
Taipei · Cape Town · Madrid · Mexico City · Amsterdam · Munich · Paris · Milan

**Pearson Education Limited**
Edinburgh Gate
Harlow
Essex CM20 2JE
England

and Associated Companies throughout the World

*Visit us on the World Wide Web at*
http//:www.pearsoneduc.com

---

First published under the Pitman Publishing imprint 1993
Second edition 1996
**Third edition 2000**

ISBN 0-273-64212-X

*British Library Cataloguing-in-Publication Data*
A catalogue record for this book can be obtained from the British Library

*Library of Congress Cataloging-in-Publication Data*

Stacy, Ralph D.
    Strategic management and organisational dynamics : the challenge
of complexity / Ralph D. Stacey. — 3rd ed.
        p.    cm.
    Includes bibliographical references and index.
    ISBN 0-273-64212-X (alk. paper)
    1. Strategic planning.    2. Organizational behaviour.    I. Title.
HD30.28.S663    1999
658.4'012—dc21
                                                99-38846
                                                CIP

10  9  8  7  6  5  4  3  2
05  04  03  02  01

Typeset by 32 in 9/12 Stone Serif
Printed and bound in Great Britain by TJ International Ltd, Padstow, Cornwall

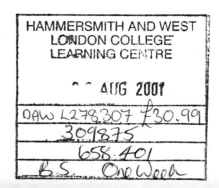

# Contents

# List of Figures

## List of Boxes

# Preface

I would like to put this third edition of *Strategic Management and Organisational Dynamics* into the context of the development of systems theory.

During the 1930s and 1940s the groundwork was being laid by a number of scientists for what was to emerge as coherent theories of systems in the late 1940s and early 1950s. These took the form of open systems theory, originating in biology, and the closely related cybernetics and systems dynamics originating in the engineer's notion of control. In the decades that followed, all of these systems theories were incorporated, in one way or another, into theories of organisation and management. At much the same time, and closely connected with the development of systems theories, there was a decisive move away from behaviourist to cognitive psychology. This movement also affected thinking in sociology, psychotherapy and organisation and management theory. Theories built, over the past few decades, on the foundations of systems theories and cognitive psychology now dominate the management discourse.

It seems to me that history is repeating itself, although in a different way. Through the 1960s and 1970s, the groundwork was being laid for what was to emerge in the 1980s and early 1990s as a new way of thinking about systems. This new way had been glimpsed by some mathematicians, such as Poincaré at the turn of the century and Turing in the 1930s and 1940s. However, it was in the 1960s, when Lorenz 'discovered' mathematical chaos with the aid of more powerful computers, that the new way of thinking began to emerge more clearly. Over much the same period Prigogine was developing his theories of dissipative structures. The 1970s and 1980s saw the development of complexity theory. By the late 1980s, then, new nonlinear systems theories with potentially radical implications had become somewhat clearer. These were theories that pointed to the limits of predictability, the processes of self-organisation and co-evolution, and the emergence of pattern and order from less ordered states. At much the same time, similar although unconnected developments were evident in sociology and psychology in the form of, for example, social constructionism, reflexivity and intersubjectivity theory. These too are concerned with self-organising and co-evolutionary processes that produce emergent patterns in human relationships.

I wrote the first edition of this book, during the course of 1991 and early 1992, with the conviction that this second wave of systems theory development was as relevant to thinking about organisations as was the first. For me, the implications were radical, although very difficult to formulate. At the time that I wrote the first edition, very little had been published on the implications of the new systems theories for organising and managing. What little there was focused on chaos theory. In the first edition, I tried to put what little there was on chaos theory into the context of the literature on strategic management. I pointed to some parts of the literature on managing and organising that seemed to me to be consistent with the new systems theories and others that I felt were not. By the time I came to write the second edition of this book in the middle of 1995, more had been written, particularly incorporating complexity theory into thinking about organisations. However, the literature was still sparse and the second edition of the book was mainly a restructuring of the material in the first edition, with some additions, primarily on complexity theory.

In early 1999, as I started to work on this third edition, it seemed to me that the situation was rather different. There has been a marked increase in the number of journal articles and books, special issues of journals and conferences, all devoted to the implications of chaos and complexity theory for organisation and management theory and practice. The Economic and Social Sciences Research Council in the United Kingdom is funding a major research programme on the implications of chaos and complexity theory for organisations. Major consultancies are exploring the implications for their work and many companies have been incorporating chaos and complexity into their management development programmes. Some managers are thinking about the meaning of these developments for them. Clear lines of difference in how chaos and complexity are to be interpreted in an organisational setting are emerging. The need to take account of this growing activity, and the different emerging interpretations it is revealing, was one of the factors that led me to undertake a major rewrite for the third edition of this book.

Another reason for this major rewriting was my experience, over the past seven years, of working with groups of managers on how they might think about their work from the perspectives of chaos and complexity. I was originally attracted to the theories of chaos and complexity because of my dissatisfaction with orthodox management theory: it simply did not help me make sense of my experience of the unexpected and the creative in organisations. More important was the deep feeling I had that there were radical implications in chaos and complexity for understanding the nature of management. However, I discovered that my ways of trying to express this intuition were far from adequate. I was trying to hold on to the paradoxical nature of complexity theory and of life in organisations. I tried to do this in the distinction I made in the second edition between ordinary and extraordinary management, arguing that complexity theory enabled a deeper understanding of the latter. However, although I stressed the paradoxical nature of ordinary and extraordinary management, namely that they were practised at the same time even though they were directly contrary to each other, the concepts were usually interpreted in a sequential manner. Managers talked about practising ordinary management most of the time and occasionally finding that they had to move into the dangerous practice of extraordinary management. I found it difficult to explain why this was not the case. Other experiences over the last few years gave me some insight into the inadequacy of the explanations that I was putting forward.

First, I came to realise that I have been trying to explain paradoxical complex human processes in language taken from a mixture of cognitive psychology and psychoanalysis. Both of these psychologies start from the position of the autonomous individual. For the former, group and society are simply formed by individuals who are then influenced by what they have formed. In the latter, group and society play a much more important role in that the individual mind is structured by the clash between individual drives and social prohibition. The social then has a much more formative impact on the individual but the motivation and energy for behaviour still comes from drives located in the individual. There is another way of thinking about human nature to be found in sociology, social constructionism, intersubjectivity theory in psychoanalysis and in group-analytic theory. From this perspective, the individual is social through and through to the core. The individual mind and social relations are simply two different perspectives on the same phenomenon. Motivation and energy for behaviour arise in relating. I have used the term relationship psychology to encompass these approaches.

When I wrote the first two editions of this book, my underlying, although poorly expressed, interest was not in how to understand complexity as an objective property of an organisation, but to understand complexity from within the system. I was interested in what it was like to be a human complex system and what it was like to be a member of a group that is a complex system. This did not come out at all clearly. I came to realise that this was because I was not being clear about the methodological position I was taking. My second realisation, then, was just how fundamental is the methodological stance one takes. Individual centred cognitive psychology and the scientific origins of systems theory make it feel natural to take the methodological position of the objective observer. The implicit prescription is that this is the position that managers should take. In this they stand outside the organisational system and either manipulate it, or understand it from a distant, uninvolved position. This is clearly the position adopted in strategic choice and learning organisation theory and to a much lesser degree by those taking a psychoanalytic perspective on organisations. An alternative methodological position is a reflexive one, namely that of the participative inquirer.

These two distinctions, namely the distinction between an individual-centred and a relationship-focused psychology, and the distinction between the methodological position of the objective observer and the participative inquirer, provide the basic structure of this third edition. The first part of the book reviews what I have called orthodox theories of organisation and management. The second part explores a radical approach. The criteria for orthodoxy are the use of the first wave of systems theories (cybernetics, systems dynamics, open systems) in combination with individual-centred psychology and the methodology of the objective observer. The theories reviewed in this part are put into categories called strategic choice theory, learning organisation theory and psychoanalytic perspectives.

The first criterion for what I have called potentially radical theories is that they take the perspective of chaos and complexity on systems. However, I argue that if they do this in a way that retains individual-centred psychology and the position of the objective observer, they implicitly subsume chaos and complexity theory into a cybernetic framework. The result is, I argue, a collapse back into management orthodoxy. In place of this, I propose taking a complexity perspective on organisation through the lens of relationship psychology. I argue that this points towards a potentially radical theory of managing and organising. This radical theory would place the self-organising conversational life of an organisation at the centre of the process through which strategies emerge. I have called these complex responsive processes in order to avoid the term complex adaptive system that has now become so associated with the autonomous individual and the objective observer. I use the term complex responsive processes to signal the danger of treating an organisation, a system, as a thing. I have also moved away from talking about complex systems in terms of feedback because of its link with and connotations of cybernetics and systems dynamics. Feedback implies reference to an external fixed point. Complex processes are more accurately thought of as self-referential.

The changes I have outlined above have made it necessary not only to restructure the book but to change its content significantly. I have removed much of the material on what I called rational and ideological theories of strategic management in the last edition. Reviews of these theories can be found in other textbooks. I have added material reviewing recent writing on chaos and complexity theory relating to organisations. I have added completely new Chapters 14 and 15 to set out what I mean by a relationship psychology and complex responsive processes of relating. The implications of these theoretical positions for understanding life in organisations are then explored in Chapters 16 and 17.

I said earlier that a number of experiences have led me to take the perspective from which I have rewritten this book. The first of these was the relationship that emerged between Douglas Griffin, Patricia Shaw and myself. Together we set up the Complexity and Management Centre at the University of Hertfordshire. The intense conversations between us over the past few years have had a powerful impact on how we are all trying to think about the nature of complexity in organisations. The structure and content of this edition owe a great deal to these conversations. During the same period, I also ran a doctoral group with my colleague Dorothea Noble. All the members of this group worked on themes to do with how they might understand their experience of life in organisations from a complexity perspective. The conversations in this group are part of the experience leading to the way I have approached this third edition. Also during the past few years, I started and completed training as a group analyst at the Institute of Group Analysis. This profound experience has much affected how I currently think.

A word about case studies. The purpose of the book is to assist people to make sense of their own experience of life in organisations. Case studies are, of course, carefully structured accounts of someone else's organisational experience, usually written with some point in mind, that a student is supposed to see. This is not consistent with the purpose of assisting readers to make sense of their own experience. Nevertheless, case studies are useful to some extent. I have retained four case studies and placed them at the end of Part One of the book. After Part Two, there are no case studies. Instead, there are six management narratives, that is personal accounts of the experience of life in organisations. Readers are invited to think about the sense they make of this experience of others. The main point, however, remains for readers to use the material in this book to make sense of their own experience.

I have already acknowledged the important part Douglas Griffin and Patricia Shaw played in what I now write in this book. I thank them very much. I must mention some others too. Morten Flatau's conversational provocation and the experience of working in groups with Eliat Aram have both had an impact, for which I thank them. I am also grateful to all the other members of the doctoral group at Hertfordshire University. I am extremely grateful to those members of the Institute of Group Analysis who undertook my training. At the end of that training I read Farhad Dalal's book, *Taking the Group Seriously*, and its impact on this edition is evident in the last few chapters. I also want to express my gratitude to Eric Miller. Working with him at Group Relations Conferences on our MBA course has been very important in my development. Finally, I am very fortunate to have the family I do.

Ralph Stacey
London
March 1999

# 1 The nature of strategy and organisational change

## 1.1   INTRODUCTION

This book is concerned with how organisations change over time. It asks how organisations have become what they are, and how they will become whatever they will be in five, ten or however many years' time.

There are many different theories that seek to explain how organisations change, or fail to change, but none of them are universally accepted. Even those that dominate academic and management discourses provide only partial explanations of life in organisations. The purpose of this book is to examine what is similar in these competing theories, and how they differ. To put it another way, the purpose of this book is to explore different ways of making sense of one's experience of life in organisations. It is from my own experience that I describe, compare and comment on the various theories I will be presenting in the chapters that follow. My own experience inevitably colours how I describe those theories and what I have to say about them. In writing this book, therefore, I am revealing how I currently make sense of my experience of life in organisations and I am inviting you to consider whether this resonates in any way with your own experience.

In the chapters that follow, I will be giving a summary of the content of the various theories reviewed, that is of their descriptions of, and prescriptions for managing, change in organisations. However, the content is not my primary interest. At a more fundamental level, I will be trying to point to the assumptions made, and reasoning processes used, in the various theories, matters that are not often made explicit by those presenting them.

### Two basic questions

What I am setting out to do in this book, then, is to review and compare different ways of explaining what strategy is and how organisations change. It is very tempting to jump straight into defining what a strategy is and how it should be formulated and implemented, or to explain immediately how organisations change and how this change should be managed. I want to avoid this temptation because, as I hope to show, the result of such haste is the obscuring of what lies behind the definitions and prescriptions. There is no universally true explanation of how organisations evolve, only a number of increasingly contested accounts. If one is to avoid blindly following one of these accounts, mistakenly taking it to be the truth, then it is necessary to stand back and ask two fundamental questions:

1   What is the phenomenon that is being talked about when the terms 'strategy' and 'organisational change' are used?
2   How do human beings make sense of any phenomenon, including the one that this book is concerned with?

The second question is important because there are different explanations of how humans make sense of anything. The particular explanation one adopts directly affects the particular account one gives of any phenomenon, including that to which the concepts of strategy and organisational change apply.

## 1.2   THE PHENOMENON OF INTEREST

Before attempting any definition of what a strategy is, or what is meant by organisational change, consider the general phenomenon that strategy and organisational change are both concerned with.

At one level, you can see what this phenomenon is simply by turning to the business section of any daily newspaper. For example, if you had turned to the business section of the *Independent* newspaper on 17 December 1998 you would have read that British Telecom had come to the rescue of its former rival, Ionica. British Telecom was to provide the finance to enable the bankrupt Ionica to continue trading until February 1999 in order to provide an orderly transition for the Ionica customers who would have to switch to other telecommunication providers. The hope was that they could be persuaded to switch to British Telecom in the time made available by the additional finance. In other words, British Telecom was cooperating with a former rival in order to enhance its own competitive advantage. On the same day, you could have read that Standard Chartered Bank would be entering the mortgage market in January 1999. Then there was an announcement that RJB Mining had signed a major deal with PowerGen to supply £1bn of coal, so securing the survival of the British coal industry. The Secretary of State for Trade and Industry announced the provision of £150m to a new Enterprise Fund whose purpose was to fund new initiatives that would help build the 'knowledge-driven economy'. It was also reported that jobless totals were rising and that the forecasts for economic growth in the UK for 1999 were getting gloomier. All of this was happening as the United States and the UK bombarded Iraqi military establishments, and proceedings to impeach President Clinton continued.

A few days later, on 21 December, you could have read that the Australian insurance group, AMP, was victorious in its battle to buy NPI, a mutual life insurer. AMP had beaten off stiff competition with its offer of £2.7bn for NPI. In addition, on that day,

Cantab Pharmaceuticals announced the purchase of two vaccines against nicotine and cocaine, offering hope to millions of addicts. There were reports that deflation would hit the UK in the year 2002 and that the market for management buyouts had collapsed. On the next day, the *Independent* reported that GEC was hoping to announce a defence tie-up with US defence contractor Northrop Grumman. GEC was also reviving its attempts to merge with British Aerospace and so create a defence giant. CRH, the Irish building materials group, rescued Ibstock, the UK brick manufacturer, from financial difficulty by purchasing it for £326m. Rexam, a packaging company, announced that it had sold most of its industrial division to SCA as part of its process of concentrating on its packaging business. Also on that day, it was reported that the gloom was deepening for textiles firms and that the IMF was pressing the Bank of England to make further cuts in interest rates. By this time, the raids on Iraq had ceased and Prime Minister Netanyahu was being forced into an election in Israel.

## A population of organisations

These newspaper reports are examples of a population of interacting organisations. Within any time period, say one, five, ten years, in any geographic region, say Europe, thousands upon thousands of new organisations are set up and within the same time frame many thousands are dissolved. In each period, there are large numbers of small organisational dissolutions and small numbers of large ones. Some organisations, however, go on for a very long time: the Roman Catholic Church is more than 1500 years old and the Swedish company Storr has survived for centuries. On average, however, the life span of commercial organisations in Western countries is about 40 years. In any time period, some organisations merge into others, as the pharmaceutical companies Smith Kline French and Beecham did some years ago. Yet others split into separate organisations as 3M and Imation did not too long ago. Many acquire others and some sell parts of their organisation to others as those reported above were doing. Organisations supply each other with goods and services. Some exert regulatory power over others.

Over the years, surviving organisations change their structures and their direction and as they do so they threaten, or create opportunities for, others. Whole new industries appear as new technologies are developed, creating niches of new activities for both new and old organisations. Many organisations reduce their workforces in downsizing, delayering activities. Many relocate their activities from one country to another. Some focus on one locality while others operate globally. There are private and public, commercial and charitable, governmental and industrial organisations interacting with each other in many different ways.

## A dynamical phenomenon

What is striking, I think, as one reads such reports day after day, is just how much change is going on. In other words, the phenomenon of interest, namely the population of organisations, is a highly dynamic one. Dynamics means movement and concern with the dynamics is concern with how the phenomenon moves, unfolds or evolves over time. A dynamic phenomenon is one that displays patterns of change over time and a study of the dynamics of any phenomenon is concerned with what generates these patterns and what properties of stability and instability, predictability and unpredictability they display. One of the key features distinguishing one theory of strategy and organisational change from another is how they deal with the matter of dynamics. I will be pointing to this in reviews of a number of theories in the chapters that follow.

It is striking how unstable the dynamics of the population of organisations is, on the one hand, but how stable it is, on the other. Or, to put it another way, what is striking is just how unpredictable are the moves made by organisations and yet how predictable they are. What I mean by this is that it is virtually certain that mergers and takeovers will take place and it is often clear in which industries they will take place. At the same time, however, it is often very surprising that one particular organisation should buy, or merge with, another. Members of an organisation, including its most senior managers, often experience such unpredictability and instability as anxiety provoking and stressful. Another striking point is how some organisations are merging with others, while yet others are splitting themselves into two or more parts. In other words, some are integrating while others are dividing.

## A paradoxical phenomenon

So, the population of organisations changes over time in ways that display both stability and instability, both predictability and unpredictability, both division and integration, both 'birth' and 'death'. What is one to make of it when the phenomenon one is trying to understand, change in the population of organisations, displays such contradictory tendencies? Is this simply an apparent contradiction, which arises for me simply because I do not understand the phenomenon fully? Or is it a paradox, the genuine, simultaneous coexistence of two contradictory forces? How one answers these questions has important implications for the kind of theory of organisational change one develops. Some theories see only contradictions to be solved by further work, while others see paradox that can never be resolved. This position on paradox will be one of the features I will use to distinguish one theory of organisational change from another. I will return to this point later in this chapter and take it up again in subsequent chapters as I review a number of theories of organisational change.

## Levels of description

Now, however, I think it is important to notice how the newspaper reports are describing and so defining the phenomenon of interest. The descriptions and the definitions are given in terms of named organisations interacting with each other in national and global economies. The description is of whole organisations interacting within a whole population as if they were individual entities. In other words, the descriptions are at the macro level, that is the level of the large, or the whole, rather than the small, or the entities that make up the whole, that is the micro level. This too will be an important feature in the comparison between different theories of organisational change in the chapters that follow. Some theories focus on the macro level, some on the micro level and yet others on both.

Moving now to the micro level, each organisation is itself a population of interacting groupings of individual people. The newspaper reports sometimes provide glimpses of what might be going on within some particular organisation. Returning to the business section of the *Independent* on 17 December 1998, you could have read that the deputy chairman of the Irish building products group, Kingspan, had resigned. The reason was that he had admitted possible responsibility for a breach of confidentiality in the run-up to a takeover. The next day, three directors of Chancery plc, a banking group that collapsed in 1991, were barred from becoming directors again after the completion of an inquiry into that collapse. Then on 21 December, it was announced that a property giant, MEPC, had come under intense scrutiny from its shareholders for a payoff of £6m to one of its directors, described as a reward for success.

### Emotion

It is necessary to call on one's own experience of life in organisations to imagine what interactions lay behind these bland announcements. I would suspect that they were preceded by intense political activity as people sought to push for, or stop, the resignation of a director or the award of a large sum of money. I would imagine that people might have become angry with each other or felt betrayed. It is not hard to imagine what kinds of conversation the directors involved had with their partners when they returned home. If you think of your experience of being promoted, having others promoted above you, having the threat of downsizing hanging over you, you can see how emotions of one kind are inseparable from interactions within and between organisations. Another feature I will be pointing to, as I review a number of theories in the chapters that follow, is just how much account they take of the emotion involved in organisational evolution.

### The objective observer and the participant enquirer

The phenomenon of interest in this book is life in organisations and this is not some interaction between abstract entities, but interactions between people that directly affect the meaning of their lives and their health. Furthermore, these interactions between people in an organisation are not richly documented either in the newspapers or in management books. To gain some understanding of these interactions you have to participate in them and your understanding will arise in your own experience. The point I am making is that it is possible to obtain some explanation and understanding at the macro level from others, second hand, as it were. Here it is possible to adopt the position of the objective observer who stands outside the phenomenon of interest and offers explanations of its behaviour. However, explanation and understanding at the micro level relies much more on one's own personal experience. Here the explanation is offered from the position of a participant in the phenomenon to be explained. This is another distinguishing feature of the theories I will review, namely the extent to which the theory is offered from the position of the objective observer as opposed to the inquiring participant.

At a macro level of description, then, the phenomenon that the concepts of strategy and organisational change relate to is that of a population of organisations interacting with each other. A theory may look for general principles governing a population of organisations, without saying much about the nature of the individual organisations themselves. Such a theory is clearly concerned with a macro level of description. A micro-level of description would require attention to differences and similarities between the organisations that make up the population. Alternatively, a theory may be concerned with a single organisation and say nothing much about the nature of the groupings of people in it. This too is a theory operating at a macro level of description. A micro level description would be one that took account of the similarities and differences between groupings of people. At a more experience near, micro level of description, the phenomenon of interest is that of a population of groupings of individuals interacting with each other. In other words, different levels of description focus on different levels of detail: the higher the level of description the more detail has been sheared away.

Furthermore, it is important to remember that macro- and micro-level events are taking place simultaneously and in moving from one level of description to another, one is simply refocusing attention. Although one may be focusing on macro events during one time period, micro-level events are still occurring. All the points I have been making about how dynamical, and possibly paradoxical, the phenomenon is, apply simultaneously to both macro and micro levels. At all levels, one finds at least the appearance of stability and instability, predictability and unpredictability, in all time spans.

## Time spans

Closely related to the level of description is the matter of the time span with which an account or theory is concerned. Most of the accounts of a change in an organisation that I have reported above will clearly have consequences stretching over a long time into the future. Levels of description and time spans are related to each other when it comes to the possibility of making predictions. Generally speaking, the higher the level of description, that is the less the amount of detail covered by the theory, and the shorter the time frame over which consequences are being considered, the greater the ability to predict those consequences. Experience teaches that there is a trade-off between level of description and time span. The longer the time span of the prediction and the higher the level of description, the smaller the amount of detail required to obtain reasonably reliable predictions. For example, it is possible to forecast accurately changes in the numbers of teenagers in a population for the next 30 to 50 years. However, if one moves from the level of the whole population to the level of this group of teenagers and asks not just how many there will be but how much they will spend on CDs, then one is hard put to make a forecast for the next 30 to 50 weeks. So, another distinguishing feature of different theories of organisational change has to do with the time spans they consider, in relation to the level of detail they focus on.

## Interaction and systems

Another important point to note about this phenomenon of a population of organisations is this: the newspaper reports I have referred to are all describing interactions. For example, one kind of interaction takes place when one company buys another and another kind of interaction takes place when one company supplies another. At the level of an individual organisation, one kind of interaction takes place when a director resigns and another kind takes place when a director is handsomely rewarded.

Furthermore, although the newspapers report one interaction, it requires only a moment's thought to see that this interaction will inevitably touch off many more. When one pharmaceutical company merges with another, it changes the competitive balance for all of the others, making it highly likely that many of them will look for merger partners. This is because they are interconnected. Interaction is usually thought of as constituting a network or a system and each individual organisation as a component of that system. However, it could be thought of as a process. Each individual organisation is also usually thought of as a network or a system and the members, and groupings of members, in that organisation as components of the system. Again, it is possible to think of these interactions as processes rather than system. Most theories of organisations think of interaction in systemic terms. Different theories of strategy and organisational change are built on different theories of the nature of a system. One of the main focuses of this book will be on different theories of systems and how these underpin different theories of organisational evolution. In the final chapters, I will look at the possibility of taking a processual rather than a systemic perspective.

This, then, is the phenomenon that this book is concerned with: a continuously evolving population of organisations, each of which is itself an evolving population of groupings of people. That population, and each of its components, is usually thought of as an interconnected system. The phenomenon can be described and understood at different levels of detail over different time spans and it has the appearance, at least, of being paradoxical. There is a striking analogy to this phenomenon, namely the evolution of species of living creatures in nature, including us. As one contemplates both of these phenomena, much the same questions spring to mind: how is one to make sense of all of this highly complex interaction and evolution?

## 1.3    MAKING SENSE OF THE PHENOMENON

The first point to note is that no individual or group of individuals can possibly make sense of the entire phenomenon I have described: there is quite simply too much of it. The reality of organisational life consists of all of the detail of all the events in all organisations' histories, as well as all of the actions of all of their members. As with any other phenomenon, human beings can only make sense by selecting certain aspects of reality for attention and ignoring the rest. In other words, people simplify reality by focusing attention at a particular level of description, or detail, over a particular time period. Furthermore, they simplify at a particular level of detail and time frame by classifying the selected details into categories. All events or objects within a category are assumed to be the same, or at least similar, while each category is different from others.

### Classifying into categories

Consider some examples of how humans simplify and classify entities and events into categories. Botanists classify flowers with particular characteristics into a category called 'roses', while flowers with other characteristics are classified into a category called 'daisies'. Economists classify some organisations into a category they call the 'coal industry', while others are classified into a category called the 'gas industry'. This simplification allows botanists to sidestep the difficulty of talking about all individual roses and to talk about the category 'rose' as if all of the members of that category were the same. A typical, or average, rose can then be compared with a typical, or average, daisy. The same goes for the economist who can then talk about the differences and interactions between the coal and gas industries. This simplification allows one to look for relationships between categories, for example the possibility that change in one causes changes in another. In this way people are able to construct explanations of the patterns they observe in the phenomenon they are interested in. Thus, in order to make sense of their experiences and so act, human beings look for patterns in entities and events at a particular level of description over a particular time period while classifying them into categories. They also look for patterns in the interactions between categories, searching for relationships, regularities and laws.

## The nature of causality

The dominant way of thinking about the relationship between cause and effect in Western culture is linear and unidirectional. There is some variable $Y$ whose behaviour is to be explained. It is regarded as dependent and other 'independent' variables, $X_1$, $X_2$, ..., are sought that are causing it. Linear relationships mean that more of a cause will lead to proportionally more of the effect.

For example, in organisations, the usual explanation for success is that it is caused by a particular culture, a particular management style, a particular control system. The more that culture, style or control system is applied the more successful the organisation will be. Opposition parties always say that the government of the day has caused recession and inflation. More of the government's policies will, they say, lead to more recession and more inflation. All of this is what is meant by straightforward unidirectional, linear connections between cause and effect.

Scientists, both social and natural, are increasingly realising that this view of the relationship between cause and effect is far too simple and leads to inadequate understanding of a system's behaviour. Greater insight comes from thinking in terms of the mutual or circular causality. The demand for a product does not depend simply on customer behaviour; it also depends upon what the producing firm does in terms of price and quality: the firm affects the customer who then affects the firm. Management style may cause success but success affects the style managers adopt. The government's policies may cause recession and inflation, but recession and inflation may also cause the policies they adopt.

When organisms and organisations are thought of as systems then complex forms of causality become evident to do with interconnection and interdependence, where everything affects everything else. In addition to the circular causality and interdependence of systems, there is also *nonlinearity*. This means that one variable can have a more than proportional effect upon another. Nonlinear systems then involve very complex connections between cause and effect. It may become unclear what cause and effect mean. The links between them may become distant in time and space and those links may even disappear for all practical purposes. If in these circumstances one proceeds as if simple linear links exist even if one does not know what they are, then one is likely to undertake actions that yield unintended and surprising results.

Many managers today think in terms of linear, unidirectional causality; and many strategic management prescriptions are based on this kind of thinking too.

## Sameness and difference: average and non-average

Note how, in the categorising I have been describing above, difference is located between categories while sameness is located within them. However, this is not reality itself, only a human simplification. Each rose is different in some respect from all others, as is each daisy, while there is a similarity between roses and daisies because they are both flowers, which, by the way, is another category. In reality, entities are simultaneously different and similar, but people seem to have a powerful tendency to classify entities into categories that polarise difference and similarity, the former being located between categories and the latter within categories. In doing this people render unconscious the differences within a category and the similarities between categories.

The discussion in section 1.2 above on the nature of the phenomenon of interest in this book is an example of the sense-making process I have just been describing. Each organisation reported on in that section was a category consisting of its members. At this macro level of description, over the time span being considered, the detail of individual differences between the members of an organisation was ignored. The implicit assumption was being made that the members of the organisation were all the same; that is, they were all assumed to be the typical or average member. Also, the interactions between them were ignored and this amounts to an assumption that these interactions are all the same, that is average, or at least normally distributed around an average (*Allen, 1998*). This is also a point that will be taken up in later chapters as different theories of strategy and organisational change are examined. The assumptions they make about sameness and difference, about average or non-average components of a system and average or non-average interactions between them, will be an important distinguishing feature between one theory and another.

Two important questions arise at this point:

1   *On what basis do people make the distinction between one category and another?*
2   *To what extent do people recognise, and how do they deal with, the paradox of sameness and difference that this act of classification conceals?*

## Competing explanations of how humans classify entities and events

There are different, competing explanations of how human beings classify their experience. One explanation is realism. Here it is the nature of reality itself that is said to determine the classification. The notion is that there is a reality external to humans that exists before they try to interpret or explain it; that is, reality is pre-given. The categories into which people classify specific instances are already there in the phenomenon they are trying to explain. A rose falls into the category 'roses' because there is a real difference between roses and other categories of flowers. An organisation falls into the category 'coal industry' because there is a real difference between organisations in this industry and those in the gas industry. If the categories exist in reality then any other classification people might make would not produce an adequate explanation, a fact that they would discover when they tried to act in accordance with that explanation. Most natural scientists would probably adopt this position in relation to the natural phenomena that they try to explain. If one adopts this position then it is quite natural to suppose that a human being can stand outside the phenomenon to be explained, taking the role of the objective observer who builds increasingly accurate explanations, or models, through experimentation. Mostly, realists do not see any inherent limitation on human ability to comprehend reality in its entirety. For them, it is only a matter of time before research progressively uncovers more and more of reality.

The opposite position to realism is idealism. Here the categories into which people classify their experiences are held to exist only in their minds, not out there in reality. Any explanations they come up with are, therefore, simply projections of their own minds. Those who hold this position maintain that there is no pre-given reality outside of humans, but that there are inherited and thus pre-given categories into which people classify their experience.

There are intermediate positions taken to explain how it is that people are able to explain and what limits that capacity. For example, constructivists hold that, because of biological evolution, humans are capable of perceiving the world in one way but not others (*Maturana & Varela, 1987*). For example, the human visual apparatus receives light waves on three channels; it is trichromate. Some other animals have dichromate (two channels) or quatrochromate (four channels) vision. Each type of creature, therefore, sees the world of colour in a different way, in effect, through biological evolution, selecting aspects of reality for attention. It is impossible for one type of creature to see the world of colour that another type sees. Similarly, constructivists would point to limitations on human capacity to perceive reality imposed by the evolved nature of the human brain. By its very nature, the human brain selects aspects of reality to pay attention to. This position has something in common with realism in that it supposes a reality that exists outside of the human organism and is not simply the result of the mind's projection. However, unlike realism, this is not an unproblematically pre-given reality but, rather, a constructed, enacted or selected reality.

Another important position taken on the nature of human capacity to explain experience is that of social constructionism (*Gergen, 1985*). Some social constructionists adopt the idealist position, holding that there is no reality out there, but others tend towards a realist position in that they hold that there is a reality outside of humans. However, the latter postulate explanations of a reality that is not pre-given but, rather, selected by those doing the explaining. In this social constructionism is similar to constructivism but with a very important difference. While constructivists focus upon the selecting nature of the individual human being, social constructionists point to social interaction, particularly in conversation, as the selecting process. The constructionist position is this: every explanation people put forward of any phenomenon is a socially constructed account, not a straightforward description of reality. If this view is held then it is impossible to adopt the role of the independent, objective observer when trying to explain any phenomenon. Instead, one could only come up with an explanation through participation in what one is trying to explain.

Constructionists and constructivists hold that it is impossible to take the position of objective observer and that those who claim to do this are simply ignoring the impact of their own participation or lack of it. This leads to the closely related notion of reflexivity (*Steier, 1991*). Reflexive entities are entities that bend back upon themselves. Humans are reflexive in the sense that any explanations they produce are the products of what they are, as determined by their histories. For example, I am trying, on these pages, to explain different ways in which humans explain their experience. If I hold the reflexive position then I cannot claim any objectively given truth for my way of doing this. Instead, I have to recognise that the approach I am adopting is the product of who I am and how I think. This, in turn, is the distillation of my personal history of relating to important other people over many years. If I accept the argument about reflexivity, I can never claim to stand outside my own experience, outside the web of relationships that I am a part of, and take the role of objective observer. Instead, I have to take the role of inquiring participant (*Reason, 1988*).

## The individual and the group

The move to a reflexive, social constructionist position is very significant in terms of what is being assumed about the relationship between the individual and the group. Realist, idealist and constructivist positions are all presented in terms of the capacities and limitations of the human individual. The individual is taken to be prior and primary to the group and groups can then only be seen as consisting of individuals. Some social constructionists see the group as prior and primary. Individuals are then the products of the group in some way. Others, however, take a more paradoxical perspective in which neither is primary. One forms and is formed by the other. This question of how to think about the individual and the group is central to the reviews of theories of strategy and organisational change in this book.

So, there are a number of different, contradictory ways of explaining how human beings come to know anything. Furthermore, there is no widespread agreement as to which of these explanations is 'true' or even most useful. The realist position probably commands most support amongst natural scientists and those social scientists, probably the majority, who seek the same status for their field as is accorded to the natural sciences. Social constructionists point to a significant difference between natural and social phenomena. Humans interpret natural phenomena, those phenomena do not interpret themselves. However, when it comes to human phenomena, we are dealing with ourselves, phenomena that are already interpreting themselves. Many constructionists hold, therefore, that while the scientific approach might be applicable in the natural sciences it is not in the human sciences.

At this point, you might be wondering why I have apparently moved so far away from the central concern of this book, namely strategy and organisational dynamics. The reason is this: any view you take of the nature of strategy and change in organisations immediately implies a view on the nature of human knowing. If you think that an organisation's strategy is the choice made by its chief executive, following a rational process of formulation, then you are assuming a realist, or perhaps constructivist, position. You are implicitly assuming that the individual is primary. Since this tends to be the dominant approach to explaining what strategy is, it is quite easy to take it for the truth. However, what I have been trying to show in the above paragraphs is that this would be a completely unwarranted move. Just how human beings know, whether the individual or the group is primary, is a hotly contested issue with no clear truth. Simply going along with today's dominant views on strategy, without any questioning of the foundations upon which they are built, amounts to shutting one's eyes to other possibilities, which might make more sense of one's experience. For example, if one shifts perspective and considers that an organisation's strategy might emerge from a conversational process in which many participate, then one would be moving towards a social constructionist position and assuming that the group is primary. Perhaps this might assist in making more sense of experience of life in organisations.

Different theories of strategy and organisational change imply different ways of explaining how human beings know or do anything. If one wants to understand just what the differences are between one explanation of strategy and organisational change and another, then one needs, I believe, to understand what assumptions are implicitly being made about how humans know anything. The key aspect distinguishing explanations of human knowing is the way they treat the relationship between the individual and the group. In the rest of this book, I will be reviewing how various ways of understanding strategy and organisational change differ. I will be pointing to how some of the most important differences relate to the implicit assumptions made about human knowing and the relationship between the individual and the group.

I want to turn now to the second question I posed earlier on. This had to do with what I referred to as the paradox of sameness and difference. I was suggesting that reality is fundamentally paradoxical in that it is always characterised by both sameness and difference. However, the human need to classify entities and acts into categories, in order to explain anything, inevitably polarises them into same and different, so obscuring the paradox. One of the comparisons I will be making between one explanation of strategy and organisational change and another will be the manner in which they deal with this, and other, paradoxes. To prepare the ground for that comparison I want here to talk more generally about the nature of paradox and how it is, or is not, dealt with. First, what do I mean by paradox?

## The nature of paradox

There are a number of different definitions of a paradox. First, it may mean an apparent contradiction, a state in which two apparently conflicting elements appear to be operating at the same time. Paradox in this sense can be removed or resolved: by choosing one element above the other all the time; or by reframing the problem to remove the apparent contradiction.

Second, it may mean a state in which two diametrically opposing forces are simultaneously present, neither of which can ever be removed. The choice is not therefore between one or the other; both must be accommodated at the same time and this can be done only by continually rearranging them (*Quinn & Cameron, 1988*).

As it is used in this book, the word paradox means the presence together at the same time of self-contradictory, essentially conflicting forces, none of which can be removed. The word is not used in the sense of a dilemma, that being a situation where a choice must be made between two equally undesirable possibilities. Dilemmas are solved by making an either/or choice. Paradoxes are orchestrated by making both/and choices at the same time, not subsequently. A state of contention is thus the consequence of a paradox in a human system. Contention is positively expressed as dialogue around the paradoxical forces and negatively expressed as unresolvable conflict. Paradoxes are mutually exclusive and simultaneously present.

Any human organisation may be said to be paradoxical for the following reasons.

In even the simplest human endeavour it is necessary for efficiency reasons to divide up the tasks that need to be done. But as soon as this is done it creates the problem of integrating the divided tasks back into a whole again – the problem of control. There is no choice between *either* task division *or* task integration. Both task division *and* task integration are simultaneously present. Paradoxes require both/and choices at the same time; either/or choices are not possible, nor is a sequential switching between them.

Each individual in an organisation has a paradoxical desire for freedom and the excitement that goes with chance and uncertainty, while at the same time fearing the unknown and wanting order and discipline. This is the paradoxical human need to fuse into a group and yet remain an individual. There are many other examples of such paradoxes. Businesses have to produce at the lowest cost, but they have to increase costs to provide quality. Organisations have to control what their employees do, but they have to give them freedom if they want to retain them and if they want them to deal with rapidly changing circumstances. All of these examples require siimultaneous both/and rather than either/or choices.

Many theories of organisation emphasise either/or choices. They prescribe either stability and success, or instability and failure. They usually do not recognise paradox as fundamental and, when they do, they prescribe some kind of harmonious, equilibrium balance between them. In this way the paradox is in effect removed; its existence is a nuisance that is not fundamental to success.

The way one perceives paradox says much about the way one understands organisational dynamics. The idea that paradoxes must be resolved, and the tension they cause must be released to be successful, is part of the paradigm that equates success with the dynamics of stability, regularity and predictability. The notion that paradoxes can never be resolved, only endlessly rearranged, leads to a view of organisational dynamics couched in terms of continuing tension-generating behaviour patterns that are irregular, unstable and unpredictable, but lead to creative novelty.

## Dialectics and dialogue

The word dialectic describes the process through which paradoxes are arranged, or orchestrated, to yield a transcending new configuration. It is a process characterised by constructive tension. For example, in an organisation it is necessary to concentrate power in order to operate efficiently. It is simultaneously necessary to distribute power in order to cope with high levels of uncertainty in a rapidly changing environment. Making an either/or choice will not do – it will sacrifice either efficiency or flexibility and both are needed. An effective organisation may continually cope with the paradox through shifting patterns of power concentrated for some purposes at some times and dispersed for other purposes at other times. This would be a dialectic process. Note that this resolution through a shifting pattern is not a solution; it throws up its own problems of continuing contention that need to be resolved, so that there is never a solution.

Dialogue is where two parties exchange views about paradoxical situations, each having the intention of modifying their position in the light of the views and evidence presented by the other. Each participant is open to being influenced by the other. Argument is simply stating positions without any intention of moving. Dialogue is thus the required process for dialectics.

I turn now to how paradoxes are understood and dealt with in various ways of knowing. What I have been calling a paradox of sameness and difference might not be seen as a simultaneously existing arrangement of contradictory forces at all. For example, from the realist position the categories people classify their experiences into are already given, out there in the world. Events, entities and acts are in a category because they really are the same and others fall into another category because they really are different. What appears to be a paradox is simply a logical contradiction due to ignorance and further efforts at understanding will remove it. From an idealist perspective, people arrive on this earth with inherited mental categories, and what I have been calling a paradox would then simply be a contradiction between these mental categories, presumably soluble by some form of logic. So, one view is that what I have been calling paradox is simply a logical contradiction that can be solved by enough work. Another approach is to regard the problem of sameness and difference not as a paradox but as a conflict or a tension. When this is done there is the possibility of relieving, or harmonising, the conflict or tension. Or, what I have been calling a paradox might be thought of as a dilemma, in which case it can be resolved. However, if sameness and difference is a paradox rather than a contradiction, conflict/tension or dilemma, then there is no solution, relief or resolution. All that can be done with a paradox is to rearrange it in a dialectical fashion.

Just as different ways of explaining how humans know anything affect how one might conceptualise strategy and organisational change, so with different ways of viewing sameness and difference. For example, take the problem of designing a reporting structure in an organisation. The central issue for organisational design has to do with dividing tasks up and integrating them into an efficient whole. How does one view the directly opposing processes of dividing and integrating? Does one see them as creating a conflict or a tension? If so, one would probably expect to be able to produce a design that relieved that tension, producing some kind of efficient, harmonious structure. The fact that organisations keep moving from centralisation to decentralisation, and back again, is then a puzzle. However, if one regards organising as a fundamentally paradoxical activity, in which contradictory forces of division and integration can only ever be rearranged but not resolved, one would adopt a different attitude towards the question of centralisation and decentralisation. The continual swings back and forth between centralisation and decentralisation would no longer be so puzzling. You would not believe that there was an optimal design and so you might change the existing one less frequently.

One of the factors I am going to pay attention to in comparing different explanations of strategy and organisational change is, therefore, going to be how they deal with contradictory forces. I will be asking whether they see them as logical contradictions, conflicts/tensions, dilemmas or paradoxes. There are a number of these contradictory forces that seem to me to be important:

- Sameness and difference.
- Individual and group.
- Division and integration.
- Predictability and unpredictability.
- Control and freedom.
- Order and disorder.
- Determinism and chance.

## 1.4   KEY FEATURES IN COMPARING THEORIES OF ORGANISATIONAL EVOLUTION

It is appropriate now to summarise the points I have been making and give you some indication of how I am going to use them in the rest of this book.

I have been describing what I think the phenomenon is that I am trying to explain when I talk about strategy, organisational change, or evolution, and organisational dynamics. That phenomenon is a population of organisations of various kinds and the population of people and groupings of people to be found within each of those organisations. It is an ever changing, dynamic population of organisations and groupings of people continuously interacting with each other. I have also been talking about how human beings come to know any phenomenon, including that of a population of organisations and groupings of people dynamically interacting with each other. In the course of describing the phenomenon and how one might come to know it, I have listed a number of factors that I want to use to distinguish between various theories of strategy and organisational dynamics. These factors are:

- How the dynamics is dealt with.
- How paradox is handled.
- What level of description the theory focuses on.
- What time frames it is concerned with.
- What part emotion is seen to play.
- How the interactive/relational nature of the phenomenon is conceptualised.
- How causality is understood.
- How sameness and difference is handled; that is, whether the theory assumes average entities and average interactions or not.
- Whether the theory assumes a pre-given reality or a constructed reality.

- Whether it takes the methodological stance of the objective observer or the reflexive, participative inquirer.
- What theory of human knowing and behaving it assumes, particularly how it deals with the relationship between individuals and groups.
- How it deals with power.

I now want to pull these factors together into four questions that I will put to each of the theories to be considered in the chapters that follow. The questions are:

1   How does the theory understand the nature of human interacting and relating? I will be considering whether the theory takes a systemic or a process perspective. I will look at what level of description and time span each theory focuses on and how it deals with the dynamics.
2   What theory of human psychology, that is ways of knowing and behaving, does each theory of strategy and organisational change assume? I will be focusing particularly on how each psychological theory deals with the relationship between individual and group and the questions of emotion and power.
3   What methodology underlies each theory of strategy and organisational change? I will be asking whether the theory takes the position of objective observer of a pre-given reality or whether it takes the position of the reflexive, participative enquirer seeking to understand a constructed reality.
4   How does each theory of strategy and organisational change deal with the possible paradoxical nature of the population of organisations and groupings of people? I will be asking whether the theory sees opposing forces simply as logical contradiction, as conflicts or tensions, as sequential alternatives, or as paradoxes.

In the chapters that follow I am going to classify different explanations into two groups according to the answers they give to the above four questions. In doing this, I immediately obliterate differences within each theory and similarities between one and another. I will try to mitigate this to some extent by pointing to different strands in each category and to similarities between them. The two category labels I propose to use are the orthodox and the radical. The distinguishing features between the two relate to:

- the theory of interaction they use. Orthodox theories are built on systems theories developed in the 1940s and 1950s. Radical theories start from the recently developed theories of chaos and complexity.
- the assumptions they make about human psychology, particularly how they deal with the question of the individual and the group. Orthodox approaches hold the individual to be primary and prior to the group while radical approaches do not.
- the methodological position. Orthodox approaches involve taking the role of objective observer of a pre-given reality while radical approaches take the role of the reflexive, participative inquirer into a socially constructed reality.
- the attitude to paradox. On the whole, orthodox approaches do not see paradox as fundamental whereas radical approaches do.
- the level of description and time span the theory focuses on and what it assumes about predictability. Orthodox theories tend to assume average entities making up a system and average relationships between them. Radical approaches focus on levels

of detail and time spans that do not allow predictability and in so doing pay attention to non-average, or deviant, individuals and relationships.

Within the orthodox category, I will distinguish between the theory of strategic choice, the theory of the learning organisation and psychoanalytic theories of organisation. In the radical category, I will distinguish between theories that start out with radical promises but end up with orthodox conclusions and theories that hold out the promise of radical conclusions.

What I am trying to do is to tease out strands of theory in order to expose assumptions and reasoning processes for comparison.

## 1.5    OUTLINE OF THE BOOK

Part One reviews three orthodox theories.

Chapter 2 describes the two pillars upon which the first of these theories, strategic choice, is built. The first pillar is cybernetic systems theory and the second is cognitivist psychology. Strategic choice theory prescribes a procedure involving the formulation of long-term strategies and then their implementation. Chapter 3 reviews the prescriptions for formulating strategies and Chapter 4 does the same for implementation. Both sets of prescription depend critically on the ability of managers to forecast. However, the theory does take account of uncertainty and Chapter 5 explores how it does so. Chapter 6 then looks at how the theory of strategic choice deals with motivation, culture, leadership and the role of groups. Chapter 7 evaluates the theory of strategic choice, examining how it answers the four key questions set out in the previous section of this chapter. It also explores how the theory focuses the attention of managers on some matters and pushes others to the periphery.

Chapter 8 turns to the foundations of the second theory to be reviewed. The theory is that of the learning organisation and the foundations are systems dynamics, cognitive and humanistic psychology. Chapter 9 reviews the theory of the learning organisation. It concludes with an examination of how it answers the four key questions set out in the previous section. It then explores how this theory focuses the attention of managers on certain issues and pushes the others to the periphery.

The final chapter in this part, Chapter 10, reviews a combination of open systems theory and psychoanalytic perspectives on human nature. It too concludes with an examination of how this theory answers the four key questions and in so doing focuses the attention of managers.

Part Two of the book moves from the systems theories developed in the late 1940s and early 1950s to those developed more recently. Chapter 11 describes the theories of chaos and dissipative structures, also making a brief reference to synergetics. Chapter 12 describes the agent-based models of complex adaptive systems.

Chapter 13 reviews some recent publications that explore the application of chaos and complexity theory to organisations. I argue that they do this from the cognitivist psychological perspective and in doing so collapse the potentially radical insights of chaos and complexity theory into another management orthodoxy.

Chapters 14 and 15 develop an alternative psychological perspective in which the individual is decentred and relationship is key to understanding human nature. Here complexity, as a theory of interaction in the abstract, coincides with relationship psychology as a theory of human interaction. Chapter 16 points to how complexity theory, understood from the perspective of relationship psychology, opens up the potential for a radical theory of organisations. This theory focuses on the self-organising and constructive nature of conversation and power relations in organisations. Chapter 17 examines how such a theory might answer the four key questions and how it focuses the attention of managers on matters that others push to the periphery. It then inevitably pushes other matters to the periphery.

## REFERENCES

Allen, P. M. (1998), Modelling complex economic evolution, in *Selbstorganisation*, Berlin: Duncker & Humblot.

Gergen, K. J. (1985), The social constructionist movement in modern psychology, *American Psychologist*, vol. 40, pp. 266–75.

Maturana, H. R. and Varela, F. J. (1987), *The Tree of Knowledge: The Biological Roots of Human Understanding*, Boston and London: Shambala.

Quinn, R. E. and Cameron, K. S. (1988), *Paradox and Transformation*, Homewood, IL: Richard D. Irwin.

Reason, P. (1988), *Human Inquiry in Action*, London: Sage.

Steier, F. (1991), *Research and Reflexivity*, Thousand Oaks, CA: Sage

# Orthodox perspectives on strategy and organisational dynamics

*[handwritten annotation: ঐতিহ্য/প্রচলিত Traditional/ঐ]*

This part reviews three theories of organisational strategy and change and examines how each directs attention in a particular way to the four key questions posed at the end of Chapter 1:

1 What is the nature of interaction?
2 What is the nature of human beings?
3 What method is used to understand human interaction?
4 How does this method deal with paradox?

Three different theories are described.

The first is the theory of strategic choice. In simple terms, this theory holds that organisations change primarily in ways that are chosen by their most powerful members. It prescribes the making of such choices on the basis of predicted future outcomes and rational selection criteria. In various forms, this is probably the theory that dominates discussions of strategy and organisational change amongst both practitioners and researchers. For this reason, Chapters 2 to 7 are devoted to describing this theory and Chapter 8 explores how it answers the four questions above. The theory of strategic choice is built on the foundations of cybernetic systems theory and takes a largely cognitivist view of human nature. Chapter 2 will explain what these terms mean and then Chapters 3 to 7 will describe how they are used in strategic choice theory.

The second theory is that of the learning organisation. In very simple terms, this theory holds that an organisation evolves through the learning processes that take place within it. It prescribes ways of thinking and behaving that are supposed to enhance this learning process. Here the systems theory is provided by systems dynamics and the psychological theory is also cognitivist with some elements of humanistic psychology. Chapter 9 explains what systems dynamics is and how it differs from cybernetics and Chapter 10 indicates how these ideas are used in the theory of the learning organisation.

The third theory explored in this part combines open systems theory with a psychoanalytic understanding of human nature. This theory is primarily concerned with unconscious processes and neurotic forms of leadership, demonstrating how these might impede rational choice and learning. It takes account of the impact on organisations of anxiety and the ways it is contained or defended against.

# The foundations of strategic choice theory

## Cybernetic systems and cognitivist psychology

## 2.1  INTRODUCTION

The purpose of this chapter is to familiarise you with the theoretical foundations of what is probably the dominant theory of strategy and organisational change. This is the theory of strategic choice and you can hear it quite clearly in the way that most management practitioners talk about strategy and change in their organisations. You can also read it in most of the books and articles written about strategy and organisational design and development.

In subsequent chapters, I will give a summary of some of the key elements of this theory but here it will suffice to give a very brief definition of what the theory of strategic choice has to say.

The theory holds that the strategy of an organisation is the general direction in which it changes over time. The general direction encompasses the range of activities it will undertake, the broad markets it will serve and how its resource base and competences will change. This general direction is chosen by the most powerful individual in the organisation, that is the person at the top of the management hierarchy, or by a small group of managers at the top of that hierarchy.

You can immediately see how this notion places the individual, and the choices made by the individual, at the very centre of the theory. It therefore immediately implies a particular theory of human psychology, that is a theory of how humans know and behave. The theory implied is that of cognitivism, a term I will explain later in this chapter.

Having chosen the general direction, or strategy, the managers at the top of the hierarchy are supposed to design an organisational structure to implement it. The structure they design is supposed to be a largely self-regulating one in which people are assigned roles and given objectives to achieve that will realise the chosen strategy.

You can immediately see how this requirement assumes a particular way in which people are thought to interact with each other, that is a particular kind of system. The particular kind of system being assumed is a cybernetic system, the nature of which I will explain in the next section of this chapter. Furthermore, the need to motivate people to achieve objectives also implies a psychological theory of motivation and this is usually based on humanistic psychology. I will also explain what this is later in the chapter.

Having set out what cybernetic systems and cognitivist psychology are, I will then pursue the four questions that Chapter 1 concluded with. I will ask how cybernetic systems theory and cognitivist psychology deal with those four questions. You should then be able to see how the theory of strategic choice, to be described in Chapters 3 to 7, displays its theoretical origins in cybernetic systems theory and in cognitivist psychology.

## 2.2    CYBERNETIC SYSTEMS

Cybernetics is an application of the engineer's idea of control to human activity. During the Second World War, the superiority of the German air force led British scientists to consider how they might improve the accuracy of anti-aircraft defences. One of these scientists, Norbert Wiener, saw a way of treating the evasive action of enemy aircraft as a time series that could be manipulated mathematically to improve the gunner's predictions of the enemy plane's future position:

> When we desire a motion to follow a given pattern, the difference between the pattern and the actually performed motion is used as a new input to cause the part regulated to move in such a way as to bring the motion closer to that given pattern. (*Wiener, 1948, p. 6*)

It is important to note how cybernetics immediately focuses attention on performing a given pattern. This is the realist position described in Chapter 1. There is an already existing, or pre-given, reality outside the entity performing the motion. What Wiener is describing here is the process of negative feedback.

### Negative feedback and equilibrium

Negative feedback simply means that the outcome of a previous action is compared to some desired outcome and the discrepancy between the two is fed back as information that guides the next action in such a way that the discrepancy is reduced until it disappears. Thus when anything at all disturbs a system from its state of stable equilibrium it will return to that equilibrium if it is governed by some form of negative feedback control. Negative feedback is the process required to produce the dynamics of stability. Consider two commonly quoted examples: a domestic central heating system and the Watt steam engine governor.

A domestic heating system consists of an appliance and a regulator. The regulator contains a device that senses room temperature connected to a device that turns the heating appliance on and off. A desired temperature is set in the regulator. When the room temperature falls below this desired level, the control sensor detects the discrepancy between actual and desired states. The regulator responds to a negative discrepancy with a positive action – it turns the heat on. When the temperature rises above the desired level the opposite happens. By responding to the deviation of actual from desired levels in an opposite or negative way, the control system dampens any movement away from desired levels. The controls keep the room temperature close to a stable level over time utilising negative feedback. *Figure 2.1* illustrates this negative feedback loop.

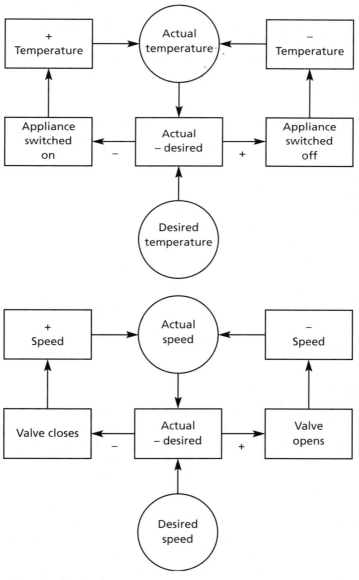

**FIGURE 2.1**    Negative feedback

The same principle applies to the steam engine governor. As the boiler of the engine is stoked, steam pressure rises causing the engine to speed up. If this speed exceeds a preset desired level, the governor responds by opening a valve to release the steam and so pull the engine speed back to the desired level. As soon as the speed falls below the desired level the valve closes, steam pressure rises, and the engine speed increases to the desired level. Here too the operation of the control system is such that fluctuations around the desired level are damped and predictable. Stable equilibrium behaviour is thus preserved through the use of negative feedback. *Figure 2.1* also illustrates this example.

Negative or damping feedback is the mechanism that is widely used in engineering for automatic control or regulation. A point of central importance about negative feedback is that it is capable of moving a system to a state of stable equilibrium.

Equilibrium is a possible state of behaviour for a system. It takes a stable form when the behaviour of a system regularly repeats its past and when it is very difficult to change that behaviour to some other state. It requires significant change to shift a system from a state of stable equilibrium. For example, in economic theory markets are assumed always to tend to a state of stable equilibrium. If there is an increase in demand, then prices will rise to encourage an increase in supply to match the demand. If demand then stays constant, so will price and supply. Any chance movement of the price away from its equilibrium level will set in train changes in demand and supply that will rapidly pull price back to its equilibrium level. It will take a noticeable change in demand or supply to alter this behaviour.

Equilibrium can take an *unstable* form. Here the system's state is easily perturbed from, and does not easily return to, its original state.

*Dynamic* equilibrium is a state in which a system continuously adapts to alterations in a continually changing environment.

The key point about all forms of equilibrium behaviour is that they are regular, orderly and predictable. Most theories of management and organisation have been developed within an equilibrium framework. Of course, to be regular, orderly and predictable, the links between cause and effect have to be clear cut. In equilibrium there are clear-cut links between cause and effect and consequently behaviour is predictable.

## Negative feedback and human action

Wiener and his colleagues saw the importance of negative feedback loops in most human actions – a loop in which the gap between desired and actual performance of an act just past is fed back as a determinant of the next action (see *Figure 2.2*).

If you are trying to hit an object by throwing a ball at it and you miss because you aimed too far to the right, you then use the information from this miss to alter the point at which you aim the next shot: you aim further to the left, trying to offset the last error. In this sense the feedback is negative – it prompts you to move in the opposite direction. You keep doing this until you hit the object. Wiener and his colleagues thought that this negative feedback was essential to controlled behaviour and that breaking the feedback link led to pathological behaviour. Those who do not correct their behaviour in the light of what they have learned about the consequences of such behaviour are in some sense ill.

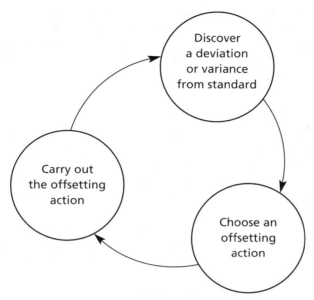

**FIGURE 2.2**    Negative feedback in cybernetics

Cyberneticists also realised that when such negative feedback becomes too fast, or too sensitive, the result could be uncontrolled cycles of over- and under-achievement of the desired state. So, for example, you may be taking a shower and find the water too hot. This leads you to raise the flow of cold water. If you do not take sufficient account of the lag between your action and the subsequent drop in temperature you may increase the cold water flow again. This may make the water too cold so you raise the flow of hot water which then makes it too hot again. Unless you get the time lag between your action and its consequence right, you may increase the hot water flow until it becomes too hot again. So, if your negative feedback control system is operating too rapidly, the temperature of the water will fluctuate in an unstable manner instead of settling down to a desired level. Negative feedback systems can be highly unstable.

Those studying such systems therefore became very concerned to establish the conditions for stability and instability in negative feedback control systems. As a result of this kind of work governments came to accept that their attempts to remove cycles in the level of activity in the economy were usually counterproductive. Just as the economy was recovering from a slump, impatient governments tended to cut taxes and increase expenditure, so fuelling an excessive boom accompanied by rapid inflation. Just as that boom was collapsing on its own, fearful governments increased taxes and cut expenditure, so pushing the economy into a deeper slump than it would otherwise have experienced. To secure stability through negative feedback you must be able to predict not only the outcome of an action but also the time lag between an action and its outcome. The design of a control system that works at the right speed and the right level of sensitivity relies upon such predictions. Given the ability to predict, it is then possible to specify in a precise mathematical way exactly what conditions will produce stability for any negative feedback system.

Having outlined what cybernetics is all about I now turn to how it has been applied to the control of organisations. Two writers have been of major importance in developing cybernetic theory, particularly as it applies to organisations: *W. Roy Ashby (1945, 1952, 1956)* and *Stafford Beer (1959/67, 1966)*. Ashby and Stafford Beer made the key points set out in the paragraphs below.

## Goal-seeking adaptation to the environment

Cybernetics postulates that two main forces drive an organisation over time. The first force is the drive to achieve some purpose: from this perspective organisations are goal-seeking systems and the goal drives their actions. The second force arises because organisations are connected through feedback links to their environments: they are subsystems of an even larger environmental suprasystem. Reaching the goal requires being adapted to those environments.

Thus, in the cybernetics tradition, organisations are driven by attraction to a predetermined desired state which is equilibrium adaptation to the environment. The state a given organisation comes to occupy is determined by the nature of its environment.

For example, on this view, a company operating in, say, the electronics industry may be driven by the goal of achieving a 20 per cent return on its capital. In order to achieve this it must deliver what its customers want. If customers have stable requirements for standardised low-cost silicon chips to be used as components in their own products, then the company has to adapt to this environment by employing mass production methods to produce standardised products at lower costs than its rivals. It will have to support these production methods with particular forms of organisational structure, control systems and cultures: functional structures, bureaucratic control systems, and conservative, strongly shared cultures. The company will look much the same as its rivals in the same market because the overall shape of each is determined by the same environment.

If, however, the electronics market is a turbulent one with rapidly changing technology and many niche markets where customers look for customised chips, then there will be very different kinds of organisation, according to cybernetics theory. A company will have to adapt by emphasising R&D and continually developing new products to differentiate itself from its rivals. It will support these production methods with particular forms of structure, control systems and culture: decentralised structures of separate profit centres, greater emphasis on informal controls, and change-loving cultures.

But how do organisations come to be adapted to their environments and achieve their goals?

## Regulators

According to cybernetics, organisations deploy regulators that utilise negative feedback in order to reach their goals and the desired states of adaptation to their environments. The central problem is how to keep an organisation at, or near to, some desired state and the answer to the problem lies in the design of the regulator, that is the design of the control system. Cybernetics is the science of control and management is the profession of control. At the heart of that science and that profession lies the design of regulators. You can see how this kind of thinking accords with a major management concern – that to do with being in control.

There are two types of regulator: the error-controlled regulator and the anticipatory regulator. In Ashby's scheme, disturbances from its environment (D in *Figure 2.3*) impact on the organisation (T in the figure) leading to an outcome (E in the figure). The problem is where to put the regulator (R in *Figure 2.3*).

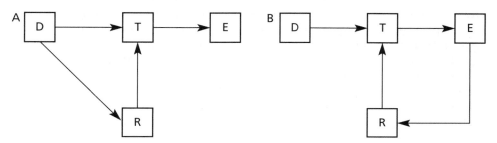

**FIGURE 2.3**    Regulation in control systems
*Source:* W. R. Ashby (1956), *Introduction to Cybernetics*, New York: John Wiley

### Anticipatory regulation

If the regulator is placed so that it senses the disturbance before that disturbance hits the organisation, then it can take anticipatory action and offset the undesirable impact of the disturbance on the outcome (part A of *Figure 2.3*).

An immediately recognisable example of this kind of regulator is of course a planning system. Such a regulator takes the form of a sensing device using market research questionnaires or analyses of market statistics. On the basis of these, realistically achievable desired states are established. These desired states are forecasts of sales volumes, prices and costs at some future point; that is, the positions and postures required to achieve the performance target or goal. Action plans to realise these forecasts are also prepared; that is, patterns in future actions are identified. As the company moves through time it continually senses the environment, picks up disturbances before they occur, and prepares planned actions to deal with them before they hit the organisation. This is the ideal control without making mistakes: preventing deviations from plan occurring in the first place.

### Error-controlled regulation

If it is not possible to establish such an anticipatory regulator, or if such a regulator cannot work perfectly, then a regulator must be placed so that it can sense the outcome once that outcome has occurred. This is the classic error-controlled regulator (part B of *Figure 2.3*).

An immediately recognisable example of this type of regulator is the monitoring, reviewing and corrective action system of an organisation. It is what a company's board of directors does each month when it meets to review what has happened to the business over the past month, monitors how the performance measures are moving, and decides what to do to correct deviations from plan that have already occurred.

It is clearly preferable to anticipate disturbances as far as possible because there are time lags: first in detecting what is happening; then in deciding what should be done; then in doing it; and then in the outcome materialising from the action. These time lags mean that relying entirely on the error-control system will not produce the intended performance. Since it takes time to correct a deviation, and since time lags can cause instability in performance, managers should aim to prevent deviation in the first place. But anticipating disturbances relies on the ability to forecast them and this can never be perfect. Therefore an organisation will have to rely on both anticipatory and error-control regulators. This is exactly what the managers of a business do when they prepare budgets and plans and then monitor and review the environment and the company's performance each month. Note, however, that even error-controlled regulators depend on some form of predictability. When a deviation between a desired and an actual outcome appears, you take action in one period. When the next period comes around and the deviation has still not been removed, do you take further action? You would only do so if the last period's action has already had its effect and that effect was insufficient. You would not do so if the effects were still working their way through. This means that when you take a corrective action you have to be able to predict the timing of its effects if error-controlled regulation is to be reliable.

## Reliance on statistics

An essential requirement for the most effective application of this whole approach to control is the availability of quantitative forecasts of future changes in the organisation and its environment, as well as forecasts of the consequences of proposed actions to deal with these changes. For self-regulating control to work adequately the forecasts need to be at a rather detailed level of description and can only function, therefore, over a time span where this is possible. The tools available for such quantitative forecasts are those derived from statistical theory. Statistical forecasting methods are based on the assumption that the disturbances hitting the organisation from its environment take the form of groupings of large numbers of closely similar events that can be described by a probability distribution. It is implicitly assumed that uniquely uncertain events will be relatively unimportant.

This distinction can be clarified by two examples. An example of a unique event is the Iraqi invasion of Kuwait in August 1990. It is of course unique because it only occurs once. It cannot be described in terms of an observed probability distribution – either it occurs or it does not. Because of its uniqueness standard statistical techniques cannot be used to forecast its occurrence. An example of a grouping of events that can be described by a probability distribution is the number of television sets a company sells each month. By looking at the records for a number of months it will be possible to say what the most likely level of demand will be. These different possibilities are illustrated in *Figure 2.4*. If the business is primarily affected by events that can be described by probability distributions it will be possible to use tried-and-tested statistical techniques to forecast them. Statistical techniques require data generated by many repetitions. If most of the events hitting a business are unique it will not be possible to rely on these techniques. If they cannot be used, then practising anticipatory and error-controlled control in the way proposed by cybernetics will not be possible.

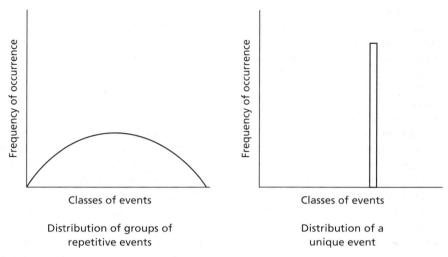

FIGURE 2.4    Distribution of events

## The law of requisite variety

However, cybernetics sees the main cause of the difficulty in designing regulators not in terms of the uniqueness of events, but in terms of their variety, or complexity. Variety is the number of discernibly different states the environment can present to the organisation and the number of discernibly different responses the organisation can make to the environment. It is the function of the regulator to reduce variety so retaining stability within a system, despite high variety outside it. That is, the huge variety of disturbances presented by the environment must be neutralised by a huge number of responses such that the outcome can match the one desirable state selected in advance that will fit the environment. In order to be able to do this, the regulator must be designed to have as much variety as the environment; the number of potential responses must match the number of potential disturbances so that they can cancel each other out and produce a single desired outcome. This is Ashby's law of requisite variety: the complexity and speed of the firm's response must match the complexity and speed of change of the environment.

Suppose an organisation faces a stable environment in which changes follow regular predictable patterns. Then it will succeed when it uses an anticipatory regulator of the comprehensive planning kind. Here it forecasts the changes that will occur and prepares a single comprehensive plan to deal with all the future changes it faces over a given time period: it decides in advance on the sequence of actions it is to follow for a particular time period and then it implements that sequence of actions.

In this case there is a simple rather than a complex environment. There is also an environment in which there is little variety: it is regular and it is possible to predict the single pattern it will follow in the future. Because the environment is simple and low in variety it is possible to design a regulator that is simple and low in variety; one single set of intended actions, the comprehensive plan, can then be followed.

Now suppose that the environment is more complex and displays greater variety. This inevitably means greater difficulty in forecasting what will happen. Using the simple regulator – one plan for the future – is likely to lead to failure because there will be a response to a great many of the unforeseeable events that are occurring. To succeed, the regulator must be given greater variety. This can be done by preparing a number of different forecast scenarios and putting together contingency plans for each scenario. As it becomes clearer which scenario is unfolding, the requisite contingency plan can be pulled from the file and implemented.

In effect, the whole planning procedure is made more flexible and long-term plans are changed every few months in order to match them to unforeseen changes as those unforeseen changes emerge. So, there may be one plan for an environment in which oil prices are low, exchange rates favourable, rates of growth in demand high, own product prices high, and competitor moves sluggish. A different plan can be developed for the reverse of all of these environmental conditions, or for only some of them.

Notice how a higher level of complexity and variety is responded to by increasing the complexity and variety of the regulator, in this case the planning system, the range of plans available, and the frequency with which they are changed.

At some point the changes in the environment may become so rapid and unpredictable that even contingency planning will not work; too many contingencies may arise to make it practicable to have a plan ready for all of them. The regulator will therefore no longer take the form of a planning system. Instead it may take the form of a loose, changing set of project teams or what Peters and Waterman called skunkworks (*Peters & Waterman, 1982*). Here each team is working on some project to deal with some possible change in the environment. Each team conducts trials to test out possible market responses. One team will be experimenting with one kind of product that might suit say a rapid-growth low-oil-price environment and another may be experimenting with a product that suits a slow-growth high-oil-price environment. The regulator takes the form of trial-and-error testing of responses that the changing environment might require. The organisation is thus developing a large number of potential responses to a large number of potential environmental changes. Those experiments that succeed are continued with and those that fail are abandoned. The more experiments conducted, the greater and faster the action, the more likely the organisation is to deal with what the environment throws at it.

Here then there is a regulator that has even more variety and complexity built into it so as to match the much higher level of complexity and variety in the environment. Orthodox views of strategic management depend crucially upon the validity of this idea.

You can see how this notion of requisite variety underlies popular approaches to success prescribed by writers such as *Tom Peters (1985)*. He presses managers to form a vision, a picture of a future state, and then reach that vision by undertaking hectic trial-and-error actions that satisfy criteria set by shared values and logical connection to the existing business.

Note how Ashby's law depends upon the proposition that it is enough to have the same number of responses as environmental shocks, not that each response to each shock has to be the right one. In other words, the mechanism is trial and error and all that is necessary is to get the level of speed of the trial and error right. What is the justification for this?

The justification is the law of large numbers, or probability. If large numbers of random shocks, or unforeseeable changes, keep hitting a system and if that system undertakes large numbers of basically random small trial actions in response, then obviously only some random actions will match some of the random shocks in the sense of being appropriate responses. Most will not but, because of the large numbers involved, the inappropriate responses will tend to cancel each other out – the law of large numbers. Provided that a system acts fast enough it will maintain stability and move towards its goal but only if shocks and responses are closely similar, or repetitive events of the kind obtained, for example, when a coin is tossed, where the result is always either heads or tails. It is only with large numbers of repetitive events that one can rely on the cancelling out of mismatches between random shocks and random actions because it is only then that the law of large numbers works.

It will be shown in Chapter 11 that a nonlinear feedback system may operate in conditions where no specific event is ever repeated in exactly the same way. The probability of any specific event occurring is therefore infinitely small. Each specific event is unique, falling only into general qualitative categories in which items bear a family resemblance to each other. An organisation does not typically get a large number of chances to repeat events that bear a family resemblance close enough to apply probability in even an approximate way.

Under these circumstances there is no guarantee that trial-and-error mismatches with random environmental shocks will cancel out. Large numbers of random actions, even within boundaries set by logical connection with the existing business and core values, cannot be relied on as a search technique that will take the business to its intended vision. Right at the outset, then, there is a problem in building a theory of organisational change on cybernetics.

## Cybernetics and causality

The law of requisite variety makes it unnecessary, according to the cybernetics tradition, to understand the internal feedback structures of the organisation and the environment. Let me explain.

Cyberneticists recognised that feedback means circular causality – event A causes event B which then causes event A. They argued that one can determine the direction this circular causality takes for any pair of events simply by observing which precedes which in a large number of cases. But when dealing with large numbers of interconnected pairs it all becomes too difficult. These internal structures are so complex that one cannot hope to understand them – they constitute a 'black box'. Note how an unquestioned assumption is being made here. Those arguing this position are assuming that there is always a specific cause for each specific outcome, the problem being that it is all too complex for us to understand. Chapter 11 will suggest that there is another way to tackle this difficulty: it may be impossible to reduce our understanding to specific cause-and-effect links because the links themselves are lost in the detail of what happens; the alternative is then to think in terms of patterns in the behaviour of systems as a whole.

The cyberneticists, however, argued that causal connections exist but one does not need to understand them because one can observe a particular type of disturbance impacting on a system and also can observe the outcome of that disturbance; that is, how the system responds. If the regulator has requisite variety, that is a large enough variety of responses to counteract the variety of disturbances, then it will normally respond to a particular type of disturbance in the same way. From large numbers of observations of such regularities statistical connections can be established between particular types of disturbance and particular organisational responses.

The importance of this notion of causal connection is that it allows the use of statistical techniques for control in a negative feedback way, despite system complexity so great that one cannot hope to understand it, at least according to the cyberneticists. What matters to them are pragmatic factors such as what is observed and what is done. It is not necessary to devote much energy to understanding and explaining, they claim, because observing and doing is what matters in a complex world. These writers were not concerned with the dynamic patterns of behaviour that organisations generated or with the complexities of the internal workings of the organisation. No importance was attached to perceptions of the patterns of behaviour generated by systems as a whole.

Note how the law of requisite variety and the view taken of complex causality amount to an assumption that the laws of large numbers, or probability, apply. Large numbers of random disturbances from the environment are to be offset by equally large numbers of responses from the organisation. But since one cannot know the complex causal relationship between these, according to cybernetic theory, it is necessary to rely on a process of cancelling out. Because causality is so complex one cannot determine exactly the right response for each disturbance, so some responses will be too weak and others too strong, but taken together the deviations from what is required should cancel out over large numbers.

Now, this is only possible if the disturbances and responses are not unique; that is, they do not take the form of a disturbance requiring one and only one response at a particular point in time if it is to be handled effectively in goal-seeking terms. If amplifying feedback could cause a tiny disturbance to escalate, then it would require an immediate response of exactly the right offsetting nature to stop this happening. If such escalation was not immediately stopped it could swamp the behaviour of the whole system – the cancelling out of inappropriate responses to disturbances would not occur. Without this cancelling out, the law of requisite variety would not be enough to secure control.

This assumption about uniqueness and large numbers is therefore of great significance to the view of control, a matter which I will be returning to in Chapter 9. There, it is shown that amplifying feedback raises problems for cybernetic ways of thinking about control.

Cybernetics, then, is an approach that seeks to control an organisation by using feedback without understanding the feedback structure of the organisation itself. It sees effective regulators as those that cause the system to be largely self-regulating, automatically handling the disturbances which the environment bombards it with. It sees effective regulators as those that maintain continual equilibrium with the environment. The result is stable behaviour, predictable in terms of probabilities of specific events and times.

These aspects of the cybernetic tradition have had an important impact on the prescriptions for designing management control and information systems.

The key points on organisational dynamics made by the cybernetics tradition are summarised in *Figure 2.5*. Whenever managers use planning, monitoring, reviewing and corrective action forms of control, they are making the same assumptions about the world as those made by cyberneticists. Whenever management consultants install such systems they too make the same assumptions. Whenever managers engage in trial-and-error actions in the belief that this will take them to an envisioned end-point

**FIGURE 2.5**    Cybernetics: main points on organisational dynamics

- Organisations are *goal-seeking*, *self-regulating* systems adapting to pre-given environments through negative feedback.
- Cybernetics thus takes a realist position on human knowing.
- The system is *recursive*. This means that it feeds back on itself to repeat its behaviour.
- It follows that causality is circular. However, although the causality is circular it is *linear*. Cybernetics does not take account of the effects of nonlinearity. Causal structures cannot be understood because they are too complex. However, regularities in the relationships between external disturbances and systems response can be statistically identified. Circular causality is thus recognised but then sidestepped by saying that it is too complicated to understand.
- Predictability of specific events and their timings is possible in a probabilistic sense. Disturbances coming from the environment are not primarily unique.
- Effective control requires forecasts and a control system that contains as much variety as the environment. Change must be probabilistic so that large numbers of random changes and random responses cancel out, otherwise unique small changes might amplify and swamp the system.
- No account is taken of positive, or amplifying, feedback. There is thus no possibility of small changes amplifying into major alterations.
- Behavioural patterns themselves, especially of the system as a whole, are not thought to be interesting enough to warrant special comment.
- The self-regulation process requires the system's actual behavioural outcomes to be compared with some representation of, or expectation about, its environment. There is an external point of reference according to which it is controlled. The system internally *represents* its environment and then responds to that representation.
- There is a clear boundary between system and environment, between inner and outer. Although the system is adapting to its environment, it is itself a closed system. It operates/changes with *reference to a fixed point at the boundary* with its environment.
- Its state is determined by flux in the environment expressed through the fixed point of reference. Instability comes from the environment.
- It is a homeostatic, or *equilibrium-seeking*, system.
- *History is not important* in that the current state of the system is not dependent upon the sequence of previous states, only on the 'error' registered at the regulator. The system does not evolve of its own accord. Any change must be designed outside the system and then installed.
- Effective organisations are self-regulating, an automatic mechanical failure flowing from the way the control system is structured.
- Success is a state of stability, consistency and harmony.

in a turbulent environment, that is whenever they implement the advice of *Peters & Waterman (1982)*, then they are assuming that the law of requisite variety is valid. The problem is that managers and consultants are normally not all that aware of what they are assuming. It is extremely important to be aware of these assumptions because if life in organisations diverges significantly from them, cybernetic systems will not work. For example, if unique tiny changes can escalate through amplifying feedback, a cybernetic system will no longer be able to self-regulate.

## 2.3   COGNITIVIST PSYCHOLOGY

The review of cybernetic theory in section 2.2 above has already brought out how cybernetics is a theory about human behaviour. It assumes that human beings are cybernetic entities and that they learn through an essentially negative feedback process. In fact, the development of cybernetic systems theory was closely associated with the development of cognitive science, or a cognitivist approach to human psychology. Furthermore, both cybernetics and cognitivism were closely associated with the development of computers. The central aim was to develop a science of mind.

In 1943, *McCulloch & Pitts (1943)* published an important paper in which they claimed that brain functioning and mental activity could be understood as logical operations. They held that the brain was a system of neurones that functioned according to logical processing principles. The brain was thought to be a deductive machine and this notion was applied to develop machines that could operate in the same way, namely computers. In essence, the claim was that human beings are cybernetic systems. So, a theory about the operation of the brain was fundamental to the development of computers and those computers then came to be taken as an analogy for brain functioning. Computers were developed to mimic what brains were thought to be and having done this the brain was then thought to be like a computer, an essentially circular argument.

The next significant development in cognitive science occurred in 1956 at two meetings in Cambridge when Simon, Chomsky, Minsky and McCarthy set major guidelines for the development of cognitive science (*Gardner, 1985*). Their central idea was that human intelligence resembles computation so much that cognition, that is human knowing, could be understood as a process of computing representations of reality, those representations being made in the form of symbols. So, just as computers process digital symbols so the human brain processes symbols taking the form of electrochemical activity in the brain. This is the central idea, just as it is with cybernetic systems. Humans are assumed to act on the basis of representations of their environment that are processes in their brains. Learning is a process of developing more and more accurate representations of external, pre-given reality utilising negative feedback processes.

*Bateson (1972)*, an important figure in the development of both cybernetics and cognitivism, distinguished between different levels of learning. He used the example of the central heating system already given in section 2.2 above. The central heating system itself is capable only of Learning Level 0; that is, no learning. The central heating system simply repeats its behaviour without change. It cannot change its own setting and so it cannot learn. He then used this example to demonstrate how a cybernetic system can be considered at a higher logical level. He introduced the resident into the room and the resident can, of course, change the temperature setting. Now the system consists of the resident and the central heating system and the environment is still, of course, the temperature in the room. The skin of the resident becomes part of the boundary of this larger system. When the skin of the resident registers an uncomfortably low temperature for a while, the resident turns the regulator setting up and the boiler is turned on. Later the resident may feel too warm and turn the setting down.

In a cognitivist approach to psychology the brain of the resident is seen to be a cybernetic device in much the same way as the heating system. Temperature variations are registered by sensing nerve cells in the skin and this perception is then represented in a specific part of the brain. The representation triggers the motor action of turning the setting on the thermometer up or down.

The structure of this larger system has changed in that the number of states it can move through is now much larger. The change in the total system is not due to one specific error, as it was before, but to a range of errors, that is a number of fluctuations that do not fit the resident's requirements. With one exception, stated below, the properties of this larger system are the same as for the logically lower system. Note particularly how there is still a fixed point of reference. The external environment is still internally represented, and the behaviour of the system is still determined by the flux of the environment as expressed through the fixed point of reference. From the perspective of the logically lower system, the heating system, the addition of the resident amounts to the appearance of an observer who can control it. The implicit assumption is that the move to a system of a higher logical level creates the observer position with regard to the system of the lower level. The one difference brought about by adding the resident to the system has to do with learning:

- The resident/heating system displays Learning Level 1 in that the resident changes the system by changing the setting, so increasing the number of alternatives open to the whole system. Note how this learning is error activated in that it is triggered by a gap between the resident's comfort level and his or her current experience.
- Furthermore, if the resident were to change his or her habits of altering the setting then the system would display Learning Level 2 because there is once more a widening of the range of alternatives open to the system. This level of learning is of a higher logical category in that it expands the range of Level 1 alternatives. Again, it is error activated in that the resident will change his or her habits because the old ones do not meet some required standard.
- The system could potentially display Learning Level 3, which expands the range of Level 2 alternatives. Bateson thought that humans very rarely achieved this level of learning and the examples he gave of it were religious conversion and personal change through psychotherapy.

What should be noted here is the importance of internal representations of the external environment and the error-activated nature of the learning process that cybernetics specifies. These are central assumptions in a cognitivist approach to psychology and they have enormous implications for how human agency, groups and organisations are understood.

Human beings are regarded, in this theory, as living cybernetic systems that can understand and control inanimate cybernetic systems. The implication is that an individual human can stand alone as a system. Implicit in a cybernetic approach to human affairs, then, is the assumption that humans are monads, that is autonomous individuals who can exist outside relationships with others. The individual is prior and primary to the group. Again, there is the assumption, dominant in Western thinking, of the primacy of the masterful, autonomous individual.

## The cognitivist perspective

From a cognitivist perspective, the brain is a network of neurones, each of which is connected to a number of other neurones. When any neurone receives a powerful enough electrochemical pulse from another, it is triggered into firing a pulse to yet other neurones it is connected to, and they in turn transmit further charges which trigger yet other neurones. Each neurone functions according to rules stipulating when to respond to an incoming impulse and when to transmit charges to particular other neurones. Neurones, therefore, transmit symbolic information, that is code in the form of pulses of electrochemical activity. The brain is thus a rule-driven mechanism that processes symbols that represent stimuli, more or less as a computer does. The notions of symbol and representation lie at the heart of the cognitivist perspective and in this perspective they have substantial ontological and epistemological implications. The main points are set out in *Figure 2.6*.

**FIGURE 2.6**   Cognitivism: main points on human knowing and behaving

- The brain processes symbols (electrochemical pulses) in a sequential manner to form representations of internal templates that are more or less accurate pictures of the world. This means that the brain is assumed to act as a passive mirror of reality. Furthermore, these mirror images are, according to cognitivists, stored in specific parts of the brain in the sense that a stimulus, say a particular light wave, would always trigger the same sequence of firing neurones. In other words, the same electrochemical pattern would be produced in a specific part of the brain when the body was presented with the same external stimulus.
- The world so pictured by the brain can be specified prior to any cognitive activity. This means that the world being perceived would have particular properties, such as light waves, and it would be these already existing real properties that would be directly registered by the brain. The world into which humans act is found, not created.
- The templates formed are the basis upon which a human being knows and acts. Repeated exposure to the same light wave would strengthen connections along a specific neuronal pathway, so making a perception a more and more accurate representation of reality. This would form the template, stored in a particular part of the brain, against which other light wave perceptions could be compared and categorised, forming the basis of the body's response. Representing and storing are, thus, essentially cybernetic processes. There is a fixed point of reference, external reality, and negative feedback of the gap between the internal picture and this external reality forms a self-

regulating process that closes this gap. Knowing, knowledge creation and learning are essentially adaptive feedback processes.

- There is a separate entity that does this representing and storing. This is a 'centred' theory in the sense that the biological individual is at the centre of the whole process of knowing and acting and also in the internal sense of processes centred in particular parts of the brain.
- Since all normal individuals have much the same biologically determined brain structures and all their brains are processing symbolic representations of the same pre-given reality, there is no fundamental problem in individuals sharing the same perceptions. The transmission of messages from one brain to another and the sharing of information between them simply do not pose significant questions.

## 2.4    BRIEF REVIEW: HOW CYBERNETICS AND COGNITIVISM DEAL WITH FOUR KEY QUESTIONS

In this section, I want to take a brief look at how cybernetics and cognitivism deal with the four questions posed at the end of Chapter 1.

### What kind of system does cybernetics posit?

First, the level of description of the system is at a macro level. The entities of which the system is composed are all the same. In other words, differences amongst the system entities are averaged out. Interactions between the entities are assumed to be average, or at least normally distributed around the average. This allows the cyberneticist to disregard the dynamics of interaction between entities of which the system is composed and concentrate on the system as a whole. What is then focused on are the regularities in the system's responses to changes in its environment. The system responds to differences between externally imposed goals and its actual behaviour. Or, it responds to differences between an expectation, or prediction, of some state it should achieve and what it actually does. In organisational terms, the focus of attention is on how the whole organisation responds to the actions of other whole organisations that constitute its environment. Little attention is paid to the differences in the people that belong to the organisation or the nature of their interactions with each other.

Second, the time span of concern is that over which the level of detail required for control is predictable. A cybernetic system's operation depends crucially on the ability to predict outcomes and time lags, or on the cancelling out of random changes.

Third, the dynamics, that is the kinds of movement over time displayed by the system, is that of an automatic move to stable equilibrium.

### What kind of understanding of human nature does cognitivism present?

Cognitivism is built on the assumption that the individual is primary and prior to the group. First, there are individuals who process symbolic representations of a pre-given world, building ever more accurate representations through the process of learning.

They arrive in the world with the inherited capacity to do this. Then there are groups composed of these autonomous individuals. The representations are of regularities extracted from behaving in an environment. They take the form of rules that govern behaviour. In later chapters I will refer to them as schemas, scripts, mental models, cognitive maps. When people use terms like these to describe how humans behave, they are making assumptions of a cognitivist kind.

From this perspective, human beings are essentially rational, logical animals. Emotion plays a rather unimportant part in how humans are held to behave. Also conspicuously absent is any notion that power and ideology structure relationships between people. There is no notion that unconscious processes might influence how people perceive and know anything.

Although the strategic choice theory to be reviewed in the next few chapters primarily assumes a cognitivist theory of human behaviour, it does take account of motivational factors in a particular way. The appeal then is humanistic psychology, represented by writers such as *Hertzberg, Mausuer & Snyderman (1959)* and *Maslow (1954)* who stress the emotional and inspirational factors required to motivate human beings. Maslow talks about the individual's need for self-actualisation. Humanistic psychology, however, retains the emphasis on the autonomous individual.

### What methodology underlies cybernetics and cognitivism?

Both cybernetics and cognitivism take a realist position on human knowing. In other words, they assume that there is a reality to be dealt with that exists before people perceive it. They take the traditional scientific perspective of looking for laws, or regularities, to explain behaviour. They seek to apply the principles of logic. In doing this they take the position of the objective observer who stands outside the system of interest and makes hypotheses about it. They build models of the system to guide behaviour. The emphasis is on the ability to control. No importance is attached to the notion that people may construct reality in their social interaction with each other. There is no notion of reflexivity and the position of understanding through participating.

### How do cybernetics and cognitivism deal with the possibly paradoxical nature of existence?

Little attention is paid in either of these theories to the possibility of paradox, that is the simultaneous presence of contradictory forces. Opposing forces would be seen as contradictions, conflicts, tensions or sequential alternatives.

### 2.5   SUMMARY

This chapter has reviewed the theory of cybernetic systems and the closely associated cognitivist theory of human behaviour. These theories are the foundations upon which the strategic choice theory of organisational change is built. Cybernetic systems depend upon the possibility of prediction over a long enough time period at a fine enough level of detail, if they are to achieve the control that is their central concern. Cognitivist psychology assumes that individuals are autonomous and that they learn in an essentially negative feedback manner. It heavily emphasises the logical capacities of the human being and it is these that enable choices to be made. These are central themes that run through strategic choice theory to which the next chapter turns.

## FURTHER READING

Richardson (1991) provides an excellent account of cybernetics and the use of feedback thinking about human systems. Baddeley (1990) provides a very good exposition of the cognitivist position and Varela, Thompson & Rosch (1995) provide a cogent critique of cognitivism.

## REFERENCES

Ashby, W. R. (1945), The effect of controls on stability, *Natura*, vol. 155, pp. 242–3.

Ashby, W. R. (1952), *Design for a Brain*, New York: John Wiley.

Ashby, W. R. (1956), *Introduction to Cybernetics*, New York: John Wiley.

Baddeley, A (1990), *Human Memory: Theory and Practice*, London: Lawrence Erlbaum.

Bateson, G. (1972), *Steps to an Ecology of Mind*, New York: Ballantine Books.

Beer, Stafford, (1959/67), *Cybernetics and Management*, London: English Universities Press.

Beer, Stafford, (1966), *Decision and Control: The Meaning of Operational Research and Management Cybernetics*, London: John Wiley.

Gardner, H. (1985), *The Mind's New Science: A History of the Cognitive Revolution*, New York: Basic Books.

Hertzberg, F., Mausuer & Snyderman (1959), *Work and the Nature of Man*, New York: John Wiley.

Maslow, A. (1954), *Motivation and Personality*, New York: Harper & Row.

McCulloch, W. S. & Pitts, W. (1943), A logical calculus of ideas imminent in nervous activity, *Bulletin of Mathematical Biophysics*, vol. 5.

Peters, T. J. (1985), *Thriving on Chaos*, New York: Macmillan.

Peters, T. J. & Waterman, R. H. (1982), *In Search of Excellence*, New York: Harper & Row.

Richardson, G. P. (1991), *Feedback Thought in Social Science and Systems Theory*, Philadelphia: University of Pennsylvania Press.

Varela, F. J., Thompson, E. & Rosch, E. (1995), *The Embodied Mind: Cognitive Science and Human Experience*, Cambridge, MA: MIT Press.

Wiener, N. (1948), *Cybernetics: Or Control and Communication in the Animal and the Machine*, Cambridge, MA: MIT Press.

# 3 Strategic choice

## Formulating the strategy

3.1 **INTRODUCTION**

Strategic choice theory makes a distinction between the formulation of a strategy and its implementation. Strategy here means a plan, that is a set of goals, the actions required to achieve the goals and forecasts of the consequences of those actions. The plan therefore plays the role of the externally set point of reference required for the operation of a cybernetic system. The plan is to the organisation what the setting of a target temperature is to the domestic heating system discussed in Chapter 2.

The plan is chosen by the most powerful individual in the organisation or by a small group of top executives. The choice is said to be made by individuals, displaying the cognitivist assumptions upon which this theory is based. The prescription is for this choice to be made following a rational sequence of logical steps, using rational evaluative criteria.

In the next chapter, I will review how a plan is supposed to be implemented. In both this and the next chapter, I will give a very brief outline of what the theory of strategic choice has to say and how it displays its theoretical foundations. The subject matter of these chapters could take a whole book and I will point to literature that goes into greater depth. I will summarise what the theory has to say with little critique, although of course the way I summarise it already expresses something of my opinion. In Chapter 8, I will express that opinion more explicitly.

The essence of strategic choice theory, I think, is that it assumes that it is possible for a powerful individual to stand outside his or her organisation and model it in the interest of controlling it. The theory assumes that organisations change successfully when the top executive forms the right intention for the overall future shape of the organisation and specifies in enough detail how this is to be achieved. It prescribes the prior design of change and then the installation of that change. Again, the cognitivist basis of this theory is clear. Autonomous individuals are assumed to be able to model their organisations from the position of the objective observer. Just as with any cybernetic systems, the ability to predict is crucial to the system's ability to cope as a cybernetic system.

## 3.2    LONG-TERM STRATEGIC PLANS

### Plans and planning

The words 'plans' and 'planning' are often used loosely by managers. For example, managers may say that they have a long-term plan simply because they have set out some long-term financial targets or because they have identified one or two specific actions that they intend to undertake, for example make an acquisition. Students of strategic management need to be more precise than this.

Managers can only be said to be planning the future of their organisation when, as a group, they share a common intention to achieve a particular future composition and level of performance for the business; that is, when they select aims and objectives for the business well in advance of acting. In addition to choosing a future state, managers must also share a common intention to pursue a sequence of actions to achieve that chosen future state, if their behaviour is to qualify as planned. Before managers can intentionally choose an intended state and an intended sequence of future actions, however, they have to identify the future environment in which they are to achieve their aims – their intentions must be anchored to a specific future reality. In other words, managers cannot possibly plan unless they can also make reasonably reliable forecasts of the future time period they are planning for. The future must not only be knowable, it must be sufficiently well known in advance of required performance. The time span and the level of detail must be that which produces the required performance.

In addition, to qualify as controlling and developing an organisation's long-term future in the planning mode, managers must set milestones along the path to the intended future state, couched in terms of results. This will enable the outcomes of actions to be checked and deviations from plan corrected. Action is both implementation of the planned sequence of actions and corrections to keep results on course. Only then is control being exercised in a planned manner. The ability to control by plan depends upon the possibility of establishing organisational intention  and making predictions at the appropriate level of detail over the relevant time span.

In order to formulate a long-term plan, managers must first identify and agree upon the performance levels, both financial and operational, that they are going to achieve by some point in the long-term future; that is, they must set the quantitative and qualitative objectives that they are going to strive for. Those objectives must satisfy the rational criteria of acceptability, feasibility and suitability that will be discussed below.

The second step in formulating a long-term plan is the specification of the future actions that will produce the performance objectives. However, before much can be said about appropriate actions for an organisation, it is necessary to find out something about the future environment in which they are to be taken; some are possible and successful in some environments but not in others. The requirement for success is that an organisation must be adapted to its environment. It follows that managers cannot plan future actions until they know something about what that environment will be.

Finding out about a future environment is a process of analysing the past and the present and then using that analysis as the basis for forecasting. Once managers know something about the nature of their future environment they can then deduce what alternative action options might deliver their performance objectives. The rational criteria of acceptability, feasibility and suitability, to be discussed below, must then be applied to evaluate each option and select that option which best satisfies the criteria. This becomes an organisation's strategy. An example of this kind of prescription is given in *Box 3.1*.

---

**BOX 3.1**

## Ansoff's strategic success hypothesis

*Ansoff (1990)* presents a strategic success hypothesis stating that a firm's performance will be optimal when:

- the aggressiveness of the sequence of actions undertaken by the firm matches the level of turbulence in its environment;
- the responsiveness of the firm's capability matches the aggressiveness of its actions;
- the elements of the firm's capability are supportive of one another.

Ansoff defines levels of turbulence in terms of rising levels of unpredictability and complexity and he distinguishes five levels: repetitive, expanding, changing, discontinuous and surprising.

Strategic aggressiveness is defined in terms of the size of the break with past strategies and the speed with which they are implemented. He identifies five levels of aggressiveness: stable, reactive, anticipatory, entrepreneurial and creative.

He then distinguishes five levels of capability responsiveness: custodial, which is precedent driven and suppresses change; production oriented, which is efficiency driven and adapts to change; marketing orientation, which is market driven and seeks familiar change; strategic, which is environment driven and seeks new change; flexible, which seeks to create the environment and seeks novel change.

Strategic logic means, for example, that flexible capability and creative action are required in surprising environments. Ansoff maintains that all these levels can be identified in advance of acting by strategic diagnosis. This amounts to a claim that there is always good enough predictability. ■

Having said something about the nature of planning, now consider the different kinds of planning that are prescribed for organisations. Since most organisations of any size consist of a collection of different activities organised into units, a distinction is drawn between corporate plans and business unit plans (*Hofer & Schendel, 1978; Porter, 1987*).

### The corporate plan

This is concerned with the actions that an organisation as a whole is to take. It is what is supposed to make the whole add up to more than the sum of its parts, a phenomenon known as synergy. The justification for grouping a number of related activities together, rather than having them operate as separate organisations, lies in the value that the corporate level adds. And it adds value by reaping synergies and by coordinating and making the parts consistent.

Corporate strategy is concerned with what activities or businesses the organisation should be involved in and how the corporate level should manage that set of businesses. In other words, corporate strategy is about a portfolio of businesses and what should be done with them. The key question for corporate strategy is: what collection of activities must be put together, and how should this collection be managed to achieve corporate objectives set by shareholders?

### Business unit plans

A business unit plan sets out how a business unit is going to build a market position that is superior to that of its rivals, so enabling it to achieve the performance objectives set by the corporate level. In other words, business unit strategy is about the means of securing and sustaining competitive advantage. The key question for business unit strategy is: how is competitive advantage to be secured so as to achieve the objectives set by the corporation?

Finally, since business units are generally organised on a functional basis – finance, sales, production and research departments, for example – the business unit strategy will have to be translated into functional or operational strategies.

### Functional and operational plans

These set out the actions that a function is to take to contribute to the whole strategy of the business unit, just as the business unit strategy contributes to the corporate one. The key question for functional plans is: what actions must be taken to contribute an appropriate share to the business unit plan?

The result is a hierarchy of long-term objectives and plans, the corporate creating the framework for the business unit, and the business unit creating the framework for the functional. Furthermore, this collection of long-term plans provides the framework for formulating shorter-term plans and budgets against which an organisation can be controlled in the short term.

The question to address now is how managers at whatever level are supposed to select the plans that will lead them to success. The prescribed way of selecting successful plans is to use analytical criteria to evaluate the options.

Evaluation criteria are intended to enable managers to conclude whether or not a particular sequence of actions will lead to a particular future state that will produce some target measure of performance. The criteria are there to enable managers to form judgements about the outcomes of their proposed actions before they take those actions; that is, judgements as to whether a choice of strategy is likely to turn out to be a good one before they do anything at all to implement it. The purpose is to prevent surprises and ensure that an organisation behaves over long time periods in a manner intended by its members and leaders. There are three very widely proposed sets of criteria for doing this:

1   acceptibility or desirability
2   feasibility
3   suitability, or fit.

Each of these will be briefly reviewed in the following sections.

## 3.3   ACCEPTABILITY OF LONG-TERM STRATEGIC PLANS

There are at least three senses, it is argued, in which strategies have to be acceptable if they are to produce success. First, performance in financial terms must be acceptable to owners and creditors. Second, the consequences of the strategies for the most powerful groupings within an organisation must be acceptable to those groupings in terms of their expectations and the impact on their power positions and cultural beliefs. Third, the consequences of the strategies for powerful groups external to an organisation must be acceptable to those groupings. Consider what each of these senses entails.

### Acceptable financial performance

If they are to be successful, managers must determine in advance of acting whether their long-term plans are likely to turn out to be financially acceptable. They are supposed to determine this by forecasting the financial consequences of each strategic option open to them: cash flows, capital expenditures and other costs, sales volumes, price levels, profit levels, assets and liabilities including borrowing and other funding requirements. Next, managers are supposed to use the forecasts to calculate prospective rates of return on sales and capital. A rate of return is calculated by expressing some measure of profit as a percentage of some measure of the sales that yield that profit or the assets used in generating it.

However, complexities arise because it is possible to define profits and assets in many different ways. Managers may be interested in profits before tax or after tax, before allowing for the depreciation of assets or after depreciation, before interest paid on loans or after interest. They may be interested in total assets employed or in net assets employed, that is after deducting amounts owed by the organisation. They may be interested in fixed assets (land, buildings, plant and machinery) or variable assets such as inventories and debtors. There are therefore many different rates of return on sales and capital and the one used depends upon the purpose of use and also on accounting conventions.

No matter what particular rate of return is selected, there will be many difficulties of measurement to be overcome. For example, it may be difficult to measure just how much of an asset has been used up in a particular period of use – the problem of measuring depreciation. Or it is often difficult to know how to allocate the costs of the corporate level of management to the business units.

### Acceptable financial performance in not-for-profit organisations

Acceptable financial performance is a relative concept and is defined in terms of the next best opportunity open to the owners of an organisation for using or investing their funds. In the case of state and not-for-profit organisations those alternatives are established through political choices and those choices depend upon the relative power of people interested in the choice.

In 1991, the UK government decided to permit British Rail to build a Channel Tunnel rail link to pass through east London rather than south London. The reason for choosing an eastern rather than a southern route was most probably because the pressure groups of people living in the east are far less powerful than the pressure groups of the much more affluent inhabitants of the southern parts of the city. Furthermore, the decision to invest government funds in this project constituted a choice not to use those funds to build, say, a refuge for the homeless. Again that choice reflected the relative power positions of industry that wanted the rail link and the homeless who needed somewhere to live.

Although the alternative uses of funds in state and not-for-profit bodies are inevitably the result of political decisions, those who wish to apply a more scientific approach prescribe the use of analytical techniques to identify and compare the costs and benefits of alternative political choices. The argument is that, even if at the end of the day the choice is made on the basis of relative power, those making the choice should at least be aware of what the costs will be of the benefits provided by each option open to them. The method for doing this is cost/benefit analysis.

- **Cost/benefit analysis.** Cost/benefit analysis (*Rowe, Mason, Dickel & Snyder, 1989; Mirsham, 1980*) attempts to place money values on all the costs and benefits of a particular strategic action option. The difficulty lies in the fact that state bodies and not-for-profit organisations are particularly concerned with intangible, non-traded costs and benefits. The analysis therefore involves many subjective judgements upon which there is likely to be disagreement that cannot be resolved by rational argument. In the end the decision has to be made by political processes of persuasion and conversion, or even force. The analysis is there to aid this process by making the factors that need to be taken into account explicit and by creating the appearance of rationality. This appearance of rationality can be instrumental in persuading people to accept a particular choice and it legitimises the decision, in effect giving it a seal of 'scientific' approval even though such rationality was not actually used to make the choice.

### Acceptable financial performance in commercial organisations

Now consider organisations in the business sector, where the ability to measure and value costs and benefits is far greater. But bear in mind that, even there, that ability to measure is far from perfect. The following are some important ways of measuring the acceptability of financial performance.

- **Performance benchmarks.** Over the long term it is the operators on the capital markets who will judge whether the performance of a business is acceptable or not and they will do so in terms of the financial return on their investment. The exception to this is family-owned private companies, where alternative investment opportunities are also determined by the capital markets, but where the shareholders have the freedom to choose some definition of acceptability other than financial return. Companies that persistently fail to achieve rates of return on assets and rates of growth in profit levels that are acceptable in these terms, and that are comparable with similar kinds of businesses, will be prime candidates for takeovers. Similar kinds of companies, therefore, provide benchmark performance measures.

- **Gap analysis.** Benchmark performance measures may be used to perform what is called gap analysis (*Argenti, 1980*). To carry out a gap analysis, the performance of a company is first projected on the basis that it continues to follow existing policies. The resulting levels of profitability, rates of return and rates of profit growth are then compared with the benchmarks and the gap between them calculated. That gap measures the contribution that will be required from the development of new strategies. It is these new strategies that must fill the gap between what is acceptable and what is likely from continuing to run the business as before. Whether a set of strategies fills the gap or not becomes a criterion for successful strategy selection. *Box 3.2* gives an example of how gap analysis is used.

---

**BOX 3.2**

## Use of gap analysis

Suppose the corporate level of a pharmaceutical company sets growth rate objectives for one of its divisions. It requires the division to achieve annual growth rates of 10 per cent in sales and 15 per cent in pre-tax profits for the next five years. The division carefully examines its product portfolio and concludes that two of its major product lines – call them X and Z – will be coming off patent towards the end of the five-year period, opening up the way for inevitable competition and loss of market share. The remaining product lines, C and D, are old ones unlikely to grow at all. The divisional managers then examine the new product development portfolio and conclude that there is no way in which new products coming on stream, E and F, could compensate for the lack of growth in revenues and profits from the existing product portfolio. It is now possible to quantify the negative gap between the corporately set objective for the division and the outcome likely to be generated by existing and new product portfolios by the end of the five-year period.

Divisional management conclude that in order to plug the gap they will have to adopt a strategy of acquiring products and/or companies. A divisional long-term plan is put together, setting out the objectives, the financial projections and the general strategy of acquisition. Here analysis of the gap between what is required and what is likely prompts plans to close the gap. ■

- **Financial models and scenarios.** Such corporate models can then be used to simulate the future of the corporation on the basis of different scenarios (*Cooke & Slack, 1984; Shim & McGlade, 1984; Beck, 1982, Rowe, Mason, Dickel & Snyder, 1989*). The use of scenarios involves specifying a number of different possible future environments for a company. Key variables specified by each of these scenarios, for example the rate of growth in the volume of market demand, are then plugged into the corporate model. The performance of the company is thereby simulated for each of the possible scenarios. This is done to assist managers to decide in advance whether a particular set of strategies is likely to result in acceptable performance or not. Simulating the performance of the company in different scenarios for the future allows different calculations of the performance gap.

- **Investment appraisal techniques.** So far the concern has been with evaluating the impact of possible strategies on the financial performance of a corporation as a whole. In addition, each of the specific elements of any strategy, that is each of the investment projects required to put it in place, also has to meet criteria of acceptability. There are a number of techniques of investment appraisal available to test whether individual projects meet the requirements of acceptable return:

  - *Payback period.* This is simply the period of time it takes to pay back the original investment.
  - *Average rate of return.* Here the profit level in the first full year of operation is estimated and used to calculate the rate of return that this represents on the original investment.
  - *Discounted cash flow analysis.* The drawback of the payback and the average rate of return methods is that they do not take account of the fact that money in the hand today is worth more than a promise of money tomorrow – if you have money today you can invest it and earn interest on it. Discounted cash flow methods meet this objection by discounting all the cash flows back to the present, using some appropriate interest rate. The difficulty of forecasting cash flows and interest rates for many years ahead is recognised by those who use that approach. Most therefore make calculations for a number of different scenarios of the environment in which an investment project may operate. Practical difficulties arise as the number of different scenarios increases. The number of scenarios required in practice to cover the most likely eventualities usually turns out to be so large that managers lose track of what they all mean. The experts preparing the scenarios and simulations end up making literally hundreds of small assumptions about prices, volumes, costs and many other matters. These are so numerous that the line managers who have to take the decision cannot be aware of what they all are. The result can be confusion as to the reasons why an investment is being undertaken. There is also, in common with cost/benefit analysis, the difficulty of incorporating important intangible, difficult-to-measure value elements.

- **Risk and sensitivity analysis.** The use of scenarios and simulations at both total corporate and specific investment project levels allows sensitivity analyses to be performed. The purpose of these analyses is to identify those variables to which performance is particularly sensitive. So a particular company, or a particular investment project, may not be all that sensitive to changes in the exchange rate, but it may be highly sensitive to changes in regulations on pollution control. Sensitivity analysis allows managers to gain some idea of how serious a change in some variable, such as the interest rate, will be for the future performance of an investment or for the corporation as a whole.

- **Financial ratios.** There are a number of indicators of the level of financial risk that are used to make judgements about the acceptability or otherwise of performance in financial terms. These indicators take the form of financial ratios and the following are among the most important:
  - *Gearing ratios.* A gearing ratio is a measure of how heavily or otherwise an organisation depends on borrowed funds. It is the ratio of some measure of borrowing to some measure of shareholders' funds. Whether this is too high or too low, and therefore whether it is particularly risky or not, is a matter of judgement by operators in the capital markets. Another measure of exposure to borrowing is provided by the ratio of profits to interest paid, a measure known as interest cover.
  - *Liquidity ratios.* Liquidity ratios provide a measure of how quickly an organisation could realise its assets. Obviously, the faster it can turn its assets into cash the more easily it will be able to deal with any financial crisis that occurs. The most liquid asset is of course cash and therefore the cash ratio is a prime measure of liquidity. This is calculated as the percentage of total assets that are in the form of bank deposits, or capital market instruments such as bonds.
  - *Inventory turnover.* This is a measure of how many times a year the inventories of a business are realised.

So much for determining whether plans will produce financial performance acceptable to shareholders and creditors in terms of both risk and reward levels. Even if plans pass this test, however, they must still pass others – they must meet the expectations of those with power in an organisation.

## Acceptable consequences for internal power groups

In addition to financial risk and reward, long-term plans have other consequences for people within an organisation. If carried out, strategic plans may well change the way people work, who they work with, what relative power they have, how they are judged by others and so on. Long-term plans could produce consequences that people believe to be morally repugnant or against their customs and beliefs in some other way. If this is the case, those plans are unlikely to succeed because people will do their best to prevent the plan being implemented. Managers must therefore submit their long-term plans to another acceptability test: they must analyse the impact of their plans on the expectations, relative power positions, and cultural beliefs of key individuals and groups within the organisation. *Box 3.3* gives an example of how managers rejected what they had calculated to be the most acceptable option in financial terms, because it conflicted with the expectations of some key individuals. Consider now what must be analysed

- **Organisational culture.** The culture of any group of people is that set of beliefs, customs, practices and way of thinking that they have come to share with each other through being and working together. It is a set of assumptions people simply accept without question as they interact with each other. In order to determine whether a plan is likely to be acceptable in cultural terms it is necessary to analyse

**BOX 3.3**

## Castings plc

Some 15 months ago Castings plc acquired a company in Colchester which produces castings using three processes:

1  sand/Shaw where wooden patterns are used to make ceramic moulds for the casting;
2  lost wax where metal moulds are filled with wax and the ferrous casting subsequently made from the wax shape;
3  lost wax used to manufacture aluminium castings.

The customers for the Colchester factory's products, large companies in the aerospace and general engineering industries, demand high-precision castings at low prices. Demand for product from the lost wax process has been growing rapidly as customers turn to the higher quality and lower cost that this process gives compared to sand/Shaw or machining. Although sand/Shaw is therefore on the wane, it is still cheaper for short runs.

When it acquired the Colchester factory, Castings plc already had another ferrous casting business using lost wax. This is located at Peterborough and it makes higher-volume less complicated castings than the new acquisition. Another Castings plc business uses lost wax to cast aluminium and it is located at Leicester. These are both very profitable businesses.

Over the first year the newly acquired company with sales of under £2m incurred a £0.5m loss. Losses over the first three months of this financial year have been stemmed, but not reversed. Now the landlord has given notice that the premises occupied by the acquisition must be vacated in nine months' time.

The board of Castings therefore considered the options open to it. The Finance Director prepared a schedule showing the sales, costs, profits and rates of return of a number of options as follows:

1  Relocating the Colchester factory to a nearby site would yield an average return on capital (ROC) for the next five years of minus 4.8 per cent.
2  Relocating the sand/Shaw business at Colchester to a nearby site, moving the lost wax ferrous business to Peterborough and the aluminium to Leicester would yield a five-year average ROC of 9.1 per cent.
3  Moving everything to Peterborough would yield a five-year average ROC of 20.9 per cent.
4  Closing Colchester down would yield a five-year average ROC of minus 0.1 per cent.

Despite the high rate of return to be gained from concentrating the whole business at Peterborough the board chose option 2. They did this because they knew that the managers of the successful Peterborough business did not want ▶

to have to deal with the problem of a declining sand/Shaw business. They would be distracted from their own profitable business. Furthermore, key personnel at Colchester would probably not move and therefore would be lost to the company. Customers too might be disaffected by the change in location. Perhaps most important of all, although it was hardly discussed at the board meeting, was the impact closure would have on operators on the stock market. The closure of Colchester would have to be made public, amounting to an admission of failure on the part of Castings plc board members who had promoted the acquisition in the first place.

The option chosen therefore met a number of people's non-financial expectations, even though it was not the best financial option according to the prescribed way of making that calculation. ∎

peoples' shared beliefs. Analysis of the culture will reveal whether options being considered fall within that culture or whether they require major cultural change. One would not necessarily reject options that require major cultural change, but then plans to bring this about would have to be formulated – a matter to be discussed in Chapter 6. The nature of an organisation's culture can be analysed by studying the stories people in that organisation tell. For example, there may be well-known stories about the organisation's founder or other memorable leaders that are always told to new joiners. The story is a way of emphasising one of the rules that all accept.

- **Power structure**. It will also be necessary to analyse the power structure of an organisation to determine whether plans are likely to be acceptable. Power flows from relationships, built up over time, between individuals and groups that determine how one affects or responds to another in making organisational choices. Power enables one person or group to force or persuade another to do something that the other does not want to do, or could not otherwise do, or would not otherwise have thought of doing. The sources of power lie in:
  - *Sanctions*. Power increases with the ability of one person or group to reward or punish another in terms of prestige, status, money or career progression.
  - *Interdependence*. One individual or group is relatively more powerful than another if it: controls more resources; has greater access to information; performs critical activities upon which the others depend for their performance; has greater access to communication channels or the more powerful; has control over communication agendas or the decision-making situations.
  - *Contribution*. Relative power increases with the personal skills and expertise of particular individuals and their ability to interpret ambiguous situations and so reduce uncertainty for others.

The source of power has much to do with the form it takes. Power can take the form of authority when it is exercised and consented to because of hierarchical position and because of the rules and regulations of the organisation. Or power can take the form of influence where it is based on interdependence between people and the contributions they make to common endeavours. Or, power can take the form of force.

Having analysed the source and form of power, the strategist has to identify its location and that means identifying the dominant coalitions in the organisation. This may be difficult because the power structure does not necessarily accord with the formal hierarchy – it will be necessary to identify which individuals and groups exercise influence even though they have less authority. It will be necessary to look for potential alliances between coalitions. *Box 3.4* gives some examples of how the power structure affects the acceptability of strategies.

### BOX 3.4
## Power and the acceptability of strategies

Some strategies will require large injections of funds that can only be obtained by the issue of new shares. This may weaken the control of particularly powerful shareholders, making the strategies unacceptable to them despite acceptable financial performance. Where the ownership of a company is concentrated in the hands of one or two individuals, then acceptability to those individuals in personal power or other terms may count for much more than acceptable performance. So the owner may tolerate below-average performance for years because it is found unacceptable to replace relatives in key positions.

It is not just acceptability to owners that counts. Some strategies may be unacceptable to a powerful subsidiary of one division of a corporation because it will undermine that division's power position in the corporation. Suppose a relatively small division proposes to expand its activities from its domestic base to foreign countries. If this is unacceptable to a larger, more powerful division already operating in foreign markets, the strategy could well fail for this reason alone. The battles between these two divisions could lead to failure as attention is diverted from the markets. Or, to take another example, for reasons that have little to do with performance, a powerful chairman may have certain preferences. For example, this chairman may favour the expansion of a house-building subsidiary because his son runs it. Because that subsidiary will require substantial investment, the chairman may be against diversification. Attempts to pursue diversification strategies are then unlikely to succeed. ■

### Acceptable consequences for external power groups

Power groups outside an organisation also determine the acceptability of that organisation's strategies. A community pressure group may find the noise level of a proposed factory expansion unacceptable. Even if the factory itself turns out to be a financially acceptable investment, the total consequences for the image of the corporation could render the strategy unsuccessful. Another example is provided by the electricity and gas industries in the UK. To succeed, strategies of companies in these sectors have to be acceptable to the industry regulators and consumer pressure groups. A further example is where the strategies of one organisation could have damaging consequences for the distributors of that organisation's products or for the suppliers to that organisation. Such damage could provoke those distributors and suppliers to retaliate in highly detrimental ways, as shown in *Box 3.5*.

---

**BOX 3.5**

## Kitchen Queen

In the 1970s a small company distributing fitted kitchens was set up in Manchester – Kitchen Queen. This company grew rapidly for a number of years because of its policy of advertising and displaying quality fitted kitchens, supporting the product with design and installation services and meeting reliable delivery time criteria. After some years of rapid growth, it was floated on the stock market and then pursued a policy of diversification. It purchased Di Lussio, a firm producing DIY flat-pack fitted kitchens of a high quality. By this move Kitchen Queen diversified into production and the profitability of Di Lussio relied on its distributors, competitors to the original Kitchen Queen business. The distributors were thus an important power group outside Kitchen Queen and the strategy of the latter would have to be in some sense acceptable to those distributors.

The acquisition worked and before long the production activity of the Kitchen Queen Group was generating most of the profit. Then a number of further diversifications were undertaken, including the purchase of a mail order company. The decision was then made to distribute all of Di Lussio's product through the mail order acquisition. When the distributors got wind of this they cancelled all their orders and dumped all their stocks of Di Lussio product onto the market at very low prices. This was one of the major causes of Kitchen Queen's bankruptcy not long afterwards. ■

*Source:* Kitchen Queen Case Study, Case Clearing House, Cranfield

---

The reactions of competitors to strategies are also of major importance. Some strategies pursued by one company could provoke more than normal competitive responses from competitors. Those competitors may regard the strategies of the first company as unfair competition and this could lead to price wars, hostile mergers, lobbying of the national political institutions, all of which could cause a strategy to fail. For example, North American and European countries have passed laws against imports from Japanese competitors or insisted on voluntary restraints.

Analysis may show that strategies are likely to be acceptable in terms of financial performance, and to major power groupings both within and outside an organisation, but yet fail because they are not feasible. To be feasible there must be no insurmountable obstacle to implementing a strategy. Such obstacles could be presented by:

- **Feasibility and financial resources.** One of the immediately obvious resources that must be available if a strategy is to be carried out is the money to finance the strategy over its whole life. If a company gets half-way through a strategy, which is on target to yield acceptable performance, but nevertheless runs out of the funds to continue, then clearly the strategy will fail. The prescription is therefore to carry out a flow-of-funds analysis of the strategy options, before embarking on any of them, to ascertain the probability of running into cash flow problems. A flow-of-funds analysis identifies the timing and size of the capital expenditures and other costs required for each project that makes up the strategy, and the timing and size of the revenues that those projects will generate. A flow-of-funds analysis makes it possible to calculate this break-even point, where a project, a set of projects constituting a strategy, or a corporation as a whole makes neither a loss nor a profit. What managers should do, therefore, to establish the feasibility of their strategy is to calculate the flows-of-funds and the break-even points for different strategic options in different scenarios. This will help them to identify the financing requirements for their strategy, the timing of those requirements, and the key conditions required for the move out of any initially negative cash flow situation.

- **Feasibility and the product life cycle.** To be feasible in market terms a strategy must take account of the stages in the product life cycle. Most products seem to follow a typical evolutionary pattern.
  - An *embryonic* stage in which the product is developed. Here market growth potential may be great but it will be very uncertain.
  - A *growth* stage in which rapid market growth materialises, attracting other competitors.
  - A *shake-out* stage in which some of the competitors who entered find that they cannot compete and therefore leave.
  - A *mature* stage in which growth in the demand for the product slows and a small number of competitors come to dominate the market.
  - A *saturation* stage in which demand for the product stabilises and competitors have difficulty in filling their capacity.
  - A *decline* stage in which demand begins to switch to substitute products.

These stages in the evolution of a product indicate different general types of strategies – different generic strategies. Which of these generic strategies is appropriate is said to be dependent upon the stage of evolution of the product's market and the competitive strength of the company producing it. So a company with a strong capability should invest heavily in the embryonic stage and establish a position before others arrive. During the growth phase it should continue investing, push for rapid growth, and so defend its strong position against new arrivals. By the time the mature phase is reached, this company should have established market leadership and, as the product gets to saturation level, the aging stage, the dominant company should defend its position but withdraw cash from the business. In a declining market it will be able to continue harvesting cash, while weaker competitors withdraw.

- **Feasibility and the experience curve.** The idea of the experience curve is based on the observation that the higher the volume of a particular product that a company produces, the more efficient it becomes at producing it. The cost per unit therefore declines as volume increases, at first rapidly and then more slowly as the learning opportunities for that particular product are exhausted. As a company moves down the learning curve it is in a position to reduce the price it charges customers for the product because its costs are falling. These price and cost curves can be linked to the idea of a product life cycle and the different strategies that strong and weak competitors should pursue. In the early stages of product evolution, a strong competitor will achieve higher volumes than a weak one and so move further down the learning curve. This will enable the strong competitor to reduce prices faster, stimulating demand and so increasing volumes even more to move even faster down the learning curve. Soon, the weaker competitor, or the latecomer, will have no chance of catching up.

- **Feasibility and the product portfolio.** The earliest and simplest form of product portfolio analysis is the Boston Consulting Group (BCG) growth share matrix (*Henderson, 1970*). To analyse their organisation in this way, managers review their whole business, dividing it up into all its different products, or market segments, or business units. They then calculate the market share they hold for each product, or market segment, or business unit, and then divide it by the share of their nearest rival. This is then the relative market share of that product, segment or business. If the relative share is much greater than 1, then the firm is dominant in that market. If the relative share is well below 1, then the firm is very weak in terms of competitive capability. The relative market share provides a measure of the firm's competitive capability with regard to that product, segment or business unit, because a high market share indicates that the firm is well down the experience curve compared with rivals. Next managers must calculate the rate of growth of the product demand or market segment. The rate of growth is held to be a good measure of the attractiveness of the market – the stage in its evolution that it has reached. Rapid rates of growth indicate the entrepreneurial and growth stages of evolution. Different combinations of market share and growth rates yield the following possibilities:

  - *Question marks* are products, market segments or business units that are growing rapidly, and the company has a relatively low share. The product life cycle and the experience curve analysis indicate that question marks will require heavy investment, are unlikely to yield profit for some time, and may face strong competitors.

  - *Stars* are products, markets or businesses that are growing rapidly, and the firm has a high relative share. Product life cycle and experience curve analysis indicate that these products will require heavy investment (negative cash flow) but may produce high levels of profit. The strategy indicated is one of concentrating effort and money on the stars.

- *Cash cows* are products in mature slow-growth markets in which the firm has a relatively high market share. The prescription is to cut down on investment in these products and harvest the cash.
- *Dogs* are products in slowly growing markets in which the firm has a low share. Both cash flow and profit could be negative. It is in a weak position and the firm should therefore withdraw.

The feasible options will be those that have some balance between the different possibilities. If a firm has enough cash cows, it will be able to use the money milked from those businesses to support the stars and perhaps try to develop some of the question marks. It can sell dogs and use the money so raised for the same purposes. An unbalanced portfolio – too many stars and not enough cows, for example – will mean that the company either has to borrow heavily or will generate big cash surpluses without knowing what to invest them in.

- **Feasibility and human resources.** In addition to financial resources, the availability of the right quality of skilled people will also be a major determinant of the feasibility of strategic options. This makes it necessary for managers to audit the human resources inside their organisation, those available outside, and the availability of training resources to improve the skills of people.

The techniques just discussed to identify financial feasibility also clearly have other messages about feasibility too. For example, it will not be feasible to enter a market already dominated by a low-cost producer, unless the focus is to be on a small niche and the strategy is one of differentiation. Product portfolios, life cycles and experience curves indicate relative market power and in doing so say something about feasibility from a market perspective as well as a financial one.

Consider now the third criterion for the evaluation and selection of successful strategies.

## 3.5    SUITABILITY OR FIT: ADAPTING TO THE ENVIRONMENT

Having established that their strategies are acceptable and feasible, the next hurdle managers must cross to achieve success is that of demonstrating that those strategies have a *strategic logic*. Strategic logic means that a proposed sequence of actions is consistently related to the objectives of the organisation on the one hand and matches the organisation's capability (including its structure, control systems and culture) to its environment on the other. The idea is that all the pieces of the strategic puzzle should fit together in a predetermined manner – the pieces should be *congruent*. When this happens we can say that the strategies fit, that they are suitable. The prescription is to use analytical techniques to determine the strategic logic of a sequence of actions, how all the pieces do or do not fit together (*Hofer & Schendel, 1978*). The analytic techniques available to do this are:

- **SWOT analysis.** This is a list of an organisation's strengths and weaknesses indicated by an analysis of its resources and capabilities, plus a list of the opportunities and threats that an analysis of its environment identifies. Strategic logic obviously requires that the future pattern of actions to be taken should match strengths with opportunities, ward off threats, and seek to overcome weaknesses.

- **Industry structure and value chain analysis.** *Michael Porter (1980, 1985)* has put the classical economic theories of market form into a framework for analysing the nature of competitive advantage in a market and the power of a company in that market, as well as the value chain of the company. These analytical techniques identify key aspects determining the relative market power of an organisation and its ability to sustain excess profits. Strategic logic entails taking actions that are consistent with and match the nature of the organisation's market power. Industry structure is held to determine what the predominant form of competitive advantage, and thus the level of profit, is. Some market structures mean that sustainable competitive advantage can be secured only through cost leadership strategies. Other structures mean that competitive advantage flows from differentiation. Strategic logic means matching actions to those required to secure competitive advantage. Value chain analysis identifies the points in the chain of activity from raw material to consumer that are crucial to competitive advantage. Since these market structure and value chain techniques have attracted widespread attention and appear in most textbooks on strategy, I will say no more about them here.

## Contingency theory

The development of contingency theory was a reaction against the idea that there is 'one best way' in management. At the time it was developed that 'one best way' was scientific management, management by objectives (MBO) and related sets of prescriptions. Contingency theory substitutes the 'it all depends' approach for the 'one best way'. The approach derived from empirical research (*Burns & Stalker, 1961; Woodward, 1965; Lawrence & Lorsch, 1967*) which showed that success was not correlated with a simple single set of factors. Instead, the effectiveness of a particular organisational structure, culture or sequence of actions is contingent upon – depends upon – a number of factors. The most important of these contingency factors are usually held to be:

- the environment, particularly the market
- the size of the organisation
- the technology it employs
- the history of the organisation
- the expectations of employees and customers.

The theory states that success will be secured when an organisation secures a good match between its situation and its strategies and structures. For example, mechanistic bureaucracies are said to be appropriate for stable environments, but flexible, organic structures are required for turbulent environments. *Child (1984)* summarises the theory as follows:

Contingency theory regards the design of an effective organisation as necessarily having to be adapted to cope with the 'contingencies' which derive from the circumstances of environment, technology, scale, resources and other factors in the situation in which the organisation is operating.

Contingency is thus a theory about the nature of cause and effect. It makes statements like these: if an organisation is operating in an environment that is very complex and changing rapidly, then it requires organic forms of organisation to succeed. If, however, it operates in simple, slow-moving environments, then it requires mechanistic structures to succeed. If an organisation is small, then it requires a simple structure. If an organisation is large, then it requires a divisionalised structure.

Contingency theory postulates a complex web of interconnections between the features of organisations and their environments in which the causal connections are linear in the sense that they run in one direction. It is a particular environment that causes a particular kind of successful strategy and that causes a particular kind of successful structure. The theory does not contemplate circular causation in which the structures of organisations cause them to follow certain strategies which then create certain kinds of environment to which they respond.

Contingency theory is based on the assumption that approximately the same cause will have approximately the same effect. It does not envisage escalation in which a tiny difference between two causes leads to two completely different outcomes. It does not, for example, allow for the possibility that two organisations operating in the same environment may develop in totally different directions simply because one gained a slightly bigger market share than the other in a particular product line at a particular point in time.

By making particular assumptions about the nature of cause and effect, contingency theory is making particular assumptions about the dynamics of organisations. Success is assumed to be a state of equilibrium and, because they are close to equilibrium, the future time paths of successful organisations are predictable. These are all assumptions that are open to question, as we shall see in Chapters 11 and 12.

The contingency concept, and its consequent prescription of consistency and congruence, runs in terms of a large number of different combinations of strategies, structures, cultures and so on, each suited to a particular environment and a particular set of objectives at a particular time. Organisations then adopt whichever of these satisfies the consistency criteria. One has to specify the circumstances rather precisely before one can identify the appropriate combination of strategy, structure and so on. On the other hand, the configuration approach, to which I now turn, tries to identify a relatively small number of typical combinations of strategies, structures and so on, into which we can classify most organisations.

## Configuration

The concept of configuration is a development of the ideas of contingency and congruence. Whereas contingency theory adopts an 'it all depends' approach, configuration is concerned with 'getting it all together' (*Mintzberg, 1989*). A configuration is some typical constellation of structural, cultural, strategy pattern, control system features and other organisational factors appropriate to a particular environment. In other words, a particular configuration is one of a limited number of categories, based on many interrelated and mutually supportive features, into which we can classify organisations. A configuration therefore describes a typical or archetypal organisational system.

**BOX 3.6**

# Examples of configuration

*Miller (1986)* describes four configurations:

1 Small firms operating in niche markets with simple structures in fragmented industries.
2 Large machine bureaucracies operating in stable concentrated industries with high entry barriers pursuing cost leadership strategies.
3 Organic adhocracies where the strategy is differentiation through innovation in embryonic or growth industries.
4 Large companies pursuing diversification strategies in mature industries with divisionalised conglomerate structures. ■

According to the configuration approach, examples of which are given in *Box 3.6*, success flows from selecting and designing an organisation and its strategies from a fairly limited number of archetypes. Empirical studies have been undertaken (reviewed in *Miller, 1986*) to demonstrate the following propositions:

1 There are only a limited number of possible constellations of strategies, structures, cultures and other organisational attributes that are feasible in any environment (*Hannan & Freeman, 1977; Aldrich, 1979; McKelvey, 1981*). Companies following these survive because they are more adapted to the environment, while other less well-adapted organisations do not survive. The environment in effect selects out various common constellations of organisational attributes. Success flows from convergence upon a viable configuration. And it is postulated that this convergence will occur in short bursts, after which the successful organisation will display stability.
2 Organisations are driven towards a few common configurations in order to achieve internal harmony and consistency between structures, cultures, strategies and contexts. Instead of an infinite number of combinations of elements, organisations tend to pursue one of a relatively small number of central themes that marshal all the elements into a coherent pattern where attributes are complementary and self-reinforcing. So a machine bureaucracy organisation with its highly specialised, routine operating tasks and highly formalised procedures can only function in stable environments in which its inflexibility is not overly limiting; but consistently stable environments enable operating procedures to be formalised, giving the advantage to machine bureaucracies. Machine bureaucracies in stable markets tend to pursue cost leadership strategies; but stable markets encourage growth to a scale that can reap cost benefits. Here the idea of configuration is stressing circular causation, whereas contingency stresses linear causation.
3 Organisations tend to change the elements of their configuration in a manner that either extends a given configuration (incrementally builds on existing strengths),

or moves very quickly to a new configuration (strategic revolution) which will then be preserved for a long time. Piecemeal moves to a new configuration will often destroy the complementarities among elements in the configuration and will thus be avoided. Only when a configuration change is absolutely necessary or extremely advantageous will organisations move rapidly to a new configuration. The rest of the time organisations will build on their existing configuration.

According to a configuration view therefore, the suitability criterion for selecting a sequence of actions is a set of closely interwoven attributes. Elements make sense in terms of the whole. Success flows from selecting patterns of action, objectives, structure and culture that all fit together as a puzzle does to produce stability, consistency and regularity, harmony and fit. The criteria for successful choice are provided by a relatively small number of rather standard patterns, not a large number of separate criteria.

## 3.6    SUMMARY

This chapter has briefly reviewed the rational, analytic sequence of steps prescribed by strategic choice theory for the formulation of long-term strategic plans. The steps involve analysing and forecasting market development, as well as the financial and power implications of alternative action options. The result should be a blueprint to guide the development of the organisation for some reasonably long period into the future. It is the template against which the actions of individual managers are to be measured. The assumption is that if the plan has been put together skilfully enough it will go a long way to ensuring the organisation's success. However, the formulated plan only provides the blueprint against which action is to be evaluated. Success requires effective implementation and it is to this that the next chapter turns.

### FURTHER READING

To obtain further information on analytical techniques and models for evaluating strategies turn to Hofer & Schendel (1978) as well as Rowe, Mason, Dickel & Snyder (1989). Also Johnson & Scholes (1999) or Bowman & Asch (1987). Also see Ansoff (1990) for a very different perspective to the one presented in this book.

### REFERENCES

Aldrich, H. E. (1979), *Organizations and Environments*, Englewood Cliffs, NJ: Prentice Hall.

Ansoff, I. (1990), *Implanting Corporate Strategy*, Hemel Hempstead: Prentice Hall.

Argenti, J. (1980), *Practical Corporate Planning*, London: Allen & Unwin.

Beck, P. W. (1982), Corporate planning for an uncertain future, *Long Range Planning*, vol. 15, no. 4.

Bowman, C. & Asch, D. (1987), *Strategic Management*, London: Macmillan Education.

Burns, T. & Stalker, G. M. (1961), *The Management of Innovation*, London: Tavistock.

Child, J. (1984), *Organisation*, London: Harper & Row.

Cooke, S. & Slack, N. (1984), *Making Management Decisions*, Englewood Cliffs, NJ: Prentice Hall.

Hannan, M. & Freeman, J. (1977), The population ecology of organizations, *American Journal of Sociology*, vol. 83, pp. 929–64.

Henderson, B. D. (1970), *The Product Portfolio*, Boston Consulting Group.

Hofer, C. W. & Schendel, D. (1978), *Strategy Evaluation: Analytical Concepts*, St Paul, MN: West.

Johnson, G. & Scholes, R. (1999), *Exploring Corporate Strategy*, Hemel Hempstead: Prentice Hall.

Lawrence, P. R. & Lorsch, J. W. (1967), *Organization and Environment*, Cambridge, MA: Harvard University Press.

McKelvey, W. (1981), *Organizational Systematics*, Los Angeles: University of California Press.

Miller, D. (1986), Configurations of strategy and structure: towards a synthesis, *Strategic Management Journal*, vol. 7, pp. 233–49a.

Mintzberg, H. (1989), *Mintzberg on Management: Inside Our Strange World of Organizations*, New York: Free Press.

Mintzberg, H. (1991), The structuring of organizations, in Mintzberg, H. & Quinn, J. B. (Eds.) (1991), *The Strategy Process: Concepts, Contexts, Cases*, Englewood Cliffs, NJ: Prentice Hall.

Mirsham, E. J. (1980), *Cost/Benefit Analysis*, London: Allen & Unwin.

Porter, M. (1980), *Competitive Strategy: Techniques for Analyzing Industries and Competitors*, New York: Free Press.

Porter, M. (1985), *Competitive Advantage: Creating and Sustaining Superior Performance*, New York: Free Press.

Porter, M. (1987), From competitive advantage to corporate strategy, *Harvard Business Review*, May–June, pp. 43–59.

Rowe, A. J., Mason, R. O., Dickel, K. E. & Snyder, N. H. (1989), *Strategic Management and Business Policy: A Methodological Approach*, Reading, MA: Addison-Wesley.

Shim, J. K. & McGlade, R. (1984), The use of corporate planning models: past, present and future, *Journal of Operational Research Science*, vol. 35, no. 10, pp. 885–93.

Woodward, J. (1965), *Industrial Organisation: Theory and Practice*, Oxford: Oxford University Press.

# Chapter

# 4 Strategic choice

## Designing the systems to deliver the strategy

## INTRODUCTION

This chapter reviews the prescriptions strategic choice theory provides for the implementation of strategic plans.

The prescriptions for implementing formulated strategies are as follows:

1  Design a hierarchical reporting structure that is appropriate to the strategy the managers have formulated.
2  Install and operate the management information and control system that will enable them to keep the organisation on its planned path.
3  Install and operate reward systems for people that will provide the monetary incentives for them to carry out the strategy.
4  Change the culture or belief system of people in the organisation to provide the non-monetary motivation for them to carry out the strategy.
5  Develop appropriate social and political behaviour that will not block the implementation of strategy.
6  Install an appropriate strategic management style.

Each of these elements of implementation will be considered further below.

4.2  ## DESIGNING STRUCTURES TO DELIVER THE STRATEGY

The structure of an organisation is the formal way of identifying:

- who is to take responsibility for what;
- who is to exercise authority over whom; and
- who is to be answerable to whom.

The structure is a hierarchy of managers and is the source of authority, as well as the legitimacy of decisions and actions. It is normally held that the appropriate structure follows from the strategy that an organisation is pursuing and that organisational structures display typical patterns of development or life cycles (*Chandler, 1962*). Chandler identified four stages in the structure life cycle:

1   Embryonic organisations have very simple structures in which people report rather informally to someone that they accept as their leader. They tend to do whatever needs to be done with relatively little separation of functions. When they embark on a growth strategy, however, they will find it necessary to change the structure to one based on more formal specialisation of functions and identification of authority and responsibility. If this is not done, managers will find it impossible to implement their strategy of growth and the organisation will probably fail.

2   As they pursue their growth strategy, managers will find that they have to carry out strategies of cost reduction to stay ahead and they will be more and more confronted with the problem of integrating specialised functions. The structure will therefore have to be made even more formal with clearer definition of lines of authority and communication. It will also be necessary to systematise and improve the techniques of marketing, manufacturing and materials procurement.

3   Then, as managers pursue strategies of diversification into new products and markets, they find it necessary to set up marketing and manufacturing organisations in different geographic areas: they install additional structures.

4   As they continue their strategy of diversification, the number of additional structures multiplies and they have to restructure to ensure a better 'fit' with the diversification strategies they are pursuing. They might secure this fit by forming a larger functionally departmentalised structure, with departments at the centre shared by many geographic areas; or by setting up largely independent subsidiaries as divisionalised or holding company structures. Another label for such organisations is the 'machine bureaucracy' (*Mintzberg, 1991*).

Implementation, then, means designing a structure appropriate to the strategy being pursued. This evolution in organisational design from simple to functional will now be considered in a little more detail.

## Simple structure

The simple structure places the emphasis on centralisation rather than decentralisation. In this structure, staff and workers report directly to a small number of managers – in most cases one person is very much 'in control'. There is relatively little division of management responsibility and little formal hierarchy.

Because it relies heavily on informal personal contact, the simple structure has the flexibility required to deal with rapid change and high levels of uncertainty. As the size of the organisation expands, however, the vague, overlapping definitions of jobs, the loose reporting relationships, and the typical absence of formal controls increasingly create anomalies: for example, the flexibility makes the system good at acquiring new customers, but the absence of a bureaucracy means that it cannot retain existing ones.

A bureaucracy consists of a set of offices or functions arranged in a hierarchy; that is, ascending levels of office-holders where authority increases with upward movement. The office-holders are bound by strict rules that establish the extent of their authority and responsibility. People in a bureaucracy do not owe allegiance to other people, but only to the impersonal duties of the office they occupy. In a bureaucracy, people take up roles under a contract; they are appointed and their functions are carefully specified. Promotion is based on qualifications and there is an established career structure. The term 'bureaucracy' is usually used nowadays in a pejorative sense to mean an overburdensome administrative machine. The term is not used in that sense in this book, but in the sense of a clear reporting structure, accompanied by clear rules, procedures and plans.

Growth demands the installation of more complex structural forms and more formal systems if control is to be effective; that is, more sophisticated bureaucracies are required.

Failure to recognise the size limitation of this structural form and the need it imposes for an efficient bureaucracy is perhaps the most frequent stumbling block encountered by the entrepreneurial founders of promising businesses.

## Functional structure

The simple structure is typically followed by the development of a functional form. This form represents a significant shift from centralisation to decentralisation. Management is divided by primary and support tasks:

- getting the work (sales and marketing);
- carrying out the work (production, delivery);
- getting the raw materials (purchasing, stock control);
- getting, retaining and developing the labour (personnel);
- developing the products and processes (research and development, design, engineering);
- recording the transactions and arranging the finance (accounting and finance).

The integrating function is performed by a superior manager: the managing director, chief executive, or chairperson, who acts as the leader of a formally appointed team of managers as shown in *Figure 4.1*.

The functional form is firmly based on specialisation and standardisation. It allows for:

- a greater injection of expertise and professionalism into the performance of each category of task in the organisation;

**FIGURE 4.1**   The functional structure

- more effective control in complex situations because it decomposes and localises the handling of disturbances to the business.

The functional form reaps the efficiency benefits of task division, but there are prices to be paid for these benefits and they become more evident as an organisation continues to increase in size and diversity. The problems encountered in the functional form centre on:

- role duality
- functional barriers
- overlap
- interdependence
- size and diversity.

These are the typical anomalies that the functional form creates and they eventually lead to contradiction and conflict, forcing a further rearrangement of the degree of division and integration. Consider how these anomalies are typically dealt with.

### Role duality, barriers, interdependence and overlap

As soon as people are divided into separately managed functional units, they are in effect being invited to take up two roles: one in relation to the function they belong to and the other in relation to the organisation as a whole. It is then inevitable that they will develop loyalties to their own particular part of the organisation, apart from, and usually stronger than, their loyalties to the organisation as a whole, so erecting barriers between one function and another. The consequence is usually conflict between functions and a tendency for their members to pursue their own functional goals. The separate functions, however, are all part of the same organisation: they are interdependent, their tasks are interconnected and quite often overlapping. If an organisation as a whole is to be effective, then coordinating devices to soften the impact of the barriers, recognise interdependence and manage overlaps are required.

### Coordinating devices

There is a spectrum of coordinating devices:

- At one extreme, coordination is permanent and formally built into the functional structure itself. One example of this is the matrix structure where role duality and interdependence is explicitly and formally recognised by two lines of authority and responsibility which build overlap into the structure (see *Box 4.1*). While this structure does deal with overlap, it can lead to confused responsibility, high degrees of conflict, and long decision-making times. It is often accompanied by complex formal committee structures to try to iron out conflicts and monitor performance, the responsibility for which is dispersed among a number of managers.
- At the other extreme, coordination takes a flexible process form. For example, special task forces or specific project teams, which are not a permanent part of the formal hierarchy, may be set up to promote communication and cooperation across functional divides in relation to a specific project.
- In between these extremes we find forms of coordination that contain both structural and process aspects (see *Box 4.2*).

BOX 4.1

# The matrix structure

In the basic functional form, lines of authority and responsibility flow from and to one manager. But the team controlled by that one manager may also be central to the tasks that have been assigned to another manager and that other manager may in turn also require the services of the team under the control of a third manager. One way of dealing with these overlapping requirements is to establish a structural form with dual authority over and responsibility for those teams. This form occurs most frequently in relation to professional or scientific expertise.

For example, the research and development establishment of a major construction company may be organised into permanent sections, each with a manager, according to scientific expertise (*Figure 4.2*):

- aggregates section
- concrete section
- plant section
- chemicals testing.

At any one time there will also be a number of development projects, each with its own project manager. Staff will be assigned to the project teams from their sections and they are then accountable to the project manager in respect of their duties on the project team, but accountable to their section manager in respect of professional competence. The section manager would carry out all managerial functions not directly related to the project. ■

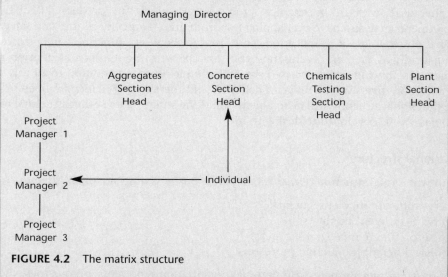

**FIGURE 4.2**   The matrix structure

> **BOX 4.2**
>
> ## Brand management
>
> Brand management is a way of dealing with the considerable production facility and market outlet interdependence of different but closely related products. For example, the producer of five different brands of chocolate may use this approach. One manager is given responsibility for the development and marketing of a particular brand but has to secure production from the production function and sales of the product through a sales force that also sells the other brands. Here the brand manager is a permanent part of the formal structure, but there is no dual reporting. Effectiveness depends on the processes the manager applies to persuading and negotiating with others. ■

### The problem of size and diversity

As the functionally structured organisation continues to grow in size without diversifying the range of its activities, the response to growing complexity may be to develop formal structures where there is even greater functional specialisation.

An essentially one-product and one-process business may therefore develop specialist engineering functions that deal with new construction and new plant, while another deals with repair and maintenance. A purchasing empire may well develop, with separate functions for different types of purchases. Separate design or development functions may develop that focus on different processes or stages of production. For example, there may be a research and development function that deals with chemical processes, while another deals with the mechanical processes relevant to the product. All of these departments may also have overlapping responsibilities for quality control and safety.

The possibilities of duplication and overlap between functions may increase dramatically as such an organisation tries to cope with the tensions of division and integration flowing from increased size and complexity. If, in addition to all this, the organisation diversifies its range of activities and the range of markets it operates in, the functional structure will be unable to stand the strain – some other structural form will have to be developed to deal with it.

## Divisional structure

In the divisional structure (*Figure 4.3*), separate business units are established to:

- serve different market segments;
- provide different products;
- focus on different geographic areas;
- utilise different production processes.

The move from a simple to a functional organisation represents a move towards the decentralised extreme of the structure spectrum. The move from a functional to a

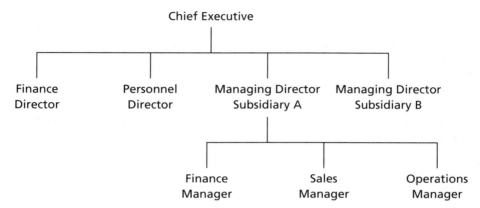

**FIGURE 4.3**    The divisional structure

divisionalised form represents a further movement towards that decentralised end of the spectrum. The organisation becomes a collection of separate, decentralised units each of which may then be functionally organised.

The further division of the management task in this way immediately raises the need for other integrative mechanisms. The first of these is provided by the establishment of a corporate head office with its own management structure headed by a chief executive.

It does not take long, however, before the anomalies of this divisional structure become apparent. As the number of business units increases, the span of control of the corporate chief executive becomes too great. The response is usually to group business units in some way under a divisional director. These divisions may develop their own management structures with their own divisional functions. In this way, the number of levels in the hierarchy proliferates, creating other centres of power and increasing coordination problems. Tensions grow between the top corporate level, the divisional barons and the business unit managers. Conflicts on how to define roles, measure performance, allocate costs and capital all increase.

The tensions create three problems:

1   Duplication of functional specialisms: corporate, divisional and business unit levels tend to develop their own separate functions.
2   Role duality, business unit barriers, interdependence and overlap: business units are profit responsible but they should meet the requirements other units have of them in the interests of the whole corporation.
3   Communication and flows of knowledge: knowledge held in one part of the organisation may be required for effective decisions in another part.

### Duplication

Each unit in a divisionalised structure might have all of its own functional specialisms or some of them could be located at the corporate or divisional levels and shared by a number of units.

### One solution: centralised corporate services

The most common centralised services are the finance and accounting functions, personnel, marketing, purchasing, research and development. The benefits of such centralisation are reduced costs, greater buying power, more marketing strength, better communication, and greater synergy between units. Furthermore, control problems may be eased by these shared services and by the usually large corporate staff.

However, there are also important disadvantages arising from this emphasis on centralisation:

- The autonomy of the business units is restricted and this could lead to inappropriate decisions.
- There is a powerful tendency for the corporate-level staff to grow in size, soon offsetting any cost benefits from shared services.
- The number of management layers in the hierarchy tends to expand, increasingly divorcing those at the sharp end of the business from those at the top.
- Centralised staff functions seek to reinforce their own power by establishing vast numbers of rules and procedures. More layers of managers with closely defined and specialised responsibilities, imposing rules and procedures on those at the sharp end of the organisation's activities, slow down responses. The consequence is much slower reaction times and much reduced ability to innovate and to anticipate change.
- Motivation of those at the sharp end is also a casualty of highly centralised structures.

### The opposite solution: self-contained business units

The opposite way of dealing with the problem of duplication is to ignore it: that is, to adopt a highly decentralised structure where each business unit is as self-contained as possible with all its own specialist functions.

The benefits of self-contained business units are:

- faster reaction times;
- more innovation;
- greater degree of anticipation of change;
- higher motivation of those at the sharp end of the organisation.

But there are also costs:

- in money terms, arising from the duplication of services in many business units;
- in the loss of synergy between different business units;
- in the increasing difficulties of communication and control of the day-to-day activities;
- in the increased need for formal systems of communication and control.

### The holding company

The extreme form of an organisation consisting of independent business units is the holding company. This operates very much as a shareholder and banker. The head office is very small and considerable autonomy is granted to the business units: they are required only to make an adequate return on the capital invested and to seek authority for all capital expenditure. But these 'only' requirements place heavy constraints upon the business units, greatly reducing their scope for strategic manoeuvre. Control is exerted by regularly monitoring financial performance and in the event of poor performance the holding company will close or sell the unit. Holding companies generally grow by acquisition and are not noted for their organic growth. See *Box 4.3*.

Most companies tend to follow cycles of shifting first towards the centralised end of the spectrum and then back again towards the decentralised end. The tension between the requirements of division and integration in the organisation leads to continual change.

**BOX 4.3**

# Hanson Trust plc

Hanson Trust plc is an acquisitive conglomerate that concentrates on acquiring businesses in basic industries with a clearly defined future. As it is acquired, each business is retained as a separate organisation. The managers of each business are set clear financial objectives and their performance is regularly monitored against these objectives. If they exceed target they are handsomely rewarded and, if they do not, they seek employment elsewhere. Capital investment is tightly controlled, with any unbudgeted item above a few hundred pounds requiring the approval of the Chairman. The corporate head office is very small, consisting of an accounts department to monitor performance against budget and a small acquisitions staff. Each business unit conducts its own affairs and is free to compete with other sister subsidiaries – there is no attempt to manage overlaps between businesses. This kind of company therefore operates very much like a group of separate businesses with only their shareholders in common. ■

## 4.3    DESIGNING SYSTEMS OF INFORMATION AND CONTROL TO DELIVER THE STRATEGY

The information and control systems of an organisation are basically procedures, rules and regulations governing:

- what information about the performance of an organisation should flow to whom and when;
- who is required to respond to that information and how they are authorised to respond, in particular what authority they have to deploy the resources of their organisation.

To implement the strategies they have formulated, managers will have to ensure that their information and control systems:

- are adequate enough for the flows of information that implementation requires;
- provide appropriate control mechanisms to enable managers to monitor the outcomes of the strategy implementation and do something if those outcomes are not in accordance with the strategy.

Management control is defined as the process of ensuring that all resources – physical, human and technological – are allocated so as to realise the strategy. It is a process in which a person or a group of people intentionally affects what others do. Control ensures proper behaviour in an organisation and the need for it arises because individuals within the organisation are not always willing to act in the best interests of the organisation (*Wilson, 1991*). The process of control involves setting standards or targets for performance, or expected outcomes of a sequence of actions, then comparing actual performance or outcomes against standards, targets or expectations, and finally taking corrective action to remove any deviations from standard, target or expectation. Control takes a *feedforward* form when corrective action is taken on the basis of predictions with the aim of avoiding deviations from expectations. It takes on a *feedback* form where the predictions cannot be accurate enough. In the *feedback* form, monitoring detects a deviation that has already occurred and then takes action to correct it. Most business control systems are a mixture of feedforward and feedback control.

The principal form taken by the control system in most organisations is that of the annual plan or budget. Strategy implementation is held to depend upon an effective budgeting system. The budget converts strategy into a set of short-term action plans and sets out the financial consequences of those action plans for the year ahead. Control is then a process of regularly comparing what happens with what the budget said would happen. Budgets allocate the resource of an organisation with which different business units and functions are charged to carry out the strategy. Budgets establish the legitimate authority for using the resources of the organisation. The budget will normally be prepared in great detail, showing what people in each business unit and function are required to bring in as revenue, what they are permitted to spend and on what, and therefore what surplus they are required to earn, or deficit they will be allowed to incur.

The budget, however, is a short-term instrument, only the first step in the implementation of the strategy. Some have therefore sought to identify the differences between short-term control and strategic control. For example, *Hurst (1982)* points out that strategic control requires more data from more sources, particularly external sources, and the data must be oriented to a longer-term future. Strategic control is therefore inevitably less precise and less formal than budgetary control. It is concerned more with the accuracy of the premises on which decisions are based and much less with quantitative deviations from standard. Strategic control has to be more flexible and use variable rather than rigidly regular time periods for reporting. The relationships between corrective action and outcome are therefore weaker in strategic control. The conclusion drawn is that although planning and control in a strategic sense is very difficult, a system to compare expectations and outcomes is even more necessary than it is for the short term.

*Goold & Quinn's (1990)* research shows that very few companies have a strategic control process that is anything like as formal and comprehensive as their budgetary control system. Even where managers do set strategic milestones that would allow them to check on their progress as the strategy was implemented, those milestones take the form of events rather than results. So the milestone might be the completion of a new factory; managers might set this for a period two years hence and then after two years check if the factory is indeed complete. If it is, they may conclude that they are keeping to their strategy. However, since this is an event rather than a result, they will not know if the financial results their strategy was supposed to achieve are in fact being achieved. The reasons for the lack of a proper results-based monitoring and control system were identified as the length of time lags between action and outcome and the risks and uncertainties that long-term plans were subject to. Despite the difficulties, however, Goold and Quinn recommend trying harder to use formal strategic control systems based on milestones for comparison.

Since effective management and information control systems are so important to the possibility of delivering chosen strategies, I will now describe them in more detail.

## Management information and control systems (MICS)

MICS is a set of rules and regulations, procedures and codified traditions that have been built up through past experience and legitimised by those in the relevant hierarchical positions. The primary purpose of MICS is the setting of objectives and standards for role-holders in the hierarchy and the processing of information on performance compared with standards and objectives, so that responsibility for corrective action can be identified and action taken.

An efficient MICS is built on a painstaking analysis of the precise detail of each step required to perform every task at all levels in the organisation. Standards of performance are established for each task at every level and the information required for the performance of each task and the monitoring of that performance are identified. In addition, the chain of authority and responsibility for carrying out every task and for dealing with variations in performance are clearly set out.

To see what this means in practical terms, consider the formal procedures typically used to control the purchasing of supplies and equipment. This is shown in *Figure 4.4.*

The starting point in that figure is the originator of a purchase: someone in the organisation requires some raw material or some piece of equipment. The originator has to follow a formal procedure to obtain the required item. In the case of raw materials, the originator fills out a requisition form and sends it to Stores. A stock sheet is used to record the raw material supplied and the remaining inventory. If inventories of that item fall below a prearranged level, a preprogrammed response is triggered and a requisition is sent to the Buyer. The procedure the Buyer is to follow is clearly laid out. There is a separate procedure, specifying levels of authorisation, for the procurement of equipment. The processes used here are those of analysis, quantification, formal rules, procedures and communication. The intervention required of the higher levels in the hierarchy is minimal.

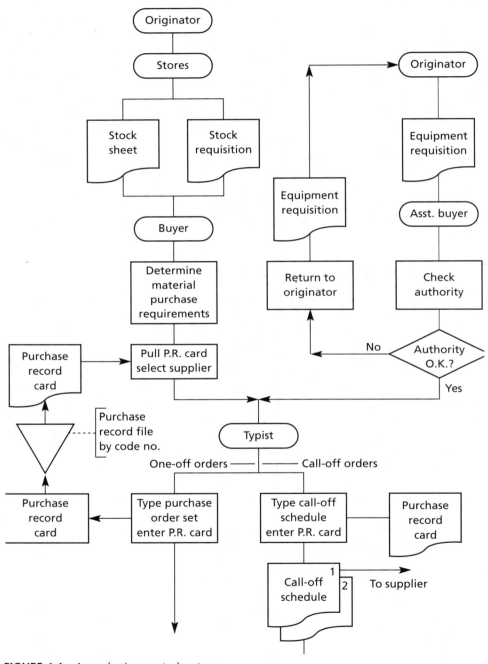

**FIGURE 4.4** A purchasing control system

The intention is to get an organisation working like a machine. But the system will never work as smoothly as planned, because some uncertainty is present in all time frames, including the very short term. More intuitive intervention will occasionally be required to satisfy an unforeseen and urgent demand for some item. Informal rules will replace the formal, and originators will persuade and negotiate directly with the Buyer to secure what they need. In other words, political activity will be deployed to handle change even in the short term – but this is the exception.

This description of a requisition procedure is, of course, an illustration of only one small part of the formal procedures employed by well-run organisations of any size. *Figure 4.5* takes a step higher up the hierarchy and looks at the activities which precede a requisition. Quarterly, weekly and daily despatch schedules for the output of some part of the organisation are prepared. These form the basis for production schedules and thus requisitions for materials and equipment. Formal procedures lay down the reports to be prepared on the actual outcomes of despatch and production and the daily review meetings to be held to compare outcomes against plan. Formal rules in policy manuals set out predetermined responses to variances. Formal action plans are prepared and implemented.

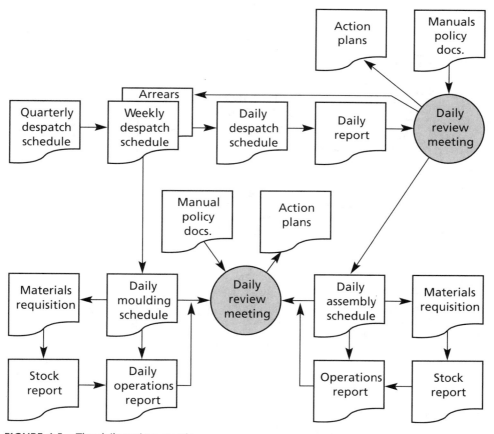

**FIGURE 4.5**    The daily review meeting

The dominant processes at review meetings are likely to be the instructing ones; effective action is usually the outcome of one-to-one contact between superiors in the hierarchy and those reporting to them, or to whom they report. But intuitive and informal negotiating processes are all used when unforeseen events occur.

A further step up the hierarchy reveals what happens to the daily reviews: there is a formal pattern according to which daily review meetings lead to weekly reports, considered at weekly review meetings by the next level up in the management hierarchy. This in turn is fed into monthly review meetings at higher management levels. Planning, monitoring and corrective action is initiated or legitimised at these meetings. (See *Figure 4.6*.)

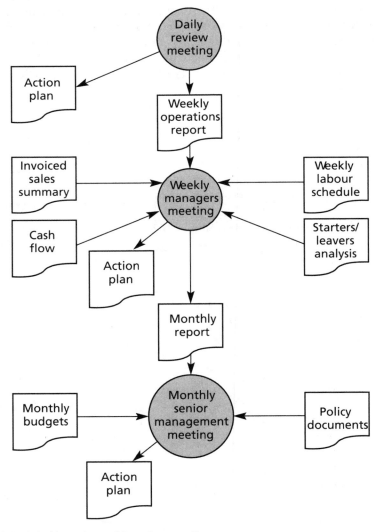

**FIGURE 4.6**   Weekly and monthly review meetings

Yet a further step up the hierarchy reveals how the formal procedures require each subsidiary to report its activities and actions by means of quarterly reports and budgets to the corporate level. Once again there are formal meetings, quantified budgets, and reports and formal policy documents which to some extent try to set predetermined responses to foreseeable changes. The process culminates in the annual meetings where budgets are set and then formally fed back down through the organisation. This is depicted in *Figure 4.7*.

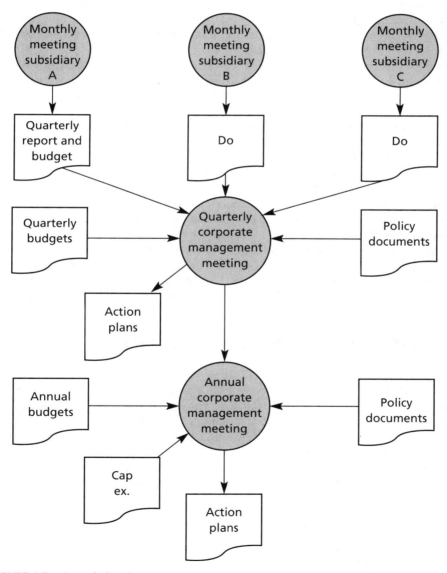

**FIGURE 4.7**    Annual planning

Note how an efficient bureaucracy is built upon simple hierarchies of managers in which roles are clearly defined. The planning and monitoring functions of the efficient bureaucracy involve the setting of hierarchies of objectives in relation to controlling and developing the existing business and the allocation of authority and responsibility for achieving them. Power in a bureaucracy is clearly derived from the rules, regulations and procedures of the organisation. The focus is therefore on administrative rather than political activity. Communication is institutionalised, rather than informal and spontaneous.

MICS is one of the main forces for stability in an organisation. In one sense it makes it more possible for people in an organisation to handle uncertainty because it provides a secure boundary. At the same time it blocks change because it reinforces the repetition of existing behaviour patterns.

Note also that the communication arenas, all the meetings and documents shown in *Figures 4.4* to *4.7*, are predetermined. They have already been set up in advance of the change; they are serially arranged with information flowing along prearranged channels from one arena to another. Those who are to participate in the arenas (meeting memberships, document circulation lists) are well defined and stable in the sense that the same group of people always participate.

The functions that each arena is to perform are quite clear. There are restricted membership meetings right at the top of the hierarchy that perform mainly symbolic functions (e.g. approving budgets and plans, thus giving them legitimacy). Other meetings may perform administrative functions. Many one-to-one meetings perform choice or decision functions from which action flows. Many of the meetings and documents perform rationalisation functions of explaining what has already happened (e.g. reviewing performance against budget). The point to note here is the importance of symbolic, legitimising, administrative, explanation of the past functions in these arenas. Making decisions is certainly not the only and may not even be the most important function of the meetings required for MICS to operate.

## 4.4   INSTALLING AND OPERATING HUMAN RESOURCE SYSTEMS

Effective strategy implementation should occur when the people required to take action to this end are motivated to do so. One of the most powerful motivators is the organisation's reward system (*Galbraith & Kazanian, 1986*). Appropriate rewards stimulate people to make the effort to take actions directly relevant to an organisation's strategy. The way in which people's jobs are graded and the pay scales attached to these grades will affect how people feel about their jobs and the effort they will make. Differentials need to be perceived to be fair if they are not to affect performance adversely. Bonuses, profit-related pay, piecework and productivity schemes are all ways of tying monetary rewards to the actions that strategy implementation requires.

Non-monetary rewards are also of great importance in motivating people. These rewards include promotion, career development, job enrichment, job rotation, training and development. They all help individuals to be more useful to an organisation while developing greater self-fulfilment. Simpler forms of reward are also of great importance, for example praise, recognition and thanks.

Training and development is an important implementation tool, not only because it motivates people, but also because it provides the skills required for strategy implementation (*Hussey, 1991*). The objectives of training and development programmes should be aligned with those of an organisation's strategy and those objectives should consist of measurable changes in corporate performance. *Lorenz (1986)* describes how ICL put 2000 managers through a development programme designed to improve ICL's competitiveness against the Japanese. Such programmes are supposed to allow managers at all levels to develop a comprehensive understanding of what their organisation's strategy actually means.

## 4.5    CULTURE-CHANGE PROGRAMMES

Just as the reporting structure of an organisation should fit the particular strategy it wishes to pursue, so should its culture, the attitudes and beliefs that people within an organisation share. *Handy (1981)* classifies organisational cultures into four categories:

1   The *power* culture is typically found in small entrepreneurial companies controlled by powerful figures. People in this culture share a belief in individuality and in taking risks. They believe that management should be an informal process with few rules and procedures.
2   The *role* culture is associated with bureaucracies where people's functions are defined in a formal way and they specialise. People here share a belief in the importance of security and predictability. They equate successful management with rules and regulations.
3   The *task* culture is found where people focus on their job, or on a project. People share a belief in the importance of teamwork, expertise and in being adaptable.
4   The *person* culture occurs where people believe that the organisation exists so that they can serve their own personal interest, for example barristers and architects, and many other professionals.

Just as structures need to fit a particular strategy and just as they tend to follow a life cycle from the simple to the functional to the divisional, so too do cultures. The power culture is appropriate to the early stages of a firm's life when its structure is simple. Later it will have to change to the role culture as it grows and installs a functional structure. Then it will have to develop a task culture to fit in with a divisionalised structure.

Implementation may well therefore require that an organisation change its culture and the conventional wisdom prescribes that such change should be planned. The reasons why people might resist a change in culture need to be identified and plans formulated to overcome the resistance. Participation, communication and training are all seen as ways of overcoming resistance. The process of overcoming resistance involves a stage called unfreezing when the existing culture is questioned and is followed by a period of reformulation where people consider what new beliefs they need to develop and share with each other. Finally there is the re-freezing stage where the new culture is fixed in place. We will be returning in Chapter 6 to these matters of planned change in belief systems – the discipline of organisation development.

## 4.6 DEVELOPING APPROPRIATE POLITICAL BEHAVIOUR

It is inevitable that people in an organisation will conflict and, when they do, they engage in political behaviour (*Pfeffer, 1981*). As an organisation differentiates into functions and units, those functions and units develop their own objectives, some of which will be different to those of the organisation as a whole. But differentiation brings with it interdependence so that no single function or unit can achieve its objectives on its own. Both will have to compete with each other for scarce resources and to cooperate with each other to reach their objective. Interdependence, heterogeneous goals and scarce resources taken together produce conflict. If the conflict is important and power is distributed enough, then people will use political behaviour, that is persuasion and negotiation, to resolve their conflict. If power is highly centralised then most will simply do as they are told – they will not have enough power to engage in political behaviour.

The kinds of political strategies people employ to come out best from conflict are the selective use of objective criteria, the use of outside experts to support their case, forming alliances and coalitions, sponsoring those with similar ideas, empire building, intentionally doing nothing, suppressing information, making decisions first and using analysis afterwards to justify them, and many more.

The above view of politics as a manipulative process of dubious ethical validity leads to the belief that steps should be taken to reduce the incidence of political behaviour. Such steps are those that reduce the level of conflict and the most powerful of these is to preach and convert people to a common ideology. Creating excess resources should also reduce levels of conflict.

I now turn to a matter closely connected with strategy implementation and strategic control – strategic management styles.

## 4.7 INSTALLING STRATEGIC MANAGEMENT STYLES

So far I have discussed the criteria managers are recommended to use to select appropriate strategies, as well as the steps they are recommended to take to implement and control the consequences of those strategies. The question now is: what part should the various levels of management play in the formulation and implementation of strategies and in strategic control? In other words, the question is to do with how managers at various levels add value to the strategy process. It is the manner in which various levels of management contribute to the strategy process that determines what we might call the management style of an organisation. In this section we will consider three well-known ways of categorising the strategic style of an organisation.

### Mintzberg's types of strategy

*Mintzberg & Waters (1985)* distinguish the following eight styles of strategic management:

1   *Planned.* Top managers articulate precise intentions and embody these in formal plans that set out what the levels of managers below them are to do. Top management then exert control by monitoring outcomes against plan.

2   *Entrepreneurial*. The organisation here is under the personal control of the leader and strategies flow from the unarticulated vision of a single leader.

3   *Ideological*. Strategies are the intended patterns in action expressed in collective beliefs. Here top managers articulate inspirational and relatively immutable beliefs that govern the actions of those lower down and so become the strategy. The ideology embodies an organisation's intention and control is through indoctrination and socialisation.

4   *Umbrella*. Here the leaders define the overall targets and set the boundaries within which managers lower down actually formulate the content of the strategy. Control is exerted by monitoring achievement against target and behaviour against the boundaries.

5   *Process*. The leaders control the process of strategy, for example the reporting structure, the planning timetable and the appointment of managers, and then leave the content to those lower down. Control is exerted through keeping people to timetables and through allocating resources, that is through exercising a final veto.

6   *Unconnected*. Here there is either no central intention or groups of people produce strategies in direct contradiction to central intention. The organisation's strategy therefore flows from a collection of unconnected strategies formed by groups within the organisation.

7   *Consensus*. People in the organisation converge on a common theme through agreement with each other, without any central managers directing them. Here strategies emerge without prior organisational intention.

8   *Imposed*. This occurs where the environment dictates what has to be done.

*Mintzberg & Waters (1985)* relate these strategic management styles to the kind of environment that managers face. For mature diversified corporations, planned strategic management styles are appropriate for stable environments, but umbrella or process styles will be more suitable in turbulent ones. This corresponds with the distinction usually drawn between top-down and bottom-up planning. For different kinds of organisation in turbulent environments we will tend to find entrepreneurial, unconnected or consensus strategic management styles.

*Mintzberg (1991)* also distinguished between five types of organisation:

1   The *simple structure* in which the entrepreneurial style of management is usually found.

2   The *machine bureaucracy* which works according to rules and regulations established by the centre of the organisation. This is appropriate for stable environments and the planned style of strategic management fits with it.

3   The *professional bureaucracy* which is bureaucratic but not centralised, such as schools, universities and hospitals. The strategic management style here will normally be of the unconnected type.

4   *Divisionalised structures* where the choice of style would lie between planned, process or umbrella.

5   *The adhocracy*, which is a highly organic organisation with little in the way of formal structures, rules and procedures. It consists of teams of specialists, for example management consultants. The strategic management style here might be entrepreneurial, consensus or ideological.

## Miles and Snow's categories

*Miles & Snow (1978)* provide another way of categorising strategic management style. They distinguish between the following four categories:

1 *Defenders.* Managers in these organisations concentrate on a relatively well-defined market area. They concentrate on increasing their expertise and improving their position in this market, rather than searching for alternative strategies.
2 *Prospectors.* Managers here are always searching for new opportunities and they often create change and uncertainty.
3 *Analysers.* Managers in this kind of organisation operate in both stable and un-stable areas; in the former they use formalised structures while in the latter they adopt a more organic approach.
4 *Reactors.* Here managers perceive change and uncertainty but are unable to respond effectively. They lack a consistent strategy and act when the environment forces them to.

## Goold and Campbell's strategies and styles

*Goold & Campbell (1987)* define strategic management styles in terms of the manner in which the corporate level of an organisation resolves a number of tensions. They distinguish between five key tensions:

1 *Multiple perspectives versus clear responsibility.* This is the dilemma created when people are given clearly defined jobs in a system that restricts them to those jobs. The result is greater efficiency at the defined job, but it leads to narrow thinking and therefore reduced ability to deal with change. If an organisation moves in the direction of multiple perspectives, however, it suffers a reduction in efficiency.
2 *Detailed planning reviews versus entrepreneurial decision making.* This presents an organisation with a similar dilemma. It can secure greater control and higher levels of efficiency if it plans carefully and regularly reviews actions against plan. But this narrows the focus of people and their motivation to act so that many new opportunities will be lost.
3 *Strong leadership versus business autonomy.* The dilemma here is that between strong central control with the synergies it brings and local autonomy with the flexibility to deal with unexpected change.
4 *Long-term objectives versus short-term objectives.* The tension here occurs because short-term profitability and cash flow is high when a company does not invest in expensive new facilities and research and development, but this failure to invest will reduce long-term profitability.
5 *Flexible strategies versus tight controls.* This dilemma is created by the need to set out precisely what people are to do in order to have a firm basis for monitoring their performance. When this is done, however, it removes the flexibility individuals have to handle unexpected changes.

Goold and Campbell argue that successful organisations resolve these tensions in a manner that matches a number of factors internal to the organisation with a number of factors external to it. The internal factors are matters such as the nature of the business portfolio, the extent to which businesses overlap each other, and the skills and personalities of people in the businesses. The external factors include the level of uncertainty the environment presents and the intensity of the competition. A strategic management style is a choice that resolves the tensions to secure equilibrium. The three most important choices of styles they identify are as follows.

### The financial control style

One choice is to operate in market segments that are highly stable so that most of the tensions described above are avoided. The organisation can then adopt an uncompromisingly simple, flat, decentralised organisational structure. It can focus firmly on short-term objectives and practise tight short-term control using quantitative management information and control systems. Unforeseen change, the strategic and the long term are all dealt with by the entrepreneurial initiative of the managers closest to the action and/or by an entrepreneurial approach to acquisitions at the corporate level.

### The strategic planning style

Here companies adopt complex, centralist structures and practise top-down long-term planning. They place great weight on the achievement of long-term objectives and are tolerant of non-achievement in the short term. They make these choices because they are pursuing interconnections and synergies; they are trying to develop competitive advantage and achieve balance in the portfolio of businesses under their control. This style choice will be appropriate where changes in customer requirements and competitor groupings are turbulent and competition intense. This choice is also appropriate where there are significant interconnections between business units in terms of shared customers or shared operational processes and technology.

### The strategic control style

These companies strike a balance between short- and long-term objectives, sacrificing short-term profit where there is a reasonable prospect of this leading to greater long-term profit. They usually choose simple, flat, decentralised organisational structures to allow effective short-term control, but try to promote collaboration to enable some interconnections and synergies to be taken advantage of. They adopt the more facilitating forms of management, relying more on the processes of persuasion and negotiation than on instruction. Planning is then of the bottom-up type. This style choice is far less clear than the other two, but it does offer advantages of flexibility. It is likely to be appropriate where the company consists of businesses that are not significantly interconnected in customer or operational and technology terms, and operates in markets characterised by rapid change arising in contained situations.

If you choose a strategy that focuses on synergy and that requires integrated operational responses and common approaches to customers, then a successful choice is the strategic planning style, with all it means in terms of structures, roles and cultures. If you choose to sacrifice some synergy and operate in rather more independent market segments, which do not have common customer bases and do not require integrated operational responses, then strategic control is the successful choice. This choice also leads to particular structural, cultural, role and systems requirements to fit or match.

## 4.8    SUMMARY

This chapter has described what in effect is supposed to be a cybernetic system. The idea is to derive detailed targets and objectives for the strategic plan. These are then operated within a hierarchical structure and detailed sets of procedures for measuring and comparing outcomes with expectations. The whole approach is one of designing cybernetic systems to ensure control. Even 'softer' elements such as belief systems, power and management style are prescribed in much the same way. I have presented the material in a rather idealised way. Of course, those who make these prescriptions and the practitioners who implement them know that the world is more uncertain and more full of conflict than the simple descriptions above recognise. The next chapter, therefore, turns to the manner in which uncertainty and conflict is dealt with within a strategic choice framework. It is also well understood that human behaviour is more complex than the descriptions of this and the last chapters suggest. Chapter 7 will therefore examine the manner in which the strategic choice framework handles motivation, culture and leadership.

### FURTHER READING

Hussey (1991) provides further material on management control and Goold & Campbell (1987) provide a thorough analysis of strategic management styles.

### REFERENCES

Chandler, A. D. (1962), *Strategy and Structure*, Boston: MIT Press.

Galbraith, J. R. & Kazanian, R. K. (1986), *Strategy Implementation: Structure, Systems and Process*, St Paul, MN: West.

Goold, M. & Campbell, A. (1987), *Strategies and Styles*, Oxford: Blackwell.

Goold, M. with Quinn, J. J. (1990), *Strategic Control: Milestones for Long Term Performance*, London: Hutchinson.

Handy, C. B. (1981), *Understanding Organisations*, Harmondsworth: Penguin.

Hurst, E. G. (1982), Controlling strategic plans, in Lorange, P. (Ed.) (1982), *Implementation of Strategic Planning*, Englewood Cliffs, NJ: Prentice Hall.

Hussey, D. E. (1991), Implementing strategy through management education and training, in Hussey, D. E. (Ed.) (1991), *International Review of Strategic Management*, vol. 2, no. 1, Chichester: John Wiley.

Lorenz, C. (1986), Metamorphosis of a European laggard, *Financial Times*, 12 May.

Miles, R. E. & Snow, C. C. (1978), *Organizational Strategy, Structure and Process*, New York: McGraw-Hill.

Mintzberg, H. (1991), The structuring of organizations, in Mintzberg, H. & Quinn, J. B. (Eds.) (1991), *The Strategy Process: Concepts, Contexts, Cases*, Englewood Cliffs, NJ: Prentice Hall.

Mintzberg, H. & Waters, J. A. (1985), Of strategies deliberate and emergent, *Strategic Management Journal*, vol. 6, pp. 257–72.

Pfeffer, J. (1981), *Power in Organizations*, Cambridge, MA: Ballinger.

Wilson, R. M. S. (1991), Corporate strategy and management control, in Hussey, D. E. (Ed.) (1991), *International Review of Strategic Management*, vol. 2, no. 1, Chichester: John Wiley.

Chapter

# 5 Strategic choice

## Taking account of uncertainty and conflict

## 5.1   INTRODUCTION

The last two chapters reviewed the theory of strategic choice, that is the view that organisations change in ways that are chosen by their most powerful executives. The strategy of an organisation, on this view, is the intention formed by an individual, or a small group of individuals. This intention is formed well in advance of change and it relates to the shape and direction of the organisation as a whole. Organisational change is the realisation of this individually formed, overall, prior intention. Such realisation is accomplished through the design, installation and operation of an essentially cybernetic system that is supposed to ensure change in financial flows and member behaviour according to the intended goals. Both the organisation and the individuals who form it are understood to be cybernetic systems. The focus is very much on control.

As Chapter 2 pointed out, cybernetic control depends on the possibility of making reasonably reliable forecasts of outcomes and timings at the required level of detail and over the required time span. When this is not possible, cybernetic control may still be effective if small and essentially random actions by the organisation can be relied upon to cancel out small and essentially random changes in the environment – the law of requisite variety. In other words, cybernetic systems require a fairly high degree of certainty about environmental change, either in the sense that a specific cause can be related to a specific effect or in the probabilistic sense of small changes cancelling out. This is the same thing as saying that cybernetic systems function effectively when they operate in rather repetitive environments.

This point about the implications of uncertainty for strategic choice has been widely recognised and various authors have put forward models of decision making under conditions of uncertainty. This chapter will review some of their work.

The review of strategic choice theory in the last two chapters also did not pay much attention to the effects of conflicting goals or conflicts between members of an organisation. This chapter will also look at what some writers have had to say about this matter.

Finally, the review of strategic choice theory in the last two chapters did not have much to say about the time path an organisation follows as it implements its chosen strategy. Is the implementation to be done in small incremental steps or as a revolutionary change? This chapter will also review that question.

What strikes me about the following ways of dealing with the pattern of change and the matters of uncertainty and conflict is this: largely they all adopt a rational, sequential, calculating approach; that is, an algorithmic approach. They remain within the strategic choice framework because they provide ways for individuals to deal with the difficulties of choosing in conditions of uncertainty and conflict.

## 5.2   INCREMENTAL AND REVOLUTIONARY CHANGE

This section will review the debate about the time path an organisation follows as it implements the strategy chosen by its most powerful individuals. One view is that implementation proceeds in small steps so that the organisation changes incrementally, converging to some state adapted to the environment. The other view is that organisations change in frame-breaking revolutions.

### Incremental strategic change

Based on his study of ten large corporations, *Quinn (1980)* identified a pattern of strategic change which he called logical incrementalism. Here managers have an intended destination for their organisation, but they discover how to reach it by taking logically connected decisions step by step. They do not make major changes but build incrementally in a consistent manner on what they already have. They sense the changes in their environment and gradually adapt to those changes so maintaining a continuing dynamic equilibrium with their environment.

### Revolutionary frame-breaking strategic change

Other studies, however, particularly those by *Mintzberg (1989)*, *Miller & Friesen (1980)*, *Greiner (1972)*, *Johnson (1987)* and *Tushman & Romanelli (1985)*, have identified a different pattern of change. Here managers resist changes that conflict with their predominant way of understanding their organisation and its environment, until some crisis makes it impossible to continue doing so. Patterns of strategic change are such that an organisation is driven down the same path by its own momentum, becoming more and more out of line with its environment. This gives rise to strategic drift. In other words, managers are caught in a fixed way of thinking. When that drift has taken an organisation too far from its environment, it then makes sudden revolutionary adjustments. These inevitably involve breaking the old frames its managers were working within and establishing new ones.

### Greiner's development model

*Greiner (1972)* presents a model of the typical pattern of development experienced by all companies. He holds that all companies must pass through a number of stages if they are to sustain acceptable levels of performance. He describes five phases of growth that are punctuated by crises. In order to make the necessary move from one phase of growth to another, an organisation must pass through a crisis. These phases and their related crises are as follows:

1   *Growth through creativity.* In the early stages of its life, when it has simple structures and is small, a company grows through the creative activity of small close-knit teams. At some point, however, they face the crisis of leadership. As the company increases in size it can no longer be managed in highly personal, informal ways.

2   *Growth through direction.* If the leadership crisis is successfully resolved through 'professionalising' the management, specialising its functions and setting up more formal systems, the company proceeds to grow in a centrally directed way. This leads to the crisis of autonomy. As the organisation gets bigger and bigger, employees feel restricted by the hierarchy and the top finds it more and more difficult to maintain detailed control.

3   *Growth through delegation.* If the autonomy crisis is successfully resolved through changing formal structures and decentralising, then growth proceeds through delegation. This brings with it a crisis of control. The top feels it is losing control and parochial attitudes develop in the divisions of the company.

4   *Growth through coordination.* If the control crisis is successfully resolved through installing systems to bring about greater coordination and cooperation, then the growth of the company proceeds. As it grows larger and more complex it is brought to the crisis of red tape. Increasingly bureaucratic controls create sharp divisions between head office staffs and operating divisions.

5   *Growth through collaboration.* Here the crisis of red tape is resolved through strong interpersonal collaboration and control through cultural sharing rather than formal controls. Greiner thinks that this growth stage may lead to a crisis of psychological saturation in which all become exhausted by teamwork. He thinks there may be a sixth growth phase involving a dual organisation: a 'habit' structure for daily work routines and a 'reflective' structure for stimulating new perspectives and personal enrichment.

These views on revolutionary change, crisis and drift point to how organisations do not change in the orderly manner implied in the last two chapters. Note, however, how resolution of each crisis is itself a strategic choice made by individuals. Note also how Greiner describes the resolution to each crisis in terms of more and more elaborate cybernetic systems.

Now consider what the literature has to say on choice in conditions of uncertainty and conflict.

## 5.3 THE EFFECTS OF UNCERTAINTY ON DECISION-MAKING MODES

*Thompson & Tuden (1959)* relate the mode of decision-making to:

- the lack of clarity in causal relationships;
- the lack of agreement over objectives.

In *Figure 5.1*, Thompson and Tuden show how managers shift from one mode of making decisions to others as the situation changes.

Where causal connections are clear and objectives shared, the conditions exist for managers to take decisions in a rational–logical way. As they move away from these conditions it becomes impossible to apply rational logic and so they have to use some other approach.

Thus, when causal connections are clear but managers conflict then the decision has to be made in a political manner – those with the greatest power will prevail. The decision-making process here will be one in which managers build coalitions (*Cyert & March, 1963; Child, 1972, 1984; Pfeffer, 1981*).

When managers are agreed on what they should be trying to achieve but the causal connections make it unclear how to do so, then they will have to use judgemental, or intuitive, modes of making a decision. They will have to reason by analogy; they will have to think laterally and use trial-and-error decision-making processes.

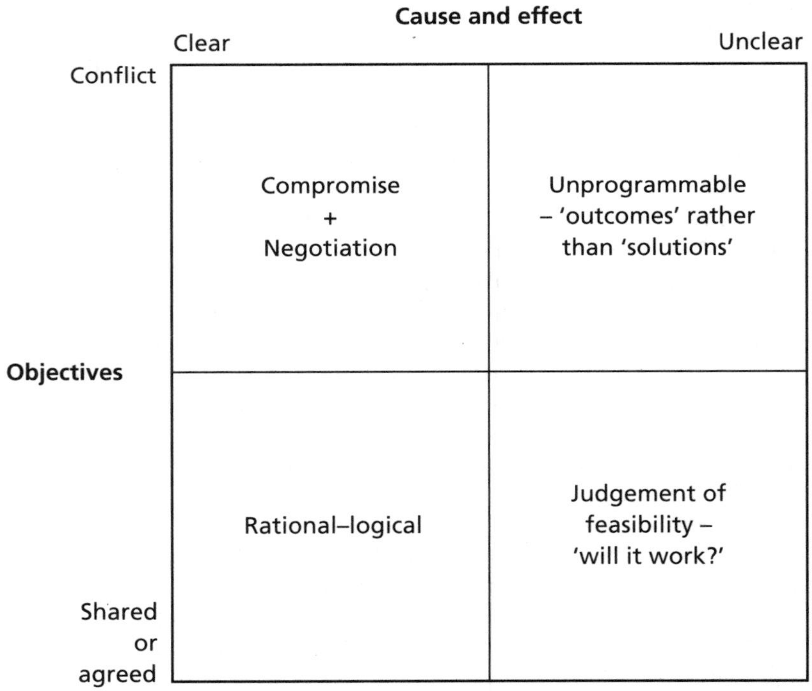

**FIGURE 5.1**  Models of decision making: types of uncertainty
*Source*: R. Turton (1991), *Behaviour in a Business Context*, London: Chapman and Hall

The most difficult situation is where causality is unclear and objectives conflict. Here managers will have to decide in a way that combines intuitive individual judgements with political interactions in a group.

## Duncan's approach

Other writers have also highlighted the connection between levels of uncertainty and modes of making decisions. *Duncan (1972)*, for example, relates modes of decision-making to degrees of environmental complexity and stability as depicted in *Figure 5.2*.

He distinguishes environments that are static from those that are dynamic, where dynamic means that the frequency, rate and extent of change are all high. He also categorises environments into those that are simple and those that are complex. In simple environments there are only a small number of variables that may change, while in complex environments there are many interconnected variables that may change. The two measures create four archetypal environments. The simplest archetype is the static and simple environment where the appropriate organisational system is the mechanistic one with its rational modes of decision making. In the most demanding of these environmental archetypes, the complex dynamic one, it is only organic organisational systems that will survive, those with flexible, political, intuitive modes of making decisions. In between, some pragmatic combination of the mechanistic and the organic is required.

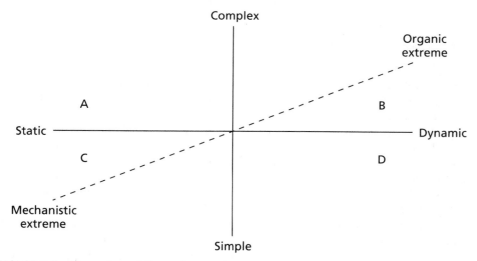

**FIGURE 5.2**    Dimensions of the environment
*Source*: R. Turton (1991), *Behaviour in a Business Context*, London: Chapman and Hall

## Perrow's model

Then, *Perrow (1972)* provides a model of the technology appropriate to different conditions, which makes much the same point. This is shown in *Figure 5.3*. The vertical axis depicts a spectrum of problem-solving procedures. At one end of the spectrum

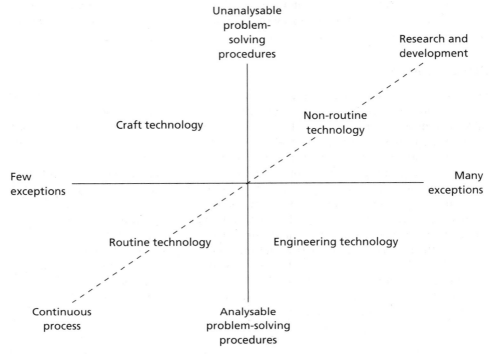

**FIGURE 5.3** The Perrow model of technology
*Source*: R. Turton (1991), *Behaviour in a Business Context*, London: Chapman and Hall

there are problem-solving procedures available that are analysable: they can be broken down into prearranged steps or rules of a logical kind. At the other end the only procedures available in a particular situation are unanalysable or unprogrammable. This means that the problem is such that one has to use some unique method of solving it, unique to that particular problem. Then on the horizontal axis there are the problem-solving situations classified in terms of the number of exceptions. Few exceptions mean that there is little variability in the situation in which decisions have to be made. Actions and responses required are familiar and repetitive. At the other end of the spectrum there are many exceptions calling for different, unique responses.

In situations where there are few exceptions and analysable problem-solving techniques are available, then routine technology is appropriate. The decision-making mode here is the rational one. As the situation and the problem-solving techniques become more complex the required technology has a higher skill content – engineering and craft skills are required. The corresponding decision-making mode calls for more judgement, but can still be reduced to step-to-step rules and procedures even though they may become very complex. But when the situation becomes complex and the techniques for solving problems become non-routine and unique, then the required technology is that of research and development. Here the decision-making mode involves unique methods of identifying new problems and finding unique solutions.

What emerges from all these analyses of decision situation and appropriate decision-making mode is this: making a decision in a rational manner is only a possibility in the most restrictive of conditions. It will not be possible in conditions of disagreement, ambiguity and uncertainty. But what does rational mean?

## Rationality

The word 'rational' can be used in a number of different ways and its use can cause confusion in discussions about management processes. It is important to distinguish one meaning from another. There are three common meanings of the word 'rational':

1   Sensible, reasonable in the circumstances, sane, not foolish, absurd or extreme. Rationality here is behaving and deciding in a manner connected to reality and judged likely to bring about desired, intended consequences.   Irrationality consists of fantasy-driven behaviour, while rationality involves testing for reality where that reality may well be of an emotional, ideological or cultural kind. I will use the term reality-testing for this kind of rationality and keep the word 'rational' for its next meaning.
2   Rejecting that which cannot be tested by reason applied to objective facts. Rationality here is behaving and deciding only on the basis of propositions that can be consciously reasoned about, rather than on the basis of customs, norms, emotions and beliefs. Irrationality here consists not only of fantasy, but also of behaviour driven by emotions and beliefs even if they are connected to an emotional and ideological reality. I will use the word rational in this sense throughout the book.
3   A method of deciding that involves setting clear objectives, gathering the facts, generating options, and choosing one that maximises or satisfices (i.e approximately satisfies) the objective. Irrationality here is any behaviour whatsoever that is not preceded by fixing objectives and weighing up options based on observable facts. I will refer to this as technical rationality.

It is quite possible, indeed highly likely, that reality testing will lead to the conclusion that technical rationality should be avoided. That is, it may be quite 'rational' in sense 1 to avoid being rational in sense 3. So, in a totally unpredictable environment, under strict time pressures, it would not be logical or sensible to try to make decisions in a painstaking manner that could never anyhow succeed in meeting all the criteria of rationality in its sense 3 meaning.

It could also be rational in terms of meaning 1 (reality testing) to avoid meaning 2. You may achieve a better response from others if you base your behaviour on emotion and belief in certain circumstances. To do so would therefore be rational in sense 1 but not in sense 2.

It is recognised, then, that in conditions far from certainty managers have to apply significantly different decision-making modes to those required in conditions close to certainty. In the next two sections I will examine in more detail what these different modes of decision making are.

## 5.4 MODELS OF DECISION MAKING IN CONDITIONS OF CERTAINTY

There are three well-known models of decision making in conditions close to certainty. These are technical rationality; bounded rationality, bureaucracies and dominant coalitions; and trial-and-error or logical incrementalism. This section examines each of these modes.

### Technical rationality

When managers know what their objectives are and agree upon them, then the effective mode of making a decision is that of technical rationality. Managers discover how their environment and the capability of their organisation are changing by gathering the facts through a continuing process of scanning, research and monitoring. They analyse the facts using the step-by-step rules of logical reasoning to generate all the options open to achieve their objectives. They calculate the effects of carrying out each option on their objectives, choose that option which maximises their objectives, and then act to implement that option. What managers are doing or should be doing is explained in terms of pure rationality, the foundation of scientific management originating in the writings of Fredrick Taylor back in the early part of this century (*Taylor, 1911*).

The previous section showed how this is possible only when the dynamics is stable; that is, when members of an organisation are both close to certainty and close to agreement. Even then, however, the limits on human cognition make pure technical rationality impossible for the following reasons.

Given clear agreed objectives in relation to clear-cut problems, pure rationality requires the decision-maker to perceive the relevant objective facts in a direct manner. Perceiving directly means not seeing the facts through some kind of lens or other means that could open up the possibility of distortion. Having perceived the facts directly, the purely rational person would then have to store them in an exact form so that they could be processed later on without distortion. This would mean storing facts in categories that are precisely defined. Having memorised the facts in this fashion and having memorised in much the same way the processing techniques required to manipulate them, the rational person would then process the facts in a step-by-step fashion according to the rules of logic and select the action option that maximises the objective. The choice is predetermined by the facts and the problem is simply one of calculation.

However, as was recognised decades ago, humans do not perceive in this manner and they cannot therefore decide using a pure technically rational mode.

### Bounded rationality, bureaucracy and dominant coalitions

Recognising the restrictive circumstance in which pure technical rationality could be applied, Herbert Simon developed the concept of bounded rationality (*Simon, 1960*). Bounded rationality is thus the weak form of what I have been calling technical rationality. He argued that managers could be rational only within boundaries imposed by resource availability, experience and knowledge of the range of options available for action. The collection, analysis and exchange of information all use resources, impose costs, and are time consuming. It will therefore never be possible, or even sensible, to gather all the information and examine all the options.

Limited economic resources and the nature of an individual brain's processing capacity together impose constraints on communication and flows of information through an organisation. All of this makes it impossible for managers to use the exhaustive process of pure technical rationality. Instead of screening all the facts and generating all the action options before making a choice, managers, in common with all humans, take shortcuts. They employ trial-and-error search procedures to identify the most important bits of information in particular circumstances; they identify a limited range of the most important options revealed by the search; and then they act knowing only some of the potential outcomes of their actions. This means that they cannot take the action which maximises their objective. Instead they satisfice: they achieve the first satisfactory outcome they can in the circumstances. What they do then depends upon the sequence in which they discover changes, make choices and take actions.

Limited resources and the nature of the brain's processing capacity are also compensated for by the use of bureaucratic procedures (*March & Simon, 1958; Cyert & March, 1963; Simon, 1960*). As managers act together they develop rules of action and standard operating procedures in order to cut down on the need to make decisions afresh each time. Precedents are established and subsequent decisions are taken without having to repeat the search process anew. Decisions and actions come to be outputs of standard patterns of behaviour. For example, next year's budget is often determined largely by uprating this year's spend. New alternatives tend to be sought only when a problem is detected: that is, some discrepancy between what is expected and what happens. Once such a discrepancy is detected, a trail-and-error search for a new solution is undertaken. Since all possible outcomes are not known, the tendency will be to make incremental decisions, that is decisions with consequences as small and containable as possible. By relying on bureaucratic roles, and incremental decision making, managers are able to reduce the levels of uncertainty they have to face. What the organisation learns will be embodied in its rules and procedures and these are used not to optimise outcomes, but to reduce uncertainty.

The lack of realism of the pure rationality model was recognised in other ways as well (*Cyert & March, 1963*). Although decisions and actions may flow from bureaucratic rules and precedent for most of the time, there are numerous occasions on which objectives and interests conflict. Which objectives are pursued will then depend on what the most powerful coalition of managers want.

The above paragraphs indicate how and why bounded-rationality/bureaucratic explanations of how managers discover, choose and act differ from pure technical rationality. But there are also similarities. Both kinds of rationality do not see problem-framing as the major difficulty. Bounded rationality is still about solving problems, even though they may not be as clearly framed. The processes described are still step-by-step or algorithmic procedures, differing from those of pure rationality only in that they are heuristic, that is, involving rules of thumb to proceed by trial and error. An organisation is still seen as searching for satisfactory attainment of known objectives according to known criteria for success and failure.

What the bounded-rationality/bureaucratic explanations do is recognise economic constraints and take a more complicated view of human cognition; they recognise the limitations of human brain processing capacity. However, they do not see the process of discovery or choice as problematic in any sense other than that of limited processing capacity. All forms of planning and budgeting in organisations employ this weak form of technical rationality as the decision-making process. Since it requires that the outcomes of different possible action options be roughly known, this decision-making process can be used only in conditions close to certainty.

## Trial and error – logical incrementation

*Quinn's (1980)* research into the decision-making process of a number of companies revealed that most strategic decisions are made outside formal planning systems, that is outside the bounded-rationality mode of decision making. He found that managers purposely blend behavioural, political and formal analytical processes together to improve the quality of decisions and implementation. Effective managers accept the high level of uncertainty and ambiguity they have to face and do not plan everything. They preserve the flexibility of an organisation to deal with the unforeseen as it happens. The key points that Quinn made about the strategic decision-making mode are as follows:

- Effective managers do not manage strategically in a piecemeal manner. They have a clear view on what they are trying to achieve, where they are trying to take the business. The destination is thus intended.
- But the route to that destination, the strategy itself, is not intended from the start in any comprehensive way. Effective managers know that the environment they have to operate in is uncertain and ambiguous. They therefore sustain flexibility by holding open the method of reaching the goal.
- The strategy itself then emerges from the interaction between different groupings of people in the organisation, different groupings with different amounts of power, different requirements for and access to information, different time spans and parochial interest. These different pressures are orchestrated by senior managers. The top is always reassessing, integrating and organising.
- The strategy emerges or evolves in small incremental, opportunistic steps. But such evolution is not piecemeal or haphazard because of the agreed purpose and the role of top management in reassessing what is happening. It is this that provides the logic in the incremental action.
- The result is an organisation that is feeling its way to a known goal, opportunistically learning as it goes.

In Quinn's model of the strategy process, the organisation is driven by central intention with respect to the goal, but there is no prior central intention as to how that goal is to be achieved; the route to the goal is discovered through a logical process of taking one small step at a time. In logical incrementalism, overall strategy emerges from step-by-step trial-and-error actions occurring in a number of different places in an organisation; for example, some may be making an acquisition while others are restructuring the reporting structure. These separate initiatives are pushed by champions, each attacking a class of strategic issue. The top executives manage the process, orchestrating it and sustaining some logic in it. It is this that makes it a purposeful, proactive technique. Urgent, interim, piecemeal decisions shape the organisation's future, but they do so in an orderly logical way. No one fully understands all the implications of what they are all doing together, but they are consciously preparing to move opportunistically (see *Box 5.1*).

---

**BOX 5.1**

## Exxon Europe

*Quinn (1978)* illustrates his concept of strategies being developed through a process of logical incrementalism as follows:

When Exxon began its regional decentralization on a worldwide basis, the Executive Committee placed a senior officer and board member with a very responsive management style in a vaguely defined 'coordinative role' vis-à-vis its powerful and successful European units. Over a period of two years this man sensed problems and experimented with voluntary coordinative possibilities on a pan-European basis. Only later, with greater understanding by both corporate and divisional officers, did Exxon move to a more formal line relationship for what became Exxon Europe. Even then the move had to be coordinated in other areas of the world. All of these changes together led to an entirely new power balance toward regional and non-US concerns and to a more responsive worldwide posture for Exxon. ■

*Source*: Quinn (1978, p. 102)

---

## 5.5    MODELS OF DECISION MAKING IN CONDITIONS OF UNCERTAINTY

When levels of uncertainty are very high, managers are by definition ignorant even of the outcomes that might possibly flow from a decision they make and an action they take. They do not know how their actions may be related in a cause-and-effect sense to the outcomes of those actions. In genuinely new situations it is not possible to assign probabilities to outcomes. In this section I will review models of decision making that do not assume knowledge either of the final destination or outcome aimed for, or of the route to that destination or outcome.

### The search for error

*Collingridge (1980)* argues that effective decision making in this situation is a search for error and a willingness to respond to its discovery. Instead of searching for the right decision as you would when using a technically rational mode close to certainty, you need to choose an option that can most easily be found to be in error, error that can most easily be corrected. In this way fewer options are closed off; you get more opportunities to adjust what you have done when the circumstances change.

For example, if you can forecast future electricity demand reliably, the right solution to increased demand may be to build one large power station now. If, however, the future demand for electricity is highly uncertain, it would be better to build a number of small power stations, spread over a few years. That way you will find it easier to check for error in your forecast of future demand and easier to correct for mistakes. You may only have to close a small power station instead of running a large one at low capacity.

This kind of approach requires a considerable psychological adjustment. Most of us are used to being judged on whether we made the right choice. If it turns out to be wrong we devote much energy to concealing this fact, or in justifying our original decision. Applying technical rationality in conditions of great uncertainty leads us intentionally to avoid the search for error and to delay its recognition. If we abandon technical rationality in these circumstances and search for error instead, we would have to admit mistakes as soon as possible and avoid trying to justify them. Here we are talking about a mature recognition that being wrong is a valuable learning exercise.

## The Mintzberg decision process model

*Mintzberg, Théorêt & Raisinghani (1976)* analysed 25 decision-making processes and formulated a descriptive model as follows. The decision-making situations they analysed were characterised by novelty, complexity and open-endedness. The research showed that a final choice was made in such situations only after lengthy periods that involved many difficult discontinuous and recursive steps.

They divided the decision process into three basic stages:

1　identification
2　development
3　selection.

Within each of the stages a number of routines were identified. I will now examine each stage and the routines it involves.

### The identification stage

It is a feature of high levels of uncertainty that the issues which have to be attended to, the problems and opportunities requiring a decision, are not at all obvious or clear. The need to make a decision therefore has to be identified or prompted by signals from the environment or from the working of the organisation. The stimulus for a decision may be the voluntary recognition of a problem or an opportunity, or the result of some pressure or mild crisis, or the consequence of a major crisis that forces a decision. Many small stimuli may need to build up to some threshold before a decision need is identified and a decision triggered. In this regard the frame of reference of the manager is important (*Johnson, 1987*). If the stimuli for a decision fall outside the currently shared wisdom on what the business is about and how it should be conducted, then managers will ignore the stimuli. It will probably require a crisis to force a decision. Where managers identify a problem to which there is no clear solution there will be a tendency to ignore it. Problems for which there are matching solutions will tend to be dealt with.

Note how the routine for recognising a problem depends upon the behaviour of individuals, is culturally conditioned, and involves political interaction.

Once managers have recognised a problem, the diagnosis routine is activated. Old information channels are tapped and new ones opened. The diagnosis may be formal or it may be very informal. It may be skipped altogether. What managers are doing here is trying to shape or structure the problems so that they may decide how to deal with them.

### The development stage

The development stage takes up most of the time and resources in the decision-making process. It involves search routines and design routines.

The search routine is an attempt to discover a ready-made solution. These routines include simply waiting for an alternative to materialise, searching the memory of the organisation, that is the solutions to problems that have worked before, scanning alternatives, hiring consultants and so on. Search is a step-by-step or incremental process beginning with the easiest search routine.

The design routine consists of the steps taken to design a solution to the problem. Mintzberg and colleagues found that organisations avoid custom-made routines for making a decision because they are expensive and require many steps. In other words, they tend not to consider large numbers of alternatives but to select one promising alternative, one that they have tried before. There is then a natural tendency to avoid innovative approaches to strategic decision making.

### Selection

Selection is often intertwined with the development stage and involves the routines of screening, evaluative choice and authorisation. The screen routine is used to screen out options that are clearly not viable. It is a superficial routine. The evaluation choice routine was not found to be one that involved the use of analytical techniques in the study that Mintzberg and colleagues conducted. The evaluation criteria were normally based on judgement and intuition. Managers dealt with information overload by using precedent, imitation or tradition. They made judgements on a proposal according to the reliability of the proposer rather than the project, on the track record of the manager.

The final routine is that of authorisation and legitimation of the choices that individuals and groups have made.

The decision-making process identified here is a number of routines that have behavioural, political and learning aspects. The routines are affected by interruptions caused by environmental factors, by scheduling and timing delays as well as speed-ups generated by those involved in the process, by feedback delays as people wait for information and authorisation, and by cycling back to earlier stages in the process.

## Dialectical enquiry

*Schwenck & Thomas (1983)* also address the process of decision making in open-ended situations. They identify three procedures for formulating problems and selecting outcomes:

1   *Brainstorming.* Here a small group of people work together to produce as many ideas as they can on what problems they should be addressing and how they should deal with them. The ideas generated can then be ranked and subjected to further study and consideration.

2   *The devil's advocate.* Here one or more persons play the role of trying to tear a proposal apart. They are performing the important function of identifying and questioning the tacit assumptions that are being made.

3   *Dialectical enquiry.* This is similar to the devil's advocate approach but involves groups of people. Two opposing groups enter into a debate on a proposed solution to a problem. Again, this focuses attention on tacit assumptions being made. From the two conflicting options being debated, a third, a synthesis of the two, may emerge.

## Muddling through, organised anarchy, and garbage-can decision making

*Lindblom (1959)* also describes the process of strategic decision making as incremental, but to him it is a form of 'muddling through'. His observations are derived from decision making in state sector organisations, but they are relevant to private sector organisations too. Because in complex situations it is not possible to identify all the objectives of different groups of people affected by an issue, policies are chosen directly. Instead of working from a statement of desired ends to the means required to achieve it, managers choose the ends and the means simultaneously. In other words, two different managers may choose the same policy or solution for different reasons.

This means that a policy cannot be judged according to how well it achieves a given end. Instead it is judged according to whether it is itself desirable or not. A good policy is thus simply one that gets widespread support. It is then carried out in incremental stages, preserving flexibility to change it as conditions change. The policy is pursued in stages of successive limited comparisons. In this approach, dramatically new policies are not considered. New policies have to be close to existing ones and limited comparisons are made. This makes it unnecessary to undertake fundamental enquiries. The procedure also involves ignoring important possible consequences of policies, a necessary evil perhaps if anything is to be done. But serious lasting mistakes can be avoided because the changes are being made in small steps.

*Cohen, March & Ohlsen (1972)* have carried this kind of analysis of state sector organisations further. They describe many of these organisations as organised anarchies and their decision-making process as garbage-can decision making.

In their research, they found that universities and some state bodies are characterised by widely distributed power and complex, unclear hierarchical structures. The hierarchical structure is such that just about any issue can be taken to just about any forum, by just about anyone. These institutions are noted for widespread participation in decision making, for ambiguous and intersecting job definitions, and a lack of shared cultural values across the whole organisation. What is found in the conditions prevailing at universities and some state bodies is the following:

- Individuals and subunits do not have clear goals.
- No individual has much power and the distribution of power is not stably determined by sanctions, interdependence and contribution. It fluctuates with the context within which decisions are being made, and consequently
- the distribution of power over time is not constant, and neither is
- the distribution of power over issue. And furthermore
- choices are often avoided, deferred, made by oversight, or never implemented.

Such organisations face high levels of uncertainty not only, or even primarily, because their environments are changing but because of the uncertainty of their technology. It is far from certain what good teaching is, for example, or what good medical care is. Such organisations therefore have to be collections of relatively free professionals. This leads to a form that the authors call organised anarchy. Here decisions and their outcomes occur largely by chance. The flow of choices over time is erratic and haphazard. There is a continuing flow of problems, opportunities, solutions and choices coming together in a largely haphazard manner. This happens because there is no simple and clear hierarchy and because the distribution of power is close to equality.

Where power is widely dispersed so that there are no powerful actors who can enforce their wills; where power is therefore unstable over time and issue; where there is little sharing of values; where there are heavy workloads on individuals and meetings; where participation in decision making is open and fluid; where access to choice situations and participation structures is open and unclear; then choice will be determined largely by chance. The choice will depend entirely upon the context in which it is attended to. It will depend upon the level of attention paid to it in the light of all the other issues; upon who was present and participated; upon how they participated and how others interpreted that participation. Looking back it will not be possible to say that the choice occurred because some individual or group intended it. In this sense intention or purpose is lacking in the choice process. There is no overall rhythm to the process and the specific sequence of choices is random and without any pattern. The sequence of specific choices can shoot just anywhere because important constraints provided by unequal power, clear hierarchies and job descriptions have been removed. Action is then the result of habit, custom or the unpredictable influence of others. It is impossible to predict the choice without knowing all the small details of the context. Intention is lost in the flow of events and goals are the product of sense-making activities after the event.

These studies have shown that where participation is widespread and power equally distributed; where job assignments are unclear and hierarchies complex; where values are not strongly shared; then sequences of choices depend largely on chance.

## 5.6    MODELS OF CONTROL

*Hofstede (1981)* defines the situation in which control is to be exerted in terms of:

- the degree of ambiguity in the objectives to be achieved;
- the measurability of the performance to be controlled;
- the extent to which the outcomes of actions are known;
- the extent to which the activity being controlled is repetitive.

Different combinations of these four factors require alternative forms of control and Hofstede distinguishes six of these.

1   **Routine control**. This applies only when there is no ambiguity in objectives, the consequences of performance are accurately measurable, the causal links are clear cut so that the outcomes of actions are known, and the activity being controlled is repetitive. The form of control in this situation is automatic negative feedback, in which information about a deviation between some desired and some actual outcome is fed back into the decision-making process to remove the deviation. An automated system to control inventory levels is an example of this.

2   **Expert control**. If we relax the last requirement to do with repetitive activities then we can no longer practise routine, that is fully automatic control. But we can come pretty close to it, if we create the possibility of expert intervention at certain points. This is the planning/monitoring form of control in which actual outcomes are reported against projections and managers then discuss the variances, identifying what to do to remove them.

3   **Trial-and-error control**. Suppose now that the only condition we set for routine control that is not met is that the outcomes of actions are not known. Then, because we cannot predict, we cannot practise routine or expert control; instead we will have to discover the effects of our interventions through a process of trial and error which is possible because actions are repetitive. This is control through trial-and-error learning about the consequences of our actions.

4   **Intuitive control**. What if the situation in which control is to be exerted becomes even more difficult in that, although objectives are unambiguous and performance is measurable, actions are not repetitive and their outcomes are not known? Then trial and error will not help much because in effect there will be only one chance to take a particular action – it is unique. In these circumstances Hofstede talks about control as intuitive, as an art rather than a science, where there are few rules to guide managers.

5   **Judgemental control**. If the control situation becomes even more difficult so that activity is not repetitive, its outcomes are unknown and now also not measurable, but objectives are still clear, then control has to take a subjective, judgemental form.

6   **Political control**. Finally, suppose that managers face unique situations in which the objectives to be achieved are unclear and the outcomes of actions are neither measurable nor known. Then the only form of control that it is possible to apply is political control. This relies on the use of power, negotiation, persuasion and manipulation, often expressed in rituals and symbols.

## 5.7   SUMMARY

This chapter first explored the time path that an organisation follows as it changes. The first view is that change takes place in small incremental steps as the organisation converges to the future state chosen by its strategists. The second view points to difficulties that managers experience in making such orderly changes. According to this view managers get stuck in particular ways of thinking and their organisation drifts away from a state adapted to its environment. It then experiences a crisis and survives only if its managers change their minds and make appropriate choices. The choices prescribed often have to do with the installation of structures and procedures that sustain control, so making the organisation a more effective cybernetic system. The writers reviewed point to difficulties in sustaining an organisation as an effective cybernetic system but they remain within the strategic choice framework with its emphasis on individual choice.

The chapter then reviewed a number of different models of decision making and control. What all of these models do is to set out a number of different situations for which different modes of decision making and control are observed or prescribed. They point to how these modes change as levels of uncertainty and disagreement rise. The researchers take the position of the objective observer of the organisational system, describing and prescribing modes of decision making and control appropriate for different situations. The implicit, and sometimes explicit, implication is that managers too should take this position of the objective observer, identify the situation that they find themselves in, and then choose that mode of decision making and that mode of control that are appropriate. This approach also remains within the strategic choice framework. Individual managers are to make choices, this time not about outcomes, but first about appropriate modes of decision making and control. What is also striking about this literature is how it describes and prescribes algorithmic modes of decision making and control. In other words, they identify sequential steps that managers follow, or are supposed to follow if they are to choose appropriately.

The alternative to strategic choice is muddled decision making, outcomes that emerge by chance and lack of control.

The next chapter turns to how human motivation, human beliefs and human emotions are taken into account within a strategic choice framework.

## FURTHER READING

Turton (1991) contains excellent summaries of decision-making modes. For even further detail on particular decision-making modes turn to Quinn (1978), Mintzberg, Théorêt & Raisinghani (1976) and Cohen, March & Ohlsen (1972).

## REFERENCES

Child, J. (1972), Organisational structure, environment and performance: the role of strategic choice, *Sociology*, vol. 6, no. 1, pp. 1–21.

Child, J. (1984), *Organisation*, London: Harper & Row.

Cohen, M. D., March, J. G. & Ohlsen, J. P. (1972), A garbage can model of organizational choice, *Administrative Science Quarterly*, vol. 17, pp. 1–25.

Collingridge, D. (1980), *The Social Control of Technology*, Milton Keynes: Open University Press.

Cyert, R. M. & March, J. G. (1963), *A Behavioural Theory of the Firm*, Englewood Cliffs, NJ: Prentice Hall.

Duncan, R. (1972), Characteristics of organisational environments and perceived uncertainty, *Administrative Science Quarterly*, vol. 17, pp. 313–27.

Greiner, L. E. (1972), Evolution and revolution as organizations grow, *Harvard Business Review*, July–August.

Hofstede, G. (1981), Management control of public and not-for-profit activities, *Accounting, Organisations and Society*, vol. 6, no. 3, pp. 193–211.

Johnson, G. (1987), *Strategic Change and the Management Process*, Oxford: Blackwell.

Lindblom, L. (1959), The science of muddling through, *Public Administration Review*, vol. 19, pp. 79–88.

March, J. G. & Simon, H. A. (1958), *Organizations*, New York: John Wiley.

Miller, D. & Freisen, P. H. (1980), Momentum and revolution in organizational adaptation, *Academy of Management Journal*, vol. 23, pp. 591–614.

Mintzberg, H. (1989), *Mintzberg on Management: Inside our Strange World of Organizations*, New York: Free Press.

Mintzberg, H., Théorêt, A. & Raisinghani, D. (1976), The structure of the unstructured decision making process, *Administrative Science Quarterly*, vol. 21, no. 2, pp. 246–75.

Perrow, C. (1972), *Complex Organizations*, London: Scott-Foresman.

Pfeffer, J. (1981), *Power in Organizations*, Cambridge, MA: Ballinger.

Quinn, J. B. (1978), Strategic change: logical incrementalism, *Sloan Management Review*, vol. 1, no. 20, Fall, pp. 7–21.

Quinn, J. B. (1980), *Strategic Change: Logical Incrementalism*, Homewood, IL: Richard D. Irwin.

Schwenk, C. & Thomas, H. (1983), Formulating the mess: the role of decision and problem formulation, *Omega: The International Journal of Management Science*, vol. 11, no. 3, pp. 239–52.

Simon, H. A. (1960), *The New Science of Management Decisions*, New York: Harper Brothers.

Taylor, F. (1911), *Scientific Management*, New York: Harper Brothers.

Thompson, J. D. & Tuden, A. (1959), Strategies, structures and processes of organisational decisions, in Thompson, J. D. et al. (Eds.) (1959), *Comparative Studies in Administration*, Pittsburgh: University of Pittsburgh Press.

Turton, R. (1991), *Behaviour in a Business Context*, London: Chapman and Hall.

Tushman, M. L. & Romanelli, E. (1985), A metamorphosis model of convergence and reorientation, in Straw, B. & Cummings, E. (Eds.) (1985), *Research in Organizational Behavior*, vol. 7, Greenwich, CT: JAI Press.

Chapter

# 6 Strategic choice

## Motivation, leadership, politics and culture

## 6.1 INTRODUCTION

This chapter reviews the literature on motivation, leadership, politics and culture in organisations. It is concerned with ideological, cultural and political processes and how they affect strategic management and organisational change.

One approach to taking these factors into account is to identify a small number of key attributes, primarily leadership and cultural factors, in successful organisations. These are then held to account for their success and the prescription is to install them in other organisations. These too should then be successful through the process of imitation. The key attributes usually relate to behaviour: working harmoniously together, strongly sharing the same culture, values, beliefs and vision of the future. The prescription is to establish a vision of the whole organisation's future, convert people into believing it, promote internal harmony by encouraging the strong sharing of a few cultural values, and empowering people.

This notion of attributes of excellence that can be imitated is explored in the next section. Then the chapter turns to questions of leadership, politics and culture.

## 6.2 ATTRIBUTES OF EXCELLENCE

In the early 1980s *Peters & Waterman (1982)* published a study of 43 major American corporations. The sample included such household names as Disney, Boeing, IBM, Mars, McDonald's, Dupont, Levi-Strauss, Procter & Gamble, 3M, Hewlett Packard, Kodak, Wang and Atari. All 43 companies were selected because they were judged to be excellent according to six financial yardsticks and because they had been innovative and adaptable over reasonably long time periods. The study reached the conclusion that the cause of the excellence displayed by these companies lay in eight prominent attributes they shared in common. The conclusion drawn was that if other companies imitated these eight attributes, they too would become excellent. The eight attributes are listed below.

## The attributes of excellence

1  **Stick to the knitting.** Excellent companies build on their strengths or core competences and they never diversify far away from these. Because successful companies stick to what they know and avoid that which they do not, senior managers can have a clear understanding of their business. It is this knowledge and experience that provides the basis of their management intuition and credibility. For example, McDonald's sticks to fast foods and avoids diversifying into hotels.

2  **Close to the customer.** Excellent companies actively listen to their customers and place great emphasis on delivering quality, reliability and high levels of service. They set very high standards in these regards and ensure their achievement through reward systems that include emotional rewards, for example reward ceremonies. The excellent companies succeed because by listening to their customers they become better adapted to their environments than their competitors.

3  **Productive through people.** Excellent companies express concern for the feelings of their people and try to foster attitudes in which people perceive themselves as belonging to an extended family.

4  **Autonomy and entrepreneurship.** Excellent companies encourage local initiative and practical risk taking; they empower people to make decisions about their own jobs. The cultural values are such that people are not penalised for the failures that must sometimes flow from taking risks. Eccentrics are tolerated, provided that they are doers.

5  **Hands on, value driven.** In their decision-making processes, excellent companies place particular emphasis on cultural values and beliefs. The leaders of the company articulate and preach a set of beliefs to which they convert others. It is this strongly shared common culture that is the principal cause of the harmony to be found in excellent companies. The role of the leaders is also to create a strong sense of direction by expressing a vision of the future state the organisation is to occupy. The vision and the core values are not open to question, other than at the fringes. Leaders are inspirational and involved in the activities of their organisation, not superior or aloof monitors of previously planned actions.

6  **Bias for action.** Excellent companies rely heavily on informal communication and employ small, temporary task forces with voluntary membership inspired by visionary product champions to progress many different projects. On this view, organisations make strategic choices in a political manner because the choice depends upon how much support the champion can build for his or her idea.

   Excellent companies are interested in tangible results, not lengthy reports; they do not wait for the results of analyses, but rather try ideas out, rapidly one after the other. They emphasise fast trial-and-error action through which they learn about their environment.

7   **Simple form, lean staff.** Excellent companies have small corporate headquarters with the rest decentralised into small autonomous units. Authority is pushed down the line. Complicated matrix forms of organisation are avoided. People are encouraged to see organisational subunits as flexible and permeable. Rigid job descriptions are discouraged.

8   **Simultaneous loose–tight properties.** Excellent companies have control systems in which there are two elements. These elements sound contradictory, but the manner in which they are used means that they are not contradictory in practice. On the one hand, excellent companies encourage simple fluid structures with high levels of autonomy and positive attitudes to risk taking where people are empowered to take their own decisions. On the other hand, excellent companies apply tight short-term financial controls to the performance of all their units and they fiercely guard the core values. But they find it possible to combine individual initiative and enterprise (the loose) with central organisational intention and control (the tight) in a consistent and harmonious way because of the belief system that all strongly share. Harmony and consistency are thus preserved, so solving the apparent contradiction between the tight and the loose.

The conclusion drawn is that if managers install these eight attributes into their organisations then people will be motivated to carry out the trial-and-error actions required to reach the vision shared by all. The top sets the vision and the values and then relies on people in the organisation to find the route to that vision. Peters and Waterman explain that rapid change and high levels of uncertainty make it impossible to forecast enough of what is going to happen to make it possible to prepare stable plans well in advance of acting; that is, to tell people well in advance what they are expected to do. It follows that managers have to discover the route to the future position they wish to occupy through trial-and-error action. The drive to undertake large volumes of trial-and-error action comes from what people believe; hence the heavy emphasis of the eight attributes on ideology, culture and vision.

Peters and Waterman argued that managers were being misled by a belief that they ought to be rational and were consequently spending too much time on research and analysis that diminished the urge to act – the result was paralysis by analysis. The argument about rationality and the extent to which managers need to use rational criteria to make decisions or to adopt some other approach still continues.

The Peters and Waterman study and the principles it identified have had a very powerful effect on companies throughout the world. During the 1980s many companies cut out layers of management to make their organisations lean and simple. They embarked on major programmes to change the cultures of their organisations and to empower people; they devoted time to forming visions and preparing mission statements; and terms such as vision, values and culture came to occupy a prominent place in the vocabulary of most business people.

The enduring contribution made by the Peters and Waterman study is the attention it focused on the important role that values, culture and beliefs play in organisational success. It also directed attention to the informal aspects of an organisation and the role that organisational politics plays in the process of strategic management by emphasising the role of leaders, product champions, project teams and task forces.

These are much the same kinds of processes that have been observed in studies of political activity in organisations.

Despite the importance of the Peters and Waterman study, however, it has not identified *the* definitive route to success. The eight-attribute plan proved to be a disappointment because, within five years, two-thirds of the companies in the sample had slipped from the pinnacle, some to return later, others to remain in the doldrums. A number of other studies followed (e.g. *Goldsmith & Clutterbuck, 1984*), but none so far can be judged to have found the one best way for all companies.

There is an important point to notice here. Peters and Waterman questioned the rational techniques of decision making and control that were reviewed in Chapters 3 and 4, pointing to their limitations in conditions of turbulence. Instead, they emphasised human motivation, values, beliefs and the importance of leadership. However, they did not depart in any way from cognitivist assumptions about human nature, nor in any essential way from the assumption that an organisation is a cybernetic system. This is evident when they talk about charismatic leaders who choose a vision of the future and certain core values that they then inspire others with, converting them into believing the vision and the values. If anything, the autonomous individual has become even more heroic in their view of organisational change. The system is still cybernetic because it is controlled by referring to the vision and the values and damping out any deviations from them.

The chapter will now go on to look at what other influential writers have had to say about motivation, leadership, politics and culture.

## 6.3   MOTIVATION

A number of different theories of motivation have been put forward in the management literature on how to secure consensus, cooperation and commitment.

### Hertzberg's (1966) extrinsic and intrinsic motivators

Hertzberg pointed out that people are motivated to work in cooperation with others by both extrinsic motivators such as monetary rewards and intrinsic motivators such as recognition for achievement, achievement itself, responsibility, growth and advancement. Intrinsic motivation is the more powerful of the motivators and is increased when jobs are enriched, that is when jobs are brought up to the skill levels of those performing them.

### Maslow's (1954) hierarchy of needs

Maslow distinguished between: basic physiological needs, such as food and shelter; intermediate social needs, such as safety and esteem; and higher self-actualisation needs, such as self-fulfilment. Maslow held that when the conditions are created in which people can satisfy their self-actualisation needs, those people are then powerfully motivated to strive for the good of their organisation.

### Schein's (1988a) and Etzioni's (1961) framework for categorising motivation

These writers distinguished three categories of relationship between the individual and the organisation. The relationship may be coercive, in which case the individual will do only the bare minimum required to escape punishment. The relationship may be a utilitarian one where the individual does only enough to earn the required level of reward. Thirdly, the relationship may take a normative form where individuals value what they are doing for its own sake, because they believe in it and identify with it. In other words, the individual's ideology coincides with an organisation's ideology. This provides the strongest motivator of all for the individual to work for the good of an organisation.

### Peters & Waterman (1982): the power of shared ideology as a driver of behaviour

These writers particularly emphasised the emotional content of motivation. They described successful organisations as ones in which people are driven by a sense of excitement and where they have strong feelings of belonging to the organisation.

### Pascale & Athos (1981): the importance of organisational culture as a motivator

Their stress on organisational culture resulted from a study of Japanese management. They recognised that people yearn for meaning in their lives and transcendence over mundane things. Cultures that provide this meaning create powerfully motivated employees and managers.

What all these studies point to is this. An organisation succeeds when its people, as individuals, are emotionally engaged in some way, when they believe in what their group and their organisation are doing, when the contribution they make to this organisational activity brings psychological satisfaction of some kind, something more than simple basic rewards. People believe and are emotionally engaged when their organisation has a mission or set of values and when their own personal values match those of the organisation. Organisational missions develop because people search for meaning and purpose and this search includes their work lives (*Campbell & Tawady, 1990*). To win commitment and loyalty and to secure consensus around performing tasks it becomes necessary to promote a sense of mission.

The development of a sense of mission is seen as a central leadership task and a vitally important way of gaining commitment to, loyalty for, and consensus around, the nature and purpose of the existing business. An organisation with a sense of mission captures the emotional support of its people, even if only temporarily. In the rest of this section I will first review what a sense of mission means, how it comes about, and how those writing about it claim that it can be managed.

## A sense of mission

A sense of mission is more than a definition of the business, that is the area that an organisation is to operate in. A sense of mission is also to be distinguished from the ideas behind the word 'vision' or 'strategic intent'. The word 'vision' is usually taken to mean a picture of a future state for an organisation, a mental image of a possible and desirable future that is realistic, credible and attractive. The term mission differs in that it refers not to the future but to the present. A mission is a way of behaving. Mission is concerned with the way an organisation is managed today, with its purpose or reason for being. Strategic intent is a desired leadership position. It too, therefore, is a desired future state, a goal to do with winning. Mission is to do with here-and-now purpose, the culture, the business philosophy. A sense of mission is an emotional response to questions to do with what people are doing, why they are doing it, what they are proud of, what they are enthusiastic about, what they believe in.

The Ashridge mission model sees a mission as consisting of four components:

1   **An inspirational definition of what an organisation is there for.** For some companies the purpose is to make money for shareholders. For example, this is quite clearly the prime purpose of Hanson plc, a purpose frequently enunciated by Lord Hanson and one which quite clearly drives the behaviour of Hanson executives. Other companies have the purpose of satisfying all their stakeholders: shareholders, employees, customers, suppliers and the community. Other companies seek to fulfil a purpose bigger than satisfying stakeholders. For example, Steve Jobs' purpose for Apple was to bring computing power to the masses. The purpose of Marks & Spencer has been expressed as that of raising standards for working people. At the Body Shop the purpose is to sell products that do not hurt animals.

2   **The organisation's strategy.** This is the commercial logic of the business. It defines the area in which the organisation is to operate, the rationale for its operation, the source of competitive advantage it is going to tap, the distinctive competence it is going to provide, the special position it is going to occupy. So one part of the Marks & Spencer business is food retailing in the UK where it seeks to secure a position as the best provider of high-quality food. Competitive advantage comes from dedication to quality.

3   **The policies and behavioural standards, defining how managers and employees should behave.** These are part of an organisation's way of doing business. For example, one of Marks & Spencer's standards is visible management – managers must be seen in the stores. Another example is given by *Campbell, Devine & Young (1990, p. 30):*

British Airways provides a good example of how the company's purpose and strategy have been successfully converted into tangible standards and actions. It promotes itself as the 'world's favourite airline' and its mission statement declares as its aim 'To be the best and most successful company in the airline industry.' The strategy to achieve this is based on providing good value for money and service that overall is superior to its competitors and having friendly, professional managers who are in tune with its staff. These strategic objectives have been translated into policies such as the need for inflight service to be at least as good as that of competing airlines on the same route, and the requirements that managers should be helpful and friendly at all times.

By translating purpose and strategy into actionable policies and standards, senior managers at British Airways have dramatically changed the performance of the airline. Central to this effort was the training and behaviour change connected with the slogan 'Putting People First'.

4   **The beliefs that constitute an organisation's culture and underpin its management style.** People do things in organisations because there is a strategic logic and because there are moral or value-based reasons for doing so.

A strong sense of mission comes about when personal and organisational values match and when the four elements are closely knitted together: when they support and reinforce each other.

Take the clothing retailing activities of Marks & Spencer. The strategy is to produce better quality classic products through close relationships with manufacturers. By selling these products at normal prices, Marks & Spencer create such a volume of sales that fixed overhead costs are much lower than for competitors and more than compensate for lower retail margins. Linked to this strategy are values based in quality, value for money, service and people care. Behaviour standards such as the company's human relations policies or visible management style tie the strategy and the values together. To sell goods in high volumes, service is critical. By looking after people well and being visibly interested in the operating issues of the business, managers create an atmosphere in which staff want to look after customers and help the business succeed. Finally, these elements of strategy, values and behaviour standards are linked together in an inspiring way by Marks & Spencer's purpose of raising the standards of the working man and woman. (*Campbell, Devine & Young, 1990, p. 5*)

The sense of mission is important because it generates trust and belief in the activities in an organisation. It gives meaning to work, motivates people, and brings about consensus and loyalty. It provides the basis for making quick judgemental decisions without having to review things from basics or exchange a great deal of information. For example, a company faced with cash difficulties might dismiss an option of selling off subsidiaries on the grounds that it is there to build businesses, not trade in them. A strong mission provides the criteria for selecting and training people who will fit. It provides self-selecting criteria for conformity. People will leave if they come to realise that they do not fit. In organisations with a strong sense of mission there is conformity, cooperation, trust and consensus.

The research that Campbell, Devine and Young carried out on missions in business led to the following conclusions:

- Creating a sense of mission is a long-term project that takes years rather than months. Missions emerge from the way people work together and those that are imposed from the top rarely take root. Top managers who wish to create a sense of mission therefore need to proceed slowly and there is little point in simply writing down intellectual statements of a mission.
- A true consensus at the top of an organisation needs to be developed before a sense of mission can be spread around an organisation.
- A sense of mission is spread through the actions of people at the top, not through their words.
- Top team visibility is essential if its views on mission are to be propagated.
- There must be continuity in the top team if a sense of mission is to be spread through an organisation.
- Any statements of mission need to be inspirational and reflect the personalities of those propounding them.
- Strategies and values should be created together.
- Managers should focus on the link between values and behaviour. Managers create meaning when they assist employees to see the link between tasks and values.

Campbell, Devine and Young maintain that a sense of mission can be managed. They draw a distinction between three approaches to managing mission:

- The first is the intellectual approach where managers go away for a weekend and write a mission statement, or they get some consulting expert to do so. The result, according to the research, is almost always a waste of time. No one believes the end product.

- The second approach is where some powerful founder of an organisation develops a business philosophy over a long period of time which takes hold in the organisation, becoming a set of timeless values that are deeply embedded in people's behaviour.
- The third approach is to focus on particular issues. These are usually rules of the organisational game as it were, values to do with service or quality or cost. People may have lost sight of the importance of these rules or values and the benefit of developing a mission lies in refocusing on them.

The authors offer this advice for developing and managing a sense of mission:

- Pick the most relevant theme in the particular circumstances, for example quality.
- Place the emphasis on action not words, for example a company-wide training programme, not a mission statement plastered on the walls.
- Focus on behaviour and stress one or two elements of behaviour such as putting people first.
- Expect it to take time.
- Build trust.

To see what this means in practice read *Box 6.1*.

## BOX 6.1
### British Airways

In November 1983 British Airways introduced a training programme called 'Putting People First'. The aim was to put 12 000 customer-contact people through a two-day course to improve their customer service skills. The programme consisted of a mixture of presentations, exercises and group discussions in which staff reviewed their personal experience as customers of other service organisations. They also examined the implications for British Airways and were pressed to identify what they would do about these implications. The response to the training programme was mixed – some were sceptical, some saw it as a brainwashing exercise, some dropped out, and others were enthusiastic. But top management continued to support the programme, demonstrating their commitment to customer service. Then non-front-line staff began asking to be included and gradually the level of cynicism faded away. Staff began identifying the obstacles, confronting their managers with the fact that resources were insufficient to deliver the levels of customer care called for. The management responded to these issues and so encouraged staff to identify others.

Then in 1984, a programme for managers called 'Managing People First' was launched to change management styles. At the time, management style was perceived to be dominated by roles and procedures and the aim of the training programme was to replace this with something more open and dynamic.

Other changes were made to reinforce the training programmes. For example, quality assurance and performance related reward systems were introduced. The services being offered by the airline were also improved, demonstrating to staff that they would get the resources required to deliver better service.

It was only once the changes in behaviour were starting to show up as better service and greater customer satisfaction that mission statements were formulated in 1986. ■

*Source*: Campbell, Devine & Young (1990)

The Campbell and Tawady research also sounds warnings about developing a sense of mission:

- The strategies and values embodied in the mission could become inappropriate as the world changes and continued reinforcement of them would then lead to failure. Over decades the British motor cycle industry stuck to its traditional values and behaviours. This blinded it to the dangers of competition from the Japanese and eventually led to the total destruction of the whole industry.
- Strong belief in a mission leads people in an organisation to resist change and to keep outsiders from occupying positions of any importance.

The authors advise that organisations should not try to develop a strong sense of mission in conditions of rapid change and great uncertainty, where the top team is divided or when the strategy is in a state of flux.

There are therefore two ways to avoid the risks: avoid creating clear values and discourage employees from becoming emotionally committed to them; or formulate a well-founded mission with values that are timeless and a strategy that can be sustained for decades. The first way of avoiding the risks is appropriate when an organisation faces extreme and temporary uncertainty. In these circumstances it may be better to wait and see how events unfold before developing a mission ... in 12 months time everything is likely to become clearer, making it possible, even advisable, to develop a strategy and build a new organisation, a new mission, around it.

For all other organisations, the pitfalls are best avoided by developing a timeless mission with values that need not change in fundamental ways. (*Campbell & Tawady, 1990, p. 13*)

In support of this conclusion the authors point to Marks & Spencer. Here the principles of good human relations and visible management have not changed, but the policy of buying British – Marks & Spencer set up an office in Hong Kong to help source product from the Far East.

The point I made about imitating attributes of excellence applies to all the theories of motivation reviewed above. The underlying assumption is that organisations succeed when individuals are motivated to perform, as individuals. The humanistic psychology that the above writers draw on accords the same primacy to the individual as cognitivism does. The difference is that the former places much more emphasis on emotional factors, predominantly of a positive inspirational kind. Note how leaders are supposed to choose appropriate motivators.

## 6.4   LEADERSHIP AND THE ROLE OF GROUPS

The hierarchy, the bureaucracy and the official ideology in effect establish formal interconnections between managers and in so doing set up formal groupings in which they will be required to work. The key point about these groups is that they have clear tasks defined by the policies and rules of the bureaucracy, or expressed in the shared ideology. Two key questions arise in relation to these formal groups:

1   What is the nature of leadership in formal task groups?
2   What is the relevance of the group, as opposed to the individual manager, in these formal groups?

### The nature of leadership in formal management groups

In formal groups, the primary focus is on the leader as one who:

- translates the directives of those higher up in the hierarchy into the goals and tasks of the group;
- monitors the performance of the task in terms of goal achievement;
- ensures that a cohesive team is built and motivated to perform the task;
- supplies any skills or efforts that are missing in the team;
- articulates purpose and culture, so reducing the uncertainty that team members face.

When leadership is defined in these terms, the concern is with the qualities leaders must possess and the styles they must employ in order to fulfil these functions effectively and efficiently. Those who have put forward explanations on the nature of leadership have differed from each other over whether the effective leader is one who focuses on the task, or one who focuses on relationships with and between people. A related area of concern is whether the effective leader is one who is autocratic, or one who delegates, consults and invites full participation. The question is which style of leadership motivates people more and thus gets the task done better. Consider three prominent theories.

#### Fiedler's (1967) Leader-Match Theory

Here managers are placed on a spectrum running from an orientation to the task at one end to an orientation to relationships at the other. Which of these orientations is more effective is said to depend upon the nature of the task, the attitudes of the subordinates, and the power of the leader. Where the task is clearly structured, and the leader has clear hierarchical authority and subordinates are supportive and willing to accept authority, then the task orientation works best. When none of these conditions is present, the task orientation still works best. The reason for this, perhaps surprising, result is that leaders with a relationship orientation would refrain from pressurising people in very unclear situations and thus not get the task done. However, where there is an in-between situation, then relationship-oriented leaders come into their own. The prescription for potential leaders is to discover their orientation and find a situation that fits.

### Vroom & Yetton's (1973) Contingency Theory

This theory presents a spectrum of leadership styles from the highly autocratic at one end to the participative at the other. It is claimed that analysis of the problem situation determines which point on this spectrum provides the most effective leadership style for that situation. So, if there is likely to be a best rational solution, if there is sufficient information to reach the solution, if the problem is structured, if acceptance by subordinates is not all that crucial, and anyway they will accept it, then an autocratic style will yield the best results. But if there is unlikely to be a best rational solution, there is insufficient information, the problem is not structured, subordinate acceptance is crucial, goals are shared, but conflict is still likely, then the best style is a highly participative one. In between, various degrees of autocracy and participation would be called for.

### Hersey & Blanchard's (1988) Situation Theory

Here, too, style and leader behaviour are to be adapted to the situation and to follower needs if they are to be effective. Task focus and relationship focus are related, however, and instead of being presented as alternatives, four leadership styles are distinguished. Leaders may adopt a 'selling' style, in which they focus heavily on both the task and relationships; or they may use a 'delegation' style, where they put a low emphasis on both task and relationships; or they may emphasise the task heavily and underplay relationships, in which case their style is 'telling'. Finally, they may focus heavily on relationships and underplay the task, in which case their style is 'participating'. The appropriate style depends upon how mature the group is. If maturity is low, then telling is the right style. As the group matures, the leader should move to selling and then to participating and finally to delegating.

According to these theories leadership styles are to be chosen by the individual manager and to be successful a style that matches certain pre-given situations must be chosen. The leader should arrive at the group with particular skills developed beforehand. The required personality, skills and styles (or, as they are sometimes called, competences) are supposed to be identified in advance since they depend upon the situation. Here leadership is about motivating people and the concern is with the appropriate role of the leader in securing efficient performance of known tasks.

## The relevance of the group

Formal groups are part of a formal hierarchy, a formal set of representative bodies, and a formal administrative bureaucracy. These are all structures that formalise the division and allocation of tasks to individuals and groups of people on the one hand, and the legitimation, integration and control of those tasks through leaders and representative groups on the other. Individuals have roles as leaders and followers, they have roles in groups. But what, if any, distinctive part does the group have to play in how managers exercise their role? I will now examine some answers to this question.

### Groups

A group is any number of people who interact with each other, are psychologically aware of each other, and perceive themselves to be a group. Formal groups in an organisation may be permanent, for example the sales department; or they may be temporary, as is the case when special task forces or multidisciplinary teams are appointed to deal with a particular task. Whether they are temporary or permanent, formal groups have clear goals and tasks; it is the purpose of formal groups to find solutions to structured problems. They usually have appointed leaders – leaders and managers have power given to them. However, they may also be autonomous, self-managing or democratic work groups that elect their own leader and design their own approach to a given structured task. Note that procedures are laid down in advance on how leaders are to be appointed and roles determined. This has sometimes been done to improve motivation and thus efficiency (*Lindblom & Norstedt, 1971*). However, even self-managing groups still have clear structures, tasks, objectives and procedures and so are formal groups, parts of an organisation's legitimate system.

Within, alongside and across the formal groups, there is a strong tendency for informal groups to develop. These may be horizontal cliques amongst colleagues on the same hierarchical level, vertical cliques that include people from different hierarchical levels, or random cliques. Informal groups develop primarily because of proximity (*Festinger, Schachter & Back, 1950*): through the contacts people make with each other given their physical location in relation to each other, the nature of their work and the time pressures they are under. The immediate concern about these informal groups is whether they will support or counter the operation of formal groups. The concern is with motivating people to cohere into functional teams that will focus on clearly defined tasks, not dissipate energies in destructive informal groups.

The concern is primarily with the authority, responsibility and performance of individual managers in carrying out their preassigned tasks. From this perspective, the interest in groups relates to the circumstances in which groups may be more effective than individuals. Groups can:

- accomplish complex interdependent tasks beyond the ability of individuals working alone;
- solve complex problems that require many inputs;
- provide a means of coordinating activities;
- facilitate implementation through generating participation and commitment;
- generate new ideas and creative solutions within the paradigm;
- provide the opportunity of social interaction that improves morale and motivation.

Groups, both formal and informal, meet human needs for affiliation and self-esteem. They provide individuals with a sense of security, they reduce anxiety and the sense of powerlessness, and they provide opportunities for individuals to test reality through discussion with others. But they also create a vehicle for individuals to pursue their own self-interested tasks and problem-solving activities.

The central concern in relation to groups is that of motivating people to perform known tasks efficiently. This requires that people should behave in a cohesive manner and develop not counterproductive but supportive informal groups. A number of factors have been identified that determine how groups will behave, how effective and efficient they will be in an ordinary management context. The factors that determine how groups behave when they have reasonably clear tasks and well-defined power structures are:

- *Environmental factors*. The nature of the work, the physical location of people and the time pressures they are under determine whether and what kinds of informal groups develop to support the formal groups. Key to the operation of both the formal and informal groups is the managerial climate. This determines whether the logically designed formal groups can satisfy emotional needs or whether there will be strong pressures to develop alternatives. The conclusion generally reached is that groups designed on purely rational task-centred factors will lead to the emergence of anti-management informal groups. When, however, groups are designed according to social criteria, the result is cohesive teams. But social groups may not be all that logically related to the task, so it is generally thought best if groups are designed on self-actualising criteria. In this way individual motivational factors can be integrated with social factors to lead to cohesive functional teams that are motivated to deal with the task. Thus informal groups in themselves are not seen as relevant to management as such; they need to be pre-empted from emerging by the design of formal groups in such a way that those formal groups meet social and psychological needs.
- *Membership factors*. How a group performs will depend upon the personalities of its members, their personal background, status, who they represent and so on. Cohesion is brought about by putting together people with common experience or by creating opportunities for them to develop that common experience.
- *Dynamic factors*. The extent to which members of the group are socialised and sensitive to the group process and the extent to which they have been trained in these.

When it comes to problem solving, groups will generally be better at it than individuals when the problem has multiple parts requiring varied skills and knowledge. The principal reason usually given for using groups to solve problems, however, is that it makes it more likely that they will then implement the solution. Drawbacks are that groups tend to take riskier decisions than individuals (*Stoner, 1968; Davis, Laughin & Komarita, 1976*) because responsibility is diluted or because a group may amplify the positive cultural value of taking risks. Another drawback is 'group think' (*Schachter, 1951*). Members with deviant views are pressurised to conform if they are to retain membership.

## The need for informal groups

It has been recognised for a long time that bureaucratic control is neither rational nor efficient outside certain limited conditions and that it produces a number of negative behavioural consequences that undermine its effectiveness. The need for an informal organisation arises, then, simply because the formal bureaucracy often cannot work. There are two major reasons why a bureaucracy fails so frequently to produce what it is supposed to.

### 1 Adverse human reactions to bureaucracy

There is a considerable literature that identifies the adverse impact and consequent reaction of people to working in bureaucracies:

- Bureaucracies have an alienating impact on people. By definition, in a bureaucracy, people are allocated to narrowly defined roles and repetitive tasks and are thus treated as the means to some end (e.g. profit). People are consequently separated from their own creativity and from social contact with their fellow human beings. This leads to feelings of powerlessness, isolation, frustration, dissatisfaction and aggression (*Blauner, 1964*).
- Bureaucracies tend to make people subordinate, passive, dependent, and lacking in self-awareness. Rule-regulated work limits people's behavioural repertoire, and confines them to interests that are superficial and cover short time spans. These are all the exact opposite of the characteristics of maturity and will therefore reduce motivation and efficiency (*Argyris, 1957*).
- Bureaucracies may lead to work that has lost its moral character and cultural significance. People then perform according to rules they do not believe in. Without shared values to govern their work, their behaviour and the sharing of rewards, people feel that their work has no meaning – a state of anomie. In this normless state, some will behave in ways that others regard as unacceptable. For example, the salaries that some company top executives pay themselves lead to envy and public outcries that escalate into strikes and other forms of disruption.
- Bureaucracies can deskill people, leading to trained incapacity (*Merton, 1957*). Merton's study shows how exclusive reliance on bureaucratic systems develops trained incapacity so that people cannot make decisions to cope with the unforeseen.
- The operation of bureaucracies can contravene or provoke certain kinds of social behaviour and so touch off vicious circles. For example, an attempt to impose bureaucratic control can lead to unintended consequences in which people stick legalistically to the rules and are therefore less efficient; or they resist and so undermine the bureaucratic controls (*Gouldner, 1964*).

### 2 The bureaucracy's inability to handle ambiguity and uncertainty

Even if the operation of a bureaucracy does not itself provoke adverse human reactions that limit its operation, there are situations where the bureaucratic form of control cannot hope to work at all.

- Bureaucracies cannot cope with complex, unstable, unpredictable environmental and working conditions because they are inevitably too inflexible and slow to respond to change (*Burns & Stalker, 1961*). Rules and regulations cannot be established in advance to deal with the unforeseen.
- Bureaucracies are filled with other functions and by their nature avoid the ambiguous. To see this consider what the functions of a bureaucracy are and on what basis people are supposed to perform those functions. The function of a bureaucracy is to divide up tasks in a predetermined way and ensure that those tasks are performed to a prearranged standard. To do this, task performance has to be regularly reported up the hierarchy and compared against standards at prescribed levels in the hierarchy. Instruction for action, or legitimation of decisions taken, has to be passed down the

hierarchy. These flows of information, decisions and instructions require a set of communication arenas (meetings, telephone calls, document circulations) to review what has just happened in the performance of current tasks, make decisions on how to respond, legitimise any deviation from the rules, policies and plans, and perform symbolic functions to generate loyalty and security (e.g. appearing to be in control even when events are occurring unpredictably). Who is to take part in each arena is determined by position in the hierarchy.

The people taking part in any one arena have many tasks and so the capacity of any one arena will be limited. It will tend to fill with its obvious and primary functions of reviewing the past, legitimising decisions, and discussing symbolic actions. The higher up the hierarchy, the more this is likely to happen. Ambiguous issues with consequences that will probably not be felt for some time, that is the real strategic issues, will inevitably therefore be delayed, if they are ever accorded any attention in the first place. This will be most true of the board of directors and other formal top executive meetings. Some other type of communication arena will therefore have to deal with open-ended issues if they are to be dealt with at all and those other arenas will be the informal ones.

People deal with these shortcomings of the bureaucratic system by colluding to operate a 'mock' bureaucracy (*Gouldner, 1964*) and acting instead within an informal organisation that they set up themselves (Blauner, 1964). The 'mock' bureaucracy is one in which all pay lip service to the rules but tacitly agree not to enforce them. The appearance of rationality and order is thus maintained, and any conflict that might have been generated by the application of inappropriate rules is avoided.

What I have presented in this section on motivation, leadership and groups represents what I understand to be the most widely held views of researchers and practitioners. They are certainly classic texts. The writers have in common, I think, an underlying assumption about the relationship between individuals and groups and a methodology. Starting with the latter point, they all take the position of the objective observer standing outside the system of interest, such as groups and teams, leaders who motivate and members who must be motivated. They then identify factors that motivate people in different situations. The explicit or implicit prescription is that leaders and managers should take this position too, identify the nature of the situation, and select leadership styles and motivational factors that are appropriate in the sense that they fit the situation. In essence, this amounts to installing appropriate feedback loops in the organisation so that it operates like a cybernetic system.

As far as the relationship between individuals and groups is concerned, again it is clear how the primacy of the individual is assumed. Groups are made up of individuals and these groups then affect those individuals, meeting some of their needs but deskilling them in other ways. In order to prevent adverse effects of groups on individuals, leaders need to pay attention to factors to do with the environment of the group, its composition in terms of members and their sensitivity to group dynamics. Formal groups are to be preferred over informal ones. It is recognised that informal groups are inevitable but the mainstream view seems to be that they threaten control. This attitude towards groups reflects cognitivist and humanistic assumptions.

I now turn to how various authors treat politics in organisations.

## 6.5   POLITICAL ACTIVITY

Conflict inevitably flows from the development of an organisation: as it differentiates into different functions and different business units, the members of these functions and units identify more closely with each other than with the organisation as a whole. They consequently develop conflicting objectives. Power and politics are resorted to as a means of dealing with such conflict in organisations. Such overt political activity is a form of negative feedback control as shown in *Figure 6.1*.

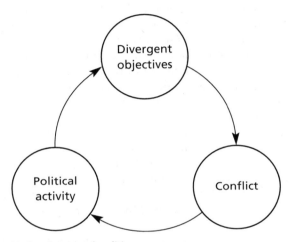

**FIGURE 6.1**   Negative feedback and politics

So, to the extent that vision and sense of mission fail to sustain conformity, managers resort to politics to restore stability and the status quo. By overt politics I mean the open interplay between vested interests and coalitions of managers and members. Also, as managers face uncertain situations they can no longer select, in advance, that sequence of actions that will realise their objections. Then they have to discover appropriate actions through trial and error and it falls to the exercise of power, to politics, to select particular trial-and-error experiments.

What does the literature have to say about the practice of politics in organisations?

Some studies of political activities in organisations have identified broad phases that managers follow as they deal with uncertainty and internal conflict. These conclusions are based on detailed studies over time of individual companies (e.g. *Pettigrew, 1985*) and cross-sectional studies of a sample of highly innovative and much less innovative companies in the United States (e.g. *Kanter, 1985*).

### Galvanising events

The cycle of political activity is triggered by some crisis (*Pettigrew, 1973, 1986*), that is a galvanising event. Examples at such events are departure from tradition, shifts in leadership, upset to existing perceptions, non-routine ways of doing things (*Kanter, 1985*). The consequence is some ideological shift, the development of different perceptions and points of view (*Srivasta & Barrett, 1986*). This increased uncertainty leads to divergent goals, conflict, and unwillingness and inability to commit to any course of action.

For example, at the beginning of the 1980s in the UK, three firms (Metal Box, Nacanco and Francis Packaging) were supplying paint cans to paint manufacturers, amongst whom ICI and Crown Paints were dominant. In the early 1980s, ICI decided to switch the packaging of its emulsion products from tin to plastic containers to increase customer satisfaction. The tin can manufacturers did not respond quickly to this new requirement, so two plastic packaging companies (Mardon Illingworth and Superfos) entered the market and took away a substantial part of the tin can market. In 1985, Francis Packaging was acquired by the conglomerate Suter plc, which removed the managing director and installed a new chief executive. These galvanising events generated great uncertainty and the remaining managers had to develop new perspectives on what their business was all about and how they should change it. They had to deal with the often suppressed conflict which ensued.

## Support building

The change in perspectives and the conflict have to be worked through before action can occur (*Pettigrew, 1986*). Particular individuals with vision are prime movers in bringing this about and they do so by developing special interests, making demands and generating support. Individuals or organisational subunits identify uncertain changes that will affect them in some way and they make demands for particular choices in their own interests. To further these demands they obtain support from other individuals and units (*Pettigrew, 1973*). From the observations of other writers, individuals and groups acquire information on what is going on, they define the problems emerging from the questioning of old ways, and build coalitions to gain attention for the problem and their solution to it (*Kanter, 1985; Quinn, 1980; Pfeffer, 1981; Bacharach & Lawler, 1980*). All this support building and coalition forming is focused not just on the problems and opportunities generated by change, but also on individual careers and subunit positions and aspirations.

This could be detected at Francis Packaging. Coalitions formed around closing some of the plants to respond to the decline in demand and this inevitably affected the career prospects of some of the managers. Others formed coalitions around the issue of updating some of the plant to improve the quality of the remaining business. The new chief executive had to build political support for proposals to develop the business.

Building support is an exercise in building power. Power is the ability of one individual or group to get others to do something against their will. Power involves overcoming resistance (*Pettigrew, 1973; Pfeffer, 1981*). Power is usually distinguished from authority. The latter derives from the structures, rules and procedures of the organisation and the former not. Power in the latter sense is seen by some as illegitimate in organisational terms (*Mayes & Allen, 1977*). Most writers define power as both authority and influence. They see the utilisation of power as an inevitable and necessary process for making organisational choices in conditions of uncertainty and ambiguity. They see it as inevitable because it arises from the very structure of the organisation itself. The division of tasks, the design of separate functions and business units, immediately leads to differing subunit goals, in turn generating conflict which can only be resolved by the application of power (*Pettigrew, 1973; Pfeffer, 1981*).

Yet others take an even more favourable view of power as the ability of one individual or group to enable others to do what they could not otherwise have done (*Srivasta & Barrett, 1986*). Here the focus is on cooperation, consensus seeking and organisational transformation. Power seen as influence is also the ability to enable others to do what they would not otherwise have done because they lacked the information or the perception (*Kanter, 1985*). Here the emphasis is on cooperative discussion to develop ideas. Further, power can take an unobtrusive form in which the decision situation or the cultural norms around decision making are manipulated to prevent different perceptions, and thus conflict, from emerging (*Pettigrew, 1986*).

Power, then, is a relationship between individuals and groups that determines how one affects or responds to the other in making an organisational choice. The relationships existing now are strongly affected by those which existed and were built up in the past (*Pettigrew, 1973; Pfeffer, 1981*). The choices that an organisation makes are determined by relative power built up over a number of periods. Once the power source of the actors involved has been identified and their relative power positions determined, the choice itself is predictable.

## Choice

Once power has been deployed to build enough support, the political cycle moves to its third phase – choice (*Pettigrew, 1973; Pfeffer, 1981*). Some writers describe this as mobilisation and completion, or the acquiring of legitimacy from higher authorities (*Kanter, 1985*). The outcome is the overcoming of conflict, or the avoidance of conflict, or cooperation. For some, this choice is part of an incremental process (*Quinn, 1980*). For others it can be a revolution (*Mintzberg, 1978*).

At Francis Packaging, the power of the Suter board and the individual power of the Francis chief executive resolved important conflicts to do with the closure of some plants, rationalisation and selective investment.

## Planned implementation or trial-and-error action

Having made the strategic choice, implementation may be realised by following an agreed plan setting out the action steps required to achieve the chosen goal; or, where the environment is characterised by great uncertainty, that goal may be reached by trial-and-error action. Here the success of each trial step is judged against criteria for success. Such criteria usually relate to the core values of the business and to some logical connection with its existing activities. Francis Packaging decided to invest in some new facilities to produce tin products for segments it had not operated in before. Some of them turned out to be reasonably successful. It also started negotiations with Metal Box to buy those Metal Box subsidiaries that competed with it. This particular trial-and-error action ended up with Metal Box buying the business of Francis Packaging instead. Not long afterwards, Metal Box sold its packaging interests to a French company.

The writers I have been reviewing hold that it is possible to establish conditions in which beneficial political behaviour will occur. This will happen when (*Kanter 1985; Srivasta & Barrett, 1986*):

- People are free and empowered: the required conditions are the wide dispersal of power, local autonomy and decentralised resources.
- People participate and collaborate with each other, and there is a willingness to share: team building and the fostering of strongly shared cultures are thus essential.
- There is a culture of commitment and pride in the organisation and its accomplishments: it must also be a culture which values and loves change.
- The cultures, structures, systems and relationships between people are integrative rather than segmentalist.
- There is open communication and networks which operate both informally and are built into the structures.
- Job assignments are ambiguous and non-routine; job definitions are loose and job territories intersecting.
- Leadership is persuasive and visionary, but also sets tough standards.
- There is an orientation to action.

It is postulated that when these conditions are established, people will participate in the kind of discovering, choosing and action that produces innovation. The negative feedback nature of these models of organisational politics is summarised in *Figure 6.2*.

Consider some other treatments of power in organisations.

---

- Messiness, difficulties and tendency to regress from cooperative activity are temporary.
- Although disorder and chance may be mentioned in passing, in most explanations of political activity they are in a shadowy background, not at the centre of the stage. Any disorder starts the process off, but does not drive how it unfolds. The impact of group dynamics, and the possibility of dysfunctional group dynamics and neurotic forms of leadership, are not part of the explanation. The interactive impact of personality differences on what choices are made is not incorporated. Thus the dysfunctional politicking, which in practice always accompanies functional political learning, is separated out as 'raw politics' (*Kanter, 1985*) and its impact on what happens is not built into the explanation in an essential way. Chance influences on political outcomes are not incorporated into the explanations.

- These models of political decision making present an orderly sequential process that occurs to overcome an initial disorderly state of ambiguity and conflict. The outcome is predictable once the sources of power have been identified and measured, once the relative power positions have been determined. Deterministic laws on power relativity yield predetermined outcomes.
- The normal state of the successful organisation is one of commitment, consensus and cooperation.
- Favourable outcomes are assumed to occur if power is widely enough dispersed, and people participate and show continuing commitment and consensus under persuasive, visionary leadership which stresses action. Disorder at an individual level does not contribute to the outcome in any essential way other than to start the whole process off.

**FIGURE 6.2**   Negative feedback aspects of models of overt political activity

### Politics and agenda building

*Huff (1988)* identifies the role of politics in strategic choice in the following terms:

- Organisational politics provides an arena for identifying and assessing new strategic alternatives which draw upon the varied experience of organisation members.
- Politics challenges organisation leaders to clarify and modify their thinking about strategic issues. In general, politics is more effective at this task than formal planning systems.
- Organisational politics identifies the individual and group commitments necessary for designing and implementing new strategy.
- Political diversity facilitates the succession of individual leaders, and promotes adaptations in the practices and beliefs which contribute to organisational culture.
- While organisation politics can be disruptive, routined decision cycles can channel potentially disrupting differences of opinion into manageable cycles of debate.

*Dutton (1988)* presents a model of decision making in conditions of uncertainty and ambiguity which he calls an issue-building process. In this model, issues attract attention if they conform to the strategy and culture of the organisation. If the issue is important and simple enough it will attract attention, otherwise the tendency will be to postpone it. This is much the same point as that made in the garbage-can model. To sustain attention an issue must be sponsored and this brings in the political process. Coalitions have to be built around the issue. Whether the issue gets onto the agenda or not will depend upon context, for example the other matters pressing for attention.

In the literature surveyed in this section politics is presented primarily as a negative feedback process. The underlying assumption is that of an organisation as a cybernetic system. Also, the assumption of the primacy of the individual is evident. Power is exerted by one individual over others. The political system is understood as one that can be objectively observed to enable identification of factors that will get it to operate beneficially.

Consider now how similar assumptions underlie discussions about culture.

### 6.6    MANAGING ORGANISATION DEVELOPMENT AND CULTURE CHANGE

The central concern of organisation development (OD) is the planning and management of changes in the beliefs, values, cultures, social interactions and behaviour of people in an organisation in order to improve its effectiveness.

Organisation development recognises that it is not sufficient to analyse the environment and then set out the planned actions logically required to achieve an organisation's goals in that environment. What actually happens in an organisation does not depend on such rational considerations alone. It depends just as much on the behavioural factors: belief systems, social interactions, cultures, group behaviour and individual psychology. It is not enough to focus on technical or primary task subsystems; it is also necessary to operate on the psychosocial subsystem. Action plans will simply not be implemented if they run counter to the belief system, or if they adversely affect social structures, or if they do not motivate people. For this reason it is necessary to plan changes in beliefs and cultures to support the required actions, according to OD.

OD is therefore a long-term programme of intervention in the social, psychological, cultural and belief systems of an organisation. These interventions are based on certain principles and practices which are assumed to lead to greater organisational effectiveness.

These principles and practices are to do with identifying those beliefs, values and cultures conducive to achieving an organisation's goals – the desired culture – and then designing a systematic and deliberate change programme to move from the current to the desired culture.

One of the pioneers of this line of thinking was *Kurt Lewin (1947, 1951)*. One can explore the main assumptions on organisational dynamics made by OD practitioners if one looks briefly at some of the key points he made. His models of the change process in organisations have had an important impact on subsequent thinking. The discipline and practices of OD, with its culture-change programmes, have been heavily influenced by Lewin's thought and are now widely accepted by practising managers.

*Lewin (1947)* saw social planning as a means of improving the functioning of organisations. He saw such social planning processes in terms of circular feedback in which goals were clarified, paths identified, and actions kept to the path, through the operation of negative feedback (see *Figure 6.3*).

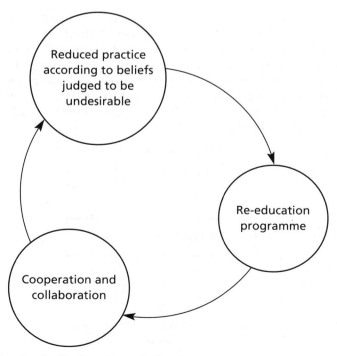

**FIGURE 6.3**    Negative feedback and organisation development

Lewin thought of the organisational change process in the following terms:

- At the beginning of any social change we can think of the organisation as being in a state of stable equilibrium: a state of harmony in which all share the same culture.
- Stable equilibrium means that the forces driving for change and the forces resisting change just balance each other. In other words, driving and restraining forces create what he called a *balanced force field*, illustrated in *Figure 6.4*.
- Then some trigger such as falling profitability, or an announcement of reorganisation, or the setting up of some programme of planned culture change, upsets the balance between the driving and resisting forces. In other words, some environmental change causes some internal change that unbalances the force field. Consequently, the existing management recipe on what the business is all about and how it should be run is challenged. This is the first stage of organisational change and Lewin called it *unfreezing*.
- When the balance between driving and restraining forces is upset, it causes confusion in which people search for new recipes. This is the second stage of organisational change, called *reformulation*. It comes to an end once a new management recipe has been identified, one that is believed to match the changed environment.
- The third stage is *refreezing* in which people are converted and persuaded to accept the new recipe. The organisation thus returns once more to the harmony and stability characterised by all sharing the same culture. If the organisation is to survive, this new recipe must be one that is more appropriate to the changed environment.

This is clearly a feedback loop, one that will keep an organisation adapted to its environment, if it functions effectively. To function effectively, the feedback loop must be negative in its operation so as to keep the organisation moving to a desired state established by the environment. The dynamics of successful change is quite clearly to do with the drive to equilibrium and it is characterised by regularity and stability.

Now, the organisational change process could just occur as the environment changed or it could be planned, and OD is based on the belief that such change should be planned along the following lines.

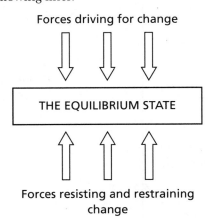

Forces driving for change

THE EQUILIBRIUM STATE

Forces resisting and restraining change

**FIGURE 6.4**   Lewin's concept of a force field

### The analysis

The first step in planned social change is that of analysing the force field existing at any one time in a specific organisation to identify what the driving forces are and what the resisting forces are.

For example, consider the problems faced by any one of the electricity utilities in the UK in 1989 as they began to prepare to operate as privately owned corporations rather than state bodies. The forces driving change were the new government policies on the ownership of the electricity industry, the European Community Directives on tighter control of pollution, and perhaps the appointment of a new chief executive from the commercial sector to oversee the change. The driving forces were creating a need for a whole new culture, one that focused on profit rather than engineering considerations. The resisting forces were created by the engineering culture of the utility, by the existing beliefs and patterns of work.

Suppose that OD consultants are hired to help with the change process. What would those consultants do? They would first form a clearer picture of the nature of the drivers of and resistances to change. They would do this by holding many discussions with managers and employees. These discussions would surface the main concerns. The consultants would start to form hypotheses about the main resistances to change and then check these by distributing and analysing questionnaires to large samples of managers and employees. The analysis would reveal much about the attitudes, the satisfactions and dissatisfaction of people throughout the organisation, the strengths and weaknesses of the organisation.

### Developing the plan

The second step in planned social change is to prepare a plan for change that strengthens the favourable driving forces and weakens the blocking resisting forces.

The OD approach to developing such a plan is one that employs process consulting. This means that the consultant does not operate as an expert selling advice to the organisation in response to a need that the organisation has already defined. Nor does the consultant act as the company doctor who diagnoses what is wrong, recommends what to do and then leaves. The process consultant (*Schein, 1987, 1988b*) helps the client to perceive and understand what is going on in the environment and within the organisation and then assists the client to develop appropriate responses. The emphasis is on clients helping themselves.

Indeed the OD approach heavily emphasises what it regards as the most effective way for clients to help themselves, namely through widespread participation. The OD process for developing plans for change is one based on an ideology of planned participation and democracy. It focuses very much on the importance of leadership in this process, but leadership of a facilitating, encouraging kind rather than authoritarian, directing kinds.

Typically therefore, OD consultants follow a sequence of activities such as the following:

- A top client group is established consisting of the most senior and politically powerful executives. Sometimes the client is simply the most powerful executive. The analysis of the driving and restraining forces described above is presented to this client and the hypotheses on them discussed. Together the client and the OD consultants identify what changes need to be brought about. So, for example, top management and OD consultants in the electricity utilities mentioned above might identify the prime need to change the culture from an engineering to a profit-centred one, to remove the old bureaucracy and cut staff levels. They might agree on a programme of regular meetings at a number of different levels in the hierarchy to set financial and staff reduction targets and then review their part of the business against those targets and take corrective action.

- The top executives might start the process off by going away for a weekend to put together a mission statement setting out what new key values are to drive the business. They might set some broad overall financial targets.
- The next step would then be to 'roll down' the mission statement throughout the organisation. The next most senior level of managers would be formed into a group and a programme of meetings arranged for it. At the first few meetings that group would examine the mission statement prepared by the top team for the whole organisation. These managers would translate that into a mission for their level.
- Then teams of managers would be established for different business units or for different functions such as sales and production. These teams would then take the mission statements and translate them into mission statements for their own business units and functions.
- As the programmes of meetings continued, members would spend time identifying how to turn the missions into more precise objectives and what plans to prepare to achieve those objectives.

In this way, an orderly hierarchy of management teams pursues a programme of clarifying objectives and roles and preparing plans for change, all in accordance with a broad framework established at the top of the organisation.

### Implementing the plan

The third and final step in planned social change is to implement the culture-change plan.

In a sense, implementation is proceeding alongside the development of objectives and plans because managers at many levels in the hierarchy are behaving in a way they did not do before. They are attending planning and reviewing meetings and working collaboratively on developing plans. The process of rolling down the mission statements and the objectives may itself be implementation in so far as the participation motivates people to accept changes in behaviour.

The planned changes in behaviour to more collaborative forms may be specifically reinforced by team-building exercises and training in group skills. So managers may be sent on presentation and assertiveness courses, or they may be sent away in groups for long weekends where they take part in team-building exercises. This may involve playing business games, or taking part in physical activities such as rock climbing, or finding the way through some wilderness. Such exercises are believed to build team spirit and establish bonds between people who have shared hardships or pleasurable activities together.

The top executive team will also probably engage in such team-building activities. These could include exercises in which the executives use questionnaires to identify the personality types to which they belong (*Belbin, 1981; Kiersey & Bates, 1978*). They then explore how these different personality types interact with other types and what impact this has on their working together as a group.

All of these OD interventions are of course a form of social engineering which could have sinister overtones, were it not for the insistence of OD that culture-change programmes will work only if they are collaborative. The culture-change programme must be one that leads the people involved to see for themselves why they should change their culture to a new desired state.

OD is therefore about a comprehensive approach to planning changes in behaviour in organisations. This kind of thinking leads to the rejection of piecemeal culture change as the effective way to alter belief systems. Simply affecting one of the driving or resisting forces is thought unlikely to move the whole system. The whole system must move if the organisation is to change enough. These thoughts lead to the current popularity of the large-scale culture-change programmes adopted by many companies.

Note how OD is built firmly on the idea that negative feedback, planning and reviewing lead to success. Note how the dynamics is described in terms of strong tendencies towards states of stability and harmony. This means that OD can be applied only in conditions reasonably close to certainty and agreement. A summary of OD is given in *Figure 6.5*.

---

- Organisations are normally in a state of stable equilibrium in terms of cultures and belief systems. The forces driving change and those resisting it balance each other.
- When it becomes necessary, analytical methods can be used to identify some new desirable state for the culture and the belief system. Analysis can also determine which driving and resisting forces to focus on in order to realise the desired change. Someone can know what an appropriate culture is. Specific actions lead to specific changes in beliefs and social structures and small chance events can be prevented from escalating into major changes in beliefs and social interactions – it is possible to prevent chain reactions and bandwagon effects (see Chapter 8, the section on positive feedback and nonlinearity in organisations).
- There are collaborative group techniques available to persuade and convert people to the new required belief system. Once rational people of goodwill see why they should change, for the common good, what they believe and how they interact socially, then they will. In other words, OD consultants implicitly assume that it is possible to ignore or overcome deeply buried unconscious group processes which lead people to behave 'irrationally'. (See Chapter 10, the section on Bion's models, which discusses sensitivity training and the Tavistock method. This approach which focuses on unconscious group processes is usually criticised by OD consultants and is very rarely used by them.)
- It is thus possible to install new belief systems and it is possible for someone in an organisation to be in control of the process.
- Once the change process is over, the organisation returns to its normal stable state.
- Successful change is planned, regular, hierarchical. It is secured through harmonious collaboration, the application of negative feedback.

**FIGURE 6.5**   Organisation development: a summary

## 6.7    SUMMARY

In this chapter I have reviewed the mainstream literature on behavioural factors in organisations. These were the motivation of people working in the organisation, the nature of leadership, the application of power in political processes and the impact of values, belief systems and culture. There were common assumptions underlying the approach in all of these areas. They were all understood in what amounts to negative feedback loops, displaying the way in which organisations are treated as if they are, or should be, cybernetic systems. In all of these areas the individual is treated as primary, displaying the underlying assumption of cognitivism and humanistic psychology. Another common assumption is that managers can and should take the position of independent observer and choose appropriate feedback loops in relation to motivation, leadership, politics and culture.

This chapter completes the review of strategic choice theory. Chapter 3 examined the rational processes of strategy formulation that provide the template against which the cybernetic system is to function. Chapter 4 reviewed the rational, designed processes of implementation that provide the feedback loops to ensure cybernetic operation. Chapter 5 explored how uncertainty and conflict are treated in the literature and demonstrated how they are held to be dealt with in rational algorithmic ways that are not fundamentally different to cybernetic operations. This chapter examined how behavioural factors are treated in essentially the same way. Throughout the assumption is that human beings behave like cybernetic systems themselves, the underlying tenet of cognitivism. Throughout the individual is unquestioningly held to be prior and primary in relation to the group.

The next chapter will review strategic choice theory in general.

### FURTHER READING

Peters and Waterman (1982) is well worth reading. More detail on organisation development can be obtained by reading any of the standard texts on organisational behaviour, for example Robbins (1986). Campbell & Tawady (1990) should be referred to for a greater understanding of the mission concept.

### REFERENCES

Argyris, C. (1957), Personality and Organization, New York: Harper & Row.

Bacharach, S. B. & Lawler, E. J. (1980), *Power and Politics in Organizations*, San Francisco: Jossey-Bass.

Belbin, R. M. (1981), *Management Teams: Why They Succeed or Fail*, Oxford: Heinemann.

Blauner, R. (1964), *Alienation and Freedom*, Chicago: University of Chicago Press.

Burns, T. & Stalker, G. M. (1961), *The Management of Innovation*, London: Tavistock.

Campbell, A., Devine, M. & Young, D. (1990), *A Sense of Mission*, London: Hutchinson.

Campbell, A. & Tawady, K. (1990), *Mission and Business Philosophy: Winning Employee Commitment*, Oxford: Heinemann.

Davis, J. H., Laughin, P. R. & Komarita, S. S. (1976), The social psychology of mixed groups: cooperative and mixed motive interaction, *Annual Review of Psychology*, vol. 27, pp. 501–41.

Dutton, J. E. (1988), Understanding strategic agenda building and its implications for managing change, in Pondy, L.R., Boland, J. R. &. Thomas, H. (Eds.) (1988), *Managing Ambiguity and Change*, New York: John Wiley.

Etzioni, A. (1961), *Complex Organizations*, New York: Holt, Reinhart & Winston.

Festinger, L., Schachter, S. & Back, K. (1950), *Social Pressures in Informal Groups: A Study of a Housing Project*, New York: Harper & Row.

Fiedler, F. E. (1967), *A Theory of Leadership Effectiveness*, New York: McGraw-Hill.

Goldsmith, W. & Clutterbuck, D. (1984), *The Winning Streak*, London: Weidenfeld & Nicolson.

Gouldner, A. (1964), *Patterns of Industrial Bureaucracy*, New York: Free Press.

Hersey, P. & Blanchard, K. (1988), *Organizational Behavior*, Englewood Cliffs, NJ: Prentice Hall.

Hertzberg, F. (1966), *Work and the Nature of Man*, Cleveland, OH: World.

Huff, A. S. (1988), Politics and Arguments as a means of coping with ambiguity and change, in Pondy, L. R. Boland, J. R. & Thomas, H. (Eds.) (1980), *Managing Ambiguity and Change*, New York: John Wiley.

Kanter, R. M. (1985), *The Change Masters: Innovation and Entrepreneurship in the American Corporation*, Englewood Cliffs, NJ: Simon & Schuster.

Kiersey, D. & Bates, M. (1978), *Please Understand Me: Character and Temperament Types*, Del Mar, CA: Prometheus Nemesis Books.

Lewin, K. (1947), Feedback problems of social diagnosis and action, Part II-B of Frontiers in Group Dynamics, *Human Relations*, vol. 1, pp. 147–53.

Lewin, K. (1951), *Field Theory in Social Science*, New York: Harper & Brothers.

Lindblom, L. & Norstedt, J. (1971), *The Volvo Report*, Stockholm: Swedish Employers Confederation.

Maslow, A. (1954), *Motivation and Personality*, New York: Harper Brothers.

Mayes, B. T. & Allen, W. R. (1977), Towards a definition of organizational politics, *Academy of Management Review*, vol. 2.

Merton, R. K. (1957), Bureaucratic structure and personality, in *Social Theory and Social Structure*, New York: Free Press.

Mintzberg, H. (1978), *Patterns in strategy formation, Management Science*, vol. 24.

Pascale, R. T. & Athos, A. (1981), *The Art of Japanese Management*, New York: Simon & Schuster.

Peters, T. J. & Waterman, R. H. (1982), *In Search of Excellence*, New York: Harper & Row.

Pettigrew, A. (1973), *The Politics of Organizational Decision Making*, London: Tavistock.

Pettigrew, A. (1985), *The Awakening Giant*, Oxford: Blackwell.

Pettigrew, A. (1986), Some limits of executive power in creating strategic change, in Srivasta, S. & Associates (Eds.) (1986), *Executive Power*, San Francisco: Jossey-Bass.

Pfeffer, J. (1981), *Power in Organizations*, Cambridge, MA: Ballinger.

Quinn, J. B. (1980), *Strategic change: Logical Incrementalism*, Homewood Ill: Richard D. Irwin.

Robbins, S. P. (1986), *Essentials of Organisational Behaviour*, Hemel Hempstead: Prentice Hall.

Schachter, S. (1951), Deviation, rejection and communication, *Journal of Abnormal and Social Psychology*, vol. 46, pp. 190–207.

Schein, E. H. (1987), *Process Consultation Volume 1: Its Role in Organization Development*, Reading, MA: Addison-Wesley.

Schein, E. H. (1988a), *Organizational Psychology*, Englewood Cliffs, NJ: Prentice Hall.

Schein, E. H. (1988b), *Process Consultation Volume II: Lessons for Managers and Consultants*, Reading, MA: Addison-Wesley.

Srivasta, S. & Barrett, F. J. (1986), Conclusions: functions of executive power, in Srivasta, S. & Associates (Eds.) (1986), *Executive Power*, San Francisco: Jossey-Bass.

Stacey, R. (1991), *The Chaos Frontier: Creative Strategic Control for Business*, Oxford: Butterworth–Heinemann.

Stoner, J. A. (1968), Risky and cautious shifts in group decisions: the influence of widely held values, *Journal of Experimental Social Psychology*, vol. 4, pp. 442–59.

Vroom, V. H. & Yetton, P. W. (1973), *Leadership and Decision Making*, Pittsburgh: University of Pittsburgh Press.

# Chapter

# 7 Review of strategic choice theory

**INTRODUCTION**

The purpose of this chapter is to reflect upon the underlying assumptions and reasoning processes of strategic choice theory. This should enable you to understand what it focuses your attention on and the extent to which it helps you to make sense of your experience of life in organisations.

In Chapter 1, I suggested that the phenomenon of interest when one talks about strategy is a population of organisations of various kinds that interact with, or relate to, each other. Each of those organisations is a population of groupings of individuals that interact with, or relate to, each other. These populations are continually changing in that new organisations and groups within them come into being, while already existing ones disappear altogether, merge with others, split apart, develop new activities, alter structurally, grow or decline. As they relate to each other in their groups, people experience enthusiasm and boredom, excitement and anxiety, anger and fear, jealousy and envy, fulfilment and disappointment, pleasure and frustration. As one reflects on this phenomenon, questions immediately spring to mind. How do new organisations come into being? Why do they cease to exist? How do they come to merge with others or split apart? Why do most organisations last for only a rather short time and why do a few survive for long periods? Why is one organisation similar to others and different from yet others? How do some organisations develop new activities? Why do other organisations simply carry on with the same activities?

Similar questions can be asked about the groupings of people within an organisation. Questions also spring to mind about individual experiences of life in those groupings. Why do people become anxious, bored or frustrated? What is it that excites and fulfils them? What impact do these emotions have on the functioning of groups and organisations?

## Making sense of the phenomenon

Strategic choice theory makes sense of this phenomenon, by answering these questions in a particular way. It does so from a realist position. In other words, it assumes that the categories discussed already exist before the discussion begins. The discussion is about a pre-given reality. If you go back to Chapter 3 on the formulation of a strategy, you can see how each step in the formulation process makes this assumption. For example, a suitable strategy is one that fits, or is adapted to a particular market. In order to determine whether or not this is so, the market must be analysed in terms of customer requirements, competitor positions, entry barriers, and so on. These factors are treated as realities that already exist, not stories about a reality that is being socially constructed by those who are participating in that market.

In addition, to establish the suitability of a strategy, managers must forecast, envision or imagine the state of these market factors some years into the future. That future is talked about as a pre-given reality too. You can hear this when people talk about getting to the future first, or use the analogy of Columbus setting sail for America, or President Kennedy announcing the dream of putting a man on the moon. These are all metaphors of a future reality that already exists, waiting to be discovered rather than created. Another example of this realist position is the discussion of leadership in Chapter 6. You will recall how different leadership styles are related to different situations and the recommendation is that individuals should choose a leadership style that fits the situation. Again, the situations and the styles already exist before any individual comes to take them up. They are not created in the act of leading but discovered and adopted in advance. As I stated in Chapter 1, this realist position is not the only one that it is possible to take.

Furthermore, strategic choice theory makes a particular assumption about the nature of causality. It assumes that linear causal links can be identified and that, therefore, predictions can be made. For example, it states that success is caused by choosing a strategy that is feasible, acceptable and suitable. Another example is provided by the understanding of groups (see Chapter 6). It is postulated that groups of people will function effectively as teams if certain environmental factors and certain kinds of members are chosen to form the group. Such linear causality is not the only possible view. Chapter 8 will review notions of nonlinear causal connections and Chapter 11 will look at theories indicating that it could be impossible to identify causal links at all in certain circumstances.

## 7.2   HOW STRATEGIC CHOICE THEORY DEALS WITH FOUR KEY QUESTIONS

The point I am making, then, is that strategic choice theory takes a particular position in relation to the way that humans know anything. As with any other position, this immediately moves the reasoning process down one avenue and excludes others. The result is to deal with the four questions I posed in Chapter 1 in a particular way. This focuses attention on particular factors in organisational life and so excludes others. Consider how strategic choice theory deals with these four questions.

## The nature of interaction

In strategic choice theory, interaction is understood in systemic terms. A system is a set of interconnected components or entities. In strategic choice theory the entities are organisations that interact with each other in industry groupings, or markets. An organisation is a system that consists of people grouped into divisions, subsidiary companies, departments, project teams, and so on. The immediate consequence is a tendency to reify, that is to think of an organisation and a system as a thing. I will take up this point again in Chapters 15 and 16.

The concept of a system in strategic choice theory is a very specific one. It is a cybernetic system, that is, a goal-driven, self-regulating system. To reiterate, the self-regulation takes the form of a negative feedback process through which an organisation adapts to its environment, that is its markets. Negative feedback is a process of referring back to a fixed point of reference established outside the organisation. The market demand to which the organisation must adapt provides the fixed point of reference. The negative feedback works through the system taking account of the difference between its offering and that market demand, so as to remove the difference. The organisation is itself also a cybernetic system consisting of groups of people. The fixed point of reference for these groups is the set of goals and targets set for them by their manager. Negative feedback operates by taking account of the difference between performance and targets, so as to remove the difference. Chapter 4 describes how negative feedback loops in information systems are supposed to control the implementation of the chosen strategy. Chapter 5 points to how uncertainty and conflict are supposed to be dealt with largely by more elaborate negative feedback loops. Chapter 6 described the thinking about motivation, political activity and culture change all in terms of negative feedback loops. Note how strategic choice theory takes no account of the effect of positive or amplifying feedback loops in human affairs.

The result is a theory that focuses primarily on the macro level. A single, whole organisation is the primary unit of analysis. Intention, or choice, is related to this whole. By focusing attention on a single organisation, 'the organisation', strategic choice theory ignores the fact that other organisations are making choices too. What happens to one depends not only on what it chooses but on what all the others do too.

You can see the importance attached to a single organisation making choices for the whole, in isolation, in the emphasis placed on: strategic intent, choosing a vision, choosing financial targets, choosing a culture, choosing strategic management styles, and so on. The possibility of making such choices successfully depends heavily on the ability to predict at rather fine levels of detail and over rather long time spans. That in turn depends upon the possibility of identifying causal links between action and outcome at a rather fine level of detail over rather long time spans.

For example, to achieve financial targets, investments must be chosen to deliver those targets. The discounted cash flow method prescribed for choosing between alternative investments requires the forecasting of detailed cash flows over periods as long as 25 years. Whether an investment is a success or not depends on the fine detail of what it costs and what revenues it generates over many years, once it is in operation. Forecasts at a coarse level of detail, or for short time periods, will then not capture the factors upon which success depends. The choice cannot then be made as prescribed, which is to make the choice in a rational way that takes account of the actual factors that lead to success. Success will not be the result of rational choice but will depend on the chance capturing of the most important factors in the coarse detailed forecasts. Much the same point applies to choices of values and cultures. If a group of people is to be reliably moved from behaving according to one set of values to another then it is necessary to make a prediction of how they will respond to some measure to persuade them to do so.

There is an alternative to prediction at fine levels of detail over long time periods required by rational choice. This is the kind of very general prediction called for in setting a direction, or articulating a vision, and trusting trial-and-error activities to carry it out. Chapter 2 made the point that this can work only if small random changes in the environment and small trial-and-error actions cancel each other out. In other words, it can only work if the law of requisite variety is valid. Chapter 11 will question this.

Strategic choice theory takes a particular view of organisational dynamics. Since it is a cybernetic theory, the dynamics is that of a move to stable equilibrium. Success is equated with stability, consistency and harmony. Instabilities arise largely in the organisation's environment.

Strategic choice theory is usually formulated in a way that focuses on the interaction between components and so ignores the richness of human relationships.


## Nature of human beings

Chapters 3 to 5 have indicated how strategic choice theory is built on a particular view of human nature. It is assumed that individuals are essentially cybernetic entities. They make representations of a pre-given reality taking the form of regularities built up from previous experience and mentally stored in the form of sets of rules, or schemas, cognitive maps, or mental models. Through experience they make more and more accurate representations, more and more reliable cognitive maps. This process is essentially one of negative feedback in which discrepancies between the cognitive map and external reality are fed back into the map to change it, closing the gap between it and reality. Strategic choice theory pays very little attention to emotion and the impact that this might have on how an organisation functions. To the extent that this theory does pay attention to emotion it does so from a humanistic psychology perspective.

Humanistic psychology was developed mainly in the United States as a reaction to what was felt to be the pessimism and conservatism of psychoanalysis. Humanistic psychology takes a basically optimistic view of human nature and its perfectibility. One of its roots was in inspirational religious revivalism and it saw the main problem of human existence as the alienation of an individual from his or her true self. From this perspective people can be motivated by providing experiences for them in which they can experience more of their true selves. You see the influence of these ideas in the theories of motivation of Maslow and Hertzberg, summarised in Chapter 6. The prescriptions for establishing visions and missions that inspire people also arise from this kind of thinking about human nature.

So, when it comes to the micro level, strategic choice theory alternates between two views of human nature, the cognitivist and the humanistic. The former tends to be predominant when the theory focuses on control systems and the latter when it focuses on motivation, leadership and culture. The way both are used, however, has an element in common. It is implicitly assumed that the individual members of an organisation are all the same and that interactions between them are all the same. It is assumed that everyone responds in the same way to the same motivational factor, for example. Another example is the implicit assumption, when talking about leadership styles, that everyone will respond in the same way to a given leadership style. Differences between individuals, deviant and eccentric behaviour have no role to play in how an organisation evolves. Indeed, they are seen as dangerous disruptions to be removed by more controls or additional motivators. The emphasis is on everyone sharing the same values to produce uniformity and conformity. The very way members of an organisation are referred to as the staff, or the management, indicates how differences within the categories are obliterated while differences between them are highlighted.

There is an important consequence of this ignoring of individual differences and deviant behaviour that will be taken up in Chapters 12 and 14. Systems in which the entities and their interactions are all the same cannot spontaneously generate anything new. For strategic choice theory this leaves the only possible explanation of creativity located in the individual's intention to do something creative. How individuals do this is not explained in strategic choice theory. It is simply assumed.

Individuals, the micro level, feature in strategic choice theory primarily in terms of how they affect the organisation as a whole, the macro level. Individuals make the choices and do the controlling. Individuals appoint people to roles and they put them into teams. They set targets for those teams and motivate and require or punish people in them according to performance. An individual forms a vision and individuals articulate missions for others. Power is possessed by individuals who exert it over other individuals. In this way the individual is consistently held to be prior and primary to the group. A group consists of individuals and may then affect how they behave.

The point I am making here is that strategic choice theory implicitly makes a number of important assumptions about human nature that should not be mistaken for the 'truth'. They are all assumptions that can quite properly be contested and when they are, the whole of strategic choice theory is questioned too.

## Methodology and strategic choice

I have pointed a number of times in Chapters 3 to 5 to how researchers writing in the strategic choice tradition and how managers talking in this way explicitly or implicitly take the position of the objective observer. They stand outside the system they are talking about and construct models of it as the basis for prescription and action. This has methodological implications for research and it has even more important consequences for how managers understand their role.

When a manager takes this position, that manager immediately assumes that it is his or her task to design and install some system, set of actions, motivators, and so on. For example, consider the discussion on culture in Chapter 6. The top executive is supposed to analyse the cultural values of an organisation. This requires the executive to step outside the value system of which he or she is a part and look at it from the outside, as it were. The next step is to design and install a new value system. Another example is provided by the discussion of leadership styles. Again, the manager is required to step outside the situation and determine whether it is one in which a particular leadership style is required. If this is different to the one the manager currently practises, then the appropriate one must be installed.

### Paradox

Strategic choice theory does not understand an organisation in paradoxical terms at all. Contradictions are to be solved, tensions and conflicts smoothed away and dilemmas resolved. In terms of what I suggested might be major paradoxes of organisational life, strategic choice consistently occupies one pole of the contradiction. So, sameness and difference are not seen to exist at the same time. One organisation is different to others but within the organisation people are the same. Individuals and groups are not paradoxical since groups simply consist of autonomous individuals. Division and integration are two functions that should be resolved by appropriate structures and procedures. They are not seen to constitute a paradox. Predictability is emphasised and the possible implications of simultaneously present unpredictability are not seriously explored. Control is emphasised and freedom to act is made consistent with it through motivational factors. Order is the requisite for success and disorder or any form of deviance or eccentricity is to be curbed and removed. Success is equated with determinism and chance with the potential for failure.

Again, the point I am making is that strategic choice theory implicitly makes assumptions about opposing forces in organisational life that cannot simply be taken for granted. It is quite possible to take a different view and so construct a different theory.

### 7.3  HOW STRATEGIC CHOICE THEORY FOCUSES ATTENTION

The primary focus of strategic choice theory is on intention and control. It prescribes a role for managers in terms of making choices and staying in control as individuals. It emphasises the installation of large numbers of negative feedback control systems relating to information, actions and behaviour. It depicts leadership as the function of directing, inspiring and choosing the shape, position and strategic direction of whole organisations. It focuses attention on stability, consistency and harmony.

In focusing attention in this way, it inevitably precludes paying serious attention to other matters. Researchers have noted, and managers themselves are usually very well aware, that strategies may emerge without any organisation-wide intention formulated well in advance. However, this is done in a way, it seems to me, that closes down any serious exploration of how this might happen. There seems to be an implicit assumption that when it is stated that a sequence of events emerges, this is tantamount to saying that there is no explanation possible. It just happens. Chapters 11 and 12, however, will present possible ways of explaining the process of emergence. The absence of organisation-wide choice and intention seems to be rapidly equated with muddled decision making and chance outcomes. This too will be questioned in Chapter 12.

One can see how strategic choice theory focuses attention by considering how it typically answers the questions posed at the beginning of this chapter:

- How do new organisations come into being? The answer is to be found in the large number of stories, often quoted in the strategic choice literature, about the founders of successful companies. A gifted individual develops an idea, makes choices and forms intentions to develop a new business, and then gathers other enthusiasts together to get it going.
- Why do they cease to exist? Because the individual's idea turned out not to be that good after all, or someone else had a better one. Another possibility is that larger organisations exert their power to prevent a new organisation from succeeding. Large organisations also fail from time to time and the answer here would be that their managers failed to change their intentions. They did not develop good enough visions. They failed to inspire and motivate their people. Other organisations made better moves and so acquired greater market power.
- How do they come to merge with others or split apart? Because their strategist chose to do so in order to maximise shareholder value.
- Why do most organisations last for only a rather short time and why do a few survive for long periods? Again, the answer would have to do with the quality of the strategic thinking and choices of an organisation's strategists.
- Why is one organisation similar to others and different from yet others? The answer is that the environment determines a small number of configurations that will succeed in a particular market. It is these configurations that determine similarities and differences between organisations.
- How do some organisations develop new activities? Because individual members have creative and innovative ideas that they are able to persuade others to pursue.
- Why do other organisations simply carry on with the same activities? Because their managers get stuck in the same way of thinking.
- Why do people become anxious, bored or frustrated? Because their tasks are not fulfilling enough.
- What is it that excites and fulfils them? Monetary and other rewards, particularly related to individual self-fulfilment.
- What impact do these and other emotions have on the functioning of groups and organisations? Positive emotions are instrumental in securing group cohesion and team spirit while negative emotions disrupt tasks.

## Making sense of experience

The question now is how this theory assists one to make sense of one's experience of life in organisations. My experience is that, despite the rational analysis, the forecasts, the visions, strategic intents, team building and so on, organisational outcomes are very frequently surprising and unexpected. I find it very difficult to make sense of this experience by taking a strategic choice perspective. The theory leads one to believe that it is possible to make choices that lead to organisational success if one follows the prescribed procedures. So when managers follow the prescriptions and the surprising, the unexpected and the downright unpleasant occur, they are left with little option but to conclude that they have been incompetent in some way. Or, more likely, that other people have been incompetent in some way. A variation on this is to blame the surprise on ignorance of enough facts. Alternatively, the blame might be placed on people who do not implement the strategic choice as required. When one makes sense of experience from the strategic choice perspective the most widespread response to the unexpected takes the form of some kind of blame.

The response is then to put more effort into gathering and analysing information to overcome ignorance. Or more intensive efforts are made to acquire the necessary competences to manage strategically and so avoid accusations and feelings of incompetence. Or new motivating and controlling systems are installed to prevent poor implementation and bad behaviour. When the surprise is a large one, these responses are usually accompanied by the removal of individuals who are conspicuously associated with the surprise from the organisation. However, none of these responses puts a stop to it all happening again. Instead, in my view, these responses raise levels of fear and place people under increasing stress. Is this inevitable or is there a problem with trying to make sense of experience from the strategic choice standpoint?

If you take the psychoanalytic perspective to be reviewed in Chapter 10, you might reach a different conclusion. It could be that many of the prescriptions of strategic choice theory are little more than defences against the anxiety of not being able to forecast and stay in control. If this is so, then they are not very good defences because, as I have just suggested, they may actually increase levels of anxiety. If you take the perspective that I will suggest in Chapter 16, you might conclude that it is the nature of organising itself that generates the unexpected and the surprising. Then it may be that no one is to blame but, rather, uncertainty needs to be accepted as an inescapable fact of life that need not provoke despair or paralyse action.

So much for theoretical perspectives, but is there reliable evidence that the application of strategic choice prescriptions works? The next section looks at this question.

## 7.4 EVIDENCE OF SUCCESS

### Do the prescriptions actually work?

If strategic choice theory succeeded in identifying a reliable set of prescriptions for strategic success, then one would expect to find at least a small sample of companies that have mastered those prescriptions. One would expect to find samples of excellent companies that remain successful for long periods of time.

In fact, it seems that no sooner does anyone identify a sample of excellent companies than most of them slip from grace. In the early 1980s, *Peters & Waterman (1982)* identified 43 excellent companies in the United States but within five years two-thirds could no longer be included in the sample. *Goldsmith & Clutterbuck (1984)* carried out a similar analysis of 25 UK companies and the same fate befell their sample. The rankings of the Fortune 500 companies and the *Financial Times* top 100 companies change dramatically over five-year periods.

It is therefore extremely difficult to find a sample of companies that have consistently mastered the task of successful strategic management for a reasonably long period of time. The usual reason given for this difficulty is that the environment is too turbulent to allow continuing success, or that companies fall from the category of excellence because they are incompetently managed. This is, however, a strange response. If the environment is too turbulent to allow the strategic management prescriptions to succeed, then clearly they should be abandoned and something else looked for. I find it rather difficult to believe that the strategic management prescriptions do not succeed because managers are not applying them competently – surely by now the business schools would have remedied this problem. Or is it possible that business schools are teaching the wrong thing when they teach the dominant view of strategy as an intentional process?

It has also proved very difficult to establish any reliable connection between the existence of formal planning in an organisation and superior performance (*Greenley, 1986*). That may be because few companies actually use long-term plans as control instruments. A survey of large companies in the UK (*Goold & Quinn, 1990*) shows that only 15 per cent of those that do have formal planning systems use them as templates against which to monitor actions. Even those 15 per cent monitor their plans against events such as building a factory rather than by results such as making a profit. It seems that most managers do not use the espoused recipes for success as they are intended to be used; and no one can establish much of a link between the use of the recipe and success.

Strategic choice prescriptions do not provide reliable answers to the question of how to create and sustain effective and long-lived organisations. Royal Dutch Shell conducted a survey in 1983 and found that the average lifetime of the largest industrial corporations was less than 40 years (*De Geus, 1988*). Corporations do not live as long as individual people! That report could only find about 30 corporations, worldwide, that had survived for more than a century and of the 50 per cent of those with reliable enough records all had significantly changed the nature of their activities a number of times. Long-term survivors do not stick to their knitting.

## The usual response

This recognition of relative failure normally provokes an intensified effort to improve a selected number of the existing prescriptions. Larger numbers of organisations are researched and the approaches to planning, envisioning, strategically controlling and consensus building are further refined.

For example, the study of large UK companies already referred to identified that only 15 per cent of those who formulated long-term plans subsequently monitored and reviewed action against them (*Goold & Quinn, 1990*). The conclusion drawn by the researchers was that managers were behaving in an ineffective way. Despite the admitted difficulties of doing so, managers were advised to devote more effort to setting strategic milestones and reviewing their actions against those milestones. The implicit assumptions the researchers were making are these:

- Companies will be successful if they formulate consistent long-term plans and then sustain stability by acting in accordance with those plans.
- Such stability can be secured only by reviewing and monitoring action outcomes against milestones.
- Levels of uncertainty are not such as to make all of this completely impossible.

But the managers in the sample of companies knew all about setting milestones and monitoring outcomes. They were doing exactly this when they used budgets for short-term control systems. Why did the majority in the sample not carry the procedure over to the long-term control of their organisation? They all knew about the importance of the long term. Perhaps they did not carry short-term reviewing procedures over to the long term because it did not make much practical sense to do so. Perhaps the level of uncertainty was too high. Repeating advice that has been heeded only superficially for decades now is surely not a useful response to a serious difficulty.

Another example of this response is the book by *Hamel & Prahalad (1994)*. It talks about the successful as the ones who 'get to the future' first, so indicating an assumption that the future already exists and the successful discover what it is and then take it for themselves. In fact, the future does not exist yet at all. It is not waiting to be discovered. It will be whatever the players make it. In that case how can anyone identify the competences that will be required to meet it, as Hamel and Prahalad propose?

## Do comprehensive culture-change programmes work any better?

Organisation development (OD) is the intentional change of a culture to be brought about through a systematic, organisation-wide, centrally planned programme of re-education. And this re-education programme has certain specific features: it is education based upon the consent and commitment of the people involved.

OD is based on the assumption that organisations will cope more effectively with change, will implement their strategies more effectively, if the creative potential of their people is unleashed. This is said to require:

- flat organisational structures;
- loose, overlapping job definitions;
- widespread participation in decision making; and thus
- the dispersion of power as authority to make decisions.

OD is about achieving planned changes in behaviour through empowering people in a particular kind of political system that we may call a democratic, collegial–consensus system (*Greiner & Schein, 1988*). The political system is collegial because it is based on dispersed power and widespread participation. It is a consensus system because it is all held together by strongly shared beliefs and decisions that are taken in a collaborative way. The aim is to move an organisation from a control model to a commitment one.

Despite the end-point of dispersed power and consensus decision making, the OD programme is in fact about reaching that point in a planned manner. Someone has to decide in advance what the change in belief systems is to be; someone is in control of the process. OD is not about changes that emerge or evolve from a pattern of interactions: it is a comprehensive pre-designed programme. And herein lies its danger, for it can all too easily become a propaganda exercise. Herein lies what may be an insuperable obstacle – it is using a control model to install a commitment one. Note the concept of leadership in the OD project: the leader decides in advance what the organisation should do and then facilitates the acceptance of these decisions by others in the organisation. Contrast this with an alternative where leadership takes the form of facilitating a learning experience in which members of the organisation, including the leader, develop a decision. That would be a commitment model being used to lead to a commitment one.

Because of its emphasis on planning, OD is based on the unquestioned assumption that an organisation is a feedback system in which negative feedback is the dominant form. It is through the negative feedback of consensus, planning and monitoring that the successful organisation is kept at, or returned to, stable states of consensus around a given culture or belief system, one that can be installed.

How well does this approach work? One study has described a long list of failed efforts at total culture change because of the neglect or lack of support from top management (*Mirvis & Berg, 1977*). Another study of a number of companies (*Beer, Eisenstat & Spector, 1990*) leads to these conclusions:

- Corporate programmes to change the whole culture of a company in a top-down planned manner do not work.
- The most effective change programmes are those that start in a number of small peripheral operations and gradually spread throughout the organisation.
- Changes to formal structures, systems and policies come at the end of successful periods of change, not the beginning. Effective culture change focuses on the tasks people have to do in business units and it spreads not because the top is in control of the spread but because the top creates the right climate for change to spread.

There is, therefore, some persuasive evidence indicating that OD programmes simply do not work consistently.

## 7.5    SUMMARY

This chapter has provided a brief review of the theoretical assumptions upon which strategic choice theory is built. It is important to remember that it is theory because it features so prominently in the discussions of researchers and practitioners alike that it is quite easy to mistake it for reality. The conclusion I reach is that this theory provides a partial and limited explanation of how organisational life unfolds. It provides powerful explanations of, and prescriptions for, the predictable, repetitive aspects of organisational life over short time frames into the future. These are indeed very prominent and important aspects of organisational life. However, if you believe, as I do, that life in organisations is woven from inextricable strands of the predictable and the unpredictable, the stable and the unstable, the orderly and the disorderly, then it provides a very partial explanation. On its own, it leaves one feeling puzzled by its constant surprise and worried about the inability to stay in control that it prescribes. Creativity and innovation remain largely mysterious if strategic choice theory is the only way to understand organisations. The richness and importance of relationships between people is absent. It prescribes predominantly top-down processes, even when empowerment and self-managing teams are suggested. They are always the result of decisions made by those at the top of the hierarchy.

## FURTHER READING

Ansoff (1990) is one of the most vociferous supporters of intentional strategy. Good summaries of counter views are to be found in Hurst (1982), Hurst (1986), Argyris (1990) and Schein (1988). A more detailed development of the arguments in this chapter may be found in Stacey (1991). Morgan (1997) and Mintzberg (1994) are well worth reading.

## REFERENCES

Ansoff, I. (1990), *Implanting Corporate Strategy*, Hemel Hempstead: Prentice Hall.

Argyris, C. (1990), *Overcoming Organizational Defenses: Facilitating Organizational Learning*, Boston: Allyn & Bacon.

Beer, M., Eisenstat, R. A. & Spector, B. (1990), *The Critical Path to Corporate Renewal*, Boston: Harvard Business School Press.

De Geus, P. (1988), Planning as learning, *Harvard Business Review*, March–April, pp. 70–4.

Goldsmith, W. & Clutterbuck, D. (1984), *The Winning Streak*, London: Weidenfield & Nicolson.

Goold, M. with Quinn, J. J. (1990), *Strategic Control: Milestones for Long Term Performance*, London: Hutchinson.

Greenley, G. E. (1986), Does strategic planning improve performance?, *Long Range Planning*, vol. 19, no. 2, pp. 101–9.

Greiner, L. E. & Schein, V. E. (1988), *Power and Organization Development: Mobilizing Power to Implement Change*, Reading, MA: Addison-Wesley.

Hamel, G. & Prahalad, C. K. (1994), *Competing for the Future*, Boston: Harvard Business School Press.

Hurst, D. K. (1986), Why strategic management is bankrupt, *Organizational Dynamics*, Autumn, pp. 4–77.

Hurst, E. G. (1982), Controlling strategic plans, in Lorange, D. (Ed.) (1982), *Implementation of Strategic Planning*, Englewood Cliffs, NJ: Prentice Hall.

Mintzberg, H. (1994), *The Rise and Fall of Strategic Planning*, Hemel Hempstead: Prentice Hall.

Mirvis, P. & Berg, D. (1977), Failures in Organizational Development and Change, New York: John Wiley.

Morgan, G. (1997), *Images of Organization*, Thousand Oaks, CA: Sage.

Peters, T. J. & Waterman, R. H. (1982), *In Search of Excellence*, New York: Harper & Row.

Schein, E. H. (1988), *Process Consultation Volume II: Lessons for Managers and Consultants*, Reading, MA: Addison-Wesley.

Stacey, R. (1991), *The Chaos Frontier: Creative Strategic Control for Business*, Oxford: Butterworth-Heinemann.

# 8 The foundations of learning organisation theory

## Systems dynamics and cognitivism

Chapters 2 to 7 dealt with strategic choice theory, showing how its theoretical foundations are to be found in the theory of cybernetic systems and a primarily cognitivist view of human nature. I now turn to another way of understanding organisational change. This is the notion of the learning organisation that has attracted increasing attention over the 1990s. This approach has much in common with strategic choice theory but there are significant differences. Most important, perhaps, is how it points to the limits of predictability. The purpose of this chapter is to explore the theoretical foundations of learning organisation theory and the next chapter will then review that theory and compare it with strategic choice perspectives. The main theoretical difference is that learning organisation theorists employ a somewhat different theory of interaction. They still see interaction in systemic terms but the systems theory is systems dynamics rather than cybernetics. The difference and the significance of the shift will be explored in the next section and how it connects with life in organisations is dealt with in subsequent sections. An important point to note at the outset is this: while the underlying systems theory changes from cybernetics to systems dynamics, the same cognitivist view of human nature is retained. Furthermore, the way systems dynamics is interpreted as feedback structures retains an essentially cybernetic perspective on control. It is this that makes learning organisation theory an orthodox perspective, in my view. The next chapter will explain what I mean by this.

## 8.2     SYSTEMS DYNAMICS: NONLINEARITY AND POSITIVE FEEDBACK

As Chapter 2 explained, cybernetics and cognitivism both developed from common origins. Essentially, cognitivism assumes that the human individual is a cybernetic entity. Cybernetic entities are driven by negative feedback towards states of equilibrium. The negative feedback process is one in which the behaviour of the entity or system is compared with some feature external to it, such as a goal, an expected sequence of behaviours, or a pre-given reality in the environment. Information on the difference between system/entity behaviour and this fixed, external point of reference is then fed back to modify the behaviour of the system/entity so that the difference is damped and removed.

Cybernetic explanations of behaviour focus on the operation of negative feedback loops and no attention is paid to the possibility of positive feedback loops. While the former dampen down differences, the latter amplify them. If amplifying feedback were applied to a steam engine it would blow up. Cybernetics also assumes linear connections between cause and effect and pays no attention to possible nonlinearities in the behaviour of a system. Consequently, it avoids the consideration of complex dynamics, seeing patterns of change purely in terms of an orderly and predictable movement towards stable equilibrium. A cybernetic system has no internal capacity for changing its state. It moves in a steady, orderly trajectory to equilibrium until some change in the environment occurs. Departures from this steady trajectory are due to errors in forecasts, particularly of time lags, not the structure of the system itself.

Systems dynamics has its intellectual roots in the same tradition as cybernetics. It is also built on the engineer's notion of control. However, from this common root and around the same time, it developed in a somewhat different way to cybernetics. While cyberneticists focused on the structure of negative feedback loops those who developed systems dynamics sought to model the system as a whole in mathematical terms. The most important figures in this development were economists seeking to model economic cycles for whole economies or some aspect of them such as inventory cycles. Some of the most important figures here were *Goodwin (1951)*, *Phillips (1950)* and *Tustin (1953)*. Systems dynamics thinking was also extended to industrial management problems (*Simon, 1952; Forrester, 1958*). It is important to note, right from the start, that when these writers referred to human beings they saw them as decision rules in a system. The understanding of human nature was essentially cognitivist as it was with cybernetics.

In their modelling work systems dynamicists used nonlinear equations that incorporated positive feedback effects and generated rather complex dynamics. These models also display some cyclical behaviour that is due to the structure of the system itself, not just changes in the environment. However, just as with cybernetics the system cannot spontaneously change its state, a matter I will return to in Chapter 12. The point is that systems dynamics makes a number of assumptions that lead it to differ in some respects from cybernetics. These are nonlinear causality, the possibility of positive, as well as negative, feedback and the possibility of internally generated cyclical behaviour and non-equilibrium. However, the interpretation of systems in terms of feedback loops retains some links with cybernetics.

This section will give a brief review of some of the key concepts in systems dynamics, starting with the nature of nonlinearity.

## Nonlinearity

Nonlinearity occurs when some condition or some action has a varying effect on an outcome, depending on the level of the condition or the intensity of the action. For example, the availability of a stock of goods in an inventory affects shipment rates of those goods, but the effect varies. When the stock is close to a desired level, there will be virtually no impact of stock levels on shipment rates. The firm ships according to its order inflow rate. However, when inventory is very low, stock availability has a powerful constraining effect on shipments.

Another example is where extra labour is hired. At first, extra labour may lead to proportionally extra output but, given fixed equipment, a point will be reached where extra labour adds proportionally less and less output. Eventually, adding extra labour causes output to decline as large numbers interfere with efficient operation. These effects cannot be captured in simple linear relationships where a cause always exerts the same degree of effect on an outcome.

Nonlinear interaction can be modelled as a system of nonlinear equations, as you can see in the following simple example. The size of a population of, say, insects is determined by the difference between birth rates and death rates so that today's population size ($P_t$) is some multiple or some fraction ($c$), of yesterday's population ($P_{t-1}$). This can be written as:

$$P_t = cP_{t-1} \qquad\qquad (1)$$

When birth rates exceed death rates, then $c$ is greater than 1 and the population grows. However, this is not the only set of forces governing the population level. As the population rises, food becomes scarcer and conflict and stress rise as overcrowding increases. This dampening impact of population increases can be represented mathematically as follows:

$$P_t = 1 - P_{t-1} \qquad\qquad (2)$$

Since both of these forces are acting upon the population at the same time, the relationship can be expressed by combining them as follows:

$$P_t = cP_{t-1}(1 - P_{t-1}) \qquad\qquad (3)$$

This is the famous logistic difference equation that has been widely used in analyses of populations of all kinds and many other phenomena besides. I will be returning to this in Chapter 11.

This equation models nonlinear behaviour in that, for the same birth and death rates, a level of population today exerts a different effect on tomorrow, depending on just how high or low it is today. It is important to note how this equation is iterative and self-referential and how it generates a history. It is iterative because it is repeatedly applied from one period to another and it is self-referential because what $P$ is today depends upon what it was yesterday. In other words, it refers back to itself in order to determine what it is and in doing so traces a path over time. I will be returning to this point in Chapters 11 and 12. I am making this point now to draw attention to the fact that this kind of structure is not spoken about in self-referential terms in the literature on the learning organisation. Instead, it is interpreted from a feedback point of view. This takes the reasoning process down a very different route to that which a self-referential interpretation takes. I will be returning to this point in Chapter 16.

Although interpreted in feedback terms, the equation itself is not a feedback structure in the cybernetic sense in that it does not feed back a difference between its behaviour and some fixed, external point of reference. You may say that it feeds back on itself but this would be a very different notion of feedback from the cybernetic one. I will use the term self-referential when referring to the kind of process that the logistic equation represents. I think that this is important because organisation theorists describe such processes in the terminology of feedback and so, I think, import a cybernetic mode of thinking into systems dynamics. The radical potential of systems dynamics is then, I believe, lost. I will explain what I mean by this in Chapter 11. In the meantime, let me explain how I see self-referential relationships of the kind depicted in equation (3) above being used as feedback loops. Consider how you might interpret that equation as a feedback model of the insect population.

Equation (1) might be interpreted as a positive, or amplifying, feedback loop. When birth rates exceed death rates, the population grows for evermore, according to equation (1). This is amplifying growth. When $c$ is less than 1, the population declines until none are left. Again, this is amplifying feedback. Equation (2) might then be interpreted as a negative feedback loop of the kind familiar from cybernetics. High levels of population dampen the growth effects of equation (1). So instead of a system that operates only according to negative feedback, as in cybernetics, there is now a system that operates according to both positive and negative feedback as shown in equation (3). These feedback loops can be represented in the diagrammatic form shown in *Figure 8.1*.

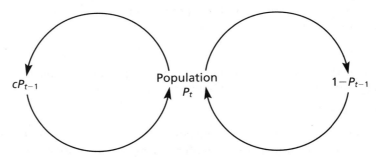

**FIGURE 8.1**   Positive and negative feedback in population growth

Systems dynamics therefore introduces the possibility that a system may display non-equilibrium behaviour as it flips between positive and negative feedback. The result is much more complex patterns of movement over time, that is much more complex dynamics. Behaviour can now be cyclical and those cycles might be very irregular if the system is perturbed by environmental fluctuations. Systems dynamics was very important in understanding the nature of economic cycles, such as cycles in inventory and other forms of investment. Systems dynamics also points to the limits of predictability by introducing nonlinear circular causality which makes it difficult to say what causes what, or what precedes what.

Before exploring further how systems dynamics ideas are used in understanding organisations I want to reiterate a point I have already made. One way of interpreting systems dynamics is to see the system as a self-referential one. The line of reasoning pursued is then to try to understand how the system determines what it is by reference to itself. Another route to take is to interpret systems dynamics in terms of feedback loops, that is to see it as a feedback system. The latter is the route that most have taken. I will be taking up the self-referential route and looking at the difference it makes in Chapters 12 and 16. I believe it has radical implications. The point I want to emphasise here, however, is that taking the feedback system route implicitly retains a conception of the system as cybernetics plus positive feedback and in doing so remains an orthodox theory of organisational change.

## 8.3    POSITIVE FEEDBACK IN ORGANISATIONS

Consider some important examples of positive feedback in organisations.

### Vicious circles

The vicious (or virtuous) circle is a widely used concept and this is a positive feedback loop. An early model of vicious circles in organisations is provided by *Gouldner (1964)*. He studied a gypsum plant in the United States and developed a model to explain what he observed. This is illustrated in *Figure 8.2*.

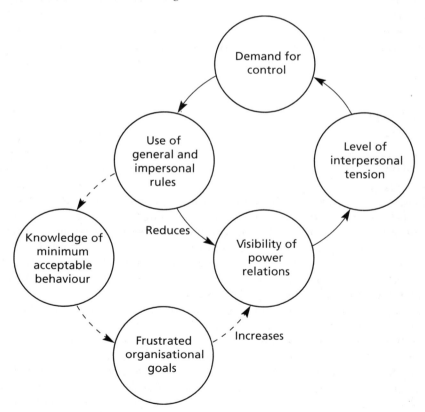

**FIGURE 8.2**    Gouldner's model of intended and unintended consequences
*Source*: R. Turton (1991), *Behaviour in a Business Context*, London: Chapman and Hall

Senior managers at the gypsum plant were concerned to manage efficiently and believed that this required reduced tension between managers and workers. Such tension could be reduced, they thought, if power relations became less visible and all behaved according to impersonal rules. The intention was to emphasise the 'rationality' of the rules and conceal the fact that power was being exercised. No reasonable person could object to rules designed to improve efficiency and those who had to enforce them could deny the personal exercise of power and simply say they were doing their job. Conflicts around the distribution of power would then be removed.

Thus, the demand by senior managers for greater control led to the use of general and impersonal rules intended to decrease the visibility of the power of senior management and hence interpersonal tension. In this way managers hoped to establish a damping, negative feedback loop producing the intended consequences of reduced tension.

These actions, however, set up another loop that produced unintended consequences. The rules created norms about minimum performance in terms of time of attendance and output levels. People stuck to the minimum norms, frustrating senior management expectations of increased performance. That led to a call for closer supervision and closer control, which had the effect of increasing the visibility of power and thus increasing the level of tension. More impersonal rules were then required. An unintended positive loop was generating unintended consequences. And that loop came to dominate what was going on, causing a vicious spiralling circle of tighter controls and more tension.

## Self-fulfilling prophecies

*Merton (1957)* developed a model of organisations in terms of self-fulfilling prophecies, another example of positive feedback at work. Many managers argue that most people are not all that competent and cannot be left to make decisions for themselves in relation to their work. They argue that efficiency requires rules. But constant compliance with rules causes individuals eventually to lose the capacity to make decisions for themselves. The constant reliance on rules leads to the rules becoming ends in themselves instead of means to ends. As a consequence of being compelled to obey rules they did not originate, employees lose the capacity for independent thought. The result is trained incapacity. Rule-bound organisations encourage unimaginative people to join them and the imaginative leave. The prophecy that people are incompetent is fulfilled by the means taken to deal with its originally supposed existence.

For example, managers may demand greater control in order to secure reliability in service terms. Employees fulfil the stipulated reliability criteria by sticking to the rules. The result is employees who stick to the rules and supply customers strictly in accordance with them. If this leads to trouble with customers, employees can show how they have kept to the rules. This is the intended feedback loop – negative and damping. But such rigid behaviour and the organisational defences it involves lead to more and more difficulties with clients. Growing customer dissatisfaction leads to top managers calling for greater reliability and more rules. So another positive loop is set up, a vicious circle with unintended consequences.

## Bandwagon effects and chain reactions

A bandwagon effect is the tendency of a movement to gain supporters simply because of its growing popularity; or it is the well-observed economic phenomenon of 'keeping up with the Joneses' – the demand for a product increases simply because more and more people see that other people have it. This phenomenon of products spreading through consuming populations is another example of a positive feedback loop, this time creating a virtuous circle for the producer of the product. A small gain in market share by one product can, through this spreading and copying effect, be escalated into market domination. So although Sony's Betamax was the technically superior video recorder, Matsushita's VHS recorder obtained a small market lead in the early days of market development. This led to more stores stocking titles in the VHS format. That led to a further increase in VHS recorder market share and therefore more stockists turned to VHS films, and so on.

A similar phenomenon is the chain reaction. Here a positive feedback process escalates a small change into major consequences. Police firing a shot into a demonstrating crowd may touch off a chain reaction which leads to a massive riot or even the overthrow of a government. *Box 8.1* gives an example from business.

There is convincing evidence that almost any human system one can think of is characterised by nonlinear relationships and by the powerful effects of positive amplifying feedback, as well as by negative feedback loops. Models that ignore this nonlinearity and the presence of positive feedback must inevitably give a very one-sided, and therefore suspect, understanding of the dynamics of organising.

---

**BOX 8.1**

## Changing the Coca-Cola formula

In April 1985, the Chairman of Coca-Cola announced that the original formula for the world-famous soft drink was to be changed to a new sweeter variety to be called 'New Coke'. This announcement followed the two years of research and planning, costing some $4m, that had gone into the development of a new strategy to counter the market share gains being made by Pepsi Cola. Market research had shown that the New Coke would boost Coca-Cola's market share and add some $200m in sales. Taste tests had demonstrated that people preferred the New Coke taste.

New Coke was launched on 23 April 1985 at a press conference attended by 200 newspaper, magazine and TV reporters. They were unconvinced by the New Coke and their stories were generally negative.

The word about the change in Coca-Cola spread quickly. Within 24 hours, 81 per cent of the US population knew about it and early results were encouraging despite the negative media response. About 150 million people tried New Coke and most commented favourably. But the protests were also mushrooming. In the first four hours, the company received 650 calls. By mid May calls ran at 5000 ▶

per day, and there was a mass of angry letters – around 40 000 letters were received that spring and summer. The company had to hire new staff to handle the complaints.

People talked about Coke as an American symbol and they felt betrayed. Some threatened to switch to tea or water. Before May, 53 per cent of sample surveys said they liked the New Coke. In July that fell to 30 per cent. Anger spread across the country, fuelled by the media. The Chairman's father threatened to disown him for tampering with a national symbol.

On 11 July 1985 the company acknowledged that it had made a mistake, top executives apologised to the public and announced the restoration of the old Coca-Cola. TV programmes were interrupted to convey the news.

No satisfactory linear cause-and-effect explanation has been found for this sequence of events. What this demonstrates is how some small change, added sweetness to a soft drink, can escalate into a major consequence through the operation of positive feedback taking the form of herd instinct, bandwagon effects. ■

*Source:* Hartley (1991)

## Feedback interactions between people

Karl Weick analysed interactions between individuals. He saw those interactions in terms of positive and negative feedback loops. His model was characterised by:

- the incorporation of both negative and positive loops in the feedback behaviour; and
- the implicit recognition of nonlinear relationships that cause systems autonomously to change from dominant positive to dominant negative feedback modes.

*Weick (1969/1979)* invited his readers to see the feedback nature of organisations for themselves by working on the diagram shown in *Figure 8.3.*

This figure depicts a number of variables that affect what happens at a meeting between two or more people in an organisation. The reader is invited to connect the phrases in the diagram with causal arrows showing the effect of one variable on the others, indicating with a plus sign when one variable causes another to increase and with a minus sign when one variable causes another to decrease. The result will be a set of interconnected positive and negative feedback loops. What happens at this meeting will depend upon whether positive or negative loops dominate, and that domination could change during the course of the meeting. The system will be stable or unstable depending upon the dominant form of feedback (see *Box 8.2*).

So right at the most basic level of an organisation, that is at the level of interactions between individuals, the unfolding of events depends upon the nature of the feedback structure that defines these interrelationships.

Because relationships between people in a group take this complicated, changing feedback form, decision making cannot be as coherent a process as rational models of any kind would lead one to believe.

1. Number of
people making
comments

2. Variety of
ideas suggested

12. My irritation
at speaker

3. My fear of
embarrassment

11. Amount of group
concentration on
problem

4. Amount of
horsing around
in group

10. My feelings
of boredom

5. Number of
ideas I think of

9. My understanding
of material that
is presented

6. My willingness
to volunteer a
comment

8. My self-
consciousness

7. Quality of
ideas suggested

**FIGURE 8.3**    Weick's model: events at a meeting
*Source*: K. Weick (1979), *The Social Psychology of Organizing*, New York: McGraw-Hill. Reproduced with permission.

**BOX 8.2**

# Feedback interactions at a meeting

Suppose we are at a meeting which I am chairing. Suppose that, as my willingness to proffer comments declines, the rest of the group engages in more horseplay (negative link between 6 and 4 in *Figure 8.3*). Then suppose that, as the level of horseplay increases, it diminishes my understanding of the material being presented at the meeting (negative link between 4 and 9 in *Figure 8.3*). As my understanding falls, my fear of embarrassment rises (negative link). And as my fear of embarrassment rises, my willingness to volunteer comments declines (negative link). The decrease in my comments leads to even more horseplay and so we continue around the amplifying, vicious circle that makes us more and more ineffective as a group. Because we have four negative links, an even number, the feedback loop as a whole is positive. With that kind of structure our meeting is unstable and we will not get much done.

But there could be other links in the loop. Suppose my level of boredom rises as the amount of horsing around increases (positive link). The more bored I become the less self-conscious I become (negative link). This fall in self-consciousness increases my willingness to comment (negative link). That willingness to    ▶

comment cuts down on the horseplay (negative link). We have here a limiting or self-regulating loop whereby the increase in horseplay sets off automatic responses that tend to hold it in check. This loop has one positive and three negative links. It is therefore a negative feedback loop. It exerts a damping effect, pushing the system towards an equilibrium.

At some point the level of horseplay may become so great that the second loop (the negative one) dominates the first (the positive one) and the meeting will move from a vicious spiral of ineffectiveness onto a path towards more effective communication. Note that the behaviour of the system moves of its own accord, because of its nonlinear feedback structure, from an unstable to a stable state. ∎

## Tight and loose coupling

Weick points to added levels of complexity in interrelationships and decision making as a move is made from single groups to the collections of groups that constitute an organisation. Organisations are typically not tightly coupled sets of groups alone. Organisations are more typically sets of groups that are tightly coupled for some purposes, but constitute a loosely coupled system for other purposes.

Groups or systems are *tightly coupled* when there are clear-cut direct connections between them; when they are so closely coordinated that a decision or action in one has immediately apparent implications for decisions or actions in another. Tight coupling is present in an efficient assembly production process, where one group assembling the components on a television set work in a highly coordinated way with another group putting the components into a plastic casing. Any failure in the first assembly operation has an immediate impact on the later operation and vice versa. Tight coupling is highly efficient while all moves according to plan. But unforeseen changes in one area have rapid and major implications for what happens in other areas. A small failure in one small part could bring the whole system down. Tight coupling is characterised by (*Perrow, 1984*):

- no delays in processing;
- no variation in sequences of events;
- only one method of achieving the goal;
- no slack in the flow of activity from one part of the system to another;
- any buffers built in at the design stage;
- possible substitution of supplies or equipment built in at the design stage.

*Loose coupling*, on the other hand, means that there is a buffer between one group and another. There is the possibility of delays and changes in the sequences of events. Parts of the system can continue to function while failures in other parts of the system are attended to. Alternative methods can be employed and additional resources called upon. Buffers and redundancies are available to deal with the unforeseeable.

Clearly, loosely coupled systems are less efficient, but they are also far safer. The more unpredictable the situation, the more helpful it will be to have a loosely coupled system. So in the assembly operation above the system could be turned into a loosely coupled one by introducing the possibility of building up unplanned inventories at each stage. If the group putting the assemblies into plastic cases fails to maintain its speed, the supervisor of the group assembling the components could decide to continue production and add to inventories, even though there is no plan to do so. Decisions or actions in one group would then not have immediate implications for another.

Because of this possibility of loose coupling, a change in one part of the system need not immediately affect the other parts. Loosely coupled systems are characterised by the possibility of delays and changes in the sequences of events. And because of this it is difficult to predict what one group will do when another takes some action. The system becomes safer in the face of uncertainty, but the safety factor itself adds a level of complexity that makes it more difficult to determine how the system will behave or why it is behaving as it does.

Loose coupling means that the connections between decisions and actions in one part of the organisation and decisions and actions in other parts are often obscure. The connections between means and ends, and between problems and solutions, also become less clear. People, problems and choice opportunities are combined in confusing ways that make it difficult to predict agendas of matters to be attended to, and the outcomes of those matters.

When they deal with the day-to-day management of their existing businesses, successful organisations set up tightly coupled systems. Modern methods of operations management and inventory control, such as just-in-time delivery and materials resource programming, are examples of this. But successful organisations always also have to face unpredictable changes to their activities. To deal with this they also evolve loosely coupled systems. Because they face both the predictable and the unpredictable, most organisations are systems that combine tight and loose coupling. The element of loose coupling often makes it very difficult to identify the events in one part of the system that are causing changes in other parts.

## Links with the environment

Weick also explains the organisation's links with the environment in terms of feedback loops. The nature of these loops is illustrated in *Figure 8.4*.

First consider what the terms used in *Figure 8.4* mean and then what the loop connections between them signify.

1  *Ecological change* means the changes occurring in the market and wider environments that an organisation operates in. Such changes are primarily the actions undertaken by actors in the environment. These external actions may lead people in an organisation to undertake actions too – hence the arrow and the + sign running from ecological change to enactment.

2  *Enactment* describes what the actors within the organisation itself do; it is the actions they undertake. The term enactment is used rather than the term action, to indicate that people within an organisation do not simply anticipate, react or adapt to what actors in the environment can be objectively observed to do. Instead,

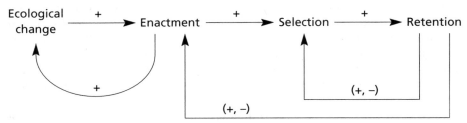

**FIGURE 8.4**   Weick's model: links with the environment
*Source*: K. Weick (1979), *The Social Psychology of Organizing*, New York: McGraw-Hill. Reproduced with permission.

people within an organisation are prompted by their subjective perceptions of what actors in the environment are doing or might do. It is those perceptions that drive their actions. Here Weick has moved from a cognitivist to a constructivist notion of human psychology. In the cognitivist perspective, an individual perceives an objective reality and then acts on that. In a constructivist perspective, an individual acts on the basis of perceptions built up through past experience and in so doing selects, or enacts, an environment. Here, the individual calls forth responses from other individuals and this constitutes his or her reality. This introduces an important notion of constraint. An individual cannot perceive objective reality but only what his or her experience makes it possible to perceive. Constructivism and cognitivism, however, both accord primacy to the individual.

Furthermore, actions of the above kind may lead environmental actors to do what they do. Those within an organisation then perceive this and undertake further action. So they all keep going around a positive feedback loop, represented by the + signs in the loop shown in *Figure 8.4* between ecological change and enactment. By taking a particular action, people within an organisation may cause people outside it to do what they do – the former are therefore in a real sense creating, or enacting, their own environment. Because they are driven by subjective perceptions it is also quite possible for people within an organisation to invent an environment and then cause it to occur. The question now is this: what causes actors within the organisation to perceive and act in the way they do? The answer lies in what they remember about what they have done before.

3   *Retention* is the process of storing what has been perceived and learned from previous actions. It is the shared memory of the collection of people constituting the organisation, built up from what they have done together over the past, reflecting their perceptions of what has worked and what has not worked. If particular actions worked in particular circumstances before, this will prompt a similar enactment now. So the link running back from retention to enactment can be positive or negative; that is, the organisational memory could prompt an action or stop it. The terms retention and organisational memory as they are used here mean the same thing as the culture of the organisation, its recipe, the paradigm its managers subscribe to, their received wisdom. These terms all have to do with the shared mental models of organisational actors, that is a cognitivist notion. The next question is this: how does retention come about? The answer lies in a process of selection.

4   *Selection* is the process through which organisational actors focus on some meanings of what they are doing and some perceptions of what others are doing, while ignoring yet others. What is selected for retention depends upon what has been done or enacted and what has been perceived (the positive arrow running from enactment to selection). And the selection itself is affected by what has been previously retained about how things should be perceived and done (the loop running back from retention to selection). What is selected to focus on now depends on the mental models already built up. These may cause people to accept or reject a perception hence the positive and negative signs in the retention–selection loop.

By looking at the interactions between an organisation and its environment in this way, Weick clarifies the concept of managers creating the reality they respond to.

## Self-designing systems

The feedback system view of how an organisation works led *Weick (1977)* to the concept of an organisation as a self-designing system. Rigid rule-bound organisations that spell out exactly how people should behave are incapable of generating new forms of behaviour to meet new situations. To be able to meet the unexpected new situation, organisations need to be loosely coupled, self-designing systems. That requires establishing the following patterns:

- valuing improvisation more than forecasts;
- dwelling on opportunities rather than constraints;
- inventing solutions rather than borrowing them;
- cultivating impermanence instead of permanence;
- valuing argument more highly than serenity;
- relying on diverse measures of performance rather than on accounting systems alone;
- encouraging doubt rather than removing it;
- continuously experimenting rather than searching for final solutions;
- seeking contradictions rather than discouraging them.

Such patterns of behaviour will make organisations less efficient but more adaptable. Weick has made a number of key points that are summarised in *Figure 8.5*.

## Hamel and Prahalad's analysis

*Hamel & Prahalad (1989)* also stress the role of organisations in creating their own environments instead of simply adapting to them. They have studied a number of global companies in North America, Europe and Japan and they suggest that what distinguishes the noticeably successful (Honda, Komatsu and Canon, for example) from the noticeably less so (General Motors, Caterpillar and Xerox, for example) are the different mental models of strategy guiding their respective actions. This research questions one of the basic tenets of strategic choice, namely the notion that successful organisations are those that fit, or adapt to, their environments.

**FIGURE 8.5**   Weick's model: key points on organisational dynamics

- Organisations are feedback systems, starting right at the fundamental level of interaction between two or more people within the organisation.
- The systematic feedback structure of the organisation itself determines the pattern of behaviour over time. The standard assumption in strategic choice theory is that the dynamics, the pattern of change, is due mainly to environmental forces outside the organisation. The proposition being made in Weick's models is that patterns of change are determined by the inherent nature of the system structure itself.
- A group of people does not necessarily have to have a shared, common purpose in order to be a group. People form groups before they have a common purpose because they have interdependent needs that require the resources of others. People group because they need each other's support, because of the means not the ends. Purpose comes later. So an organisation is not necessarily driven by goal-seeking behaviour, that is achieving a given goal. It may well be driven by searching for a goal in the first place. This is a very different perspective from strategic choice theory.
- Meaning for an organisation is retrospective not prospective. People can only understand what they are doing by interpreting what they have done. They impose meaning on what they have done. So a vision would not be a picture of a future state but an interpretation of where they have now got to. Meaning, purpose, vision and mission emerge from what people have done and are doing – they are not prior organisation-wide intentions.
- Organisations create and invent their own environment in the sense that the environment is their perception of what is happening and in the sense that their actions impact on the environment which then impacts back on the organisation. This is different to the simple adaptive view that is common in strategic choice theory.
- Predicting what feedback systems will do is very difficult. It is difficult to guess what people's preferences will be in the future and it is these preferences that will drive what they do.
- But despite the unpredictability and the complexity, people can operate as part of a system that is too complex for any one person alone to understand. Each plays a part in the complex unfolding of events, understanding only a part, and relies on others to play their parts.
- Loose coupling is important in the ability of such complex systems to remain flexible, but that loose coupling adds to system complexity and makes it even harder to understand and predict its behaviour.
- Such systems are essentially self-designing.
- Positive feedback, self-reinforcing processes play a very important part in what happens. Instability is an essential part of what goes on and one cannot simply ignore it or write it off as something to be banished by negative feedback controls. There is too much evidence that this focus on negative feedback alone leads to unintended positive loops and unintended consequences.

Hamel and Prahalad found that the less successful companies follow strategic choice prescriptions and so seek to maintain strategic fit. This leads them to trim their ambitions to those that can be met with available resources. Such companies are concerned mainly with product market units rather than core competences. They preserve consistency through requiring conformity in behaviour, and they focus on achieving financial objectives. These companies attempt to achieve their financial objectives by using generic strategies, selected according to criteria of strategic fit, in order to secure sustainable competitive advantage. Hamel and Prahalad report that this approach leads to repetition and imitation.

On the other hand, Hamel and Prahalad found that successful companies focus on leveraging resources, that is using what they have in new and innovative ways to reach seemingly unattainable goals. The main concern of these companies is to use their resources in challenging and stretching ways to build up a number of core competences. Consistency is maintained by all sharing a central strategic intent and the route to this successful state is accelerated organisational learning, recognising that no competitive advantages are inherently sustainable. Here, managers are not simply matching their resources to the requirements of the environment, leaving to others those requirements their resources are incapable of delivering. Instead, managers creatively use the resources they have, they create requirements of the environment which they can then meet, they push to achieve stretching goals, and so they continually renew and transform their organisation.

While these authors question some assumptions of strategic choice theory, they preserve others. In particular, they continue to see organisational success as flowing from clear, prior organisation-wide intention. They stress what they call strategic intent, a challenging shared vision of a future leadership position for the company. This strategic intent is stable over time. It is clear as to outcome but flexible as to the means of achieving the outcome. It is an obsession with winning and winning on a global scale cannot be secured either through long-term plans or through some undirected process of intrapreneurship or autonomous small task forces. Instead success is secured by discovering how to achieve a broad, stretching, challenging intention to build core competences.

This study questions the idea of adapting to the environment, proposing instead creative interaction. But in other respects – intention, harmony and consistency – it falls within what I have called orthodoxy.

## 8.4    SYSTEMS THINKING

Perhaps the most important development of systems dynamics models for application to organisational and social policy issues has been by *Jay Forrester (1958; 1961)*. His background was that of a servomechanisms engineer, digital computer pioneer and manager of a large R&D effort. He developed an approach to understanding human systems that is based on concepts of positive and negative feedback, nonlinearity and the use of computers to simulate the behaviour patterns of such complex systems. Feedback is the basic characteristic of his view of the world:

Systems of information feedback control are fundamental to all life and human endeavour, from the slow pace of biological evolution to the launching of the latest satellite. A feedback control system exists whenever the environment causes a decision which in turn affects the original environment. (*Forrester, 1958, p. 4*)

Here human decision making is firmly linked to the feedback concept.

### Production and distribution chains

Forrester has illustrated his approach by modelling the behaviour of production–distribution chains. A factory supplies a product, say beer, to a number of distributors who then ship it to an even larger number of retailers. Orders for the product flow back upstream from retailers to distributors and from them to the factory. The factory, the distributors and the retailers form a system and the links between them are flows of orders in one direction and flows of product in the other. Each part of the system tries to do the best it can to maintain inventories at minimum levels without running out of product to sell. Each attempts to ship product as fast as possible. They all do these things because that is the way to maximise their individual profits.

But because of its very structure – the feedback and lags in information flows – this system shows a marked tendency to amplify minor ordering disturbances at the retail level. An initial 10 per cent increase in orders at the retail level can eventually cause production at the factory to peak 40 per cent above the initial level before collapsing.

*Peter Senge (1990)* reports how he has used this example as a game with thousands of groups of managers in many countries. Even when people know about the likely consequences of this system, he has always found that the consequences of a small increase at the retail level are, first of all, growing demand that cannot be met. Inventories are depleted and backlogs grow. Then beer arrives in great quantities while incoming orders suddenly decline as backlogs are reduced. Eventually almost all players end up with large inventories they cannot unload. It is exactly this kind of cyclical behaviour we observe in real-life businesses.

Only by being aware of how the system as a whole functions, rather than simply concentrating on one's own part of it, can the extreme instabilities of the cycles be avoided. It seems, however, that these cycles can never be removed altogether.

### The lessons of systems thinking

The lessons of the game are that:

- The structure of the system influences behaviour. The cycles in ordering, inventory levels and production in the game are really the consequence of the structure of the system. But, when people play the game in a classroom, or in real life, they blame others in the system for what is going on. For example, the retailers blame the distributors for running out of stock and not delivering fast enough.
- Structure in human systems is subtle. Structure is the set of interrelationships between people and, because of negative and positive feedback loops, that structure can generate unintended results.

- Coping effectively often comes from a new way of thinking. If one simply focuses on one's own part in the system, thinks for example always as a retailer, then one's behaviour of over- and under-ordering will simply contribute to the system's instability. If, instead, players think in terms of the whole system, they will behave differently. For example, they will realise that widespread over-ordering is likely to occur. They will realise that doing so themselves in this situation will not help them much in the short run, but will eventually lead to stock levels that are too high. They will avoid doing what everyone else is doing, even if this reduces profitability in the short run.

## Principles of systems dynamics

By running computer simulations of a great many different human systems, researchers in the systems dynamics tradition have identified a number of principles about complex human systems. These are set out below.

1   Complex systems often produce unexpected and counter-intuitive results. In the beer game, retailers increase orders above their real need expecting this to lead to bigger deliveries, but because all retailers are doing this, and because of lags in information flows, the unexpected result is lower deliveries. Simulation of other situations suggests that increased low-cost housing in an inner city will exacerbate rather than arrest the decline of inner cities, because it creates ghettoes where social mobility is impossible. Policies of demolishing slum housing and discouraging the construction of cheap housing make the centre more desirable for the better off, but also create a more balanced social system in which there is the opportunity for upward mobility.

2   In complex systems – nonlinear relationships with positive and negative feedback – the links between cause and effect are distant in time and space. In the beer game, the causes of increased demand appeared at the retail end, distant in space from the factory and distant in time because of the lags in order flows. Such distance between cause and effect makes it very difficult to say what is causing what. Those playing the beer game always think that the fluctuations in deliveries are being caused by fluctuations in retail demand when in fact they are due to the manner in which the system operates. The problem is made worse by many coincident symptoms that look like causes but are merely relational. This means that it is extremely difficult to make specific predictions of what will happen in a specific place over a specific time period. Instead, quantitative simulations on computers can be used to identify general qualitative patterns of behaviour that will be similar to those one is likely to experience, although never the same. Simulation here is being used not to capture the future specific outcome within a range of likely outcomes, but to establish broad qualitative features in patterns of behaviour. *Senge (1990, p. 73)* puts it like this:

> The art of systems thinking lies in being able to recognise increasingly (dynamically) complex and subtle structures, … amid the wealth of details, pressures and cross-currents that attend all real management settings. In fact, the essence of mastering systems thinking as a management discipline lies in seeing patterns where others see only events and forces to react to.

3   Complex systems are highly sensitive to some changes but remarkably insensitive to many others. Complex systems contain some influential pressure, or leverage, points. If we can influence those points we can have a major impact on the behaviour of the

system. The trouble is that these are difficult to identify. Note how this concern with leverage points relates to the ideas introduced at the beginning of this chapter on chain reactions, bandwagon effects and virtuous circles of behaviour. In the beer game, the leverage points lie in the ordering practices of retailers and distributors. Unfortunately these pressure points, from which favourable chain reactions can be initiated, are extremely difficult to find. More usually, it seems, complex systems are insensitive to changes and indeed counteract and compensate for externally applied correctives. So when retailers find that deliveries from the distributors are curtailed, they respond by ordering even more and so make the situation worse. When aid programmes provide more dams and water pumps to halt the expansion of the Sahara, tribesmen simply enlarge their herd sizes, leading to overgrazing and the even more rapid encroachment of the desert.

Because of this natural tendency to counteract and compensate, that is to move to stability, it is necessary to change the system itself rather than simply apply externally generated remedies. By their very nature, complex systems often react to policy changes in ways that are the opposite to those which policy-makers intend; and complex systems tend to a condition of poor performance because they resist change.

The above points lead inevitably to the conclusion that, because an organisation is a complex system, attempts to plan its long-term future and plan changes in its culture and behaviour patterns are all likely to prompt counter-forces and lead to little change at all or to unexpected and unintended changes.

## Archetypes of feedback processes

Once the strong possibility that complex systems will counteract correctives and produce unintended consequences is recognised, it becomes essential to analyse and understand the feedback connections in the system, to understand the system as a whole. It becomes vital for effective intervention in the behaviour of the system to understand the dynamics of the system.

Through their simulations, systems dynamicists have built up a set of templates, or archetype feedback processes, that are very commonly found in organisations of all kinds. The purpose of these archetypes is not to make specific predictions of what will happen, but to recondition perceptions so that people are able to perceive the structures at play, to see the dynamic patterns of behaviour, and to see the potential leverage in those structures. The templates are meant to be used in a flexible way to help understand patterns in events. You have to use the template as an analogy with which to build your own explanations of each specific situation you are confronted with. Some examples of these templates are as follows.

### 1  Limits to growth (Figure 8.6)
Limits to growth occur when a reinforcing positive feedback process is installed to produce a desired result (a positive growth loop) but it inadvertently creates secondary effects (a negative limiting loop) that put a stop to the growth. The 'limits to growth' structure is found wherever growth bumps up against limits.

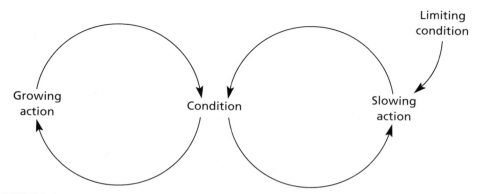

**FIGURE 8.6**   Limits to growth
*Source*: P. Senge (1990), *The Fifth Discipline*, New York: Doubleday

The most immediate response to this structure is that of pushing harder on the factors that cause growth. In fact this is counterproductive because it causes the system to bump even more firmly against the limits. The solution is to work on the negative loop, on relaxing the limits.

For example, a company may grow through introducing new products flowing from its R&D efforts. As it grows it increases the size of the R&D department which becomes harder to manage. Senior engineers then become managers and the flow of new product ideas slows. Pressing for more new product ideas will simply lead to a bigger R&D department and that will exacerbate the management problems, so reducing the flow of new ideas. Instead, there is a need to rethink the whole process of developing new products and running R&D activities. The leverage point is the way in which the actual R&D effort is organised and to see how this should be done one needs to understand the whole system of which R&D is a part.

### 2  Shifting the burden (Figure 8.7)
Shifting the burden happens where some underlying problem generates a number of symptoms. Because the underlying problem is difficult to identify, people focus on the symptoms. They look for the quick, easy fix. While these temporarily relieve the symptoms, the underlying problem gets worse. People do not notice at first how the underlying problems are getting worse and as they avoid dealing with these problems the system loses its ability to solve them.

An example is bringing an expert into an organisation to solve a problem. This may leave a manager's ability unaltered and when related problems arise again the manager will be unable to cope without the expert.

### 3  Eroding goals (Figure 8.8)
Another template is that of eroding goals, where a short-term solution is effected by allowing fundamental goals to decline. This happens when managers accept a decline in performance standards as a temporary measure to deal with a crisis.

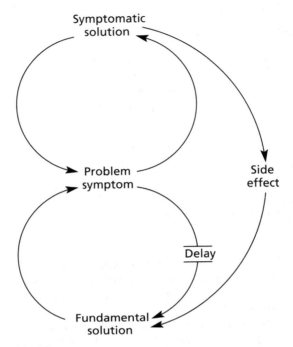

**FIGURE 8.7**   Shifting the burden
*Source*: P. Senge (1990), *The Fifth Discipline*, New York: Doubleday

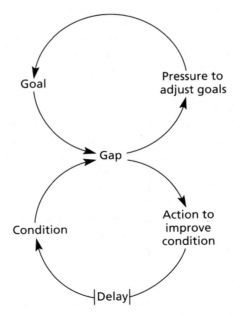

**FIGURE 8.8**   Eroding goals
*Source*: P. Senge (1990), *The Fifth Discipline*, New York: Doubleday

So, for example, a company producing a good product attracting high levels of demand increases its delivery time to accommodate a backlog crisis. It then does little to increase production capacity. The next time it goes around the circle, it experiences even bigger backlogs and so it extends delivery time even further. This goes on until customer dissatisfaction suddenly reaches a critical point and demand falls away rapidly.

Simulations show that when firms allow their goals for quality and delivery time gradually to slip it has dramatic effects on their profitability, as shown in *Box 8.3*. The message is to beware the symptomatic solution and seek to understand how the system is working.

---

**BOX 8.3**

## Peoples Express

Peoples Express provided an innovative low-cost airline service between the United States and Europe and within the United States. It was a no-frills service, but it was reliable. However, Peoples Express found that it could not build its service capacity to keep pace with the exploding demand. Instead of slowing its growth (by increasing prices) and focusing on training to increase service capacity, it continued to grow as fast as it could. Service levels declined more and more rapidly, staff morale collapsed, and competition became more fierce. Eventually customers no longer found Peoples Express attractive. ■

*Source*: Senge (1990)

---

### 4  Growth and underinvestment (Figure 8.9)

This occurs when new investments in capacity are not made early enough or on a large enough scale to accommodate continuing growth. As growth approaches limits set by existing capacity, the attempts made to meet demand result in lower quality and service levels. The consequence is customer dissatisfaction and declining demand.

### Another example of systems thinking: Porter's analysis of the competitive advantage of nations

*Porter (1990)* puts forward an explanation of how nations develop competitive advantage. This approach sees a particular company as part of a complex system consisting of other competing, supplying, supporting, customer and governmental organisations. The pattern of change any one company in this system displays depends upon a self-reinforcing interplay between what all of them are doing. Clusters of supporting and competing companies emerge in particular areas as a result of

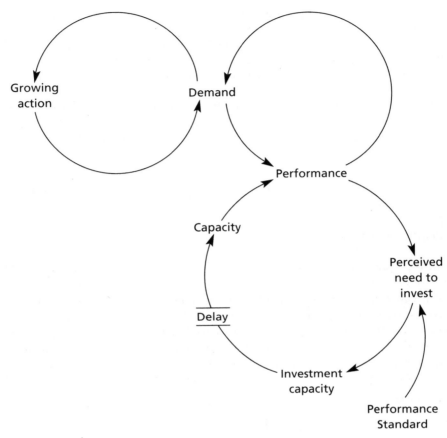

**FIGURE 8.9** Growth and underinvestment
*Source*: P. Senge (1990), *The Fifth Discipline*, New York: Doubleday

spreading benefits between them – a form of feedback between them that amplifies advantages and disadvantages and sets off virtuous and vicious circles of development. In this process, partly affected by chance, the cause and effect of individual determinants becomes blurred.

Porter's industry structure and value chain analysis mentioned briefly in Chapter 3, paints a picture of managers in an organisation who analyse a given environment and then choose a particular strategy that they then implement. If they choose the right strategy, that is if they formulate the right organisational intention and then actually carry it out, they will succeed. This is a picture of orderly, intentional adaptation to the environment. In the later analysis being discussed here, however, each firm is part of a system and therefore what happens to any individual firm will be a consequence, not of the shared intention of its top managers, but of the evolution of the whole system of which that firm and its top managers are a part.

The analysis is conducted in terms of what Porter calls the 'national diamond' reproduced as *Figure 8.10*. A nation, and therefore any individual firm within it,

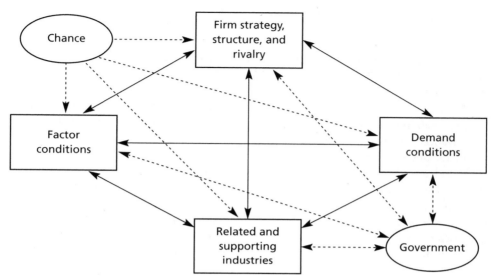

**FIGURE 8.10**    Porter's model for analysing the competitive advantage of nations
*Source*: M. Porter (1990), *The Competitive Advantage of Nations*, London: Macmillan

achieves success in a particular industry when it develops a favourable configuration between the following:

- *Factor conditions* such as skilled labour, the transport and education infrastructure, knowledge resources.
- *Demand conditions* such as the size of markets and the sophistication of buyers.
- *Related and supporting industries*. The point here is that one firm has competitive advantage when it is part of a whole value chain that is competitive. So Italian shoe manufacturers have advantages because they are part of a cluster of industries containing support in the form of leather suppliers and designers. This support industry is made possible by the existence of related firms such as handbag manufacturers.
- *Firm strategy*, structure and rivalry. The way firms are managed and formulate their strategies affects their competitive advantage. The more intense the rivalry between firms the more effective and efficient they will have to be to survive and therefore the more internationally competitive they will be.

In addition to these four determinants, the development of firms in a cluster depends on chance and on the government. Chance inventions or other events outside the control of companies or their governments create discontinuities that can reshape an industry. Government policies are part of the system too because they can add to or detract from competitive advantage (see *Box 8.4*).

These determinants create a system within which the nation's firms are born and develop. They gain advantage when the cluster they are part of is more favourable than competing clusters. This is a self-reinforcing system because the effect of one determinant depends upon the state of the others. Favourable demand conditions only lead to success if the state of rivalry is such that firms respond.

**BOX 8.4**

## Silicon Valley and the Italian shoe industry

Research centres of excellence in microelectronics and information technology at Stanford and Berkeley, together with the availability of skilled labour, played an important part in the development of Silicon Valley in California. The availability of advanced technology made this an attractive location for electronics manufacturers in the early stages of that industry's development. These businesses in turn attracted component suppliers and other support companies. What we can observe is a feedback process through which a particular constellation of industries is built up.

A similar process can be observed around Cambridge in the UK. Once again a research centre of excellence has played an important part in the initial attraction of electronics and information technology firms. Feedback connections attracted others to establish a whole new industrial area. Similar developments are to be observed between Reading and Bristol, for similar reasons.

But the specific composition of the industries, which have grown up around San Francisco, around Cambridge and between Reading and Bristol, are quite different. For example, neither of the two UK areas contains silicon chip manufacturers. These differences may be due to government policies, to some other factor, or even to small chance differences between locations and the way people responded.

Similar patterns of geographic development in fashion clothing and shoes can be observed in northern Italy around Milan. The process is the same. Some initial advantage attracts a small cluster of companies. Through feedback, support industries are attracted and so the pattern develops. ■

## 8.5    HOW SYSTEMS DYNAMICS DIFFERS FROM CYBERNETICS

*Figure 2.5* in Chapter 2 summarised the key features of cybernetic systems and *Figure 8.11* presents a similar summary for systems dynamics. By comparing them you will be able to see that the key differences are as follows. While cybernetics assumes linear causality, systems dynamics takes account of nonlinearity. Cybernetics deals only with negative feedback processes through which self-regulating control is maintained while systems dynamics also incorporates the effects of positive feedback as well. Consequently, non-equilibrium is a highly likely state according to systems dynamics while systems move to equilibrium according to cybernetics. The possibility of prediction is not seen as problematic from the cybernetic perspective but it is from a systems dynamics one. Discussions about organisations from a systems dynamics perspective, therefore, present much more complex dynamics and much more problematic possibilities for control than do discussions from a cybernetic perspective.

**FIGURE 8.11**  Systems dynamics: main points on organisational dynamics

- Organisations are goal seeking but amplifying feedback loops and nonlinearity mean that they are not self-regulating in the cybernetic sense. Instead, they are self-influencing and this may take a self-sustaining or a self-destructive form. They may be adapting to pre-given environments through negative feedback or diverging from them through positive feedback.
- Systems dynamics takes a realist position on human knowing.
- The system is recursive. This means that it feeds back on itself to repeat its behaviour.
- It follows that causality is circular. However, in systems dynamics causality is nonlinear. Causal links are distant and often difficult to identify.
- Predictability of specific events and their timings is very difficult and this makes it important to recognise qualitative patterns.
- Control becomes difficult but if the structure of the system is understood, leverage points can be identified. These are points where efforts to change behaviour have the most effect. These points are difficult to find. Changes there might simply provoke compensating and offsetting behaviour.
- Positive, or amplifying, feedback is seen to be of great importance.
- Behavioural patterns of the system as a whole are of great importance. Behavioural patterns can emerge without being intended; in fact they often emerge contrary to intention. The result is unexpected and counter-intuitive outcomes.
- Because the analysis is conducted in feedback terms there is still the notion of an external point of reference. The system still operates on the basis of representations of its environment.
- There is a clear boundary between system and environment, between inner and outer. Although the system is adapting to its environment, it is itself a closed system. It operates/changes with reference to a fixed point at the boundary with its environment, either amplifying or damping in relation to that fixed point.
- Its state is determined by its own structure as well as flux in the environment expressed through the fixed point of reference. Instability comes from within the system as well as the environment.
- The system is no longer homeostatic, or equilibrium seeking, but far more likely to be in non-equilibrium. However, left to its own devices, the system has a tendency to stabilise and so deteriorate in the face of change.
- History is important in that the current state of the system does depend upon the sequence of previous states. However, the system does not evolve of its own accord. Any change must be designed outside the system and then installed.
- Effective organisations are self-regulating, an automatic mechanical feature flowing from the way the control system is structured.
- The goal is still to achieve as much stability, consistency and harmony as is compatible with changing to adapt to the environment.

## 8.6 SUMMARY

This chapter introduced systems dynamics theory and clarified how it differs from systems dynamics. The most significant difference relates to the introduction of nonlinearity and positive feedback. The way in which positive feedback processes have been used to understand life in organisations was reviewed. From this it can be seen that a systems dynamics perspective presents a richer more complex insight into the dynamics of life in organisations. The next chapter carries this review further to see how systems dynamics underlies the theory of the learning organisation.

### FURTHER READING

Richardson (1991) provides an excellent account of the use of feedback thinking in human systems and Senge's (1990) book is an excellent summary of systems thinking. Turton (1991) provides discussion in more depth of much of the material in this chapter.

### REFERENCES

Forrester, J. (1958), Industrial dynamics: a major break-through for decision-making, *Harvard Business Review*, vol. 36, no. 4, pp. 37–66.

Forrester, J. (1961), *Industrial Dynamics*, Cambridge, MA: MIT Press.

Goodwin, R. M. (1951), Econometrics in business-style analysis, in Hansen, A. H. (Ed.) (1951), *Business Cycles and National Income*, New York: W. W. Norton.

Gouldner, A. (1964), *Patterns of Industrial Bureaucracy*, New York: Free Press.

Hamel, G. & Prahalad, C.K. (1989), Strategic intent, *Harvard Business Review*, May–June, pp. 63–76.

Hartley, R. F. (1991), *Management Mistakes*, New York: John Wiley.

Merton, R. K. (1957), Bureaucratic structure and personality, in *Social Theory and Social Structure*, New York: Free Press.

Perrow, C. (1984), *Normal Accidents: Living with High Risk Technologies*, New York: Basic Books.

Phillips, A. W. (1950), Mechanical models in economic dynamics, *Econometrica*, vol. 17, pp. 283–305.

Porter, M. (1990), *The Competitive Advantage of Nations*, London: Macmillan.

Richardson, G. P. (1991), *Feedback Thought in the Social Sciences and Systems Theory*, Philadelphia: University of Pennsylvania Press.

Senge, P. M. (1990), *The Fifth Discipline: The Art of Practice of the Learning Organization*, New York: Doubleday.

Simon, H. A. (1952), On the application of servomechanism theory in the study of production control, *Econometrica*, vol. 20, p. 2.

Turton, R. (1991), *Behaviour in a Business Context*, London: Chapman and Hall.

Tustin, A. (1953), *The Mechanism of Economic Systems*, Cambridge, MA: Harvard University Press.

Weick, K. (1969/1979), *The Social Psychology of Organizing*, Reading, MA: Addison-Wesley.

Weick, K. (1977), Organizational design: organizations as self-organizing systems, *Organizational Dynamics*, Autumn, pp. 31–67.

# 9 The learning organisation

## 9.1  INTRODUCTION

This chapter explores how those who provide theories of the learning organisation employ systems dynamics. Strategic choice theory held that organisations change when their managers make choices about a wide range of issues. According to the theory of the learning organisation change flows from a process of organisational learning. It is when people in an organisation learn effectively together that it changes.

The chapter first summarises the key points of learning organisation theory made by *Senge (1990)* and then explores them in later sections. The key notions focused on are to do with mental models and their connection with learning, how learning in an organisation may be blocked, and the role that leaders and groups play in this learning.

## 9.2  SENGE'S CONCEPTION OF THE LEARNING ORGANISATION

One of the most influential expositions of the concept of the learning organisation is that given by *Senge (1990)*. Senge believes that an organisation excels when it is able to tap the commitment and capacity of its members to learn. He sees this capacity as intrinsic to human nature and he locates it in the individual, although he does see such learning as occurring when individuals experience profound teamwork. He identifies five disciplines required for an organisation that can truly learn.

### Systems thinking

Senge understands organisations from the perspective of systems dynamics and holds that a learning organisation requires its people to think in systems terms. The last chapter reviewed at some length what he means by that. People should not think about their work purely in terms of their own roles. Instead, they should develop an understanding of the negative and positive feedback structure of the system they are part of. This should enable them to obtain some insight into the unexpected consequences of what they are doing. The purpose of thinking in systemic terms is to identify leverage points: that is, those points in the web of negative and positive feedback loops where change can have the largest beneficial effects. As in strategic choice theory, the purpose is to stay in control as much as is possible in a very complex system. This chapter will say no more about systems thinking because it was covered in the last chapter.

## Personal mastery

The second discipline required in a learning organisation is personal mastery. Senge does not mean by this some form of domination but, rather, a high level of proficiency such as that possessed by a master craft worker. Those who have personal mastery consistently obtain the results that they want and it requires commitment to lifelong learning. It is a process of continually deepening one's personal vision, focusing energy, developing patience and seeing reality objectively. He links it with spiritual foundations. The strongly humanistic flavour of his view of human nature is evident and takes the same line of inspirational motivation described in Chapter 6 in relation to strategic choice theory.

## Mental models

The third discipline required for the learning organisation is an understanding of the notion of mental models. These are deeply ingrained assumptions, or generalisations, often taking the form of pictures or images. Individuals are mostly not aware of their mental models. They are hidden, or unconscious, mental constructions. Senge emphasises how mental models restrict perceptions and points to Royal Dutch Shell, claiming that it developed the skill of surfacing and challenging the mental models of managers. Mental models are internal pictures of the world and he claims that individuals can learn to surface them and subject them to rigorous scrutiny. Institutional learning is a process in which management teams work together to change their shared mental models of their company and its markets.

This is, of course, pure cognitivism of exactly the same kind as that assumed in strategic choice theory. The whole topic of mental models and learning to change them will be the subject of the next section.

## Building a shared vision

The fourth discipline of the learning organisation is that of building a shared discipline. A shared vision inspires people to learn. It is a lofty goal and requires the skill of identifying inspiring pictures of the future. It is important that this vision should not be dictated but developed by people working together. Again, the humanistic foundations of this idea are evident.

## Team learning

The final discipline of the learning organisation is that of team learning. Senge maintains that teams can learn and when they do the intelligence of the team exceeds that of the individual members and produces extraordinary results. When this happens the individuals learn more rapidly too. The basis of team learning is dialogue. This is a free flow of meaning through a group that enables the group to make discoveries that individuals on their own could not do. Team learning also requires skill in identifying factors that block true dialogue. These blockages must be recognised and surfaced. He claims that it is teams rather than individuals that learn.

The points about blockages to learning and about the role of groups in that learning will be taken up in later sections of this chapter. It is important to signal here, though, how Senge handles this question of the individual and the team. It sounds as though he is making the group primary to the individual. However, this is not so. Although he says that it is the team that learns, when he develops what he means by team learning it is clear that he is saying that an effective team provides the context within which a number of individuals together learn more than they could on their own. It is still the individuals who learn. They arrive to form a team and the atmosphere of that team then affects their capacity for learning together. He is not according formative capacity to the group in the manner I will discuss in Chapter 15 in that he does not see individual minds actually being formed by the group while they form it.

The key points that Senge makes will now be explored more fully in the sections that follow, starting with mental models and the notion of single- and double-loop learning.

## 9.3   MENTAL MODELS: SINGLE- AND DOUBLE-LOOP LEARNING

One of the foundations upon which the notion of single- and double-loop learning is built is research on human cognitive ability. According to this research, humans are capable of retaining only up to 7 bits of information in the short-term memory at any one time. A bit is a digit, or a letter of the alphabet, or some chunk of them such as a word. The new information-processing capacity of the human brain is thus limited. The capacity of the long-term memory is apparently infinite, but it takes seconds to store new information in that long-term memory. Human ability to absorb and process new information is therefore painfully slow, much slower than computers. However, their ability to recognise patterns in information and to extract new meaning from them is considerably greater than that of computers. Note how it is assumed that brains store information in much the same way as computers – the cognitivist position.

Humans are therefore compelled by their limited brain capacity for processing new information to simplify everything they observe; they are unable to know reality itself; all they can do is construct simplifications, that is mental models of reality. What they discover and therefore what they choose and how they act, all depend upon the mental model they bring to the task. When they look at a particular situation, they see it through the lens provided by the mental models built up through past experience and education. Humans approach each situation every day with a mindset, a recipe they have acquired from the past, that they use to understand the present in order to design actions to cope with it. When they take actions that fail to have the desired result, the reason often lies in the way the problem is perceived in the first place. The remedy is to amend the mental model, the perspective, the mindset, the paradigm with which the task is being approached.

The methods used to store mental models and to use what has been stored for subsequent discovery and choice have important implications. Research on cognitive ability claims that people do not normally store what they have previously observed and processed in any detailed form. They only store items and recall them in exact detail in exceptional circumstances, for example when they learn the lines of a play or prepare for certain kinds of examination. Normally people store and recall only some important category features of the items observed. It is as if people label items according to the category they belong to, according to the strength of association they have with other similar items. People are said to store schemas, frames or scenes, particularly noting exceptions. Mental models are sketchy, incomplete constructs used in a feedback way to affect what is discovered next (*Baddeley, 1990*). When confronted by some situation people do not observe its complete detail. They select certain items and fill in others using previously stored frames or scenes. Experiments have shown that people can be quite convinced that they have witnessed an event, even though it has not occurred, simply because that event normally occurred in a particular situation the experimenter now presents (*Baddeley, 1990*).

These points about how people build partial, loose, flexible mental models based on similarities and irregularities in the patterns of events observed, and then use them later partially to reconstruct what they then observe, are of great importance to an understanding of management. These points mean that managers will not simply observe a given environment and a given organisational capability – the facts. They, like all other humans, will sometimes inevitably invent what they observe. The whole process of simplifying and selecting means that the environment is in a real sense the invention and the creation of the managers observing it. It will then only be possible for managers to make sense of what they are doing after they have done it (*Weick, 1969/79*). In highly complex and uncertain situations, then, explanations of strategic management need to take account of the possibility that environments may be invented or created in managers' minds and that they can often only make sense of what they are doing with hindsight.

## Mental models

So far, a number of ways in which humans compensate for their limited brain-processing capacity have been referred to. They simplify complex reality by constructing mental models of that reality in which data are classified in loose categories. They store those models and use them later to understand the next situation and indeed to fill in some of the detail of the next situation. They do not always use algorithmic step-by-step reasoning, but sometimes make intuitive jumps. In this way they can handle far greater levels of complexity and uncertainty, as well as far faster rates of change, than a straightforward use of processing capacity would allow.

But the consequence of this way of operating is that people may invent the reality around them.

In addition to all this there are two further means of great importance that are said to be used to compensate for the limited capacity of the brain to process new information in a complex world. First, mental models are automated, so speeding up the process of recall and application to a new situation. Second, those automated models are shared with others to cut down on the need to communicate before acting together.

## Experts and unconscious mental models

A person would function very slowly if for every action that person had consciously to retrieve and examine large numbers of previously acquired mental models and then choose an appropriate one. Experts therefore push previously acquired models below the level of awareness into the unconscious mind. One aspect of learning is through repetition of an action in order to make the design of later similar actions an automatic process. The expert seems to use some form of recognisable pattern in a new situation automatically to trigger the use of past models developed in relation to analogous previous situations. Experts do not examine the whole body of their expertise when they confront a new situation. Instead they detect recognisable similarity in the qualitative patterns of what they observe and automatically produce models which they modify to meet the new circumstances.

For example, an expert chess player differs from a novice in terms of the richness of his or her mental store of patterns and relationships between the pieces on a chess board. On being confronted with some new juxtaposition of pieces, the expert perceives patterns missed by the novice. It is from these perceptions that the expert derives superiority. This conclusion is supported by the fact that the expert is no better than the novice in deciding what to do when the pieces have been set out randomly. It is not therefore that the expert has a better short-term memory or can process information faster. The expert's superiority arises because models of the moves appropriate to different patterns are stored in the expert's memory and drawn on as required through some form of analogous reasoning.

Analogy has been found to pervade thought. People use analogies to make the novel seem familiar by relating it to prior knowledge. They use analogies to make the familiar seem strange by viewing it from a new perspective. These are fundamental aspects of human intelligence used to construct new scientific theories, design experiments, and solve new problems in terms of old ones (*Gick & Holyoak, 1983*).

One form of learning, then, is that which uses some form of repetition to push mental models into the unconscious where they can be recalled and used very rapidly. The richer the store of unconscious models the more expert the person. This is single-loop learning. Each time people act they learn from the consequences of the action to improve the next action, without having consciously to retrieve and examine the unconscious models being used to design the action.

But expert behaviour based on single-loop learning and unconscious mental models brings not only benefits; it carries with it significant dangers. The fact that the mental models being used to design actions are unconscious means that they are not being questioned. The more expert one is, the more rapidly one acts on the basis of unconscious models. This means that one more easily takes for granted the assumptions and simplifications upon which the mental models are inevitably built. This is highly efficient in stable circumstances but when those circumstances change rapidly it becomes highly dangerous – in other words, it is an appropriate way to learn in conditions close to certainty and agreement, but more and more dangerous the further one moves away from certainty and agreement. Mental models used without question can rapidly become inappropriate in rapidly changing conditions. The possibility of skilled incompetence (*Argyris, 1990*) then arises. The more expert people are, that is, the more skilled they are in designing certain actions, the greater the risk that they will not question what they are doing. It follows that they are more likely to become skilled incompetents. This gives rise to the need for double-loop learning. Here people learn not only in the sense of adjusting actions in the light of their consequences, but in the sense also of questioning and adjusting the unconscious mental models being used to design those actions in the first place.

To summarise, mental models are the simplifications that humans construct and store in their brains of the world they encounter. These models are the lenses through which they perceive the world they have to operate in, the constructions they make to explain how it and they are behaving, the structures they use to design their actions. These models are based on loose flexible categories of information, where categories appear to be defined in terms of similarity and irregularity. In totally new situations, people use processes of analogous reasoning to construct new mental models using those already stored. Coping with the world can be seen as a continuing feedback from one set of models to another.

People automate mental models by pushing them into the unconscious – this is the process of becoming an expert. Some models, the expert ones, are therefore implicit and hardly ever questioned while others are explicit and are more likely to be questioned. The latter are the explanations of what people are doing that they articulate. People share the expert unconscious models when they work together in a group. Automation and sharing lead to the strong possibility of expert incompetence and groupthink when conditions are changing rapidly. In the literature a number of words are used to mean much the same thing as mental models – paradigms, mindsets, frames of reference, company and industry recipes, schemas, scripts. Note that the culture of a group is its shared mental model according to this perspective.

## Teams and shared models

Managers do not choose and act as isolated individuals. They interact with each other, choosing and acting in teams or groups. Simply by being part of a group, individuals learn to share the mental models they use to discover, choose and act. In this way they cut down on the communication and information flows that are required before they can act together. In particular, the more they share those implicit, expert models that have been pushed into the unconscious, the less they need to communicate in order to secure cohesive action. This sharing of implicit models is what is meant by the culture of the group or the organisation. Groups and organisations develop cultures, company and industry recipes or retained memories, as they perform together, in order to speed up their actions.

Individuals who are part of any group are put under strong pressure by group processes to conform, that is to share the mental models of the other members. While this may have great benefits in terms of efficient action in stable conditions, it becomes a serious liability when conditions are changing rapidly. It then becomes necessary to question the implicit, unconscious group models that are being used to design actions. As conditions change the unquestioned models may well become inappropriate. The powerful pressures that grow up within groups of experts to accept rather than question very fundamental values opens up the strong possibility of skilled incompetence in group behaviour, of groupthink.

## Espoused models and models in use

People overcome limited brain working capacity to produce unlimited mental capacity by simplifying and selecting, building models, automating those models by pushing them below the level of awareness, and learning to share them with others in their group. They use qualitative similarities and dissimilarities between one situation and another to develop more appropriate models in new situations. Managers design their expert actions in this way, just as physicians and physicists do. The more expert an individual or a group the more actions are designed in ways determined by unconscious, implicit models. Because the assumptions underlying those models are not surfaced and questioned it is quite possible that experts will articulate one model while designing their actions according to another. There may well be a difference between espoused models and models in use (*Argyris and Schon, 1978*). Experts are quite likely to say one thing and do another. The more expert people become in working together as a group the more prone they are to do this too. Ask managers what they do and most will say that they organise and plan. Observe what managers actually do and they dash from one task to another in a manner which is not all that planned or organised.

When it is recognised that there are frequent differences between what expert managers say they are doing and what they are actually doing, differences which they themselves are not usually aware of, it can be seen how easy it is for managers to play games and build organisational defences against facing up to what is really happening (*Argyris, 1990*). For example, most managers espouse a rational model of action and believe that they should uncover the facts and consider a sensible range of options before they take action. Most espouse free and open discussions because that is a rational position to take. But at the same time there is a widespread norm in organisations requiring subordinates to withhold the truth from their superiors, especially if they believe that the superior will find the truth unwelcome and accuse them of being negative. Games of deception and cover-up are therefore played. All know they are being played but none openly discuss what is happening, despite espousal of rational behaviour. Managers sometimes say one thing, do the direct opposite, and rarely find this strange. Add to this the existence of skilled incompetence and you can see how very difficult it will be to change these games and break down these defences. Attempts to explain how strategic management is actually carried out and attempts to prescribe how to do it better will be misleading and perhaps dangerous unless they explicitly recognise the existence of skilled incompetence, the difference between espoused models and models in use, and the behavioural dynamics these lead to. These are matters that I will deal with in more detail later in this chapter. I turn now, however, to how a further examination of mental models are used and changed; that is, the process of learning and the single- and double-loop forms that it takes.

## Single- and double-loop learning

The single-loop form of learning can be illustrated by the activity of reviewing a budget and taking corrective action. There is a monitoring, or discovery, step in which an actual profit outcome is compared with the desired outcome set in the budget. If actual is below budget, the reason is discovered, a choice of corrective action is made, and action is taken. That action affects profit in the next period as do external changes, leading to the need for the next round of discovery, choice and action. Managers involved in this single loop are controlling and they are also learning. They are discovering the consequences of their actions and amending their behaviour according to what they discover. This kind of learning is single loop because managers are not questioning what they are doing in any fundamental sense. The budget, for example, is not questioned. Taking another example, General Motors thought that high fuel costs and therefore smaller cars were the key issues and Japanese competence in offering small cars the key reason for their success in the 1970s. General Motors' managers focused on this explanation, never questioning their assumptions, and so missed the importance of quality as the source of competitive advantage. This kind of single-loop learning is depicted in *Figure 9.1*.

Now consider what these managers would do if they were to learn in a double-loop way. When they analyse why profit is coming in below budget, they do so using their expertise, that is the implicit unconscious mental models they have built up through

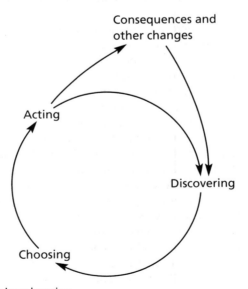

**FIGURE 9.1**    Single-loop learning

past experience and have come to share through working together. They have a recipe on how their organisation and its industry or environment work. The reasons they produce to account for poor profit performance will be determined by these unconscious shared mental models. Consequently their choice and their action will also depend on these mental models. In the single-loop case they do not surface what the model is or question it; they simply use it. In double-loop learning they would, as part of the discovery stage, surface and question that model. They would be discovering not only what is changing outside and what the consequences of their actions are, but also what this all means for the unconscious models they are using, for their recipes and received wisdom. This simultaneous journey around two loops is depicted in *Figure 9.2*.

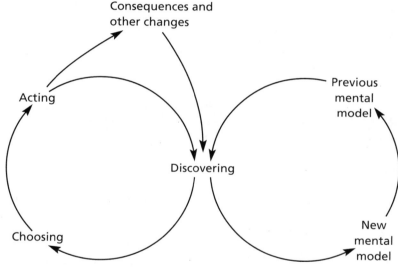

**FIGURE 9.2**    Double-loop learning

Double-loop learning, then, involves changing a mental model, a recipe, a mindset, a frame of reference or a paradigm. It is a very difficult process to perform simply because one is trying to examine assumptions one is not normally even aware one is making. People will therefore keep slipping into single-loop learning because that is easier. But it is important to encourage double-loop learning since it is this that produces innovation. Managers who would innovate need constantly to be shifting, breaking and creating paradigms – they must engage in double-loop learning.

To summarise, single-loop learning is when one learns from the consequences of previous actions to amend the next action. It is a feedback process from action to consequence to subsequent action, without questioning the mental model driving the action.

Double-loop learning involves another feedback loop. It occurs when the consequences of actions lead to a questioning of the mental model, the underlying assumptions, that have been driving the actions. That questioning may lead to the amendment of the mental model, the reframing of the problem or opportunity, before action is amended. There is a double loop in which not only are actions amended, but the model driving the actions is too. Double-loop learning requires destruction – old ways of viewing the world have to be destroyed. Double-loop learning also involves creation – new ways of viewing the world have to be developed. Double-loop learning is the shifting, breaking and creating of paradigms.

- Single-loop forms of organisational learning take the form of negative feedback loops in which groups of people review and learn from the actions they have just undertaken.
- Single-loop forms of learning are conducted within a given paradigm and sustain the group learning in a state of stability, moving towards the realisation of a vision or the achievement of a goal.
- Double-loop learning is partly the negative feedback learning about the consequences of actions, but also partly an amplifying, positive feedback loop of questioning the underlying assumptions.
- Double-loop learning is therefore potentially destabilising and revolutionary, but it is vitally necessary for innovation.

## 9.4   COVERT POLITICAL PROCESSES AND THEIR IMPACT ON ORGANISATIONAL LEARNING

Double-loop learning begins when people question their own unique mental models and when together they start questioning the mental models they share with each other. As soon as they do this they arouse fears to do with failing to produce anything that functions in place of what they are destroying, as well as the fear of embarrassing themselves and others with questioning and discussion that may appear incompetent, or threatening, or even crazy. As soon as such fears are aroused people automatically defend themselves by activating defence routines of one kind or another. The raising of such defensive routines in an organisational setting is what I mean by covert politics. It is a form of game playing that all are aware is going on but all agree, tacitly, not to discuss (*Argyris, 1990*).

### Organisational defence routines

One of the main reasons for the failure of groups of people to engage in double-loop learning is that the questioning of deeply held individual and shared assumptions about the world they are operating in may well provoke and reinforce powerful organisational defence routines that are very difficult to identify and even more difficult to deal with effectively (*Argyris, 1990*). The activation of such defence routines is a specific example of a general point: namely, that complex systems tend to counteract planned changes to the system because they also unintentionally provoke positive feedback loops called organisational defence routines.

For example, top managers may try to abandon a command and control model of managing in the belief that this will make their organisation more flexible and entrepreneurial. This may be an example of double-loop learning if they are genuinely trying to question the assumptions underlying their currently shared mental model of management – the command and control one. Consider first what is meant by a command and control model of managing. It is one in which:

- the manager's power is derived from position in the hierarchy;
- people are motivated by the task; and
- people respond most to short-term rewards in relation to task achievement.

These beliefs about the source of power and the way to motivate people are closely associated with the suppression of negative feelings and judgements about people's performance. Such judgements are usually not publicly exposed and tested in case they upset and demotivate others, so reducing levels of task performance. Instead evaluations are made privately and covered up in public – covert politics. All understand that this is what is happening but they accept it as a necessary defence against hurting people's feelings and against the consequent organisational inefficiency.

When a manager is fired, this is frequently presented as a resignation due to health reasons or some other factor. Memoranda are distributed thanking the fired person for years of valued contributions. All know that this is a tissue of lies but none publicly says so. This is an example of a defence routine, a game people play to protect each other from having to face unpleasant organisational truths in public. As a result, the real reason for firing the person, a judgement that the person is incompetent, is never properly examined; it could well have been unjustified and turn out to be harmful to the performance of the organisation.

These kinds of beliefs about control lead to win/lose dynamics in which people adopt tactics of persuasion and selling, only superficially listening to others. People driven by win/lose behaviour also tend to use face-saving devices for themselves and each other. They save face by avoiding the public testing of the assumptions they are making about each other's motives or statements. This behaviour produces skilled incompetence: skilled in that the behaviour is automatic; incompetent in that it produces obstacles to work, real learning, effective decision making. These obstacles take the form of organisational defence routines that become embedded in behaviour and are extremely difficult to change.

Defence routines become so entrenched in organisations that they come to be viewed as inevitable parts of human nature. Managers make self-fulfilling prophecies about what will happen at meetings, because they claim it is human nature; they indulge in the game playing, so confirming their belief in human nature. The defence routines, game playing and cover-ups can become so disruptive that managers actually avoid discussing contentious issues altogether. Even if this extreme is not reached, the dysfunctional learning behaviour blocks the detection of gradually accumulating small changes, the surfacing of different perspectives, the thorough testing of proposals through dialogue. When they use the control management model with the organisational defence routines it provokes, managers struggle to deal with strategic issues. They end up preparing long lists of strengths and weaknesses, opportunities and threats that simply get them nowhere. They produce mission statements that are so bland as to be meaningless, visions not connected to reality, and long-term plans that are simply filed. Or they may decide on an action and then not implement it.

Managers collude in this behaviour and refrain from discussing it. They then distance themselves from what is going on and blame others, the chief executive or the organisational structure when things go wrong. They look for solutions in general models, techniques, visions and plans. All the while the real causes of poor strategic management – the learning process itself, the political interaction and the group dynamic – remain stubbornly undiscussable.

People within an organisation collude in keeping matters undiscussable because they fear the consequences if they do not. Consultants too find themselves sucked into defence routines because they are nervous of the consequences of exposing them – they may be fired. The result of the defence routines I have been talking about is passive employees and managers, highly dependent upon authority, who are not well equipped to handle rapid change. In these conditions, managers produce vague, impractical prescriptions as a defence against having to do anything in difficult situations, such as 'we need more training' or 'we need a vision'. The organisation loses out on the creativity of people because of the management model it uses.

The way out of this impasse, proposed by Argyris, is for managers and managed to reflect jointly, as a group, on the processes they are engaged in. If this can be perceived as a challenge rather than a potential source of embarrassment and fear, then managers are able to engage in double-loop learning. For example, joint reflection might lead them to consider the extent to which:

- power flows from expertise and contribution, not simply position in the hierarchy;
- people are motivated primarily by their own internal commitment; and
- people respond to long-term rewards.

These beliefs about power and motivation are said to encourage the public exposure and testing of relevant feelings and judgements, even if they are negative, in order to ensure that decisions are being taken on valid data. Behaviour according to such a 'commitments' model should lead to cooperative dynamics and mutual control, allowing people to put their own creativity to use for the organisation.

The problem is that the attempt to move to such a 'commitment' model is itself likely to provoke the damping feedback loops of organisational defences. When people behave according to the control model, they set off damping loops of organisational defence which have the effect of blocking the double-loop learning process, so trapping an organisation in a state of stable equilibrium – that is, within the same mental model.

One of the main fears touching off such damping loops is the fear managers have of losing control. This can quite easily completely immobilise learning, decision making and action, as *Boxes 9.1* and *9.2* show.

## The fear of losing control

If people are to engage in double-loop learning then they must expose relevant negative feelings, the basis of the judgements they make on the performance of others, the cover-ups and games they are playing.

Such learning is therefore bound to upset people and to arouse management fears of losing control. Such fears will reduce commitment to double-loop learning, and

**BOX 9.1**

## The *Challenger* disaster

In 1986 a Presidential Commission inquired into the disaster that had occurred when the *Challenger* shuttle had exploded soon after launching. It concluded that NASA had sound structures, policies and rules to secure safety. What had gone wrong was that those most intimately involved with the launch had focused so heavily on the launch itself that they neglected safety matters. The conclusion was that there was nothing wrong with the organisation: the disaster was due to human failures. These were to be addressed in the future by making it compulsory for all launch constraints, and waivers of launch constraints, to be considered by all levels of management. In other words there was to be more referral up the management hierarchy.

*Argyris (1990)* analyses this episode to show how the disaster was actually due to organisational defence routines, which both NASA and the Presidential Commission were unwittingly covering up. The recommendation of more referral to higher management levels would do nothing to remove those organisational defence routines. It would therefore most probably be ineffective in preventing another accident.

Using the testimony presented to the Commission, Argyris shows the following. Before the launch, engineers had indicated that the launch should be delayed because of problems with rings, problems that ultimately caused the disaster. At a meeting with the engineers, one manager understood them to be advising a delay, but his superior concluded that they were simply raising some questions. The two managers did not explore their different understandings with each other; they did not test them publicly. The superior manager decided, without discussing it with anyone, not to report on the meeting with the engineers to higher levels of management. The engineers sounded a number of warnings and then stopped when they realised that no one would listen. Engineers never questioned management as to why they would not listen; that would have been regarded as an affront to management capability.

At each level, the engineers and managers were covering themselves. The engineers raised the problem, but the next level did not heed them. Engineers were defending themselves by drawing attention to a problem and then giving up when it became clear that the next level would not listen. Engineers would not themselves take the matter further up the hierarchy because they knew that this would antagonise their immediate superiors. So they adopted the routine of raising the matter, knowing it would be ignored, and then dropping it, all in order to defend themselves – if anything went wrong, they would not be to blame. The first manager heard the message but bowed to his superior. He was covered because he was doing what the superior wanted. The superior was covered because he interpreted the points made by the engineers as simply raising    ▶

questions and no one contradicted him. He probably made this interpretation because he knew that those above him did not want bad news that they would have to convey to the President. In the end the disaster was due to all of these organisational defence routines and cover-ups. All knew that what was being covered up was important. They do not need rules to tell them this. Introducing rules is therefore unlikely to prevent this kind of thing from happening again. No rule can stop some manager from interpreting a warning as a question. If it is a warning it has to be conveyed up the hierarchy. If it is a question it does not. The only way around this is to require everything to be conveyed up the hierarchy and that is impossible. The real solution is to uncover the defences and discuss them, despite the anxiety and difficulty this involves. *Argyris (1990, p. 43) concludes:*

Organizational defense routines make it highly likely that individuals, groups, intergroups, and organizations will not detect and correct the errors that are embarrassing and threatening because the fundamental rules are to (1) bypass the errors and act as if that were not being done, (2) make the bypass undiscussable, and (3) make its undiscussability undiscussable.

These conditions, in turn, make it difficult to engage the organizational defense routine in order to interrupt them and reduce them. Indeed, the very attempt to engage them will lead to the defensive routines being activated and strengthened. This, in turn, reinforces and proliferates the defensive routines. ■

BOX 9.2

## The culture-change programme

In early 1988, the senior managers at Apex Engineering were driven by increased international competition to find significant and permanent cost reductions. The management team examined the problem and decided to reorganise from a functional structure to one of profit-responsible business units. They employed consultants to identify international cost standards and set benchmarks relating to the level of inventories, product completion times, sales per employee, added value per square metre of space occupied, and people employed per project. They also employed consultants to develop a strategy to achieve the cost standards by 1994.

In early 1989, the management team, in conjunction with the consultants, set out its mission. That mission was to become the prime world-class manufacturer of its main product and the strategy to achieve this consisted of installing just-in-time inventory control systems and cellular manufacturing; that is, small multidisciplinary teams responsible for clearly specified parts of the total product.

In addition, a leaner, flatter organisation was to be created by removing a rung of middle management.

The senior managers recognised that the strategy represented a major change in the way people worked and therefore set up a culture-change programme. A change champion was appointed and management groups set up to deal with initiatives, problems and issues. The intention was to promote collective problem solving and decision making. But the role of the change champion was specified as that of ensuring that key people did in fact attend the groups. No one seemed to think it odd that managers were to be compelled to cooperate. Right at the beginning a control model was to be used to install a commitment model.

The result was a network of people who were committed to the change but they tended to be located in the former department of the change champion – the personnel and purchasing functions. Little real support existed in the manufacturing function because so many managers stood to lose power from a switch to cellular manufacturing.

Senior managers in discussion with each other stated that, without careful communication and selling to the workforce as a whole, the strategy would be viewed with scepticism, mistrust and outright rejection. So the managing director gave propaganda talks to people, a three-dimensional model of the new site configuration was built for all to see and questions were invited. This whole exercise might be viewed as a defence routine: senior managers are making presentations calling for group problem solving, but they are presenting a solution that has not been arrived at in this way. Those listening to the presentation know this but do not point it out.

The next step was to negotiate changes in work practice with the trade unions. When the unions asked what the mission and cost standards set for 1994 meant for work practices, the senior managers said that they could not readily be translated into specific work practices. They also said that the vision did not allow specific savings to be identified and so they could not identify any rewards for introducing new work practices. Managers are promoting a commitment model, but they are not being open with the unions. Or they are telling the truth and their missions and plans are so general and vague as to be meaningless.

In view of this the unions would not support the change programme and a small pilot programme was mounted instead. This was supposed to emphasise management commitment (but in fact the managing director showed little interest in it) and to test the cellular method of manufacturing. The pilot team was set up and received awareness training, diagnostic skills training and teamwork skills training. The pilot project was said by many to be a success, but no hard evidence to support this was produced and it did not run for its full time period – it was halted by a strike. Nine months later the unions agreed to cellular manufacturing but by this time, late 1990, the economy was in recession and the whole project was petering out. ∎

consistent with the control model they are still using, even though they are trying to get away from it, people will also tend to conceal the diminishing commitment. The effect is to reduce the effectiveness of any attempt to engage in double-loop learning and the possibility of switching to some other model of control. The harder they try, the more it provokes the fears that impede it.

The result is a positive feedback loop running from the control mental model to anomalies and contradictions that weaken the control model and build up an alternative model. But movement around this loop itself touches off movement around another loop. This is a negative, damping loop that undermines the complex learning process and therefore strengthens the control model. This is depicted in *Figure 9.3*.

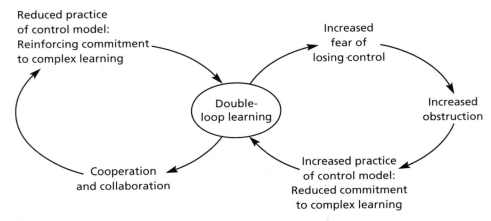

**FIGURE 9.3**   Fear of losing control

The problems I have been talking about in this section are primarily due to the fact that all of us try to hang onto our existing model of how to learn as we learn: we all try to kill our own learning for one reason or another. How can we overcome this? Well, one popular prescription for promoting the learning organisation is that of empowering people throughout the organisation, where empowerment is equated with democracy, dispersed power and widespread participation. However, simply dispersing power, inviting widespread participation, is no guarantee whatsoever that the organisation will function more effectively or make better decisions. First, widespread participation means that, although more people are being invited to take part in decision making, they are all still using the control model. There are simply more people behaving incompetently. There is no guarantee that lower managers or employees behave better than top executives. While the larger numbers involved in decision making continue to use the control model they simply spread the win/lose dynamics more widely. The negative damping loops of organisational defences will be reinforced. Widespread participation is no guarantee of more effective learning or better decision making at all. People first have to learn how to operate on the basis of continuing complex learning and that is very difficult to achieve. Simply inviting people to do so will not have the required result. Widespread participation is no guarantee of better learning.

- The behaviour of people in organisations is dominated by what Argyris has called the control model of management. This is usually operated within a pluralistic political system, in which a number of groupings have countervailing power.
- Use of the control model, the existence of different power groups, leads to win/lose behavioural dynamics. Here people employ a number of organisational defence mechanisms to protect themselves and others from the consequences of the win/lose pressures. They play games and make matters undiscussable. Consequently, decisions are often not made on valid data, implementation of decisions is often obstructed, small changes go undetected for lengthy periods. In short the ability of the organisation to develop strategically is severely impaired.
- But movement from the control model/pluralistic political system is fraught with difficulty. The most widespread idea of what to move to is a commitment model of control operating within a collegiate political system. This is the OD programme (and also the prescriptions of writers such as Peters, discussed in Chapter 6). Movement away from the control model, and particularly movement to the collegial model, touches off many positive amplifying feedback loops which undermine that movement.
- These positive feedback loops are activated because any attempt to change an organisation in a fundamental way upsets the balance and nature of power and raises the levels of uncertainty and ambiguity. All of these changes increase anxieties of one kind or another. And it is the anxiety that provokes positive feedback loops.

**FIGURE 9.4**   Defence routines and covert politics: main points on organisational dynamics

Emotion plays a major role in this double-loop learning process. As soon as people embark upon double-loop learning they must confront their own fear of failing. This triggers avoidance of the fear, and hence the learning, altogether by engaging in organisational defence routines – summarised in *Figure 9.4*. If people can hold the fear, see it as a challenge, then they can proceed with the double-loop learning.

## 9.5   THE IMPACT OF VESTED INTERESTS ON ORGANISATIONAL LEARNING

The previous section looked at how attempts to learn in a double-loop way can give rise to a number of fears, such as the fear of failing, of being embarrassed and of embarrassing others. These fears tend to trigger defensive routines, game playing and covert politics that block the learning. The whole point of double-loop learning is to bring about organisational change and it is highly likely that change of an important kind will alter power relations between people. Change threatens vested interests and the prospect of losing power is likely to trigger action to prevent this from happening. That action is also likely to block the process of double-loop learning. In other words, the nature of an organisation's political system, the way in which power is used, is likely to have an important impact on its capacity to learn.

### Authoritarian use of power

The authoritarian use of power may be relatively benign when it is based on legitimate positions in the hierarchy and exercised according to the accepted procedures of the organisation. This is likely to be accompanied by a group dynamic of compliance, especially when followers strongly share the same ideology. Compliance amounts to the suspension of intellectual and moral judgement about the appropriateness of superiors' choices and actions. People then willingly do what the powerful want (*Bacharach & Lawler, 1980*). Clearly this is incompatible with double-loop learning. Where power is exercised as force over unwilling followers the dynamics tends to be much more volatile. It is characterised by sullen acceptance, covert resistance and at time outright rebellion. Again, this is inimical to double-loop learning.

### Collegiate use of power

Highly authoritarian political systems based on mechanistic rules are, however, rather rare in practice. There is far more likely to be a complex pluralistic political system in which power is already spread around an organisation in groups with vested interests (*Greiner & Schein, 1988*). Thus, the typical modern corporation does not have a political system in which one or two powerful executives at the top control what goes on throughout the company. Instead there are powerful subsidiary companies and powerful departments in many different parts of the organisation and those at the top have to sustain enough support to govern. Any change of any significance is going to affect the balance of power, making one department, subsidiary company or management grouping weaker or stronger than it was before. Any sign of change will touch off fears that such power shifts might occur even before it is clear what they might be. People and groups will therefore start taking protective action as soon as they get wind of any possible change.

Any attempt to engage in double-loop learning, to change mental models, is likely to be just such a change, one that is directly concerned with changing power positions. It is therefore highly likely to touch off damping feedback loops of a political nature that will undermine and perhaps eventually destroy it. The more people are persuaded to move to a consensus collegiate way of making choices, the more powerful groups with vested interests are threatened and the more likely they are to put a stop to the programme. The more managers try to head off this threat, the more they have to play by the rules of the political system they are trying to replace. If they do this they simply reinforce what they are trying to remove. This is shown in *Figure 9.5*.

Once again, initiatives will fail if they do not recognise and deal with the damping feedback loops that are always present in organisations. And how to deal with these loops is far from clear.

### Power vacuums and organised anarchies

If managers do succeed in installing a collegiate political system and the commitment management model, yet other damping feedback loops may be activated by the shift in the distribution of power.

As authority and other forms of power are dispersed, as organisational structures are flattened, as job descriptions become looser, and as the establishment of widespread

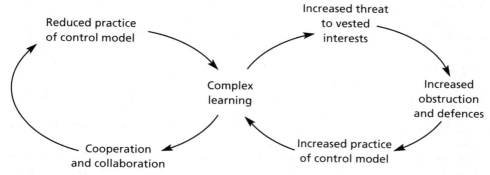

**FIGURE 9.5**    Threats to vested interests

consensus comes to be required before decisions are possible, so the likelihood of a power vacuum at the centre increases. It becomes more and more difficult for anyone to exercise much authority; more and more people have to be able to handle their own independence. In situations in which most people seek the comfort of dependency this could create serious difficulties. One way of understanding the consequences of changes in power distribution is provided by *Greiner & Schein (1988)*.

Greiner and Schein use the device given in *Figure 9.6* to relate changes in willingness to assert and to accept power to the consequent group dynamic. When both leaders and followers consent freely to the exercise of power, there is a high probability of active consensus. When the leader exerts power but the followers do

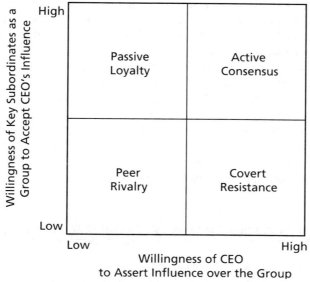

**FIGURE 9.6**    Power and group dynamics
*Source:* L. E. Greiner & V. E. Schein (1988), *Power and Organization Development: Mobilizing Power to Implement Change*, Reading, MA: Addison-Wesley

not consent, then we get the behaviour of covert resistance. You will see from *Figure 9.6* that as the leader becomes less able or willing to exert power, while followers still look for a lead, then the behaviour is that of passive loyalty. If, in the same circumstances, the followers too become less willing to accept the exercise of power, the group's behaviour is characterised by peer rivalry.

So the dispersal of power and the spread of participation could set off feedback loops in which declining central power leads to greater rivalry throughout the organisation, or to passive loyalty, both of which will block double-loop learning. Indeed events could be much more complex than this if at the same time levels of uncertainty and ambiguity are raised by loosely defining people's jobs.

Others have studied the decision-making processes in organisations such as universities, hospitals, as well as other public sector and professional bodies, that are characterised by the collegiate-type political system. They have described these organisations as organised anarchies and their decision-making processes as 'garbage-can' decision making (*Cohen, March & Ohlsen, 1972*).

The point to be made here is this. When decision-making procedures are highly unstructured, as they tend to be when power is dispersed and widespread participation invited, then the particular decision taken on a particular occasion will depend almost entirely on the detailed context at the time. Here context means details such as: who attended the meeting at which the decision was taken; how important those attending were; what other matters they had on their minds. In this sense the particular decision made comes to depend upon chance. And in these circumstances there is a high level of probability that decisions will be postponed and, even if made, not implemented.

The main points are summarised in *Figure 9.7*.

---

- Positive feedback loops are activated by any attempt to change an organisation in a fundamental way. This is because change upsets the balance and nature of power and raises the levels of uncertainty and ambiguity. Consequent anxiety provokes offsetting negative feedback loops.
- One feedback loop has to do with the fears of existing power groups that they will lose control. As change programmes are pushed, so these fears are increased, leading usually to covert undermining of the programme. Organisational defence routines are then strengthened rather than weakened.
- Dispersing power and weakening central authority can set off loops leading to peer rivalry or passive loyalty. Both determine creativity and decision-making ability.

---

**FIGURE 9.7**   Vested interests: main points on organisational dynamics

## 9.6   THE ROLE OF GROUPS IN THE LEARNING ORGANISATION

The kind of group that learning organisation theory focuses on is the team and the key question is what kind of team performs double-loop learning effectively.

*Argyris (1957)* stressed the conflict between the individual and the group. He maintained that there is a conflict between the needs of healthy individuals and the demands of formal organisation. Chains of command and task specialisation require people to be passive and dependent, but psychologically mature individuals seek to be unique and different. The conflict leads to frustration, hostility and rivalry and a focus on a part of the organisation rather than the whole, as well as a focus on short-term objectives. To adapt, individuals develop defence routines that then feed back into the organisation and reinforce the adverse effects. Argyris' learning theory, summarised in the last two sections, is built on this view that a group is made up of individuals and that there is a fundamental conflict between being an individual and being in a group.

From this perspective, the key concern is that of understanding how a group can evolve into a functioning team in which individuals can learn. The basic premise is that this will happen when people can engage in true dialogue rather than in the kind of defensive conversational cover-ups discussed in the previous section. This requires that members of a group trust each other enough to expose their shared assumptions to public scrutiny. It is held that this is possible only when the team is cohesive, that is when there is good team spirit. Today, organisations spend considerable sums of money to provide social and training events where teams can be together in the belief that this fosters the required team spirit. In addition, attention is paid to the composition of the team in terms of different personality types. It is believed that a balance of different personality types will enable a team to function and learn effectively. This section looks at what has been written about phases in group development and about the effect of different compositions of membership in terms of personality type.

## Patterns in small-group development

*Gibbard, Hartman & Mann (1974)* distinguish between three models of group development: linear progressive, life-cycle and pendular models. They describe each of these types of models in the following terms.

### Linear progressive model
In this kind of model the explanations of group behaviour run in terms of progressive stages that the members of a group pass through and the resolutions they achieve in each stage before they can work effectively together. One of the best known descriptions of group development (*Tuckman, 1965*) identifies the four sequential steps that all groups are claimed to follow during the course of their development:

1  *Forming.* When people first come together to form a group, they go through a hesitant testing stage in which they begin to identify their task, form relationships and develop roles. It is a stage in which people are typically dependent and look for guidance.
2  *Storming.* Having acquired some sense of security, the members of a group then conflict over what it is they should be doing, how they should do it, and what roles each should occupy. This is a stage of emotional expression.
3  *Norming.* The next stage is that of working through the conflict and developing shared values or norms to govern how they are to operate together. The outcome is conformity and cohesion.
4  *Performing.* This is the stage in which the group produces what it has gathered together to produce; it performs its primary task.

You will recall from Chapter 6 that Lewin described the stages of change in an organisation and a group in terms of a period of 'unfreezing' (similar to forming and storming), followed by a period of 'reformulation' (similar to norming), followed in turn by 'refreezing' (similar to performing). Another model identifies two phases in group development, each of which consists of a number of subphases (*Bennis & Shepard, 1956*):

1   *The authority phase.* When people first come together to form a group they are preoccupied with the question of authority; that is, who is to be in charge, who is to be looked to for guidance, who is to be depended upon in performing the primary task? This phase is typically divided into subphases. First, people in the group behave in a submissive way, looking for and being willing to take guidance on what to do and how to do it. The hope is that some leader will provide the solutions that will allow the group to work. This is followed by the next subphase in which people rebel against those they have at first depended upon, hoping that conflict will provide a solution to the problems of group life. The third subphase is one in which members find a compromise solution and partial resolution of the dependency–authority/submission–rebellion issue, one that accepts their simultaneous presence.

2   *The interpersonal phase.* Once the group has at least partially worked through the questions of authority and dependence, submission and rebellion, the concern then becomes that of interdependence between the members of the group. The first subphase here is one in which members of the group identify with each other, the subphase of 'enchantment'. The psychological force here is a desire on the part of individuals to find the security that comes from fusing themselves into the group. This is a primitive defence in which members seek the route to performing their primary task through group cohesion. This gives way to the second subphase in which members of the group experience 'disenchantment' with their interdependence and seek to establish their own individuality and independence of the group. The third subphase here is one in which there is some resolution of the fusion–individuation tension, one in which fusion and individuation are both present.

It is easy to see how these models assume that groups move to stable equilibrium when they are effective. These models appear to assume that a group reaches a peak of efficient work and then ends or continues at that level.

### Life-cycle models

These models are an elaboration of the linear progressive models, the principal addition being the emphasis on the terminal phase for small groups. Thus *Mills (1964)* adds a stage of 'separation' in which the group begins to face and cope with its own death and members assess the success or failure of their efforts.

Having discussed how small groups develop, we now turn to the roles people take up in those small groups.

## Roles and leadership in groups

In the formal system, leaders are appointed to an office in a bureaucracy, or perhaps elected to a position in some representative body, where they take charge of a group of people who have also been appointed or elected in some formal way. People come to their roles in a formal fashion in groups that already have structures, procedures, norms, cultures, systems, goals and relatively clear primary tasks. In these circumstances the important question quite clearly is one of identifying how groups can most effectively and efficiently perform the task and reach the goal. When it is observed that people have a natural tendency to develop informal social groupings as they work together in addition to the formal, the concern becomes one of harnessing that informal group to support and not obstruct the performance of the main task. The concern is with motivation and the prime role of the leader is to motivate, form the vision and clarify the cultural values. One then looks to personality traits, styles and skills as the determinants of good leaders. One reaches the conclusion that techniques and programmes can be installed to develop good leaders and cohesive groups, ones that are aware of the social and psychological self-realisation needs of individuals.

Jung stressed the differences between people that flow from the many archetypes that drive them. He identified a number of common psychological types, preferred ways of behaving, or temperaments. From this perspective, patterns in the behaviour of small groups would be explainable from the manner in which different temperaments typically interact.

## The impact of personality

Jung distinguished between preferences that go to make up different temperaments (*Kiersey & Bates, 1978*). First, people express preferred modes of behaviour somewhere between extroversion (E) and introversion (I). The E person derives energy from contact and interaction with others, while the I person is exhausted by such contact and seeks energy from internal, reflective sources.

Second, people have a preference along a spectrum that stretches from sensation (S) at one end to intuition (N) at the other. The S person prefers facts and knows through experience; such a person is firmly anchored to reality. The N person lives in anticipation and looks for change, skipping from one activity to another; such a person values hunches and prefers speculation.

The third pair of preferences are thinking (T) and feeling (F). The T person prefers the logical, impersonal basis for choice, while the F person prefers the personal, emotional basis.

Finally, there is the spectrum running from perceiving (P) to judging (J). The P person prefers to keep options open and fluid, seeing things from different points of view, while the J person prefers closure, that is narrowing choices down and reaching solutions.

The four pairs of preferences lead to 16 possible temperament types and the possibility of having evenly balanced preferences adds a further 32 combinations to these. All these temperaments, however, can be sorted into four broad categories:

1   **The Dionysian or SP person.** As a manager this type of person prefers not to be tied down by routine, but focuses on the present, seeks action and tends to be impulsive.

2   **The Epimethean or ST person.** As a manager this type of person is dutiful and desires to belong to the organisation. Such a manager is careful, thorough and accurate, a giver rather than a taker.

3   **The Promethean or NT person.** As a manager this personality type is interested in power, control and predictability. They avoid the personal and emotional and want to be competent and in charge.

4   **The Apollonian or NF person.** As a manager this type makes intuitive decisions, seeks to be unique, and finds it difficult to take negative criticism.

When people come together, their temperamental differences lead to misunderstandings and the widest gulf is that between the sensing and the intuitive types – the one insisting on logic and the facts, the other pushing proposals based on intuition and experience. People with the same personality type can also clearly have difficulties – a whole group of NT types all trying to control the group, for example, is a recipe for destructive conflict and inactivity. But differences bring contributions to relationships that would otherwise be lacking and some similarity provides the basis of understanding each other.

The behaviour patterns of groups of people would on this view be driven by the understanding and misunderstanding generated by the range of temperaments of the people constituting the group. The implication is that effective groups can be designed if one finds out enough about the personality composition of sets of people, or group functioning can be improved by becoming more aware of the difficulties and contributions flowing from temperamental preferences.

### Belbin's classification

Belbin has used teams of managers playing business games to identify the effects on group performance of different personality types (*Belbin, 1981*). He showed how some types work effectively together while others do not and that this has a greater impact on performance than the individual abilities of the people involved. Teams made up of people simply on the basis of their ability – how clever they are – do not make winning teams. Teams designed to include a balance of different personality types are much more likely to win even if they do not contain the most able individuals; it is actual contribution and interdependence that determines performance.

In Belbin's terms the basis of a good team is the Company Worker types – the conservative, dutiful and predictable, even if inflexible, people (much the same as the Epimethean manager above). These Company Workers are the basis of a good team because of the stability they provide and the steady work contributions they make.

This is not enough for superior performance, however. In addition a team needs members paired into the 'Chairman' (Promethean) and the 'Shaper' (Apollonian) types. The 'Chairman' is calm, self-confident and controlled, arouses the contributions of many types, has a strong sense of objectives, but is average in creative ability. The 'Chairman' therefore needs to be balanced with a 'Shaper' who is highly strung and dynamic, challenges complacency and self-deception, and is impatient and irritable.

The team is strengthened by the addition of the 'Plant' (Apollonian) and the 'Resource Investigator' (Dionysian). The 'Plant' is an unorthodox individualist who contributes new ideas but is apt to be 'up in the clouds'. The 'Resource Investigator' is an enthusiastic extrovert, eager for challenge but apt to lose interest quickly. These two types need to be balanced with sober and prudent 'Monitor Evaluators' and the orderly, conscientious 'Completer Finishers' (both Epimethean). Finally, superior teams contain 'Team Workers' who are socially oriented but tend to be indecisive in times of crisis (Apollonian, perhaps).

## 9.7 HOW LEARNING ORGANISATION THEORY DEALS WITH FOUR KEY QUESTIONS AND FOCUSES ATTENTION

At the end of Chapter 1, I posed four questions that I would ask of each of the theories of organisational change that this book is concerned with. They were:

1   How does the theory view the nature of interaction?
2   What view does it take of human nature?
3   What methodology does it employ?
4   How does it deal with paradox?

Then in Chapter 2, I examined the answers to these questions suggested by cybernetics and cognitivism. They are summarised in *Figures 2.5* and *2.6*. In Chapter 7, I looked at them again in relation to strategic choice theory as a whole. *Figure 8.11* in Chapter 8 sets out the key points made in systems dynamics theories and by comparing it with *Figures 2.5* and *2.6* you will be able to see how the theories differ. In this section I will briefly review the questions again in relation to learning organisation theory. First, how does learning organisation theory deal with the nature of interaction?

### The nature of interaction

Learning organisation theory sees interaction in systemic terms just as cybernetics does. It is concerned with how components, entities or individuals interact to produce patterns of behaviour. It understands the system in the terms of systems dynamics and this, like cybernetics, is a theory that focuses on the macro level. It identifies the feedback structure of the system. It does not attempt to model the micro detail of the entities constituting a dynamical system. Two assumptions are implicitly made about these entities, events or individuals in systems dynamics (*Allen, 1998*):

- First, it is assumed that micro events occur at their average rate and that it is sufficient to take account of averages only. Interactions between entities are then homogeneous.
- Second, it is implicitly assumed that individual entities of a given type are identical, or, at least, that they have a normal distribution around the average type. The entities, or events, are thus implicitly assumed to be homogeneous. Within a category, distinctive identities and differences are not taken into account.

These assumptions make it possible to ignore the probabilistic dynamics governing the micro entities, events or individuals and model the system at the macro level. This is done by specifying the structure of negative and positive feedback loops that drive the system. For example, the beer distribution system, described in the last chapter, is specified in terms of damping and amplifying loops between orders, inventories and shipments between the different components of the system, namely customers, retailers, wholesalers and producers. Nothing is said about how customers, retailers, wholesalers and producers are organised or how they make decisions. This kind of model yields insight into the dynamics of the system as a whole and the possibility of unexpected outcomes. The way systems dynamics is used in learning organisation theory amounts to adding positive feedback loops to a cybernetic system. Systems dynamics is not used in a self-referential sense. I will explore in Chapter 11 how developments of systems dynamics point to how this might be done.

However, there are also major differences compared to cybernetics. Because of the presence of positive feedback loops the dynamics is no longer an automatic movement towards an equilibrium state. Instead, the system is a non-equilibrium one with the dynamics of fluctuating patterns that create considerable difficulties for prediction over longer time periods. However, it is claimed that if the feedback structure of the system is understood, then leverage points can be located. Action at these leverage points makes it possible to control the system.

## The nature of human beings

Learning organisation theory draws on cognitivist, constructivist and humanistic psychology to understand the nature of human beings. The cognitivist assumptions are particularly clear in that individuals are understood to act upon the basis of mental models built from previous experience and stored in the individual. They are representations of the individual's world. Part of each individual's model is shared with others and this forms the basis of their joint action together. The focus on the individual nature of these models, their representation function, the claim that they are stored and shared, the belief that they can be surfaced and subjected to rational scrutiny, are all hallmarks of a cognitivist psychology. However, the way in which mental models select some aspects of reality for attention and exclude others is a feature of a constructivist approach to psychology. The emphasis placed on individual vision and fulfilment, as part of the learning process, is evidence of the humanistic leaning in the theory of the learning organisation.

In all of these psychological theories the individual is held to be prior and primary to the group. Mental models are individual constructs that are shared with others. Effective teams are composed of a balance of different types of individual. Note, however, how differences between individuals do not feature in a fundamental way in the learning organisation theory. A small number of different categories may be identified but the difference is located between categories, while within those categories everyone is implicitly assumed to be the same. This is consistent with a systems dynamics approach in which micro entities are all assumed to be average and their interactions are assumed to be homogeneous. What I am trying to emphasise is this: cohesion and sharing are seen as the foundations of effective learning. There is no notion that deviant and eccentric behaviour might be essential to any creative and innovative thinking and behaving. In Chapter 16 I will be arguing that organisations change in novel ways through deviant behaviour.

The group is treated in a particular way. It consists of individuals and develops in phases, only some of which are conducive to members learning together as individuals.

So, learning organisation theory uses the same psychological theories as strategic choice theory but does place more emphasis on emotion and relationships between people. It also identifies more clearly what may block people from changing and learning. Perhaps the importance of power receives more attention but power is still located in the individual. However, there is no fundamental change in the view of human nature as one moves from the one theory to the other.

## Methodology and organisational learning

The methodological stance in learning organisation theory is the same as that in strategic choice theory. It is a realist position in which managers are assumed to be able to stand outside the system they are a part of and think systemically about it. They are also supposed to be able to stand outside their own mental models, rigorously scrutinise them and then rationally change them.

## Dealing with paradox

As far as I can see, the notion of paradox does not play a fundamental part in learning organisation theory. Tensions, contradictions and dilemmas are certainly recognised but they are thought to be resolvable. As with strategic choice theory, learning organisation theory takes a position at one of the poles of what seem to me to be fundamental paradoxes of organisational life. This is very clear in the case of the individual of the group. I argue above that this is not seen as a paradox at all. The individual is given primacy and understood to be in fundamental conflict with the group. This conflict must be resolved through building relationships of trust in teams if learning is to take place. Sameness and difference are not held in mind at the same time. For example, individuals within a personality category are treated as if they were all the same and all different from individuals in another category. Although unpredictability is pointed to, it is predictability and the possibility of control that is emphasised. As with strategic choice theory, order, stability, consistency and harmony are all seen as prerequisites for success and the role that the opposites of these might play in creativity is largely ignored.

## How learning organisation theory focuses attention

As with strategic choice theory the primary focus of learning organisation theory is on intention and control. Intention takes the form of a vision. Control is to be sustained not simply through installing negative feedback loops, but also through understanding the positive feedback nature of organisations and identifying the leverage points at which they can be controlled. The role of leaders is to inspire and to create conditions in which people feel motivated to learn.

In Chapter 7, I tried to indicate how I think strategic choice theory answers a number of key questions. I will pose the same questions in relation to learning organisation theory. I know that the answers I give to each of these questions is very simplistic. I give them more in the spirit of suggesting that you reflect on how you think the questions are answered by the theory.

- How do new organisations come into being? I think the answer is the same as that which strategic choice theory suggests. A gifted individual develops an idea, makes choices and forms intentions to develop a new business and then gathers other enthusiasts together to get it going.
- Why do they cease to exist? Because the organisation fails to learn while others do.
- How do they come to merge with others or split apart? The answer seems to be the same as for strategic choice theory, namely that leaders choose to do so in order to maximise shareholder value.
- Why do most organisations last for only a rather short time and why do a few survive for long periods? Again, the answer has to do with the quality of learning that takes place in the teams of which the organisation is composed.
- Why is one organisation similar to others and different from yet others? Because their managers have different mental models.
- How do some organisations develop new activities? They do so through the process of organisational learning.
- Why do other organisations simply carry on with the same activities? Because their managers fail to alter their mental models. Learning is blocked by defence routines and politics.
- Why do people become anxious, bored or frustrated? Because their tasks are not fulfilling enough and team spirit is poor.
- What is it that excites and fulfils them? Profound learning experiences in cohesive teams.
- What impact do these and other emotions have on the functioning of groups and organisations? As with strategic choice theory, positive emotions are instrumental in securing group cohesion and team spirit while negative emotions disrupt tasks.

## Making sense of experience

At this point, I invite you to reflect on how this theory assists you to make sense of your experience of life in organisations.

For me, the focus on learning, and what blocks it, provides a rich addition to strategic choice theory when it comes to making sense of my experience. I certainly recognise my own involvement in defence routines and political struggles. I also recognise the difficulty of learning in a fundamental way. However, I think the theory holds out a rather idealised picture of what it is possible for people in an organisation to do.

For example, Argyris reports that he has worked with large numbers of managers in many countries, coaching them to engage in double-loop learning. He reports that they find it difficult and rarely engage in it when they return to their workplace. Instead, they carry on with their win/lose dynamics and their defence routines. I think this immediately raises a question mark over his theory on learning as a change in mental models. Many organisations clearly do change, often in quite creative ways. How does this happen if double-loop learning is such a rarity? Furthermore, I wonder whether it really is possible for people to surface their mental models and change them. Where are they located? It is far from clear that brains store anything that could be correlated with a map or a model. If it is possible for people to identify assumptions they are unaware of and change them, then why is mental illness so prevalent and difficult to deal with? I greatly doubt my own ability to identify whatever it is that makes me think the way I do, and then simply change it.

In the hurly-burly of organisational life, with its political intrigues and the possibility of losing one's job, is it at all wise to expose the defence routines that one is taking part in? If it is so important to do so, why is it so rare to find people doing it?

When I ask myself questions such as these I have serious doubts about the practicality of the prescriptions this theory presents for successful organisational learning.

## 9.8    SUMMARY

This chapter has reviewed learning organisation theory. According to this theory, organisations are systems driven by both positive and negative feedback loops. The interactions between such loops tend to produce unexpected and often counter-intuitive outcomes. Perfect control is not possible but it is possible to identify leverage points where control may be exerted. Perhaps the most important loops relate to learning. Organisations learn when people in cohesive teams trust each other enough to expose the assumptions they are making to the scrutiny of others and then together change shared assumptions which block change. The theory identifies some important behaviours that block this learning process. Although learning organisation theory uses a different systems theory to strategic choice theory, its conceptualisation of that systems theory in terms of feedback loops keeps it close to cybernetics. Learning organisation theory is built on the same psychological theories as strategic choice theory. Control and the primacy of the individual are central to both.

### FURTHER READING

Rush, White & Hurst (1989) explain how personality types affect decision making, as does Belbin (1981). Kiersey & Bates (1978) give a questionnaire that you can use to identify your own personality type. Senge (1990) and Argyris (1990) are important reading.

### REFERENCES

Allen, P. M. (1998), 'Evolving Complexity in Social Science', in Altmann, G. & Kock, W. A., *Systems: New Paradigms for the Social Sciences*, Berlin: Walter de Gruyter.

Argyris, C. (1957), *Personality and Organization*, New York: Harper & Row.

Argyris, C. (1990), *Overcoming Organizational Defenses: Facilitating Organizational Learning*, Boston: Allyn & Bacon.

Argyris, C. & Schon, D. (1978), *Organizational Learning: A Theory of Action Perspective*, Reading, MA: Addison-Wesley.

Bacharach, S. B. & Lawler, E. J. (1980), *Power and Politics in Organizations*, San Francisco: Jossey-Bass.

Baddeley, A. (1990), *Human Memory: Theory and Practice*, Hove, Sussex: Lawrence Erlbaum Associates.

Belbin, R. M. (1981), *Management Teams: Why They Succeed or Fail*, Oxford: Heinemann.

Bennis, W. G. & Shepard, H. A. (1956), A theory of group development, *Human Relations*, vol. 9, pp. 415–57. [Republished in Gibbard, G. S., Hartman, J. & Mann, R. D. (Eds.) (1974), *The Analysis of Groups*, San Francisco: Jossey-Bass.]

Cohen, M. D., March, J. G. & Ohlsen, J. P. (1972), A garbage can model of organizational choice, *Administrative Science Quarterly*, vol. 17, pp. 1–25.

Gibbard, G. S., Hartman, J. J. & Mann, R. D. (Eds.) (1974), *Analysis of Groups*, San Francisco: Jossey-Bass.

Gick, M. L. & Holyoak, K. J. (1983), Schema introduction and analogical transfer, *Cognitive Psychology*, vol. 15, pp. 1–38.

Greiner, L. E. & Schein, V. E. (1988), *Power and Organization Development: Mobilizing Power to Implement Change*, Reading, MA: Addison-Wesley.

Kiersey, D. & Bates, M. (1978), *Please Understand Me: Character and Temperament Types*, Del Mar, CA: Prometheus Nemesis Books.

Mills, T. M. (1964), *Group Transformation: An Analysis of a Learning Group*, Englewood Cliffs, NJ: Prentice Hall.

Rush, J. C., White, R. E. & Hurst, D. C. (1989), Top management teams and organizational renewal, *Strategic Management Journal*, vol. 10, pp. 87–105.

Senge, P. M. (1990), *The Fifth Discipline: The Art and Practice of the Learning Organization*, New York: Doubleday.

Tuckman, B. W. (1965), Developmental sequences in small groups, *Psychological Bulletin*, vol. 63, pp. 384–99.

Weick, K. (1969/1979), *The Social Psychology of Organizing*, Reading, MA: Addison-Wesley.

# 10 Obstacles to strategic choice and organisational learning

## Open systems and psychoanalytic perspectives

Chapters 2 to 7 explored the foundations upon which the theory of strategic choice rests. These are a theory of interaction to be found in cybernetic systems theory and a theory of human nature to be found primarily in cognitivism, but also in humanistic psychology. Then Chapters 8 and 9 examined the theoretical foundations of learning organisation theory. Here there is some shift from a theory of interaction based on cybernetics to one based on systems dynamics. However, the way systems theory is used retains a link with cybernetics through the conceptualisation of systems dynamics in feedback terms. There is much less of a shift in the basic theory of human nature. This remains heavily cognitivist, although with the addition of a constructivist slant in that mental models are seen to select features for attention, so constructing rather than purely representing experience. The reliance on humanistic psychology seems to be even stronger than it is in strategic choice theory.

   In this chapter I am going to review a theory of organisational change that is built on both a different theory of interaction and a different theory of human nature. Interaction continues to be seen in systemic terms but this time from the perspective of open systems theory. The theory of human nature is provided by psychoanalytic perspectives. I will first review open systems theory, then turn to relevant psychoanalytic notions, before showing how they can be combined to shed light on life in organisations.

## 10.2    OPEN SYSTEMS THEORY

Around the same time as the development of cybernetics and systems dynamics, there also appeared the closely related ideas of general systems theory. In a number of papers and books between 1945 and 1968, the German biologist von Bertalanfy put forward the idea that organisms, as well as human organisations and societies, are open systems. They are systems because they consist of a number of component subsystems that are interrelated and interdependent on each other. They are open because they are connected to their environments, or suprasystems, of which they are a part (see *Box 10.1*).

**BOX 10.1**

## The organisation as an open system

*Kast & Rosenzweig (1970)* conceived of the organisation in terms of suprasystems and subsystems:

- *Environmental suprasystem*. This can be divided into general societal and specific task systems. The general environmental system covers the culture of the society of which the organisation is a part, its general level of technology, its politics, and so on. The task systems include customers, suppliers, competitors, and so on. The more complex and unstable the environmental system, the more complex and differentiated the internal structuring of the organisation will have to be to cope.
- *Goals and values subsystems*. These flow from relationships between five levels: individuals within the organisation; groups of people within the organisation; the organisation as a whole; the task environments; and society at large.
- *Technical subsystem*. This relates to the knowledge required to perform tasks. It includes the technology of production specific to the organisation, the degrees of specialisation and automation required and applied, and the extent to which tasks are routine and non-routine.
- *Psychological subsystem*. This is created by individuals and groups in interaction. Individual behaviour and motivation, status and roles, group dynamics and political interactions are all part of this subsystem. It is clearly influenced by all the other subsystems and suprasystems.
- *Structural subsystem*. This covers the ways in which tasks are divided up and then integrated again. Organisational charts and job definitions, as well as formal communication flows, are the more visible manifestations of this subsystem. It also includes the informal organisation with its networks of personal contacts and casual information flows.
- *Managerial subsystem*. This spans the entire organisation and it relates the organisation to its environment, developing goals and plans, designing structures, and establishing control processes. Its primary role is an integrating one. ■

Each subsystem within a system and each system within its environment has a boundary separating it from other subsystems and other systems. For example, the sales department in an organisation is a subsystem separated by a boundary from the production and accounting departments. One organisation such as IBM is a system separated by a boundary from the other organisations and individuals that form its environment.

Within each system or subsystem, people occupy roles, they conduct sets of activities, and they engage in interrelationships with others. They do this both within their part of the system and in other parts or other systems.

Each subsystem within a system and each system within an environment is open. It imports materials, labour, money and information from other subsystems or systems. It also exports outputs, money and information to other subsystems and systems.

Open systems explanations of managing and organising therefore focus attention on:

- behaviour of people within a subsystem or system;
- nature of the boundary around a subsystem or system;
- nature of the relationships across the boundaries between subsystems and systems;
- requirements of managing the boundary.

The open systems concept provides a tool for understanding the relationship between:

- the technical and the social aspects of an organisation;
- the parts and the whole organisation (e.g. the individual and the group, the individual and the organisation);
- the whole organisation and the environment.

## Negative feedback

Changing one component in an open system will clearly have knock-on effects in many other components because of the prevalence of interconnection. Changes in the environment will have an impact on changes in the subsystems of an organisation. What happens in one system will affect what happens in another system and that in turn will affect the first.

You can see the importance of the insight provided by open systems theory if you consider how the technical subsystem of an organisation is interconnected with its social subsystem (*Trist & Bamforth, 1951*).

Scientific rational management tends to concentrate on the technical subsystem. This system consists of the primary tasks that the organisation is there to carry out: for example, the techniques, technology and sets of tasks required to produce coal in the case of a coal mining business. The prescription for success made by the scientific management is to make the task subsystem as efficient as possible. So, if you introduce the latest technology for mining coal together with rules and regulations about quality and efficiency to govern the work of coal miners, then you should succeed according to scientific management. Success here depends primarily on the technical subsystem.

The behavioural school of management, on the other hand, focuses primarily on the psychosocial subsystem. Its prescriptions for success stress the establishment of a social system in which people are motivated and participate in making decisions about the nature of the tasks and the technology. To succeed you must consult those who perform the organisation's primary tasks, involve them in decision making, and introduce reward structures that will motivate them to operate efficiently. Success here depends primarily on the social subsystem.

The insight that comes from open systems theory is that the technical and social systems are so interconnected that it makes no sense to regard one as dominant and the other as subordinate. Both subsystems have to be handled together in a manner that takes account of their interdependence.

The importance of this interconnection was demonstrated many years ago in a study of the coal mining industry in the UK by *Trist & Bamforth (1951)*. In the late 1940s, the British coal industry introduced the more efficient long-wall method of mining coal. This technology, however, required changes in the set of tasks performed by coal miners. These changes broke up the cooperative teams in which miners were accustomed to working, teams that reflected their social arrangements in the coal mining villages in which they lived. Because of the consequent resistance to working in the new way, the technology failed to yield its technical potential.

The message is that, if changes are to succeed, then they have to be based on a realistic understanding of the interconnection, or feedback, between the social and the technical subsystems. And that interconnection is not simply taken account of by introducing  participation or reward schemes for individuals. Instead, general systems theory prescribes a match between the two subsystems, one that establishes stable equilibrium.

Like cybernetics and systems dynamics therefore, the general systems strand of thinking sees an organisation as a feedback system. It also sees that feedback system as one that maintains equilibrium with its environment, and between its parts, by utilising the mechanisms of negative feedback.

## Conflicting subsystems

In general systems theory, open systems are thought of as having maintenance subsystems to sustain orderly relationships between the parts of the system (*Lawrence & Lorsch, 1967*). In an organisation this would be the management information and control systems and the cultures that keep people working harmoniously together. However, it is recognised that these maintenance systems are conservative by nature. They are intended to hold the system together; to prevent it from changing too rapidly; to keep it efficiently carrying out its main tasks. The inevitable consequence of this maintenance form of control is that the overall system and its subsystems become out of balance as time goes by and things change. They become out of balance with each other and with the environment.

But organisations also have adaptive mechanisms that promote change so as to keep them in dynamic equilibrium with the environment. These two subsystems, the maintenance and the adaptive, inevitably conflict, but successful organisations sustain a stable balance between them, according to general systems theory. Note that general systems theory recognises fundamental conflict inherent in the structure of the system, but assumes that successful systems deal with this by sustaining equilibrium.

## Differentiation and integration

*Lawrence & Lorsch (1967)* used the conceptual approach of open systems to research the functioning of a number of large organisations. They concluded that as organisations increase in size they differentiate into parts, and the more they differentiate, the more difficult becomes the consequent task of integration.

So as the environment becomes more complex and as they grow in size, companies differentiate into functions – finance, operations, sales, and so on. But each part or function then faces the problem of relating to the other parts, if the firm is to operate effectively. Integrating what people in the production department do with what those in the sales or finance departments do then becomes more and more of a problem.

As organisations deal with their external environment they become differentiated into separate units, each dealing with a part of the environment. Think of large multinational companies, such as ICI or IBM, with perhaps hundreds of different subsidiary companies across the world. They have reached advanced stages of differentiation and face well-known and very difficult-to-solve problems of integrating all their activities.

The authors found a relationship between variables external to the organisation and the states of differentiation and integration within that organisation. They found that organisations become more differentiated as their environments become more diverse.

Citibank operates in a large number of countries, a complex environment, through a great many national subsidiaries. This is a differentiated organisation. Since the environment demands more interdependence and cooperation, the organisation responds with greater integration. So, Citibank superimposes upon its national subsidiaries a central activity to serve its multinational clients wishing to deal with one central point, not hundreds of subsidiaries (*Buzzell, 1984*).

As environments become more diverse and organisations more differentiated, the tasks of integration become greater, leading to a proliferation of complex integrating devices. Citibank finds that conflicts grow up between the national subsidiaries and the central body dealing with multinational clients. It has to set up rules and systems to try to resolve the conflicts.

Lawrence and Lorsch also found that the more unpredictable the environment becomes the more decentralised the organisation becomes, pushing the locus of decision making down the hierarchy. This kind of reasoning was encountered in Chapter 3 when discussing contingency theory. The general systems approach is also a contingency theory.

Note how general systems theorists recognise fundamental conflicts in organising: the need to divide tasks up and to integrate them; the need for maintenance control systems for stability but the inevitable drift from the demands of the environment as such maintenance control is applied. Note how they interpret organisations dealing with these conflicts. They, in effect, see them as solving them, the solutions being dictated by the need to adapt to the environment.

General systems theory has made an important contribution to an understanding of the nature of managing and organising in a number of ways. It focuses attention on:

- interdependence, interaction and interconnection between parts of an organisation and between organisations;

- the importance of the boundaries between parts of an organisation and between one organisation and others;
- the roles of people within and across the boundaries and the nature of leadership as management of the boundary.

These ideas, summarised in *Figure 10.1*, have been important in developing an understanding of group dynamics within an organisation and in the discipline of organisation development which was reviewed in Chapter 6.

---

- An organisation is an open system: a set of interconnected parts (individuals, informal groups, formal groups such as departments and business units) in turn interacting with other organisations and individuals outside it.
- Interconnection means that a system imports energy and information from outside itself, transforms that energy and information in some way, and then exports the transformed result back to other systems outside of itself.
- An organisation imports across a boundary separating it from other systems, transforms the imports within its boundary, and exports back across the boundary. The boundary separates a system from its environment but also links it to its environment.
- Relationships across the boundary are always changing, the environment is always changing. The boundary therefore exercises a regulatory function: on the one hand it protects the system from fluctuations in the environment and on the other it relays messages and prompts changes within the boundary so that the system adapts to its environment.
- It is the role of leadership to manage the boundary, to regulate so that the system is protected and changes adaptively.
- Successful management keeps an organisation adapted to its changing environment through a process of negative feedback producing stable equilibrium.
- Adaptation to the environment determines the stable equilibrium balance between differentiation and integration, between maintenance control systems and change, required for success. Organisational paradoxes are thus solved in a unique way determined by the environment.
- Success is therefore a state of stability, consistency and harmony.

---

**FIGURE 10.1**    General systems theory: the main points on organisational dynamics

I now want to move on from open systems theory to some relevant psychoanalytic concepts. I will return to it in section 10.4.

## 10.3    PSYCHOANALYSIS AND UNCONSCIOUS PROCESSES

Psychoanalysis originated in the work of Freud. One of its most basic concepts is that of the unconscious. It is believed that people repress dangerous desires and painful memories. However, repression does not get rid of all this. It remains in the unconscious as determinants of behaviour. Repression is one of the major defences against anxiety, that is a painful state of unease for which no clear reason can be found. It is also held that peoples behaviour can be driven by unconscious group processes.

## Unconscious processes in organisations

An unconscious group process is one in which a group of people engage without consciously agreeing to it or even realising that they are doing it. When groups of people are in this state they find what is happening to them both puzzling and upsetting and it makes it impossible for them to engage in double-loop learning. Covert politics is a defence against anxiety that people are more or less conscious of practising but unconscious processes are defences they indulge in quite automatically without being aware of what they are doing.

So, anxiety triggers an automatic negative feedback loop, a damping process that inhibits movement away from a currently shared mental model so trapping a group of people in stability. A group of people can only learn in a double-loop way when they are able to hold the anxiety such learning provokes, as opposed to avoiding it through covert politics, on the one hand, or becoming overwhelmed by it in the form of unconscious processes, on the other hand.

When people's ways of thinking are challenged, they become anxious. That anxiety may rise to such high levels that people swing into automatic basic assumption behaviour – an unconscious process. This is a notion developed by Wilfred Bion that I will review in some detail in this section. When groups are dominated by basic assumption behaviour they cannot learn and therefore their organisation cannot develop new strategic direction. On the other hand, if there is a good enough holding environment so that people can contain rather than submit to or avoid the anxiety, then insight and creativity may be generated by and accompany the anxiety of learning.

I now go on to consider the work of Bion, and others, on the nature of unconscious group processes.

## Bion's models: unconscious group processes

The nature of interaction between people depends upon the extent to which those people are aware of the nature of their own and each other's behaviour. This point is made in *Figure 10.2*, a diagram known as JOHARI's window.

When people are aware of their own behaviour and those with whom they are interacting are also aware of that behaviour, then interaction between them takes on a Public form – they all know what they are doing together and why. But one group of people may be doing something that they are completely aware of to others who are unaware of what is going on. Such behaviour is labelled Hidden in *Figure 10.2*; some are manipulating others. Again, one group may be performing in a particular way, for reasons that they are unaware of, but their behaviour is transparent to others. Such behaviour may be called Blind: some pretend they are doing one thing while they do another, but other people can see through this. The figure also shows a quadrant that is cross-hatched, depicting behaviour where those behaving and those responding are unaware of the true nature of their interaction. This is unconscious behaviour.

When individuals behave in such a way that they are not explicitly aware of the nature, or the quality, or the causes of that behaviour, then one can say that they are behaving unconsciously. For example, when I react in a hostile manner to a total stranger I have never heard about or met before, then I am behaving unconsciously – there is no

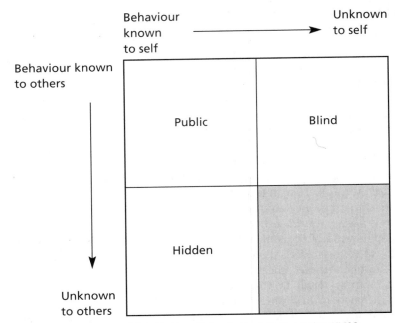

Source: P.B. Smith (1969), *Improving Skills in Working with People: The T Group*, London: HMSO

**FIGURE 10.2    JOHARI window**

obvious reason, no clear connection with external reality, to explain my reaction. The reason for such a reaction is held by pschoanalysis to lie in the unconscious mind; the particular person has activated a response from some other experience in the past that has been pushed into the unconscious. Whenever people react to some stimulus in a manner which others, and later they themselves, perceive to be out of all proportion to the stimulus, then in all probability the cause of that behaviour lies in their unconscious.

When you lose your temper at a typist for making a small spelling error, the true source of the anger is most probably not the typist at all; you are simply projecting anger felt for someone else, who might well be yourself, onto the unfortunate typist. This kind of projection is an unconscious process in which all humans regularly indulge, according to psychoanalysis.

Since all people behave in ways that are directed by unconscious as well as conscious processes, it is inevitable that, when they come together as a group, at least part of their behaviour in that group will be determined by those unconscious processes. In other words, unconscious group process will inevitably be part of most decision-making processes in an organisation.

This proposition is not recognised in most explanations of managing, organising and decision making. The role of unconscious processes is also firmly denied any explicit attention by the many management practitioners. Such considerations tend to be dismissed as peripheral concerns for mature managers who are supposed to make decisions in largely rational ways. When unconscious processes are discussed they are normally seen as peripheral influences on a decision, usually adverse influences, which must and can be removed.

More careful reflection, however, suggests that unconscious processes are so deeply embedded in human behaviour that it is only some completely inhuman, and therefore non-existent, decision-making process that can occur in the absence of unconscious processes, or with those processes occupying a position of only peripheral importance. It is therefore a matter of importance for the effectiveness of strategic management to explore what impact these processes may have and how they come about. First consider one way of becoming aware of what the processes I am talking about are.

## Group relations conferences

A very powerful way of experiencing what unconscious group processes actually feel like is provided by what is known as group relations conferences, (*Miller, 1989*). This approach to training in group awareness was popular in the 1960s but fell from favour largely because it did not produce predictable, longlasting changes in people's skills in building cohesive teams. From a psychoanalytic perspective, this is not the only aim, so the criticism need not deter one from learning from this approach. I would therefore like to describe some of the kinds of behaviour that always emerge in such events and then outline the explanations that have been put forward to account for it.

What I am going to describe is based on three separate conferences, each lasting two days over a weekend. The participants on each occasion were about 30 part-time MBA students, average age around 35. Some points on the composition of these groups are as follows: about 15 per cent were female; perhaps 10 per cent of the total were from minority groups; about 70 per cent of the total were from the commercial and industrial sector and the remainder from public sector and charitable bodies; over 90 per cent had degrees or professional qualifications. All of these intelligent people held responsible managerial positions in their organisations.

Participants arrived at the residential weekend with some feelings of apprehension because they had heard rumours from others about the strange happenings likely to occur. At the start of the weekend, all of the participants met in a plenary session with the staff who were to act as consultants to groups of participants. The staff consisted of three visiting consultants with considerable experience in running such conferences and two teachers from my own institution who played a relatively minor consulting role. The task of the weekend was briefly outlined: it was to study group processes, particularly unconscious processes, so enabling each individual to examine the part he or she plays in those processes, including the exercise of authority.

Participants were then divided into study groups of 10–12 members each and the task of the study group was stated to be that of studying intra-group processes in the here and now, when they happen and as they happen. It was clearly explained to the participants that each study group would be attended by a consultant, who would not be there to teach, but to provide working hypotheses about the processes occurring in groups. It was quite clearly stated that participants must take responsibility for their own learning.

The study groups were therefore set up in such a way that there was nothing that the managers involved recognised as the kind of objective and task they were used to. Managers do not normally simply examine their own behaviour in a group – the behaviour normally lies in the background of dealing with an objective and a task. Here the behaviour itself is brought out of the background actually to provide the, rather unfamiliar, objective and task. The role that the consultants steadfastly occupy is also not one that the participants are used to. The consultant clearly occupies some position of authority as far as the participants are concerned, but that consultant abandons the participants in the sense that the consultant refuses to occupy the expected role of teacher, expert or leader. Then, however, having abandoned them in this sense, the consultant nevertheless keeps intruding in the role of consultant to offer interpretations of what the participants are doing (*Gustafson & Cooper, 1978*).

These two changes, the removal of what is normally regarded as a task and the removal of what is normally regarded as a teacher or leader, always provoke high levels of anxiety in the participants, anxieties which they are reluctant to recognise. Those anxieties find expression in all manner of strange behaviours. Group discussions may take on a manic form with asinine comments and hysterical laughter. In a remarkably short space of time the participants attack the visiting consultant for not playing a more usual and active role and openly question whether they are earning their consulting fees. Participants become incredibly rude to the consultants, behaviour they would not normally display to a visitor, no matter how poor the visitor's performance might be. Significantly, however, participants never attack the two teachers, perhaps because they represent the ongoing authority figures for the MBA course.

Members of study groups might try to find a leader to replace the non-functioning consultant but they rarely seem to be successful in this endeavour for very long. They begin to pick on an individual, usually some highly individualistic or minority member of the group, and then treat this person as some kind of scapegoat. They all become very concerned with remaining part of the group, greatly fearing exclusion. They show strong tendencies to conform to rapidly established group norms and suppress their individual differences, perhaps because they are afraid of becoming the scapegoat.

The study group events are followed by the inter-group event. Here the participants are invited to organise themselves into groups and then study inter-group behaviour in the here and now as it happens. The sight of these mature people organising themselves into groups is quite astonishing. They do so without any forethought, all seemingly in a panic at the thought of being left out of a group. Within seconds the room is cleared of people who have all rushed off, away from the consultants, in one group or another. Then they begin to interact and within minutes the win/lose dynamic takes powerful hold. Even though there is no specific objective, other than studying behaviour, even though the groups have formed without any common purpose whatsoever, some groups at least start to talk about dominating the others. They then proceed to try to do so, brushing aside any quiet, puzzled voice that might ask why they are doing this. In their pursuit of domination, group members lie to each other, spy on each other, and play one deceitful game after another.

The one thing they hardly do at all is examine the behaviour they are indulging in, the task they have actually been given. Individuals and whole groups become scapegoats, set up by others and collaborating in that set-up. Very real emotions of anger and fear are evoked by what goes on, despite the fact that all know that this is 'only a training weekend'. Rumours spread about what other groups are doing, fantasies that participants afterwards realise are completely false. But at the time little effort is made to check on the data: all is wild assertions, building up fantasies of attacking and being attacked, rejecting and being rejected. People talk all the time about the group as some real thing separate from themselves as individuals. They place enormous store on being part of the group and on the group being cohesive. They talk about belonging to the strongest, most cohesive group, the best group, in a fantasy-like manner.

I personally found it most surprising that undoubtedly competent, mature people in responsible managerial positions react so strongly to two rather small changes from the normal. After all, there is a task: it is to study group processes as they happen and there is certainly much happening. There is assistance in performing the task in the form of comments and guidance from the experienced consultants, even though they refuse the role of teacher. But it seems that the original stimulus of two rather unusual changes sets off some kind of amplifying feedback loop in the behaviour of the groups of participants from which they seem incapable of escaping during the whole weekend. They, and even I as a rather peripheral consultant, become totally caught up in very strong and difficult-to-understand amplifying processes. The fact that the magnitude of the response is out of all proportion to the stimulus is a sign of unconscious processes. Throughout the experience it becomes apparent to many participants that processes of this kind occur every day within their own real life organisation, although usually at a much lower level of intensity. I personally found it even more surprising that I too behaved in this way when I joined a group relations conference as a member.

How is one to explain the nature and cause of these unconscious processes that make it virtually impossible for a group of intelligent and competent managers to work on a task for a whole weekend? A psychoanalytical explanation is that, when humans are confronted by high levels of anxiety provoked by unfamiliar tasks and lack of leadership, they revert very easily to infantile mechanisms. They begin to behave according to patterns they learned as infants. So first look briefly at an explanation of how infants cope with their world provided by the object relations school of psychoanalysis (*Klein, 1975*).

## Infantile mechanisms

According to Melanie Klein's explanation (1975), infants are born with two powerful drives: the libido, or life force, which is the drive to love; and the morbido, or death wish, which is the fear of death and destruction, the feeling of persecution. The inner life of the infant is very simple – it is dominated by these two extremes of love on the one hand and persecutory fear on the other.

The infant's perception of its external world is also very simple, consisting of two part objects: a good part of the mother that feeds and comforts it and a bad part that denies it food and comfort.

The infant copes with this simple and also powerfully distressing world by splitting its inner life into a loving part that is projected onto the good part of the mother. The infant then identifies itself with that good part and introjects it back into itself. The same thing is done with the persecutory feelings and the aggression and hatred they arouse. These are all projected onto the bad part of the mother, and the infant identifies its own violent impulses with that bad part – it then introjects that bad part of the mother back into itself.

The infant projects its feelings and then perceives those feelings as coming from the outside object. It therefore reacts to the object in a manner provoked by the feelings which originally come from itself. So it projects its own fears of persecution and then reacts to the object projected upon as if that object is actually persecuting it. This leads to a reaction of hate and aggression, strengthening the feeling of persecution. If the projection affects the behaviour of the object, then the whole feedback process becomes even stronger. It is through this feedback that the character of the infant is formed. If it experiences loving responses to its loving projections then the loving side of its character is strengthened. If the persecutory projections are reinforced by lack of love and actual persecution then this side of the character is reinforced. Right at the earliest stages of behaviour, then, positive and negative feedback loops play major parts in the development of an infant.

This first stage of infantile development is known as the paranoid–schizoid position. It is schizoid because the infant splits the external world and it splits its own internal world too. It is paranoid because of the persecutory fears of the infant. The infant deals with these fears by using the mechanisms of splitting and projective identification, putting what is inside its own mind out into some external object or person and then identifying with and reacting to what it has projected. It copes with harsh reality by creating a fantasy world of separate objects, some of which are persecuting it. It is idealising the good parts and denying its own bad parts by projecting them, so building the external bad into a demon.

The infant who develops normally works through this position and comes to realise that the bad and good objects in its external world are really one and the same whole person. But having learned how to defend against the earliest anxieties, these defences remain in the unconscious. In later life when people confront anxiety again, they are highly likely to regress to the infantile mechanisms of splitting the world and themselves into extreme and artificial categories of the good and the bad, projecting the parts of themselves we do not like onto others, so creating fantasies that have little to do with reality.

Once the infant realises that it loves and hates the same person it is filled with anxiety because of the feelings of anger and hatred previously projected into the mother. This causes the depressive position. The normal infant works its way through this position too, developing strong feelings of love and dependence on the mother, while seeking to make amends for previous bad feelings. It experiences hope from the maturer relationship with the mother. Once the infant can hold the depressive position, that is hold in the mind the paradox of simultaneously loving and hating, then that child can go on to make reparative acts and have reparative feelings. If these are responded to with love then a lifelong cycle of experiencing guilt, making reparation and receiving forgiveness is put in place. Melanie Klein saw this as the basis of all later creative behaviour. So, it is when people are in the depressive position, when they can hold in their minds the paradoxes and ambiguities of organisational life, that they are able to engage in double-loop learning. When they regress from that depressive position to the paranoid–schizoid position they become trapped in primitive ways of thinking and behaving. And this, it is held, happens to all of us when we cannot contain the anxiety of learning and when our environment provides us with no anxiety containment either.

## Transitional objects, learning and play

*Winnicott's (1971)* work gives further insight into the development of the ability to learn and be creative. He identified child development with a process of separation from the carer and he stressed the vital importance of 'good enough holding' by the carer in this process. He defined the good enough carer as one with a fine judgement of just how much to gratify the child to sustain a sufficient degree of security, and just how much to frustrate that child to provoke exploration of and relation to the environment: that fine balance constitutes 'good enough holding' and comes from the instinctive empathy the carer has with the child. Good enough holding enables children to cross the boundary of their own minds and begin to explore, relate to and manipulate the real world outside their minds.

However, eventually the child has to develop its own holding mechanisms as it were, since reliance cannot be placed on the carer to do this all the child's life. Winnicott proposed that such holding mechanisms take the form of what he called transitional objects. As they mature children develop the ability to compensate for short absences of their carer by developing a very powerful relationship with some special object such as a blanket or a teddy bear. Winnicott suggested that this object stands for the carer: it is treated for short periods as if it were the carer and so it provides enough security for the child to continue exploring the environment. In this sense the object is a transitional one: it is a transition from a present carer to an absent carer; it stands for the carer although it is not the carer. This is how the child begins to use symbols, the beginning of all language and reasoning powers.

In fact the teddy bear soon comes to stand for anything the child wants it to be, providing experiences of play which develop the imagination and the ability to manipulate symbols. It is through this experience of play that the child learns and develops imaginative, creative powers. The child discovers how to control and manipulate objects outside the mind, first by manipulating the transitional object and then by controlling real objects. The play takes place in a transitional space between the inner fantasies of the mind and the outer reality of a concrete world, as depicted in *Figure 10.3*. Here the child holds ambiguity and paradox: the transitional object is one thing but stands for something else. In this sense the transitional space is close in meaning to the depressive position (*Miller, 1983; Gordon, 1993*).

Play continues to be a major source of learning and it continues throughout life to be closely associated with creativity. It is when individuals are able to play, when they are able to manipulate symbols, when they are able to occupy the illusionistic world, that they are able to be creative. Winnicott argued that the transitional space continues throughout life to be the area in which people develop cultures, myths, art and religion. So, double-loop learning in organisations would have to do with creating the space for play and with creating the conditions that will hold the anxiety such creative play arouses.

**FIGURE 10.3**    The creative space
*Source:* Adapted from Miller (1983)

## Groups and infantile mechanisms

When mature, competent managers come together as a group, each brings along the infantile mechanisms of dependence, idealisation, denial, splitting, projection and fantasising that have been learned as an infant and laid down in the unconscious.

Anything that raises uncertainty levels and thus anxiety levels could provoke regression to those infantile mechanisms.

Bion has provided an explanation of how these mechanisms are manifested in group behaviour, leading to the kinds of behaviour at the group relations conferences described earlier (*Bion, 1961*).

Bion distinguishes between two important aspects of any group of people. The first aspect is the sophisticated work group. This is the primary task that the group has come together to perform. So a team of top executives has the primary tasks of controlling the day-to-day running of the business of the organisation and also the strategic development of that organisation.

All groups are also at the same time what Bion called 'basic assumption groups'. A basic assumption group is one that behaves as if it is making a particular assumption about required behaviour. The assumption becomes most apparent when uncertainty and anxiety levels rise. What Bion is talking about here is the emotional atmosphere, the psychological culture, of the group. All groups of people have these two aspects: some task they are trying to perform together, accompanied by some emotional atmosphere within which they are trying to perform their task. That atmosphere can be described in terms of a basic assumption they are all making.

So, at any one time, a group of people may constitute a sophisticated work group characterised by a basic assumption on behaviour that occupies a kind of low-level background position, influencing the conduct of the primary task but not dominating or blocking it. Then when uncertainty and anxiety levels rise markedly the group can become suffused with and dominated by the basic assumption; a strong emotional atmosphere, or group culture, that blocks the group's ability to function as a sophisticated work group. The primary task will not be carried out, or it will be carried out in an ineffective manner.

Bion distinguished between three basic assumptions:

1  **Dependence.** Here the group behaves as if it has come together to depend on some leader. The members of the group seek a leader on whom they can depend. They abandon their individuality and critical faculties in favour of some kind of adoration of a charismatic leader. They actively seek a charismatic person who will tell them what to do. Charisma lies not in the person of the leader but in the interrelationship between the followers and the leader.

   In this state, members of a group will idealise the leader, expecting completely unrealistic performance from the leader. Groups working on this assumption are destined to be disappointed and will quickly abandon the leader. This dependence is an infantile mechanism because the members of the group are projecting their requirements for something to depend upon onto someone else. This projection will in effect select the leader. Note how this raises a possibility not normally thought of. When a group is behaving in this mode it is creating its own leader through projecting demands onto a person – it is not the leader who is creating the group. If the person selected for this projection does not cooperate or disappoints, then members of the group project their frustration and fear onto that person and begin to attack. This brings us to the second basic assumption

2  **Fight/flight.** Here it is as if the group has come together for the purpose of fighting some enemy or for the purpose of fleeing from some enemy. Members project their desire for fight or flight onto someone to lead them in fight or flight. Once again they may rapidly become disappointed with and attack the leader. Groups in this state invent fantasy enemies in some other department or some other organisation. The energy goes into competition and win/lose dynamics.

3  **Pairing.** Pairing is another mode a group might operate in. Here it is as if the group has come together to witness the intercourse between two of their number which will produce the solution to their anxieties. The atmosphere here is one of unrealistic hope that some experts will produce all the answers.

*Turquet (1974)* has added a fourth basic assumption:

4  **Oneness.** Here it is as if the group has come together to join in a powerful union

with some omnipotent force which will enable members to surrender themselves in some kind of safe passivity. Members seem lost in an oceanic feeling of unity.

## The dynamics

The explanation presented so far is summarised in *Figure 10.4.*

Once a group of people come to be dominated by one of the basic assumptions, they enter into volatile dynamics in which they switch, for apparently no reason, from one basic assumption to another. While people in a group are behaving like this they are incapable of performing the primary task or acting as a work group. They cannot remember what they have just discussed; they go around and around in incompetent

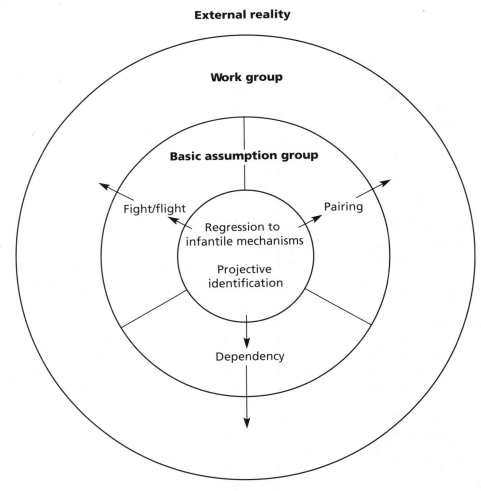

**FIGURE 10.4**  Unconcious group processes
*Source:* R. de Board (1978), *The Psychoanalysis of Organizations*, London: Tavistock

circles; they suck unsuitable people into leadership positions; they create scapegoats; they act on untested myths and rumours; they build fantasies and lose touch with reality. Individuals sink their individuality in group uniformity and become deskilled.

What provokes the switch from a work group with some background basic assumption, being used in a sophisticated way to support their task, to a group dominated by a basic assumption? The provocation seems to have a great deal to do with levels of ambiguity and uncertainty on the one hand, and with certain styles of exercising power on the other. If leaders abandon groups in times of great uncertainty and ambiguity then they will develop into basic assumption groups and become incapable of handling the uncertainty and ambiguity.

But note that this is not clear-cut causality between a specific action, say the withdrawal of power, and specific outcomes in behavioural terms. All one can say is that, when the nature of power in a group is changed so that people's requirement for dependency is frustrated, they will display general patterns of behaviour that can be labelled as fight/flight or some other label. It will not be possible to say what form such fighting or such flight may take, or when it will occur. The key points about the dynamics and unconscious processes are summarised in *Figure 10.5*.

---

- Positive feedback loops are activated by any attempt to change an organisation in a fundamental way. This is because change upsets the balance and nature of power and raises the levels of uncertainty and ambiguity. Consequent anxiety provokes positive feedback loops.
- Increased anxiety unleashes unconscious processes of regression to infantile behaviour. Work groups become swamped with basic assumption behaviour in which they are incapable of undertaking strategic developments.
- A group of managers facing strategic issues is tuning up the levels of uncertainty and ambiguity since these are characteristics of strategic issues. Such issues threaten power positions. It is therefore inevitable that strategic issues themselves will touch off the positive amplifying loops of basic assumption behaviour. Such behaviour is an inevitable part of the process of making strategic decisions.
- In these circumstances it is quite likely that long-term plans, mission statements, visions and the like are simply being used as defence mechanisms. Perhaps people cling to a dominant paradigm despite all the evidence to the contrary because it is their main defence mechanism against anxiety.
- The dynamics of any real-life organisation is inevitably unstable, unless it is completely dominated by rules, fears or force, in which case it will atrophy and die. Strategic management proceeds as part of this unstable dynamic.
- Success has to do with the management of the context or boundary conditions around a group. The main factors that establish the context are the nature and use of power, the level of mutual trust, and the time pressures on people in the group. The purpose of managing the context, or the boundaries, is to create an emotional atmosphere in which it is possible to overcome defences and to test reality rather than indulge in fantasy. In other words, the context must be managed to create an atmosphere that enables double-loop learning.

---

**FIGURE 10.5**    Unconscious group processes: main points on organisational dynamics

## 10.4   OPEN SYSTEMS AND UNCONSCIOUS PROCESSES

The combination of open systems theory and psychoanalysis originated in the Tavistock Institute of Human Relations. This was set up London in 1946 by a group of psychoanalysts from the Tavistock Clinic and social scientists from other institutions. During the 1950s and 1960s a distinctive approach to understanding life in organisations was developed by members of this Institute, for example Trist, to whom I have already referred, Rice and Miller (*Miller & Rice 1967*).

As I have already said, an open system exists by importing energy/materials from its environment across a boundary, transforming them, and then exporting them back across the boundary (*Miller & Rice, 1967*). This boundary is seen as a region in which mediating, or regulating, activities occur to protect the system from disruption due to external fluctuations but also allow it to adapt to external changes (*Miller, 1977*). The boundary region must therefore exhibit an appropriate degree of both insulation and permeability if the system is to survive. This makes regulatory functions at the permeable boundary region of central importance. In organisational terms, these regulatory functions are performed by leaders/managers at the organisation's boundary with other organisations. It is the activities of leaders and managers at the boundary who are key to the process of change. It then becomes quite logical to think about change in terms of rational design and to look for what might inhibit such rational designing activity. Disorder is seen as an inhibitor that must be removed. The disorder is due to the unconscious processes described in the last section.

*Miller & Rice (1967)* used *Bion's (1961)* insights to see a group of people as an open system in which individuals, also seen as open systems, interact with each other at two levels. At one level they contribute to its purpose, so constituting a sophisticated (work) group, and at the other level they develop feelings and attitudes about each other, the group and its environment, so constituting a more primitive (basic assumption) group. Both of these modes of relating are operative at the same time. When the basic assumption mode takes the form of a background emotional atmosphere it may well support the work of the group, but when it predominates it is destructive of the group's work. So, individuals are thought of as open systems relating to each other across their individual boundary regions. In this way they constitute a group, which is also thought of as an open system with a permeable boundary region. Furthermore, Miller and Rice argue that it is confusing to think of organisations, or enterprises, as open systems consisting of individuals and groupings of individuals. So, an intersystemic perspective is adopted in which an enterprise is thought of as one open system interacting with individuals and groupings of them as other open systems.

Enterprises are seen as task systems – they have primary tasks that they must perform if they are to survive. There are various definitions of the primary task. It may be the task that ought to be performed. It may be the task people believe that they are carrying out. It may be a task that they are engaged in without even being aware of it and this probably means that it is a defensive mechanism. The primary task requires people to take up roles in order for it to be carried out and the enterprise, or task system, imports these roles across its boundary with the system consisting of individuals and groupings of them. Roles, and relationships between roles, fall within the boundary of the task system. However, groups and individuals, with their personal relationships, personal power plays and human needs not derived from the task system's primary task, fall outside it: they constitute part of the task system's environment. So, there is one system, a task system, interacting with other systems, individuals and groups, and the groups are always operating in two modes at the same time: work mode and basic assumption mode.

When the individual/group system has the characteristics of a sophisticated group with basic assumption behaviour as a supportive background atmosphere, then it is exporting functional roles to the task system and the latter can perform its primary task. The enterprise, or task system, is thus displaying the dynamics of stability – that is, equilibrium or quasi-equilibrium. When, however, the individual/group system is flooded with basic assumption behaviour it exports that behaviour into the task system so disrupting the performance of the primary task. The dynamics is then that of instability or disintegration. *Miller (1993, p. 19)* argues that this intersystemic view encourages one to focus on interdependence: people supplying roles to enterprises and those enterprises requiring performance in role from people in order to survive. He argues that when individuals and groups are seen as parts of the whole enterprise the focus shifts to a subordinate–superior relationship.

Part of the task system, a subsystem of it, might be set up to contain imported basic assumption behaviour such as fight. Its primary task is then to operate as an organisational defence that allows the rest of the task system to carry out its primary task. Without such organisational defences, the task system as a whole would import fantasies and behaviours that are destructive of the primary task – the dynamics of instability. These undesirable imports are to be diminished by:

- clarity of task;
- clearly defined roles, and authority relationships between them, all related to task;
- appropriate leadership regulation at the boundary of the task system;
- procedures and structures that form social defences against anxiety (*Jacques, 1955; Menzies Lyth, 1975*);
- high levels of individual maturity and autonomy.

Most of these factors seem to me to emphasise design and some joint intention relating to the system as a whole. Furthermore, there is, it seems to me, a strong implication that the dynamics of stability is a prerequisite for a functioning task system, while the dynamics of instability is inimical to that functioning. There is little sense in this formulation of the creative potential of disorder. I am making this point here because the theory to be presented in Chapter 16 takes a different view on these matters.

*Shapiro & Carr (1991)* employ the above model in their interpretation of the role of the consultant. The consultant uses counter-transference feelings to formulate hypotheses about the transferential and projective processes at work in an organisation, and about the impact of basic assumption behaviour on the work of that organisation. They see the function of the consultant as one of feeding back those hypotheses into the life of the organisation and so fostering a collaborative, negotiated understanding and verbalisation of the unconscious, irrational processes at play. It is believed that this process enables the reclaiming of projections and distorted impressions of reality, so restoring to the group its work function. The consultants engage with and understand the complexity of organisational life by adopting an interpretive stance. This stance is seen as the most important element in creating a holding environment and they draw an analogy with a therapeutic setting: 'containment and holding ordinarily refer to symbolic interpretive ways in which the therapist manages the patient's (and his own) feelings' (*Shapiro & Carr, 1991, p. 112*).

Another feature of the holding environment, one that interpretation aims to secure, is the clarity of task, boundary and role. This is seen as containing, for example, sexual and aggressive feelings. Empathic interpretation affirms individuals in their roles and the resulting containment establishes a holding environment. This provides for safe regression, a shift from rationally organised words to the primitive distortions of fantasy images and simple metaphors which can then be articulated and so disarmed. The aim of interpretation is to move people from states of irrational anxiety and fantasy that distort work to the more reality-based taking of roles that support it.

According to Shapiro and Carr, the aim of the consultant's work is to identify whether an organisation is functioning according to its design. This will happen when members of the organisation understand their tasks so that roles within and across parts of the organisation can be legitimately authorised and fully integrated. This, in turn, requires clarification of authorisation from one level to another in the hierarchy and a structure of meetings to promote effective communication. Shapiro and Carr stress the need to develop a culture in which people bring their work-related feelings to legitimate forums where they can be made available for examination in relation to the work rather than discharged in informal subgroups. What they mean by an interpretative stance, then, is a collaborative verbalisation of unconscious processes leading to withdrawal of projections that might be adversely affecting task performance. The objection to informal subgroups seems to be based on the belief that, since they are based purely on personal relationships rather than task, they are fertile ground for projections and basic assumption behaviour. Note how this model of organisational functioning leads to a focus on the legitimate relationships in an organisation.

## 10.5   LEADERS AND GROUPS

In both strategic choice and mainstream learning organisation theory, leaders are assumed to be perfectly healthy, balanced people, who set the direction of the organisation for others to follow. However, as soon as it is reorganised that basic assumption groups can very quickly emerge from work groups, the possibility arises that leaders can also be the creations of the group. It is quite possible that leaders are vainly trying to act out the fantasies that those in the management team are projecting. Leaders affect what groups do, but groups also affect what leaders do through processes of unconscious projection.

### Leadership

*Bales (1970)* identified the emergence of two kinds of leaders in small task-oriented groups: the task leader who gives suggestions, shows disagreement and presses the group to focus on task completion; and the social–emotional leader who asks for suggestions, shows solidarity, and soothes tempers by encouraging tension release. (The leadership theories discussed in Chapter 6 also focused on this dilemma of the task and the people.) These leadership roles are mutually supportive in that each helps the group solve different problems, provided that the role occupants can work together. Sometimes one person can combine both roles – the 'great man' leader (*Borgatta, Couch & Bales, 1954*). When specialist leaders of this kind do not emerge or cannot work together, then members begin to deal with their frustration in unconscious ways that lead to the emergence of scapegoat roles, enemy roles, messiah roles and so on. *Bion (1961)* distinguishes between different types of leader in the basic assumption group: the fight leader, the flight leader, the dependency leader, and the leader who symbolises some unrealistic utopian, messianic, or oceanic hope. Bion points to the precarious position these leaders occupy. The important point here is that the leader is sucked into that position by the group and is controlled by the group, not the other way around as we usually believe.

An important distinction is that between the leader of a work group and a basic assumption leader. An effective leader is one who maintains a clear focus on and definition of the primary task. That task determines the requirements of the leader, who must continually struggle to synthesise, participate and observe. The effective leader operates on the boundary of the group, avoiding both emotional immersion and extreme detachment. Leaders are there to regulate transactions between their groups and other groups. Both immersion and distance make this impossible. When a group is dominated by basic assumption behaviour it sucks into the leadership position one who is completely immersed in the emotional atmosphere, the basic assumption behaviour of the group. This leader is subjected to conflicting and fundamentally impossible roles – to provide unlimited nurturance, to fight and subdue imaginary enemies, to rescue the group from death and dissolution, to fulfil utopian or messianic hopes.

One of the most intriguing aspects of relatively unstructured and ego-involving small groups is the evolution of a constellation of informal roles that serve important social and psychological functions for the group. Most small-group research has addressed itself to groups that do not have formal statuses and ascribed social positions. The roles that emerge are usually described as 'behaviour patterns,' 'individual roles,' or 'interpersonal styles.' Under relatively unstructured conditions, psychological factors, conscious and unconscious, become increasingly important as determinants of role structure . . . Explicit and formal social prescriptions are replaced by fantasy conceptions of norms and sanctions. At the same time, it is assumed that such roles are not simply expressive of idiosyncratic needs but perform necessary and recurrent functions for the social system – such functions as impulse expression, group maintenance, tension release. (*Gibbard, Hartman & Mann, 1974, p. 179*)

The kinds of roles that have been distinguished are those of the aggressor, the seducer who tries to seduce people into exposing their feelings and positions, the scapegoat, the hero, the resistors, the anxious participators, the distressed females, the respected enactors, the sexual idols, the outsiders, the prophets (*Dunphy, 1968*). These informal roles develop in order to contain and deal with internal conflict, the tension of fusion and individuation. One of the key roles is that of leader.

Managers' choices and actions may have more to do with unconscious processes than any rational consideration. The example given in *Box 10.2*, based on actual events, demonstrates what is meant.

### BOX 10.2

## Choosing a training programme

David, the manager of a particular department, met with Judy, the personnel director, to talk about a possible training programme for his department. The idea had arisen casually before that in a conversation between David and Judy. David wanted to mount a team development weekend similar to one that he and his senior management colleagues had been on. During that weekend they had operated competitively in teams to win points in each of a series of events such as rock climbing, finding their way back to base over rough terrain and so on. He and his colleagues had enjoyed the event and felt that it had increased the team spirit among them.

Judy was supportive and so they involved David's secretary and the most senior supervisor in his department, Chris. As soon as he became involved, Chris suggested that they use a firm set up by his friends to run team training events on a yacht – crewing together develops team spirit. David opposed the idea on the grounds that many of the staff in the department were women who would not want to spend the weekend on a yacht. Privately he told Judy that Chris was an accomplished yachtsman and was pressing his idea simply so that he could win, something not all that good for the rest of the department.

In the end the yacht idea was dropped for what sounded like fairly rational reasons. However, frank discussions with David revealed completely different reasons. David was a sensitive, rather individualistic person who felt somewhat guilty about not being an enthusiastic member of the team who worked for him. Chris, on the other hand, was a boisterous, outgoing, macho man who was quite clearly a full member of the team. David felt threatened by Chris and his real reason for ensuring that the yacht weekend idea was quashed had to do with fears, probably about his own sexual prowess, in relation to Chris. In this way conscious and unconscious processes covered over with rational-sounding reasons often determine what happens. ■

### Neurotic forms of leadership

Strategic choice and mainstream learning organisations theory focus on what leadership means when it is functioning well, however, leaders often do not function all that well and quite often they are definitely dysfunctional. Such dysfunctional leadership has not attracted all that much attention in most of the management literature, but it occurs frequently and it is therefore a matter of importance to understand something about it. Functional leaders assist in the containment of anxiety and thus help to create the possibility of double-loop learning, but dysfunctional, neurotic leaders may well get caught up, and drive others to get caught up, in neurotic defences that will block such learning.

*Kets de Vries (1989)* explains the nature of neurotic leadership in the following way. Everyone behaves in a manner that is affected by what one might think of as an inner theatre. That theatre consists of a number of representations of people and situations, often formed early in childhood, and those that have come to play the most important roles are core conflictual relationships. It is as if people spend much of their lives re-enacting conflicts that they could not understand in childhood, partly because they are familiar to them, and partly, perhaps, because they are always seeking to understand them. What they do, then, is project this inner play with conflictual situations out onto the real world they have to deal with. Leaders do this just as others do, the difference being that they project their inner conflicts onto a much larger real-world stage that includes their followers. A leader projects internal private dialogues into external public ones and these dialogues are about core conflictual themes from childhood. The particular neurotic style a leader practises will be determined by the nature of these core conflicts.

Followers also project their inner plays onto the leader and these leader/follower projections keep leaders and followers engaged with each other in a particular manner. Followers project their dependency needs into leaders and displace their own ideals, wishes and desires into them too.

The inner theatre in which leaders and followers join each other contains scenarios which are the basis of imagined, desired and feared relationships between them. There are typical scenarios that are found over and over again and they constitute typical dispositions, typical ways of defending against, repressing, denying and idealising particular leader/follower relationships. Everyone uses such devices and everyone has a number of prominent dispositions that constitute that person's neurotic style. This is quite normal and it becomes a problem only when people massively, compulsively and habitually use a rather small number of defences. This blocks their ability to relate to reality effectively and it is then that they might be labelled 'neurotic'.

*Kets de Vries (1989)* distinguishes between a number of such dispositions or neurotic styles as follows. Every leader will display a combination of some of these styles and it becomes a problem only when a rather small number of these come to dominate the behaviour of the leader and the followers.

1   The **aggressive** disposition tends to characterise many who become leaders and rather fewer who are followers – aggression is often acceptable in leaders but creates problems for followers. Tough chief executives who are socially forceful and intimidating, energetic, competitive and power oriented fall into this category. People are not important to them and they want to dominate. They tend to be impulsive and to believe that the world is a jungle. They expect people to be hostile to them and they become aggressive in advance to counteract such expected hostility. Of course their behaviour may well provoke the hostility they expect. Such leaders probably experienced parental rejection or hostility.

2   The **paranoid** disposition is found frequently amongst leaders and less amongst followers. Such people are always looking for hidden motives and are suspicious of others. They are hypervigilant, keep scanning the environment and take

unnecessary precautions. They deny personal weakness and do not readily accept blame. They tend to be restricted and cold in relationships with little humour. They are fond of mechanistic devices to measure performance and keep track of people. Such people may have had intrusive parents and may feel uncertain of themselves.

3   The **histrionic** disposition is characterised by a need to attract the attention of others at all costs. Such people are alert to the desires of others, they are sociable and seductive with their sense of self-worth heavily dependent on the opinion of others. They love activity and excitement and tend to overreact to minor incidents, often throwing tantrums. Such people may have had difficulty attracting the attention of parents.

4   The **detached** disposition is displayed when people find it difficult to form close relationships. They tend to be cold and aloof and this may be a response to parental devaluation.

5   The **controlling** disposition is high in leaders and low in followers and it is displayed by people who want to control everything in their lives. They have an excessive desire for order and control. This is a way of managing hostile feelings that may have arisen from the behaviour of controlling parents. The resultant hostility may emerge as tyrannical ways of behaving or its opposite of submission.

6   The **passive–aggressive** disposition tends to be found more in followers than in leaders. Such people are highly dependent but tend to attack those they depend upon. They resist demands for performance, they are defiant, provocative and negative, complaining all the time and demanding much from their leaders. They tend to blame others all the time, they are ambivalent and pessimistic. This difficulty might arise because such people find it difficult to assess what is expected of them. They are likely to have parents who presented them with conflicting messages.

7   Other dispositions are the **narcissistic** one when people see themselves as exceptional and special; the **dependent** disposition in which people are excessively dependent upon others; and the **masochistic** disposition.

It is not just the style of the leader or the style of the followers on their own that determines how their joint behaviour unfolds. It is how the styles engage each other that will create the environment within which they have to work. So, an aggressive, controlling leader interacting with dependent, masochistic followers will produce a rather different context and pattern of behaviour compared with such a leader interacting with, say, passive–aggressive followers. These patterns of interaction will have a powerful impact on how effectively an organisation learns. Such neurotically based interactions, therefore, have to be understood as processes of extraordinary management.

## 10.6   HOW OPEN SYSTEMS/PSYCHOANALYTIC PERSPECTIVES DEAL WITH FOUR KEY QUESTIONS AND FOCUS ATTENTION

This chapter now turns to how open systems/psychoanalytic perspectives answer the four questions posed at the end of Chapter 1. These were:

1   How does the theory view the nature of interaction?
2   What view does it take of human nature?

3   What methodology does it employ?
4   How does it deal with paradox?

You can compare how the theories surveyed in this chapter answer the questions with the kind of answers found in strategic choice theory (section 2.2 and *Figures 2.5* and *2.6*, and section 7.3). You can also make comparisons with learning organisation theory (section 8.5 and *Figure 8.11*, and section 9.7). Consider now how open systems/psychoanalytic perspectives deal with the questions.

## The nature of interaction

Interaction within and between organisations is understood in systems terms as with strategic choice and learning organisation theory. While cybernetics analyses a system in terms of self-regulating negative feedback loops and systems dynamics takes account of amplifying positive feedback loops, open systems theory focuses attention on regulatory functions at the system's boundary. Essentially, these functions regulate the flows of imports into, and exports out of, the system so that the system adapts to its environment. The dynamics, the way the system moves, is therefore the same as for cybernetics, that is a tendency to move towards stable equilibrium when it is succeeding.

Open systems theory pays more attention to the micro level than cybernetics and systems dynamics do. In other words, it pays attention to the subsystems of which the whole is composed. This is especially so when it is combined with psychoanalytic perspectives because they are very much concerned with the individuals and the groups that make up an organisation. The disorderly dynamics generated by individuals relating to each other in groups then becomes very important as an obstacle to the successful movement towards adaptive equilibrium. Those writing in the Tavistock tradition distinguish between the task/role system and the system of individuals/groups. The task/role system is a subsystem of the organisation that is open to the other subsystem consisting of individuals and groups, and also open to the environment consisting of other organisations. When the imports from the individuals/groups subsystem are adequately regulated then the task/role subsystem can make rational choices about adapting to the environment of other organisations.

So, this is a theory that pays considerable attention to both macro and micro levels and it envisages both orderly and disorderly dynamics. The former is equated with successful adaptation to the environment and the latter as an obstacle to this process. The orderly operation of the task/role system is understood in much the same way as strategic choice or learning organisation theory. However, the attention to micro detail brings in very important processes that can disrupt the rational processes.

## The nature of human beings

The theory reviewed in this chapter takes a very different view of human nature to the mainly cognitivist and humanistic perspectives on which strategic choice and learning organisation theories are built. The main difference is the emphasis it places on unconscious processes, the effects of anxiety, and the ever present possibility of defensive and aggressive behaviour. Human ability to behave rationally and altruistically is seen as highly problematic and the capacity for learning as very fragile. Attention is focused on power and dysfunctional behaviour in a way that the use of cognitivist and humanistic assumptions in the other theories largely ignores.

However, there are also significant similarities. First, the notion of representation is as central in psychoanalysis as in cognitivism. In other words, in both of these theories it is assumed that individuals somehow form inner mental representations of outer reality and then act on the basis of those representations. However, the nature of the representations and the processes through which they are formed are very different. Consider what representation means in most psychoanalytic theories:

- In classic, Freudian drive theory, a representation is a conscious or unconscious idea that represents an instinct and as such it is the expression of some basic, inherited body function. So, here there is no notion of a more or less accurate picture of a pre-given external world. Instead, there is a unique expression of general bodily functions internal to the individual body, developed from the interaction of inherited instincts and actual experience. In early object relations theory (*Klein, 1975*) the notion of representation is developed in a different way. Representations are of part objects and objects encountered in relationships. Object here is mainly a person or some part of a person and the nature of the representation is highly complex. It is not at all a more or less accurate picture of an external reality but rather an internal construct developed through experience on the basis of inherent, inherited phantasies common to all humans. The earliest object is that of the mother's breast and what is being represented is not so much the object itself as the experience and phantasied relationship with the object. Later object relations theorists (Bion, Winnicott, Fairbairn) placed much more emphasis on the relationships as did attachment theorists (Bowlby, Balint), self psychologists (Kohut) and relational psychologists (Sullivan, Stern), for all of whom representations are primarily of relationships with other human beings.

- As with cognitivism, representations are made up of symbols that form 'internal' templates (drive derivatives, forbidden wishes, objects, relationships) which are the basis upon which a human being knows and acts. 'Internal' here refers not to the brain but to a mental apparatus or process. This is described in terms of mental components or agents – the ego, the id and the superego, various object and self-object representations, relational interactions that have been generalised. The question of where such an apparatus might be located, or where the phantasies and other psychological processes might actually be, is never addressed.

- As with cognitivism, representations are built up through a process of symbol processing but there is no suggestion that this is like a computer. Indeed, the process through which the representations are constructed becomes highly complex. Drive theory emphasises processes of defence and suppression. Object relations theory presents highly complex mental processes of splitting, projecting, introjecting, identifying, idealising, denigrating, making reparation, and so on. Attachment theorists, self and relational psychologists talk about processes of evocation, resonance, mirroring, attunement and empathy. All of these processes build up representations of objects and relationships.

- As with cognitivism, representing is a process of recovering or reconstructing templates from a memory bank but these now take different forms. They could be drive-driven wishes that are permissible in terms of external reality or of suppressed wishes expressive of the pleasure principle. Or, they could be recoveries of past object relationships. Representing as a process of comparing new stimuli with past representations of external, environmental features receives little emphasis. Instead the representations are used to interpret reality and may well distort it in various transferential and projective processes.

The above usage of 'representation' clearly carries with it substantial implications. It postulates that the individual human mind is formed by the clash of inherited drives and social constraints, out of which there emerges a mental apparatus that mediates the clash. Later developments in psychoanalytic theory increasingly see humans occupying a world formed by relationships with other human beings with representations of these relationships emerging from them and coming in turn to govern them. There is a separate entity that does this representing, namely a mind or psyche. These separate entities cannot easily share the same representations because each uniquely constructs its own. However, psychic processes are postulated that allow some degree of sharing of mental contents or states. These processes include projective identification, resonance, mirroring, empathy, attunement and, of course, talking. The world into which the human acts is primarily created rather than found. This, of course, is the reverse of the cognitivist implication.

There is a decentring of the individual in an inner sense in that the individual is not clearly in control of his or her mind, but, rather, is buffeted about by the id. However, in any external sense there is no significant decentring of the individual. It is true that the social prohibition is part of the process of structuring the psyche, particularly in the form of the superego, but groups arise when members identify with the same leader. There is no sense of individuals and groups co-creating each other. The social plays a part only in terms of the reality principle. This curbs the limitless drive for pleasure on the part of the individual, a drive which has to be mediated first by an ego and then by a superego. The process of mental structuring is essentially the feat of the individual infant as it copes with unconscious phantasy, proceeding from primitive dependency to autonomy. This is very much within the dominant Western paradigm of the autonomous individual.

To summarise, in both cognitivism and psychoanalysis, the individual is prior and primary to the group. In both theories individuals build representations of reality. However, they do so in very different ways and build very different kinds of representations. In doing so, they present very different views on human nature and the ability of an individual to control his or her own mental processes. The impact of unconscious group processes on the individual's ability to think and act rationally receives a great deal of attention in this theory. The individual is primary in the sense that he or she is born with inherited drives and phantasies that are constrained by social forces. The individual is not primary if one takes the view that an individual mind is socially constructed within the constraints provided by biological inheritance. If one takes the latter view then a different theory of organisations is arrived at. I will be discussing this possibility in Chapters 15 and 16.

## Methodology

In strategic choice and learning organisation theory the researcher, consultant and manager are assumed to be able to stand outside the organisational system and take the position of the objective observer. The perspectives in this chapter take a similar methodological stance but with an important difference. The consultant, researcher and manager are assumed to stand at the boundary of the organisational system. In this position one is not so immersed in the organisational culture that one loses a rational, objective perspective. However, one is immersed enough to experience how being in that culture feels. These feelings are part of the information that can be used to understand the organisation.

## Paradox

While strategic choice and learning organisation theory do not recognise paradox, it is central to a psychoanalytic perspective. The struggle between ego, id and superego is never resolved, only continually rearranged. The capacity to think and learn requires an individual to take the depressive position where it is possible to hold ambiguity and paradox in the mind. Creativity requires the individual mind to occupy the transitional space. This is essentially paradoxical since it is both fantasy and reality at the same time.

## Focusing attention

The theories in this chapter lead to an important shift in focus of attention. This is done by emphasising how unconscious processes of defending against the anxiety of work take the form of many defensive behaviours that block rational thinking and the possibility of learning. As in Chapters 7 and 9 I will now briefly indicate the way attention is focused by psychoanalytic perspectives by posing the same questions as I did in those chapters. Again, the answers are very simplistic and given more in the spirit of encouraging you to give your own answers.

- How do new organisations come into being? I think the answer is the same as that which strategic choice and learning organisation theory suggest. A creative individual develops an idea, makes choices and forms intentions to develop a new business, and then gathers other enthusiasts together to get it going. Their reasons for doing this and the emotional difficulties they will find as they work together would be of great interest from a psychoanalytic perspective, but probably receive little attention if one took the strategic choice and learning organisation perspectives.
- Why do they cease to exist? Because the organisation fails to learn while others do, particularly because people get sucked into unconscious processes to defend against anxiety.
- How do they come to merge with others or split apart? Here the answers could be very complicated and would probably be cast in terms of the unconscious needs of leaders to play out some drama in their inner theatres.
- Why do most organisations last for only a rather short time and why do a few

survive for long periods? The answer here would probably have something to do with the great difficulties individuals experience in group life and also with the possibly neurotic behaviour of leaders.

- Why is one organisation similar to others and different from yet others? Organisations will be similar to each other in that all groups of people are prone to basic assumption and defensive behaviour. They will differ because some will have better holding environments than others and less neurotic leadership than others. They will also differ as they adapt to different environments.
- How do some organisations develop new activities? They do so through individuals who are capable of the creative processes of play and learning.
- Why do other organisations simply carry on with the same activities? Because their members are caught in defensive behaviours of dependency, fight, flight and other basic assumption behaviour.
- Why do people become anxious, bored or frustrated? Because the holding environment is not good enough.
- What is it that excites and fulfils them? Creative learning and the move towards greater individual autonomy.
- What impact do these and other emotions have on the functioning of groups and organisations? It depends upon how intense they are and whether they are responses to anxiety that cannot be held. When the holding environment is good enough people can think and learn, but when it is not basic assumption behaviour blocks them.

## Making sense of experience

The perspectives in this chapter are particularly useful when it comes to making sense of experiences that feel stressful or bizarre. It might be possible to understand them by paying attention to the effects of anxiety on people's behaviour and how they are defending against it. It also offers ways of understanding the nature and impact of dysfunctional leadership and inappropriate applications of power. It is important to bear in mind that the processes I have been describing affect how an organisation evolves. They are as important as rational choice in determining what happens to an organisation.

## 10.7    SUMMARY

This chapter has reviewed open systems theory and psychoanalytic perspectives pointing to how they focus attention on aspects of life that do not feature in strategic choice and learning organisation theory.

The open systems/psychoanalytic approach opens up insights like these:

- Charismatic leaders and the strong cultures of dependence they provoke in followers may well be extremely unhealthy for organisations. Researchers (e.g. *Peters & Waterman, 1982*) may therefore note the presence of charismatic leaders and superficially conclude that this is the reason for success, when it might well be a neurotic phenomenon that is about to undermine the company.

- A cohesive team of managers may not be a healthy phenomenon at all. It may be an unhealthy and unproductive reflection of the fantasy of basic assumption groups acting out dependence or oneness assumptions. Again researchers not considering an organisation from a psychoanalytic point of view may well conclude that such neurotic cohesion is a reason for success.
- The idea of the group or the management team may itself be a defence mechanism. So, faced by high levels of strategic uncertainty and ambiguity, managers may retreat into the 'mother figure' of the team for comfort and in so doing fail to deal with the strategic issues.
- Groups clearly do not have to have a purpose or even a task to function very tightly as a group, even if it is a misguided one. Again, signs of close teams should provoke suspicion, not praise.
- Groups or teams are a two-edged sword. People need them to establish their identity. They need them to operate effectively. But they can also deskill people.
- The desire for cohesion may well be a neurotic phenomenon.
- Plans and rigid structures and rules may all be defences against anxiety instead of the rational way of proceeding usually considered.
- One aspect of culture is the emotional atmosphere, the basic assumption, that a group of people create as they interact.

## FURTHER READING

Hirschorn (1990) provides an important exposition of the role of the informal organisation as a defence against anxiety. I would also recommend Shapiro & Carr (1991) and Kets de Vries (1989), as well as Miller (1993) and Oberholzer & Roberts (1995). They all give deeper insight into the psychodynamics of organisations. Winnicott (1971) is also well worth reading.

## REFERENCES

Bales, R. F. (1970), *Personality and Interpersonal Behaviour*, New York: Holt.

Bion, W. R. (1961), *Experiences in Groups and Other Papers*, London: Tavistock.

Borgatta, E.F., Couch, A. S. & Bales, R. F. (1954), Some findings relevant to the great man theory of leadership, *American Sociology Review*, vol. 19, pp. 755–9.

Buzzell, R. D. (1984), Citibank: marketing to multinational customers, in Buzzell, R. D. & Quelch, J. A. (Eds.) (1988), *Multinational Marketing Management*, Reading, MA: Addison-Wesley.

De Board, R. (1978), *The Psychoanalysis of Organizations*, London: Tavistock.

Dunphy, D. C. (1968), Phases, roles and myths in self analytic groups, *Journal of Applied Behavioural Science*, vol. 4, pp. 195–226.

Gibbard, G. S., Hartman, J. J. & Mann, R. D. (Eds.) (1974), *Analysis of Groups*, San Francisco: Jossey-Bass.

Gordon, R. (1993), *Bridges: Metaphors for Psychic Processes*, London: Karnac Books.

Gustafson, J. P. & Cooper, L. (1978), Toward the study of society in microcosm: critical problems of group relations conferences, *Human Relations*, vol. 31, pp. 843–62.

Hirschorn, L. (1990), *The Workplace Within: Psychodynamics of Organizational Life*, Cambridge, MA: MIT Press.

Jacques, E. (1955), Social systems as a defence against persecutory and defensive anxiety, in Klein, M., Heinmann, P. & Money-Kyrle, P. (Eds.) (1955), *New Directions in Psychoanalysis*, London: Tavistock. (Also published in Gibbard, G. S., Hartman, J. J. & Mann, R. D. (1974), *Analysis of Groups*, San Francisco: Jossey-Bass.)

Kast, P. & Rosenzweig, F. (1970), *Management and Organization*, New York: McGraw-Hill.

Kets de Vries, M. F. (1989), *Prisoners of Leadership*, New York: John Wiley.

Klein, M. (1975), *The Writings of Melanie Klein*, London: Hogarth Press.

Lawrence, P. R. & Lorsch, J. W. (1967), *Organization and Environment*, Cambridge, MA: Harvard University Press.

Menzies Lyth, I. (1975), A case study in the functioning of social systems as a defence against anxiety, in Coleman, A & Bexton, W. H. (Eds.) (1975), *Group Relations Reader*, Sausalito, CA: GREX.

Miller, E. J. (1977), Organisational development and industrial democracy: a current case-study, in C. Cooper (Ed.), (1977), *Organisational development in the UK and USA: A joint evaluation*, London: Macmillan, pp. 31–63.

Miller, E. H. (1983), *Work and Creativity*, Occasional Papers, London: Tavistock.

Miller, E. H. (1993), *From Dependency to Autonomy: Studies in Organization and Change*, London: Free Association Books.

Miller, E. J. & Rice, A. K. (1967), *Systems of Organization: The Control of Task and Sentient Boundaries*, London: Tavistock.

Miller, E. J. (1989), *The Leicester Conference*, Occasional Papers, London: Tavistock Publications.

Oberholzer, A. & Roberts, V. Z. (1995), *The Unconscious at Work: Individual and Organizational Stress in the Human Services*, London: Routledge.

Peters, T. J. & Waterman, R. H. (1982), *In Search of Excellence*, New York: Harper & Row.

Shapiro, E. R. & Carr, Wesley A. (1991), *Lost in Familiar Places*, New Haven, CT: Yale University Press.

Smith, P. B. (1969), *Improving Skills in Working with People*: The T Group, London: HMSO.

Trist, E. L. and Bamforth, K. W. (1951), Some social and psychological consequences of the long wall method of coal getting, *Human Relations*, vol 5, pp. 6–24.

Turquet, P. (1974), Leadership: the individual and the group, in Gibbard, G. S., Hartman, J. J. & Mann, R. D. (Eds.), (1974), *Analysis of Groups*, San Francisco: Jossey-Bass.

Winnicott, D. W. (1971), *Playing and Reality*, London: Tavistock. Reprinted in 1993 by Routledge.

# Case studies

**ENIGMA CHEMICALS**

Enigma Chemicals is a large company producing a limited range of chemical products from three sites in the UK, mostly for the domestic market, although it does export about 20 per cent of its output. The chemicals that Enigma produces are important inputs into the production processes of a number of other major companies. Although the Enigma products are important to its customers' production processes, they do not constitute a major cost component in the final products of those customers. Furthermore, through control over a vital raw material and through various patent arrangements, Enigma occupies an almost monopoly position in the UK and has done so for many years.

Another fact about Enigma's products is also important: they are of a hazardous, environmentally threatening nature and this makes Enigma an ideal target for environmental pressure groups. The company is frequently attacked by the media, despite the fact that it has, on the whole, a rather good safety record – its policies and monitoring systems certainly place tremendous importance on these matters. However, over the past few years there have been two serious incidents of a rather dramatic nature: in one of these incidents pollutants were accidentally released into the atmosphere causing health problems for people living in the vicinity of the plant concerned; and in another serious incident pollutants leaked into a river, killing fish, birds and other wildlife over an area of many miles. Periodically, there were fires in the manufacturing plants and some former employees were suing the company on the grounds that the manufacturing process had damaged their health. These incidents had created a public image that Enigma was experiencing great difficulty in changing.

The patents that afforded Enigma a near monopoly position were due to expire in ten years' time, after which Enigma could expect fierce competition to cause a dramatic decline in its sales. Over the past few years, Enigma's managers and employees had experienced a foretaste of what this might be like: the long recession of the early 1990s had caused a significant decline in sales and for the first time in its 30-year history Enigma had been forced to reduce its workforce. Although the reduction in the numbers of both managers and employees had been accomplished entirely through early retirement and voluntary redundancy, it had unsettled people at Enigma, the great majority of whom had come to believe that they had 'jobs for life'.

As part of the strategy for coping with the new commercial realities, the management reporting structure of Enigma had been reorganised. Before the reorganisation, there had been a monolithic functional structure: main Board Directors were responsible for personnel, R&D, health and safety, finance, engineering and production. The production function, by far the largest employer, was subdivided according to geographic sites, each of which was run by a General Manager to whom a number of works managers reported. These works managers were responsible for a number of plant managers; in turn responsible for supervisors, to whom foremen reported. After the reorganisation, Enigma consisted of five divisions, each responsible for its own profitability and having a wide range of its own functional activities such as personnel and engineering. The corporate level still had functional responsibilities, but in theory at least, much of the responsibility and the authority had been devolved to the divisions.

At the time of the reorganisation, the Board had also reviewed its strategic planning process and decided to devolve much of the responsibility for this to the divisions. Whereas the central planning function had in the past prepared five- and ten-year plans with little involvement of managers at the site level, it was now to act more as an adviser to divisional management which was charged with preparing the five- and ten-year plans for the approval of the main Board. In future, the Chief Executive would lay down a general framework to establish future direction and he would articulate some important strategic thrusts, but then it would be up to divisional managers to develop the strategy.

The Chief Executive, Harry Bream, had spent his entire career at Enigma and consequently knew it well. He could recall previous reorganisations and previous attempts to change strategic direction, none of which had actually done a great deal to change the way people at Enigma worked. He knew from experience, therefore, that simply reorganising and pushing strategic responsibility further down the hierarchy would not necessarily lead to the strategic actions that a more hostile world and the eventual running out of the patents would create. He therefore contracted with a team of consultants to advise how the inevitable obstacles to implementation might be removed. The consultants conducted a series of interviews with a sample of managers and staff at all levels in order to identify what the issues were and what sort of company Enigma was. The notes that follow on three of these interviews turned out to be rather typical of all of those conducted with top management and the views of supervisory and middle management are indicated in a summary of interview notes prepared by one of the consultants, which is given below after the interview notes. The consultants now faced the task of formulating an approach to assisting their client.

## Notes on an interview with Adrian Sinclair, Director of Division X

Adrian Sinclair had been with Enigma since he left university with an engineering degree some 20 years ago. In his interview with the consultant he started by describing how the organisation had changed since he joined it. Twenty years ago it had been an extremely bureaucratic, status-conscious organisation. Thus, there had been a sharp divide between the shop-floor workers on the one hand, and the staff on the other. Staff in turn were divided into professional and scientific streams; people entered the company either as a technician or as an administrator and tended to remain in the stream they had joined, moving regularly up the strictly graded structure. Relationships between people at different levels were very formal – you always addressed a more senior person as 'Mr', and you always communicated in strict hierarchical order. No one ever went around their boss to a higher level.

The system had changed when the distinction between the professional and the scientific grades was abolished. All new entrants now came into a unified stream and then progressed up the grades according to experience. As they progressed, they encountered two important break-points in the pay grading structure. At the first of these points, those promoted were given significantly better terms and conditions. So, when entrants joined from university, they had terms and conditions set out in a staff handbook with a brown cover and at the first important break-point, the ranks of middle management, they acquired the terms and conditions set out in a green staff handbook. Then, when a person reached senior management status, the terms and conditions changed once more and this time they were set out in a blue staff handbook. Managers therefore came to be classified into clear-cut groups known as 'Greens' and 'Blues'. Everyone knew to which group a manager belonged and every year there were separate conferences for 'Greens' and 'Blues'.

One thing had not changed, however, and that was the open-interview procedure for promotions up the grade structure. Competent people could expect promotion as a matter of course. All openings were publicly advertised throughout the company and applications were invited from anyone with the right qualifications. Those selected had to attend a Promotions Committee consisting of three people, two of whom were outside the department in which the promotion was to be made. In this way, said Adrian, 'We can be seen to be fair and it prevents people from promoting their blue-eyed boys'. With this system, everyone got a fair chance and the company benefited when new talent was unearthed.

Adrian outlined how it was everyone's ambition to reach 'Blue' status and how he had thought of the 'Blues' as a kind of 'club' or 'secret society' until he had joined it. Once one reached the 'Blue' level, one was entitled to the BMW grade of car, a secretary, personally selected office furniture, private medical assurance and other benefits.

Adrian reiterated how the company had changed, how people had become much more flexible and less status conscious than they were, but he did say that there were 'many images of old ways of behaving still lurking about', and it was these that he saw as the major obstacles to achieving the low-cost regimes and the entrepreneurial behaviour that were called for in the ten-year corporate plan.

According to Adrian, one of the principal images of the past, which were still 'lurking about', related to the manner in which managers at Enigma typically handled poor performance. There was a system in which people's performance was appraised each year. Although the system allowed people to be placed into one of five performance categories, ranging from the 'completely unsatisfactory' to the 'excellent', in fact managers tended to put almost everyone into the average performance category. Most people consequently got the average level of bonus and incentive pay. It was very difficult to fire non-performers because of agreements with powerful unions and because of the complex procedures that had to be followed before anyone could be fired. But quite apart from this, managers did not like to apply sanctions to anyone anyway. There was therefore a widespread perception that managers avoided tough decisions and personal confrontation. 'We do not like to go home at night feeling that we have been unpleasant to people', is how Adrian put it. He also felt that if managers lower down were suddenly given the right to appoint and fire staff without going through all the laborious procedures, they would simply not take up that responsibility.

Adrian did point out, however, that if he was determined to do something, then the bureaucratic systems simply did not stop him. He got around the bureaucracy through his informal contacts. He felt that those who complained that they could not manage because of bureaucratic systems imposed on them by the corporate centre, were simply using this as an excuse for not managing. When he had a staff member who did not perform he usually managed to find someone inexperienced enough to take that person, or he privately convinced the non-performer to go, or he just found the non-performers something else to do, usually a promotion that got them out of the way. He felt that managers at Enigma did not sack people because they had not got the stomach for it. They all felt that they had a job for life and if that was changed in one case, who knew where it might stop. Anyway, it was a bad idea to do anything that would provoke a strike because that would simply attract media attention and the old environmental scares would simply be revived.

## Notes on an interview with Adam Frusquin, Director of Division Y

Adam had joined the company 25 years ago after completing his doctorate in chemistry. He described how for years people at Enigma had seen their company as a good employer operating in a stable industry, giving people jobs for life. He described the family atmosphere that prevailed and gave examples of the caring attitude the company adopted to its people. He also described Enigma as a not particularly demanding employer.

In his view this was a company in which, even nowadays, 'people tended to know their place' in a clearly structured hierarchy. It was also a company in which everything was done by negotiation rather than instruction. The result was a relatively comfortable, conflict-free and content organisation. However, Adam was convinced that these attitudes would have to change and he talked about the need 'to be seen to be more commercially aggressive'. Instead of operating strictly according to hierarchical position and following well-established negotiating procedures, Adam believed that people at all levels would have to be empowered to take their own decisions. But he recognised that many managers would find this threatening and would not want the responsibility.

### Notes of an interview with Anita Cummings, Director of Human Relations

Anita was a highly unusual manager at Enigma: first, she was the only woman in a senior position; and second, she had been at Enigma for only a year. Harry Bream had brought Anita on to the Board as his way of signalling that he wanted change in behaviour throughout the organisation and that personnel practices and systems were going to change to bring this about. He 'was tired of having everything he tried to do disappearing into a fog'. Anita's arrival had caused quite a stir because she had previously been the Personnel Director of AMR, a ruthless conglomerate, and in that position she had acquired a reputation for being tough with non-performing managers.

In the interview with the consultant, Anita confessed that she was still surprised at the lack of focus on costs and financial performance generally. She found the style of management to be highly bureaucratic, proceduralised and very slow moving. As far as she was concerned, people did not seem to recognise any pressures for change, but channelled much of their energies into what she called 'sibling rivalry'. She explained how people tended to form fairly cohesive teams in the department or immediate project group they worked in, but built up animosities against other groups and did their best not to cooperate with them. She spoke with some amusement about the classification of managers into the 'Greens' and the 'Blues'. As far as she was concerned these were secretive 'men's clubs' that were not open to her and were, anyway, irrelevant as far as the business was concerned. She said that people at Enigma 'react to newcomers with fear'. She said that managers felt that 'they had to be seen to be members of the "Blue" club'.

She still found it surprising that senior managers kept starting new initiatives that somehow always required a committee, a task force or a workshop and often the assistance of consultants. There was so much activity examining everything and suggesting changes in everything and yet so little change itself.

She described the culture of the organisation as a comfortable family atmosphere in which people saw their roles in terms of the pay grade they had reached.

### Summary notes on interviews with middle managers

In almost all the interviews managers stated their support for the company which they viewed as a good employer that provided them with job security. However, they were also critical of more senior managers who, they said, avoided tough decisions. Senior managers tended to communicate with them using memos rather than walking around. Despite all the efforts to promote participation, most middle managers saw it as a sort of front – they believed that decisions were really taken in a rather autocratic way. Middle managers complained about communication with higher levels where they had to rely on the grapevine and they thought this was wrong. They called for more detailed and precise information on the company's objectives and strategies. When the consultant pointed out that they had been sent summary copies of the ten-year plan, some said they could not remember what it said, others said it was in a drawer somewhere, others said it was not detailed and precise enough. They claimed that top managers had no sense of direction and they, at the middle level, needed to be told what this direction was before they could function properly.

As far as the outside world was concerned, few middle managers talked about the prospects facing the company as its monopoly hold on its chief product weakened. But they all mentioned the unreasonable way in which pressure groups and the media pilloried them for what they felt were imaginary environmental dangers.

## CASE STUDY 2    APEX ENGINEERING PLC*

Apex plc is an internationally diversified corporation with a portfolio of activities in the heavy engineering, control systems and information technology markets. The corporation has undergone many transformations during the past 20 years as a result of mergers and acquisitions as well as organic growth. One of the larger subsidiaries, the one in the heavy engineering industry, is called Apex Engineering Ltd and it operates from a number of factory sites in the UK.

In 1988 a new Chief Executive was appointed to run Apex plc and one of his first steps was to announce a rationalisation strategy for Apex Engineering Ltd: this would involve closing three sites and reducing costs by 30 per cent within four years at the remaining three sites. Between 1988 and 1990 those three sites were indeed closed and, in accordance with the cost-cutting strategy, many thousands of people were made redundant at the others.

The recession of the early 1990s made life even more difficult and by mid-1992 it was clear that a further site would have to be closed. Sites at Warrington, Newcastle and Birmingham were therefore vying to secure a position as one of the survivors.

This case is concerned with events at the Warrington site, the principal activity of which was the manufacture of heavy equipment. In 1988 the production process was one of batch manufacture of components and flowline assembly. The site was run by a General Manager and reporting to him there were a number of Directors of support functions (Finance, Engineering and Personnel) and also a Production Director. The General Manager and the Directors together formed an Operations Executive Committee (OEC). A number of Production Managers reported to the Production Director and to each of them, a number of works managers reported. Each works manager had a number of product managers reporting to them and they in turn had supervisors to whom foremen reported.

## The Warrington strategy

In 1988, in response to the Apex Chief Executive's strategy on rationalisation, Warrington's OEC appointed consultants to assist in formulating a strategy for the survival of the Warrington site. About a year later, the strategy agreed upon was that of dividing the operations function at Warrington into smaller, more manageable units, flattening the reporting structure of the manufacturing activity by reducing the levels of management to three, and empowering people at lower levels to make decisions and become accountable for their actions. The new organisational structure was therefore to be one in which a number of workshop managers were to report to the Production

Director. Each workshop was to consist of a number of cells, each with its own cell supervisor, and each manufacturing cell was to be given responsibility for a section of the final product. Each cell would include staff from the support function and they would report to the cell supervisor, retaining only a functional link to the old support function departments, which would become advisory in nature. So, instead of some people manufacturing parts of a component while others assembled them all, components would in future be manufactured and put together into subassemblies before going on to a higher-level assembly operation. In addition, the manufacturing cells were to operate just-in-time (JIT) inventory policies, pulling their supplies from other units as they needed them. And the way accountants, controllers and personnel people would work would, of course, be significantly changed because they would now relate to cell teams.

## The old performance reporting system

These changes in work practices in turn required changes in the way that performance was measured, controlled and rewarded. Under the batch production and flowline assembly system, performance measures were built up from data collected at the level of the individual operator to construct work hour and cost indicators for batches of components. Reporting for monitoring and control purposes was against batch cost standards and the performance measures were therefore cost accounting measures. It was, consequently, the function of the site's Finance Department to set the standards, collect the cost data and report on performance.

In 1988, the key performance measures were:

- batch delivery times to outside customers;
- work hour costs per batch;
- actual hours against standard;
- number of quality defects per batch.

Although these measures were generally considered adequate, it was known that the reporting system was not distributing costs into the right cost categories, but because the interest was only in cost at a higher level of aggregation, the system was not changed.

Throughout the history of the Warrington plant the accounting system measured shop-floor workers' output against standard packages of work and the individual bonus schemes and payments by results systems were tied to this. Both shop-floor operators and managers were thus interested in maintaining 'accurate' data. Although the data were perceived to be 'accurate', the operators' bonuses grew each year until in 1978 they had become unacceptably high. The bonus payment system had then been replaced with one based on components delivered to outside customers and applied to all people in the company. This meant that operators away from the final assembly activity could not relate their performance to the final product and so they had lost the incentive to work against target. They also lacked the motivation to collect accurate data since they could not see what purpose it served. The recorded work hours against the job increased and performance deteriorated.

## The project to develop and apply new performance measures

Operating a strategy of cellular manufacturing and JIT would clearly require a different system for measuring performance and monitoring and controlling it. It would be essential to measure not the batch cost, but the cost of each item that a manufacturing cell produced. Without this information, cell team members would not be able to identify areas for improvement. In the new system information would not simply be reported up the hierarchy for attention by senior managers. Instead, cell team members would monitor their own performance and decide how to keep to target. For this new method of control to work faster information feedback to team members themselves would have to be ensured.

OEC members recognised the pivotal importance of performance measures for the new manufacturing strategy and so appointed a project leader to design a new set of performance measures. The project leader appointed consultants to design appropriate new performance measures and the consultants' proposals for a new set of six measures was accepted.

## The pilot cell

The first step in implementing the new manufacturing strategy was to set up a pilot manufacturing cell. A joint union/management committee was set up to monitor the progress of this pilot over a three-month period, after which the committee was to review the conditions under which the trial would continue. The trial was to include a shift from an external department, measuring individual performance, to the cellular team, measuring themselves and then doing what was needed to improve performance. It was necessary, however, to ensure that links were maintained between the old method of measuring performance and the new one during the trial period. Therefore, an informal management review board, including representatives of all site functions, was set up to monitor the use of the new performance measurements. This board sent a project leader into the pilot cell to work with the cell team to design and implement new performance measures.

Before the three-month trial was up, however, the unions withdrew their support, ostensibly because of a disagreement on overtime in another part of the site, and the informal board refused to approve the specific performance measures that cell members proposed. The operators in the trial cell then withdrew their cooperation with the engineers and controllers who had been allocated to the team from the site's support functions. The operators continued to produce the performance data in the form they had recommended to the informal board, but of course, the data were not used for anything.

Six months later, the objection to the pilot cell was withdrawn and the trial continued. A formal initiative called Performance Management and Reporting (PMR) was established to look at performance reports. A new project leader was appointed and he set up an informal working group, consisting of the support departments. A number of meetings were held but little progress was made because individuals had other priorities. One meeting resulted in a slanging match between Finance and Operations – both complained about each other's ability: Finance accused Operations of not managing its people, while Operations claimed that financial reporting was useless because it was so out of date and not at the level of detail required to understand the problems. The informal group was also criticised for not including operators and cell supervisors. In the end the frustrated project leader defined his own set of performance measures, but these too failed to secure senior management approval.

Shortly after this, senior Apex Engineering Ltd management arranged for a group of experts to present their ideas on performance to the management of all sites in the company. The presenters were highly critical of the Apex approach to performance measurement and those attending reacted with disbelief to the adverse comparisons made with their competitors. When the Apex Finance Director arrived to close the day's event, he presented a message that conflicted with the presenters' emphasis on long-term thinking – the Finance Director stressed the importance of short-term financial results.

By late 1990 the Operations function at Warrington had initiatives of one kind or another running into double figures. Senior managers became concerned at the number of changes that were being examined and the PMR board was called together to try to obtain an understanding of what all these initiatives were and what they were supposed to achieve. A small working group was asked to define a ten-point plan to prioritise the initiatives. When this plan was discussed it was decimated and no action was taken. Instead people said things like, 'This topic is already covered by another initiative', or 'That has already been completed', or 'This topic is something that needs to be looked at in the future'.

After these failed PMR meetings, Operations circulated a list of performance measures defined by an engineering support function leader. In response to this, a number of memos were issued by the Finance Department on cell accounting. Operations did not respond to these memos – they said the memos were not comprehensible – and so Finance let the matter drop.

## Consultant intervention

Then in January 1991, the Managing Director of Apex Engineering Ltd suggested that consultants be appointed to define performance measures at the Warrington site. A joint Consultant–Operations team was set up and, after eight weeks' work, the following set of performance measures, to be taken at the manufacturing cell level, was agreed by the PMR board, with the exception of the cost statement that required the agreement of the Finance Department and this was not forthcoming:

- delivery time compared with plan;
- order–delivery response time;
- capacity utilisation against plan;
- stock levels;
- costs.

These were designed to be simple measures that operators and management could understand at a glance. The measures were to be displayed on charts on the wall for all to see. The data for the charts were to be collected by team members themselves. Problems were to be reported up the hierarchy only on an exceptions basis.

A senior operations manager then requested that an analysis be made of all current performance reports so that some could be dropped when the new measures came into force. The consultant did not want to be involved in a discussion of what were the best measures so the analysis was conducted by another group. This analysis showed that 90 people in Operations and Finance were generating data in 85 reports coming mostly from support departments that had no relevance to the manufacturing cells. The reports were too complex to understand quickly and were the result of years of *ad hoc* accumulation. This confirmed what had been known for years – that there was too much irrelevant information.

## Implementation

The next step was that of setting up a Performance Reporting Board to manage the implementation phase of the now agreed performance measures. The consultant left and a new project manager was appointed. Implementation was seen as the joint responsibility of Operations and Finance, but gradually Finance withdrew and eventually the Finance Director stopped attending meetings of the Performance Reporting Board. The fifth agreed performance measure, the cost statement, was therefore not developed further or applied.

In the meantime, as we have seen, union resistance to cell manufacturing had been overcome and a number of Manufacturing Centres and their constituent cells had been set up. In the absence of site-wide agreed performance measures, each cell was using its own.

**CASE STUDY 3**     # MANAGING CREATIVITY IN THE PHARMACEUTICAL INDUSTRY*

Pharmex Research plc[†] is the research and development arm of Pharmex Products, a highly profitable transnational pharmaceutical organisation. The Pharmex group has grown rapidly in recent years from a middle-sized company to one of the largest in the world. Pharmex Products has a strong research and development orientation and this has been concentrated almost exclusively within Pharmex Research plc (PR plc), a multidivisional organisation with the role of discovering, developing and carrying out clinical trials upon new pharmaceutical products. Reflecting the organisation of the rest of the Pharmex group, PR plc has sites in the UK, throughout Europe and in the United States.

Within the UK, PR plc has concentrated its operations in the southeast of England on the sites of pharmaceutical companies taken over during the apparently inexorable rise of Pharmex Products to its current position. The recent growth of the company has meant that operations are now constrained by lack of space and several years ago a decision was taken to move them to a single site. After considerable research into suitable sites had been undertaken, Greenfields was chosen – a previously undeveloped

100-acre area about 60 miles away from the existing London head office. There are four major subdivisions within PR plc in the UK (two on each of the existing main sites) and these represent the traditional divisions within scientific disciplines, although changes in the nature of science brought about by developments in scientific understanding and in biotechnology have begun to blur the edges of these functional divisions.

## The existing sites

A visit to the laboratories at either of the main Pharmex Research sites is revealing. The white-coated scientists working at their rather cramped, equipment-covered benches are young and casually dressed, giving the laboratories the feel of those in the universities many will have recently left. Pharmex's growth, much of it during periods of high demand for well-qualified scientists, means that some 60 per cent of the workforce have been in the company for five years or less. Many of the buildings are old and consist of long corridors with laboratories leading off on both sides. The size of the laboratories to a large extent determines the size of the research teams based within them. Generally there will be a team of six in each laboratory supervised by a research leader.

During periods of high employment Pharmex could expect an annual labour turnover of between 10 and 14 per cent, although this was always highest amongst the less well-qualified ancillary and technician staff. By spring 1993 average labour turnover had dropped to around 3–4 per cent and growth in staff had largely come to an end. Pharmex was seen as a good employer in terms of pay, deliberately placing itself in the top quartile.

Industry analysts have identified three key strategic considerations which are seen as acting upon Pharmex (as well as upon other companies in the sector) and which appear to have contributed to the decision to develop Greenfields:

### 1 Increasing competition in the world pharmaceutical industry

The time taken to discover, develop and carry out clinical trials on a drug before it can be marketed widely is lengthy. After a drug is patented there is a time limit, after which competitors are free to develop the 'generic' product (i.e. the chemical substance which is the drug's active component). In order to recoup the investment made at the research and development stage, aggressive marketing is important to convince medical practitioners to prescribe the product. Increasingly, however, the most successful companies will be those able to shorten the development period of a product and hence exploit the longer period before the generic drug can be manufactured by others in the industry. Where all of those involved in the design of a new drug can be gathered together Pharmex management believes that the discovery process can be expedited.

### 2 Changes in pharmaceutical technology

The traditional division in pharmaceutical science is based on the separation of biology and chemistry. Developments in, for instance, biotechnology have begun to break down these divisions. There is a developing understanding of cell biology due to improved biotechnology. At a senior level Pharmex is keen to encourage scientists from different disciplines to talk to each other and separation of the disciplines on several sites militates against this.

### 3 The need for greater efficiency in the process of drug discovery

A squeeze on profits over the next few years seems inevitable with the tightening on price controls by governments and public health authorities across the globe.

A fourth consideration, specific to Pharmex, was identified by senior managers within the company:

### 4 Recent growth of the company has put pressure on laboratory space

Growth in employee numbers has led to cramped working conditions with a number of scientists, for instance, sharing a fume cupboard in each laboratory and having to search for bench space to write up reports.

There are now some 1500 employees of PR plc. Over 50 per cent are graduates and one in six has a doctorate. One looming problem lies in the impact the combined problem of rapid growth and low labour turnover will have upon perceptions of career opportunities for younger scientists.

## The Greenfields site

The new site will cater for the increased numbers of staff and a tour reveals a development on an impressive scale. The architect's design documents make reference to a 'campus-style' development. Asked what kind of an image Pharmex wished to promote on its newest site the Human Resource Director replied, 'something modern, young, not a factory, not an office, something that looks exciting to go to … the sort of thing that reflects what we're trying to do, what we are as a company, modern, flexible, innovative'.

The electronic attendance monitoring machines apparent on the walls of each floor at the existing sites and essential to the current flextime system will not be used at Greenfields. Members of the senior management of Pharmex have been consulted during the design process in the hope that the resulting site will meet the needs of a modern scientific research organisation into the twenty-first century. The result is a set of buildings designed to promote interaction between its occupants. There will be 'nodal points' (coffee machines and informal seating areas) and each laboratory can be approached from two sides. From one side a 'clean corridor' will lead into the office side of the work space containing each researcher's desk. From the other side a 'dirty corridor' used for the transportation of materials and equipment will lead into the laboratory. This half of the work space will contain the fume cupboards where experiments are carried out. Each scientific worker will have a fume cupboard to him- or herself – a major improvement upon the situation at the existing sites.

## Management of innovation

At Pharmex the management of research rests in the hands of highly qualified scientists with good track records in research themselves. Gary Brice, Head of Research, argued:

Most of our management is done through science. You don't want a heavily structured or heavily organised environment if you want people to be creative. I always say its like running an opera house. You've got to make sure that the toilets are clean, you've got to make sure that the tickets are sold, the ice creams are there in the interval, your gin and tonics are available, but if the fat lady don't sing, it's all a waste of time. And what is important is generating an environment where the prima donnas perform, because it's the prima donnas who actually make the invention, who take you to places you couldn't otherwise go. There's a few people out there who are really a bit special, who put things together in a different way. What we've got to create is something that allows them to perform, not something that necessarily satisfies the aspirations of the masses, because you can do that by making it run very smoothly. Everyone will say 'it's a fantastic place to work', but you never make inventions. What the hell good's that?

The impending move to Greenfields had prompted a new approach to the management of working time which is currently being piloted in certain divisions. Gary Brice put it as follows:

When you move house you are awfully conscious of the fact that you've got a lot of things in the loft or in the top of the garage that you don't actually have a use for any longer and you get shot of them, or you take them down to the tip, or you send them to a jumble sale ... I'm quite keen on looking at flextime. Twenty years ago we adopted flextime as a liberalising influence. Prior to that everybody was getting in at 8.45 and signing in before the line was drawn across the page. Flextime was a big step forward, but then we had the whole business of time recorders and people signing that they had done so many hours and then had not had the opportunity to have the days off that they had accumulated over the flex period. What I'm saying is do you really, as creative people, as professional people at the beginning of the twenty-first century, want all this paraphernalia associated with time, because it doesn't get us any new drugs and I'm not bothered about it. What I want is for people to feel committed and I want to work towards this end.

'Flexible working', the new system, is based on self-management in which scientific staff will be expected to be present at work during core hours of 10.00–12.00 and 2.00–4.00, but this is not formally monitored. They are not expected to account formally for the remaining $17\frac{1}{2}$ hours' attendance per week for which they are contracted. Managers believe the flextime system encouraged an instrumental approach to work where employees who needed to put in hours to meet the system's requirements simply clocked in early for a day or two but might not then spend the time engaged in useful activity. Clocking in and flextime were concerned with 'control' and 'bureaucracy'. This was not an appropriate or fruitful way to encourage well-qualified people to make use of their creative ability. As another senior manager said:

We don't want to have clocks in our new environment, in Greenfields, because we don't think it's compatible with a professional environment, and also it makes people conscious of time, and they should really be conscious of what they are doing and how they're doing it. Time management is really irrelevant to research when you think about it. It's the management of ideas, and how you produce them in practice and the quality of your goals, and whether they are practical or not or how innovative they are, things like that, those are key issues.

What was required, it was felt, was to make maximum use of the commitment to the process of scientific innovation which the young scientists brought with them from their universities and which led them not to count hours at work but to concentrate on achieving scientific goals. Under the old system employees were allowed up to 12 'flex' days per year off if they built up time credits. Under the new system such credit could not be 'banked', as such, but line managers had the ability to award days off to employees who they felt had done something to deserve it.

Pharmex operates a performance-related pay system, but the scheme has not been popular with staff and both this and a high degree of stress were identified during attitude surveys carried out during 1992. A human resource manager asserted:

Most people say they like performance-related pay, but they never seem to like it when it is applied to them ... PRP is a very hot area for discussion at the moment.

Much of the work carried out by scientific staff necessarily involves significant individual autonomy within a teamworking environment. Measuring the output from work is extremely difficult, as only a tiny proportion of compounds created ever reach the market. A human resource manager commented on the problem of rewarding performance in a research environment:

You find that in research targets are much woollier than they are, say, in IT. In research you might have a target today of finding a new nasal spray to prevent the common cold, and two months later Wellcome publish a patent and there's no point in doing it anymore. Your entire project switches to something new and, of course, many researchers are in a position year in, year out where they produce a whole bunch of failures. I mean, when you think that one compound makes it to the market out of every 10 000 compounds, one each year, and we've got 3700 research scientists across the globe pursuing it, it's not surprising that you get a lot of people whose life is a whole bunch of failures, and the supervisor has the job of subjectively assessing how good they were at getting those failures out. It's quite a difficult task. How do you assess someone's innovation or motivation or energy or drive? It's not all about how many hours they've spent at the bench, because you've got some people who can spend twelve hours a day at the bench and get a 'fair' appraisal ranking and you can get someone else who can spend six hours there but the way their brain and luck works they can achieve a 'special award'.

The pay review system involves line managers in judging their staff as performing somewhere on a scale from 'poor' to 'exceptional' without many formal guidelines as to what constitutes each category.

Taken together the PRP system and flexible working appeared to be putting a high degree of subjective power in the hands of line managers. The result was a heightened awareness amongst research workers of the need to convince line managers of the value of the work that they were doing. Line managers were not necessarily project leaders and so did not always have direct evidence of an employee's day-to-day performance. One scientist put it this way:

We're very task orientated here and we're working towards goals. Maybe there isn't so much freedom because I think we all spend a lot of time communicating what we are doing and making sure that, if you like, our managers and bosses can see the positive aspects of our work.

Good employee relations at Pharmex Research were seen as achievable by senior managers without recourse to recognising trade unions. A significant proportion of employees (about 1 in 4) were members of MSF (the Manufacturing, Science and Finance union), but this was recognised only for the purposes of representation of employees in, for instance, grievance procedures. Collective bargaining did not occur. However, at Greenfields Pharmex was intending to withdraw recognition for even this limited purpose. On the whole derecognition seemed unlikely in itself to represent an issue with research staff. Salaries were good, conditions at Greenfields were likely to be an improvement on the existing sites, jobs were seen as being secure and staff still had a high degree of autonomy about how they carried out their work. Indeed, there was some degree of freedom to choose *where* work was carried out and in many respects scientists were expected to operate like their peers who had chosen to remain in an academic environment. As a senior manager pointed out:

You must remember that scientific grades are contracted to work $37\frac{1}{2}$ hours per week and we would expect employees on average to be sorting their lives out such that they work those hours. But that doesn't necessarily mean at the bench, that just means contributing to GGR for $37\frac{1}{2}$ hours on average a week, and there's a hint that it doesn't have to therefore even be in the building. It can be contributing elsewhere in a library, in an institution somewhere else, whatever. But overall, contribution will not be measured on the hours you have your card in the machine in the future, but on the part that you play in achieving the objectives of the company.

However, the road to drug discovery is not an easy one, or one which has guaranteed success at its end. In many ways it is a game of chance. Pharmex has been seen as overdependent on one or two very successful products, so-called 'blockbuster drugs', and with nothing of the same magnitude yet in the pipeline to replace these when the patents expire. The increasingly competitive nature of the industry means that whilst resources will be put behind potential scientific leads by investing in projects likely to lead to new products, those that are seen as unlikely to give competitive advantage are shut down promptly and their members integrated into new or continuing projects. This can be a source of frustration to project team members as there may be knowledge of scientific interest still to be gained from the work. This market orientation can clearly be seen to differentiate work in the industrial and academic environments and to a significant number of scientists working at the bench the attempt to make the new site 'more like a university' was viewed with cynicism.

Greenfields, then, represents an attempt by Pharmex management to develop an environment conducive to the needs of the new product discovery side of the pharmaceutical industry as it approaches the twenty-first century. In order to work creatively scientists are seen as needing a degree of autonomy, and managers, nearly all of them accomplished scientists in their own right, appear to recognise the need to build this into working practices. However, it is possible to identify tensions in the company arising out of the necessity of directing activity towards the production of a marketable product. The question remains whether such a tension can be managed in a way which can ensure Pharmex a continuing place amongst the leading companies in the industry.

## CASE STUDY 4    THE COOPERATIVE ALLIANCE BETWEEN THE BANK OF ST HELLIER OF THE UK AND BANCO REAL OF SPAIN*

In late 1988, the UK bank the Bank of St Hellier (BSH)[†] and Banco Real of Spain[†] announced plans for a wide-ranging commercial cooperation, backed by a cross-holding of shares of an equivalent market value in each other's organisation.

This alliance was intended to be the backbone of EC strategy for both banks. Real

* Copyright © Dorothea Noble, University of Hertfordshire Business School
[†] Not the companies' real names

was already well established in Latin America, and both banks had some presence in the USA. Both felt unable to develop a Europe-wide strategy of their own, when faced with the established presence and resources of the larger EC banks. For BSH particularly, the possibility of takeover could not be ignored; substantial family ownership and strong liquidity served to protect Real from that threat.

## The banking environment

Until the country became an EC member in 1985, Spanish banking was closed to non-Spanish banks, with the exception of very few with a long history of banking in the territory, pre-dating Franco. The need to make the sector more competitive in the early 1980s encouraged the Spanish government to stage-manage the takeover of some weaker institutions by foreign banks. However, with the issue of the Second Banking Coordination Directive in 1988, a single market in EC banking came closer, and those not positioned to compete at this level could prepare for takeover. The directive provides for a 'single banking licence' whereby any credit institution authorised to act as such in one EC market is automatically qualified to carry out those same activities in any other member state. This, controversially, applied to non-EC financial institutions too. The directive also changes, among other things, minimum capital requirements and capital adequacy arrangements by stating minimum levels to be met by all, in part to avoid use of the least strictly regulated country as the channel for entry by non-EC firms.

Given these changes, financial institutions throughout Europe were conscious of the need to build a position in the EC that would be of sufficient substance to meet the growing competition from outside the region, as well as maintain their relative position vis-à-vis local rivals. Hence the search by BSH and Real, both smaller European operators with limited non-domestic presence, for partners in a European growth strategy.

## Reaching agreement

One executive commented on the apparent mismatch of image between the 'careful' north European banker counting and protecting his reserves, and the dashing Spanish patron taking care of his friends and leaving everything to *mañana*. However, both banks had carried out a structured search for potential partners in the four main EC banking countries; they had found banks too large, and too politically influenced, to be considered potentially 'equal' partners. Real as a family-owned bank was freer from political influence than many Spanish institutions, and participation in the market was attractive because of its recent liberalisation, the dynamism of the national industry, and the continuing availability of high margins; the Spanish are accustomed to paying for their banking services.

From the Spanish perspective, the UK was attractive as an advanced competitive market, open to international competition on many fronts for a long time and with a reputation for product developments that could have immediate application in Spain. Also links between the north of Spain and the UK are long established, through trade mainly, and the more recent developments of emigration and tourism. 'When we chanced upon the BSH it seemed to fit, happily.'

BSH was in the final phase of restructuring in the UK at the time; its position was fragile and it was vulnerable to hostile takeover; BSH needed to have 'a good friend on board' according to one manager at Real. With an important presence in the UK, and an international outlook, it was an attractive target at a time when all EC banks were on the acquisition trail. Real's 10 per cent holding in BSH gave something of the 'white knight' role to the alliance, 'giving them time to get to know each other and see whether merger may eventually be a good thing'. The bank stressed that this was a secondary motive, however, with the main focus on the benefits of joint action in specific areas.

The banks were about the same size at the time, with just over £1 billion equity each, and profits of £200 million. Assets were valued at approximately £15 billion for Real and £20 billion for BSH, according to a BSH press release at the time. Market valuation for Real was higher, so equivalent financial investment would eventually give BSH 5 per cent of Real and Real 10 per cent of BSH, the exchange to be phased over an agreed period.

Their motives were based on the realisation that increasingly their existing customers' market would be Europe, and that both banks would have to be able to provide those services currently available at home in other EC markets. By each giving immediate access to the other's domestic branch networks their range was greatly extended. In addition, BSH bought 50 per cent of the equity of two small banks in Belgium and Germany that Real had acquired the previous year from Bank of America, and they became 50 per cent partners in operations in Gibraltar and Portugal. Each of these joint ventures was to be managed under the leadership of either BSH or Real to simplify reporting structures and to exploit the most appropriate experience. BSH had concluded that parity and the existence of complementary skills and opportunities would be essential to the success of the alliance; these projects seemed to be prime examples of that.

The nature of the agreement developed through a series of conversations between the presidents and chief executives of the two banks. From discussion of the theme of providing services to each other's customers as a starting point one executive reported how other ideas came, and some have flown, and others have not flown as we've talked and come together'. The alliance 'wasn't set up with any particular structured plan in mind; it was very much set up to be in a position to cooperate, to jointly take advantage of opportunities as they came along'. (One manager likened it to the Treaty of Rome – 'designed to accommodate every eventuality'.) The discussions threw up broad areas of interest, in addition to those of servicing each other's customer base through existing branch networks, and specialist subsidiaries. Prospective areas included technology development, the consideration of joint acquisitions, exploration of ways to improve cross-border financial services, and possible joint action in the Far East. The resulting agreement was 'something looser than acquisition, with the potential to be something else, as and when it became necessary'.

The press reported the scoffing of securities analysts: 'How will it benefit shareholders; when will they see a return on their investment?' The straight-talking Chairman of BSH, tired of being quizzed on the relationship's bottom line, has repeatedly stated: 'We are taking a 10-year view. This is not about making profits 12 months from now!'

Some have viewed it more favourably. 'They are starting out small with broad objectives rather than attempting to instantly smash themselves together ... I think that has a better chance of success'. One manager queried the validity of other banks' strategies:

We've just sold two of Real's secondary bank brands to a major French institution [Crédit Lyonnaise] for a massive premium. I'm intrigued to know how they expect to recoup that investment. They would say the same as us – that they take a long-term view – but the bill they're facing is substantially larger than the one we face.

## Getting organised

Initial contacts and negotiations had involved the most senior executives of the banks, and their involvement continued to be of major importance once the agreement became official. Their stated objective was to allow the development of both groups throughout Europe to proceed more rapidly than either could achieve alone by:

- developing profitable customer bases in Europe;
- marketing improved cross-border financial services;
- providing services to corporate and personal customers of both Groups through a larger number of locations in Europe (press release, 1988).

Interpreted by one of their managers three years later, these become:

- To serve our domestic customer bases in foreign countries through close cooperation with our respective partner.
- To look for opportunities and approaches to the rest of Europe to achieve that service to our domestic customer base in the other European countries too.
- To cooperate jointly to take advantage of niche opportunities that may arise in third countries.
- Where possible, to transfer product ideas, technological ideas, management ideas between ourselves in order to position ourselves better in our domestic markets.

These reflect the two banks' philosophy that banking is essentially local in each market. Their need for EC-wide presence was based on their domestic customers' interest in receiving services over a wider geographic area than previously, not on the belief that they could offer domestic banking to the nationals of each country where they had a presence. Their expansion would therefore be by acquisition of small banks serving local niches, and offering some established branch network which could be accessed straight away for the partners' own customers, and which would continue to operate locally for its existing customer base. These would subsequently gain access to the wide service base offered by the alliance and its network throughout the EC. 'Any commercial customers of ours should know that we can service them anywhere in Europe.' This contrasts with the strategies of other UK clearing banks, Barclays and National Westminster for instance, who have expanded under their own names in all EC markets, often gaining access by initial acquisition, and subsequently expanding organically.

Certain ground rules were established for the alliance partners to follow too. Both banks were committed to remaining independent; therefore shareholdings would not be increased by either party without prior reference to the other bank. Shares would not be sold without offering the partner bank first refusal on the holding; and each would support the other's strategy by voting the shares it holds according to the recommendation of the other's Board (press release, 1988). These developed to include giving each other first refusal on sharing any further investments either may wish to make in any other European country; and that alliances with other banks from their respective territories would only be undertaken with the full knowledge of their partner.

Development of the alliance became the responsibility of a surveillance committee, which met every six weeks and was made up of the chief executives and presidents of the two banks, and several senior managers. Their initial role was to identify the broad areas of greatest potential for commercial cooperation and operationalise the process of investigating them. Six broad areas of interest were defined:

1  Access for all customers to services via each other's branches.
2  Shared ownership of operations in other EC countries.
3  Collaboration between the two investment banking arms of each group.
4  Technology development, with priority for electronic home banking, self-service terminals, and enhanced branch technology.
5  Joint acquisitions in countries where neither bank has access to a branch network, with one of the partners being designated in each case as lead management.
6  Exploration of ways to enhance service to customers in the Far East.

This committee set a framework for the alliance, formed a hub for the exploration of ideas and the identification of those to receive priority treatment. The seeds of cooperation and trust would be nurtured and spread from this centre, as these were the senior people who had sensed the initial rapport, and had had confidence in the ability of the two organisations to collaborate.

Audit teams were proposed for each of the areas of interest, with representatives from each partner; they would work with internal teams in the partners' offices to discover specific systems, products and techniques that could be applicable in the operations of the other partner; identify areas of development where work was complementary and worth coordinated action; and report back to the surveillance committee with recommendations for priority attention. Overall priorities and budget allocations were approved by the committee, with operations managers ensuring that appropriate task forces and project teams would take up the agreed actions.

In addition to these meetings, the chief executives and presidents of the two banks were members of the other's Board, so information exchange at the strategic level was formally well established.

As one manager put it: 'We are trying to build a flexible management structure, a flexible branch network, a flexible management information system, in order to be able to compete in whatever situation arises.'

## Operation of the alliance: making it work

The technological audit jointly carried out in both banks generated many opportunities for shared development; the most notable to the international customer must be their work on speeding international movements of money.

### The inter-bank transaction network

A senior manager described how this idea developed in the following terms:

We had had this idea floating around for a while to link our computer systems in order to provide same-day transactions, real-time transactions between Spain and Britain. We looked at that idea and thought about it, referred it to various technological bods in Spain and in the UK, who talked together and reported to the surveillance committee; I wonder if it would work – but maybe it won't; I tell you what, we'll try it with our cash point network first. So this time last year [1990] we linked the two computers together and now you can withdraw money from your UK account here in Spain just using your BSH card in a Spanish machine.* Right; that works so can we extend it to provide a similar service, or even a more complicated one to medium-sized corporate customers? And we examined that idea and eventually decided it was feasible; and now [1991] we're launching an inter-bank system and will be grafting on more complicated corporate-oriented products as we check that it works ... This has allowed us to do things today in a way that was impossible just a few months ago.

Since 1991, this inter-bank transaction system has expanded steadily. It moved from project status with four-month exchanges of IT staff, to become a joint venture between the two alliance banks, the joint venture being charged with the responsibility of developing the service and marketing it to other interested parties. The service offered the virtually instant transfer of funds among banks who are members of the network, without reference to existing financial infrastructures; initially it was targeted at small transfers, but established operators in the transfer of large sums saw this as the first step in a progress towards competing for large transfers.

At first the network was extended to link BSH and Real to their other joint ventures; subsequently, they envisaged that one bank in each EC country could join and be the access point for all national subscribers; by mid 1993 they were having some difficulty in deciding how best to extend the network. Five US banks were showing interest in joining. Limiting access meant that competitor products were being developed, not only by alternative EC bank networks, but also by the 'American interlopers', Visa and American Express. It seemed that the two banks' resources were not sufficient to tackle its further expansion alone.

The alliance partners had drawn on British Telecom and Digital Equipment Corporation for support with the initial phase of development. Early in 1994 a US computer services giant took a 30 per cent share in the network, bringing in expertise to boost its expansion – a digital superhighway for the banking industry. With a director of global business in place, and letters of intent from a further eight international banks wanting to join the network by the end of 1994, the venture's goal was to capture 10 per cent of the international payments market by the end of the decade, and have a customer base of 500 banks.

### Additional technological benefits

Other areas were identified for transfer between the banks, and adaptation to suit other markets or internal systems. Real was seen to be 'leading the pack' with management information systems, particularly for tracking the profitability of individual branches, customers and products. BSH's insurance technology system,

---

* For Spanish people operating in the UK it was slightly more difficult because exchange controls were still in place, but it was still technically possible for them to access Spanish accounts from the UK.

telephone insurance, was seen as having great potential in Spain; and both studied the German joint venture's practice on consumer credit products to exchange ideas on applications over a wider market. 'We're promoting interchange of people at the technology level, and looking for every single opportunity where we can do technological or product transfers.'

Despite the potential from their shared ideas, both banks were convinced that at the individual and small corporate customer level, products and services would be different from one country to another.

There will be a natural process of convergence as we put new products on the market, as they do the same, as we gain each other's ideas, and as products across Europe become more standardised. But I think we'll see two different sets of products for the foreseeable future. As we go up the tree in terms of customer size, you'll see an increasing convergence and standardisation of the products that both banks provide, but we're always independently seeking UK solutions to UK problems, and Spanish solutions to Spanish problems. That's one advantage we have from this alliance format – no-one at the top, as head of European branch banking, has any crazy idea that we should be able to standardise lending products for all customers across Europe.

### International expansion

On setting up the alliance, BSH had bought into existing branch networks that Real already owned in Portugal, Germany and Belgium, and Real had bought into BSH's existing operation in Gibraltar. These continued therefore as joint ventures with one of the partners being lead management in each case. 'We have representatives on the boards of all of them and each is confident that the other can manage the day to day operational management as well as anyone else – and we talk very openly'. The plan was to continue to expand through the acquisition of small branch networks, with the initial focus being on France and Italy.

As other developments take place, consideration is given to the possible benefits of joint action. Both banks had investments in the United States, not originally planned as an area for cooperation, but 'these things get talked about, is there anything we can do together in America? There's no formal consultation structure, there's just lots of chat.'

### New product development

The same applied to the development of banking products: the UK had more experience of interest-bearing current accounts in 1988, 'so there were conversations between the consumer people here and the consumer people in the UK about the pitfalls and possibilities of that; we're bringing experience to bear in each other's marketplace and we hope there will be opportunity for product interchange'.

Evidence of the influence exists: Real is attributed with starting the war of the 'supercuentos' when it sought to expand its domestic customer base by announcing interest-bearing current accounts in 1990, causing something of a shake-up in traditional Spanish personal banking. The press in 1994 talked also of how Real had 'built up an international reputation for innovation – in fields such as telephone banking, a probable offshoot of BSH's long experience in the direct selling of financial services.

The City's questioning of BSH's dual strategy in direct and branch banking is enlightening. According to an analyst at SG Warburg quoted in the *Financial Times:*

Doubts about it having overlapping distribution methods ... are easing. As more banks reduce their branches and turn to telephone and direct selling methods, BSH's dual delivery approach appears increasingly sensible. BSH's ability via direct selling to attract reliable, well-off customers means they can take market share cheaply, and with little risk. 'People do not realise the value of having more than one brand.' BSH has the ability via direct selling to price personal loans differently according to its assessment of how credit-worthy the borrower is. The branch bank could not do it because it would be socially unacceptable.

### Day-to-day operation

Management information systems tend to be applied to the overall management of branch networks within each bank separately, with adaptations to suit each other where interactive systems are necessary. The operation of the alliance itself relies on informal contacts and conversations that tap into the experience of project team members, staff exchanges – anyone that has had contact with the partner organisation.

We have continuous contacts at the highest levels, at levels lower down it's not so well developed yet; it's more difficult to talk to our colleagues where the levels of confidence and trust aren't there yet. We would tend to route through those channels where we have confidence. If someone here in the retail banking side wants to know something about some bit of technology or some work going on in the UK, it will generally get passed up the line, until we find some point where 'oh yes, I know that guy in London, he's good, he'll help us with that', and it will be done by phone. There's not much need for formal information flows ... the channels are found on a very *ad hoc* basis. Because we're not a subsidiary, we don't have the fall-back position of saying 'we're the boss – do it!' We have to make personal contacts. We're finding an advantage here through this structure that we wouldn't have if we had direct ownership.

One of the things that developed from the exchange of expert teams to carry out audits, working on identified projects, was the idea of exchanging staff simply with the idea of getting to know each other.

This was a specific idea, that we should get to know each other at the strategic level and we should let people have a broad idea of what their partners were doing; so we got swapped. One of the problems for staff interchange is that everyone in Spain's head office speaks English, but no-one in the UK speaks Spanish.

They have got round this by having someone from Spain in the UK while projects are going on; he can speak to counterparts in both offices and problems can be solved that way.

Visits to each other's territory automatically mean visiting partner offices.

I've done a survey and there's someone here [Madrid] from BSH virtually every day; the marketing people come, the technology people, and you'll bump into somebody in the corridor because they're doing a presentation on information systems, or mortgage products, or we're sharing ideas on branch networks.

## Management opinion

Managers interviewed expressed a range of views regarding the benefits of the alliance, its success, difficulties associated with it, and perceptions of its value.

*Benefits*

From the point of view of jointly developed products, and of building up the customer base, there were examples of a high level of success either achieved already, or with increasing potential as time goes by:

The alliance has created opportunities for differentiating our product that didn't exist before. For example, the ability to make same-day transfers, with fixed fees quoted in advance and the absolute certainty that it's going to arrive that same day is an incredible new product for the European market; I can't see anyone doing the same thing. Banking though is more than simply the products; it's very much a question of building relationships with clients, but we believe that the technological base that we're building will provide an excellent foundation for gaining new customers and also developing new products for those customers. We'll be able to do – no-one really knows, it's like trying to take a crystal ball.

The aliance's role in the expansion of both banks within the EC remains:

We believe that the alliance is a key building block in the strategy of maintaining a profitable operation here in Spain, and looking for niches in the rest of Europe; the alliance is key to that.

The value of London as a financial centre, and of an experienced presence there for intelligence about what is going on across Europe, was acknowledged:

London is for the time being the most important financial market in Europe; what is most important are the informal flows of information – people coming, talking; by just being here you hear things, know what's going on.

*Success factors*

The significance of an intuitive sense of being able to do business together was repeated often:

So much of establishing the alliance has really been down to the chemistry between the two sides. The alliance probably wouldn't have happened if the two managements hadn't hit it off; we've been very lucky and the chemistry worked.

The importance of top-level support was indicated too:

In our bank there's only one person that really matters and that's the Chairman – it's not very democratic.

A manager with Real saw the alliance in 1991 as having worked out well for BSH; it had given them the chance to focus on their restructuring without concern for a hostile takeover, although he questioned whether they could be giving time to European expansion, while preoccupied with restructuring at home. For Real he was not so sure:

It's hard to say; the intangibles that are building up can't be measured in NPV terms; but at senior level it is taking up a lot of time; however, things may develop over the long term.

*Difficulties*

Managers repeated the advantage of the alliance in representing a much lower financial commitment, and therefore exposure, than is involved in merger or acquisition:

There have been painful moments, and pleasant ones, but we're not carrying the same risk, we're not carrying the same weight of expectations.

Even with that, however, the attitude of city analysts has not been helpful; they have criticised the high premiums paid to acquire financial services companies, seeing little prospect of an appropriate return to shareholders in the short term. Yet the lesser commitment of the alliance is viewed with suspicion:

If there's been one disadvantage of doing it so early, it's been that everyone said great, now what are you going to do, let's see some results, some numbers; let's see your increased profits, and as time goes by analysts say we haven't seen any benefit from this, when are we going to see something credible from the alliance; so if there's a problem it's the perceptions of the market in the very short term.

A manager with Real had a problem in believing the partners would cooperate in areas of strength; in his view, people would only want to cooperate in areas of weakness that they could not progress alone. This demonstrated a lack of trust and confidence in the partnership – it was not easy for him to believe that a good opportunity would be shared: 'Why are they going to give you a piece of their business – only if it is bad!'

### Perceptions

A manager with BSH agreed that within the two organisations there was some scepticism about the alliance and its significance. He felt there were two main reasons for this:

One is that the European market isn't developing quite how we saw it in 1988; it's not developing as fast as we thought, and we realise that cultural factors and national boundaries are still going to play an enormous part in business post-1992. So there aren't the opportunities to gain massive amounts of new business that maybe we thought were there in 1988, which we were afraid of losing. The other reason is that working across borders within whatever structure, be it acquisition or through an alliance, is a lot more difficult that anyone can ever tell you in advance, and it does take time; it takes time to build the trust, it takes time to build the communications. For example, no-one in the BSH speaks Spanish. So, OK, we can do business at the highest level with people who speak English, and we can use people from Spain who can speak English to speak to the BSH; but at the computer level, for example, it takes time for the right people to do the jobs.

The same manager had experienced a conversion regarding face-to-face contact with colleagues and collaborators.

One thing I was sceptical about when I was working in London was the value of personal contacts. 'What are these people doing, jetting off to Spain, going there for a three-day meeting; I'm sure that isn't necessary, we need to control costs!' What I realise now is that in this kind of business, this kind of structure, personal contact, personal confidence is a number one priority.

As one of the directors exchanged to encourage alliance contacts, he felt there was wide optimism about the alliance, and a strong conviction as to its value:

We're definitely satisfied with the way it's progressing, despite internal questioning and the scepticism of the analysts; we're satisfied that we're building something quite special and unique, and we're reaching those targets that exist.

# Towards radical perspectives on strategic management and organisational dynamics

Part One of this book has described how the 1940s and 1950s saw the development of a number of closely related ideas. At much the same time engineers, mathematicians, biologists and psychologists were proposing the application of systems theories taking the form of open systems, cybernetics and systems dynamics. These systems theories were closely related to the development of computers and cognitivist psychology. Over the decades that followed, all of these theories and applications were used, in one way or another, to construct ways of making sense of organisational life. The central themes running through all of these developments are probably those of the autonomous individual who is primary and prior to the group, and the concern with the control of systems. In the three theories of organisation surveyed so far, namely strategic choice, learning organisation and psychoanalytic perspectives, there is a clear focus on the individual and how powerful individuals make rational choices about the purpose and direction of their organisations. It seems to me that the key differences between these three theories relate to how they understand the blockages to the process of rational choice, organisation-wide intention and control. These ways of talking about, understanding and acting in organisations are now so taken for granted that many people talk as if they are objective facts about organisations.

The 1970s and 1980s bear some striking similarities to the 1940s and 1950s in terms of the development of systemic theories. During those two decades, physicists, meteorologists, chemists, biologists, economists, psychologists and computer scientists have been working across their disciplines to develop new theories of systems. Their work goes under titles such as chaos theory, dissipative structures, synergetics, complex adaptive systems, nonlinear dynamics. What they have in common is the centrality they give to nonlinear relationships. Independently of this work in the natural sciences, similar ideas have also been appearing in sociology and psychoanalysis.

Part Two of this book will consider what these developments are and how they are being taken increasingly seriously in the field of management and organisational theory. This increasing interest is demonstrated in the number of special issues on chaos and complexity in the major management and organisation journals; the growing number of academic papers; a major research programme being mounted by the UK's Economic and Social Research Council; the investments being made by major consulting organisations; the interest being shown by major corporations; and the growing number of management books on these topics.

This part of the book first reviews the theories of chaos, dissipative structures, synergetics and complex adaptive systems. It then explores how these theories are being used by writers on management and organisation. There is now enough of this writing to be able to suggest how different perspectives are developing and what the nature of those differences is. I will be suggesting that the principal differentiator is the assumption made about the relationship between the individual and the group. One strand in the use of chaos and complexity theories retains the cognitivist understanding of human nature and the notion of the objective observer. I will argue that this loses the potentially radical nature of the insights coming from complexity theory. The themes of individual autonomy, organisation-wide intention and control continue to be central, just as they were in what I have called the orthodox theories. I will be suggesting that if complexity theory is interpreted through an understanding of human nature in which neither the individual nor the group is primary, then the potential for a more radical theory of organisational life is opened up.

The theories of organisation outlined in Part One have been developed and used for decades now. The development of the theories I will outline in this part are in their infancy. It follows that their implications for action in organisations are far from clear at this point. However, they do hold out the possibility of making sense of life in organisations in a different way.

# 11 Chaos theory, dissipative structures and synergetics

## 11.1 INTRODUCTION

In the review of systems dynamics in Chapter 8, I pointed to how it differed from both cybernetics and open systems theory in the emphasis that it placed on nonlinearity and non-equilibrium states. The system was mathematically modelled using nonlinear relationships. In other words, systems dynamics took account of relationships where the effects of a cause could be more or less than proportional and where there could be more than one effect for a single cause. When systems dynamics came to be used in learning organisation theory, the nonlinearity was incorporated by adding positive feedback loops to the negative feedback that formed the basis of cybernetic systems. Systems dynamics was used, I suggest, as an extension of cybernetics. This chapter is concerned with much the same kind of nonlinear relationship that systems dynamics was originally concerned with. These relationships, just as those explored in systems dynamics, are deterministic. This means that the relationships themselves do not change or evolve. To put it another way, these are systems that do not learn. It follows that they cannot be applied in any direct way to human relationships since humans do learn and evolve, but they may have some value as metaphors. Chapter 12 will examine systems that do evolve, namely complex adaptive systems. This chapter outlines the development of three theories of nonlinear deterministic systems. These are chaos theory, the theory of dissipative structures and synergetics. The chapter will explore the potential implications of these theories.

## 11.2 CHAOS, DISSIPATIVE STRUCTURES AND SYNERGETICS

If you go back to section 8.2, you will find that I used the logistic equation to illustrate the nature of systems dynamics. The equation was used to model the dynamics of population growth and decline, explaining how the dynamic is internal to the system and might be explained in terms of a switch from amplifying to damping feedback. To illustrate the theory of chaos I want to return to that equation and look more closely at its properties. In case you are wondering why I want to do this, remember that populations of organisations and populations of groups of people also display the dynamics of growth and decline. Insight into these dynamics, no matter where they come from, may therefore be potentially useful. Furthermore, remember that one of the key disciplines of the theory of organisational learning is systems thinking and this notion comes directly from systems dynamics, of which the logistic equation is illustrative. Developments in systems dynamics may well have implications for what systems thinking in organisations means.

I am going to use the logistic equation as a model of a ridiculously simple organisational interaction. I am not claiming in any way that this is a model of any organisational reality. I am simply using it to explain the properties of a particular dynamical system.

## 11.3   CHAOS THEORY

Suppose that the profit level $P$ of a particular company in a time period $t$ depends exactly upon its advertising outlay in that period. Suppose further that there is a simple nonlinear relationship between profit and advertising. The relationship would be such that increased advertising has a diminishing impact on consumers until eventually some increase in advertising brings in a profit which is smaller than the outlay, so that the total profit falls. Therefore, sometimes profit grows and sometimes it declines, just as the insect population did in Chapter 8. The logistic equation already encountered in Chapter 8 can therefore be used to model this behaviour.

$$P_t = cP_{t-1}(1 - P_{t-1})$$

This nonlinear relationship will generate a sequence of profits over time for any value of $c$. The question is what patterns will profit follow as the value of the parameter $c$ (bigger impact of advertising on profit and/or bigger proportion of profit devoted to advertising) is raised.

At low levels of $c$, profit will settle into stable equilibrium paths of straight lines over time (values for $c$ between 0 and 3), or of regular, repetitive cycles (values for $c$ between 3 and 3.5). At high values for $c$ (above 4), profits will show an unstable but uniform pattern of explosive growth to infinity. So, there are states of stable equilibrium at first and later on states of explosive growth that would lead to the disintegration of any real-world system. What happens at the borders between stable equilibrium and the highly unstable state (values for $c$ between 3.5 and 4)?

To answer this question it is necessary to perform thousands of calculations on a computer, gradually increasing the value of $c$. For example, at $c = 3.2$, profits fluctuate along a regular two-period cycle with one peak and one trough. At a value for $c$ of 3.5, a period four cycle appears – two peaks and two troughs. If the parameter is 3.56 then the period doubles again to an eight-period cycle. By 3.567 the cycles are to period 16. Thereafter there are rapid period doublings until the parameter $c$ takes the value of 3.58 (*Stewart, 1989*).

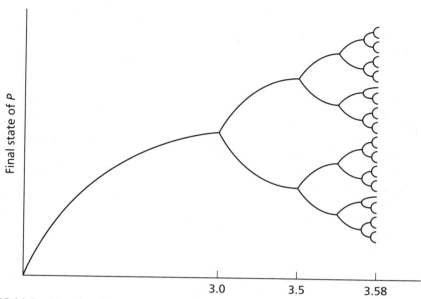

**FIGURE 11.1**    Mapping the logistic equation
*Source*: R. Stacey (1991), *The Chaos Frontier: Creative Strategic Control for Business*, Oxford: Butterworth–Heinemann

So, for low values of *c*, the system displays one form of behaviour. Chaos theorists call this a point attractor. An attractor is the state of behaviour to which a system is drawn. To put it another way, it is the final state of behaviour which a system settles into. The point attractor is a state of stable equilibrium. As the parameter *c* is increased the system's attractor changes to two forms of behaviour known as a periodic or cyclical attractor. Further increases to *c* result in further changes in attractor to more and more complicated cyclical attractors. These are all perfectly predictable states of equilibrium, of the kind open systems and cybernetics focus on.

The pattern described above is shown in *Figure 11.1*. Here the final values reached by profit are plotted (on the vertical axis) against the value of the parameter *c* (on the horizontal axis). So for each value of *c* between 0 and 3 there is a single stable point, a higher point for each value of the parameter shown by the rising curve from 0 to 3. At 3 there are two final values for profit: the peak and the trough of the cycle. The line splits into two, or bifurcates. And the peaks and troughs diverge as the parameter moves from 3 to 3.5. At 3.5 there is a further bifurcation to show two peaks and two troughs. They in turn bifurcate and soon at 3.58 there are infinitely many bifurcations. This diagram has been called a figtree diagram, showing how, at successive values of the parameter, the trunk of final values splits into boughs, the boughs into branches, the branches into twigs, the twigs into twiglets, and so on. The behaviour of the system is far more complicated than one could have imagined.

What happens as the parameter *c* continues to be tuned up? At the parameter value of 3.58 the behaviour of the system becomes highly irregular (instability), within fixed boundaries (stability). There are no regular cycles; the values from each iteration shoot all over the place (within boundaries) and never return to any value they previously had. No matter how many thousands of iterations are tried, this remains true. There are cycles that one can recognise as cycles, but they are always irregular. This is mathematical chaos, also known as a strange attractor. This is not a state of equilibrium but one of non-equilibrium. You could say that it is far from equilibrium. The key point about a strange attractor is that it has a shape, or qualitative pattern, but the path it traces over the long term is unpredictable. This is because tiny changes in the environment the system is operating in can be escalated into completely different paths over time. You would have to be able to detect every tiny change and measure it with infinite precision in order to make long-term predictions. For this example this property, known as sensitive dependence on initial conditions, means that you will not be able to forecast what will happen to profit over the long term if the parameter value is 3.58 – and that has nothing to do with environmental changes or random shocks. Nothing changes outside the equation: the same constant rule is followed and the parameter value sticks at 3.58, but the consequence is an unpredictable path in profit over the long term, although there is predictability over the short term.

*Figure 11.2* shows a representation of many thousands of iterations for parameter values between around 3.3 and 4. The black areas are mathematical chaos and the white stripes within chaos are windows of order.

You can now examine the first white stripe in the top part of *Figure 11.2* by iterating for very small intervals of the parameter value which yields that white stripe. In effect, you 'blow up' the picture within the window of order, and you find that this magnified portion resembles the whole diagram. This is shown in *Figure 11.3*. If you repeat the

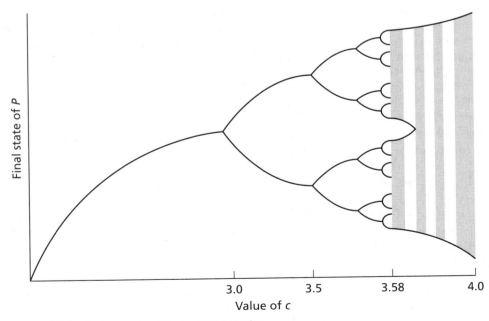

**FIGURE 11.2** Further map of the logistic equation
*Source*: R. Stacey (1991), *The Chaos Frontier: Creative Strategic Control for Business*, Oxford: Butterworth–Heinemann

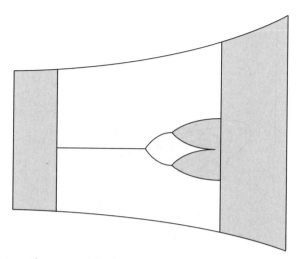

**FIGURE 11.3**   Yet another map of the logistic equation
*Source*: R. Stacey (1991), *The Chaos Frontier: Creative Strategic Control for Business*, Oxford: Butterworth–Heinemann

blow-up procedure for the first white stripe in *Figure 11.3* you will once again find a picture that resembles the whole diagram. The structure is infinitely deep; there are pictures within pictures forever and they are always similar.

The conclusion, then, is that a very simple nonlinear relationship, a perfectly deterministic one, produces a highly complex pattern of behaviour over time. Between stability and instability there is a complex border that combines both stability and instability. Note that although the word chaos is being used, it does not mean the utter confusion, the complete randomness, it usually means in ordinary conversation. On the contrary, mathematical chaos reveals patterns in phenomena previously thought to be random. It is just that the patterns are paradoxically regular and irregular, stable and unstable.

## Chaos in nature's systems

Chaos exists outside abstract mathematical equations, for example in the earth's weather system. The weather is patterns in interdependent forces such as pressure, temperature, humidity and wind speed that are related to each other by nonlinear relationships.

To model its behaviour, the forces have to be measured at a particular point in time, at regular vertical intervals through the atmosphere from each of a grid of points on the earth's surface. Rules are then necessary to explain how each of the sets of interrelated measurements, at each measurement point in the atmosphere, move over time. This requires massive numbers of computations. When these computations are carried out they reveal that the weather follows what is called a *strange* attractor, another name for a chaotic pattern. The shape of that attractor is shown in *Figure 11.4*.

What this shape means is that the weather follows recognisably similar patterns, but those patterns are never ever exactly the same as those at any previous point in time.

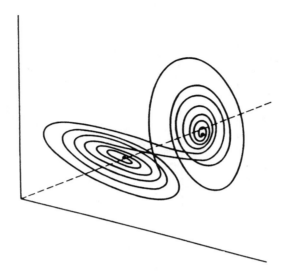

**FIGURE 11.4**   The strange attractor for the weather system
*Source*: R. Stacey (1991), *The Chaos Frontier: Creative Strategic Control for Business*, Oxford: Butterworth–Heinemann

The system is highly sensitive to some small changes and blows them up into major alterations in weather patterns. Chaotic dynamics means that humans will never be able to forecast the weather at a detailed level for more than a few days ahead. The theoretical maximum for accurate forecasts is two weeks, one meteorologists are nowhere near reaching yet.

Although the specific path of behaviour in chaos is unpredictable, that behaviour does have a 'hidden' pattern, a qualitative shape. *Figure 11.4* gives a simplified picture of that shape, the strange attractor which the weather follows.

That figure shows how the weather, described in terms of air pressure, humidity, temperature, and so on, varies over time, moving around one of the lobes of the shape and then suddenly switching to the other. The weather system moves endlessly around this shape, never once returning to any point it previously occupied; the lines never intersect. (They appear to do so in *Figure 11.4* only because this is a two-dimensional representation of a three-dimensional figure.)

So the specific path of the weather is unpredictable in the long term, but it always follows the same global shape. There are boundaries outside which the weather system hardly ever moves and, if it does so, it is soon attracted back to the shape prescribed by the attractor. Some weather conditions are not allowed – snow storms in the Sahara desert or heat waves in the Arctic. There is an overall shape to weather behaviour because it is constrained by the structure of the feedback relationships generating it.

Because of this 'hidden' order, the system displays typical patterns, or recognisable categories of behaviour. Even before people knew anything about the shape of the weather's strange attractor, they always recognised patterns of storms and sunshine, hurricanes and calm, and seasonal patterns. These recognisable patterns are repeated in an approximate way over and over again. They are never exactly the same, but there is always some similarity. They are similar to what went before and similar to what is occurring elsewhere in the system.

The category winter follows the category autumn and within a particular winter there are typical patterns of temperature, rainfall and wind speed. As one enters a particular winter, one does not know whether the temperature will be very low or very high for that time of the year, the rainfall heavy or light, the wind speed moderate or at gale force.

This means that it is not possible to identify specific causes that yield specific outcomes, but the boundaries within which the system moves and the qualitative nature of the patterns it displays are known. The very irregularity of the weather will itself be regular because it is constrained in some way – it cannot do just anything. The resulting self-similar patterns of winter weather can be used to prepare appropriate behaviour. One can buy an umbrella or move the sheep off the high ground. People can cope with the uncertainty and the lack of causal connection because they are aware of self-similar patterns and use them in a qualitative way to guide specific choices.

Throughout the 1970s and the 1980s the principles of chaos have been explored in one field after another and found to explain turbulence in gases and liquids, certain pathological conditions of the heart, the eye movements of schizophrenics, the spread of some diseases, and the impact of some inoculation programmes against some diseases. The body's system of arteries and veins follows patterns determined by feedback rules with chaotic properties. The growth of insect populations has chaotic characteristics. The leaves of trees grow through a process of iterating deterministic rules contained in their spores; they are fractal and self-similar enough to allow us to distinguish one kind from another but no two of a kind are ever exactly the same. You can reproduce similar individuals, clearly belonging to one category, on a computer using the rules and iteration. The reason for no two snowflakes ever being the same can be explained using chaotic dynamics. The orbit of the moon Hyperion around Saturn follows a path which can be explained using the principles of chaos as can the Great Red Spot of Jupiter. Water dripping from a tap has been shown to follow a chaotic time pattern, as does smoke spiralling from a cigarette. For me, one of the most intriguing discoveries is that healthy hearts and healthy brains display mathematical chaos. The heart moves into a regular rhythm just before a heart attack and brain patterns during epileptic fits are also perfectly regular. It seems that chaos is the signature of health.

The properties of low-dimensional deterministic chaos have been found to apply to nonlinear feedback systems in meteorology, physics, chemistry and biology (*Gleick, 1988*). Economists and other social scientists have been exploring whether these discoveries are relevant to their disciplines (*Baumol & Benhabib, 1989; Kelsey, 1988; Anderson, Arrow & Pines, 1988*). There are some indications that chaos explanations give insight into the operation of foreign exchange markets, stock markets and oil markets (*Peters, 1991*).

At this stage, I want to return to the point that I made in Chapter 8 on how the logistic equation is interpreted in systems dynamics. The description ran in terms of feedback loops. First, the system follows an amplifying loop when the population is low and then it flips into negative feedback when the population is high. There it is the level of the population that is causing the nature of feedback to change. This method of analysis in systems dynamics was taken into the way systems thinking is understood in the theory of the learning organisation. The system is understood as alternating between positive and negative feedback. The model is essentially cybernetic with the addition of the possibility of positive feedback. The analysis in chaos theory is different. It is the parameter $c$, which reflects the rate of information or energy flow in the system, that causes the dynamics to change at any level of the population. For low values of $c$ the dynamics is stable and for high values it is unstable. At a critical range, the dynamics is mathematically chaotic. It follows the pattern of a strange attractor. The strange attractor is paradoxically stable and unstable, regular and irregular, predictable and unpredictable, at the same time. This is a very different notion to that of a sequential flip from one dynamic to another and back again.

The point I am making is that if you interpret the operation of a dynamical system in feedback terms you are likely to introduce this sequential pattern. The insight that behaviour between stability and instability is a completely different dynamic, one that is simultaneously amplifying and damping or constraining, tends to get lost. This is not a notion of some sequence, but one of a continuously present tension between amplification and constraint.

It seems to me that it is not appropriate to use the concept of feedback when interpreting the meaning of nonlinear relationships such as the logistic equation. The system is not referring to some outside point and then amplifying or damping differences between its behaviour and that reference point. Instead, it seems more meaningful to interpret the system as referring back to itself. It is a self-referential system, not a feedback one. In other words, its state now depends only on its state last time, not on any comparison with an external reference point. I think that this distinction is important because if you interpret nonlinear systems in feedback terms, as I did in previous editions of this book, you are in danger of losing the insight about paradoxical behaviour. There is then very little difference between chaos theory and systems dynamics if you do this. Utilising chaos theory as a metaphor in theories of organisation will then rapidly lead to the same conclusions as systems dynamics and learning organisation theory.

There is another important point to notice. Systems dynamics pointed to the possibility of unexpected and unanticipated outcomes. Chaos theory provides an explanation of why this might be so and takes a further step by pointing to the impossibility of long-term prediction. It therefore makes a much stronger statement about dynamical systems.

This section now continues the exploration of deterministic dynamical systems by briefly describing the theory of dissipative structures.

## The theory of dissipative structures

Prigogine (*Prigogine & Stengers, 1984; Nicolis and Prigogine, 1989*) has shown how nonlinear systems develop unpredictable new forms of behaviour when they operate far from equilibrium. He points to a fundamental relationship between the dynamics of chaos on the one hand, and the development of new forms, on the other.

Chaos performs the important task of amplifying small changes in the environment, causing the instability necessary to shatter existing behaviour patterns and make way for the new. Systems may pass through states of instability or crisis and reach critical points where they may spontaneously self-organise to produce some new structure or behaviour that cannot be predicted from a knowledge of the previous state. The new more complex structure is called a dissipative structure because it takes energy to sustain the system in that new mode.

For example, as energy is pumped into a particular gas the molecules are put into a more and more excited state. They all move randomly in different directions – a state of instability. This instability performs the function of amplifying or spreading the energy or information around the molecules in the gas. The instability also shatters any relationship the molecules bore to each other before the energy was pumped in. In this state the gas emits a dull glow. As further energy is pumped into this system, it reaches a critical point. At this point the molecules suddenly and spontaneously organise themselves so that all point in the same direction. The result is a laser beam casting its light for miles. The sudden 'choice' of molecules all to point in the same direction is not predictable from the laws of physics. There is no central law prescribing this behaviour; it emerges out of instability through a self-organising process.

Consider another example in a little more detail.

A liquid is at thermodynamic equilibrium when it is closed to its environment and the temperature is uniform throughout it. The liquid is then in a state of rest at a global level, that is there are no bulk movements in it, although the molecules move everywhere and face in different directions. In equilibrium, then, the positions and movements of the molecules are random and hence independent of each other. There are no correlations, patterns or connections. At equilibrium, nothing happens and the behaviour of the system is symmetrical, uniform and regular. This means that every point within the liquid is essentially the same as every other and at every point in time the liquid is in exactly the same state as it is at every other. Time and space do not matter.

When the liquid is pushed far from equilibrium by tuning up the control parameter heat, then the system amplifies small fluctuations throughout it. So, if one starts with a layer of liquid close to thermodynamic equilibrium and then begins to apply heat to the base, that sets up a fluctuation or change in the environmental condition in which the liquid exists. That temperature change is then amplified or spread through the liquid. The effect of this amplification is to break the symmetry and to cause differentiation within the liquid.

So, at first the molecules at the base stop moving randomly and begin to move upward, those most affected by the increase in temperature rising to the top of the liquid. That movement eventually sets up convection so that those molecules least affected are displaced and pushed down to the base of the liquid. There they are heated and move up, in turn pushing others down. The molecules are now moving in a circle. This means that the symmetry of the liquid is broken by the bulk movement that has been set up. Each point in the liquid is no longer the same as all others: at some points movement is up and at other points it is down. There is diversity at the micro level.

After a time, a critical temperature point is reached and a new structure emerges in the liquid. Molecules move in a regular direction setting up hexagonal cells, some turning clockwise and others turning anti-clockwise: they self-organise. What this represents is long-range coherence where molecular movements are correlated with each other as though they were communicating. The direction of each cell's movement is, however, unpredictable and cannot be determined by the experimenter. The direction taken by any one cell depends upon small chance differences in the conditions that existed as the cell was formed.

As further heat is applied to the liquid, the symmetry of the cellular pattern is broken and other patterns emerge. Eventually the liquid reaches a turbulent state of evaporation. Movement from a perfectly orderly, symmetrical situation to one of some more complex order occurs through a destabilising process. The system is pushed away from stable equilibrium in the form of a point attractor, through bifurcations such as the limit cycle, and so on towards deterministic chaos. The process is one of destruction making way for creation of the new.

So, self-organisation is a process that occurs spontaneously at certain critical values of a system's control parameters and it involves the system organising itself to produce a new pattern without any blueprint. Emergence means that the pattern produced by self-organisation cannot be explained by the nature of the entities that the system consists of or the interaction. What is important is that there should be diversity, otherwise the system cannot spontaneously jump to a new attractor. The new pattern that emerges is a dissipative structure in that it easily dissolves if the system moves away from critical points in its control parameters. An equilibrium structure requires no effort to retain its structure and great effort to change it, while a dissipative structure requires great effort to retain its structure and relatively little to change it.

Prigogine (*Nicolis & Prigogine, 1989; Prigogine & Stengers, 1984*) has established that nonlinear chemical systems are changeable only when they are pushed far from equilibrium where they can become dissipative systems. Dissipative systems import energy/information from the environment that then dissipates through the system in a sense causing it to fall apart. However, it also has structure taking the form of irregular patterns and it is capable of renewal through self-organisation as it continues to import energy/information. A dissipative system is essentially a contradiction or paradox: symmetry and uniformity of pattern are being lost but there is still a structure; dissipative activity occurs as part of the process of creating a new structure. A dissipative structure is not just a result, but a process that uses disorder to change, an evolving interactive process that temporarily manifests in globally stable structures.

Thus, when nonlinearity and constraints are introduced into a system the result is to hold the system far from equilibrium in a state of some instability. In other words, the system is prevented from becoming adapted to its environment and this enables it to amplify small changes. That amplification makes it possible for the whole system to change. Stability dampens and localises change to keep the system where it is, but operation far from equilibrium destabilises a system and so opens it up to change.

It is important to note here that the kind of system described in the section on chaos theory cannot spontaneously move of its own accord from one attractor to another. Something outside the system has to alter the parameter for this to happen. However, with the kind of system described in this section such a spontaneous move is possible because the system is sensitive to non-average interaction with its environment (fluctuations) and the internal process of symmetry breaking creates microdiversity within it. The suggestion is that a creative system is one that is constrained from settling down into equilibrium. It is one characterised by non-average relationships and entities. You can see how this would have considerable implications for management practice if it said anything at all about organisations. Most management theory talks about success as a move to equilibrium and seeks to remove differences between entities, by getting everyone to share the same culture.

## Synergetics

Synergetics is the name applied to a field of research that seeks to understand how patterns form in non-equilibrium systems (*Haken, 1977; Kelso, 1995*). Synergetics is concerned with how the interaction between large numbers of parts of a nonlinear system cooperate to create novel forms. Here similar concepts to those in dissipative structure theory are employed. Synergetics points to the importance of instability in generating new form through a process of spontaneous self-organisation. Much of the research in this area is concerned with the brain. It suggests that the brain is a self-organising system subject to nonlinear dynamical laws. Since the concepts employed in synergetics are close to those used in the theory of dissipative structures I will not go into further detail. I did think it important, however, to at least refer to this body of work.

I want to turn now to the potentially radical implications of the theories presented in this section.

## 11.4    RADICAL POTENTIAL

Since the times of Newton, Bacon and Descartes, scientists have tended to understand the natural world in terms of machine-like regularity in which given inputs are translated through absolutely fixed laws into given outputs. For example, if you apply a force of 5 newtons to a ball weighing 10 kilograms, the laws of motion will determine exactly how far the ball will move on a horizontal plane in a vacuum. Cause and effect are related in a straightforward linear way. On this view, once one has discovered the fixed laws and gathered data on the inputs to those laws, one will be able to predict the behaviour of nature's systems. Once one knows how the system would have behaved without human intervention, one can intervene by altering the inputs to the laws and so get nature to do something different, something humans want it to do. According to this Newtonian view of the world, humans will ultimately be able to dominate nature.

This whole way of reasoning and understanding was imported into economics, where it is particularly conspicuous, and also into the other social sciences and some schools of psychology. This importation is the source of the stable equilibrium paradigm that still today dominates thinking on managing and organising. That thinking is based on the belief that managers can in principle control the long-term future of a human system. Such a belief is realistic if cause-and-effect links are of the Newtonian type described above, for then the future of a system can be predicted over the long term and its future can be controlled by someone.

If one takes the perspective presented in the last section, nature is still understood to be driven by laws. The laws, however, are not ones of straightforward unidirectional causality; rather, they take the form of nonlinear relationships in which the system refers back to itself so that causality is circular.

More specifically, these theories say that, when a deterministic nonlinear system moves away from stable equilibrium towards the state of explosive instability, it passes through a stage of *bounded instability* in which it displays highly complex behaviour. One might think of this stage as a border area between stable equilibrium and explosive instability; that is, a state of paradox in which two contradictory forces, stability and instability, are operating simultaneously, pulling the system in opposing directions. While the system is in this border area neither of these contradictory forces can ever be removed; instead, the forces are endlessly rearranged in different yet similar patterns. When the system is in the border area it never behaves in a regular way that leads to equilibrium. Instead, it generates patterns of behaviour that are not only irregular but also unpredictable over the long term. Nonetheless, such behaviour has an overall, 'hidden', qualitative pattern.

These properties may be fundamental to all nonlinear systems no matter where they may be found. They may be consequences of the nonlinear structure of the system itself, not due to any environment the system may operate in.

## Bounded instability far from equilibrium

So a key discovery about the operation of deterministic nonlinear systems is that stable equilibrium and explosive instability are not the only *attractors*. Nonlinear systems have a third possibility: a state of bounded instability far from equilibrium in which behaviour has a pattern, but it is irregular. That pattern emerges through self-organisation. These are properties of the system itself, not the consequences of some external agent first applying positive feedback and then applying negative feedback. Either the system is driven by negative feedback and then it tends to stable equilibrium, or the system is driven by positive feedback and then it tends to explosive instability. If that instability is to be removed, then some agent or condition outside the system would have to 'step in and put a stop to it'. However, when systems are held far from equilibrium, they automatically apply internal constraints to keep instability within boundaries. This is so because of the nonlinear structure of the system.

When it operates in the border between stability and instability, the behaviour of the system unfolds in so complex a manner, so dependent upon the detail of what happens, that the links between cause and effect are lost. One can no longer count on a certain given input leading to a certain given output. The laws themselves operate to escalate small chance disturbances along the way, breaking the link between an input and a subsequent output. The long-term future of a system operating in the borders between stability and instability is not simply difficult to see: it is for all practical purposes, unknowable. It is so because of the structure of the system itself, not simply because of changes going on outside it and impacting upon it. Nothing can remove that unknowability. If this were to apply to an organisation operating in the border area between stability and instability, then any decision-making process that involved forecasting, envisioning future states, or even making any assumptions about future states, would be ineffective. Those applying such processes in conditions of bounded instability would be engaging in fantasy activities.

Although deterministic nonlinear systems may generate unpredictable specific behaviour over the long term, that behaviour nevertheless has an overall qualitative pattern to it. Perhaps the easiest way to think of this is as follows. Dynamic feedback systems generate sequences of specific behaviours or events that fall into categories recognisable by 'family resemblance' types of features which the behaviour or events share with each other. But within those very general, rather vague and irregular categories, each piece of behaviour or event is different. There is endless individual variety within broad categories. If this applied to organisations, one would raise questions about decision-making techniques that involved step-by-step reasoning from assumptions about the future. One would have to rely instead on using qualitative patterns to *reason by analogy and intuition*. Those who succeeded in the borders between stability and instability would be those who saw patterns where others searched for specific links between causes and events.

## Cause and effect

The discovery of the state of bounded instability has implications for the nature of cause and effect. These important conclusions about cause and effect might apply to organisations. In a state of deterministic chaos a system operates to amplify tiny changes in starting conditions into major alterations of consequent behaviour. That sensitivity is so great that differences in the value of a variable or parameter to the thousandth or even the millionth decimal point can eventually alter the complete behaviour of the system. Tiny changes that could not possibly be detected, measured or recorded could lead the system to completely different, qualitatively different, states of behaviour. This means, for all practical purposes, that the links between cause and effect are lost in the detail of what happens. For all practical purposes the links have disappeared, making it impossible to identify the specific consequences of a specific action and to identify the specific cause of a specific event. Instead, it is necessary to think in terms of general qualitative patterns related to the system as a whole.

System dynamics recognises that the links between cause and effect become distant in complex systems and are hard to detect. Chaos theory suggests that it might be more extreme than that – the links can disappear altogether if the system operates in the area of bounded instability.

## Chaos, cybernetics and statistical relationships

You will recall that those who developed cybernetics (see Chapter 2) were concerned with what feedback meant for cause-and-effect links. They sidestepped the problem by saying that a feedback system is so complex that one cannot establish what the causal links are. But the way cybernetic models operate is based on the assumption that the links generate clear connections between inputs to the system and outputs from it. It is only because of this assumption that cybernetic control can be based on statistical relationships. Chaos theory suggests that this connection is broken when a system operates in deterministic chaos. This would make cybernetic control impossible. When the cause-and-effect links are in effect lost in the complexity of specific experience strong statistical associations in data from the past may be detected, but those associations will not continue into the future.

## Going back in time

Consider what this loss of the ability to identify cause-and-effect links means. Suppose a system has moved from a particular state A many periods ago and now occupies another state B. Could one take control of this system and take it back to state A? One could, if it were possible to identify the links between the causes and effects of its behaviour and one had a record of those causes over the past periods. The system could then be made to retrace its steps and go back into its own history. If perfectly accurate records of past causes and precisely specified causal links were not available, the system could still be taken back to a position approximating A, provided that it did not escalate tiny differences. So, one could only take a system back to some previous state if it was operating in equilibrium. Only then are there the detectable connections between cause and effect and only then do tiny differences not escalate in an unpredictable way.

If, however, the system operates in bounded instability it will be impossible to make it retrace its steps. For, on its journey through time from state A to state B, it will have lost some information. It will have been impossible to keep infinitely accurate records of everything that happened to it, to measure with infinite accuracy to the millionth decimal place. This inability to retain every single scrap of information as the system moves from A to B is of great importance when the system operates in deterministic chaos. For, as the system moves backwards, it inevitably makes tiny mistakes in reproducing what happened to it. Before long those tiny mistakes take over and the system misses the state A that one is trying to take it back to. Time is irreversible and one can never give an entirely accurate explanation of why the system is where it now is (*Prigogine & Stengers, 1984*).

## Going forward in time

The same points apply if one wants to control the movement of a system to a fixed point in the future. There is no fundamental problem of principle in doing this if the system is an equilibrium one. But, to control movement to a future point when the system is boundedly unstable, one would have to specify with infinite accuracy each event, each action, required to reach that future state. If one makes some tiny error in specification the system could well amplify this and end up somewhere completely different. One cannot then decide on some future state for the system, say C, and identify the events required to take it there. It is not possible to measure or record in the infinitely accurate detail required to allow this to happen. The tiniest error could escalate and swamp the behaviour of the system. Nor could one fix on some future point and then get there by trial-and-error action, because errors would not cancel out.

One could imagine this desirable state C and stipulate that that is where one wishes to go, but there is an infinitely small chance that one will actually reach it. Stipulating the future state is then an illusion, a waste of time, when the system is operating in bounded instability. Making some assumptions about what that future state might be is also rather pointless because one will have to keep changing those assumptions. If an assumption is made about the specific future of a chaotic system, then the only useful thing to be said about that assumption is that it will not happen. It then becomes difficult to see how the assumption helps one to make a decision. The real drivers of behaviour become what has just happened, not some hypothetical and unrealisable assumption about what might (see *Box 11.1*). There is no option but to create where the system is going through action and discovering where it is going as it is going there. This is a process of learning in real time, provoked by paradox and conducted through reasoning by analogy.

---

**BOX 11.1**

## Making assumptions about the future

Take a very abstract case. Suppose we have to decide now whether we are going to invest in a particular project or not. The project will make a lot of money if certain conditions prevail in five years' time but lose a great deal if certain other conditions prevail then. We decide that we cannot forecast what the situation is likely to be in five years' time because of the level of uncertainty, but we believe that we must at least make some assumptions before we can take the decision and that we should make the decision on the basis of these assumptions.

Suppose that after much research and discussion we decide that the most reasonable assumptions are that conditions ABCD will prevail. On this basis we decide that the project will make money and we go ahead, even though we know that ABCD will not be what actually materialises. We believe we can live with that if we keep updating our assumptions as time passes. So we make the investment.

Nearly a year later, some way through to completion of the project, we review the situation and find that we need to change the basic assumptions – ABCZ is now a much more reasonable scenario, we think. But three months later the project runs into a hitch and we review the situation again. Now we think that conditions XBCW make a more reasonable scenario. Even if these conditions indicate that we are unlikely to make much money, the project is now almost complete so we continue. Some three months later the project is complete and further reviews reveal that YPCW is now the likely scenario. This looks better so we set the project running. A month later we review the first month of full-scale operation and find that the situation likely to prevail at the end of our original five-year period is now assumed to be ZPNX.

Two years ago we decided to go ahead on the basis of assumptions ABCD, knowing that they would not actually prevail. Now, looking three years ahead, we are saying that the conditions will be ZPNX, completely different as we suspected all along. And no doubt we will continue to change the assumptions during the next three years. When we look back we have to admit that we decided to do something for reasons that were completely invalid and, furthermore, we knew we were doing this at the time.

In what possible sense can we say that it was sensible or reasonable to make the decision on the basis of ABCD in the first place? The answer must be none. If we know that a set of conditions will not prevail it makes no sense at all to make a decision on the basis of such a fantasy. Yet this is what boards of directors do when they use discounted cash flow calculations to make investments. ■

It follows that no one can be 'in control' of a system that is far from equilibrium in the way that control is normally thought about, because no one can forecast the specific future of a system operating in bounded instability. No one can envision it either, unless one believes in clairvoyance or prophecy. No one can establish how the system would move before a policy change and then how it would move after the policy change. There would be no option but to take a chance, make the change and see what happens. Note that the long-term future of the system is inherently unpredictable. It is unknowable. It is not just that it is difficult to forecast accurately. It is impossible to do so. Such systems are an unravellable record of their own histories. You can see that if organisations were to display similar properties to the dynamical systems being discussed here, it would have major implications for how people think about and act in organisations.

## More orthodox perspectives

There is by no means widespread agreement on the kind of radical potential I have outlined above. Some scientists working in the field of nonlinear dynamics do take a radical perspective. For example, Prigogine speaks of a new dialogue with nature in which the purpose of science would not be that of dominating and controlling nature. Others, and they may well be the majority, do not see the kind of radical potential that Prigogine does. As an example, consider how *Holland (1998)* interprets chaos theory.

For Holland emergent patterns are predictable and regular. He points to how chaos theory is used to explain why it is that the long-term future of nonlinear systems is unpredictable. He accepts this but then takes the example of the weather system and says:

Because meteorologists do *not* know the values of all the relevant variables, they do not work at a level of detail, or over time spans, in which chaos would be relevant … Moreover, rather than trying to develop predictions based on remote initial conditions, as with the butterfly effect, meteorologists start anew each day, using the most recent data. These observations continually bring the state of the model into agreement with what has actually occurred. Under this regime chaos theory has little relevance. (p. 44)

However, the procedure Holland describes still does not enable long-term prediction, only short-term prediction. What Holland does, then, is to dismiss the importance of long-term unpredictability and holds that it is possible to get by through focusing on the short term. In organisational terms it may be impossible to follow this advice. Sometimes organisations must make investments that take a very long time to produce results and those results depend on the fine details of what happens over long periods. Holland's approach is of little assistance in these circumstances because some method of making long-term decisions is still required. How is one supposed to do this if the long-term future is radically unpredictable?

## 11.5  COMPARISONS WITH OTHER SYSTEMS THEORIES

Open systems theory models a system at both the macro and micro levels while cybernetics focuses on the macro level. Both assume that systems naturally tend to states of stable equilibrium. Systems dynamics models systems at the macro level and assumes nonlinear relationships between variables in a system that does not move rapidly to equilibrium. The models are specified in mathematical terms in which the values of the variables (micro events) affecting the system are set externally by the environment. These variables, or micro events, are assumed to occur at their average rate. In other words, 'noise', or 'fluctuations', in the variables are assumed away, leading to the assumption that the most probable trajectory is the only one. This allows the modeller to use a deterministic, mechanical description of the system. It is also assumed that individual components in a given system are identical, or have a normal distribution around an average, or vary in a fixed, exogenously imposed manner. Models built on these assumptions display different dynamics; they occupy different attractors, at different parameter values, as set by the modeller. The assumptions made in systems dynamics models are such that the system itself cannot move of its own accord from one attractor basin to another but must await manipulation by the modeller, the objective observer who stands outside the system. Because the model of the system cannot move attractors of its own accord, it lacks the vitality of most of the systems we see around us.

How do the systems models discussed in this chapter compare?

## Chaos theory

Chaos theory is an extension of this kind of systems dynamics. It demonstrates that the kind of equations used by systems dynamics modellers have:

- different possible stationary states;
- different possible cyclical states;
- chaotic motions of various kinds.

For different parameter values there are different basins of attraction. The modeller can alter the parameters and move the system from one basin to another. However, the system model can only follow trajectories within the basin of the initial conditions and cannot of its own accord jump from one basin to another. The model does not display self-organisation. There is no place for intrinsic novelty.

Various strange attractors can be shown to occur, given certain initial conditions/parameter values. The insight is that, in certain conditions, dynamical systems are characterised by sensitive dependence on initial conditions and radical long-term unpredictability at some level of description. At other levels of description and over the short term, predictability is still possible. Some modellers play down the property of radical unpredictability and focus on the short term and that level of description where some predictability is still possible. This is because the equations used in chaos theory are the same as those used in systems dynamics. They model at the macro level and they assume average relationships with the environment and average micro events and entities.

## Dissipative systems

Prigogine's theory of dissipative structures takes a radical step from systems dynamics and chaos theory. Like systems dynamics, Prigogine's models are cast in nonlinear equations that specify changes in the macro states of a system and like systems dynamics the system is assumed to be a non-equilibrium one. In addition, however, the assumption that micro events occur at their average rate is dropped. In other words, the 'noise', or 'fluctuations', in the form of variations around any average are incorporated into the model. Prigogine's work demonstrates the importance of these 'fluctuations', showing how fluctuations impart to a nonlinear system that is held far from equilibrium the capacity to move spontaneously from one attractor basin to another. He calls this 'order through fluctuations' and shows how it occurs through a process of spontaneous self-organisation. This order takes the form of a dissipative structure.

It is important to note how the nature of self-organisation and emergence is conceived in these theoretical developments. Self-organisation and emergence are thought of as the collective response of whole populations. The process is described in terms of correlations and communication at a distance.

### Insights

The move from systems dynamics and chaos theory to a theory of dissipative structures offers a number of insights:

1  Nonlinear systems operating in conditions far from equilibrium are sensitive to initial conditions and fluctuations and their long-term future development is radically unpredictable.
2  The capacity of a system to self-organise depends upon fluctuations in its environment and the diversity of its micro entities. Non-average behaviour is a requirement for the production of novelty.
3  The notion of an individual trajectory is replaced by that of collective, adaptive responses. Attention is thus focused on populations rather than individual entities or single paths of development.
4  Emergence and spontaneous self-organisation are central features of these models.

## 11.6  SUMMARY

This chapter has reviewed a number of developments in theories of systemic behaviour, namely chaos, dissipative structures and synergetics. These developments suggest a number of radical possibilities, which not everyone working in the field accepts. It is important for those trying to understand organisational life to consider the implications of these new systems theory developments. This is because current ways of understanding management and organisation were derived from the systems theories developed just after the Second World War, namely open systems theory, cybernetics and systems dynamics. If these are being superseded, in some sense by chaos and dissipative structure theory, then this could have important implications for theories of organisation. What if the future of a creative organisation is radically unpredictable over the long term? What if those long-term outcomes emerge from processes of self-organisation? What if difference, disorder and chance are essential to the creative evolution of an organisation? These are questions I will return to in Chapter 16. At this point, however, the next chapter will outline the nature of complexity theory.

## FURTHER READING

On chaos there is the classic account of how chaos was discovered and what it means by Gleick (1988), and also Briggs & Peat (1989) and Kellert (1993). A more mathematical but accessible treatment is Stewart (1989). On self-organisation it is useful to read Prigogine & Stengers (1984), Davies (1987), Nicolis & Prigogine (1989).

## REFERENCES

Anderson, P. W., Arrow, K. J. & Pines, D. (1988), *The Economy as an Evolving Complex System*, Menlo Park, CA: Addison-Wesley.

Baumol, W. J. & Benhabib, J. (1989), Chaos: significance, mechanism and economic applications, *Journal of Economic Perspectives*, Winter, vol. 3, no. 1, pp. 77–105.

Briggs, J. & Peat, F. (1989), *The Turbulent Mirror*, New York: Harper & Row.

Davies, P. (1987), *The Cosmic Blueprint*, London: William Heinemann.

Gleick, J. (1988), *Chaos: The Making of a New Science*, London: William Heinemann.

Haken, H. (1977), *Synergetics: An Introduction*, Berlin: Springer.

Holland, J. (1998), *Emergence: From chaos to order*, New York: Oxford University Press.

Kellert, S. H. (1993), *In the Wake of Chaos*, Chicago: University of Chicago Press.

Kelsey, D. (1988), The economics of chaos or the chaos of economies, *Oxford Economic Papers*, vol. 40, pp. 1–31.

Kelso, J. A. Scott (1995), *Dynamic Patterns: The self-organization of brain and behaviour*, Cambridge, MA: MIT Press.

Nicolis, G. & Prigogine, I. (1989), *Exploring Complexity: An Introduction*, New York: W. H. Freeman.

Peters, E. E. (1991), *Chaos and Order in the Capital Markets: A New View of Cycles, Prices and Market Volatility*, New York: John Wiley.

Prigogine, I. & Stengers, I. (1984), *Order out of Chaos: Man's New Dialogue with Nature*, New York: Bantam Books.

Stacey, R. (1991), *The Chaos Frontier: Creative Strategic Control for Business*, Oxford: Butterworth–Heinemann.

Stewart, I. (1989), *Does God Play Dice? The Mathematics of Chaos*, Oxford: Blackwell.

# 12 Complex adaptive systems

## 12.1 INTRODUCTION

In Chapter 11, I described how chaos theory identifies a dynamic between stability and instability, namely bounded instability. This paradoxical dynamic is both stable and unstable at the same time and it displays variety as opposed to the repetitive, uniform behaviour of the dynamics of stability. When a system operates in the dynamics of bounded instability, its short-term behaviour is predictable at a fairly detailed and quantitative level. Its long-term behaviour is predictable in a qualitative sense because it displays recognisable patterns called strange attractors and it may be predictable in a quantitative sense, but only at a coarse level of detail. However, prediction at a fine level of detail over the long term is impossible for all practical purposes. Long-term unpredictability and variety seem to go together.

This matter of variety and long-term unpredictability is of central importance in relation to the possibility of controlling a system. Suppose that the production of variety is a requirement for the successful evolution of a system. In other words, it must operate in the dynamic of bounded instability. Suppose also that the long-term success of any change made to the system depends only on the qualitative pattern and coarse level of quantitative detail produced by that change. Then, it will be possible for someone standing outside that system to determine in advance which changes should be made so as to secure outcomes selected well in advance of making the change. It will be possible to control the system over long time periods and actualise a comprehensive long-term intention in relation to that system as a whole.

However, if the long-term success of any change to the system depends upon the fine detail of the outcome, then the situation is completely different. Someone standing outside the system, or inside it for that matter, will not be able to predict outcomes to the required level of detail. It will be impossible to determine what system-wide outcomes will be in advance of action and so ensure success well in advance of making a change. The only alternative will be to make the change and deal with what happens. As chaos theorists put it, there is no shorter way than to run the program; that is, there is no shorter way of discovering the nature of an experience than that of having it. I argued, in the last chapter, that the success of some organisational change depends upon the outcomes of that change at a fairly fine level of detail. The question then becomes: how is one to understand the nature of management and the process of organisational change when the long-term future is unpredictable at the required level of detail?

One way of thinking about this question is provided by further developments in systems theory. Chaos theory is a theory of systems that focuses on the same level of description as systems dynamics; that is, both focus on the level of the system as a whole. They both make assumptions about the entities comprising a system and their interactions, particularly with the environment. The assumption is that both the entities and their interactions are average, or normally distributed around an average. Dissipative structure theory develops the notions of self-organisation and emergence. It models the system of interest in terms of nonlinear mathematical equations governing state changes at the macro level of the system, just as systems dynamics and chaos theory do. However, unlike the latter, the former models incorporate fluctuations, or variety, in exogenous variables, or micro events. In other words, fluctuations in the sense of non-average behaviour in the system's environment are incorporated in the former and not in the latter. The result is the phenomenon of self-organising order through fluctuations. In addition, unlike systems dynamics and chaos theory, the dissipative structure model incorporates fluctuations in the sense of diversity in the system. The result is the possibility of evolution, that is the emergence of radically unpredictable novelty.

This is a very important point. It is only in the presence of non-average behaviour, that is diversity and difference of entities and their interactions, that a system has the internal capacity to move spontaneously from one attractor to another and to evolve new attractors. Note also that self-organisation in dissipative structure theory is a collective response of the whole system. It takes the form of correlations and resonances between the entities comprising the system that emerge as new patterns or order.

Another approach to understanding complex behaviour is that taken by scientists working at the Santa Fe Institute in New Mexico, who formulate systemic behaviour in agent-based terms. Here there are no equations at the macro level. Instead, the system is modelled as a population of agents interacting with each other according to their own local if–then rules. Note how this theory of systems differs from all of those so far surveyed in that it focuses attention at a lower level of description, namely the level of the individual agents that form the system. The models demonstrate how local, self-organising behaviour yields emergent order for the whole system and also, in certain conditions, evolution in the form of emergent novelty. These models focus on a system's internal capacity to evolve spontaneously. Here self-organisation refers to local interactions between agents in the absence of a system-wide blueprint, rather than the collective response of the whole system as in dissipative structure theory.

This chapter will be concerned with complex adaptive systems theory. I think it is important to look carefully at what the theory of complex adaptive systems is stating and how it is interpreted. I think this is important in order to avoid drawing loose and unjustified conclusions about organisations on the basis of complexity theory.

## 12.2   COMPLEX ADAPTIVE SYSTEMS

A complex adaptive system consists of a large number of agents, each of which behaves according to some set of rules. These rules require the agents to adjust their behaviour to that of other agents. In other words, agents interact with, and adapt to, each other. For example, a flock of birds might be thought of as a complex adaptive system. It consists of many agents, perhaps thousands, who might be following simple rules to do with adapting to the behaviour of neighbours so as to fly in formation without crashing into each other. A human being might be seen as a network of 100 000 genes interacting with each other. An ecology could be thought of as a network of vast numbers of species relating to each other. A brain could be considered as a system of 10 billion neurones interacting with each other. In much the same way, an organisation might be thought of in terms of a network of people relating to each other. Complexity science seeks to identify common features of the dynamics of such systems or networks in general.

Key questions are these: how do such complex nonlinear systems with their vast numbers of interacting agents function to produce orderly patterns of behaviour? How do such living systems evolve to produce new orderly patterns of behaviour?

The traditional scientific approach to answering these questions would be to look for general laws directly determining the order and governing the evolution observed. The expectation would be to find an overall blueprint at the level of the whole system according to which it would behave. The approach taken by complexity scientists is fundamentally different. They do not look for an overall blueprint for the whole system at all but, instead, they model agent interaction, with each agent behaving according to their own principles of local interaction. In such a structure, no individual agent, or group of agents, determines the patterns of behaviour that the system displays or how those patterns evolve and neither does anything outside of the network. This is the principle of self-organisation: agents interact locally according to their own principles, or 'intentions', in the absence of an overall blueprint for the system they form.

A central concept in agent-based models of complex systems is that of self-organisation, which involves the emergence and maintenance of order, or complexity, out of a state that is less ordered, or complex. Self-organisation and emergence lead to fundamental structural development (novelty), not just superficial change. This is 'spontaneous' or 'autonomous', arising from the intrinsic nonlinear nature of the system, sometimes in interaction with the environment. Some external designer does not impose it, rather global behaviour emerges from simple, reflex-like rules. Self-organisation is a bottom-up process in which detailed input of the system itself determines what happens.

Since it is not possible to experiment with living systems in real-life situations, complexity scientists use computers to simulate the behaviour of complex adaptive systems. Some scientists argue that computer simulations are a legitimate new form of experiment but others hold that they show nothing about nature, only about computer programs.

## How complex adaptive systems are studied

In the computer simulations, each agent is a computer program. This computer program is a set of operating rules and instructions concerning how that program should interact with other computer programs. It is possible to add a set of rules for evaluating those operations according to some performance criteria. It is also possible to add a set of rules for changing the rules of operation and evaluation in the light of their performance. Another set of rules can be added according to which the whole computer program is copied to produce another one. That set of replicating rules could take the form of a rule about locating another computer program to mate with. Another rule could instruct the first to copy the top half of its program and the second to copy the bottom half of its program and then add the two copies together. The result would be a new, or offspring, program. This is known as the genetic algorithm, developed by John Holland of the Santa Fe Institute.

You can see how such a procedure would model important features of evolution in that a population of computer programs interact with each other, breed and so evolve. The result is a complex adaptive system in the computer consisting of a collection of agents, each of which is a computer program. Each of the agents in the simulation, that is each computer program, is made up of a bit string, a series of ones and zeros representing an electric current that is either on or off.

Take a simple example, namely a flock of birds. Whenever I ask a group of managers how they think it is that thousands of birds manage to fly in formation, the usual reply is that they are following the leader. The following simulation indicates that this may not be the case. *Reynolds (1987)* simulated the flocking behaviour of birds with a computer program consisting of a network of moving agents called Boids. Each Boid follows the same three simple rules:

1  Maintain a minimum distance from other objects in the environment including other Boids.
2  Match velocities with other Boids in the neighbourhood.
3  Move towards the perceived centre of mass of the Boids in the neighbourhood.

These three rules are sufficient to produce flocking behaviour. So, Boids interacting with each other according to their own local rules of interaction produce an emergent, coherent pattern for the whole system of Boids. There is no plan, or blueprint, at the level of the flock. There is no overall intention in relation to the flock on the part of any Boid. Each does its own thing and orderly behaviour for the whole emerges. Flocking is an attractor for a system in which entities follow the three rules given above.

Another example of the operation of an adaptive system is provided by the trail-laying behaviour of ants. Ants set off from their nest in search of food and those who find it lay down trails of a chemical called pheromone. Other ants learn to follow the trail and find the food. This behaviour has also been simulated using what are called cellular automata. In the Vants simulation (*Langton, 1996*) each agent moved across a grid according to rules such as 'if you move into a square coloured blue then turn right and change the colour of that square to yellow'. As they did this, they left coloured trails that other Vants could follow just as ants do. The simulation starts from a random position in which the Vants simply move without pattern. There is no 'boss' or central programmer. However, once the table of rules has been established, bottom-up self-organisation takes over and coherent patterns of behaviour emerge out of the chaos of randomness: the Vants learn to follow a trail. This bottom-up process and its emergent outcomes are fundamental properties of complex adaptive systems. Trail-following behaviour is an attractor for a system whose entities follow the rules set out in the table of rules.

Note, in these examples, how all agents follow the same rules. Each agent is the same as every other agent and there is no variation in the way they interact with each other. Emergence here is therefore not the consequence of non-average behaviour, as was the case with dissipative structures in the last chapter. Instead, emergence is the consequence of local interaction between agents. Unlike dissipative structures, and because of the postulated uniformity of behaviour, these simulations cannot spontaneously move, of their own accord, from one basin of attraction to another. Instead, they stay always with one attractor and show no evolution. However, more complicated simulations of complex adaptive systems do take account of differences in agents or classes of agents and different ways of interacting. These simulations do then show the capacity to move spontaneously from one attractor to another and to evolve new ones. This is demonstrated by the simulation called Tierra (*Ray, 1992*).

## The Tierra simulation

Organic life utilises energy to organise matter and it evolves, developing more and more diverse forms, as organisms compete and cooperate with each other for light and food in geographic space. An analogy to this would be digital life in which central processing unit (CPU) time organises strings of digits (programs) in the space of computer memory. Computer programs are used as the analogue of living organisms. Would digital life then evolve as bit strings compete for CPU time? This is the question explored by Ray in his simulation.

### What the programmer sets
In this simulation the programmer:

- sets aside a block of RAM in a computer, designating it as the space within which the digital organism can operate and evolve. The space is divided into blocks available for occupation by digital organisms.
- designs the first digital organism, hereafter referred to as a creature. This creature is a self-replicating assembler-language program. All programs are converted into machine code since it is this that directly manipulates bits, bytes, CPU registers and something called the instruction pointer. Ray likened assembler language to amino acids in biology. The first, or mother creature, is 80 instructions long; that is, it is a string of digits of a particular length with its beginning and end marked by a template. The code enables this creature to write, read and execute. In order to replicate it has to examine itself to identify where in memory it begins and ends. It calculates its size and allocates a block of adjacent memory of the same size for its daughter. It then copies, or writes, its code into this space and executes a divide

instruction so that the daughter is now independent. After this, the mother cannot write in the daughter's space but can proceed to replicate again. The daughter too can now replicate. However, the independence is not complete because although no creature can write in another's space, it can read and execute code in spaces that are near enough to it. Interaction between creatures is thus possible.

- determines that the evolution of this system is to be driven by random mutations taking the form of bit flipping, some of this occurring in a background way and some occurring during replication. These mutations affect the process whereby the creatures examine themselves and calculate their size, thus potentially causing the production of offspring of different sizes.
- introduces a constraint taking the form of scarce computer time which works as follows. Agents are required to post their locations in the computer memory on a public notice board. Each agent is then called upon, in turn according to a circular queue, to receive a slice of computer time for carrying out its operational and replication tasks.
- introduces a further constraint on agent life span. Agents are lined up in a linear queue according to their age and a 'reaper' lops off some of these, generally the oldest. However, by successfully executing some parts of their programs agents can slow down their move up the linear queue while flawed agents rise quickly to the top.

The only task agents have is that of replicating in a regime of scarce CPU time and what happens is that new modes of doing this evolve. In other words, different categories of replication method appear. These changes in numerical terms can be observed by watching changing patterns of dots on a computer screen. An analogy is then drawn between this digital interaction and the biological evolution of species and the simulation is described in these biological terms. For example, categories of agents are said to develop their own survival strategies. It is important to remember that this is an analogy drawing attention to changes in categories of agent in the digital medium and changes in categories of species in the biological medium.

### What happens in the simulation

The simulation was set off by introducing a single agent consisting of 80 instructions. Within a short time, the computer memory space was 80 per cent occupied by these agents but then the reaper took over and prevented further population growth. After a while agents consisting of 45 instructions appeared, but they were too short to replicate. They overcame this problem by borrowing some of the code of longer agents in order to replicate. This strategy enabled them to replicate faster within their allocated computer time. In other words, a kind of parasite emerged. The use of the term 'parasite' is obviously an analogy. What actually happens in the computer simulation is as follows. Through random mutation, code representing a template at either end of an agent appears in the middle of the bit string. When the instruction to identify the beginning and end of the string is carried out, the middle is mistaken for the end and a shorter version is copied into an adjacent space. This copy does not have all the required code. However, because it can read and execute in adjacent spaces it can match its template with code in an adjacent space.

Returning to the analogy, although the parasites did not destroy their hosts, they were dependent on them for replication. If they became too numerous in relation to hosts then they destroyed their own ability to replicate and so declined. In the simulation, the parasites suffered periodic catastrophes. One of these catastrophes occurred because the hosts stopped posting their positions on the public notice board and in effect hid so that the parasites could no longer find them. Some hosts had, thus, developed an immunisation to parasites by using camouflage as a survival strategy. But, in hiding, the hosts had not retained any note of their position in the computer memory. So, they had to examine themselves to see if their position corresponded to the position being offered computer time, before they could respond to that offer. This increased the time they needed for replication. However, although not perfect, the strategy worked in a good enough way so that the parasites were nearly wiped out.

Then, however, the parasites developed their own memories and did not need to consult the public posting board. Once again, it was the parasites' turn to succeed. Later, hyperparasites appeared to feed off the parasites. These were 80 instructions long, just like the hosts, but they had developed instructions to examine themselves for parasites and feed off the parasites by diverting computer time from them. These hyperparasites worked symbiotically by sharing reproduction code: they could no longer reproduce on their own but required cooperation. Although this was not yet cross-over replication, analogous to sexual reproduction, something close to it had emerged spontaneously as a strategy for survival without anyone programming it.

This cooperation was then exploited by opportunistic mutants in the form of tiny intruders who placed themselves between replicating hyperparasites and intercepted and used hyperparasite code for their own replication. The cheaters could then thrive and replicate although they were only 27 instructions long. Later, the hyperparasites found a way to defeat the cheats, but not for long.

### How the simulation is interpreted

I would like to emphasise, once more, what is happening in this simulation. I think that this is important because it is all too easy to slip into rather cavalier interpretations of what simulations like this mean for biological evolution and the evolution of human organisations. I know this because in previous editions of this book, and in other publications, I have been as guilty of this as anyone else. In terms of the computer simulation, this is what I understand to be happening. After the simulation has run for some time there are a number of bit strings, each arranged into operating instructions requiring them to replicate in a particular way, often in interaction with other bit strings. These bit strings fall into categories and all within a category replicate in the same way while bit strings in another category replicate in a different way. In complexity language, each of these categories is an attractor and there are a number of different attractors in the system. To put it another way, there is microdiversity in the total population of bit strings. During one round of replication, that is during a given short time period, the bit strings carry out their instructions, one after the other, and as they do so bits in some of the strings are randomly flipped. Over a series of runs the bit flipping and the interaction between the bit strings, that is self-organisation, result in rearrangements in the bit strings themselves. In other words, new arrangements of bit strings appear, that is new categories of replicating instructions. At the same time older categories disappear because of the procedure of competitive removal of some of them.

In summary, the population of bit strings is a population of algorithms, or logical procedures. What running the simulation demonstrates is the logical properties of iteration (replication) and local interaction of algorithms (self-organisation in the absence of a blueprint for the whole) in the presence of random mutation and competitive selection. The simulation shows that it is logically possible for self-organisation, mutation and selection operating iteratively to display evolution – that is, emergent novelty that is radically unpredictable. This evolution is characterised by both destruction of some categories and emergence of new ones.

Anything more that is said about the simulation is an interpretation by way of analogy. So, Ray uses the simulation as an analogy for biology and calls the bit strings creatures. One category of bit strings are called hosts and another are called parasites. If the interpretation is done carefully, it may provide insight. For example, it may indicate that new biological forms can emerge from a process of self-organisation. If done carelessly it could produce unwarranted claims. For the purposes of this book, therefore, it is important to take great care in using insights about self-organisation and emergence in relation to organisations. The question becomes one of how to interpret, in organisational terms, the logic of iterative, nonlinear interaction between replicating algorithms and their self-organising and emergent properties. Even more fundamental is the question of whether it even makes sense to try to do this.

So, this simulation displays digital evolution. The digital forms are self-organising and new forms of interaction emerge. What emerges is unpredictable. Many other simulations display the same processes of self-organisation, emergence and unpredictability.

How is one to interpret the significance of these findings? What implications do they have for thinking about organisations? Increasingly researchers at universities are turning to complexity theory for a new frame of reference. Practising managers are also increasingly being exposed to these ideas. It is important, therefore, to look rather carefully at just how various people are interpreting the meaning of self-organisation and emergence. As soon as one does this, it becomes clear that there are significant differences between complexity scientists themselves. This section will consider the nature of these differences. In the next chapter I will explore how those differences appear in the way researchers and writers are using the concepts in relation to organisations.

## 12.3 DIFFERENT INTERPRETATIONS OF COMPLEXITY

It seems to me that there are at least four important matters on which those working in the field of complexity take different positions. These four matters are:

1 The significance of self-organisation.
2 The nature of emergence.
3 The importance of unpredictability.
4 The implications for the scientific method.

To illustrate how views on these matters differ (*Griffin, Shaw & Stacey, 1998*), I will now review the positions of five leading figures in the field of complexity, namely, *Langton (1996), Gell-Mann (1994), Holland (1998), Kauffman (1995)* and *Goodwin (1994)*.

## Langton

*Langton (1996)* puts his work into the category of artificial life (AL), carefully distinguishing it from artificial intelligence (AI). He locates AL historically in the development of mechanical control systems that have complicated internal dynamics, such as clocks. He describes how clockwork mechanisms were used to make automata that imparted life-like movements to mechanical figures, such as the mechanical figures which strike a bell to mark the hours. Process control developed from this, leading to programmable controllers. Then, in this century there was the formalisation of logical sequences of steps that is the essence of a mechanical process. It was realised that the essence of a mechanical process was an abstract control structure or program, that is a sequence of simple actions selected from a finite repertoire. The essence of the control structure could be captured in an abstract set of rules, a formal specification, without regard to the material out of which the machine was constructed. This logical form is an algorithm, that is a step-by-step procedure for manipulating information. It is then a short step to viewing these abstract, formal specifications, or algorithms, as potential machines, or universal computers. Programmable controllers (cybernetics), calculating engines and universal computers (formal theory of machines) come together in the form of the general-purpose computer. Note how the origins of complexity theory, in Langton's view, can be traced through cybernetics.

### Limits of computers

Langton then points to the limits of computers. First, there is the limit to computability in principle. There are some behaviours for which no formal specification can be given for a machine that will calculate that behaviour. In principle, an algorithm cannot be specified for such behaviour. Then there is the limit to computability in practice. Here, although algorithmic in principle, there are many behaviours for which an algorithm cannot yet be identified in practice. This makes it necessary to draw a distinction between the logical structure of a machine and the logical structure of that machine's behaviour. It may be possible to specify the structure of the machine but not the structure of its behaviour and the only way to understand its behaviour will then be to run the machine and observe its behaviour. In essence, this is what those studying AL do: they specify the structure of a system whose behaviour cannot be generated by an algorithm because of its nonlinear complexity and then they observe the behaviour that emerges.

So, Langton specifies the simple rules of interaction that each agent in his system will follow and then observes the behaviour that emerges, as in the Vants simulation described above. He stresses the radical unpredictability of the pattern that emerges. The inability to provide a global rule, or algorithm, for changes in the system's global state makes it necessary to concentrate on the interactions occurring at the local level. It is the logical structure of the interactions, rather than the properties of the agents themselves, which is important.

Langton sees organisms as extremely complicated and finely tuned biochemical machines and AL as the science devoted to abstracting the logical form of an organism. The fact that the organisms on earth are carbon-based constructions is not seen as essential and so the same logical form can be exhibited by silicon-based computer organisms (programs). In AL, life is thought of as an information structure, encoded for example in the DNA. This genetic information is manipulated to generate carbon-based life while computers are thought of as incubating information structures in silicon. Langton distinguishes AL from the AI project:

AI has based its underlying methodology for generating intelligent behaviour on the computational paradigm. That is, AI uses the technology of computation as a model of intelligence. AL, on the other hand, is attempting to develop a new computational paradigm based on natural processes that support living organisms. That is, AL uses insights from biology to explore the dynamics of interacting information structures. AL has not adopted the computational paradigm as its underlying methodology of behaviour generation, nor does it attempt to 'explain' life as a kind of computer programme. (*Langton, 1996, p. 50*)

The advantage of working with information structures is that information has no intrinsic size. The computer is *the* tool for the manipulation of information, whether that information is a consequence of our actions or a consequence of the actions of the information structures themselves. Computers themselves will not be alive, rather they will support informational universes within which dynamic populations of informational 'molecules' engage in informational 'biochemistry'. (*p. 50*)

It is important to notice, I think, how AL retains the processes of information manipulation, of computation, but locates them at the level of the agents rather than the global level as AI does. This establishes a strong link with cybernetics and cognitivism. In both of the latter, the manipulation and processing of information is a central concept. The system as a whole is no longer a cybernetic one but it is composed of cybernetic entities which function in a cognitivist manner in that they process information. Algorithms drive the behaviour of the agents, although no algorithm can be identified for behaviour at the global level. This retention of an essential cognitivist view of the world has important implications for the ease with which the insights generated by AL can be assimilated into the orthodox management discourse.

## Methodology

Langton makes this statement on methodology:

The field of Artificial Life is unabashedly mechanistic and reductionistic. However, this *new mechanism* – based as it is on multiplicities of machines and on recent results in the fields of nonlinear dynamics, chaos theory, and the formal theory of computation – is vastly different from the mechanism of the last century. (*Langton, 1996*)

What Langton appears to mean by this is that the old mechanism is one in which the components could be added to arrive at the whole in a linear manner. Parts have functions that fit together uniquely to determine the whole. The new mechanism he is talking about is one in which the parts interact according to recursive rules to produce a whole that is radically unpredictable. However, the system remains mechanistic in the sense that the recursive rules are computed and it is this running of the program that yields the resultant whole. The mechanism is the rules and the reduction is to the rules, so that there is nothing left unexplained. The system has subparts and the rules of the system specify how to modify the most elementary subparts. The rules are recursive to the context in which the subparts are embedded. There is an important feedback mechanism between levels of description. Intervention at local levels gives rise to global-level dynamics and this affects the lower levels by setting the local context within which each entity's rules are involved. The behaviour of the whole system does not depend upon the internal details of the entities, only on the details of the way they behave in each other's presence.

So, Langton's position on methodology is one that stays close to scientific orthodoxy. The methodology remains deterministic, reductionistic and mechanistic. However, he stresses the radically unpredictable nature of emergent order. For him, self-organisation is an algorithmic interaction of a cybernetic kind and emergence is a fundamentally important phenomenon.

## Gell-Mann

*Gell-Mann (1994)* gives a number of examples of complex adaptive systems: biological evolution; the behaviour of organisms; learning and thinking; the evolution of human societies; the functioning of markets; the use of computers to make predictions on the basis of past observations and to prepare strategies.

The common feature of all these processes is that in each one a complex adaptive system acquires information about its environment and its own interaction with that environment, identifying regularities in that information, condensing those regularities into a kind of "schema" or model, and acting in the real world on the basis of that schema. In each case, there are various competing schemata, and the results of the action in the real world feed back to influence the competition among those schemata. (*p. 17*)

… complex adaptive systems … are collectives of co-adapting adaptive agents, which construct schemata to describe and predict one another's behaviour. (*p. 318*)

The cognitivist frame of reference, and its cybernetic underpinnings, could hardly be put more clearly than this. Furthermore, the emphasis on evolution as competitively selected adaptation also clearly stands out. He then goes on to define effective complexity of a system in algorithmic, informational terms as the length of the schema used to describe its regularities, relative to the complex adaptive system that is observing it. He locates effective complexity as intermediate between order and disorder, stating that it is only here that a complex adaptive system can function. Order is defined as too much regularity and disorder as too little.

Conditions between order and disorder characterize not only the environment within which life can arise, but also life itself, with its high effective complexity and great depth. (*p. 116*)

Gell-Mann does not talk a great deal about self-organisation and emergence, at least not in the book that most now use when importing his ideas into organisation theory. Typical of his references to self-organisation and emergence is the following quote:

In an astonishing variety of contexts, apparently complex structures or behaviors emerge from systems characterized by very simple rules. These systems are said to be self-organised and their properties are said to be emergent. The grandest example is the universe itself, the full complexity of which emerges from simple rules plus the operation of chance. (*p. 100*)

It is important here to note the use of the word 'apparently' to limit the notion of the complex and the emphasis that he places on self-organisation as a process of following 'simple' rules. It is important to note this, I think, because the emphasis on apparent complexity and simple rules makes it very easy indeed to assimilate what Gell-Mann says into the orthodox discourse on the nature of organisations. What Gell-Mann is doing is downplaying the importance of self-organising process and emergence and focusing on competitive selection as the driver of evolution in complex adaptive systems. This is made clear by the importance he attaches to 'frozen accidents':

The tree-like structure of branching histories involves a game of chance at every branching. Any individual coarse-grained history consists of a particular outcome of each of those games. As each history continues through time, it registers increasing numbers of such chance outcomes. But some of those accidents become frozen as rules for the future, at least for some portion of the universe. Thus the number of possible regularities keeps increasing with time, and so does the possible complexity. (*p. 229*)

So like Langton, Gell-Mann stays with orthodox scientific methodology. He emphasises the importance of chance in the evolution of complex adaptive systems. Although this implies long-term unpredictability, Gell-Mann seems to me to downplay the implications of this and focuses instead on regularities and predictability. His emphasis on 'frozen accidents' and competitive selection is close to the orthodox ideas of neo-Darwinism, as is his lack of emphasis on self-organisation and emergence, which he clearly does not see as radical concepts in any way. Despite talking about the importance of interaction, he retains the primacy of the autonomous individual in the sense of agents and systems that individually represent a world and then act autonomously on those representations. For me, the potentially radical implications of complexity theory are readily assimilated by Gell-Mann into scientific orthodoxy. Complexity theory, in his version, is an interesting extension of orthodoxy. This, and the explicitly cognitivist frame of reference he works within, makes it almost inevitable that the importation of his work for theorising about organisation will not pose any radical challenge.

## Holland

Modelling lies at the heart of Holland's way of understanding life:

Among living forms on earth, the construction of objects and scripts that serve as models is a uniquely human activity ... It is less apparent that models are a pervasive part of everyday activity. Driving to or from work is model directed; we have a kind of internal map of the principal landmarks and turning points along the way. We are typically unaware of this map until we have to search for an alternative route ... In that search we carry out virtual experiments, rather than actually testing the alternative routes. Herein lies a major value of models: we can anticipate consequences without becoming involved in time-consuming, possibly dangerous, overt actions. (*Holland, 1998, p. 10*)

Holland is particularly concerned with nonlinear agent-based models and he sets out the procedure for designing such models. The first step is to shear away irrelevant detail because the model must be simpler than that which it models. He then talks about specifying the mechanisms through which entities, or agents, relate to each other and how these mechanisms form the building blocks of the model. The configuration of the building blocks determines the state of the model at any particular moment and transition functions determine how it changes state.

... the art of model building turns on selecting a level of detail that admits simple laws ... (*p. 46*)

It is our ability to discern and use building blocks that makes the perpetual novelty of our world understandable, and even predictable. (*p. 25*)

The program is fully reducible to the rules (instructions) that define it, so nothing remains hidden; yet the behaviours generated are not easily anticipated from an inspection of those rules. (*p. 5*)

If the model is well conceived, it makes possible prediction and planning and it reveals new possibilities. (*p. 11*)

Holland's cognitivist frame of reference is quite explicit, as is his deterministic and reductionistic approach to science. He clearly takes the position of the independent observer of a system and talks about models needing to follow the designer's intent. Also, the model need bear no resemblance to what is being modelled. Repeatedly he talks about focusing on the time spans and the levels of detail that allow the uncovering of regularities and unchanging laws. He stresses how simple rules of interaction yield emergent pattern, how rules generate perpetual novelty. However, he rapidly follows such statements with others in which he says a phenomenon is emergent only when it is recognisable and recurring, although it may not be easy to recognise or explain. So, he points to chance, unpredictability and novelty and then rapidly backs away from these notions to advocate concentrating on time spans and levels of detail where predictability is possible and 'novelty' is regular.

The emphasis he places on the autonomous individual also comes out very clearly when he describes the individual agents in his models. He says that these agents must have strategies, that is prescriptions telling them what to do as the game unfolds, approximating a complete strategy that tells them what to do in all possible situations.

... It is next to impossible to predict the course of the game. Emergence and perpetual novelty are ever present in games where the opponents are adapting to each other. (*p. 10*)

This view of opponents' adapting to each others' strategies, encourages a more careful look at emergence in rule-governed systems. A computer, once supplied with the rules of the game, and the rules that determined the players' strategies and changes in strategies (setting aside chance moves), can, move by move, determine the course of the game. So the overall system is fully defined. Despite this, an outside observer will be hard put to determine what happens next, even after extended observation ... what, if anything, shows the regularity and predictability we expect of emergent patterns? (*pp. 10–11*)

Above all, we've seen that models give us a way of compensating for the perpetual novelty of the world. (*p. 243*)

What I see here is someone pointing to radical unpredictability, emergent novelty through a radical notion of self-organisation and then immediately assimilating it into orthodox science and so neutering its implications. Again, I would argue that the principal route through which this is achieved is the retention of a cognitivist perspective on human knowing. As with Gell-Mann, I would argue that in the hands of Holland, complexity theory represents an interesting development of orthodoxy in the natural sciences. I am not trying to say that this is unimportant. I am simply pointing to the reasoning process being employed. Holland's views, even more so than Gell-Mann's, are immediately and easily assimilated into management orthodoxy.

## Kauffman

Kauffman's work has much in common with that of Gell-Mann and Holland but in some important respects it is radically different: his work holds much of the radical implications of complexity while that of the others slips into orthodoxy. The similarity is in his method. He simulates abstract living systems consisting of large numbers of autonomous adaptive agents in terms of information-processing systems. What he does is quite close to Langton's work on cellular automata. Once again, the agents and their rules of interaction are simple and, from this simplicity of interaction, complex novelty emerges. As with the others, his agents are cybernetic entities, cognitivist in nature. His methodology and the underlying cognitivist assumptions make it just as easy to import his modelling approach into orthodox theorising about organisations. However, the conclusions he draws from his work are radical.

Biology has come to seem the science of the accidental, the ad hoc, and we just one of the fruits of this ad hocery ... We humans, a trumped-up, tricked-out, horn-blowing, self-important presence on the globe need never have occurred ... Since Darwin, we turn to a single, singular force, Natural selection ... Without it we reason, there would be nothing but incoherent disorder. (*Kauffman, 1995, pp. 7–8*)

I shall argue ... that this idea is wrong ... the emerging sciences of complexity begin to suggest that the order is not all accidental, that vast veins of spontaneous order lie at hand. (p8)

The first theme is self-organization. Whether we confront ... the origin of life ... or the patterns of co-evolution ... we have found the signature of law. All these phenomena give signs of nonmysterious but emergent order ... Selection is the second theme ... powerful, but limited ... the inevitability of historical accident is the third theme. (*pp. 185–6*)

So, Kauffman is taking a radical stand. This is one which places emergent novelty at the centre of life and as a consequence he accepts that one has to give up the dream of predicting the details. Instead, one has to pursue the hope of explaining, understanding and, perhaps, predicting the emergent generic properties of a system.

If I am right, the very nature of co-evolution is to attain this edge of chaos, a web of compromises where each species prospers as well as possible but where none can be sure if its best next step will set off a trickle or a landslide. In this precarious world, avalanches, small and large, sweep the system relentlessly ... At this poised state between order and disorder, the layers cannot foretell the unfolding consequences of their actions. While there is law in the distribution of avalanche sizes that arise in the poised state, there is unpredictability in each individual case ... In such a poised world, we must give up the pretense of long-term prediction. (*p. 29*)

The radical position Kauffman takes up here is directly contrary to management orthodoxy and it is this perspective I will be interested in exploring in relation to organisations.

## Goodwin

*Goodwin (1994)* also holds the radical implications of complexity theory, particularly emphasising relationship and participation. He points to two aspects of the development of form: an individual developmental cycle (Aristotelian evolution) and the evolution of species, or new forms. Neo-Darwinists see the individual development cycle as being determined by genes and markers on genes. In other words, the typical phases and features of individual development have causes that are to be found in the genes. Evolution of the genome then occurs through random mutation and competitive selection. The result is infinite variety, novelty, that is partly history determined and partly due to chance, all cobbled together without any internal, inherent order. Like Kauffman, Goodwin rejects this view and presents the following argument.

Goodwin takes the organism, rather than the gene, as the fundamental unit in biology. He thinks in terms of a network of interacting genes located within an environment, or context, which he calls the morphological field. This context is a constraint on the possible patterns of expression by the genetic network. The field limits the set of possible sequential trajectories. The field, as a constraint, is then a source of order. The field is a spatio-temporal order, a dynamic process with distinctive properties that result in the emergence of progressively more complex spatial patterns as development proceeds. The action of the genes takes place within, and contributes to, a context of spatio-temporal order, the morphogenetic field. Networks of genes lie at the interface between individual development and the evolution of form. For individual development to be stable, it must be insensitive to developmental and mutational noise. However, for evolution to occur, gene interactions must be plastic and capable of generating a large variety of dynamic sequences, which can be selected and stabilised. Paradox is at the heart of his explanation.

According to neo-Darwinism, one would expect a huge variety of leaf arrangements. In fact, there are only three: whorls, as in mint or a rose; distichous – that is, alternating from side to side of a stalk – as in maize and grass; spiral, as in ivy and most plants. He suggests that the mechanical behaviour of the meristem (stalk) constrains the leaf trajectories to three. Furthermore, 80 per cent of the 250 000 higher plant species have spiral pattern leaves. He thinks that this probably reflects the relative probability of morphogenetic trajectories. All three forms, however, might be good enough light collectors and so one does not confer greater survival benefit than another. Here natural selection does not generate form but is simply one factor in stabilising it.

By ensuring that parameter values fall within certain domains, genes contribute to the stability and repeatability of a life cycle, the biological memory, or heredity. But, organisms are entities organised dynamically by developmental and morphogenetic fields. Such fields are powerful particulars: that is, things with a particular kind of agency or causal power. Fields are wholes actively organising themselves. They are agents but they are also acted upon. Organisms influence, and are influenced by, their environment. He sees a species life cycle as an attractor and claims that genetic networks can undergo extensive reorganisation as the whole organisation responds to the environment.

What Goodwin is doing here is, to my mind, quite radical. Unlike all the others I have reviewed above, he relocates agency away from interacting individual components and places it at the level of the whole. This whole is the morphogenetic field, the interface between a network and its context. This is radical because the Western mind overwhelmingly locates agency in individuals. This shift in the location of agency can be seen quite clearly if one consider levels of description. It is common to regard physics as one level of description, from which emerges chemistry. The latter is constrained by the former but cannot be reduced to it. Similarly, the genetic could be thought of as a level of description that emerges from chemistry, being constrained by, but not reducible to, chemistry. One could then see biological organisms as a level of description that emerges from the genetic but is not simply reducible to it. What Goodwin is proposing, it seems to me, is the biological as one level of description. This is the morphogenetic field constituted by the interaction of genome and context, one forming and being formed by the other, at the same time, in the field.

I see a parallel between what Goodwin is proposing and what I will later present (Chapter 15) as a relationship psychology approach to the social and the psychological. It is usual, in the social sciences, to regard the biological as one level of description. The individual mind is then seen as a higher level that is constrained by, but not reducible to, the biological. The group and the social are seen as a yet higher level of description that is constrained by, but not reducible to, the individual mind. The debate then arises as to whether the individuals form the group or whether the group/social forms the individuals. The former is the position of cognitivism and psychoanalysis and the latter the position of the social constructionist. What I will be suggesting in Chapter 15 of this book, under the label of a relationship psychology approach, is that the individual and the group are one level of description. I will be suggesting that the individual is the singular and the group the plural of one phenomenon, namely the matrix of relationships and communication between people. As Goodwin locates agency in the genes and the morphogenetic field, so I locate agency in the individual and the group matrix. I will argue that individual minds form and are formed by groups, just as groups form and are formed by individual minds, at the same time.

## A summary

I have gone to some length to separate out what I see as different perspectives on the nature of complex adaptive systems. On the one hand, there is what seems to me to be an orthodox perspective, typified by the views of Holland and Gell-Mann and to some extent by those of Langton. From this perspective, a complex system is understood in somewhat mechanistic, reductionist terms and is modelled by an objective observer in the interests of predicting its behaviour. Self-organising emergence is not seen to be a new ordering principle in the evolution of the system. Evolution occurs through random mutation and competitive selection. The radical unpredictability of emergent new forms is not emphasised. The system is modelled as a network of cybernetic and cognitivist agents: they represent regularities in the form of schemas, the equivalent of mental models; they store those representations in the form of rules and then act on the basis of those rules. On the other hand, there is what seems to me to be a radical perspective on the nature of complex systems. This is typified by the views of

Kauffman and, even more so, those of Goodwin. From this perspective, self-organisation, rather than random mutation, plays the central role in the emergence of new forms. Those new forms emerge and they are radically unpredictable. Agency lies not at the level of the individual agent but at the level of the agent and the morphogenetic field.

This distinction becomes a very important issue when organisational theorists use insights from agent-based modelling. The more orthodox viewpoint on complex adaptive systems can be brought to bear on organisational issues within a cognitivist view of human psychology. The result, I hope to show in the next chapter, is a theory of organisation that uses the terminology of complex systems but stays firmly within the orthodox discourse. Potentially radical insights from complexity theory are easily assimilated into the orthodox discourse. This is done by selectively concentrating on time periods and levels of detail that are predictable and talking about self-organisation and emergence as if they could be controlled by managers. When this is done, what is lost is the invitation to explore what managers do when time spans and levels of detail are radically unpredictable. In the next chapter, I will be exploring how some writers have been doing just this, in my view. In the chapters after that I will be exploring the consequences for organisational theory of the radical perspective on complexity within a framework of human psychology that is different to both cognitivism and psychoanalysis. Before doing that, however, I would like to return to the Tierra simulation described and look at the insights it brings if one takes a radical perspective. In that interpretation I will use Ray's interpretation in terms of biology.

## 12.4 INSIGHTS INTO THE DYNAMICS OF COMPLEX ADAPTIVE SYSTEMS FROM A RADICAL PERSPECTIVE

Returning now to the Tierra simulation in section 12.2, I would like to draw your attention to some of the major insights that this simulation provides on the nature of complex adaptive systems when one takes a radical perspective.

**First**, this system produces order of a changeable and diverse kind that comes about in a spontaneous, emergent way. It has not been programmed and there is no blueprint, grand design or plan. Furthermore, this spontaneous self-organising activity, with its emergent order, is vital for the continuing evolution of the system and its ability to produce novelty. However, what form that order takes – that is, the global pattern of behaviour, the system-wide strategies – cannot be predicted from the rules driving individual agent behaviour. In that sense the system is disorderly. This system continuously operates in a state of bounded instability: periods of stability are followed by upheavals as particular strategies for the survival of both hosts, and parasites emerge from spontaneous self-organising processes that appear to be so close to market competition. The experimenter is not introducing them and neither is an agent taking over and formulating the strategy.

The strategies are emerging unpredictably in a co-evolutionary arms race occurring in a dynamical, somewhat disorderly environment, driven partly by chance. First the strategy is small size, but then parasites change the rules and the most successful strategy becomes feeding off others. Then the hosts change the rules and the better strategy is camouflage. But the parasites change the rules of the game again and the best strategy becomes the development of a local memory. Competition and conflict emerge and the evolution of the system is driven by agents trying to exploit each other, but the game can go on only if neither side succeeds completely, or for long, in that exploitation.

This is self-organisation, or the collapse of chaos, in that the environment was at first random but as soon as an agent is introduced the collapse begins. From this perspective, the evolution of life in the universe does not occur primarily through random mutations selected for survival by the forces of competition, but primarily through an internal, spontaneously self-organising, cooperative process that presents orderly forms for selection by the forces of competition. Selection is not made by freely operating competition that chooses between random little pieces, but by a competitive process constrained to choose between new forms emerging from a cooperative process. Life in the universe, and life in organisations, arises from a dialectic between competition and cooperation, not from an unconstrained competition! The implications are both profound and, of course, contentious.

**Second**, this system has discovered, quite spontaneously, the importance of competition. But not competition all on its own, rather competition in tension with cooperation. Through an internal process of spontaneous self-organisation this system produces parasites and something approaching a predator–prey dynamic. This is behaviour that is, paradoxically, both cooperative and competitive.

**Third**, this system has discovered symbiotic reproduction.

Note the common thread running through these three insights about complex adaptive system dynamics. Each is a paradox. Each is the simultaneous presence of stability and instability, order and disorder, tidiness and mess. Take the first. There is emergent order but it is unpredictable. Take the second. There is the tidy harmony of cooperation but it operates in tension with the dissonance of destructive and messy competition. The system has not yet discovered cross-over replication, that is sexual reproduction. However, when this is added to the system it produces even more novelty. Why is this? Well, in cloning an agent gets to copy itself only if it is relatively successful, so that less successful code is incrementally weeded out and the system moves progressively in the direction of improvement. In cross-over replication, however, a male agent copies half his code and splices it to a copy of half of a female's code, thus mixing up the code. This makes it possible for some inefficient and ineffective code to be passed on to the next generation, as well as effective code. Evolution is, then, not an incrementally progressive affair, but a rather stumbling sort of journey in which a system moves both forwards and backwards. And this, as I will now explain, is the most effective way to proceed.

## Fitness landscapes

You can see why this is so if you think in terms of fitness landscapes, a concept *Kauffman (1993, 1995)* has used to give insights into the evolutionary process. Picture the evolution of a particular species, say leopards, as a journey across a landscape characterised by hills and mountains of various heights and shapes, and valleys of various depths and shapes. Suppose that movement up a hill or mountain is equivalent to increasing fitness and moving down into a valley is equivalent to decreasing fitness.

Deep valleys would represent almost certain extinction and the high peaks of mountains would represent great fitness for the leopards. The purpose of life is then to avoid valleys and climb peaks.

### The shape of the landscape

What determines the shape of this landscape, that is the number, size, shape and position of the peaks and valleys? The answer is the survival strategies that other species interacting with leopards are following. So, leopards could potentially interact with a large number of species in order to get a meal. They could hunt elephant, for example. However, the elephant has a survival strategy based on size and if leopards go the elephant-hunting route they will have a tough time surviving. Such a strategy, therefore, is a move down into a rather deep and dead-end sort of valley. Another possibility is to hunt rather small deer. In order to achieve this the leopard might evolve the strategy of speed, competing by running faster than the deer. To the extent that this works it is represented by a move up a fitness hill. Or, the leopards may specialise in short-distance speed plus a strategy of camouflage. Hence their famous spots. This strategy seems to have taken them up a mountain to a reasonably high fitness peak.

The evolutionary task of the leopard, then, is to journey across the fitness landscape in such a manner as to reach the highest fitness peak possible, because then it stands the greatest chance of surviving. To get caught in a valley is to become extinct and to be trapped in the foothills is to forego the opportunity of finding one of the mountains.

### Moving across the landscape

So, how should the leopards travel across their landscape to avoid these pitfalls, given that they cannot see where the high peaks are? They can only know that they have reached a peak when they get there. Suppose the leopards adopt what strategy theorists call a logically incremental strategy. That is, they adopt a procedure in which they 'stick to the knitting' and take a large number of small incremental steps, only ever taking a step that improves fitness and avoiding, like the plague, any steps that diminish fitness. This rational, orderly procedure produces relatively stable, efficient, progressive movement uphill, consistently in the direction of success. Management consultants and academics in the strategy field would applaud leopards following this procedure for their eminent common sense. However, a rule that in essence says 'go up hills only and never downwards' is sure to keep the leopards out of the valleys, but it is also almost certain to get them trapped in the foothills, unless they start off with a really lucky break at the base of the highest, smoothest mountain, with no crevices or other deformities. This is highly unlikely, for a reason I will come to.

The point to note here is that the rational, efficient way to move over the short term is guaranteed, over the longer term, to be the most ineffective possible. What is the alternative? This is where the mess comes in. The alternative is to abandon this nice, neat strategy of logically incremental moves and travel in a somewhat erratic manner that involves sometimes slipping and tumbling downhill into valleys out of which a desperate climb is necessary before it is too late. This counter-intuitive and somewhat inebriate method of travelling across their fitness landscape makes it likely that the leopards will stumble across the foothills of an even higher mountain than the one they were climbing before. So the mess of cross-over replication, sex to us, makes it more likely that we will find higher mountains to climb than, say, bacteria who replicate by cloning precisely because of the disorder of mixing the genetic code rather than incrementally improving it.

The whole picture becomes a great deal more interesting when you remember that the fixed landscape I have been describing for the leopard is in fact a fiction, because the survival strategies of the other species determine its shape and they are not standing still. They too are looking for peaks to climb and every time they change their strategy then what was a peak for the leopard is deformed and could become a valley. So, if the leopard increases its short-distance speed and improves its camouflage then it moves up towards a fitness peak on its landscape. But, if the deer respond by heightening their sense of smell, then that peak certainly subsides and may even turn into a valley.

The evolutionary journey for all species, therefore, is across a constantly heaving landscape and it is heaving about because of another mess, namely competition. The mess of competition ensures that life itself never gets trapped. Species come and go but life itself carries on, becoming ever more complex. It is this mess of competitive selection that is one of the sources of order, the other being the cooperative, internal process of spontaneous self-organisation.

The insight is this. Systems characterised by dynamics that combine order and disorder, that operate at the edge of disintegration, are capable of learning faster than those that are purely orderly, those that operate well away from the edge of chaos in the stable zone. At the edge of chaos, at the edge of disintegration, systems are capable of endless variety, novelty, surprise – in short, creativity. Systems that get trapped on local fitness peaks look stable and comfortable, but they are simply waiting for destruction by other species following messier paths.

## Redundancy or loose coupling

Another insight follows from the study of complex systems. Life survives at the edge of disintegration because of massive inbuilt redundancy. It is redundancy flowing from self-organising cooperation that is the source of constancy and order. Some kind of mess, or inefficiency, is required to enable faster discovery and other kinds of mess, redundancy, are required to be able to survive that disorder. The human brain, for example, is characterised by redundancy in that one part of it is capable of carrying out functions normally carried out by some other parts. Humans can, therefore, survive the destruction of fairly large parts of their brains. Slack resources, multitasking, overdeterminancy and loose coupling are what make systems resilient enough to cope with the pressures of creativity at the edge of system disintegration. This certainly raises a question mark over the huge drive over the past decade to remove redundancy in organisations across the world.

## Dominant and recessive schemata

In complexity theory, each agent is a set of rules. It is according to these rules that each agent adjusts its behaviour to that of others. Agents' rules also evolve. The rules are expressed in code. In the case of a computer simulation the code is digital. In an organism the code is genetic.

The important point about this code in both cases is that part of it is arranged into that set of rules governing an agent's current engagement with its environment. This code takes the form of rules governing the stable, predictable conduct of everyday tasks, the implementation of the current survival strategy. I call this the dominant schema. However, the dominant schema does not use up all the available code. There is part left over constituting what might be called a recessive schema. It is possible to study what happens to this recessive schema in computer simulations as a system evolves and that study yields what is to my mind a very exciting discovery (*Hillis, 1992*). While the agent and the system are continuing to move in a stable, more or less steady fashion from iteration to iteration, from day to day as it were, following dominant schemata, the recessive schemata are more or less randomly rearranging themselves. The recessive schema is in a continual state of flux and it is evolving a replacement for the dominant schema. What then happens is that the dominant schema is quite suddenly replaced by a new one that has quietly accumulated in the recessive one. It looks as if the system is jumping from one stable equilibrium position to another, but in fact this is only apparent, because the replacement has been gradually prepared, behind the scenes, subversively, in the recessive schema.

While part of the system is getting on with the serious task of carrying out its day-to-day survival in a stable manner, another part is engaged in play. Play without a clear purpose, play that is spontaneously self-organising, can ultimately lead to a kind of *coup d'état* in which the dominant schema is replaced by a new one. Innovation in the dominant schema follows creative activity, play, in the recessive one. The important point is that these two systems are working in tension with each other and creativity is intimately linked to destruction.

This links to Prigogine's important notion of dissipative structures. You will recall that he has shown how certain chemical systems, certainly those upon which life is based, have a structure but one that continually dissolves. Take our bodies – over a two-year period every cell in my body, so I am told, is replaced with others and yet the structure, me, is preserved, although unfortunately in a subtly altered, increasingly aged, form. I read recently that cancer is not caused by the excessive growth of malformed cells, as had been previously thought, but by the suppression of the instruction to die. Survival, it seems, requires death as well as birth.

## The importance of mess

Those who have developed the study of complex adaptive systems have been most interested in the analogy between the digital code of computer program agents and the chemical code in the genes of living creatures. One of their principal questions has been this: if in its earliest days the earth consisted of a random soup of chemicals, how could life have come about? You can simulate this problem if you take a system consisting of computer programs with random bit strings and ask if they can evolve order out of such random chaos. The amazing answer to this question is that such systems can indeed evolve order out of chaos, and even more amazingly this chaos, or mess, is essential to the process.

Contrary to some of our most deep-seated beliefs, mess is the material from which life and creativity are built and it seems that they are built, not according to some overall prior design, but through a process of spontaneous self-organisation that produces emergent outcomes. If there is a design, it is the basic design principles of the system itself, namely a network of agents driven by iterative nonlinear interaction to produce emergent outcomes that do have pattern. There is inherent order in complex adaptive systems simply waiting to unfold through the experience of the system, but no one can know what that experience will be until it does unfold in real time. There are deep reasons why, in certain conditions, agents interacting in a system can produce, not anarchy, but creative new outcomes that none of them ever dreamt of, if they self-organise in what looks like a mess most unlikely to contain within it an implicate order. It seems that even if no one can know the outcome and even if no one can be 'in control', we are not doomed to anarchy. On the contrary, these seem to be the very conditions required for creativity, for the exciting journey into open-ended evolutionary space with no fixed, predetermined destination.

## 12.5    COMPARISONS WITH OTHER SYSTEMS THEORIES

Part of what I have been doing in previous chapters is reviewing the theories of interaction upon which various theories of organisation and management are based. All of them, including the complex adaptive system theory reviewed in this chapter, are systemic theories of interaction. They are about entities interacting within a system, or systems interacting with each other.

The first of these systems theories was reviewed in Chapter 2, namely cybernetics. It models a system at the macro level; that is, without paying attention to the nature of the entities comprising the system. They are implicitly assumed to be homogeneous, or average. The central concept is that of feedback. This is a process in which the system's output is compared with some fixed reference point outside and the difference between that fixed reference point and its output is fed back as input into the next iteration of the system. In cybernetics, the only type of feedback considered is that of negative, or damping, feedback. This means that the system is self-regulating and its dynamic is that of a movement towards stable equilibrium. Such a system has no internal capacity to change spontaneously by moving to a different attractor or evolving a new one. It can move only within one attractor, that of equilibrium. Change has to come from outside the system. The methodology employed in studying such a system is that of the objective observer who is able to control the system by designing a move from one attractor to another.

The point was also made that the cognitivist view of human nature is essentially a cybernetic one. This is the basis of strategic choice theory.

The second systems theory reviewed was that of systems dynamics. Here the system of interest is also modelled at the macro level, but this time using mathematical models consisting of nonlinear equations that can be interpreted in both negative and positive, or amplifying, feedback terms. Again, the entities comprising the system are assumed to be homogeneous as are the interactions between them. These models produce the dynamics of non-equilibrium movement. These systems are rather unlikely to move to equilibrium because they are nonlinear, or as some interpret this, because they also take account of amplifying feedback. This system also has no internal capacity to move from one attractor to another and so change has to come from outside it. The methodology is once again that of the objective observer. This systems theory is the basis of the theory of the learning organisation.

The third systems theory surveyed was open systems theory. This theory takes account of the entities of which a system is composed, its subsystems. However, nonlinearity is not a central feature and the system is assumed to move towards stable equilibrium in the absence of obstacles. The focus of this theory is on regulation at the boundary of the system to sustain it in equilibrium adaptation to its environment. Iterative replication does not feature in this systems theory. This forms the systemic foundations of psychoanalytic perspectives on organisations.

Fourth came the review in the last chapter of nonlinear dynamical systems, namely chaos theory and dissipative structure theory. Chaos theory employs the same mathematical approach as systems dynamics, models at the macro level, and makes the same assumptions about entities. It goes further than systems dynamics in identifying the different attractors that such a system can move to – most importantly, the possibility of strange attractors at critical parameter values. This theory clarifies the possibilities and impossibilities of prediction. However, as with systems dynamics such a system has no internal capacity to move spontaneously from one of its attractors to another. The impetus for change has to come from outside the system.

Dissipative structure theory also models systems at the macro level by means of nonlinear mathematical equations. Here, however, fluctuations and symmetry breaking mean that there is non-average relationships between micro entities and the entities are not homogeneous. In other words, small, chance variations in relationships between a system and its environment, the fluctuations, can amplify through the system when it is held far from equilibrium. The effect is to break the symmetry or uniformity of behaviour within the system. The consequence is a move to a new attractor and the possibility of evolving a new one. So, once microdiversity is introduced into the model it acquires the internal capacity to change spontaneously. Change need no longer be imposed or triggered from the outside but can emerge from spontaneous self-organisation at certain critical points. Note how different this is from the nature of a cybernetic system. In every respect a dissipative structure is the opposite of a cybernetic system, other than that, like all the systems models mentioned so far, the methodology is that of the objective observer. Despite this, however, dissipative structure theory is a radical theory of systems, and if it were to form the basis of a theory of organisation, one might expect that to be a radical theory of organisation.

Finally, there are the complex adaptive systems reviewed in this chapter. They differ from all of the others in locating the focus of analysis primarily on the micro level. They are concerned with the behaviour of the entities comprising the system. Some complex adaptive system models assume that the agents are homogeneous and that their interactions are all the same. Such systems have no internal capacity to move from one attractor to another. Self-organisation in these systems produces an emergent attractor that the system follows until some change is introduced from outside. Other models of complex adaptive systems do include agent diversity and the system shows the internal capacity to move from attractor to another and evolve emergent, radically unpredictable new attractors through the process of self-organisation. The new emerges in these models when the system displays the dynamics of the edge of chaos, or bounded instability. Here the system produces not only the new but avalanches of destruction as well, with many small and few large extinction events. The methodology remains that of the objective observer. Some scientists do not see anything radical in this and some do. If this systems theory formed the basis of a theory of organisation and management would that be an orthodox or a radical theory?

In the review of all of these systems theories there has been a move from models that are linear, equilibrium seeking and lacking in any microdiversity to those that are nonlinear, far from equilibrium and full of microdiversity. The most striking change in the properties they display is the capacity for spontaneously developing new forms. Many would say that this is one of the hallmarks of living systems.

## 12.6    SUMMARY

This chapter has reviewed complex adaptive systems theory. This theory models interaction between many agents comprising a system. It sets out the logical structure of algorithmic, that is digital-code-based, interaction and derives the properties of such interaction through the method of computer simulation. The digital code interaction is then used as an analogy for some other kind of interaction. For example, digital code is used as an analogy for the genetic code of biological organisms. The properties of digital code interaction are then inferred to apply to biological code. In other words, an act of interpretation is required in order to utilise the insights derived from the logic of digital code interaction in relation to some other kind of interaction.

I have distinguished between what seem to me to be orthodox and radical interpretations of the implications of digital code interaction. From an orthodox perspective, the insights yielded by complex adaptive system simulations do not represent a radical departure from previous scientific theories. Predictability is stressed and self-organisation is not seen as a new ordering principle. Other scientists, however, take a more radical perspective, stressing unpredictability and the radical importance of self-organisation.

From a radical perspective, the key insights yielded by agent-based modelling of systems are as follows:

- The dynamic at the edge of chaos. This is understood to be a dynamic of paradox, that is simultaneous stability and instability. This dynamic between stability and instability is a requirement for the emergence of novelty. It occurs when certain key parameters are at a critical point. The parameters relate to information/energy flow, connectivity between agents and diversity of types of agents. When information/energy flow is high but not too high, when the numbers of connections between agents are high but not too high, when the diversity of agents is rich but not too rich, then the system displays the dynamic at the edge of chaos.
- Emergence of the new and extinction. Although the dynamic at the edge of chaos is required for novelty to emerge it does not provide a guarantee of survival. In addition to the emergence of the new there are many small and a few large extinction events.

- Diversity as a prerequisite for the emergence of the new. A system displays the internal capacity to change spontaneously only when agents display difference.
- Radical unpredictability over certain time spans and levels of detail, which renders problematic the possibility of top-down control. What agent-based modellers have consistently identified is that, in certain critical conditions, complex adaptive systems, consisting of large numbers of interacting agents, display a paradoxical dynamic of simultaneous stability and instability. Some call it effective complexity lying between order and disorder; others call it the dynamics of the 'edge of chaos'. When a system operates in this dynamic it displays radical unpredictability over certain time spans at certain levels of detail. The insight is that uncertainty is inevitable in an evolving system.
- The self-organising capacity of a complex adaptive system and its ability to produce emergent novelty when it operates in the dynamic at the edge of disorder. Self-organisation here means interaction between agents on the basis of local organising principles. Emergence means the appearance of novel forms arising from this local interaction, in the absence of any overall program or design, in a context that may be characterised by chance events. An insight here is that the creative and the new arise in relationships in the absence of any overall design. Those relationships create the context within which they themselves take place. Complex adaptive systems co-evolve, participating in the collective production of their own future in the absence of any external imposition. The system is recursive and causality is mutual. Another insight is that creativity is a collective phenomenon and the collective, the group, is therefore primary.
- The paradox of stability and instability. This is linked to the possibility of making predictions for some time spans and levels of details and at the same time, with regard to the same system, the impossibility of making predictions for other time spans and levels of detail. Another interesting form this takes is demonstrated in simulations by Hillis. Here particular forms emerge and remain stable for some time before suddenly jumping to new forms. This looks like punctuated equilibrium but what happens in this simulation is that redundant code, that code not required to produce current forms, is randomly forming alternative forms that might suddenly displace the existing ones. The insight here is that redundant, non-essential activity is, in a sense, exploring and preparing replacement possibilities. Self-organising, unstable, redundant activity, occurring behind the screen, as it were, of stable forms is the source of novelty.
- Most agent-based modellers locate agency at the level of interacting individual entities in a complex adaptive system, that is at the level of the autonomous agent. A more radical perspective locates it at the level of the interaction of system and context. System and context form and are formed by each other at the same time.

It is these insights that I wish to explore in relation to organisations because I believe that they have the potential for making more sense of life in organisations than the orthodox approaches do. I do not believe that the modelling and simulating approach of agent-based modellers holds much potential for understanding the nature of organising and managing. I think that it is the insights about the nature of systems that hold the potential, rather than the methodology.

Why might these insights be important? Their importance lies, I think, in the possibility of a radically different theory of organisation. This can be seen by comparing the above insights with the organisational theories reviewed in previous chapters.

Strategic choice theory holds that an organisation changes because its top managers choose new strategic directions. Learning organisation theory holds that organisations develop in new ways because top managers identify leverage points in the system from which they can control it. This theory also holds that new directions flow from changes in the mental models of people in an organisation and that these changes can be managed. From the psychoanalytic perspective, an organisation changes when its managers can regulate the boundary between their psychic lives and their roles so that task performance is not impaired.

The insights listed above suggest a completely different possibility. Managers may be making strategic choices, operating at leverage points and managing boundaries. However, from a radical complexity perspective they are agents in the system, not external observers of it. They cannot therefore know the long-term outcome of the choices they are making. Instead new directions for an organisation emerge from both their choices and the patterns of responses this evokes from others in a self-organising way.

In many ways, an approach like this reverses orthodox theories. I think it is important to consider whether there is anything to this radical interpretation.

## FURTHER READING

Useful reviews of complexity theory are provided by Waldorp (1992), Casti (1994), Cohen & Stewart (1994), Goodwin (1994), Kauffman (1993, 1995), Levy (1992). Boden (1996) provides a useful review of the philosophy and methodology of complex adaptive systems.

## REFERENCES

Boden, M. A. (Ed.) (1996), *The Philosophy of Artificial Life*, Oxford: Oxford University Press.

Casti, J. (1994), *Complexification: Explaining a Paradoxical World through the Science of Surprise*, London: Harper Collins.

Cohen, J. & Stewart, I. (1994), *The Collapse of Chaos: Discovering Simplicity in a Complex World*, New York: Viking.

Gell-Mann, M. (1994), *The Quark and the Jaguar*, New York: Freeman.

Goodwin, B. (1994), *How the Leopard Changed its Spots*, London: Weidenfeld & Nicolson.

Griffin, D., Shaw, P. & Stacey, R. (1998), Speaking of complexity in management theory and practice, *Organization*, vol. 5, no. 3, pp. 315–34.

Hillis, W. D. (1992), Co-evolving parasites improve simulated evolution as an optimization procedure, in Langton, G. C., Taylor, C., Doyne Falmer, J. & Rasmussen, S. (Eds.) (1992), *Artificial Life II, Santa Fe Institute Studies in the Sciences of Complexity, vol. 10*, Reading, MA: Addison-Wesley.

Holland, J. (1998), *Emergence from chaos to order*, New York: Oxford University Press.

Kauffman, S. A. (1993), *Origins of Order: Self Organization and Selection in Evolution*, Oxford: Oxford University Press.

Kauffman, S. A. (1995), *At Home in the Universe*, New York: Oxford University Press.

Langton, C. G. (1996), Artificial Life, in Boden, M. A. (Ed.) (1996), *The Philosophy of Artificial Life*, Oxford: Oxford University Press.

Levy, S. (1992), *Artificial Life*, New York: First Vintage Books.

Ray, T. S. (1992), An approach to the sythesis of life, in Langton, G. C., Taylor, C., Doyne Farmer, J. & Rasmussen, S. (Eds.), *Artificial Life II, Santa Fe Institute, Studies in the Sciences of Complexity, vol. 10*, Reading, MA: Addison-Wesley.

Reynolds, C. W. (1987), *Flocks, Herds and Schools: A Distributed Behaviour Model*, Proceedings of SIGGRAPH '87, Computer Graphics Vol. 21/4: 25–34.

Waldorp, M. M. (1992), *Complexity: The Emerging Science at the Edge of Chaos*, Englewood Cliffs, NJ: Simon & Schuster.

# Chapter

# 13 How organisational theorists are using chaos and complexity theory

## 13.1 INTRODUCTION

Something of an intellectual revolution took place during the late 1940s and the 1950s. People in many disciplines began to think about the phenomena of interest to them in rigorous systemic terms. The biologist von Bertalanfy developed general (open) systems theory and pointed to how it could be employed in thinking about social as well as natural phenomena. At much the same time Wiener, Ashby and others developed the theory of cybernetic systems. They too were scientists, this time drawing on engineering notions of control to develop a theory that could be applied to human affairs. This period also saw a move in psychology from behaviourism to cognitive psychology, a view of human perception, knowing and behaving that was closely connected to the development of cybernetics. In addition, at much the same time, other scientists developed systems dynamics. It too was developed from the engineer's notion of control and was applied to human affairs.

All of these theoretical developments were also closely connected to the early development of computers. There was a reciprocal relationship between designing machines that could 'think' like the human brain and conceptualising the human brain as a thinking machine. The brain was assumed to be an information-processing machine rather like the computer and a computer was thought to be an information processing machine rather like the brain. The information-processing individual is central to the cognitivist view of human knowing and behaving. The emphasis on control is central to cybernetics and systems dynamics.

The period since then has seen very little further fundamental conceptual development in open systems theory, cybernetics or systems dynamics. Instead, this period has seen the application of these ideas to theorising about the nature of organisations, sometimes quite explicitly, but frequently only implicitly. One or other of these systems theories, combined with a cognitivist and sometimes a humanistic view of human nature, now dominates the theory of organisations and the prescriptions for management. It constitutes what I have called the orthodox perspective and it is very difficult for anyone, I believe, to think about organisations in any different way because the orthodox perspective is so much taken for granted.

However, it seems to me that during the 1970s and 1980s there have been developments of a fundamental conceptual nature in the thinking about systems. In the last two chapters, I have summarised and reviewed what I think are the main features of this development, namely chaos theory, the theory of dissipative structures and synergetics, and the theory of complex adaptive systems. These systems theories, like the earlier ones, have also been developed by natural scientists. I have argued that they are potentially radical in that they point to the self-referential, self-organising capacities of such systems. What this means is that agents in a complex system interact locally with each other on the basis of their historically evolved identities. They do so without knowing in advance how the whole system is going to evolve, or even understanding its current state as a whole. However, despite lack of knowledge about the whole and its future, local self-referring, self-organising capacity itself generates emergent new forms. These insights are a radical departure from what has become the orthodox view of systems in that new forms are now seen to emerge from interaction, but only in the presence of diversity. The emphasis is placed on relationships between entities rather than on the nature of the individual entities themselves. This potentially displaces the cognising individual from the central position occupied in the earlier systems theories. Furthermore, the creative novelty that emerges is unpredictable. This raises question marks over the nature of control, another central feature of the earlier system theories. However, in the last two chapters I have also tried to show how the theory of complex systems in the natural sciences does not depart completely from cybernetics. This is because, in some formulations, the agents making up a complex adaptive system are defined in cybernetic and cognitivist terms. Despite its radical potential, stressed by a few, most of the natural scientists working in this area seem to me to remain, more or less, with a basically orthodox perspective. In the main, as I hope to show, organisational theorists using chaos and complexity theory focus on those expositions in which the notion of feedback is used as an explanatory device and those simulations in which agents are cybernetic entities.

## The objective observer

There is another important sense in which those developing complex systems theory seem to me to be continuing in the cybernetics and systems dynamics traditions. This is the matter of methodology. Just as the earlier systems theorists did, most complexity theorists in the natural sciences adopt the stance of the objective observer who stands outside the 'real' system and models it.

What I mean by this is the following. Flocks of birds and colonies of ants existed long before Reynolds and Langton constructed models to mimic and explain their behaviour. Reynolds and Langton were concerned with a pre-existing reality. They stood outside the flock of birds and the colony of ants and observed the patterns in their behaviour. They had to do this, of course, because they are not birds or ants. They then experimented with different computer simulations of the behavioural rules that individual birds and ants might be following as they interacted with each other. They were able to identify a small number of simple rules, which if followed by the birds and the ants would lead to the emergence of flocking and trail setting. In doing this, they were able to show that it is, in principle, possible for processes of self-organisation to produce emergent global order. Ray did a similar thing when he considered how species might evolve. He observed what is known about a pre-existing reality, the species that have evolved over the past, and constructed a computer simulation to demonstrate how processes of self-organisation could, in principle, lead to the unpredictable emergence of new species.

In the main, organisational theorists adopt the same methodology. They stand outside what is assumed to be the pre-given reality of an organisation and observe its behaviour. Some use computer modelling and simulation techniques and can quite rapidly incorporate chaos and complexity into their work. Others research organisations, describing how successful organisations function and in effect constructing qualitative models of them. They then derive prescriptions for the successful conduct of all organisations. The great majority build models and make prescriptions on the implicit assumption that organisations are cybernetic systems, or systems of the systems dynamics type, made up of individuals who behave according to the principles of cognitivism. So, orthodox organisational theorists share a methodology with what I have called orthodox complexity scientists and they share the same view about the nature of the agents constituting the system. What they have not shared, until some recent writings, is the same view of systems, namely the processes of self-organisation and the possibility of unpredictably emergent new forms. However, the fact that organisational theorists and complexity scientists share the same fundamental methodology, and the same views about individual agents, makes it comparatively easy for the former to incorporate a complex system perspective into their models. In doing this, as I explain in the next sections of this chapter, they lose the radical implications of complexity theory.

For me, the problem in adopting the position of the external, objective observer of a pre-existing organisational reality is this: according to complexity theory, new forms emerge unpredictably in a complex system through the process of self-organisation. To reiterate, this means that the agents in the system interact with each other at their own local level on the basis of their historically evolved identities. In other words, they are always participants and the system evolves only because they participate in this local way. It is the very essence of self-organisation that none of those individual agents is able to step outside the system and obtain an overview of how the whole is evolving, let alone how it will evolve. It is the very essence of self-organisation that none of the agents, as individuals, nor any small group of them on their own, can design, or even shape, the evolution of the system other than through their local interaction. In their interaction with each other, they are co-creating its evolution but none of them, individually or in small groups, is organising the interaction, the self-organisation, across the system. No agent is setting the simple rules for others to follow and then 'allowing' them to self-organise. If they were, the system could no longer be described as a self-organising one.

The methodological position of the external observer is a possibility if I want to study birds and ants because I am neither. However, if I want to study the behaviour of a group of people, it seems to me that I have to take account of the fact that I am one of them. As soon as one loses sight of this and talks about a complex system of human beings from an external position, it is easy to slip into the tendency of prescribing this external position as the management role. The question then becomes how the manager needs to be able to identify whether the organisation is operating in the dynamic of bounded instability so that it has creative potential. Or whether it is operating in stable equilibrium and needs to be nudged, by the manager, into bounded instability. Or the prescription becomes to find the set of simple rules and prescribe them for the members of the organisation. This is supposed to ensure that they self-organise to produce the emergent pattern that the manager wants. That immediately implies a pre-given reality and the possibility of prediction rather than the emergence of new forms. In other words, the tendency is to focus on an individual who is able to exert some kind of control or impart some kind of coherence to a self-organising system.

As soon as this is done, it seems to me, it results in the loss of the radical implications of complexity theory for understanding life in organisations. If a human group or organisation is a complex adaptive system then the questions become: What is it like to be an agent in such a system? What is it like to be such a system? What does diversity mean in human relationships and how do people respond to it? How does an agent in such a system cope with radical unpredictability? What is it like to participate in self-organising processes? To what extent can agents in such a system articulate emergent patterns? How does doing this help?

The point I am making is this. I think the insights about the nature of systems coming from complexity theory offer an opportunity to theorists and practitioners to explore a different way of thinking about life in organisations. However, this opportunity is rapidly lost if the insights are imported into organisation theorising from the methodological position of the external observer, implicitly based on the assumption of the powerful, autonomous individual so central to cognitivism. I will illustrate what I mean first by looking briefly at some recent books and papers that use notions from complexity theory and then in more detail at the work of *Nonaka (1991)*.

## 13.2  MODELLING COMPLEX SYSTEMS IN ORGANISATIONS

One approach to using the theories of chaos and complexity in relation to organisations is to apply the mathematical and modelling techniques used by the natural scientists. I point to some of these in this section.

### Forecasting of financial markets

A number of writers and researchers (*Hsieh, 1989; Schenkman & Le Baron, 1989; Peters, 1991*) have explored the hypothesis that the financial markets exhibit low-dimensional deterministic chaos and are attempting to build forecasting models using nonlinear equations. This involves accepting that long-term developments cannot be predicted but offers the hope that well-specified models might enable superior short-term forecasting.

## Production and inventory scheduling

Here researchers (*Morley, 1993, 1995*) employ some of the simulation techniques of complexity theory, such as the genetic algorithm, to develop methods of production and inventory scheduling. The approach is to regard production processes as complex systems that are capable of learning. In the genetic algorithm computer programs breed new computer programs so evolving in a manner akin to learning. So instead of preparing a comprehensive design or plan for the production line or inventory levels the computer programs are left to find beneficial schedules themselves. This holds the promise of a more flexible approach more suited to customised production methods. These developments are in their infancy.

## The psychology of perception and learning

Here, researchers (*Abraham, 1995; Guastello, 1995*) apply nonlinear mathematics to the measurement of perception and learning. This is, of course, firmly grounded in cognitivist psychology.

## Modelling industries

Another approach is to model the dynamics of whole industries. This section looks at two examples of this. The first uses Prigogine's work and the second employs chaos theory.

Prigogine's theory of dissipative structures, briefly described in Chapter 11, represents a potentially radical shift in the domain of the natural sciences. I argue, however, that when these radical theories are imported into the domains of social, economic and organisational theory they are subtly transformed into orthodoxy, cast in a new vocabulary. I suggest that this happens because those making the transfer adopt an essentially cognitivist view of human psychology, emphasising the primacy of the individual who knows through making representations of reality and behaves on the basis of these representations. As I keep reiterating, this is an essentially cybernetic view of human knowing and behaving, one that is entirely compatible with orthodox management and organisational theory. The result is that the potentially radical implications of Prigogine's theory are not realised in relation to the management of organisations.

## Allen

To illustrate what I mean, take *Allen's (1998)* analysis of the fishing industry. He contrasts the conclusions produced by equilibrium (cybernetic), systems dynamics and what he calls self-organising and evolutionary models of that industry. The equilibrium model produces a policy recommendation to constrain fishing effort at, or just below, the maximum that yields a sustainable fish population. However, the dynamics of the fish population and fish markets rapidly render any selected sustainable level of fishing highly inaccurate. A systems dynamics model allows for variations in fish populations and in economic conditions. However, the model uses average data for all of these factors.

Allen then introduces 'noise' into the equations to represent random fluctuations in fish populations and the model produces boom-and-bust oscillations in fishing fleet catches. He concludes that management should concern itself with overcoming this cyclical behaviour rather than discussing fishing quotas. He introduces a variable to represent the rate of response of the fleet to fish availability, another for the level of technology and yet another for price responsiveness. Now there is still a boom-and-bust attractor, but in addition, another attractor emerges, one of small high-priced niche where fish becomes a luxury food. He offers this as the kind of strategic insight modelling can yield.

He then goes on to incorporate different levels of information acquired by each fishing fleet and different attitudes to risk. He assumes that fishing fleets are boundedly rational decision-makers and so imports cognitivism as his theory of human psychology. The model demonstrates that optimal use of information increases profit in the short term but not necessarily in the long term. Cautious optimisers get locked into the existing situation while more adventurous risk-takers open themselves to the possibility of finding new strategies. The model identifies a tendency to follow short-term profit-maximising strategies at the expense of the long term.

Finally, Allen specifies what he calls an evolutionary complex model:

…Not only do we have uneven and changing patterns of fish stocks in the system, but we are also not going to consider that the "taxonomy" of boat types and fleet behaviours is fixed. We can now develop a model that will explore the relative effectiveness of different strategies, and will search for success, not just in geographic space, but also in strategy space, and will discover robust fishing strategies for us. (*p. 33*)

From this analysis, he reaches the conclusion that sustainability does not lie in efficiency, or in allowing free markets, but in creativity. Creativity is rooted in diversity, cultural richness and the will and ability to experiment and take risks. Another conclusion is that uncertainty is inevitable:

Innovation and change occur because of diversity, non-average individuals with their bizarre initiatives, and whenever this leads to an exploration into an area where positive feedback outweighs negative, then growth will occur. (*p. 36*)

Allen very clearly demonstrates the importance of diversity in generating new forms as he moves from one way of modelling the fishing industry to another. He clearly identifies the radical nature of models that incorporate high levels of diversity. However, what he suggests as application in terms of management falls quite easily into the orthodox management discourse. For example, his whole methodology implies a cognitivist view of human beings that use rational constructs to explore scenarios in the interest of gaining insight. This easily allows one to sidestep the possibility that management itself is an evolving system. The implication is that managers can step outside their system and model it as the basis of making decisions to manipulate it. The insights he produces are radical but the prescriptions are not.

## Levy

*Levy (1994)* simulates an industrial supply chain using nonlinear equations of the type that can produce mathematical chaos and concludes:

As well as illustrating the volatility of the supply chain and its associated cost, the model can be used to guide decisions concerning production location, sourcing and optimum inventory levels.

Used for this purpose the model demonstrates how complex systems need to be understood as a whole, and how goals can be achieved through indirect and nonobvious means. For example, the model enables the cost of offshore sourcing to be estimated in terms of the incremental inventory needed to maintain demand fulfillment at some level.

So, here chaos theory is being used to model an operational system at the macro level in order to aid decision making. Levy clearly equates the manager's role with that of the model builder or programmer who stands outside the system and controls it.

I think that the radical potential of theories of chaos and dissipative structures for organisational theory tends to be obscured by simulations of this kind because the agents in the system are treated in an impersonal way. This is a problem if you are interested, as I am, in the nature of organising and managing in terms of human relationships. Attempts to model people as agents driven by rules immediately introduces cognitivism and loses the rich texture of emotional and embodied relating.

## 13.3   SEEING ORGANISATIONS AS COMPLEX SYSTEMS

In this section, I will look briefly at a number of recent publications that import theories of chaos and complex adaptive systems into theorising about organisations in a qualitative way.

### Complexity: a new answer for managers

As examples of this approach, I am going to take two books published in 1998. The first is by *T. Irene Sanders (1998)* and is called *Strategic Thinking and the New Science: Planning in the midst of chaos, complexity, and change.*

#### Sanders

Sanders starts her book like this:

In the last decade, scientists attempting to understand chaos, complexity, and change, and organizations trying to survive them, reached the same conclusions: Chaos, complexity, and change are everywhere! Mastering them requires new ways of seeing and thinking. (*p. 6*)

... at the heart of the new science is the discovery that beneath what appears to be disorder there is order – a type of self-organizing pattern that emerges through the rich web of tangles, connections, and interrelationships in the system observed. And the most exciting discoveries relate to the dynamics, or "hows" of this process.

By applying the insights from the new science to our lives and businesses, I believe that I have found a way to show you how to anticipate, respond to, and influence change as it is emerging and before a crisis arises. ... And at last we have a way to develop the much-needed skill of strategic thinking. (*pp. 6–7*)

Note how she talks about observing the system, so implicitly taking the position of manager as objective observer rather than participant. She defines dynamics as hows, that is as prescriptions. Dynamics, however, refers to patterns of movement and to the stability and instability characteristics of this movement. It is difficult to see what is prescriptive in this. She also claims to have found the answer. The basis of the claim seems very unclear to me.

The book depicts and describes the Lorenz strange attractor of a simplified model of the weather that I also described in section 11.3. It is then claimed that this picture allows 'scientists to *see*, for the first time' (*p. 59*) the order hidden in disorder. She concludes from this image that it is possible to identify any system's initial conditions because it is deterministic, but that it is difficult to predict its future state because it is nonlinear. If you return to Chapter 11, you will see that this statement is wrong. It is in practice impossible to forecast the long-term state of the kind of system she is talking about precisely·because it is not possible to identify the initial conditions to the infinite exactness required. Infinite precision is required because the nonlinear structure of the system may amplify even the tiniest failure to identity and precisely measure the initial conditions. Without this, long-term prediction would be possible because the system is deterministic. Determinism is a theory of causality and it implies nothing whatsoever about the ability to measure initial conditions.

She then says that despite an inability to make predictions of long-term states it is possible to provide qualitative descriptions of whole system behaviour over time. This is true, but only for the attractor the system is currently drawn to. It would not be possible to describe any new attractor that some system was capable of spontaneously jumping to, until the jump occurred. This is Prigogine's point about bifurcation, also described in section 11.3. Furthermore, human systems are not deterministic because even if there are 'rules' governing them, these rules change over time. Human systems learn, they are adaptive, they evolve and produce new forms. In other words, they move to entirely new attractors, the 'shape' of which cannot be 'seen' before the move is made, according to complex adaptive system simulations capable of generating new forms. So, you can only 'see' the shape of the attractor you already know about. To the extent that strategy is about producing creative, innovative new forms of business, it would not be possible, in terms of complexity theory, to 'see' that form before it emerges.

Sanders tries to get around this by saying:

"Perking" information is the term I use to identify the new initial conditions to which your system may be sensitive – changes or developments that are already taking shape just below the surface, and which can only be seen with peripheral vision or well developed foresight skills ... The key to foresight is learning to recognize your system's initial conditions as they are emerging, so that you can see change coming, respond early, or influence it to your advantage. It's important to recognize your system's initial conditions BEFORE they erupt as an unexpected strange attractor. (*p. 74*)

...if you want to influence the future, you need to identify your system's perking information or changing initial conditions – and apply your resources here. These are your new leverage points. (*p. 77*)

This attempt runs into the same problem as before. It is not possible to identify all of the initial conditions and measure all of them with infinite accuracy. There are too many and they may be very small indeed. It follows that objective detection and measurement cannot be relied upon. Instead, she proposes peripheral vision and foresight. What is the former? How can you have foresight if you cannot predict? All the radical potential is lost and all that is left is straightforward strategic choice theory. Managers can carry on identifying leverage points and there is no threat to the possibility of control. The use of chaos theory is quite unnecessary and simply amounts to a change of vocabulary.

As far as I understand it, what I have summarised above is the conceptual core of the whole book and underlies all the prescriptions it makes. Sanders clearly takes the stance of external objective observer who sees an organisation as a chaotic system. Implicitly, she is prescribing this as the stance that a manager should take too. Managers are supposed to look at the system as a whole and then identify the pre-existing order, the strange attractor, hidden in apparent disorder. Then they are supposed to detect new initial conditions and take hold of them, master them she says, before they do something that is unexpected or not wanted. Not only is the manager to be the objective external observer but also the heroic individual who can master chaos and find hidden order. Unpredictability is mentioned and then, in effect, ignored. The words are from complexity science but the concepts are from cybernetics and cognitivism. In the process, any new insight is lost and orthodox prescriptions are simply presented in different language.

Consider now how *Shona L. Brown & Kathleen M. Eisenhardt (1998)* apply complexity theory to management in their book, called *Competing on the Edge: Strategy as Structured Chaos*.

### Brown and Eisenhardt

Brown and Eisenhardt start their book as follows:

Given the pervasiveness of change, the key strategic challenge is managing that change. ... Given this challenge, what strategy is successful in rapidly and unpredictably changing industries? (*p. 3*)

The answer is a strategy that we term *competing on the edge*. (*p. 4*)

At its heart competing on the edge meets the challenge of strategic change by constantly reshaping competitive advantage even as the marketplace unpredictably and rapidly shifts. The goal is reinvention through a relentless flow of competitive advantages. In terms of strategy, competing on the edge ties "where do you want to go?" intimately to "How are you going to get there?" The result is an unpredictable, uncontrollable, and even inefficient strategy that nonetheless ... works. (*p. 4*)

Again, the authors claim to have found the answer using complexity theory. The questions posed, however, are the conventional ones of strategic choice theory: where do 'you', the masterful individual, want to go and how will you get there?

Having stated that their strategic solution involves a strategy that is unpredictable and uncontrollable they then immediately state what managing change means. It means reacting to the unexpected as a defensive tactic. It also means anticipation:

By anticipation we mean gaining insight into what is likely to occur and then positioning for that future ... Anticipation means looking ahead to the needs of the global market and then lining up ahead of time the right resources ... Or it could mean foreseeing the emergence of a new customer segment (p. 4)

This is still seen as defensive, however, so they claim that the highest level of managing change is leading change by dominating markets, setting the rhythm and pace for the others. So, on the same page they talk about a strategy that is unpredictable and uncontrollable and then prescribe foresight and the domination of markets. They imply that this is a choice that it is possible for managers to make all on their own. Having said that the future is unpredictable, they immediately call for anticipation and foreseeing the emergence. Surely, this is a logical contradiction. This is straight back to the theory of strategic choice. It implicitly assumes the presence of the heroic individual manager who can do all of these things in a cognitivist fashion. How do they use complexity theory?

The central concept they employ from complexity theory is that of the "edge of chaos", which they define as being only partially structured. Notice how the notion of paradox is immediately lost. This is not a state of contradictory forces that can never be resolved. It is simply a balance: not too much structure and not too little. Too much structure produces stability and too little produces chaos. Being at the edge also means letting a semicoherent strategy emerge from the organisation, that is, one that is not too fixed, nor one that is too fluid. Of the edge of chaos they say:

> The power of a few simple structures to generate enormously complex adaptive behaviour – whether flock behaviour among birds, resilient government (as in democracy), or simply successful performance by corporations – is at the heart of the edge of chaos. The edge of chaos captures the complicated, uncontrolled, unpredictable, yet adaptive (in technical terms *self-organized*) behaviour that occurs where there is some structure but not very much. The critical management issue at the edge of chaos is to figure out what to structure, and as essential, what *not* to structure. (*p. 12*)

It is worth spending a little time unpicking what is being said here. The notion of the dynamic at the edge of chaos is a rather sophisticated one. It is a dynamic to which a system evolves, or self-organises. This is the notion of self-organising criticality. The edge of chaos is a dynamic that occurs when certain parameters fall within a critical range. For example, at critical rates of flow of information, critical degrees of connectivity between agents, and critical degrees of agent diversity, the edge of chaos dynamic occurs. These authors take the notion of the edge of chaos across into organisations and immediately collapse these parameters into one of organisational structure and it then becomes a choice for managers to make. The choice is to install just enough structure to move their organisation to the edge of chaos where it can experience relentless change. Self-organisation is equated with adaptiveness and the notion of local interaction amongst agents producing emergent outcomes is lost. The analogy of the birds is used and then quite effortlessly coupled with successful organisations.

However, flocking is one attractor for bird behaviour, one that already exists. The few simple rules that produce it will not produce spontaneous jumps to new attractors. Surely, success for corporations over the long term requires just such a move to new attractors. Furthermore, a key feature of the edge of chaos is the power law. This means that small numbers of large extinction events occur periodically while large numbers of small extinctions occur. There is no guarantee of survival at the edge of chaos, only the possibility of new forms emerging that might survive. Nowhere do the authors mention this power law. Instead, they make a simplistic equation between being at the edge of chaos and success.

Among the prescriptions they derive from complexity theory there is, first, the injunction to improvise:

> ... successful managers rely on a few key rules to innovate adaptively while consistently executing products and services on time, on target and on budget. These managers neither fall into rigid

routines nor do they become chaotically undisciplined. Rather, they solve the dilemma of how to achieve adaptive innovation and consistent execution. Here *improvisation* is the first building block of competing on the edge. (*p. 22*)

In the managerial situation, improvisation is about extensive, real-time communication in the context of a limited structure with a few sharply defined responsibilities, strict priorities, and targeted deadlines. Improvisation is what enables managers to continuously and creatively adjust to change and to consistently move products and services out of the door. (*p. 33*)

Human behaviour is reduced to a few key rules. It is assumed that they can ensure success. And it is assumed that managers solve dilemmas rather than face paradoxes. The authors provide a questionnaire that managers can use to identify whether they are at the edge of chaos or trapped in one of the other dynamics (*pp. 30–310*). They give examples from their research of a company in each of these states and, of course, the only successful one is reported to be at the edge of chaos. They then give prescriptions for moving to the edge, if they are not already there. Managers should foster frequent change in the context of a few strict rules. They should keep activity loosely structured but at the same time rely on targets and deadlines. They should create channels for real-time, fact-based communication within and across groups.

So, the strategic choice now relates less to outcomes and more to a few strict rules, frequent changes to keep people on edge and fact-based communication channels. Why is it necessary to appeal to complexity theory for these prescriptions?

I think I have said enough to show that, once again, researchers have made some very loose interpretations of what complexity theory means and quite easily subsumed it into orthodox organisational theory. The prescriptions and the descriptions rely implicitly on cybernetics and cognitivism, even though the language is drawn from complexity theory. The result is a watered-down strategic choice theory.

## Chaos theory and organisations: analysis at the macro level

In this section, I am going to look briefly at how three authors use chaos theory to analyse organisations. These are analyses at the level of the organisations as a whole and they explore the implications of viewing whole organisations as chaotic systems.

### Thietart and Forgues

The first paper (*Thietart & Forgues, 1995*) reviews chaos theory and concludes that mathematical chaos can be found 'when there is the simultaneous influence of counteracting forces' (*p. 23*). The authors then review relevant literature on organisations to show that organisations are characterised by counteracting forces. Some of these forces push an organisation to stability, namely the forces of planning, structuring and controlling. Other forces, however, push an organisation towards instability and disorder. These forces include innovation, initiative and experimentation. They argue that when these forces are coupled they produce the chaotic organisation. On this basis, Thietart and Forgues present a number of propositions based on the theory of chaos, such as:

- Organisations are potentially chaotic.
- Organisations move from one dynamic state to another, namely stable equilibrium, periodic equilibrium, or chaos.

- Forecasting is impossible, especially at a global scale over the long term. Change, therefore, has an unpredictable long-term effect.
- When in the chaotic state organisations are attracted to an identifiable configuration.
- Similar actions taken by the same organisation will never lead to the same state.

They conclude as follows:

The combination of the forces of stability and change can push the organization towards the chaotic domains where deterministically induced random behavior is the rule. Furthermore, because of the dissipative nature of open systems such as organizations, chaos has an underlying order: the strange attractor or the organizational configuration. As a consequence chaos contains the seeds of new stabilities. It is an organizing force. Thus, organizations face two contradictions: first, let chaos develop because it is the only way to find new forms of order. Second, look for order but not too much, because it may be a source of chaos. (p. 28)

There are a number of points to note about this kind of analysis. First is the level at which the analysis is conducted, namely the macro level of the organisation as a whole. Second, it combines notions from chaos theory and the theory of dissipative structures. Third, it adopts the position of the objective observer. Fourth, there is a hint of an underlying cognitivist perspective in that organisations, presumably those who manage them, are assumed to be able to choose how much chaos or order to have. Again, there is the notion that the role of managers is to move their organisation between different dynamic possibilities. I would like to sound a note of caution in pursuing this kind of analysis. Chaos theory is a theory of deterministic systems but human systems are not deterministic. The behaviour of people is not driven by unchanging rules. The 'rules', if that is what they are, change as people learn.

### Levy

The second paper, (*Levy, 1994*) focuses the analysis at an even higher macro level, that of the industry. Levy argues that industries can be modelled as dynamic systems that exhibit both unpredictability and underlying order. He notes the point that human systems are not deterministic:

Human agency can alter the parameters and the structures of social systems, and it is perhaps unrealistically ambitious to think that the effects of such intervention can be endogenized in chaotic models. Nevertheless, chaotic models can be used to suggest ways that people might intervene to achieve certain goals. (p. 169)

He concludes that, although short-term forecasting is possible, long-term planning is impossible and says that this has 'profound implications for organisations trying to set strategy based on their anticipation of the future' (*p. 170*). He concludes that strategic plans should take account of a number of scenarios and that firms should not focus too narrowly on core competences. For him, strategy becomes a set of simple guidelines that influence decisions and behaviour. Furthermore, firms need to change these guidelines as industries and competitors change. He also says that the system as a whole must be understood if one is to understand indirect and counter-intuitive means to an end.

Notice again how this argument proceeds. It recognises the impossibility of long-term prediction. However, instead of asking how managers are actually now proceeding in the absence of forecasts or foresight, Levy says they should foresee a number of scenarios and set simple guidelines. Again the notion seems to be that complex systems can be managed if one can identify the right set of simple rules. He also recommends, just as the systems-dynamics-based theory of the learning organisation does, that organisations must be understood as a whole and that this can be done by computer simulation. Clearly, Levy takes the position of the external observer and is implicitly recommending that this is the position managers should also take. The idea that an organisation can be modelled and then influenced and controlled is implicitly cognitivist and cybernetic. What is lost here is the question of what it is like for a manager to be a member of a complex system, interacting at a local level, when it is not possible to see the organisation as a whole.

### Morgan

*Morgan (1997)* uses chaos and complexity theory as the basis of one of his metaphors for organisations, namely the organisation as flux and transformation. Having outlined the key elements of chaos and complexity theory he draws a number of conclusions with regard to organisations. First, he states that:

But the message of chaos and complexity theory is that while some kind of ordering is *always* likely to be a feature of complex systems, structure and hierarchy can have no fixed form, hence cannot function as predetermined modes of control. (*p. 266*)

He repeats this *always* on a number of occasions. However, this is not necessarily so. A complex system can self-organise into disintegration just as it can into a rigid, repetitive pattern. Furthermore, even when it operates at the edge of chaos there is the potential for the emergence of a new form, the shape which no one can know of in advance, and it may well not be one that leads to survival. Remember the power law. There is no guarantee of survival.

Like most of the other writers already surveyed here, he then points to the order that can emerge from interaction governed by a few simple rules. He equates this with his notion of 'minimum specs': that is, avoiding a grand design and specifying a small number of critical variables to attend to. He says the minimum specs define an attractor and create the context within which the system will move to it.

I have already referred to the problems with this idea. If the requirement is some new form then the rules, or the context, that will produce that form do not exist yet. If the emergence depends critically on small changes then there is no way to specify what they are in advance. You could not ensure that you have detected all of them or measured them accurately enough. Morgan passes over this and recommends that managers should manage the context and allow self-organisation to do the rest. Here again there is the notion of manager, not as participant in a difficult-to-understand complex system but one who stands outside it, identifies the minimum specs and then creates the context for it to produce self-organisation. Note the talk about a manager 'allowing it to happen'. This seems to assume that self-organisation is some new form of behaviour rather than a different way of understanding how people have always behaved. The question is whether such self-organising behaviour produces patterns that block or enable change.

Morgan also recommends identifying the small changes, or leverage points, that will transform the system. I have already explained above why I think that this does not fit with the notion of a complex system. He also recommends identifying the existing attractor that is locking an organisation into a stable position and identifying whether it should be changed. If it is to be changed, then managers are supposed to work out how the transition is to be achieved and how small changes can be used to do so. In advance, they are supposed to identify what the new ground rules are supposed to be. They must consider how they are going to manage through the 'edge of chaos'.

For me, the essentials of cybernetics and cognitivism are all firmly in place in this argument. The focus is on the autonomous individual who stands outside the system and in effect controls it, even if in a much looser way than is usually supposed. The reasoning remains, I think, firmly within orthodoxy and the invitation to explore a radical perspective is passed by.

## 13.4  COMPLEXITY AND KNOWLEDGE CREATION

Nonaka's (*Nonaka, 1988; 1991; Nonaka & Takeuchi, 1995*) use of chaos theory has been influential in the study of the creation of knowledge in organisations and for this reason, I will devote this section to reviewing it.

### Creating new knowledge

According to *Nonaka (1991)* new knowledge is created when tacit knowledge is made explicit and crystallised into an innovation, that is a recreation of some aspect of the world according to some new insight or ideal. New knowledge, according to Nonaka, comes from tapping the tacit, subjective insights, intuitions and hunches of individuals and making them available for testing and use by the organisation as a whole. For him tacit knowledge is personal and hard to formalise. It is rooted in action and shows itself as skill, or know-how. In addition to technical skills, tacit knowledge lies in the mental models, beliefs and perspectives ingrained in the way people understand their world and act in it. Tacit knowledge is below the level of awareness and is therefore very difficult to communicate. The nature of explicit knowledge, however, is easy to understand: it is the formal and systematic knowledge that is easily communicated, for example product specifications or computer programs.

#### Tapping tacit knowledge

Nonaka gives an example of how tacit knowledge is to be tapped. In 1985, product developers at Matsushita could not perfect the kneading action of the home bread-baking machine they were developing. After much unhelpful analysis, including comparison of x-rays of dough kneaded by the machine and dough kneaded by professionals, one member of the team proposed a creative approach. She proposed using a top professional baker as a model, so she trained with a top baker to acquire his kneading technique and after a year of trial and error she was able to help her colleagues reproduce a mechanical kneading action that mimicked that of the professional. This example describes a movement between different kinds of knowledge, the tacit and the explicit:

- tacit to tacit as the product developer acquires the skill of the professional baker through observation, copying and practising, so internalising it and learning;
- tacit to explicit as the product developer articulates the foundations of her newly acquired tacit knowledge to her colleagues;
- explicit to tacit as the colleagues internalise the knowledge made explicit by the product developer and use it to alter their own tacit knowledge or mental models – in other words, they learn;
- explicit to explicit as the newly formulated product specifications are communicated to the production department and embodied in working models and final production processes.

Innovation then flows from a form of learning, that is new knowledge creation, that in turn flows from moving knowledge between one type and another.

New knowledge starts with an individual, according to Nonaka. Tacit knowledge has to travel from one person to another, in a way that cannot be centrally intended because no one knows what is to travel, or to whom, until it has travelled. New knowledge can therefore only be created when individuals operate in self-organising teams.

A key difficulty in the creation of new knowledge is that of bringing tacit knowledge to the surface of individual awareness, conveying tacit knowledge from one person to another, and finally making it explicit. This is so difficult because it requires expressing the inexpressible and this needs figurative rather than literal language.

*Metaphors*    Metaphors have to be used to link contradictions to each other. It is when people juxtapose seemingly illogical and contradictory things that they are stimulated to look for multiple meanings, to call upon tacit knowledge, and so develop new insights. The ambiguity of metaphors provokes and challenges people to define them more clearly. Metaphors are formulated through intuition, a form of tacit reasoning that links images that may seem remote from each other. Nonaka describes how, in 1978, top management at Honda inaugurated the development of a new car concept with the slogan 'Let's gamble', indicating the need for a completely new approach. The development team expressed what they should do to deal with this metaphor in the form of another slogan: 'Theory of Automobile Evolution' (a contradictory idea of a car as both a machine and an organism). This posed the question: if a car was like an organism how would it evolve? The designers discussed what this might mean and produced another slogan: 'Man–maximum, Machine–minimum'. This conveyed the idea that the car should focus on comfort in an urban environment. The idea of evolution prompted the designers to think of the car as a sphere, a car that was 'short' and 'tall'. This gave birth to the idea of a 'Tall Boy' car, eventually called the Honda City.

*Analogy*    Once metaphors have provoked new ideas, analogies between one thing and another can then be used to find some resolution of the contradictions that have provoked people into thinking new things. Analogy is a more structured process of reconciling opposites and making distinctions, clarifying how the opposing ideas are actually alike or not alike. To illustrate this, Nonaka recounts the story of Canon's development of the mini-copier. To ensure reliability, the developers proposed to make the copier drum disposable – the drum accounted for 90 per cent of maintenance problems. Team members were discussing, over a beer, the problem of how to make the drum easily and cheaply, when the team leader held up his beer can and asked how much it cost to make one. This led the team to examine the process of making cans to see if it could be applied to the manufacture of photocopier drums. The result was lightweight aluminium copier drums.

*Models*   Finally, models are used actually to resolve the contradiction and crystallise the new knowledge: for example, a prototype kneading machine, or a prototype small photocopier.

As new knowledge is dispersed through a group and an organisation, it must be tested – that means that there must be discussion, dialogue and disagreement.

The distinction Nonaka makes between tacit and explicit knowledge (*Griffin, Shaw & Stacey, 1999*) is derived from Polanyi (*Polanyi & Prosch, 1975*). Nonaka and Takeuchi maintain that 'knowledge is created and expanded through social interaction between tacit and explicit knowledge' (*1995, p. 61*) in the four modes of knowledge conversion described above. However, as Tsoukas points out, Polanyi was actually arguing that tacit and explicit knowledge are not two separate forms of knowledge, but rather that:

Tacit knowledge is the necessary component of *all* knowledge; it is not made up of discrete beans which may be ground, lost or reconstituted ... to split tacit from explicit knowledge is to miss the point – the two are inseparably related. (*Tsoukas, 1997, p. 10*)

Another point to note is how *Nonaka & Takeuchi (1995)* talk about knowledge as embodied, rooted in experience and arising in interaction between individuals:

Our dynamic model of knowledge creation is anchored to a critical assumption that human knowledge is created and expanded through social interaction between tacit knowledge and explicit knowledge. We call this interaction "knowledge conversion." It should be noted that this conversion is a "social" process *between* individuals and not confined *within* an individual. (*p. 10*)

They emphasise the importance of dialogue and discussion in this conversion process (*p. 13*), pointing to the importance of intuition, hunches, metaphors and symbols (*p. 12*). They see knowledge as essentially related to action and arising from a process in which interacting individuals are committed to justifying their beliefs. They talk about knowledge as justified belief closely related to people's values. They talk about the context of ambiguity and redundancy in which knowledge is created (*p. 12*). However, they then take their argument in a direction that leaves the importance of relationships and the social undeveloped and unexplored. Having emphasised the social, they locate the initiation of new knowledge in the individual:

In a strict sense, knowledge is created only by individuals. The organization supports creative individuals or provides contexts for them to create knowledge. Organizational knowledge creation, therefore, should be understood as a process that "organizationally" amplifies the knowledge created by individuals and crystallises it as a part of the knowledge network of the organization. The process takes place within an expanding "community of interaction," which crosses intra- and interorganizational levels and boundaries ... Tacit knowledge is personal, context-specific, ... (*p. 59*)

In this way of seeing things, tacit knowledge is possessed by individuals and the knowledge creation at an organizational level is the extraction of this already existing tacit knowledge from individuals and spread across the organisation by socialising processes. This leads to a rather linear sequential view of individuals passing tacit knowledge to others, primarily through imitation, then formalising and codifying it so that it can be used.

This is very different to the view I will be exploring in Chapters 15 and 16. There, individual selves and their knowledge emerge from, are socially constructed in, relationships where the processes are far more wide ranging and complex than simple imitation. In my view, tacit, unconscious, pre-reflective knowledge is never had by anyone but is rather a potential continually unfolding in actual experience.

I will be emphasising the emergent, self-organising, intertwined character of individual, group and organisational knowledge in Chapters 15 and 16. The emphasis of Nonaka and Takeuchi on the individual as the origin of knowledge, on the other hand, leads them to emphasise the organisation-wide intentional character of knowledge creation:

The knowledge spiral is driven by organizational intention, which is defined as an organization's aspiration to its goals. Effort to achieve the intention usually takes the form of strategy within a business setting. From the viewpoint of organizational knowledge creation, the essence of strategy lies in developing the organizational capability to acquire, create, accumulate, and exploit knowledge. The most critical element of corporate strategy is to conceptualize a vision about what kind of knowledge should be developed and to operationalize it into a management system for implementation ... Organizational intention provides the most important criterion for judging the truthfulness of a given piece of knowledge. If not for intention, it would be impossible to judge the value of information or knowledge perceived or created. (*p. 74*)

Having emphasised the ambiguity of the situation in which knowledge arises, Nonaka and Takeuchi leave this behind and move to the strategic choice view of strategy. Insights about the radical unpredictability of emergent new knowledge, and the social ways in which it arises, are lost. Nonaka and Takeuchi also use the words 'self-organising' but in a very different way to my understanding. They see self-organisation, not as the local interaction of agents that produces emergent patterns, but rather as autonomous or free individuals. They describe a self-organising team as a structure in which individuals can be free to diffuse their ideas in a team (*p. 76*). They link this with *Morgan's (1997)* 'minimum critical specification'. In complexity theory, self-organisation is a process in which agents interact locally on the basis of their historically evolved identities. This does not necessarily imply freedom to diffuse ideas.

A key insight from complexity theory is that of the paradoxical dynamics of stability and instability at the 'edge of chaos'. Again Nonaka and Takeuchi use similar words but for them they have little to do with characteristics of relationships that generate the dynamic. Rather, they equate chaos with crisis and assign top management the role of injecting it into the organization in order to break down routines, habits and cognitive frameworks. I cannot see any justification for equating mathematical chaos with human crisis, a matter I briefly take up below.

Furthermore, Nonaka and Takeuchi do not pay much attention to the ever present possibility of groups of people becoming stuck in some stable dynamic, or some fragmenting one that kills off the knowledge-creating process. In my way of understanding the evolution of organisations it is important to understand something of the responses people make to the inevitable anxiety aroused by emergent new knowledge.

What Nonaka and Takeuchi end up with, then, is a process for knowledge creation that can be managed and controlled. Nonaka and Takeuchi use the language of chaos to restate the concepts of orthodoxy. From a radical perspective, the knowledge creation process cannot be controlled or managed from outside of that process. Rather, it is a self-organising process that 'manages' itself if the characteristics of relationships are such as to allow this to happen.

## 13.5 HOW THE ABOVE APPLICATIONS OF COMPLEXITY THEORY DEAL WITH FOUR QUESTIONS AND FOCUS ATTENTION

In the above sections, I have given a brief review of some of the growing literature dealing with a complex systems view of organisations. Some employ the simulation methods of complexity scientists to model organisational processes at the macro level of the organisation as a whole. Others use the theory of complex systems as a metaphor that gives insight into the management of organisations. The analysis here is usually at the macro level, but sometimes at a more micro level. In the latter case, the emphasis is on prescription rather than analysis.

I would like now to do what I did in relation to the three theories of organisation reviewed earlier in this book. I want to examine how the theories surveyed in this chapter deal with the four questions posed in Chapter 1.

### The nature of interaction

As with strategic choice, organisational learning and psychoanalytic perspectives, interaction in organisations is seen in systemic terms, this time in terms of chaotic or complex systems. Analysis of these systems may be at a macro level in which diversity in agents and their interactions is not postulated. In that case, the system may follow equilibrium attractors or some strange attractor, but it does not have the internal capacity to move from one attractor to another. In this regard, there is relatively little difference from systems dynamics. What is different is the identification of strange attractors and the use of the concept of self-organisation to explain how movement around the strange attractor emerges. Alternatively, the system may be modelled with a focus on the micro level to include agent and interaction diversity. In this case, the system does display the internal capacity to move spontaneously from one attractor to another or to evolve new ones. Self-organisation is now understood as the process that produces emergent novelty. This is a major difference from all of the other systems models reviewed in this book.

It seems to me that the literature reviewed in this chapter uses the first of the above complexity models, namely the one that does not place microdiversity at the centre. This is evidenced by the focus on identifying a few simple rules and on someone operating on the conditions, or model parameters, to move the system to the edge of chaos. Apart from Allen, none of the above approaches utilising complexity theory talk about the importance of diversity, which in human terms amounts to deviance and eccentricity and this is central to that kind of self-organisation that might produce emergent novelty.

Complex systems at the edge of chaos display the dynamics of order and disorder, stability and instability, regularity and irregularity, all at the same time. When this is interpreted in organisational terms, by the authors reviewed in this chapter, it is often translated as 'crisis'. I suppose that from an orthodox perspective it might be crisis. However, the dynamics of the edge of chaos is not at all the dynamics of crisis, but rather, of paradox and ambiguity. For me, this connotes a mature ability to hold a difficult position, not a state of crisis. Equating the edge of chaos with crisis leads on to the prescription to inject crisis into an organisation. Surely, this is a misinterpretation of what mathematical chaos or complexity might mean in human terms.

## The nature of human beings

The above applications of complexity theory to organisations all make implicit assumptions about human psychology. These are drawn from cognitivist psychology. This is evident in the emphasis placed on the individual. It is the individual who learns and chooses, even though that individual may be part of a team. Further evidence is given by the use of the notion of mental models and the idea that people can pass tacit knowledge from one individual to another, quite separately from explicit knowledge. This means that the notion of a complex system is being interpreted in organisational terms from the same psychological perspective as those theories based on cybernetics and systems dynamics. Given the tendency also to interpret complex systems from the orthodox perspective, it would be surprising to find enormous differences between the theories surveyed above and those of strategic choice and organisational learning.

## Methodology and paradox

The methodological position of the theorists reviewed above is no different to those proposing strategic choice and learning organisation theories. They all take the position of the objective observer who stands outside the system and models it in the interest of controlling it. The prescriptions derived from these theories all implicitly place the manager in the same position. It is the manager who must produce and impose the few strict rules that will produce the desired attractor. It is the manager who must alter the parameters, or create the conditions, that create the edge of chaos dynamics. This is then simplistically equated with success.

Although paradox seems to me to be at the heart of what the dynamics at the edge of chaos means, it does not feature at the centre of the theories developed above.

## Focusing attention

- The methodological position taken is that of the external observer who objectively models the system in either a quantitative or a qualitative way. I think it is always implicit that this is the position managers should take too. The invitation to explore what it means to be a participant in a complex system is then not taken up.
- There is a tendency to state the potentially radical insights coming from complexity theory to do with unpredictability, self-organisation and emergence. However, these implications tend not to be taken seriously and descriptions and prescriptions are presented that do not differ fundamentally from those of strategic choice or learning organisation theory.
- The notion in complexity theory that seems to be most attractive is that agents following a few simple rules can generate highly complex emergent behaviour. This is taken as the basis of a prescription to do with identifying and setting the rules that will yield the required complexity. This, however, is at odds with the emergent nature of new forms. It rather assumes a pre-existing reality that can be identified and then achieved through simple rules.
- It is implicitly assumed that human behaviour can be adequately explained by cognitivist theory.

The approaches using chaos and complexity theory reviewed in this chapter focus attention on much the same factors as the three orthodox theories reviewed in the first part of this book. There is the same emphasis on the agency of the autonomous individual. There is the same concern with control. There is the same downplaying of the importance of unpredictability and diversity. There is the same belief in the possibility of an organisation moving according to some organisation-wide intention.

It seems to me that what is happening is this. The starting point is a systems theory that potentially differs quite radically from cybernetics and systems dynamics. This potentially radical systems theory is then combined with a cognitivist theory of human behaviour. Cognitivism has close links with cybernetics and systems dynamics and as soon as the cognitivist perspective is brought to bear cybernetics and systems dynamics assumptions come with it. The result, I think, is theoretical developments that start off with radical promise but then rapidly slip back into orthodoxy. It seems to be very hard to hold on to the radical perspectives of complexity as a theory of systems while retaining the assumptions of cognitivism and continuing to adopt the methodology of the independent, external observer.

I think these points apply not just to the literature I have reviewed here but also to what I have written over the past seven years on this topic. In the *Chaos Frontier (Stacey, 1991)*, I rather stridently claimed that organisations were nonlinear systems that displayed chaotic behaviour when they were creative. I repeated that claim, less stridently I hope, in the first edition of this book (1993). By the time I came to write the second edition (1996), and *Complexity and Creativity in Organizations (Stacey, 1996)*, I had come to think that this was wrong. This was because mathematical chaos is a property of deterministic systems and humans are not deterministic systems. So, in these later books I wrote about organisations as complex adaptive systems. However, I can now see that in all of these books and other publications (*Stacey, 1992; 1995*) I was doing just what I am suggesting is a problem in the literature reviewed in this chapter.

I was struggling to hold on to the radical implications of a new systems theory, complexity, while trying to explain it in the language of cognitivism and psychoanalysis. In other words, I was trying to explore the implications of a theory that is essentially relational at the systems level in combination with theories of human behaviour that grant primacy, not to relationship, but to the autonomous individual. In the chapters that follow, I want to explore a very different understanding of human behaviour, one that sees individuals and groups as one phenomenon rather than two different levels of description. I will be trying to combine a radical theory of systems with a radical theory of human behaviour.

What are these radical implications?

First, groups of people are creative only when their behaviour displays the dynamics of bounded instability. Both stability and, of course, disintegration are inimical to creativity. In psychological terms, bounded instability has to do with the ability to hold the ambiguity and paradox of life and contain the anxiety they generate.

Second, the creative process is also destructive. It involves not only cooperation, but also competition that takes place in the medium of ideas, communication and power relations. The creative process in human networks is, therefore, inevitably messy: it involves difference, conflict, fantasy and emotion; it stirs up anger, envy, depression and many other feelings. To remove the mess by inspiring people to follow some vision, to indoctrinate them to share the same culture, is to remove the mess that is the very raw material of creative activity.

Third, neither the messy creative processes nor their outcomes can be planned or intended because long-term outcomes are unknowable in the dynamics of bounded instability. Links between people's next actions and their long-term outcomes disappear so that no one can be 'in control'. This becomes far less anxiety provoking once it is accepted that the consequence is not necessarily randomness and anarchy. This is because spontaneous self-organisation produces emergent strategies; that is, the interaction itself creates patterns that no agent individually intends or can foresee. Emergence means that it is not possible to foresee the global outcome of interaction between individuals, nor is it possible to reduce the global pattern to the behaviour of the agents.

For me, the key message coming from the science of complexity is this. It is possible, with much effort, for someone, or some small group of powerful people, to predict the outcomes of group, organisational and societal behaviour, therefore, to remain 'in control' of them. However, this is possible only while there is enforced stability in behavioural dynamics. The result could be stability for a long time, but it will be the death of creativity and innovation and hence, ultimately, the death of the system. So, organisations cannot survive by following some blueprint. Instead, the potential for, but not the guarantee of, survival is created by the capacity to produce emergent new outcomes. This is controlled by the process of spontaneous self-organisation itself.

## 13.6  CHAOS, COMPLEXITY AND ANALOGY

Before turning to how complexity theory might lead to a radical theory of organisations, I would like to set out how I think chaos and complexity theory need to be interpreted as analogies for organisational life.

## Chaos

I would like to explain what I understand the theory of chaos to be. Chaos theory reveals the properties of iterating mathematical, or algorithmic, deterministic nonlinear relationships, in which the output of one iteration becomes the input of the next. This is not a cybernetic relationship and it cannot be called feedback. In cybernetic, or any other, feedback, the output of one iteration is compared with some target, or some environmental state, outside the iterative process and the difference between the target/environmental state becomes the input for the next iteration. The relationship between this input and the subsequent output is such as either to dampen or amplify the input. The system can either amplify or dampen, or alternate sequentially between the two.

In the relationships relevant to chaos theory, it is the whole output of one iteration that becomes the input for the next iteration. There is no comparison with an outside reference point. This is more accurately described, therefore, as self-reference rather than feedback. In other words, the current state is determined by referring, through a deterministic nonlinear algorithm, to its own previous state. When a control parameter is held, by some external force, at a critical point, then this self-referential relating takes the form of a strange attractor. While the control parameter is held at that critical point, the pattern of relationships takes one, and only one, form, namely that of the particular strange attractor generated by these particular algorithmic relationships. This is the simultaneous operation of amplification and constraint – that is, a paradox. It is not a sequential alternation between constraint and amplification.

## Complexity

Complexity theory reveals the properties of iterating the interaction between separate algorithms. One form of iteration consists of a population of algorithms that are all the same, for example the Boids simulation described in Chapter 12. These algorithms are cybernetic entities. This is so because the output of one, say its velocity in the case of the Boids, is compared with that of a neighbour, and the difference is fed back so as either to increase or decrease its velocity. The agents in complex adaptive systems of this kind are deterministic, cybernetic algorithms. What the iteration of their interaction reveals is the emergence of a coherent collective pattern, that is an attractor for the whole system. Such a system has no capacity to move spontaneously from one attractor to another.

Another form of complex adaptive system is one in which the interacting algorithms can change from one iteration to another through random mutation and/or cross-over replication. This means that the algorithms in the population fall into different categories, so that difference is located between categories and sameness within a category. An example of this kind of system is provided by the Tierra simulation in Chapter 12. At the start of that simulation, one algorithm copies itself to generate another algorithm of the same kind. The output of the algorithm's operation is another algorithm, not an input into its next iteration. Instead of taking a previous output as the input for the next operation, the algorithm is simply repeated, with some random mutation. Here there is no feedback, rather the algorithm refers to itself in order to operate. Exactly the same point applies to its copy. The only possibility of any change, or evolution, lies in the random mutations. In the case of cross-over replication, two algorithms produce an output that is combined to form another one. This new one is not utilised as input into the next iteration of the original two. Therefore, there is no feedback, only reference by each to itself. Now variety can arise in the system because of the mixing of code to produce another algorithm. The nature of the system, namely the scarce CPU time and the limited number of iterations allowed for each algorithm, provides a constraint on the possibility of each algorithm performing its iteration.

Note that the agents are not cybernetic entities and note that they are not deterministic but rather probabilistic relationships due to the presence of random mutation. What the iterations reveal in this kind of system is the emergence of new forms, new attractors.

## Interpretation and analogy

The question is how these theories of algorithmic interaction are interpreted in organisational terms to say something about organisational life. Remember that this algorithmic interaction has to be taken as an analogy for some kind of interaction in organisations.

So what, in organisations, is taken to be the analogue of an algorithm – that is, an agent? Remember that in the complexity simulations the agent is an algorithm. What, in an organisation, is taken to be the analogue of the output of the iteration of an algorithm? What is the analogue of the input into the next iteration? When someone uses chaos theory, are they doing so in a self-referential sense or are they interpreting it approximately as a cybernetic system that alternates between positive and negative feedback? When they use complexity theory are they using insights drawn from simulations in which agents are all the same, or ones in which there are different categories of agents? It makes a significant difference because the former cannot evolve while the latter can. What is the analogue of an attractor? What is the organisational analogue of the programmer of the simulation?

What is becoming more apparent as more people take chaos and complexity theory over into organisations is that these questions are not being carefully considered. Instead, immediate and often simplistic jumps are made from algorithmic interaction to human interaction and this produces unjustifiable conclusions.

For example, the analogue of the algorithmic agent in a complex adaptive system is often unquestioningly taken to be an individual human being. The translation of agent as cybernetic entity in a computer simulation to human being as a cognitive entity is all too easy to make. A rapid jump is then made to prescribing a few simple rules that all agents should follow. No account is taken of the implication. It means that the system can follow one and only one attractor. It then lacks the capacity to change spontaneously that is so characteristic of life and creativity. Instead, any change has to come about through someone standing outside the system and altering parameters, creating conditions, so that the whole system can move to the edge of chaos. The prescription implies that the organisational analogue for the programmer of the simulation is the manager of the organisation. This translation occurs, probably, because it all fits so well into orthodox management discourse. The result, however, is old recipes in new vocabulary.

At every step, what I have described in the previous paragraph is a questionable procedure. Are humans analogous to algorithms and cybernetic entities as cognitivism suggests? Are managers analogous to simulation programmers? What about the capacity of living systems to change spontaneously?

What I hope to do in the following chapters is begin exploring the implications of taking a self-referential view of human beings rather than a feedback/cybernetic one. I want to explore what happens when organisational analogies are sought for simulations in which there is agent diversity and hence the spontaneous capacity to change. It will be necessary to consider what in organisations is analogous to the probabilistic algorithms of complex adaptive systems where there is diversity. It will also be necessary to ask what the analogues for random mutation and cross-over replication are, as well as what the analogue for an attractor is. Instead of thinking about the manager as the analogue of the programmer I would like to consider the consequences if the manager is the analogue of an agent in the system. I am also going to ask whether groups of human beings are at all analogous to a system or a network. What if human interaction is thought of, not as a system or a network, but as processes? What if humans do not always adapt to, or fit in, with each other? It might then be useful to think of human relating, not as adaptive, but as responsive. I will suggest that the analogue for complex adaptive systems in the simulations are complex responsive processes in an organisation. I will explain what I mean by this in Chapter 16.

## 13.7 SUMMARY

This chapter has reviewed the way in which a number of writers are interpreting chaos and complexity in organisational terms. It has suggested that the common approach is to retain a cybernetic and cognitivist approach and to interpret chaos and complexity from that perspective. This amounts to retaining the assumption of the autonomous, even heroic, individual and the prescription of the manager as the objective observer of the organisation as a system. I have argued that the result is the re-presentation of strategic choice and learning organisation theory in a different vocabulary. The emphasis on control and organisation-wide intention remains intact. For me, that means that the opportunity to explore what it means to operate as a participant in a setting in which the future is unknowable is lost. No further understanding of the process of how strategy might emerge from local interaction is obtained. The interpretation of chaos and complexity thus remains within management and organisational theory orthodoxy.

The remaining chapters of this book suggests some steps toward a radical interpretation of the implications of complexity theory for organisational evolution.

### FURTHER READING

The publications reviewed in this chapter are examples of the most recent work in this field. For further reading I suggest Axelrod (1984), Goldstein (1994), Goerner (1994), Hurst (1995), Kiel (1994), Nilsen (1995), Wheately (1992) and Zimmerman (1992). If the applications to economics are of interest the following are suggested: Anderson, Arrow & Pines (1988), Arthur (1988), Baumol & Benhabib (1989) and Kelsey (1988).

# REFERENCES

Abraham, F. D. (1995), *Chaos Theory in Psychology*, Westport, CT: Praeger.

Allen, P. M. (1998), Evolving Complexity in Social Science, in Attmann, G. & Koch, W. A. (Eds.) *Systems: New Paradigms for the Social Sciences*, Berlin: Walter de Gruyter.

Anderson, P.W., Arrow, K. J. & Pines, D. (1988), *The Economy as an Evolving Complex System*, Menlo Park, CA: Addison-Wesley.

Arthur, W. B. (1988), Self-Reinforcing Mechanisms in Economics, in Anderson, P. W., Arrow, K. J. & Pines, D. (Eds.) (1988), *The Economy as an Evolving Complex System*, Menlo Park, CA: Addison-Wesley.

Axelrod, R. (1984), *The Evolution of Cooperation*, New York: Basic Books.

Baumol, W. J. & Benhabib, J. (1989), Chaos: significance, mechanism and economic applications, *Journal of Economic Perspectives*, Winter, vol. 3, no. 1, pp. 77–105.

Brown, S. L. & Eisenhardt, K. (1998), *Competing on the Edge: Strategy as Structured Chaos*, Boston: Harvard Business School Press.

Chakravarty, B., Van de Ven, A. and Roos, J. (Eds.) *Implementing Strategic Processes: Change, Learning and Cooperation*, London: Blackwell.

Goerner, S. J. (1994), *Chaos and the Evolving Ecological Universe*, Langehorne, PA: Gordon Breach.

Goldstein, J. (1994), *The Unshackled Organization: Facing the Challenge of Unpredictability through Spontaneous Reorganization*, Portland, OR: Productivity Press.

Griffin, J. D., Shaw, P. & Stacy, R. D. (1999), *Knowing and Acting in Conditions of Uncertainty: A Complexity Perspective*, Systemic Practice and Action Research.

Guastello, S. J. (1995), *Chaos, Catastrophe, and Human Affairs*, Hillsdale, NJ: Lawrence Erlbaum Associates.

Hsieh, D. (1989), Testing for nonlinear dependence in daily foreign exchange returns, *Journal of Business*, vol. 62, no. 3.

Hurst, D. (1995), *Crisis and Renewal: Meeting the Challenge of Organizational Change*, Boston: Harvard Business School Press.

Kelsey, D. (1988), The economics of chaos or the chaos of economics, *Oxford Economic Papers*, vol. 40, pp. 1–31.

Kiel, L. D. (1994), *Managing Chaos and Complexity in Government*, San Francisco: Jossey-Bass.

Levy, D. (1994), Chaos theory and strategy: theory, application, and managerial implications, *Strategic Management Journal*, vol. 15, pp. 167–78.

Morgan, G. (1997), *Images of Organization*, 2nd edn., Thousand Oaks, CA: Sage.

Morley, D. (1993), Chasing chaos in Santa Fe, *Manufacturing Systems*, February, p. 40.

Morley, D. (1995), Chaos 3.0, *Manufacturing Systems*, August, p. 14.

Nilsen, T. H. (1995), *Chaos Marketing*, Maidenhead: McGraw-Hill.

Nonaka, I. (1988), Creating organizational order out of chaos: self renewal in Japanese firms, *California Management Review*, Spring, pp. 57–73.

Nonaka, I. (1991), The knowledge-creating company, *Harvard Business Review*, November–December, pp. 96–104.

Nonaka, I. & Takeuchi, H. (1995), *The Knowledge-Creating Company: How Japanese Companies Create the Dynamics of Innovation*, Oxford: Oxford University Press.

Peters, E. E. (1991), *Chaos and Order in the Capital Markets: A New View of Cycles, Prices and Market Volatility*, New York: John Wiley.

Polanyi, M. and Prosch, H. (1975), *Meaning*, Chicago: The University of Chicago Press.

Sanders, T. I. (1998), *Strategic Thinking and the New Science: Planning in the midst of chaos, complexity, and change*, New York: Free Press.

Schenkman, L. & Le Baron, B. (1989), Nonlinear dynamics and stock returns, *Journal of Business*, vol. 62, no. 3.

Stacey, R. (1991), *The Chaos Frontier: Creative Strategic Control for Business*, Oxford: Butterworth–Heinemann.

Stacey, R. (1992), *Managing the Unknowable: The Strategic Boundaries Between Order and Chaos*, San Francisco: Jossey-Bass.

Also published in the UK as *Managing Chaos*, London: Kogan Page.

Stacey, R. (1993), *Strategic Management and Organisational Dynamics*, London: Pitman.

Stacey, R. (1995), The science of complexity: an alternative perspective for strategic change processes, *Strategic Management Journal*, August.

Stacey, R. (1996), *Complexity and Creativity in Organizations*, San Francisco: Berrett-Koehler.

Thietart, R. A. & Forgues, B. (1995), Chaos theory and organisation, *Organisation Science*, vol. 6, no. 1, pp. 19–31.

Tsoukas, H. (1997), The firm as a distributed knowledge system: a constructionist approach, *Complexity and Management Papers*, no. 10, Complexity and Management Centre, University of Hertfordshire Business School.

Wheatley, M. J., (1992), *Leadership and the New Science: Learning about Organisation from an Orderly Universe*, San Francisco: Berrett-Koehler.

Zimmerman, B. J. (1992), The inherent drive towards chaos, in Lorange, P., Chakravarty, B., Van de Ven, A. & Roos, J. (Eds.), *Implementing Strategic Processes: Change, Learning and Cooperation*, London: Blackwell.

# Chapter

# **14** Complexity

## The problem with the notion of the autonomous individual

## 14.1　INTRODUCTION

In the first part of this book, I distinguished between a number of theories of organisational change. I suggested that each combines a theory of interaction with a theory of human psychology. Strategic choice theory combines a theory of interaction defined in terms of cybernetic systems and a cognitivist psychology. Learning organisation theory combines a theory of interaction defined in terms of systems dynamics, also with a cognitivist and to some extent humanistic psychology. Then there is the combination of a theory of interaction in terms of open systems and psychoanalysis. Chapter 13 looked at how a number of writers on organisation and management are applying chaos and complexity theory. I suggest that they combine a theory of interaction in terms of laws generating mathematical chaos, or in terms of complex adaptive systems, with cognitivist psychology. I believe that in doing this, their arguments remain in the orthodoxy represented by strategic choice and learning organisation theory. I have suggested that this is basically due to the retention of the cognitivist assumptions of the primacy of the individual and the position of the objective observer. This is what I term the problem with the notion of the autonomous individual. Retention of this assumption stops further exploration of the potentially radical insights coming from chaos and complexity theory.

This chapter looks for an alternative psychology, one that does not assume the primacy of the autonomous individual, but also does not move to the opposite pole to place the group, society or the collective above the individual. The latter position loses the importance of each of us as unique individuals. I call this alternative, relationship psychology. The next chapter takes this exploration further and indicates how relationship psychology coincides with a theory of interaction derived from complexity theory in a move towards a radical theory of organisational change.

This chapter starts with a return to the issue raised at the end of the last chapter, namely that of how complexity theory might be interpreted.

## 14.2    INTERPRETING COMPLEXITY THEORY

I want to go back to the material in Chapters 11 and 12, namely the theories of chaos, dissipative structures, and particularly agent-based modelling, in order to examine carefully what they are.

### Interpreting the theories of chaos and dissipative structures

Chaos and dissipative structure theories present abstract mathematical models of nonlinear interactions between entities that form a system. They are sets of mathematical equations whose properties are identified through analysis and iteration. The mathematical models are not reality but simply logical structures created by mathematicians. The physicist, meteorologist, chemist, biologist, or any other scientist in any other field, then has to interpret how these abstract logical structures might apply to the field they are interested in. They do this by calling upon what is already known, through scientific experiments, about the phenomena in their field of study. They also perform new experiments suggested by the new theories in order to provide empirical support for the claim that the abstract mathematical models they have developed do apply to the phenomena in their field of interest.

I referred briefly to the work of economists and some organisational theorists who adopt exactly the same approach. They use data on macro events, such as foreign exchange rates, to explore whether the mathematical equations of chaos theory, say, fit the data. As soon as they do this, they make implicit assumptions about the nature of human interaction. They assume that human beings are such that patterns in their interaction can be described at the macro level in terms of equations. Alternatively, other organisational theorists use the concepts expressed in the mathematical models as metaphors to describe organisations. For example, Chapter 13 reviewed the work of a number of researchers who describe an organisation as chaotic. As soon as they do this, they too are making implicit assumptions about the nature of human interaction. It is very important not to jump straight from a mathematical model to an application in a particular field without examining how the model is being interpreted in that particular field.

### Interpreting agent-based systems with homogeneous agents

Exactly the same point applies, of course, to the use of the agent-based models, that is complex adaptive systems, described in Chapter 12. In this section, I want to look at the nature of complex adaptive system models and how they are being interpreted to apply to organisations. Instead of using macro-level mathematical models, agent-based modellers construct computer models consisting of large numbers of interacting agents and then explore their behaviour through simulation.

#### Boids

Take the Reynolds' simulation of boids, described in Chapter 12. The system consists of a number of computer programs, each comprising the same three instructions that organise the interaction of each computer program with other programs. Each instruction is a bit string, a sequence of ones and zeros. This model, then, is a number of bit strings, symbols, that are arranged in a particular sequence specifying an agent interaction with others. In other words, the model is simply a large number of symbol patterns. Each symbol pattern interacts with other symbol patterns.

The simulation then reveals that this interaction between each separate symbol pattern with some others yields an overall pattern in the relationship between all of them. They clump together. When each bit string is represented as a dot on the computer screen, the clumping pattern can be seen and the programmer can observe how it persists in various forms over time. Reynolds then makes an interpretation. He calls each bit string, or symbol pattern, a 'boid' and he calls the pattern they produce 'flocking'. He makes a further interpretation when he suggests that the boids are logically equivalent to real birds and that the model points to how real birds produce flocking behaviour. He then points to how a few simple rules can yield emergent patterns of a very complex kind, without the need for any overall blueprint to determine them. Each symbol pattern interacting with a few others at their own local level of interaction is sufficient to produce an overall pattern of relationships between them.

Let me emphasise the point. The boids simulation simply reveals the logical consequences of the interaction between separate symbol patterns. It demonstrates the overall pattern that unfolds, the attractor, as symbol patterns of a very specific kind interact. The attractor is enfolded, as it were, in the interacting symbol patterns and revealed by iterating their interaction. One interpretation of this phenomenon is that as soon as the symbol patterns, or rules, are specified, they imply a given reality. However, that reality cannot be logically deduced or predicted from the rules and there is no blueprint for it. It emerges. Once the program has been run, the programmer can predict that these particular symbol patterns will lead to the emergence of a particular type of overall pattern that might then be called flocking. However, the programmer cannot predict the specific qualitative form that the flocking will take as the symbol patterns interact since this depends upon the specific context in which they interact. This system of separate, interacting symbol patterns is described as a self-organising system.

But what is organising itself in the boids simulation? Each separate boid is a little blueprint, doing only what the program enables it to, and it is constrained by that program from doing anything else. Therefore, it cannot be they, as separate individual symbol patterns, that are organising themselves. Instead, it is the overall pattern of interaction that is organising itself because there is no blueprint for that. The pattern of interaction called flocking turns back on itself, so recreating itself through the interaction of the separate symbol patterns and providing the context within which the separate symbol patterns interact.

There is a very important point to note about simulations, such as the boids one, where each interacting symbol pattern is the same as all the others. This is interaction where there is no diversity amongst the symbol patterns, no non-average interaction between them, no noise, no fluctuations in Prigogine's terms. Because of this lack of diversity, the simulation cannot display spontaneous moves from one attractor to another, nor can it spontaneously generate a new attractor. The symbol patterns, or rules, always yield the same attractor and change can occur only when the programmer changes the individual symbol patterns.

I have made this point a number of times before in previous chapters. I repeat it here because I believe that it is very important when it comes to interpreting complexity theory in the setting of human organisations. This touches on another very important point that is worth continually emphasising, namely that any use anyone makes of a simulation is an interpretation that they are making.

### Organisational interpretations

Consider how some organisational theorists interpret simulations like boids. They use the simulation to justify the following conclusion. If a manager wants his or her organisation to produce an overall pattern, or strategy, of a highly complex kind then it is not necessary to formulate and implement an overall strategy. It is not necessary to provide a blueprint that sets out what the strategy is and how it is to be implemented. Instead, the manager should establish a few simple ground rules and this is held to unleash the power of self-organisation. In this interpretation, the manager is, without any explicit justification, equated with the programmer. Reynolds, the programmer, took the position of the objective observer, standing outside the pre-given reality of birds flocking, and induced rules that might produce flocking. He then simulated them in the computer and showed that they do produce the equivalent of flocking. This is what the manager is now supposed to do. Implicit in the prescription to formulate a few simple rules that all in the organisation are to follow is the notion that the manager must first choose which attractor he or she wants the organisation to be drawn to. The manager then has to induce the few simple rules that will produce it.

However, note the consequence of this. Suppose that the manager succeeds in identifying the right set of rules and people do follow them. Then the required attractor will indeed emerge. However, that is all that will emerge. The organisation will follow this attractor until the manager changes the rules because a system in which the separate entities are all following the same rules does not possess the capacity for spontaneously moving to another attractor, nor does it possess the capacity to generate new attractors spontaneously. The prescription ensures that the organisation will not be creative. The only change from strategic choice theory is that the manager is now relieved from having to formulate detailed overall plans. This is not a radically different insight since it was long ago concluded that detailed long-term plans were not all that helpful in turbulent times and that what managers needed to do was set the direction in the form of a few guidelines.

## Interpreting agent-based models with heterogeneous agents

Now consider another simulation in which the agents do not all follow the same rules.

### The Tierra simulation

In the Tierra simulation, Ray designs one bit string, one symbol pattern. This is not a few simple rules but 80 instructions specifying in detail how the bit string is to copy itself. He then introduces a mechanism to generate diversity. This is random mutation in the bit string and a selection criterion, namely speed of replication. He does this by limiting the computer time available for replicating and limiting the total time period over which an individual bit string has the opportunity to replicate. In other words, he designs rules to generate random mutation in, and impose constraints on, the replicating system that come from outside that system. He is imposing conditions that both enable and constrain, and in doing so, he introduces chance, or instability, into the system. This instability within constraints makes it possible for the system to generate novel attractors, as follows.

An overall pattern of interaction rapidly emerges in the form of an increase in the number of bit strings encoding the 80 instructions. The attractor is that of exponentially increasing numbers, which eventually impose a constraint on further replication. The overall pattern is continually moving from sparse occupation of the computer memory to overcrowding. The bit strings are also gradually changing through random bit flipping. In other words, they are gradually differing from each other and increasing diversity is appearing.

### A new attractor

Soon, this random mutation and the selection pressure of limited computer time in the presence of large numbers provide the context for the emergence of a new attractor. This is the appearance of smaller bit strings. Now there are distinctively different kinds of bit strings, namely long ones and short ones. The constraints on computer time favour smaller ones and the overall pattern is now decline in long bit strings and increase in numbers of short ones. The system has spontaneously produced a new attractor.

New forms of individual bit string and new overall patterns have emerged at the same time. There can be no pattern of increase and decline without simultaneous change in the length of some individual bit strings. There can be no sustained change in bit string lengths without the overall pattern of increase and decline. Individual bit string patterns, and the overall pattern of the system, are forming and being formed by each other, at the same time.

### Another new attractor

Later, another kind of bit string emerges, that is another symbol pattern, taking the form of instructions to read the replication code of neighbouring bit strings. Another new attractor has emerged.

At the overall level this is a pattern of fluctuating numbers of the new kind of bit string and the old kind. The new bit strings are very short and require the presence of the others in order to perform their replication task. If the short ones increase in numbers too much, then they cannot find enough partners to replicate with and so they decline. This is the new attractor that has emerged at the level of the population of bit strings as a whole. However, at the same time new kinds of bit string have emerged. The new attractor is evident both at the level of the whole population and at the level of the individual bit strings themselves at the same time.

The important point is that the programmer has not programmed the new attractors in advance. They emerge because the system is organising itself within the constraints that the programmer has set, but the programmer is not able to predict what they will be before they emerge. Once they have emerged, the programmer can of course repeat the program and the same attractors will emerge again. However, now they are not new. The new comes about through self-organisation, not design.

### The pattern of interaction organises itself

So, what is organising itself here? It seems to me that it is the pattern of interaction that is organising itself and doing so simultaneously at the level of the individual agents and the population as a whole. Indeed, it now seems rather problematic to separate them out as levels, since they are emerging simultaneously. They are forming while being formed at the same time. The argument for claiming this is as follows. No individual bit string can change in a coherent fashion on its own. This is because continual random mutation in an isolated bit string would eventually lead to a completely random one. In interaction with other bit strings, however, advantageous mutations are selected and the others are weeded out. What is organising itself, through interaction between symbol patterns, is then the changes in the symbol patterns themselves. Patterns of interacting are turning back on themselves, imperfectly replicating themselves, to yield changes in those patterns of interaction and this is possible only because there is a mechanism for generating diversity. New attractors can only emerge when the process of replication is imperfect.

When Ray introduces another form of generating diversity, the bit strings evolve in ways that are more complex. This other form of diversity generation is that of cross-over replication, the genetic algorithm referred to in Chapter 12. Here bit strings are mixed up in replication, so that replication is even more imperfect.

So, this simulation is very different to the boids one. The latter displayed only one attractor and could not spontaneously move to another. The programmer had to change the symbol patterns for this to happen. In the Tierra simulation, the system does spontaneously move to other attractors and indeed spontaneously produces emergent new ones. The programmer had, however, to introduce a mechanism for generating diversity in the replication process.

Ray, the objective observer external to this system, then interprets the changes in symbol patterns in his simulation in terms of biology. He points to the evolution of life and claims that life has evolved in a similar, self-organising and emergent manner. Other simulations have been used to suggest that this kind of emerging new attractor occurs only at the edge of chaos where there is a critical combination of both stability and instability.

### Organisational interpretation

I want to turn now to how ideas such as this are used by organisational theorists. The unquestioned assumption of the primacy of the individual results in implicitly equating the manager, especially the most powerful executive, with the programmer. It is then deduced that, like the programmer of the simulation, the manager must introduce some mechanism for generating sufficient instability and variety and a mechanism for selection. The prescriptions for introducing instability are to set stretching targets, put people under pressure and create crises. The equivalent to cross-over replication is to promote mental cross-fertilisation through cross-functional contacts and multidisciplinary teamworking. The selection mechanism is increased competition between individuals and groups. Having put these mechanisms in place managers are then supposed to leave the teams to operate in what is called a self-organising way. The factor that receives little serious attention is that the new behaviours that will emerge are unpredictable according to the very complexity theory these writers are using to justify their prescriptions.

The problem, as I see it, lies with the equation of manager and programmer. In other words, the problem is with the notion of the objective observer. What the agent-based modellers are trying to show is how a complex system operating within enabling constraints has the capacity to organise itself, from within itself, into emergent new attractors. They are trying to point to the plausibility of novelty emerging in the absence of a design or a designer. Of course, they cannot avoid some initial designing activity themselves because they are dealing with computers and not the reality they are trying to model. However, if an organisational theorist is trying to keep to the spirit of what they are trying to do, namely understand the internal capacity of a system to produce novelty spontaneously, then it is necessary to avoid equating the chief executive, or any other manager, with the programmer. Instead, all managers, no matter how powerful, need to be understood as agents participating in the system. I turn now to the implications of this view.

## Managers as participants in self-organising systems

I find that there is a typical response whenever I suggest to a group of managers that they might think of themselves, and also their chief executive officer (CEO), as participants in self-organising processes. They claim that if they cannot be the designer and if they cannot know the outcomes of what they are doing then they have no role. They claim that they would simply give up if they thought that this was true. Alternatively, they point to examples of CEOs who do form overall intentions for their organisation, who set out compelling visions and missions and do thereby transform their organisation. They conclude that the notion of self-organisation does not apply to them. Why do they think this?

It seems to me that they are immediately understanding self-organisation in terms of the individual: the unquestioned assumption of the primacy of the individual again. Self-organisation is taken to mean that it is the individual members of the organisation who organise themselves. This then leads to the view that self-organisation means all or some of the following:

- Something that happens no matter what anyone does. This means that there is no point in doing anything. One should simply sit back and just wait for fate or destiny.
- Full-blown democracy in which all agents are equal and nothing is done without complete consensus.
- Anarchy in which everyone does whatever they please.
- The empowerment of the lower echelons in the organisation and then leaving them to get on with it.
- The disempowerment and incapacitation of the higher echelons who no longer have a role.

It is important to stress that the notion of self-organisation as it is employed in complexity theory does not mean any of these things. People think it does because they hear these words from the perspective of the autonomous individual and think that it means that individuals are organising themselves without any constraint. However, if you look carefully at the simulations intended to demonstrate the nature of self-organisation you will notice two points. First, there very clearly are conditions that both enable and constrain the operation of the system at the same time. Take the Tierra simulation. Agents are enabled to replicate because computer time is allocated to them, but this is also a constraint because they only have limited time. In organisations, all managers are both enabled and constrained by the availability of resources. In the simulation, agents are constrained by the mode of replication and by the competitive selection applied to them. In the simulations, the programmer imposes all of these constraints but in the reality he or she is trying to model, they all emerge within the system as it evolves. So self-organisation is certainly not a constraint-free form of behaviour.

Second, that which is organising itself is not the separate individuals on their own. It is the overall pattern of relationships that is organising itself at the same time as the nature of the agents is changing (*Griffin, 1998*). The agents are forming and being formed by the overall pattern of relationships. They are, I think, the same phenomenon viewed from different perspectives. The system and its agents are emerging together, simultaneously constraining and being constrained by each other. Once this perspective is taken there is no justification for making any of the interpretations of self-organisation in the bullet points above. Instead:

- Far from there being no point in doing anything, everything one does, including nothing, has potential consequences. Far from the outcome being a matter of fate or destiny, it is the co-creation of all interacting agents.
- There is no reason at all why agents should be interacting in a democratic way. They might, but they might not. Furthermore, they are not all equal in a simulation such as Tierra. Some are pursuing more powerful strategies than others, in terms of survival. There is certainly no requirement for consensus but, rather, the tension between competition and cooperation.
- There is no anarchy because no agent can do whatever it pleases. There are a number of constraints, not least those provided by the actions taken by other agents.
- There is no connection whatever between empowerment of the lower echelons in an organisation and self-organisation, a matter I will explore next.
- There is also no connection whatever between disempowering the higher echelons and self-organisation, also to be explained in the next section.

### The Roles of the most powerful

Self-organisation means that the agents in a system interact with each other according to their own local principles of interaction. This means that they respond to others according to their own capacity to respond. They are enabled to respond in certain ways and constrained from responding in others by that capacity, which has emerged from their histories of interacting with others. There is no reason whatever why some agents should not have wider ranging capacities than others do. Indeed the evolution of the system virtually ensures this. Some have capacities that enable them to respond more effectively and more successfully than others do. This can be translated into organisational terms by saying that some members have more knowledge, more understanding and more power than others do.

Furthermore, there is nothing in the notion of self-organisation that says that each agent should interact with the same number of agents, nor that they have to be nearby in spatial terms. The simulations tend to limit the number of connections and specify them in relation to spatially nearby agents, but this is simply a matter of convenience. So, there is no reason why some agents in a self-organising system should not be much more powerful than some others, nor any reason why some agents should not interact with many more agents than some others.

In organisational terms, the top executives have more power than others, that is a greater capacity to instruct, persuade, or even force others to do what they want. Furthermore, those top executives interact with a great many more people than the less powerful. A CEO may communicate with, and issue instructions to, hundreds of thousands of others in his or her organisation through email, for example. If they all responded according to some blueprint the CEO, or others, had designed, then there would clearly be no self-organisation. However, if they responded according to their own local capacities, and their responses had some effect on the CEO, leading to further responses from the CEO, then this would be self-organisation.

### Understanding the whole system

Greater understanding also confers power. Unlike agents in computer simulations, human beings are able to stand back and understand something of the whole process of which they are a part. Note that this is not the same thing as stepping outside those processes and understanding them from the perspective of the objective observer. A human being trying to understand a human process cannot stop being human. Human emotion and the impact of the one trying to understand on those that he or she is trying to understand make it impossible to step outside. What I am talking about is standing back, as a participant, to reflect on the nature of what is happening as a whole. Humans are able to reflect on, and articulate something about, the whole that is emerging.

However, such articulations, or even models of the whole system, are always inevitably partial. Constructing a model of a whole system involves shearing away detail and focusing on what is judged to be important. The model can, therefore, never encompass the whole. In other words, the whole is always absent, not least because the whole is evolving. Such articulations, or models, then form part of a person's capacity to respond. So, a CEO might form certain views about the nature of his or her organisation, the nature of leadership, the direction the CEO would like it to go in, a vision or a mission for it, and so on. These are all actions the CEO is taking that are likely to call forth some kind of response from many others in the organisation. A small group of powerful people at the top of an organisation might take a decision to enter a new market or to negotiate with a small group of powerful people in another organisation to merge with it. All of these actions would evoke and provoke a multitude of responses from others, both within and outside the affected organisations. If the pattern of these responses were simply the expression of some overall blueprint then the system could not be called self-organising. However, if others were responding according to their own local capacities to respond, it could be self-organising.

The point I am making is this. Small groups of very powerful people at the top of an organisation allocate resources and in so doing both enable and constrain other members of the organisation. They design sets of procedures and hierarchical reporting structures. They legitimise some actions and not others. They communicate with very large numbers of others. They make statements about visions and missions. They make decisions and take actions that greatly affect a great many others. What they cannot do, however, is program the responses those others will make. The powerful may identify what kind of responses they would like by making statements about values and required cultures and behaviours. They may try to motivate others to adopt all of this. However, people will still only be able to respond according to their own local capacities to respond and the most powerful will find that they have to respond to the responses that they have evoked and provoked. This is what I think self-organisation means in human terms. It is a process of interaction that is ever present in all human situations and would only cease if people really did respond like automatons to statements about the values and behaviours they were supposed to display.

There is another aspect to the self-organising nature of what I have just been describing. I have been talking about powerful people who state and implement intentions that affect many others in an organisation. How did they come to have such intentions? They would doubtless have emerged in numbers of conversations and political interactions that, I will be arguing later, are themselves self-organising processes.

In this section I have been stressing how one group of people takes actions that evoke and provoke responses from many others, the latter in turn evoking and provoking yet further responses from the first group. Since all are acting according to their own local capacities, it is impossible to predict how this pattern of responses will unfold past a certain point in the future. All together will be forming and being formed by this overall pattern of responses. In describing behaviour in this way I have, in effect, avoided taking the perspective in which the individual is primary. Instead I have been suggesting that neither the individual nor the group is primary since they form and are formed by each other at the same time. The next section will explore the justification for this statement.

## 14.3    THE INDIVIDUAL AND THE GROUP

Chapter 2 described how the cognitivist approach to understanding human behaviour placed the individual as prior to, and primary over, the group, so that groups are seen as collections of individuals. Those collections might then affect how individuals behave. There is no notion of individual minds being somehow constructed in group relationships. Chapter 10 described the dominant psychoanalytic perspectives. These also give primacy to the individual in that inherited drives provide the energy and the motivation for behaviour. However, psychoanalysis does see individual minds as emerging from the clash between inherited drives, or inherent phantasies, and the external reality of the group. Once again, groups consist of individuals but from this perspective their minds are structured by the clash between their inheritance and the conformity required by the group. Furthermore, the individual's behaviour, indeed his or her thinking capacity, is affected by the group context. Groups play a far more important role from this perspective than they do from a cognitivist one.

There are other perspectives that ascribe much more importance to the role of the group in creating individual minds. These are social constructionism (*Gergen, 1982, 1985, 1991; Harre, 1983, 1986; Shotter, 1993*), intersubjectivity theory in psychoanalysis (*Stolorow, Atwood & Brandschaft, 1994; Atwood & Stolorow, 1984*) and radical group-analytic perspectives (*Dalal, 1998*). All three of these approaches see relationship as primary. In relating to each other people create, and are created by, their social reality. Here the mind is not structured by a clash between an inherited, internal force and an external reality. Instead, the mind is seen as emerging in relationship and the notion of a mind inside someone disappears. An individual's mind arises between that individual and the others with whom he or she is in relationship. It is between them, not in one of them. Mental phenomena, including the sharing of meaning with others, all arise in social, or group, relationships, although they may be experienced as phenomena pertaining to the individual. It is this perspective, which I will refer to as a relationship psychology, that I want to describe in this section.

From this perspective, genetics and biology create the potential for the fundamental human attribute, namely the need, and the capacity, to form social relationships. However, it is the experience of relating that actualises this potential in terms of unique individual minds, thoughts and behaviours and the capacity to resonate to a common meaning and hold similar beliefs. The sociologist *Mead (1934)* argued that an individual mind is an inner conversation, the internalisation of social processes, where internalisation does not imply within an individual body, but within a private, silent, secret conversation that the individual holds with him- or herself. You might like to stop reading this page for a few seconds and reflect upon what is going on in your mind. Is it a thought that triggers a thought, which triggers another, endlessly all day long? This is what Mead meant by mind as a silent conversation.

## Silent, secret conversations

Behaviourist psychology focused on the behaviour of the isolated individual, explicitly excluding any mental phenomena and implicitly excluding the importance of social relations between individuals. From this perspective behaviour is the response of the individual to a stimulus, and whether the stimulus is provided by a thing or another human matters little. The meaning here lies in the stimulus, for if it rewards, the human responds in one way, and if it punishes, the human responds in another way.

Mead argues that humans cannot be understood in isolation and that the phenomenon of mind cannot simply be ignored. He explains the phenomenon of mind in the context of the evolution of the human animal and its emergence in behaviour, but social rather than isolated individual behaviour. The fundamental unit of analysis then becomes the social act: that is, not simply a stimulus or a response but the sequence of both together. This is important because, for all social organisms, other organisms provide most of the stimuli each organism responds to and each response is itself the stimulus to yet other responses. He held that the meaning of a stimulus lies not in the stimulus itself but in the response to it. Most stimuli are gestures made by one animal and most responses are returned gestures made by another animal. The stimulus calls forth the response and the meaning lies in this response. For example, one dog may approach another and bite it and this may call out a violent response in the other. This social act then means aggression, attack and anger. Alternatively, the first dog might bite the second in a manner that calls forth the response of a counter nip. The meaning of this social act is then play. The stimulus on its own is not sufficient to establish what the meaning is. The gesture, then, is the first phase of an act. It carries with it the attitude of the one making the gesture, that is the emotion that underlies it. The gesture means this attitude, it is a symbol of it, and it calls forth the response of the other.

In this way Mead shows how all social animals communicate with each other through a conversation of gestures, movement, touch, sound, visual display and odour. At this point, however, while there is meaning, there is no mind or consciousness. Mead argues that mind evolved in humans when they came to use vocal gestures more and more. This is because the vocal gesture, more than any other, can be experienced by the one making it in the same way as it is experienced by the recipient. We cannot see the facial expressions we are making to another but we can hear the sounds we make just as they do. This opens up the possibility that the vocal gesture can call forth the same response in the one making it as in the other. This then becomes what Mead calls a significant symbol because it means the same thing to the maker of the gesture and the recipient.

It is now possible for the maker of the gesture to be aware, in advance, of the likely response of the recipient. The maker of the gesture is, thus, conscious and can think; that is, hypothesise likely responses to a gesture. The maker of the gesture now has a mind. Mind means being conscious of the possible consequences of actions and exploring them, in advance of action, by means of a silently conducted conversation of gestures in the form of significant symbols. The maker of the gesture has a mind in the sense that he or she can have some notion of the consequence of his or her actions, can think, can reflect in the pause between stimulus and response.

All of this is possible only because of the evolution of significant vocal symbols, that is language. Mead is at pains to stress that he is providing an explanation of how a gesture can come to call forth the same response (meaning or idea) in the one making it as in the one receiving it. He is saying that meaning is shared through social relationships conducted in significant symbols. The shared meaning arises, and continually rearises, in the conversation of gestures, in the action and interaction. Meaning is not something that is going on in a mind or that even requires a mind. Mind is a silent conversation about the meaning in an action so making it conscious. The silent conversation needs to take place externally before it can be 'internalised' and in this sense mind is always a social phenomenon even though it is an individual conducting the silent conversation. Mead's theory of mind is also firmly linked to the body because mind as a silent conversation of gestures requires a body.

## Reflexivity and self-consciousness

The explanation of mind as conscious thinking in the form of a private 'inner' conversation is one based on reflexivity. This is so in the sense that the conversation is about the response one's own stimulus is calling out in one's self as well as in the other.

This kind of reflexivity gives humans consciousness but not yet self-consciousness. To become self-conscious one must, as a subject, become an object to oneself, a further reflexivity.

Mead explains the process that makes this possible. To be an object to himself, an individual man or woman must experience himself or herself from the standpoint of others; they must talk to themselves as others talk to them. This happens as they learn to take up the roles of others in a form of play with themselves, eventually becoming able to take the position within themselves of the whole group. They move from taking the attitude of specific individuals towards themselves to taking the attitude of the whole group towards themselves. Mead calls this taking the attitude of the 'generalised other'. When she does this, the individual here takes the attitude of the whole community towards herself, as well as the attitude of others towards herself and the attitude of others towards each other. It is through this generalised other that the community exerts control over the individual. This is a social process and is possible only in language. It follows that the self is a social construction and only animals that possess language can possess a self. This does not mean that an individual cannot have the solitary experience of a self. One can never start life as a hermit, but once having evolved a self one can go off and be a hermit.

Note here how in this theory, the social is not a constraint and the mind or self does not emerge out of a clash between something that is already there in the individual and that constraint. Mind is emerging in social relationships and it is the 'internalisation' of those social relationships. It needs to be stressed that this is a very different notion of mind to that in cognitivism, humanistic psychology and psychoanalysis. The individual mind is not primary and prior to the group. Instead, the individual mind and the web of relationships that are a group are emerging simultaneously. Individuals are forming and being formed by the group at the same time. Note how similar this is to the description of complex adaptive systems given above. There never was a time when there was just an individual, nor was there ever a time when there was just a group. Both have to be there at the same time. The individual is social to the core (*Foulkes, 1948*). The individual is the singular, while the group is the plural of the same phenomenon, relationship (*Elias, 1978, 1989*).

## Language, ideology and power

Another sociologist, *Elias (1978, 1989)*, also held that human beings were born with an inherited, instinctual nature, but as a constraining potential rather than a determining force. Humans were enabled to see and hear what they saw and heard because of this inherited potential and that inheritance also constrained them from seeing or hearing in any other way. Like *Maturana & Varela (1992)*, and like *Mead (1934)*, he emphasised the selecting or enacting nature of biology and evolution.

Part of the inheritance was a species-specific set of reactions and symbols, such as smiling and grimacing. Another part was the capacity for learning that broke the rigid link between instinct and behaviour. The key element in this capacity to learn was the ability to develop a community-specific symbol system in addition to the species-specific one. The community-specific symbol system is, of course, language. He was of the view that symbols did not represent the world but were rather a medium of social orientation within the world and within the self. He also claimed that experience was multidimensional and could not be reduced to symbols. Symbols allowed humans to take a view of their world that was somewhat detached and could have some distance from their fears, but only somewhat. Experience was always invested with emotion to some extent. Elias defined the human mind in terms of the capacity to utilise symbols to explore potential reactions to an action before undertaking that action. He also stressed the use of language and symbols of all kinds in the elaboration of private fantasies.

He saw people interacting with each other through the use of both species- and community-specific symbols to form what he called figurations. By figuration, he meant the pattern of interdependence, a kind of order. These figurations were formed by the competitive and cooperative relationships between people and reflected power disparities between individuals and groupings of them. Relationships constrain and constraint is what power is about. Note how power is located in the relationship. It is not, here, one individual imposing his or her will on another. Power relations are co-created. Elias pointed to how particular uses of symbols, particular ways of talking, could be used to signal and enhance power:

By figuration we mean the changing pattern created by the players as a whole – not only by their intellects but also by their whole selves, the totality of their dealings in their relationships with each other. It can be seen that this figuration forms a flexible lattice-work of tensions. The interdependence of the players, which is a prerequisite of their forming a figuration, may be an interdependence of allies or of opponents. (*1978, p. 130*)

In this way, people are emotionally bound together through the medium of symbols. (*p. 137*)

So, figuration is the pattern of bonding, that is the web of interdependence, between people upon which human existence utterly depends. Individuals cannot develop, and having developed they can only rarely exist, outside a web of relationships. The immediate consequence of such interdependence is that the behaviour of every individual is constrained by the demands of others. Constraints are what power is about and as soon as one sees this, it becomes clear that figurations are structured by power. What Elias is presenting here is a clearly self-referential, reflexive process in which individual minds are formed by the power relationships while they are, at the same time, forming those power relationships. He writes about these processes in a way that shows how he thought about them as self-organising processes that produced emergent patterns in themselves. He was very alive to the paradoxical nature of the processes he was describing. For example, he defines individuals as interdependent people in the singular and he defines society as interdependent people in the plural, so emphasising the point that he sees individual and society as two aspects of the same phenomenon.

Elias then explains how the interdependence between people in a figuration is expressed in symbolic form. He insists that language, reason and knowledge, speaking, thinking and knowing are different words for exactly the same phenomenon: they all have to do with handling symbols. For him, language is not a tool used to express a thought because a thought is already in language. Thinking is born of concrete activity that takes place between people. It is because people are interdependent that they must communicate if they are to survive and the means of communication is language. Language, therefore, expresses the power relations of the social figuration. Language orients one in the world – that is, it is knowledge – and its themes organise experience. Elias equates mind with inner conversation, just as Mead did before him, and mind, therefore, emerges in social relationships. In fact mind is the internalisation of social relationships and is, therefore, just as much structured by power relationships as social figurations are.

## Ideology and the preservation of power relations

One of the principal ways that power differentials are preserved is the use of differences to stir up hatred (*Elias & Scotson, 1994*). It is not that a racial or religious difference generates hatred of itself, but rather that such differences are used to stir up hatred in the interests of sustaining power positions. Elias and Scotson studied the events following the influx of a working-class group into a new housing estate adjacent to an older estate, also occupied by working-class people. Although there was no material difference between the two groups, hostility soon appeared in which the older inhabitants denigrated the newer ones.

Elias and Scotson explained this in terms of the cohesion that had emerged over time in the already-established group of inhabitants. They had come to think of themselves as a 'we', a group with common attachments, likes, dislikes and attributes that had emerged simply because of the passage of time. They had developed an identity. The new arrivals lacked this cohesive identity because they had no history of being together and this made them more vulnerable. The more cohesive group therefore found it easy to 'name' the newcomers and ascribe to them hateful attributes such as being dirty or liable to commit crimes.

So, although there was no obvious difference between the two groups, one group used the fact that the other was newly arrived to generate hatred and so maintain a power difference. This was, in a sense, 'accepted' by the newcomers who took up the role of the disadvantaged. *Dalal (1998)* points to this as an unconscious social process. The hatred between the groups emerged from an essentially self-organising process that no one was really aware of or actually intended.

Another, and closely related, way in which power differentials are preserved is through the use of what Elias and Scotson called the 'weapon' of ideology, also an unconscious process that emerges in a self-organising way. A key aspect of ideology is the binary oppositions that characterise it and the most basic of these is the distinction between 'them' and 'us'. Ideology is thus a form of conversation that preserves the current order by making it seem natural and in this way, just like all other conversation, it organises the experience and behaviour of the group. As a form of conversation, as an aspect of the power relations in the group, ideology is internalised into that silent conversation which is mind in individuals. It is important to note how these authors are talking about ideology as a mutually constructed conversation that is continually repeated, not a 'thing' that is shared or stored. The ideology exists only in the speaking of it.

Elias and Scotson point to how ideology emerges in a self-organising process of gossip. Streams of gossip stigmatise and blame the outsider group while smaller streams of gossip praise the insider group. The gossip builds layer upon layer of value-laden binary pairs such as clean–dirty, good–bad, honest–dishonest, energetic–lazy, and so on. The result of the gossip is to attribute 'charisma' to the powerful and 'stigma' to the weak. In this way the power differences are reinforced. In established, cohesive groups, streams of gossip flow along well-established channels that are lacking for newly arrived groups. The stigmatisation, however, only sticks where there is already a sufficiently large power difference. Again these are social relations that are internalised into the inner conversation that is mind, conferring feelings of superiority on the powerful and feelings of inferiority on the weak.

## The social unconscious

Dalal further develops the notion of the social unconscious in relation to the structure of language. Humans categorise or partition experience in order to deal with it and this act of naming is intrinsically binarising: the deep structure of language is a binary logic in that things are categorised as 'A' or 'not-A' . There seems to be an inevitable tendency, as humans frame their experience, to binarise and polarise it. The next point is that there seem to be two different forms of logic used by humans to frame their experience, forms that *Matte-Blanco (1975, 1988)* called asymmetrical and symmetrical logic. Asymmetrical logic establishes difference in that it distinguishes things from each other and locates them in time and space, much as in Freud's secondary process thinking. Symmetrical logic, on the other hand, treats all objects as the same, rather as in Freud's primary process thinking. Symmetrical logic homogenises everything and recognises no contradictions, no negation and no degrees of certainty or uncertainty. There is no difference, no space, no time. Matte-Blanco argued that both forms of logic are applied in all forms of thought at the same time.

We can now make a general statement and say that all thinking consists of fracturing the continuum of experience, of breaking it up into different parts, and relating those parts to each other. Thus between the parts, difference is emphasised, and similarity is obliterated – asymmetric logic. Whilst within each part, similarity is emphasised and difference obliterated – symmetric logic. (*Dalal, 1998, p. 166*)

Conscious thinking tends to be more asymmetrical than symmetrical and unconscious thought tends to be more symmetrical than asymmetrical. Dalal argues that the very act of naming or categorising inevitably binarises and polarises an experience and at the same time the process of thinking makes the experience both heterogeneous (asymmetrical and conscious) and homogeneous (symmetrical and unconscious). So, when some in a group are named 'British', the others all become 'not-British' and symmetrical thinking is immediately applied to both 'British' and 'not-British' in that homogeneity is imposed on each group. Within each group the differences between members are obliterated and the fact that this is being done is unconscious. At the same time there is asymmetrical thinking in that a difference is being drawn between the two groups: 'every sentence contains globules of homogeneity, which are connected by heterogeneity … *Thus all thought could be said to consist of a weaving together of islands of unconsciousness*' (Dalal, 1998, pp. 190–1).

Dalal then makes a very important point about identity and difference. At the centre of identity there is symmetry, an unconscious symmetry that cannot be tested without destroying that identity. He sees this as an aspect of the social unconscious and links it with discourse. Within each discourse there are certain categories taken to be natural, the equivalent of identities, and these are homogenised and so hidden from questioning. It is these categories that constitute the social unconscious and what is being made unconscious is the power differential. People cluster around their similarity – the symmetrical – to hide the difference of power. I will return to these points about power, ideology and the social unconscious in Chapter 16 when I talk about 'shadow' relationships.

Consider now how Elias's analysis extends Mead's notion of mind as 'inner' conversation. Elias places great emphasis on fantasy, the propensity of individuals to elaborate 'inner' conversation in highly imaginative ways. Individuals do not simply take 'real' social relationships into their private, secret conversations with themselves. Whatever is so taken in is subjected to a process of elaboration that can rapidly diverge from external conversations and actions. Of course, those 'inner' elaborations may well find expression in external gestures, so evoking responses in others in the same way as any other gesture.

## More on power

Elias also introduces a fundamental aspect of social relationships, namely the constraints they impose on members of a group and, therefore, the power differentials they create. He points to a basic social impulse, namely to maintain power differentials and how this is exercised by using any difference between groups to arouse the hatred needed to preserve power. He links this to the role of ideology, which categorises groups into binary opposites, making power preserving behaviour feel natural. He identifies how that form of conversation known as gossip plays a central role in constantly reinforcing the ideology and so preserving power differences. What Elias has done, therefore, is put power, ideology and emotion at the centre of social relationships and therefore at the centre of conversation. All of the factors will, thus, characterise the silent conversations individuals have with themselves. Minds too will be taken up with power relationships, ideological and emotional interchanges between the inner conversationalists, some of which will be the voices of group opinion.

*Dalal (1998)* has drawn on Elias and Matte-Blanco to develop *Foulkes' (1948)* notion of the social unconscious. Key elements of this social unconscious are:

- when members of a group collectively employ, in their talk and their actions, differences between themselves and other groups to stir up hatred against the others in order to preserve unconsciously sensed power differences;
- when members of a group collectively categorise their experience into binary opposites that become entrenched as ideologies, which make their behaviour seem right and natural;
- when members of a group collectively obliterate some differences and highlight others, so polarising experience.

These socially unconscious processes are all self-organising and they produce emergent patterns of social relationships. Furthermore, they will be taken into the silent conversations that are individual minds to constitute individual unconscious processes.

The main point I am trying to make is that mind is silent conversation. If this is so, mind must be organised in much the same way as ordinary everyday conversations between people are organised. Mental processes must, therefore, be equivalent to conversational processes. There is only one difference. Public conversation between people requires vocalisation that is directed towards other people with the purpose of evoking responses from them. The private conversation that is mind is silent gestures from one 'voice' evoking responses from others. Public conversation discloses to others, while private conversation conceals from others, at least initially. However, in terms of nature and structure, public and private conversation, it seems to me, must be equivalent. Understanding the nature of ordinary, everyday conversation then becomes crucial to an understanding of human behaviour, of group processes, and of organisations.

## How conversation constructs social realities

Bhaktin wrote in the 1920s and, after a long period of official banishment during the Stalinist regime, again in the 1950s and 1960s. His thinking bears some striking similarities to that of Mead and Elias, although as far as I know he was not aware of their work, nor they of his. As for Mead and Elias, so for Bhaktin, all social phenomena are constructed in the ongoing dialogical relationships between people. He stressed the multiplicity of discourses, symbolising practices and speech genres that are to be found in any culture. He talked about language as simultaneously structuring and being structured by people so that individuals were not simply the effects of social relations but nor were social relations simply the sum of individuals.

Bhaktin stressed the unpredictable and unfinished nature of dialogue and its capacity to produce the novel:

An utterance is never just a reflection or an expression of something already existing and outside it that is given and final. It always creates something that never existed before, something absolutely new and unrepeatable, and moreover, it always has some relation to value … (*Bhaktin, 1986, pp. 119–20*)

He also stressed the paradoxical, tension-filled nature of dialogue. The tension was between centripetal forces seeking expression in unity, merging, agreement and monologue, on the one hand, and centrifugal forces seeking expression in multiplicity, separating, disagreement and dialogue, on the other. This is similar to Matte-Blanco's symmetrical and asymmetrical logics and to the properties of language that make binarising and polarising inevitable. These forces that characterise dialogue account for the emergence of official ideologies: centrifugal forces push towards unity and order giving voice to particular beliefs while the centripetal forces of multiplicity and diversity come to be denied expression. This is the point about power again. Power relations determine which words can be used officially and which can only be used unofficially.

## Official and unofficial ideologies

Bhaktin paints a picture of official ideological unity on the surface that covers over a multiplicity of unofficial ideologies. He places considerable emphasis on what he calls 'carnival' as the process that subverts the official ideology and is thus a force for change. By carnival he means humour and parody, the grotesque and the sensuous, all of which are means of turning the official ideology on its head. Bhaktin saw this as a non-violent process of change. Carnival stands for the processes that create the conditions of fluidity and ambiguity that are required if change is to occur. It may be argued that carnival is not a good metaphor because carnivals are officially sanctioned and that what they actually do is allow people to discharge emotion so working to sustain the official ideology. It seems to me that the grotesque, the humorous and the sensuous could work either to sustain or undermine the official ideology depending on the context. I will be returning to this matter later. Here I want to point to how Bhaktin focuses attention on the processes he calls 'carnival'. He claims that they give a voice to those at the margins and that this is associated with the potential for change in some way.

*Shotter & Billig (1998)* build on Bhaktin's distinction between official and unofficial ideologies to talk about a 'dialogic unconscious' that is very similar to Dalal's suggestions for a theory of the social unconscious:

We see it as operating, not within the heads of individuals, but in our use of certain words at certain times in certain ways, while repressing or ignoring the use of others. In such a view there would be a dialectical relationship between consciousness and unconsciousness, for, as the very words we use in our dialogues with others draw attention to certain issues, it is drawn away from others. As dialogic consciousness, or attention, is focused on particular aspects of language, so others slip by, as it were unnoticed. (*p. 20*)

They are arguing that ideology is reproduced in the unconscious aspects of language and they point to how the very ability to continue in dialogue with others requires repression of impulses to rudeness. The intricate codes and rituals of polite relating and conversing must be observed if one is to stay in the dialogue and this underlies the unconsciously repressive aspect of language.

The final point I want to mention in relation to Bhaktin is how he stressed that although dialogue constructs meaning, that meaning does not lie in the words themselves. Dictionaries may set out the common features of words but the meaning always resides in a communication made by a specific person in a specific context. The meaning is not, however, in the intention or control of the speaker. This is because a word has already been spoken by someone else and what it means will also depend on the one to whom the word is addressed. Meaning is determined by whose word it is and for whom it is intended. In order to fill a word with meaning the speaker uses particular intonations and places words in different relationships to each other. For the other to whom the word is addressed to understand it that other must recognise these context-dependent novelties. Understanding meaning depends upon understanding the novelty of the communication rather than the abstract identity of the word. I think this is a very important point to which I will return later. What it is saying is that the sophisticated negotiation of meaning in ordinary everyday life depends heavily on the human capacity to detect difference and novelty in the communications of others, rather than the capacity to extract regularities from an environment that cognitive psychology emphasises so much.

## 14.4    TOWARDS A RELATIONSHIP PSYCHOLOGY: HOW IT COMPARES WITH OTHER PSYCHOLOGICAL THEORIES

In Chapter 2, I briefly outlined the view of human knowing and acting presented by cognitivist psychology. The immediate focus of attention from this perspective is a single individual, particularly a single individual brain. Cognitivism postulates that the human brain is an information-processing mechanism in much the same way as a computer. While a computer processes symbols taking the form of on/off electric currents, the brain processes electrochemical discharges between the neurones of which the brain consists. In computer language terms, the on/off electric current is represented as digital symbols, ones and zeros. In mental terms, the brain's electrochemical discharges are represented in symbols mainly taking the form of sounds and pictures.

The symbols are representations of an external reality that already exists before the representation is made. That representation is made through the senses of seeing, hearing, smelling and touching. The representations are stored in the brain/mind, as they are in computers, in short- and long-term memory banks. Through repeated experience of similar sensations the individual brain/mind builds up a more and more accurate picture of external reality taking the form of a template, a map, a model, schemas, scripts or rules relating to behaviour. These rules, maps, models, schemas or scripts then form the basis upon which the individual acts. These models are assumptions about the world, including other people. They are predictions of the reaction of others to any action a person takes.

When one individual interacts with another, he or she does so in a manner determined by his or her mental model. An individual acts on the basis of the assumptions and predictions of which the model consists. A group of people is a collection of individuals who are interacting with each other on the basis of their mental models. Those mental models will include assumptions and predictions of how groups of people behave. It is through mental models that an individual interprets the response of other individuals in a group and it is in this way that the group affects the individual. Group and individual are two different levels of analysis. First there are individuals and then there are groups composed of individuals.

Individuals, according to this theory, are essentially cybernetic entities who can take the position of objective observer of an external reality, although that observation might be distorted by their mental models. I have argued that this view of human psychology is fundamental to the theories of strategic choice and the learning organisation. I have also argued that it underlies the way most people seem to be interpreting chaos and complexity theory in an organisational setting.

In Chapter 2, I mentioned humanistic psychology and then in Chapter 9, I pointed to how it plays an important role in the theory of the learning organisation. Humanistic psychology also immediately focuses attention on the individual, but in a way rather different to cognitivism. The central tenet here is the belief that the human individual is fundamentally motivated by self-realisation, or self-actualisation. Human knowing and acting, and therefore human learning, are driven by the need to find the self. Others, in the form of community, are very important to emotional well-being but it is not postulated that the group or the community actually forms the individual. In fact, the self-actualising individual has to find his or her self despite group pressures to conform.

In Chapter 10, I briefly summarised the psychoanalytic understanding of human beings. Again, the primary focus is on the individual. An individual is born with instincts and these provide the energy and the motivation for living. The instincts are represented as drives in the psyche and they seek satisfaction through discharge. Individuals, however, also need others to survive and so cannot discharge any drive in any way they please. Individuals are constrained by the prohibitions of society and this clash between drives and social prohibition structures the mind. Later developments in psychoanalysis stressed the importance of inherited mental phantasies and how these were shaped in relating to others. So the later developments of psychoanalytic theory increasingly emphasised the importance of relationships in forming the psyche of an individual. Mostly, however, the primacy of the drives as the source of energy and motivation has been retained, with the exception of intersubjectivity theory, which I will mention again later.

In psychoanalytic theory the group consists of individuals but exerts a far more powerful effect on how individuals behave than is the case in cognitivism and humanistic psychology. Individuals anonymously contribute emotions to groups and are then affected by them in the form of basic assumption behaviour.

The way of thinking that I have described in this chapter, drawing primarily on the work of the sociologists Mead, Elias and Bhaktin, points to what I will call a relationship psychology. There are strong similarities between this and intersubjectivity theory in psychoanalysis (*Stolorow, Atwood & Brandschaft, 1994*). This holds that one person is not an object that affects another, but that they are subjects interacting with each other. In their interaction, they form the experience of each other. The work of the psychoanalyst and developmental psychologist *Stern (1985, 1995)* also emphasises the importance of relationship in the formation of the infant mind. Group-analytic theory, which I will turn to in the next chapter, also emphasises the formative importance of the group and the social. In one way or another, I suggest, all of these developments fall within or near to what I am calling relationship psychology.

The essence of relationship psychology is the notion that an individual mind is a silent conversation of voices and feelings, more or less hidden from others. This secret, silent conversation arises in relationships between people, while being experienced in their bodies. Relationships between people are expressed in the same medium as mind, namely conversation and feeling states. The two – relationships between people and relationships between voices in a silent, secret conversation – are equivalent to each other. They form and are formed by each other at the same time. Unlike any of the other psychological theories, this one does not see individuals at one level of description and groups at another. They are the same phenomenon seen from different angles: one is the singular of relationship and the other the plural of relationship. This does not mean that all individuals are the same. First, each develops unique, private fantasies around public conversation. Furthermore, I suggest that the development of mind is sensitive to small misunderstandings, or differences in understandings, which can easily escalate into very different silent conversations, that is very different minds.

As I said in the introduction to this chapter, cognitivist, humanistic and psychoanalytic psychology all postulate the individual as primary. For cognitivists, relationships between people do not play any fundamental part in how humans know anything. Each individual knows in the way he or she does because of the architecture of the brain. Humanistic psychology attaches importance to relationships between people in so far as a sense of community is part of the actualisation of an individual self. Psychoanalysis puts relationships in a much more central position but retains the assumption that psychic energy and the motivation are located in an individual's inherited drives or inherited fantasies.

Relationship psychology, as I have explained above, makes a radical departure from all of these by decentring the individual, without moving to the opposite extreme of giving the group, or the social, primacy either. It does so by postulating that individual minds are formed by and form relationships at the same time. The energy and the motivation for individual and joint action arise simultaneously in relationship. Relationship immediately constrains and so establishes power relations. Relationship is communication and it is this communication that forms and is formed by power relations.

From the perspective of an individual-centred psychology, the analogue of a complex adaptive system in human terms is easily assumed to be a group of individuals. The analogue for an agent in that system is easily assumed to be an individual human. The analogue for self-organisation is then individuals organising themselves in a group, or, more likely, a team. The analogue of the complex adaptive system programmer is easily taken as the manager. Through this route, people immediately think that complexity theory applied to organisations implies the manager standing outside the complex system; altering the conditions so that the dynamics of the edge of chaos is obtained; setting the rules to secure the desired attractor; and then leaving the members of a team to organise themselves. These prescriptions are no different from those of strategic choice or the learning organisation. They are simply presented in a new vocabulary.

What happens, however, if one looks for analogues from the perspective of relationship psychology? The analogue for the digital code in a simulation is the symbols people use to communicate with each other. Since the agents of a complex adaptive system simulation are nothing other than arrangements of digital code, it seems reasonable to say that the analogue in the case of humans is arrangements of symbols, that is themes, stories and propositions. In other words, the analogue of agents is the themes organising conversation, communication and power relations. What is organising itself, therefore, is not individuals but the pattern of their relationships in communicational and power terms in the public vocal arena and, at the same time, in the silent, private arena that is mind. The analogue of a complex adaptive system in human terms is then the processes of communicating in power relations.

The next chapter will explore this analogy more fully.

## 14.5    SUMMARY

The mind, that private conversation a body has with itself, is made possible by social relationships. The mind and the social are two facets of the same phenomenon. One cannot exist without the other. Mind is conversational in nature. It continuously arises between bodies while being experienced in an individual body. The silent, private world of mind is, however, essentially social in nature, the symbols having been taken into this private sphere through actual experience of social relationships in conversation.

Mind, as a mental process, always arises between people but, at the same time, is always experienced in an individual body. Mind is thus paradoxical in that it is at the same time between individuals but experienced in their individual bodies. Mind is also paradoxical in another sense: it is formed by the social/the group at the same time as it is forming the social/the group.

The mind does not process symbols to produce representations of a pre-given reality and nor does the ordinary everyday conversation that gives rise to mind. Gestures people make to each other, the vocal ones of language as well as the cues of body movements, are symbols and in that sense they represent something other than themselves. However, they are not symbols or representations in the cognitivist sense of an accurate picture of an already existing reality that is stored as a template, map or program. Rather the symbols of language and body cues are gestures, that is a phase in an act that points to the later unfolding of that act, in effect warning and signalling to another how the act will unfold. Such symbols convey meaning to both the presenter and the recipient of the symbol and in doing so call forth responses that are the meaning of the gesture. Symbols of this kind, gestures and responses that together create meaning, do not have to be stored anywhere for the meaning is in the act. Nor is there any 'thing' that needs to be shared in order for people to have common beliefs and undertake joint action. This is because there is no 'thing' to share. All there is are continuously emerging patterns of social relationship emerging in conversation that is being taken into the private sphere of conversation called mind. It seems unlikely that any two individuals will 'take in' to their private spheres of conversation exactly the same themes. Even if they did the capacity for fantasy would soon lead to variety. This does not cause a difficulty for joint action because joint action does not mean that all do exactly the same thing – it means that all more or less fit in with each other. The way they do this is the continual negotiation of ordinary everyday conversation.

The important point about this silent conversation is that it is reflexive. The maker of the gesture is turning its meaning back on him- or herself. The inner conversation is frequently even more reflexive than this when it becomes an inner conversation about how the maker of the gesture takes the perspective of others to talk about him- or herself. This is self-consciousness. To understand what a phenomenon is it is also necessary to understand what it is not. An understanding of what consciousness means requires an understanding of how the unconscious arises. This chapter has presented arguments suggesting that the very structure of language, the categorising processes and the very logics of thought render some matters unconscious in order to render others conscious. What is unconscious is thus first and foremost a social phenomenon arising in language. The social unconscious is also the process of concealing the power relations that language reflects and creates as well as the ideology it emergently produces to make those power differentials feel natural and unquestionable. The replication of these social relationships as silent conversation absorbs the social unconscious into the individual unconscious, where it is open to even further elaboration and variety through the process of fantasising.

## FURTHER READING

Useful further reading is provided by Burkitt (1991), Bell & Gardiner (1998), Dalal (1998), Shotter (1993), Steier (1991), Stolorow, Atwood & Brandschaft (1994) and Turner (1994).

## REFERENCES

Atwood, G. E. & Stolorow, R. (1984), *Structures of Subjectivity: Explorations in Psychoanalytic Psychology*, Hillsdale, NJ: Analytic Press.

Bell, M. M. & Gardiner, M. (Eds.) (1998), *Bhaktin and the Human Sciences*, Thousand Oaks, CA: Sage.

Bhaktin, M. M. (1986), *Speech Genres and other late Essays*, Austin, TX: University of Texas Press.

Burkitt, I. (1991), *Social Selves: Theories of the Social Formation of Personality*, London: Sage.

Dalal, F. (1998), *Taking the Group Seriously: Towards a post-Foulkesian Group Analytic Theory*, London: Jessica Kingsley.

Elias, N. (1978), *What is Sociology?*, London: Hutchinson.

Elias, N. (1989), *The Symbol Theory*, London: Sage.

Elias, N. & Scotson, J. (1994), *The Established and the Outsiders*, London: Sage.

Foulkes, S. H. (1948), *Introduction to Group Analytic Psychotherapy*, London: William Heinemann Medical Books.

Gergen, K. J. (1982), *Toward Transformation in Social Knowledge*, New York: Springer.

Gergen, K. J. (1985), The social constructionist movement in modern psychology, *American Psychologist*, vol. 40, pp. 266–75.

Gergen, K. J. (1991), *The Saturated Self: Dilemmas of Identity in Contemporary Life*, New York: Basic Books.

Griffin, J. D. (1998), *Dealing with the paradox of culture in management theory*, Unpublished thesis, University of Hertfordshire.

Harre, R. (1983), *Personal Being: A Theory of Individual Psychology*, Oxford: Basil Blackwell.

Harre, R. (1986), An outline of the social constructionist viewpoint, in Harre, R. (Ed.) (1986), *The Social Construction of Emotions*, Oxford: Basil Blackwell.

Matte-Blanco, I. (1975), *The Unconscious as Infinite Sets: An Essay in Bi-Logic*, London: Duckworth.

Matte-Blanco, I. (1988), *Thinking, Feeling and Being*, London: Routledge.

Maturana, H. R. & Varela, F. J. (1992), *The Tree of Knowledge: The Biological Roots of Human Understanding*, Boston and London: Shambala.

Mead, G. H. (1934), *Mind, Self, & Society: From the Standpoint of a Social Behaviourist*, Chicago: Chicago University Press.

Shotter, J. (1993), *Conversational Realities: Constructing Life through Language*, Thousand Oaks, CA: Sage.

Shotter, J. & Billig, M. (1998), A Bhaktinian psychology: from out of the heads of individuals and into the dialogues between them, in Bell, M. M. & Gardiner, M. (Eds.) (1998), *Bhaktin and the Human Sciences*, Thousand Oaks, CA: Sage.

Steier, F. (1991), *Research and Reflexivity*, Thousand Oaks, CA: Sage.

Stern, D. N. (1985), *The Interpersonal World of the Infant*, New York: Basic Books.

Stern, D. N. (1995), *The Motherhood Constellation: A Unified View of Parent-Infant Psychotherapy*, New York: Basic Books.

Stolorow, R., Atwood, G. & Brandschaft, B. (1994), *The Intersubjective Perspective*, Northvale, NJ: Jason Aaronson.

Turner, S. (1994), *The Social Theory of Practices*, Cambridge: Polity Press.

# 15 Complexity

## Self-organising experience

## 15.1 INTRODUCTION

Chapter 14 outlined the basis of a relationship psychology. The basic proposition of this theory of human knowing and acting is that people relate to each other in the medium of symbols. These symbols are gestures that call forth responses, which are themselves symbols that call forth further responses in a conversation of gestures. Mind and group are one. I argued that these symbols are the human analogue of the digital symbols, or code, that are the medium of computer simulations of complex adaptive systems.

The simulations reveal a number of possibilities. First, random collections of interacting digital symbols can self-organise into orderly patterns. Second, interaction between a number of homogeneous digital symbol patterns (e.g., boids) can produce particular emergent collective patterns, or attractors (e.g., flocking). These attractors are patterns of interaction so that interaction is producing emergent patterns in itself, through self-organisation. Third, interaction between a number of heterogeneous digital symbol patterns can produce novel emergent patterns of interaction. In other words, new attractors can emerge and they are simultaneously new patterns of collective interaction and rearrangements of the individual symbol patterns. Interaction is producing new patterns in itself, through self-organisation. In the last chapter, I suggested that there is a human analogue for this process of digital symbols organising patterns in themselves. The analogue is to be found in another fundamental notion in relationship psychology. This is the proposition that human experience is organised by themes, stories and conversations. This chapter will explore what is meant by this proposition.

## 15.2 THE ORGANISATION OF EXPERIENCE

It might be useful to start the exploration of how human experience is organised right at the beginning.

## Symbols

*Stern (1985, 1995)* has drawn together a body of experimental evidence to offer an explanation of how an infant's self emerges in the mutual relationships between the infant and his or her family members. As soon as an infant is born, the conversation of gestures begins. Parents hold the infant. They make sounds and they look at the infant. These gestures evoke responses from the child who cries, stops crying, makes noises and returns the parental gaze. In this manner infant and parents, as well as other people, communicate with the infant who communicates with them in ever more elaborate ways. This communication is the infant's experience just as it is the experience of those relating to the infant.

It is important to note how these are bodily experiences, or feeling states. Feeling states can be thought of as rhythms in the body (*Damasio, 1994*): rhythms of breathing, heart beating, digestion, brain functioning, and so on. There is never a time when a living body is without feeling states. Furthermore, as bodies interact with each other, the feeling state of one body affects those of other bodies. One might say that bodies resonate with each other. For example, a crying infant immediately evokes feeling states in the bodies of caregivers. The same thing happens, of course, between adult bodies. Emotions are heightened feeling states of a specific kind, such as anger or pleasure. At the start of life, then, communication is in the medium of gestures and responses take the form of looking, vocalising, listening, touching and smelling, all expressive of feeling states in bodies. These gestures and their evoked responses are symbols that constitute the meaning of interactions. A cry when responded to with food that brings satisfaction means hunger. I will call symbols of this kind protosymbols; that is, the first, original or elementary symbols.

Stern presents a picture of an infant in a family whose members are continuously responding to each other. He suggests that each member relates to other members in accordance with principles that organise their experience of being with each other. He calls these organising principles schemas-of-being-with. Stern uses the cognitivist language of schemas and suggests that they are representations of relational experiences. I think it is important to avoid using this cognitivist language in a psychology of relationship. It is possible to do so by interpreting what Stern is saying using the terminology of intersubjectivity theorists (*Stolorow, Atwood & Brandschaft, 1994*). They talk about principles that organise the experience of a person interacting with another.

Stern's schemas-of-being-with then become principles that organise the interactive experience of being-with a particular person in a specific, repetitive way. For example, an infant would repeatedly experience being hungry and waiting to be fed. As the infant's experience of relating to others continues, that infant develops more and more organising principles and some of them become tied together by a common theme or feature. For example, they may cluster around the themes of feeding, playing or separation. Another possibility is that they become organised around particular emotions, for example being-sad-with or happy-with. Alternatively, they may be organised around particular people.

### Qualities of relational experience

The important point to notice is this: Stern is suggesting that, in the infant's experience of relating to others, themes emerge around the *qualities* of that relational experience. These are reinforced by repeated experience and become expectations and so come to structure the infant's responses to the gestures of others. In other words, themes of being-with others that have emerged in a particular history of relating to others then organise the subsequent experience of relating. These themes are the infant's emerging self, always arising in relationship while being experienced in the infant's body. Themes that organise the experience-of-being-with trigger others, which trigger yet others. At some point, particularly when the infant begins to talk, its gestures come to call forth the same response in itself as in the others to whom they are directed. At that point one might say that the infant is conscious and the symbols being used are what Mead called *significant symbols*. However, the child does not abandon the use of protosymbols and use significant symbols instead. Both are present together. In fact it is not possible to communicate in significant symbols alone because it is a body that is communicating and bodies always have feelings. Communication has moved from the medium of protosymbols alone to an inseparable intertwined medium of protosymbols and significant symbols.

Later as the child develops and comes to take the attitude of others towards itself, one may say that it is self-conscious. *Meares (1992)* has related the fullest sense of a self to that point, around 4 years old, when a child discovers that he or she can have a secret. In other words, the child comes to know that he or she has thoughts that others do not know about until he or she discloses them. The development of mind, consciousness and self in Stern's studies is quite consistent with Mead's theorising.

From this perspective, then, self is a process of 'internalising' social relations into patterns of interacting themes, rather than some mental apparatus, such as a mental model. It is not only infants and their caregivers that interact in the manner I have just described. This is how people relate to each other throughout their lives.

It is important to notice the difference between interactive themes that organise experience, on the one hand, and the notion of mental models (see Chapter 9), on the other. The former arises in relationship *between* people, while the latter are located *in* individuals. In the former, self and mind are not located in a person; rather, they both continuously arise out of the relationship between them. Mind/self and relationship are forming and being formed by each other at the same time (*Griffin, 1998*). I think that this is a radical perspective because the individual is no longer prior to the group, nor is the individual primary. From the perspective I am proposing the individual and group continuously and simultaneously co-create each other. Furthermore, the notion of human experience being organised by interactive themes captures more of the rich texture of human relationship, I think, than the idea of individual mental models consisting of simple or even complicated rules.

Stern's descriptions show how organising themes evolve in the interactive experience of the infant being with the mother, the father and other family members, and their being with him or her. His descriptions demonstrate how an infant self emerges in this evolution. The mother's experience is also organised by themes-of-being-with, for example her infant, mother, husband, herself. These interact with her infant's themes that organise the experience-of-being-with her. The personality emerges from the continuous interaction between all of these themes. Furthermore, mind, self, personality are not formed in this way and then fixed for life. They continuously evolve throughout life, always arising in the relationships with others. As the pattern of relationship changes so the selves, the minds and the personalities change too. At the same time minds, selves and personalities exhibit long-term stability. Here the notions of mind and self are paradoxical, displaying the interwoven stability and instability that is typical of complex systems of all kinds.

As I have already mentioned, it is not only Stern who talks about themes organising experience. Those writing from an intersubjective psychoanalytic perspective adopt a similar formulation. *Stolorow, Atwood & Brandschaft (1994)* talk about recurring patterns of interaction that result in the establishment of invariant principles that unconsciously organise an infant's subsequent experiences. They see these principles as the process of personality development and this process as continuous throughout life. The organising principles provide distinctive configurations of self and other that shape and organise a person's subjective world. They think of these configurations as systems of ordering or organising principles, through which a person's experiences assume their characteristic forms and meanings.

### A social constructionist perspective

Some social constructionists take a similar view in some respects. For example, *Shotter (1993)* talks about experience being organised in what he calls the rhetorical-responsive conversations of ordinary, everyday life. What he means by this is that people continually account for themselves to each other. They continually respond to what others are doing and try to persuade others to take the position they want. This conversational activity organises experience. Shotter explores how groups of people come to a more articulate grasp of their practices from within their ongoing conduct of them. *Shotter & Katz (1997)* talk about a relational–responsive form of understanding between people in their ordinary everyday conversation. In their ordinary forms of language they:

deconstruct the routine links and relations between things once constructed and then taken for granted. In this way, new possibilities are revealed. People do this in the directive use of words: by saying 'Look at that', 'Look at this', people can lead others and themselves to notice important features of their circumstances. In ordinary conversation, people arrest or interrupt each other in order to deconstruct and destabilise so that they can make new distinctions and so create new knowledge. They also use analogies, metaphors, and other ways of making comparisons to develop new ways of talking. It is in talk like this that people are moved. (*Shotter & Katz, 1997*)

This is a very important point: new knowledge can emerge in ordinary, everyday talk.

The point I am making is that throughout life people's experience is organised by interactive conversational themes in the medium of protosymbols and significant symbols. These themes endlessly trigger other themes that trigger yet others in turn. Later in this chapter, I will return to how these themes take a narrative form, but here I want to refer to another form of symbol in which communication takes place.

Returning to the development of a child, the child is taught to read and write at some point and then goes to school. I think that the symbols that constitute reading and writing lead to what I will call *reified symbols*. These are symbols taken to be the reality they point to. People use written symbols to construct models and frameworks of many kinds and the tendency is to equate the model with the reality being modelled. The reified symbol becomes a thing in itself rather than just a means of communication. While protosymbols and significant symbols are arranged into narrative themes, reified symbols are arranged into propositional themes. *Tsoukas*

*(1997)* draws a distinction between propositional and narrative knowledge that is relevant here. Propositions make causal and prescriptive statements about experience, such as if you shout then people will get angry. Since reified symbols are also made by bodies, they too will be interwoven with protosymbols. The point is that experience may be organised by both narrative and propositional themes.

## Themes organising the experience of being together

*Foulkes (1948)*, the founder of group-analytic psychotherapy, used the term 'group matrix' to describe the web of relationships and communication between people in a group. He used the term 'personal matrix' to mean an individual mind. Group and personal matrices can be interpreted in the language of themes organising experience that I have used above (*Stacey, 1999a, 1999b*).

Each member of the group has his or her own personal organising themes that have been taken into the silent conversation, or mind, of that individual. They reflect his or her own personal history of relations with, and between, others. The 'personal matrix', or mind, means the personal themes that organise the private, silent conversation of the individual. As soon as members of a group meet each other, they all actively, albeit largely unconsciously, select and so organise their own subjective experience of being in that place with those people at that time. They do this according to personal organising themes that reflect their own individual histories. However, what those particular themes are at that particular moment will depend just as much on the cues being presented by others as upon the personal history of a particular individual. Each is simultaneously evoking and provoking responses from others so that the particular personal organising themes emerging will depend as much on the others as on the individual concerned. Put like this, it becomes clear that no one individual can be organising his or her experience in isolation because all are simultaneously evoking and provoking responses in each other. Together they immediately constitute intersubjective, recursive processes. These are continuous back-and-forth circular processes and in which themes emerge that organise the experience of being together out of which further themes continuously emerge.

Relationships between people in a group can then be defined as continuously replicating patterns of *intersubjective themes that organise the experience of being together*. These themes emerge, in variant and invariant forms, out of the interaction between group members as they organise that very interaction. I want to stress, however, that I am not suggesting that these themes are disembodied interactions. Although the themes emerge between people, and therefore cannot be located 'inside' any individual, the experience is nevertheless always a bodily experience. I am suggesting, then, that both personal and group themes always arise between people but are always at the same time experienced in individual bodies as changes, marked or subtle, in the feeling tones of those bodies. Consider an example of what I mean.

### An example

During a social meeting between three people, one person, Mary, may complain that the other two are taking no account of how she feels about a troublesome relationship with her boyfriend. Her friend, Helen, may take this as a direct criticism of her and aggressively suggest that there is nothing stopping her from talking about this relationship. Helen's partner, Fred, may support her and complain about Mary always wanting to be the centre of attention. Mary may then slump back into her seat, adopting a silent, sulky pose. She may then announce that their remarks have simply confirmed what she already knew, namely that they do not like her. Therefore, remarks by one person evoke feelings and remarks from another, which in turn trigger other remarks and feelings in others in a self-organising way. The personal and group themes are so intertwined that they cannot be separated. There may be an invariant and, therefore, largely predictable strand in the themes that emerged here. On many occasions before, Mary may have complained to Helen and Fred that people do not take account of her feelings and they may usually have responded angrily. However, on each occasion, the particular form this sequence takes, and when it occurs, may well be very different and so quite unpredictable.

This simple example makes it clear that the interweaving of organising themes of being together does not mean that all share the same theme. Each member is responding differently around a theme that has to do with dissatisfaction with each other, of being liked or not liked. This clarifies why there is no need to postulate the sharing of any kind of mental content. Nothing is being shared as people resonate individually around a common theme to do with being together. They are responding to each other in a meaningful way, not sharing something.

I am suggesting, then, that a large number of themes organise the experience of being together in the group. The entities in this interaction are these themes that organise experience and they are simultaneously arising between people and being experienced in their individual bodies. The entities are not simply individuals. Thus, in the case given above, Helen's feeling that she is being criticised is evoked by Mary's comment. Her remark in turn evokes a reaction from Helen and a statement from Fred, and as he makes his remark, she slumps in her chair. Even where there is no apparent change in posture, I am suggesting that there will always be subtle changes in body rhythms as changes in feeling states accompany the emergent themes organising experience. From the perspective I am suggesting, the themes interact in a self-organising manner so that patterns of relating continuously emerge. These patterns are changes in the themes organising local interaction as group members seek to negotiate with, and respond to, each other in some way. The pattern of organising themes is continually recreating itself in a self-referential, reflexive way as people continuously experience these changes in their bodies.

These themes create power relations. In fact, they are power relations. Remember that power is not simply an individual imposing his or her will on others. Relating is a process of constraining and constraints are power. It is not an individual imposing power but the process of relating that inevitably creates power relations. The pattern of relating is thus also a pattern of power relations. It is another way of describing the same phenomenon.

Another important point to be made here about organising themes is that they arise in a particular place at a particular time. The bodies interacting with each other in a group are located in a wider context of a community and a society that has a history. This means that the group/individual themes are resonating with wider themes that organise the experience of being in a community and a society at a particular point in its history. The themes arising in a particular group, at a particular time, will thus be influenced by the figuration of power relations in the wider grouping. They will also reflect the pattern of control over economic resources and, therefore, the material, technological and physical nature of the place at a particular historical moment. The focus on the importance of a particular group at a particular time can easily lead to neglecting the constraining nature of the social and material and technological world that the group themes are arising in.

So, organising themes are continuously arising in the interaction between people, while simultaneously being experienced in their bodies, located in a particular community, in a particular place, at a particular point in the history of community and group. Note that this is very different to saying that members of a group share the values of the community and the society they are located in. It is saying that at a particular time there will be salient themes organising the experience of being together in a community. They will evoke themes organising the experience of being together in a particular group. The theme evoked in the group might be quite different to the theme in the community. For example, a theme organising the experience of being together in a community might have to do with condemning gypsies. Groups of residents and groups of gypsies in the community will not be sharing a common theme. However, both groups will be responding to the theme in a different way.

## The analogy with complex adaptive systems

I want to return now to how complexity theory might provide an analogue of human behaviour. Computer simulations are the equivalent of laboratory experiments for those studying complex adaptive systems. The simulations are conducted in the medium of digital symbols.

There is one feature of computer simulations for which there is no analogue in human interaction. The computer simulations are to some limited extent designed by programmers and those programmers take the position of objective observer, drawing insight from running the program. In human interaction, there is no objective observer who prepares a minimal design and then watches the program running. Even the most powerful human is a participant in human interaction.

The first analogue has to do with the digital code. In human terms, the analogue of digital symbols is the protosymbols, significant and reified symbols that are the medium of human relating. The symbolic medium of human relating and communicating is therefore very much more complicated than the digital symbols of the computer simulations. However, the logic of interaction revealed by the interaction in the medium of digital symbols may nevertheless provide further analogies for human interaction and thus further insight.

Second, the digital symbols in the computer simulations are arranged into patterns taking the form of algorithms, that is if–then calculating procedures. These algorithms, or agents, interact with each other and in the presence of diversity they self-organise to produce emergent changes in themselves. Overall, patterns of interaction and the individual symbol patterns evolve simultaneously in the absence of an overall blueprint. The analogue in human terms could be described in the following way. Protosymbols interwoven with significant symbols are arranged primarily in the form of narrative themes that organise people's experience of being together with others and with themselves. Protosymbols interwoven with reified symbols are arranged into propositional themes that organise people's experience of being with others and with themselves. These themes interact with each other in the presence of diversity in a self-organising way to produce emergent changes in themselves. Themes organising the experience of being together in a group and themes organising the silent conversation of mind evolve simultaneously in the absence of an overall blueprint. In other words, public, vocalised conversations between people and the private, silent conversations of mind evolve simultaneously. The analogue of agents in human interaction is themes that organise experience.

Note again how very much more complicated it all is in the case of humans. Some of the themes organising human experience may take an algorithmic form, namely, what I have called propositional themes. However, human experience is mainly organised by narrative themes in conversation and this is not algorithmic at all. Nevertheless, insights drawn from the logic of interaction between algorithms may illuminate interaction between narrative themes.

Third, the computer simulations reveal patterns of interaction that are called attractors. The analogue of an attractor in human interaction would be a recognisable pattern in sequences of organising themes triggering organising themes. So, in the example given above, the attractor would be Mary complaining that people do not take account of her feelings, triggering an angry response from those she is complaining to, triggering in turn further complaints that they do not take account of her feelings.

Fourth, in the computer simulations, diversity and thus the capacity to evolve spontaneously is provided by random mutation and cross-over replication. The analogue in human interaction would be the imperfect communication between people, misunderstanding, and the partial taking into silent conversation by one person of ways of conversing acquired from others in the course of public conversations. I will return to this matter later in this chapter.

The fifth analogue has to do with the notion of a complex adaptive system. What is the analogue of this in human terms? The analogue would be human interaction itself. However, I think it necessary to signal very clearly the difference between a computer simulation and human interaction. Human interaction is certainly complex, but to describe it as adaptive is to miss the full complexity. People do not simply fit in with, or adapt to, each other. Often they negotiate a lack of fit with each other. I suggest then that the key feature of human interaction is that it is responsive, and in this responsiveness it may be adaptive or it may not. I think it is also problematic to put the label 'system' or even 'network' or 'matrix' on human interaction. This is because these words produce an immediate tendency to reify, as if human interaction was a thing. To signal that the notion of a complex adaptive system is a rather crude analogy for human behaviour I will use the term complex responsive processes in relation to human interaction. The analogue of a complex adaptive system in human terms is thus complex responsive processes. I am suggesting that experience, that is communication within any group of people and communication of any one of them with him- or herself, is complex responsive processes, analogous to complex adaptive systems.

Finally, in computer simulations it is the pattern of digital symbols that is organising itself. The analogue of this in the case of human interaction is the manner in which themes organising experience are organising themselves. In fact, human experience is these themes. So to say that the themes organise experience is to say that they organise themselves. The primary medium for this self-organisation is conversation. Conversation organises itself through bodies.

To ground what I am talking about I now recount an experience I shared with two of my colleagues when we were employed to run a workshop at a major company, which I will call Excel. After that, I will return to the important matter of conversation.

### The workshop at Excel

We were working with human resource executives of Excel's European subsidiary and with members of another institution to develop ways of introducing managers to the insights of complexity theory. Through some contact we were unaware of, a senior executive in the management development function at the head office in the United States, Stan, got to hear about this work and asked us to run a workshop there. Initially, the workshop was to consist of a group of line managers. However, when Stan's boss, Steve, heard about this he insisted that novel material of this kind had to be seen first by himself and his colleagues before they risked it with people outside the department. There was some discussion between them and us around this point but we eventually agreed to go ahead on Steve's terms.

We drove from the airport to one of Excel's locations, which consisted of a number of low stone and glass buildings in parkland with a rather severe, grim appearance. We entered the building through two sets of automatic doors and went to a reception desk where a very sharp young woman told us we would have to pay for our stay. We managed to get her to understand that we had come as speakers whose costs were being paid for by Excel. She did not appear very interested in this because the subcontractor who ran the building on behalf of Excel employed her. Then she gave us instructions to the effect that we had to park the car in a particular car park, unpack our luggage and then wait for transport to take us to our rooms. She told us, rather severely, that we were not allowed to drive cars to the building where the rooms were. The three of us felt that we had been treated like children and all of us felt rather depressed.

After unpacking, we met Stan in the room we were to use. It was a long narrow room with a long narrow table of such weight that it could not be moved. One of my colleagues and I felt so depressed by this time that we pleaded jet lag and went to our rooms, leaving our other colleague, by now rather alarmed, to make preparations. Later, the other colleague and I returned and Stan found us a room that we could rearrange and took us out to dinner. Stan seemed rather disconcerted by our room rearrangement.

So, a number of cues were presented to us, in the form of the building itself, the infantilising reception, the rigidity of the room, and the surprise of Stan at our wanting to rearrange it. These cues directly conveyed tones of the themes that organise experience at Excel. Our experience of being together on that evening at those Excel offices was being organised, most importantly, by protosymbolic themes to do with the rhythm of the place and the rhythms, or feeling states, being evoked in us. One might say that, as a group, we were resonating in some way with the experience of the Excel community. We experienced a rather rigid and depressing quality of life there.

On the next day, the morning workshop went quite well. It was interesting how Steve, a striking, powerful-looking man, came in and immediately moved his chair. At first, he looked almost angry and withdrawn but eventually asked quite a number of questions and became very involved with the material. After lunch, we tried to link what we had been talking about in the morning to a particular project we knew about at Excel. We asked the person who was most concerned with this project to talk about it. Steve objected to this, saying it was not how he wanted to spend the afternoon. This silenced the person we had invited to speak.

Steve then aggressively asked us how complexity theory was to be applied. I felt irritable about the way he twisted his chair and body away from the group in a rejecting manner and then made aggressive demands. It may have been this irritation that prompted me to stand up and give a short lecture. Steve and some of the others liked this and it sparked some discussion. The pattern we then fell into, for nearly an hour and a half, was quite striking. The three of us tended to give long speeches, one after the other, with interjections from Steve. We tended to look at him and the others hardly ever said anything. We kept talking about the importance of conversation, but none of us really engaged in one. I noticed what we were doing and formulated it as basic assumption dependency behaviour (see Chapter 10) that we were very much colluding with, but I felt it impossible to say anything like this.

My colleagues later said that they too felt disabled. We do not usually work in this way and we do not usually feel powerless to point to, or stop colluding with, this kind of group dynamic. We were not really relating to each other or using our relationship in our work. We were simply making speeches, one after the other. We were talking about complexity as an intellectual construct and not working at all with the psychological implications and the behaviour in the room.

One might understand this as follows. This session was characterised by a push to use intellect to cover up feelings. We were caught in a power dynamic in which the more powerful have to provide for others who take up a dependent position. There was something disabling about the atmosphere in this company when it came to anything but an intellectual approach. There was something about the relative unimportance of relationships compared with doing a task. These are all recognised aspects of Excel's culture, confirmed for us the next morning by Stan and Steve. Steve arrived for this meeting rather later and we learned that he had been at Excel, noted for its long-serving employees, for only a year. As we talked about these matters, he eventually disclosed how tired and depressed he is at constantly having to justify what his department does. He felt pressed by those above him and unsupported by his staff. He talked about how tiring it all was and how lonely he felt. This felt to us like a real shift. Apparently, he had not spoken like this before.

So, how was it that the three of us came to be so totally sucked into the themes organising this company's experience, to the point where we seemed to have little power to avoid its organising our experience? Culture is often thought to be transmitted by imitation, as something people share. However, our experience on this occasion points to some direct way that one rapidly becomes part of a culture. The whole context of building, room settings, the manner in which one is treated, the ways in which members of the group and their managers respond to us and to each other, are all protosymbolic. They were rhythms that evoked bodily rhythms, feeling states, in us.

In this account, I have been stressing the relevance of protosymbols but of course we engaged in ordinary conversation and in the use of reified symbols organised into theoretical propositions in a lecture. There were a great many narrative themes organising our experience of being together with each other and with the members of Excel. For example, the difficulties Steve was having in adjusting to the culture of Excel.

I return now to the important matter of conversation, which I have suggested is complex responsive processes.

## 15.3    THE ANALYSIS OF CONVERSATION

Ethnomethodologists (*Goffman, 1981; Garfinkel, 1967*) study the finely ordered detail of local action, including an analysis of the detailed flow of ordinary conversation (*Sacks, 1992; Shegloff, 1991; Jefferson, 1978*).

### Self-organising turn taking

Conversation analysts have used recordings of ordinary conversations to build up a picture of how such conversations are structured and how they produce orderly interactions between people. What they point to, as the fundamental organising principle of conversation, is the process of turn taking. Starting with Mead's notion of the conversation of gestures between animals, and between human infants and their caregivers, this principle is everywhere in evidence. Turn taking is at the heart of all social activity in that it establishes a temporal and spatial location for social interaction. From it flows the back-and-forth rhythm of social relationships. Turn taking:

... creates the rhythms of daily life, from the formal, public rituals and ceremonies of ancient religions and national states to the most intimate of human intercourse. (*Boden, 1994, p. 66*)

Sack's research pointed to the way in which turns to speak are valued, distributed across speakers, competed for, abandoned and held onto. Turn taking is, thus, one of the important ways in which power differentials are established and sustained in conversations, very much a reflection of the process Elias points to. The process also has all the hallmarks of self-reference as participants respond to each other in a back-and-forth way. The response of one calls forth a further response from another, in turn calling forth a response from the first. It is also a reflexive process since none of the participants can get outside the conversation, observe it and control it, at least without destroying its very nature as ordinary, everyday conversation. Furthermore, the process is very clearly a self-organising one that produces emergent patterns of meaning for participants. I am suggesting, then, that conversations are complex responsive processes. Speakers take turns that are organised by certain principles that have themselves emerged out of the history of interaction in the community of speakers to which they belong.

The principles I am referring to have to do with: how one person speaks at a time; how it may, or may not, be permissible to interrupt or talk over others; how the number and order of speakers varies; how turn sizes vary; how turn transition is accomplished; what kind of gaps and overlaps occur in turn taking; how the turns themselves are allocated. These organising principles evolve, and so come to differ from one historical period to another and from one locality to another.

Sacks and others have also pointed to the manner in which turns tend to be organised into what they call 'adjacent pairs'. So conversational exchanges may be organised into greeting–greeting, question–answer, invitation–acceptance (rejection), summons–answer, request–response, and so on. Speakers create turns with recipients in mind and listeners are motivated to hear their turn, all in a self-organising manner. Speakers tend to pursue a response until they are acknowledged and those being addressed are under pressure to respond to the meaning. This requirement to respond does not mean that grammatical sentences are always used. In fact, ordinary conversation is characterised by grunts, other noises like 'mm', pauses, and fragments of sentences. The listener is thus creating the meaning by a constructive process of filling in. The result is the highly associative nature of ordinary, everyday conversation.

Boden talks about different kinds of conversation:

From the basic elements of conversational turn taking, what Sacks and his collaborators proposed was that other speech exchange systems such as meetings, classrooms, interviews, debates, and even the most ritual of ceremonies would span a kind of continuum. The central differences between casual, freely occurring conversation and the kinds of exchanges listed depend primarily upon such issues as: allocation and duration of turns, selection and order of potential speakers, and designation and order of topic, as well as a specific method for ensuring that each speaker is heard and that discussion does not break down into mini conversations. In meetings and on conference calls, the structuring methods of turn-taking are indeed modified ... but the core of organizational communication remains this simple, reciprocal and self organizing system. (*Boden, 1994, pp. 72–3*)

The self-organising nature of ordinary, everyday conversation can be very easily seen by asking a group of people to play a word game. One member of the group is asked to start with any word he or she chooses and the others are asked to respond. What always happens is this. One word triggers a response, usually by association, from another person and that response triggers yet another, and so on. Within a very short time, a theme emerges. For example, the theme may have to do with the weather, with body parts, with places, with moods, or whatever. Some people may try to break the associative links and if they succeed another theme begins to emerge. Even when people try very hard not to associate but to keep breaking the links, it turns out to be rather difficult to keep it going. This is exactly what happens in conversation: a theme emerges and the talk swirls around this theme, until some remark triggers the emergence of some other theme.

## Dynamics of conversation: attractors

So far, I have been stressing how complex responsive processes of relating in conversation are self-organising processes analogous to processes in complex adaptive systems. The evolution of complex adaptive systems is usually explained in terms of movement in state space from one attractor to another. State space, as described in Chapter 12, is a kind of landscape of possibilities, sculpted into basins of attraction and peaks of repulsion.

One might think of conversation in a similar way. It moves through state space, where state space is the range of all possible conversational themes. As a particular grouping of people converse together, recurrent themes will inevitably emerge and so begin to sculpt conversational state space into basins of attraction. Particular words around the edges of this basin will immediately trigger repetitions of the conversational themes associated with that basin. As new people join the group, or as the group encounters new experiences together, new basins of attraction will form. In addition, some themes will become repellers for the group, taking the topological form of peaks in state space. Some words will trigger rapid avoidance of a conversational theme because it has become taboo, or is likely to arouse hostile responses, for example. Therefore, attractors in the conversation are patterns of themes that are triggered by certain associations. Again, I feel it necessary to re-emphasise that I am not talking here about a conversational network that is in any way whatsoever disembodied. Conversation is always interwoven with feelings and emotions. The complex responsive processes that I am talking about are conversations embedded in and suffused by the bodily rhythms that accompany it and are an irremovable part of it. Conversations are not possible without bodies and bodies are never without feelings.

## Free-flowing conversation

Consider how the conversational life of a group can be thought about in a dynamic way. As people participate in a conversation, the details of the context of place and time those people are embedded in may change. Others may join in the conversation while some leave it, for example. In terms of the topography of conversational state space, the landscape will be heaving about, changing the breadth and depth of basins of attraction and peaks of repulsion in conversational state space. This is what happens in lively, energising conversation. However, a group of people may get stuck in a particularly deep basin of attraction and find it difficult to get out of it. The result will be repetitive, emotionally dulling exchanges between people. *Foulkes (1948)* made a strong association between this kind of stuckness and mental ill health. He defined health as free-flowing communication through a group or community. He saw mental illness as, at its roots, a disturbance, a blockage, in the free flow of communication and he pointed to how this blockage could become located in one or more of the members of a group or community. This was one of his key concepts, ill health as a blockage in communication that may become located in one or more of the members of a group. This process of location and blockage is clearly self-organising and, I suggest, can be understood as a group's conversation caught in a basin of attraction from which it cannot escape. Such a group is caught in repeating a similar conversation repeatedly.

Now, since the mind is an inner conversation, the internalisation of the experienced social process, then that inner conversation must have the same features of the social interaction discussed in the above paragraphs. I think that my own efforts at introspection, and the reports of others about the results of their introspection, provide ample support for this claim. People often talk about different parts of themselves and they frequently refer to voices in their minds talking to each other. Introspection reveals a stream of thoughts, which as *Elias (1989)* emphasises are exactly the same as conversations, one thought triggering others in a manner that one cannot design or control. There is a kind of turn taking shown by the great difficulty, at least for me, of sustaining a consistent train of thought. In fact, the distinction rapidly blurs between the vocal conversation of each person engaged in an interaction and their silent conversations that are going on at the same time. What I am talking about is the same phenomena, viewed from different vantage points. If one takes the viewpoint of the individual one identifies an inner, silent conversation and if one takes the group viewpoint one identifies an external, vocalised conversation. However, they are so intimately interlinked with each other that they cannot be separated.

The point about mental disturbance can be seen from the group point of view, as was done above. Alternatively, one can view it from the point of view of the individual. Not surprisingly, there is no real difference because the phenomenon is the same. It is only the perspective that is different. So, mental disturbance displays itself in an individual as a blockage in the free flow of inner conversation; that is, as a repetitive attractor. The topology of the state space of inner conversation is such that this conversation is stuck in a deep basin of attraction from which there is no escape. This is an extremely distressing and painful state to be in. It is a state of a silent conversation that has lost its free-flowing nature and come to alternate repetitively between a few positions. The number of inner voices has been severely curtailed. So, for example, one obsessively ruminates about some slight or even about some deep hurt. Peace and happiness are states of fluid free-floating silent conversation. The link with the social is ever present because the silent conversation resonates with vocalised conversations throughout life. Note the analogy here between the dynamics of stability in complex adaptive systems and the repetitive attractor or blockage in conversation. Note also the analogy between the dynamics at the edge of chaos for a complex adaptive system and the dynamics of free-flowing conversation amongst people.

### Conversation and power

I have been arguing then that conversations are complex responsive processes of themes triggering themes through self-organising association and turn taking that both reflect and create power differentials in relationships. These conversational processes are organising the experience of the group of people conversing and from them, there is continually emerging the very minds of the individual participants at the same time as group phenomena of culture and ideology are emerging. Individual and group phenomena emerge together in the same process, co-creating each other. In fact, one can say that they are the same phenomena simply looked at from different standpoints. This is a very radical view of the nature of the relationship between the individual and the group. It is saying that change in the behaviour of a group and change in the behaviour of individual members is exactly the same phenomenon. Furthermore, it is saying that change can only occur when the pattern of conversation changes. Individual behaviour can only change when individuals' silent conversation changes because it is this that organises their experience. However, that silent conversation can only change through a process of internalising conversational change in a group. It is only as individuals experience change in social relationships that they can change psychologically and, of course, their relating to others can only change as they change psychologically. It is in this sense that change in groups and in individual is the same thing. They can only occur together since both are forming and being formed by each other at the same time. This view of culture change or change management has far reaching implications that will be explored in a later chapter. Briefly, it means that it is only when people in an organisation talk differently to each other that their organisation will change. Facilitation of change is facilitation of different forms of conversation.

I want to return now to the notion of conversation as a self-organising process from which themes emerge. Ordinary, everyday conversation is themes organising themes into stories and narratives.

## Stories and narratives

A story is an account of a sequence of specific actions, feeling states and events, while a narrative is a story line linked by reflections, comments upon, and categorisations of, elements of the story line. So, a narrative contains within it a story but it is a more complex form of communication than a story because it involves some kind of evaluation. It seems to me that the associative, turn-taking processes of ordinary, everyday conversation produce emergent, co-created narrative. One person tells an anecdote that evokes some evaluative comment from another and an associated anecdote from a third as together they spin narrative themes. These narrative themes structure their historic experience and their current experience of being together, so creating personal and group realities (*Gergen, 1982; Shotter, 1993*).

Bruner has identified some of the key features of narrative processes of constructing experience. Narratives create a sense of temporality in experience, linking present experience to past ones and pointing towards the future evolution of the experience. They focus upon departures from what is expected, from what is taken for granted as ordinary and acceptable, and thereby they reinforce cultural norms. Stories that simply recount expected routines are not all that interesting, but those that describe the unexpected are, and such stories usually have a 'moral' that reinforces the culture or ideology of the group. Stories also impart something about the subjectivity of the narrator or about the subjectivity of the characters in the story. In other words they disclose some aspects of individuals' silent conversations and provide the means for people to experience each other's subjectivity.

People also use stories to describe and deal with ambiguity. *Bruner (1990)* points to the essential ambiguity of stories themselves in that it is quite difficult to tell just what is fact and what is fiction in a story, thereby opening up the possibility of the fantasy potential that Elias attached so much importance to. An essential aspect of narrative, therefore, is the scope it offers for the exercise of imagination and the spinning of fantasy. Bruner also emphasises the constructive role of the listener in story-telling, because people do not just listen to stories. They select and fill in meanings and indeed story telling techniques employ devices to encourage this active participation in the co-construction of meaning in narratives. Bruner talks about stories as 'trafficking in human possibilities rather than settled certainties' (*1986, p. 28*).

*Sarbin (1986)* points out the link between narrative and feelings – emotional states are located in narratives and passions are 'storied'. *McCleod (1996)* emphasises the problem-solving function of stories in that they are used to put chaotic experiences into causal sequences, explain dilemmas and deviations:

In co-constructed narratives, the listener or audience may feed their own alternative accounts into the story that emerges, or may seek clarification by asking questions. So, the act of telling a story makes available a communication structure that not only conveys a sense of a world of uncertainty and ambiguity, but also provides a means of reducing dissonance and re-establishing a sense of control and order, by assembling an account that becomes more complete or ordered through the process of being told. (*p. 37*)

I wish to emphasise the self-organising character of narratives and the emergence of meaningful themes in their telling. Conversations, stories and narratives are complex responsive processes of symbols interacting with each other to produce emergent themes of meaning that organise the experience of those engaged in the conversational activity.

Furthermore, if mental phenomena are simply social processes taken into the silent conversations of individuals then mind can also be usefully thought of as having the same characteristics as social interaction. In other words, an individual's mind can be thought of as complex responsive processes of symbols, that is language and feelings, self-organising into narrative themes that organise the experience of the individual concerned. This is a web of social experience taken into a silent conversation. The psychoanalyst *Schafer (1992)* points to how people construct story lines to account for important events in their lives and how one of the most important of these story lines is the self-narrative. As with social constructionists, he sees the self as an autobiographical story a person tells about him or herself, a story that is endlessly retold and can change in the retelling.

## Intention

One response to the theory I have outlined in the previous chapter, and in this one, is that it leaves no room for intention, choice and free will. This, however, is not so.

Intention is a communication between people, and like any other communication it is expressed in the medium of symbols. It is a particular kind of theme and it organises experience just as any other theme does. An intention may be expressed explicitly or implicitly in a propositional theme. For example, if you do this for me, then I will do that for you; or we are going to buy a car. When managers communicate statements about strategic direction, mission, vision and values, they articulate propositional themes. An intention may also be expressed explicitly or implicitly in a narrative theme. All of these intentional themes are gestures that provoke or evoke responses in others. Those articulating the intention then find that these responses, in turn, evoke or provoke responses from them and they will not be able to know in advance just how these responses, and response to responses, will unfold.

The question arises as to where intention comes from. The theories of strategic choice, the learning organisation and psychoanalytic perspectives on organisations take intention for granted. They assume that the formation of an intention is not problematic. People simply decide. However, when one comes to regard intention as a theme that organises the experience of being together it becomes clear that intentions emerge in relationship just as any other organising theme does. Intention, then, emerges in the conversational life of a group of people. A single individual does not simply 'have' an intention. Rather the intention an individual expresses has emerged in the conversational interaction with others. Intention and choice are not lonely acts but themes organised by and organising relationships at the same time.

Where does this leave human free will? The response that any individual can make to a gesture is both enabled and constrained by the history of that person's relationships with others, as reflected in his or her current silent conversations with him- or herself. I am not free to choose to do what I am not able to do. However, I am free to respond to a gesture in a number of different ways that do fall within the repertoire available to me. Thinking about human relationships as self-organising complex responsive processes does not therefore mean that individuals have no free will. It simply means that people have the freedom to respond within the constraints of who they are and the relationships they are in.

## The dynamics of complex responsive processes

This section explores the insights that complexity theory brings to human relationships. Complexity theory demonstrates that the dynamics of a complex network of interacting agents is determined by the nature of the relationships across the network. In general, as information/energy flows increase, as connectivity between agents and diversity in the nature of agents increases, the dynamics of the network shifts from repetitive, predictable stability towards the dynamics of randomness and disintegration. At some critical range in information/energy flow, connectivity and diversity, the dynamics of bounded instability appears, that is the simultaneous presence of stability and instability, order and disorder. It is in this dynamic, at the edge of disintegration, that novel forms of relationship may emerge. I think that these factors have immediate and quite obvious relevance to groups of people. It is widely known that groups of people fall into repetitive patterns of behaviour when they have little access to information or to the stimulation of high enough interaction with others who are sufficiently different to be stimulating. In other words, the themes organising experience are impoverished through too little content, connection and diversity. It is also well known that people can be incapacitated by information overload and by too many contacts with people who are too different from each other to form any kind of agreement. In these conditions human relating disintegrates. In other words, themes organising experience are so diverse, interconnected and full of content that communication is random. It is in the dynamic in between that free-flowing conversation arises.

In human terms of course, other factors affect the dynamics. There are two such factors which seem to me to be of particular importance (*Stacey, 1996*). The first of these is power difference. Those who exaggerate power difference by behaving in an autocratic manner, or even in too directing a way, are likely to evoke either compliance in group members, the dynamics of stability, or rebellion, the dynamics of instability and disintegration. On the other hand, ignoring or abdicating from the position of power altogether is likely to provoke the dynamics of 'sibling' rivalry as members seek to fill the power vacuum. Part of the skill of managers and leaders, therefore, lies in exercising power difference in a manner that steers between directing and abdicating. There will also be power differences between people because some are more persuasive, more frightening, more dominant than others and the manner in which these differences are exercised could have similar effects to those outlined above.

The second major factor influencing the dynamics of the human system has to do with the holding of anxiety. Where anxiety is avoided, the group dynamic is one of stability and regularity. This is evident when a group moves into a conversational mode similar to that of a dinner party – here there can be no change or evolution in the pattern of themes organising the experience of being together. On the other hand a group can become so suffused by anxiety that it defends against by engaging in basic assumption behaviour of dependency, fight–flight or pairing (*Bion, 1961*). This produces an unstable dynamic disintegrative of work as the group shifts in a volatile manner between the different basic assumption behaviours, operating almost entirely on the basis of fantasy. The patterning of themes of being together fluctuates in a virtually meaningless way. However, when the pattern of relationships can contain the anxiety in a 'good enough manner' then there is the possibility of change. What changes then is the pattern of themes that organise the experience of being together and by being taken into the inner conversation of the individuals involved, this changes them too.

## 15.4 SUMMARY

This chapter explored how complexity theory might provide a framework for thinking about the process of mind and self-formation. A complex adaptive system consists of a great many agents interacting with each other according to their own local rules and in doing so they are adapting to each other. When this is interpreted in a human context it is easy to postulate a human system in which the agents are individual people adapting to each other according to their own mental models. I suggested another interpretation. First, humans are not simply adapting to each other according to given mental models. I find it more useful to think of humans as continuously responding to each other. Humans continuously make gestures that evoke and provoke responses from each other. The word responsive, therefore, seems more apt than the word 'adaptive' when it comes to humans. I also want to move away from the notion of human interaction constituting a 'system' because of the mechanistic connotation this word has. I therefore proposed using the concept of process instead. Human relating is complex responsive processes.

Complex responsive processes are interacting themes that organise human experience and they largely take a narrative form. Each individual mind is many narrative themes that are interacting with each other and with those of other people to produce emergent patterns of family, and any other group, relationships that constitute the further evolution of their narrative themes. These relational, responsive narrative themes are continuously replicated, or recreated, and as this happens there is the possibility of novel emergent relational patterns. In other words, as people relate to each other, the complex responsive network of relational themes evolves. Those networks consist of protosymbols, significant symbols and reified symbols. These symbols are all intricately interwoven with, and endlessly triggering, each other to form narrative themes, and also propositional rules, that organise the experience of being together in a particular place at a particular time. Distinguishing between these categories of symbols in this way is important, I think, in emphasising the way in which themes, both personal and group, organise experience. The conversational experience is not organised in language or significant symbols, alone. It is also organised through the medium of body, that is protosymbols, and in the context of a material, technological world expressed in reified symbols.

These complex responsive processes take the form of coherent thought and communication. By demonstrating the possibility of self-organising processes and the emergent coherence they produce, complexity theory offers a way out of having to postulate some designer, program, or group mind to explain how the coherence comes about.

What I am suggesting here is a very different interpretation of complexity theory in relation to humans to those reviewed in Chapter 13. I described there how there seems to be a general tendency to interpret human affairs from a complexity perspective in the following way. It is unquestioningly postulated that the agents in a human complex adaptive system are the individual members of a group or organisation. Each of the individual agents then possesses a mental model according to which they adaptively interact with others. I think that this general tendency is based on the unquestioned assumption of the autonomous individual, prior and primary to the group. I suggested that this leads to the incorporation of complexity theory into orthodox management and organisational theory. When one moves to the relational view I have been describing it become impossible to equate agency with individuals. Instead, agency lies simultaneously with individuals and the group since they form and are formed by each other. It is because I want to signal this shift that I want to use the term complex responsive processes. The term 'complex adaptive system' has now come to mean one in which individuals are the agents. I am proposing that in complex responsive processes, the entities are themes that organise experiences of relating. The individual person and the group are simply different aspects of the one phenomenon, namely relating.

## FURTHER READING

The book by Boden (1994) is highly recommended.

## REFERENCES

Bion, W. (1961), *Experiences in Groups and Other Papers*, London: Tavistock.
Boden, D. (1994), *The Business of Talk: Organizations in Action*, Cambridge: Polity Press.
Bruner, J. S. (1986), *Actual Minds, Possible Worlds*, Cambridge, MA: Harvard University Press.
Bruner, J. S. (1990), *Acts of Meaning*, Cambridge, MA: Harvard University Press.
Damasio, A. R. (1994), *Descartes' Error: Emotion, Reason and the Human Brain*, London: Picador.
Elias, N. (1989), *The Symbol Theory*, London: Sage.

Foulkes, S. H. (1948), *Introduction to Group Analytic Psychotherapy*, London: William Heinemann Medical Books.

Garfinkel, H. (1967), *Studies in Ethnomethodology*, Englewood Cliffs, NJ: Prentice Hall.

Gergen, K. J. (1982), *Toward Transformation in Social Knowledge*, New York: Springer.

Goffman, E. (1981), *Forms of Talk*, Philadelphia: University of Pennsylvania Press.

Griffin, J. D. (1998), Dealing with the paradox of culture in management theory, Unpublished thesis, University of Hertfordshire.

Jefferson, G. (1978), Sequential aspects of storytelling in conversation, in Shenkein, J. (Ed.) (1978), *Studies in the Organization of Conversational Interaction*, New York: Academic Press.

McCleod, J. (1996), Qualitative research methods in counselling psychology, in Woolfe, R. & Dyden, W. (Eds.) (1996), *Handbook of Counselling Psychology*, London: Sage.

Meares, R. (1992), *The Metaphor of Play: On Self, the Secret and the Borderline Experience*, Melbourne: Hill of Content Publishing Co.

Sacks, H. (1992), *Lectures on Conversation*, Ed. Jefferson, G., Oxford: Blackwell.

Sarbin, T. R. (1986), The narrative as a root metaphor for psychology, in Sarbin, T. R. (Ed.) (1986), *Narrative Psychology: The Storied nature of Human Conduct*, New York: Praeger.

Schafer, R. (1992), *Retelling a Life: Narration and Dialogue in Psychoanalysis*, New York: Basic Books.

Shegloff, E. A. (1991), *Reflections on Talk and Social Structure*, in Boden, D. & Zimmerman, D. H. (Eds.) (1991), *Talk and Social Structure*, Cambridge: Polity Press.

Shotter, J. (1993), *Conversational Realities: Constructing Life through Language*, Thousand Oaks, CA: Sage.

Shotter, J. and Katz, A. M. (1997), Articulating a practice from within the practice itself: establishing formative dialogues to the use of a 'social poetics', *Concepts and Transformations*, vol. 2, pp. 71–95.

Stacey, R. D. (1996), *Complexity and Creativity in Organizations*, San Francisco, Berrett-Koehler.

Stacey, R. D. (1999a), Complexity and the group matrix, Group Analysis.

Stacey, R. D. (199b), Reflexivity and the group matrix, Group Analysis.

Stern, D. N. (1985), *The Interpersonal World of the Infant*, New York: Basic Books.

Stern, D. N. (1995), *The Motherhood Constellation: A Unified View of Parent-Infant Psychotherapy*, New York: Basic Books.

Stolorow, R., Atwood, G. & Brandschaft, B. (1994), *The Intersubjective Perspective*, Northvale, NJ: Jason Aaronson.

Tsoukas, H. (1997), The firm as a distributed knowledge system: a constructionist approach, *Complexity and Management Papers*, no. 10, Complexity and Management Centre, University of Hertfordshire Business School.

# Chapter

# 16 Understanding organisations as complex responsive processes

## 16.1 INTRODUCTION

In the last chapter, I suggested that the human analogue for a complex adaptive system is complex responsive processes. The theory of interaction I propose as the foundation of a radical approach to theorising about organisations is that of complex responsive processes. I also pointed to what relationship psychology takes as fundamental to human nature, namely the complex responsive processes through which people relate to each other. While the other theories reviewed in this book combine a theory of interaction with a theory of human psychology, what I am proposing, therefore, is a theory of human psychology that is also a theory of interaction. There is no need to combine anything. Interaction and human nature are the same phenomenon. While the other theories distinguish between individual and group as different levels of analysis, relationship psychology proposes that the individual is the singular of relating while the group is the plural of relating. This perspective can be expressed in the following propositions:

1 Humans relate to each other in the medium of symbols, which are always gestures and responses interwoven with feeling states or emotions.

2 These symbols form themes that organise people's experience of being together and being alone. The themes interact with each other in a self-organising way. Themes trigger themes that trigger themes so that they are continuously reproduced and transformed in relationships through conversations between people.

3 An individual mind is a silent, private conversation resonating with vocal, public conversations. Mind and group/society are the same phenomenon. They form and are formed by each other, at the same time, in an essentially self-referential process. That process is also reflexive in that people evoke, provoke and resonate with each other in ways that are both enabled and constrained by their own histories of relating.

4  The organising themes are dynamical. They may display stable attractors in which the same themes are continually reproduced in a stable way. They may also display the analogue of attractors at the edge of chaos in which there is both stability and change in their reproduction so that there is the potential for some kind of transformation. Conversation then takes a spontaneous free-flowing form.

5  The organising themes of one moment emerge from interaction between themes of the previous moment and what so emerges may take propositional or narrative forms. Both are emergent but the former takes a more stable and often more persistent form while the latter form is more fluid and fleeting. Both forms of theme are expressed in conversation. Intention is an organising theme that emerges from conversation and organises experience. The intention of one is a gesture and its meaning lies in the response it evokes from others.

6  Relationships organised in conversation by propositional and narrative themes both enable and constrain what may be said, done and even thought. In other words, conversations configure, and are configured by, power relations between people.

7  Ideology is organising themes that either justify current power relations or justify the undermining of these current power relations. Dominant ideology makes current power relations feel natural, while ideologies at the margin make opposition feel natural. Official ideology is themes organising what may be openly and safely talked about. Official ideology legitimises some kinds of conversation and banishes others. Unofficial ideologies are themes organising the relationships and conversations banished from the legitimate arena. They may either collusively support current power relations or potentially undermine them.

8  Ideological themes organising experience, whether official or unofficial, binarise and polarise experience into sameness and difference, them and us, in and out.

9  This leads to the notion of the social unconscious. People are usually unaware of how ideology polarises experience and makes differences seem natural in the interest of sustaining or opposing current power relations.

10  Another aspect of the social unconscious is the fantasies that groups and individuals develop around power relations and take into their silent conversations that are mind.

11  Official ideologies are sometimes maintained and sometimes undermined through processes of gossip and ridicule.

12  Change in individuals and groups means change in the themes organising the experience of being together and hence change in power relations.

13  The responsive nature of the processes of relating means that the evolution of relationships displays the paradox of predictability and unpredictability common in complex systems. Since any gesture could call forth a variety of responses, and those responses could provoke a variety of further responses, the possibility of predicting how they will unfold rapidly diminishes. Human responses are sensitive to small variations in gesture.

This chapter will explore how an organisation, as part of a population of organisations, might be understood from the perspective of relationship psychology, as complex responsive processes. What I am seeking to do in this chapter is to present some pointers to the direction that a radical theory of organisational dynamics and strategic management might take.

## 16.2    ORGANISING THEMES, POWER RELATIONS AND IDEOLOGY

The theoretical perspective I am suggesting draws on complexity theory to posit that organisations are complex responsive processes analogous to complex adaptive systems but also significantly different from them. I do this because the logical properties of interaction revealed by simulations in digital symbols provide, I believe, a powerful analogy for interaction in the protosymbols, significant and reified symbols that are human communication.

Digital symbols are arranged in algorithmic forms that organise interaction between themselves, that is they self-organise. This is analogous to the arrangement of protosymbols, significant and reified symbols into propositional and narrative themes that organise themselves as people's experience of relating to each other. Instead of taking a cognitivist, humanistic or psychoanalytic view of human psychology that leads straight to defining organisations as complex adaptive systems in which the entities or 'agents' are individual humans, I am taking a relationship psychology perspective. Consequently, an organisation is not immediately thought of as an adaptive thing-like system or network but, rather, as responsive processes. The self-organising entities are then not individual human beings but the symbols, arranged as propositional and narrative organising themes, through which they relate to each other. What emerges is the reproduction and potential transformation of the propositional and narrative themes themselves, that is the pattern of relationships between people. This is closely analogous to the computer simulations of complex adaptive systems in which the self-organising entities are arrangements of digital symbols in the form of algorithms that interact with each other. What emerges here is the reproduction and potential transformation of the algorithms, that is the pattern of relationships between them.

### Algorithmic and human interaction

Given this close analogy, I suggest that the insights about nonlinear interaction in complex adaptive systems point to a radically different way of thinking about creative change in organisations. The insights I am referring to have to do with the self-organising, emergent nature of the interaction, the paradoxical dynamic at the edge of chaos and the potential for creativity, and the radical unpredictability arising in that dynamic. I am suggesting, then, that the similarity between algorithmic interaction and human relating resides in the nonlinear nature of both, implying a similar logic to, and similar properties of, interaction in both cases. I believe that a careful exploration of these similarities is a fruitful theoretical strategy, but one requiring detailed attention to the enormous differences.

The enormous difference between algorithmic and human interaction relates to the significant difference between digital symbols and the symbols humans use in communication. The symbols in human communication are not digital, they are primarily not algorithmic in form, and they are not processed or disembodied. The symbols of human communication are arranged as narrative and propositional themes that organise the responsive experience of those individuals in their being and doing together and their experience is these themes. It is the themes, not the individuals, which interact. Furthermore, these themes are always experienced in individual human bodies. In other words, an organisation is thought of, not just as a group of individuals, but as responsive processes of relating, that is communication between them.

Organisational action, then, is never simply the act of an autonomous individual but always occurs in the relationships that people have with each other. Drawing on the analogy of complex adaptive systems, I want to suggest that the complex responsive processes of human relating are self-organising. By this I mean that the interacting responsive processes, operating at any one time, organise themselves, with reference to themselves, into emergent processes of relating at the next point in time. Responsive processes of relating continuously reproduce and transform themselves. This in no way denies the possibility of an individual choosing or intending anything. It simply posits that such choice and intention is itself a theme-organising experience that emerges in the same way as any other theme. Intentions emerge from conversations as gestures that call forth responses from others in an ongoing conversation. This may sound as if I am saying that processes of relating between people organise themselves in some abstract way not involving individual bodies. However, I am not saying this at all for reasons that follow.

People relate to each other through gestures made by one body to another that evoke responses in other bodies that are gestures to the first. There can be no relationships without this circular connection between gesture and response. As soon as the connection is broken the relationship ceases. All gestures and all responses are the actions of bodies. They can take place either directly between bodies in the presence of each other, or through the medium of some technology or artefact. Whether the self-referential, reflexive gesture–response cycle takes place directly or through technology or artefact, it does so in the medium of symbols.

I have distinguished between protosymbols, significant and reified symbols. To recapitulate, protosymbols are body rhythms experienced as feeling states. They are bodily responses to gestures made by the body itself, by other bodies and the material environment of the body.

Significant symbols are bodily gestures potentially calling forth the same response in oneself as in others. The most important form of significant symbol is vocal language. Since significant symbols are bodily gestures, they are always interwoven with protosymbols and they are organised into narrative themes that organise the experience of being together. Narrative themes are always interwoven with emotion in that people care, often passionately, about the narratives that organise their experience. Narrative themes have the potential of organising experience of a fluid kind with multiple meanings.

Reified symbols are those that tend to be used as if they are the reality that they symbolise. They are arranged into propositions that organise the experience of being together. Usually, reified symbols are stated in written form or vocal recordings. Through this means there may be a long delay between the gesture and the response.

However, the words or recordings have no meaning until someone reads or hears them, responding with an interpretation. Since bodies express and, after some delay, bodies interpret propositional themes, they too must be the interweaving of reified and protosymbols. People may be no less passionate about certain propositional themes organising their experience than they are about narrative ones. Propositional themes may be arranged in the form of procedures, maps of role relationships, flows of tasks, models of organisational activity and organisational environments. Experience organised in this way tends to be rather stable.

## Organising themes

Narrative and propositional themes, both conscious and unconscious, organise themselves into conversations, both the public and vocal and the private and silent of mind, and can take a number of forms, for example:

- fantasies
- myths
- rituals
- ideology
- culture
- gossip
- rumour
- discourses and speech genres
- dialogues
- discussions
- debates
- presentations.

In all of these forms of relating, narrative and propositional themes are organising that experience of relating in a number of ways, for example, by:

- selecting what is to be attended to;
- shaping how what is attended to is to be described;
- selecting who might describe it;
- accounting by one to another for their actions;
- articulating purpose in the form of themes expressing intentions;
- justifying actions in the form of themes that express ideology.

Organising themes of an ideological nature are fundamental to human relating because it is these themes that make current power relations feel natural, so justifying them. Relationships always impose constraints on what may be done, what feelings may be acknowledged and even on what may be thought. Such constraint is power. The narrative and propositional themes express and are expressed by, they shape and are shaped by, power relations between people in organisations. Power, from this perspective, is not located in one individual who somehow manipulates or dominates others, but in the relationship between people. Relationships between people constrain all of them. The patterns of constraints arising in relationship is what is meant by the figuration of power relations.

From this perspective, then, an organisation is complex responsive processes of relating, that is various forms of communicating, in the form of conversation. Conversation is complex responsive processes of organising themes or, to put the same phenomenon in different words, relational constraints. I am suggesting that it is useful to think of an organisation as a pattern of conversation and organising and managing as responsive processes of relating in conversation. How people talk, what patterns that talk displays, is of primary importance to what the organisation is and what happens to it. The processes of conversation are also of great importance to how individual members of an organisation experience themselves. This is because the silent, private conversation with oneself is one's mind and self, and this conversation inevitably resonates with the vocalised, public conversations taking place in an organisation.

If one takes this perspective, that an organisation is a pattern of talk (relational constraints), then an organisation changes only in so far as its conversational life (power relations) evolves. Organisational change is the same thing as change in the pattern of talk and therefore the pattern of power relations. Creativity, novelty and innovation are all the emergence of new patterns of talk and patterns of power relations. In other words, the strategic direction an organisation follows emerges as a pattern in the way people talk and so configure power relations. Note that public, vocal conversations (group relationships) and private, silent conversations (individual minds) are both aspects of the same phenomenon. Change in one means some kind of change in the other. Organizations and their individual members change together. It is not a matter of changing the people first and then changing the organisation. Change is possible when conversational life is free flowing and flexible and impossible when conversational life remains stuck in repetitive themes. The key questions then become: How do themes organise the experience of organisational life? What facilitates and what blocks the emergence of new patterns of talk?

I now want to explore how themes organise experience of life in organisations, starting with how they organise what can, and what cannot, be talked about.

## 16.3 LEGITIMATE AND SHADOW THEMES

If there is one thing that everyone knows about life in organisations, or any other grouping of people for that matter, it is this: it is not possible to talk freely and openly to just anyone, in any situation, about anything one likes, in any way one chooses, and still survive as a member. Relationships impose powerful constraints on what it is permissible to say, to whom and how. There is another thing that everyone knows about life in organisations and it is this: it is sometimes quite acceptable to act but quite unacceptable to discuss freely and openly the reasons for doing so. Alternative reasons that cover up the 'real' reason are disclosed instead. This is the basis of the distinction I make between legitimate and shadow themes that organise relationships in organisations.

Legitimate themes organise what people feel able to talk about openly and freely. They organise conversations in which people give acceptable accounts of themselves and their actions, as well as imputations about the actions of others. They are the kind of conversation you readily engage in with others, even if you do not know them well.

Shadow themes organise conversations in which people feel able to give less acceptable accounts of themselves and their actions, as well as of others and their actions. They are the kind of conversations you would only engage in informally, in very small groups, with others you know and trust. Shadow themes organise what people do not feel able to discuss freely and openly.

The distinction between legitimate and shadow themes is intimately related to ideology, which can be either official or unofficial. It is ideology that legitimises a conversation. In particular, it is the ideology sustaining current power relations that makes conversation feel natural, acceptable and safe – that is, legitimate. One would normally expect that ideology to be official; that is, the values that are publicly pronounced as those people are to live by. This official ideology may well exert a powerful influence on what may or may not be freely spoken about. However, it need not necessarily determine what may or may not be done. Despite the official ideology, people may act in ways consistent with unofficial ideologies, even though they cannot talk about how their actions are justified by unofficial ideologies. Instead, they will have to find some other, plausible, factual reason consistent with the official ideology. When people engage in shadow conversations, they also do so on the basis of some ideology that makes it feel natural and justifiable to talk as they do, but this time secretively. Here too, the underlying ideology could be official or it could be unofficial.

Let me give an example to clarify the distinction. Although the organisation I am about to describe is a fiction, it is nevertheless constructed from experiences in a number of real organisations.

## Example: equal opportunities

This company's board of directors consists of eight men. The group of 30 senior executives who report to them also consists entirely of men. There are some 150 senior managers reporting to them, and of these, 12 are women, mostly in the human resources, public relations and marketing functions. For the past ten years, the directors have emphasised the company's formal equal opportunities policy for recruitment and promotion and its policy on the harassment of women and minorities. Virtually everyone in the organisation is aware of this official ideology of equality, for example between men and women, and it exercises a powerful constraint on what may be talked about freely and openly. It is widely felt to be unacceptable to talk freely and openly about whether women, for example, are in general suitable for the most senior positions. It is also unacceptable to ask openly why there are no women in the upper echelons despite the equal opportunities policy. Even the 12 senior women managers in the company do not feel that it would be wise to talk to directors about this matter. The fear seems to be that such comments would be interpreted as accusations of hypocrisy. The organising theme has to do with it being unwise to point to openly, let alone question the policies of equal opportunities and harassment in any way.

This is what I mean by themes organising the legitimate experience of being together. Some of these themes are formal, propositional and quite conscious in nature, such as the policy statements on equal opportunities and harassment. Others are narrative, informal and possibly unconscious in nature. The unconscious aspect may lie in the reasons why the women managers do not challenge top executives. For example, it might be a fantasy that the latter would interpret any comment as an accusation of hypocrisy. It is legitimate in this organisation to talk openly and freely only in terms of the equality that is part of the official ideology but it is also quite legitimate to appoint only men to the upper echelons. In other words, it feels right and natural to appoint men only, but it does not feel right to talk openly about this. Note here how the ideology underlying current power relations is a mixture of official and unofficial ideology.

However, people do talk about inequality in private, but only to those who they trust and expect to agree with them, or in the form of a joke. For example, some of the directors and senior managers can be heard to tell disparaging jokes about women, occasionally in the presence of one of the 12 female managers. Female managers also sometimes make disparaging remarks about men, often in their presence. Because the exchange takes place in the form of jokes, any serious intention underlying them can be denied if need be. Privately a few men express their unwillingness to report to a woman. Although women are sometimes interviewed for director and senior executive posts, a good reason has so far always been found for not appointing them. In each separate case, the reasons produced are indeed plausible but the pattern over a long period of time is curious. The senior women managers also talk in private, often amongst themselves but also with male colleagues who are known to be sympathetic. They talk about glass ceilings and hypocrisy.

These are all examples of what I mean by shadow themes that organise the experience of being together. They organise conversations that can only be conducted in private with people whom one knows and trusts, or in the form of jokes. These conversations express the organisation's unofficial ideologies. Unofficially, some have an ideology that does encompass discrimination and yet others believe that top executives are hypocrites. Note how the themes organising shadow conversations are mainly narrative in nature. Also, note the unconscious aspect. Those making decisions to appoint women are usually not cynically ignoring the equal opportunities policy and most of them would strenuously, and probably quite genuinely, deny that they are discriminating. After all, they provide very careful and convincing reasons why they have not appointed a woman in each separate case. The female managers may not be aware of how they are colluding in maintaining the situation by their public silence. Note how the ideologies underlying shadow conversations are usually unofficial but could be official. The official ideology of equality underlies some of the shadow conversations.

Clearly, unofficial ideologies are undermining official ideology. It is also easy to see that one powerful unofficial ideology, in part unconscious, is sustaining current power relations in which men get the top jobs. It can also be argued that the unofficial ideology of the women and some of the men who support them contributes to sustaining current power relations. It looks as if official ideology is about changing current power relations and unofficial ideologies are resisting this. However, a different argument can be made. In today's social climate, it would be unacceptable not to have public policies about equal opportunities and harassment. It is also probably helpful to have them from a legal point of view. The policies may well be providing an official ideology that meets the requirements of public opinion and in the process covers up the unofficial ones that really make action feel right. This interpretation is strengthened when one of the human resources directors recounts how he raised the topic of equal opportunities over the two years before it was incorporated in personnel policies. He did so privately with a few of his colleagues to get the necessary support to take it to the board. His most persuasive argument was the weight of public opinion.

I am using this example to argue that it is neither the official nor the unofficial ideologies on their own that are sustaining current power relations. Rather, it is the complex interplay between them, between legitimate and shadow organising themes, that sustains current power relations. I am also using it to point to how what is the officially stated ideology today in fact emerged from shadow conversations some time ago.

I want to take this example one step further. A few of the female managers become increasingly frustrated and begin to talk privately about how they can influence the situation. Some of them talk, as people do, at dinner parties about their experience of discrimination in the workplace. A guest at one of these dinner parties is an influential journalist, well known for her championing of women's rights. She interviews the chairman and writes a sarcastic piece in a major newspaper about the all-male management cast at this particular company. Most people in the company talk about the article and they now feel able to talk more openly and freely about why there are so few women in top management. What was a shadow conversation has now emerged into the legitimate arena. A few months later two women are appointed to the senior executive ranks and a prominent businesswoman is appointed to the board as non-executive director. Clearly, the meaning of the equal opportunities policy has changed and with it the pattern of power relations.

Again, what I am illustrating here is the complex interplay between shadow and legitimate themes organising experience in an organisation and how new themes, new meanings, can emerge in this interplay. This interplay has generated greater diversity and variety in the management of the company.

## Another example

Consider another example of the interplay between legitimate and shadow themes. Fonseca (see *Management narrative 1* in this book) reports a development in a water utility in Lisbon. The manager and his colleagues in the Operations and Maintenance Department talked about the waste involved in having to consult many different maps showing the location of utilities in the streets before they could carry out any repairs on the water supply system. They decided that it would be a good idea to digitalise all the existing maps so that repair crews would only have to consult one up-to-date map. However, the manager of the department knew that investment priorities lay elsewhere and that any request for funds for the digitalisation project would be turned down. Without approval, the manager nevertheless started the project, freeing up some time for the four engineers who were enthusiastic and finding small amounts of funding from other budgets.

The project could not be talked about openly and freely to anyone because it was not in the legitimate arena. This did not mean that no one else knew about it. Senior managers did know about it and tolerated it. However, it still could not be talked about openly. Conversations about it were organised by shadow themes. The reason is obvious. The official ideology on control was one in which the use of resources had to be approved by senior executives. It is immediately evident how such a control ideology sustains current power relations and how going around the approval procedures subverts them. After some time, the project reached a stage at which there was enough evidence of its potential usefulness to seek and obtain official approval. As it further developed, it led to significant shifts in power relations between different departments in the organisation. The complex interplay of shadow and legitimate themes led to the emergence of a new technology.

A key point to notice here is how shadow themes can organise collusive maintenance of existing power relations or subvert them. The complex dynamics of interactions between legitimate and shadow themes, between official and unofficial ideologies, establishes the power relations of who is 'in' and who is 'out', who is at the 'centre' and who is at the 'margin'. I will return to this below when the importance of diversity and deviance is discussed.

The distinction between legitimate and shadow themes is not one that is made in the theories reviewed earlier in this book. The distinctions made there were between formal and informal, conscious and unconscious aspects of organising. Consider first how they are defined and then how one might understand the relationship between them and the distinction between legitimate and shadow.

## Formal and informal

All of the theories reviewed in this book draw much the same distinction between the formal and the informal aspects of an organisation. The formal is identified in terms of an organisation's purpose, its mode of fulfilling its purpose, that is its task, and the individuals who are assigned roles in carrying out the task. The formal organisation is defined in terms of the role it promises to fulfil in its larger community and the boundary around it is clear cut and definable in terms of those formally authorised to be its members. The organisation's identity here is defined in terms of formal propositions as to membership, roles and relationships between roles, tasks and purposes.

The informal organisation consists of all relationships not formally defined by their roles or clearly related to their tasks. All personal and social relationships fall within this category. These personal relationships extend into other organisations making it difficult to define the boundary between one organisation and another. As everyone knows, no organisation can function without these informal relationships and an organisation, therefore, has to be understood in terms of both formal and informal relationships.

In the terms I am using in this chapter, some of the themes that organise the experience of being together, and therefore some aspects of power relations, may be described as formal. These are primarily propositional themes, frequently expressed in written form setting out reporting structures, procedures and policies of various kinds. The propositions model the hierarchy and the bureaucracy and set out the official ideology. However, the formal organising themes also encompass some of a more narrative kind. For example, there are unwritten understandings of how people should conduct themselves at formal meetings and the kind of deference they should display in conversations with those more senior to them in the hierarchy. The themes that organise informal experience take a narrative form.

Note that this distinction between formal and informal is very different to the distinction between legitimate and shadow. The former distinction relates to the degree of formality and the latter to the degree of legitimacy.

## Conscious and unconscious

Learning organisation theory distinguishes between assumptions people are aware of and those that they are not aware of. The concept of mental models used in this theory postulates that most of the content of the models is below the level of awareness. A distinction is also drawn between tacit and explicit knowledge. Psychoanalytic perspectives distinguish between what members of an organisation do consciously and what they do unconsciously and it attaches particular importance to the notion of unconscious group processes. This theory pays particular attention to the impact of unconscious fantasy on organising how people experience being together and to the unconscious deployment of defences against anxiety. In terms of this chapter's focus, there is the notion of the social, or dialogic, unconscious in which people are unaware of how they use ideology to justify power relations.

People are usually conscious of the formal propositional statements that organise their experience of being together. Reflective members of a group are also usually aware of a number of the narrative and protonarrative themes that are organising their experience of being together. However, most of the themes organising experience are likely to be unconscious. It is unusual for people to struggle publicly to identify what these themes are. Certain categories of themes are particularly likely to be unconscious and will be linked with other themes that protect them from exposure to consciousness. In Chapter 14 one such category was identified around the unconscious preservation of power relations through talking and acting on differences that are used to stir up hatred.

This is the dynamic of those who are 'in' and those who are 'out'. While people will be aware of who is 'in' and who is 'out', what they tend to be unaware of is the purpose this categorisation is serving. People in groups also unconsciously categorise experience into binary opposites that become entrenched as ideologies, which make their behaviour seem right and natural. Here the ideology will be conscious but its dubious basis will be unconsciously excluded from consideration. Then the very categorising and logical procedures of language work to highlight certain differences and obliterate others in what is ultimately an arbitrary way. The difference is conscious but what it obliterates becomes unconscious.

To summarise, people in a group will normally be conscious of the propositional statements organising their experience of being together. They will also normally be conscious of some of the narrative themes organising their experience of being together. In particular they will be conscious of themes that include certain people in informal groupings but exclude others and they may be conscious of the ideological reasons for doing this. What they are far less likely to be aware of is that the reason for their classification of who is in and who is out is to preserve power differences. They will be unaware of how they exclude any examination of the ideological basis on which they are discriminating between those who are in and those who are out. Of potentially great importance is the manner in which logic itself unconsciously obliterates differences within categories of people and focuses attention on arbitrary differences between categories of people.

## How organising themes interact

This section examines how organising themes of the formal–informal, conscious–unconscious and legitimate–shadow type relate to, and interact with, each other. The connections between them are depicted in *Figure 16.1*. The key point I hope to make in using this diagram is that although one may focus attention on a part of it, the processes it points to are always simultaneously operating in any organisation. Each category in the diagram is a description of themes that organise the process of relating and together they constitute the complex responsive processes of relating that are the organisation. All of the categories have to do with the reproduction and potential transformation of power relations.

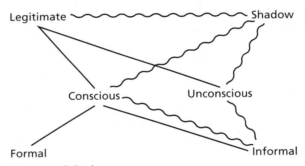

**FIGURE 16.1**    Legitimate and shadow

The straight lines in the diagram identify all the interconnections between organising themes that can be described as legitimate, while the wavy lines describe those that can be described in terms of shadow themes. I have already described how the complex interplay between legitimate and shadow organising themes, official and unofficial ideology, either supports or undermines current power relations. This interaction is depicted by the wavy line running between legitimate and shadow in the diagram. The following subsections examine other important interactions.

### Legitimate interactions

From the definition given above, it is obvious that all formal themes organising experience are also conscious and legitimate. This is depicted in the diagram as the straight line connections between these categories. These are the organising themes that strategic choice theory focuses attention on. The organising themes here are primarily propositional in nature and are arranged in models and maps of one kind or another. Plans and budgets, management information and control systems, reward systems and all the other systems and techniques discussed in the chapters on strategic choice theory take this form.

However, the formal–conscious–legitimate themes never interact in isolation from the others. To illustrate this, I suggest that you turn to *Management narrative 2* in this book. This is an account of a perfectly normal formal meeting to review a budget submission that is to be made to senior executives. It is about propositional themes falling into the conscious and legitimate categories described above. The problem is how to deal with a substantial budget overrun. The first striking point is how personal ambitions and interpersonal rivalries are all part of the process. This immediately brings in organising themes of an informal and even a shadow nature. The story reveals the emotional undercurrent and the anxiety, first of not knowing just how realistic the figures are, and, second, of not knowing how senior management is going to receive them. This points to the probability of unconscious organising themes as a response to anxiety. The story also points to the way in which interaction between various organising themes supports or threatens current power relations. The point is that even as routine and rational an activity as reviewing a budget cannot be understood purely in terms of formal, conscious, legitimate interaction. What emerges from the budget meeting emerges from the interaction of all the categories of themes.

This example also helps to clarify the nature of intention and control. All arrive at the meeting with an intention, namely to reduce the budget estimate. This is their response to the gesture made by senior management. Each participant also arrives with an individual intention, namely to reduce his or her part of the budget as little as possible and hopefully even increase it. Whether this intention is materialised, or not, depends upon the response it evokes from the others. These intentions and the response they evoke are all themes organising their experience together. It is relatively predictable that they will reduce the budget estimate. However, what they are all well aware of is that they might find themselves in a similar position next year. After all, when they prepared the original estimate some time ago they did not intend that it should quadruple. What happens over the next year will emerge, just as what happens to the detail of the estimate emerges in this meeting. The self-organising interaction of the themes organising their experience and the emergent outcome does not imply in any way that people are interacting without intention.

A similar point applies to the issue of control. A prime requirement of managers' role is that of controlling their activities and the expenditure they generate. It is the purpose of this meeting to carry out that requirement. However, the managers are well aware that they have not succeeded in controlling the expenditure since the last estimate and they clearly realise that this might happen again. Nevertheless, they do not take this as a cause of despair and so abandon the whole attempt. They, and the situation they are in, cannot be described as out of control. This is what *Streatfield (1998)* refers to as the paradox of control. In situations of great uncertainty managers are in control and not in control at the same time.

Returning to *Figure 16.1*, you will see that I have connected informal, conscious and legitimate with straight lines. This is because some organisations are run on informal lines and carry out informally what others would do formally. I have also connected informal, unconscious and legitimate with straight lines indicating that some legitimate organising themes can be informal and unconscious. What I have in mind here is the point made above, namely that people may be interacting informally with each other according to quite legitimate ideology but be unconscious of how in doing so they are sustaining current power relations.

I now want to turn to the wavy line connection between informal, conscious and shadow organising themes in *Figure 16.1*.

### Covert politics

In learning organisation theory, reviewed in Chapter 9, *Argyris (1990)* identifies behaviour in organisations that blocks learning. He calls it organisational defence routines. For example, people make certain issues undiscussible, and they also make undiscussible the fact that they are undiscussible. They do this, according to Argyris, because they fear embarrassing, and being embarrassed by, others. He ascribes this behaviour to a defective mental model of the learning process located in the minds of individuals. This model is one in which a person enters a discussion with assertions about others that are not disclosed, knowing that others are doing the same. Each also assumes that they are engaging in the discussion to win and not to lose. His prescription is then that individuals should become aware of their defective mental model of the learning process and change it. The new model requires them to enter into open dialogue and disclose the assertions they are making about each other. He recognises that this will be very difficult and reports that, despite training, people hardly ever do this.

From the perspective I am pointing to this finding is hardly surprising. People hardly ever move to the learning process Argyris recommends because it is a completely unrealistic requirement. It amounts to requiring people to disclose the shadow themes organising their experience, so making the shadow public and legitimate. However, they cannot do this without taking the chance of openly undermining the current power relations and incurring the retaliation of those they threaten. Some ideologies are unconsciously justifying current power relations and others are unconsciously justifying covert attempts to undermine them. People are passionate about these ideological underpinnings. Requiring people to move to the kind of position Argyris has in mind is the same as requiring them to abandon passion and expose not only their ideological position but the largely unconscious purpose they serve. This is only remotely plausible if you put the individual at the centre of your theory of psychology.

Once you place relationship at the centre, it is evident that the basic nature of human relating, the power relations it immediately implies and the ideologies that underpin these relationships would all have to change completely before the Argyris prescription could work. I cannot imagine that human beings will stop engaging in the kind of covert politics that Argyris has so perceptively identified. These complex responsive processes are always likely to characterise life in organisations. However, while they cannot be removed they can be understood as can their impact on how an organisation evolves.

Covert politics is clearly informal, shadow themes organising experience and the themes are mostly conscious, although the underlying reasons for them may not be. However, it is not organising experience in isolation from or as an alternative to other combinations of theme. For example, over many months I and the colleagues I worked with engaged in just the kind of covert politics Argyris talks about. One faction in the company I worked for formed around the chief executive and favoured a strategy of investing in the existing business while another faction formed around another powerful figure and favoured diversification by acquisition. I found myself in the latter faction. The chief executive did not publicly dismiss the diversification strategy, although we all knew that he did not favour it. Instead, he called for it to be carefully examined and commissioned a paper on acquisition criteria. After discussion of this, a lengthy report was prepared on possible acquisition targets. At the end of the discussion on this report the chief executive called for a rewording of the acquisition criteria. By the time this had been discussed most of the acquisition targets had been bought by other companies. A further report was prepared. This went on for many months during which time one small investment after another was made in the existing business.

Everyone engaged in this process knew what was going on and knew that others, including the chief executive, knew what was going on too. No one, however, spoke about this at executive meetings, only privately. Conversations about what was going on were organised by shadow theme while legitimate themes organised silence. Note how the themes were informal, quite conscious and of the shadow. However, the reasons for keeping the conversation in this form were probably less conscious and much of the interaction between the two factions took place at formal meetings organised by legitimate themes. It was all going on at the same time.

From the perspective I am suggesting, covert politics is a social process. In ordinary conversations, legitimate and shadow themes interact in complex ways as people bolster, undermine and shift power positions. Action to remove people from their positions, from the chief executive to the office clerk, all begin as ordinary conversations organised by shadow themes. The important point here is that this form of conversation can shift power relations and patterns of talking but it can just as easily block any such shifts. Obviously this affects how an organisation evolves.

### Unconscious themes

Consider now how relationships might be organised by themes that are informal, unconscious and have shadow characteristics.

An example of what I mean occurred during a meeting of a group in which I was a consultant. The chief executive for this company expressed considerable frustration with a group of his most senior executives, claiming that he had empowered them to get on with meeting their targets. Instead of doing this, he said that they still kept referring everything to him and he felt that this was a cause of their company's falling profits. He was unwilling to reflect on why this was happening. Instead, he instructed the managers to attend a meeting at which they were to define their roles in such a way that they took more responsibility. I was to be a consultant at this meeting. He started the meeting by berating them for their lack of initiative and then left them to go through the exercise of defining their roles. They refused to do this and spent the entire day in an emotional attack on the chief executive's leadership style. They complained about the unreasonableness of being required to meet conflicting targets. One reported overhearing the chief executive promising to fire the next executive who failed to meet any target whatsoever. This provoked outrage on the part of the managers. How could they be held responsible for changes over which they had no control? During this time, any comment I made was simply ignored and they decided that when the chief executive returned on the next day they would confront him.

However, the next morning one of the executives advised caution and gradually their resolve to confront him ebbed away. Instead they prepared a number of colourful overhead projector foils and made a presentation to the chief executive about some rather safe business issues. He responded with a lecture. During the course of this lecture it became clear that there was little truth in the rumour that he would remove anyone who failed to achieve all targets no matter what happened. It was only on the following day, in a somewhat depressed state, that they were able to reflect on what they were doing. We talked about some of the themes organising their experience of being together at that time. For example, one clear theme that they seemed to be unconscious of was one that might be summarised as follows: 'Every casual remark the chief executive makes is an instruction or at least about to become one.' An example was the statement all took to be true that they had to achieve all targets or they would be fired. Other themes were those around flight from their task, the fight dynamic around the chief executive and the dependency on presentations of safe issues. These, of course, are the basic assumption behaviours of the psychoanalytic perspective, reviewed in Chapter 10. On the chief executive's next visit they were able to discuss their relationship with him.

The themes organising the experience for much of this meeting were informal, unconscious and of the shadow. However, the meeting took place legitimately and when the chief executive appeared it took formal, conscious and legitimate form. However, even when this happened the feelings and silent communications between the senior executives clearly reflected the informal, unconscious and shadow themes organising their experience. Again, interaction between all the kinds of theme differentiated in *Figure 16.1* are taking place simultaneously. What emerges does so through the complex interplay of legitimate and shadow, conscious and unconscious, and formal and informal themes. How all this is at the same time forming and being formed by power relations is also evident in the example. Again, these processes affect how an organisation evolves.

One of the most important aspects of shadow organising themes is the socially unconscious form they take. What is unconscious here is how members of a group collectively employ, in their talk and their actions, differences between themselves (senior executives in the above example) and other groups (the chief executive and his immediate reports) to stir up anger (even hatred) against the others in order to preserve unconsciously sensed power differences. They do this by collectively categorising their experience into binary opposites (meet all the targets or get fired) that become entrenched as ideologies, which make their behaviour seem right and natural. Furthermore, they collectively use the logics of symmetry and asymmetry to obliterate some differences and highlight others, so polarising experience.

## 16.4   THE IMPORTANCE OF DIVERSITY

Let me reiterate what I mean by shadow themes that organise experience. Legitimate themes are legitimate because they conform to official ideologies. The opposite of legitimate is, of course, that which is illegitimate or illegal. This is not what I mean by the organisational shadow. Shadow themes form conversations, that is power relations, that arise between the legitimate and the illegitimate or illegal. The shadow is neither legitimate nor illegitimate. In a sense, one might say that it is both legitimate and illegitimate at the same time. Shadow themes/power relations are shadow because of the manner in which they are expressed in conversation. Such conversations always take place informally between small numbers of people and their distinguishing feature is that they do not conform to the official ideology. Some unofficial ideologies may collusively support current power relations while others seek to undermine them and both can be taking place at the same time. This does not mean that such conversations only take place between the less powerful. The most powerful participate in them too.

In using the term shadow, I am trying to capture some of the points reviewed in Chapter 15. The first is that made by *Elias (1989)* when he talked about people challenging the official ideology from the margin. Conversations in the shadow are conversations at the margin. I am also trying to capture the point *Bhaktin (1986)* made about 'carnival'. Frequently, conversations in the shadow take humorous forms. Conversations in the shadow are a form of play, transitional phenomena in the sense of *Winnicott (1965)*. It is in the complex interplay of legitimate and shadow themes that ordinary everyday conversations create organisational reality (*Shotter, 1993*).

To summarise, organisations exist to enable joint action and people can only act jointly through their relationships with each other. People relate to each other through complex responsive processes that can be understood in terms of interacting propositional and narrative themes. It is these themes that organise the experience of relating between people. The themes take many forms. They may be ideological themes. They may take the form of intentions, expressions of emotion, descriptions, and so on. Simultaneous interaction between many themes taking different forms constitutes the conversational life of an organisation. The process of relating through conversation constrains that relating and so establishes power relations. Conversation and power relations are simply different words for the same phenomenon, namely that of relating between people. An organisation is processes of relating, that is its pattern of power relations, that is its conversational life. Conversational life cannot develop according to an overall blueprint since no one has the power to determine what others will talk about all the time. Conversation is thus a self-organising phenomenon and this self-organisation continuously produces emergent patterns in itself. In other words, themes organising the experience of relating in conversation continuously reproduce themselves and in so doing may transform themselves. Creativity, innovation and learning are all transformations of organising themes as they reproduce themselves. It is important, therefore, to understand how such transformation occurs. The key to transformation is diversity.

## The reproduction and transformation of conversational themes

In the language of complexity theory, system transformation means that the system moves from one attractor to another. More fundamentally, transformation is movement not just from one attractor to another that already exists, but to a new one that is evolving. Chapter 12 described the conditions that must be satisfied if a system is to display the internal capacity to move spontaneously from one attractor to another and to evolve new ones. These conditions have to do with the heterogeneity of the entities comprising the system and the heterogeneity of their interactions. Transformation is possible only when the entities, their interactions with each other and their interaction with entities in the system's environment are sufficiently heterogeneous, that is sufficiently diverse. The fundamental requirement for transformation is non-average, deviant, maverick or eccentric behaviour on the part of the entities comprising a system (*Allen, 1998a, 1998b*). In simulations of complex systems, such diversity is generated in the course of reproduction through random mutation, that is chance changes, in the digital code and through cross-over replication, that is the mixing of two sets of digital code. Of course, if the rate of mutation is too high, the system becomes totally disorganised. Transformation therefore requires a rate of mutation within a critical range where it is neither too high nor too low. A similar point applies to cross-over replication. If the mixing of the code during replication is totally random the system will soon become completely disorganised. However, cross-over replication, as with sexual reproduction, is not a totally random mixing of digital, or genetic, code. Blocks of code from one 'mate' are joined to blocks of code of the other, so preserving some structure, but not too much.

What is the analogue of random mutation and cross-over replication in the conversational life of an organisation?

### Misunderstanding

As everyone knows, human communication is far from perfect. When people converse about any matter that is at all complicated, they only partially understand each other, at first anyway. The back and forth movement of conversation is a process of trying to clarify meaning. In other words, there is usually some degree of misunderstanding in human communication. This is the analogue of random mutation. Meaning, that is themes organising conversational life, has the potential for being transformed when there is a critical level of misunderstanding (*Fonseca, 1998*). If misunderstanding is too extreme, then communication fails, and if it is very mild, then nothing novel is being communicated. The analogue for cross-over replication is the interaction of different patterns of conversation. This occurs, for example, when people from one discipline, say biology, talk to people from another, say management (*Fonseca, 1998*). These two groups of people use different vocabularies and concepts but in talking to each other, trying to understand each other's ways of talking, new meaning may be generated. This is cross-fertilisation and emergent transformation in the reproduction of conversation.

I am suggesting that it is through the diversity generated by misunderstanding and cross-fertilisation of different ways of talking that transformation in organising themes and thus patterns of conversing occur. Individuals and small groups become identified with this diversity, attracting the labels of conforming and deviant, normal and eccentric, responsible and maverick, orthodox and radical, us and them, and so on. This is clearly the identification and description of power relations in terms of what conversational themes and which people are 'in' and 'out'. All of these distinctions are ways of describing the distinction between legitimate and shadow. That distinction between legitimate and shadow is important because the tension between the two is the potential source of the diversity that is critical to the capacity to change spontaneously in novel ways.

The organisational shadow, then, is those organising themes/power relations that are in some sense deviant and this deviance encompasses the despicable and the destructive, on the one hand, and the heroic and the creative, on the other. Shadow communications take the form of ordinary, everyday conversations, gossip, rumour, inspirational accounts, stories that express humour and the grotesque, tales that take the form of elaborate social fantasies or touching personal contacts. Shadow communications shape and are shaped by power relations, some of which collusively support and others of which covertly undermine the legitimate. I am suggesting that it is important to distinguish between legitimate and shadow organising themes because the potential for the emergence of new organisational direction arises when legitimate and shadow themes are in tension. In other words, creative potential arises from the subversion of legitimate organising themes by shadow themes. What emerges then is new forms of conversation, that is shifts in power relations. In other words, just as with any complex system (*Allen, 1998a*), an organisation's internal capacity to move spontaneously to a new organisational attractor depends upon the degree of diversity in its conversational themes.

## The dynamics of conversation

Chapter 12 described the different dynamics characteristic of complex adaptive systems, namely the dynamics of stable equilibrium, bounded instability at the edge of chaos, or disintegration. It also pointed to the conclusion that such systems produce novel emergent forms when they operate in, or near to, the dynamics of the edge of chaos. That dynamic occurs at critical rates of information flow, critical degrees of connection between agents and critical levels of diversity in agents and their interactions. I think that convincing analogues for the dynamics of complex adaptive systems and the factors that alter this dynamics are to be found in the complex responsive processes of human relating, that is in patterns of conversation.

You can see this when you reflect upon how changes in patterns of conversation sometimes arise spontaneously and at other times get caught in patterns of repetition where change is blocked. Repetitive patterns of conversation that block change are the analogue of equilibrium attractors in complex adaptive system. Free-flowing, flexible conversation that spontaneously shifts to new patterns (*Shaw, 1998*) is the analogue of the complex attractors at the edge of chaos. Highly emotional miscommunication would be the conversational analogue of the dynamics of disintegration. Organisational health has to do with the capacity to change, to produce new forms, and this depends crucially on free-flowing, flexible conversation, that is conversation displaying the dynamics of bounded instability. Organisational illness, on the other hand, is an inability to change that occurs when conversational life follows stable attractors in which themes are simply repeated with only superficial change.

Consider now the analogues for those factors that determine whether the dynamics is that of stable equilibrium, bounded instability or disintegration. The first two are the rate at which information flows through the system and the number of connections between agents. The human analogues of information flow and connectivity in complex adaptive systems are the number and quality of the connections between themes that organise the experience of relating. In other words, the richness of the themes organising the experience of relating have an impact on the dynamics of conversation. When relationships between people are organised by a small number of loosely connected themes, conversational patterns become repetitive, the dynamics of stable equilibrium. For example, neighbours may see each other regularly as they come in and out of their homes but the themes organising their relating may be few in number and they may not trigger many associations with other themes. They may organise the conversation around how the others are, what they feel about the weather and sometimes a report about some local matter, such as planning permission for some building alteration. These conversations are repetitive and predictable. They lack any spontaneous and free-flowing qualities.

Relationships between colleagues in work situations, on the other hand, may be organised by a large number of themes triggering many associations with other themes. The complex interaction of these themes is likely to produce conversations of a free-flowing nature. When conversation is organised by very many themes triggering very many associations with others, communication is likely to become highly disorganised. The conversational equivalent of bounded instability at the edge of chaos is thus likely to occur in some critical range of richness in organising themes. If the themes are too impoverished then the dynamics is stable and if they are too rich then the dynamics is disintegrative.

### Diversity

The third determinant of the dynamics in a complex adaptive system is the diversity in agents and their interaction. The analogue in human relating is the diversity in organising themes. As discussed above, that diversity arises in misunderstanding and in the cross-fertilisation of concepts through interaction between different patterns of conversation. Again, the dynamics of free-flowing conversation is associated with critical levels of misunderstanding and cross-fertilisation. If there is little misunderstanding between people forming a group with well-established concepts and ways of talking to each other, their conversations are likely to be repetitive. If there is too much misunderstanding between people drawn from very many disparate groups then there is the disintegration of communication, a 'tower of Babel'. The conditions for creative, free-flowing conversations lie in some critical range between these extremes. This is where the tension between legitimate and shadow themes becomes important in that this tension expresses the relationship between orthodoxy and deviance. It is this deviance that imparts the internal capacity to evolve spontaneously new patterns of conversation, that is new conversational attractors.

There are some additional factors affecting the dynamics of human relating that are not evident in simulations. Human relationships are relationships between bodies and the medium of relating is symbols that are always felt in bodies. It is essential then, in understanding the dynamics of relating, that is of conversing, to understand the impact of bodily interactions. I suggest that the most important additional aspects to incorporate in thinking about complex responsive processes of relating are the nature and impact of anxiety and the emotional responses to power relations.

### Anxiety

Anxiety is a generalised form of fear. While fear has a known cause, anxiety is a very unpleasant feeling of general unease, the cause of which cannot be located. Chapter 10 on psychoanalytic perspectives reviewed the important contribution that psychoanalytic perspectives make to an understanding of the organisational effects of anxiety. First, there are the defences people use to avoid feeling anxious. These may take the form of structures and procedures having the ostensible purpose of enabling some rational task, but actually operating as defences. For example, people may prepare forecasts of future states that are impossible to predict and develop strategic plans on the basis of these forecasts. Such plans may then have little impact on what is actually done but by creating a sense of certainty defend people against the anxiety of feeling uncertain. The result is stable, repetitive conversational dynamics around strategies that are simply a continuation of what is already being done. An alternative form of defence is what *Bion (1961)* called basic assumption behaviour. Here people in groups are overwhelmed by volatile fight, flight, dependency and other dynamics that disable their thinking capacity. Conversations are organised by fantasy themes that produce highly unrealistic conversational stability or conversational disintegration. The former are present when the basic assumption is dependency and the latter when it takes the form of fight–flight.

Chapter 12 also introduced the important psychoanalytic concept of 'good enough holding'. Here conditions are such that people are able to hold the simultaneous excitement and anxiety of conversations that test the boundary of what they know. The 'good enough holding' of anxiety is an essential condition for the free-flowing conversational dynamics that is the analogue of the edge of chaos. I suggest that 'good enough holding' is a quality of the themes organising the experience of relating. When these take the form of trusting interaction, they are themselves then forms of 'good enough holding'. In other words, when the quality of relating is characterised by trust, conversation can take free-flowing forms. This interpretation of 'good enough holding' differs from the psychoanalytic interpretation in that it does not locate the 'good enough' in a leader or a consultant (*Stapley, 1996*) but in the quality of conversational interaction itself.

Closely related to the 'good enough holding' of anxiety there is the matter of the quality of power relations. Themes organising relating between people may be highly constraining so that power relations have the qualities of force, authoritarianism, dictatorship, and so forth. The responses that these qualities evoke are either submission or rebellion. The former produce highly repetitive, stable conversational patterns, while the latter produces disintegration in communication. Sometimes, the themes organising the relating between people impose very little constraint. This is equivalent to saying that relational ties are very weak and, therefore, patterns of conversation are likely to be disrupted. The conversational dynamics is disintegrative. Again, it is a critical range that is associated with free-flowing conversation, this time a critical range in the constraining qualities of relating. This is a quality of the themes that organise relating.

### Free-flowing conversation

The crucial distinction I am making here is that between free-flowing conversation and patterns of conversation that take on a repetitive, stuck form. This is crucial, because it is only in the former that potential creativity, that is emergent new patterns of conversation, lie. A healthy, functioning organisation is one that continually responds; that is, provokes and evokes responses from other organisations and reacts to the provocations and evocations of other organisations so as to survive and prosper. For this to happen, communication must flow freely and not get caught in repetitive themes. This means that the themes organising experience must interact so as to flow continually along new pathways and this will happen only if new shadow themes emerge to become legitimate. An ailing organisation is one in which communication is blocked.

This is essentially the same as *Foulkes' (1948)* view of mental ill health. He defined health as the free flow of communication between people in a group. For him illness was a state in which communication was blocked and he argued that this blockage gets located in an individual or group of individuals. That individual or group is then said to be ill but it is really the whole pattern of relationships that is ill, the illness merely being located in particular people or groups. The 'cure' is to attend to the blockage and free it.

In organisational terms, I suggest that the quality of free-flowing conversation is closely associated with the interplay between legitimate and shadow themes organising conversational life. Conversations arise in the organisational shadow as a response to the inhibition that legitimate power relations, and the official and unofficial ideologies that support them, impose on talking. They take place, often in fleeting snatches, in small groups of people, usually as they are going about other, legitimate business. They occur in corridors, on aircraft, in cars, in someone's office, in the bar, over dinner, around the photocopier, and so on. Their key feature, however, is that they are expressions, and explorations, of deviations, eccentricities and other matters that do not fit with what is legitimate. In such conversations, people question the wisdom of decisions made, they complain, they suggest other possibilities, they talk about highly personal differences and difficulties, they spread gossip and rumour, they express cynicism, they fill gaps in their knowledge with fantasies, they tell jokes, they express their feelings of anger and frustration, enthusiasm and excitement, hatred and affection, pride and disappointment, trust and mistrust. Conversations in the shadow provide a means to vent emotion and to test the boundaries of what is acceptable. They deal with the unexpected and the ambiguous. They are a form of play.

The kinds of conversation I am describing are, from an orthodox management point of view, an unproductive waste of time at best, and normally even worse than this, a destructive deviation from consensus and the capacity for joint action. What purpose do they serve from the more radical perspective I am suggesting? Ordinary conversations are complex responsive processes evoking and provoking responses in a continuing back and forth rhythm. Each response is made on the basis of local organising principles in the absence of any overall blueprint. Complexity theory suggests that it is just this kind of interaction that has the potential, in certain conditions, for producing emergent new forms.

I suggest, then, that an organisation's potential for creativity lies in these shadow conversations and their tension with the legitimate. Complexity theory also suggests that the dynamics of creativity is also that of destruction. So, conversations in the shadow are potentially both creative and destructive. The key condition of the kind of free-flowing ordinary conversations to have the potential for creativity, and destruction, is that of trust. When people who trust each other engage in shadow conversation they feel able to test boundaries, particularly those of current power relations, talk about what is possible and what is not, and how the impossible might be rendered possible.

The kinds of conversation arising in the shadow are therefore crucial to an organisation's capacity to produce novel strategic directions. When shadow conversations collusively support the legitimate then the organisation cannot change. The potential for change lies in the extent to which shadow conversation undermines current power relations and legitimate forms of talk.

The capacity for emergent new ways of talking is fundamental to organisational creativity. If this is so, then it is a matter of considerable strategic importance to pay attention to the dynamics of ordinary conversation, particularly those in the shadow. The purpose of this attention is not to control the conversation or somehow produce efficient forms of it, but to understand it and particularly to understand what blocks it. So what are its chief characteristics?

Conversation in the shadow is always informal and it is organised by complex and subtle principles. It is a self-organising, rhythmical process of vocal gestures and response. This turn taking is organised by implicit principles relating to who may speak next, who may interrupt who, and so on. Although a response to the inhibition opposed to the official ideology, it too is organised by power relations expressed in ideology, this time deviant, or even subversive, ideologies covering up deviant power relations. The content of these conversations is organised by narrative themes, rather than propositional ones.

The conversational life of an organisation displays stable attractors when people repeat the same kinds of shadow conversation over and over again in ways that never emerge as shifts in legitimate conversations; for example, repetitive complaints about poor management and lack of direction; or repetitive complaints about poor-quality staff who do not do as they are told. Unstable attractors occur when people engage in highly destructive attacks on others, undermining their credibility and tearing their reputations apart. New attractors may emerge at the edge of chaos in free-flowing conversations that begin to appear in legitimate form. The conditions for this to happen are trust and the holding of anxiety, power relations that are both cooperative and competitive, and conversational practices that do not block exploration.

What conversational practices block the kind of flexible, exploratory conversations characteristic of the dynamics of the edge of chaos? What practices trap groups of people in highly repetitive conversations? Some of the answers to these questions are provided by paying attention to the rhetorical ploys that people employ in their conversations.

All ordinary conversations employ some kind of rhetorical ploy. In such conversations, people are giving accounts of themselves to others, explaining to each other why they feel as they do and why they want to do what they want to do. Rhetoric is the conversational art of giving such accounts persuasively. They are conversational organising principles.

### Rhetoric

*Springett (1998)* categorises rhetorical ploys as follows. Amongst the many he identifies, there are moves that:

- influence the path of conversation. Under this heading, he includes statements that invoke a sense of purpose, as when someone says, 'these are *the* objectives'. Then there are silencing moves such as not responding to a point made but rapidly raising another. There are also moves that bound the path, such as 'this is really Stone Age stuff'. Some moves contract the line of conversation, such as 'let's concentrate on the key points'. Other moves expand the line of conversation, such as 'there must be other ways to think about this'. Yet other moves give emphasis, such as 'this is the way we must go'.

- provide frames of reference. This takes place when someone uses other companies as examples of the successful application of their ideas.
- make claims to be the truth, such as 'the latest research shows', or 'customers feel'.
- destabilise, such as 'Does that really add anything?'
- influence beliefs about what is real and possible. Examples are making the intangible seem tangible, such as talking about a merger as a 'marriage', referring to a company as if it were a person, and using statements like 'let me walk you through this'. Another example is a move that implies pre-existence, such as talking about unlocking a company's potential.
- construct urgency, such as 'there is a short time window'.

The point is this: without even being aware of it, people in ordinary conversation may be using conversational devices to dismiss the opinions of others and close down the development of a conversation in an exploratory direction. If this way of talking to each other is widespread in an organisation, it will inevitably keep reproducing the same patterns of talk. The use of some rhetorical device is therefore one of the most important blockages to free-flowing, flexible conversation and thus the emergence of new knowledge. Other usages of rhetorical devices could have the effect of freeing these blockages.

I want to draw attention to one further analogy between complex adaptive systems and human complex responsive processes. The dynamics of the edge of chaos in relation to complex adaptive systems is characterised by a power law (see Chapter 12). This means that there are a large number of small extinction events and a small number of large extinction events during some time period. In other words, a system at the edge of chaos has the potential for emergent new forms but there is no guarantee of survival for these new forms. Some will survive and others will not because of competitive selection. The same point applies to complex responsive processes. The dynamics of bounded instability displayed in free-flowing conversation in organisations creates the potential for the emergence of new forms of conversation, power relations and thus activities. However, the pattern of conversation and activity that emerges will be subjected to selection in competition with other patterns emerging in other organisations. Some will succeed and others will not. There is no general recipe for success. While stability guarantees ultimate extinction, bounded instability creates the potential, but not a guarantee, of survival. Notice how frequently I have used the word 'quality' in talking about the conditions in which an organisation displays the internal capacity to change spontaneously.

*Figure 16.2* summarises the key points that this chapter has made about the dynamics of complex responsive processes. You might like to compare this with similar figures relating to other theories of organisation in previous chapters (*Figures 2.5, 2.6, 6.5, 8.11, 10.5*).

> - Organisations are complex responsive processes of relating between people. Since relating immediately constrains, it immediately establishes power relations between people. Complex responsive processes take the form of propositional and narrative themes that organise the experience of relating and thus power relations. The themes organise the conversational life of an organisation.
> - These themes take many forms. Of great importance are the official ideological themes that determine what it is legitimate to talk about in an organisation. Of even greater importance are the unofficial ideological themes that make current power relations feel natural and the unofficial themes that organise the subversion of current power relations. In other words, unofficial ideologies may be supporting or subverting official ideologies. This dynamic is an aspect of the organisational shadow.
> - Themes organise patterns of conversation and power relations. These patterns are the analogues of attractors in complex adaptive systems.
> - Conversational attractors may take stable forms of repetitive patterns of conversation in which people are stuck. They may also take the form of strange attractors, that is more free-flowing patterns. This is the dynamics of bounded instability.
> - Change occurs in novel ways through the presence of sufficient diversity in organising themes. This is expressed in free-flowing conversation in which shadow themes test the boundaries of the legitimate.
> - The evolution of free-flowing conversation and the emergence of creative new directions are radically unpredictable.
> - Free-flowing conversation becomes possible when the pattern of relating has the quality of good enough holding of anxiety.
> - It is qualities of relationship that determine whether an organisation has the internal capacity for creativity.
> - There is no guarantee of success.

**FIGURE 16.2**   Complex responsive processes: main points on organisational dynamics

## 16.5    SUMMARY

One of the important insights contributed by the theories of dissipative structures and complex adaptive systems, reviewed in Chapters 11 and 12, relates to the importance of diversity. A system only has the internal capacity to move spontaneously from one attractor to another, and to evolve new attractors, when it operates in the presence of diversity. In other words, a system can produce novel, creative behaviour only when it has the internal capacity to generate and respond to variety. Variety arises through processes such as cross-over replication, random mutation, internal and external fluctuations or 'noise', or heterogeneity in the entities comprising a system. In terms of human organisations this means that organisations can only evolve new strategic directions, change in creative ways, produce innovations if they have the internal capacity, that is enough diversity, to generate and respond to variety.

This internal capacity to sustain diversity and generate variety has to do with the nature of the complex responsive processes that are an organisation. Organisational change is change in the themes organising the experience of being together in an organisation. Novel change takes place when these themes self-organise to produce emergent changes in themselves. In other words, organisations change in novel ways when new patterns of conversation and the power relations embedded in them emerge. The required diversity and variety, and the emergent change conditional on their presence, can be understood by making a conceptual distinction between two inextricably intertwined forms of organising theme. The distinction is that between themes that are felt to be legitimate and those that I describe as shadow themes. Creative change arises in the tension between shadow and legitimate themes that organise the experience of relating.

The next chapter will explore the implications of taking the approach I am suggesting.

## REFERENCES

Allen, P. M. (1998a), Evolving complexity in social science, in Altman, G. & Koch, W. A. (Eds.) (1998), *Systems: New Paradigms for the Human Sciences*, New York: Walter de Gruyter.

Allen, P. M. (1998b), Modelling complex economic evolution, in Schweitzer, F. & Silverberg, G. (Eds.) (1998), *Selbstorganisation*, Berlin: Dunker and Humblot.

Argyris, C. (1990), *Overcoming Organizational Defenses: Facilitating Organizational Learning*, Needham Heights, MA: Allyn & Bacon.

Bhaktin, M. M. (1986), *Speech Genres and other late Essays*, Austin, TX: University of Texas Press.

Bion, W. (1961), *Experiences in Groups and Other Papers*, London: Tavistock.

Elias, N. (1989), *The Symbol Theory*, London: Sage.

Fonseca, J. M. L. (1998), Innovation: a property of complex adaptive social systems, Unpublished thesis, University of Hertfordshire.

Foulkes, S. H. (1948), *Introduction to Group Analytic Psychotherapy*, London: William Heinemann Medical Books.

Shaw, P. (1998), An exploration of the role of organisation development intervention in fostering emergence and self-organisation, Unpublished thesis, University of Hertfordshire.

Shotter, J. (1993), *Conversational Realities: Constructing Life through Language*, Thousand Oaks, CA: Sage.

Springett, N. (1998), Producing strategy in the 1990s: the rhetorical dynamics of strategic conversation, Complexity and Management Centre Working Paper no. X, University of Hertfordshire.

Stapley, L. F. (1996), *The Personality of the Organisation: A Psycho-dynamic Explanation of Culture and Change*, London: Free Association Books.

Streatfield, P. J. (1998), *Informal self-organising transformation of manufacturing organisation: a management practitioner's perspective*, Unpublished thesis, University of Hertfordshire.

Winnicott, D. W. (1965), *The Maturational Processes and the Facilitating Environment*, London: Hogarth Press.

# 17 The implications of understanding organisations as complex responsive processes

## 17.1 INTRODUCTION

In Chapter 1, I suggested that this book would be dealing with the following questions. How do populations of organisations, and the individual members of those populations, change and evolve over time? How do these populations and their members come to be what they are and how will they come to be whatever they come to be? How can one make sense of the observation that new organisations are continually forming while many small and a few large ones disappear or merge into others? In other words, how does one explain the dynamics of populations of organisations and their members? What does strategy, strategic direction and strategic thinking mean? How does a strategy come into being and how is it manifested? I also suggested that the way one answers these questions depends upon the frame of reference from which one approaches them and I reviewed a number of different frames of reference.

In this chapter, I want to explore how a theory of organisation as complex responsive processes deals with questions like these and in so doing compare this theory with the others reviewed in this book.

## 17.2 HOW THE THEORY OF COMPLEX RESPONSIVE PROCESSES ANSWERS FOUR KEY QUESTIONS

Four important questions were posed in Chapter 1 and used to reveal important features of a number of theories of organisation. These questions relate to:

1  How the theory in question understands the nature of interaction.
2  What views the theory takes on human nature.

3   The methodological position that the theory adopts.
4   The manner in which it deals with paradox.

This section will examine how a complex responsive process theory of organisation deals with these questions and how this differs from other theories.

## The nature of human interaction

Strategic choice theory is built on a systemic notion of interaction in which organisations adapt to their environments in a self-regulating, negative feedback (cybernetic) manner so as to achieve their goals. The dynamics, or pattern of movement over time, is that of attraction to states of stable equilibrium. Prediction is not seen as problematic. The analysis is primarily at the macro level of the organisation in which cause and effect are related to each other in a linear manner. Microdiversity receives no attention and interaction is assumed to be uniform and harmonious.

Learning organisation theory also adopts a systemic perspective on human interaction, but one that takes account of positive as well as negative feedback. From the systems dynamics perspective the dynamics is that of non-equilibrium in which unexpected outcomes appear. However, this theory holds that when managers understand the positive and negative feedback structure of the whole system they will be able to identify leverage points through which they can control it. This theory does not explore the implications of radical unpredictability. Here too, the analysis is at the macro level of the organisation but this time connections between cause and effect take nonlinear forms in which the connections might be distant over time and space. Again, little attention is paid to microdiversity and successful interaction is still assumed to be harmonious, although this theory does recognise obstacles to the achievement of such harmony.

The third theory reviewed also takes a systemic perspective on interaction, this time open systems theory, which focuses on regulation at permeable boundaries between system and environment and between subsystems of the system. The dynamics of human open systems is somewhat turbulent and the importation of primitive human behaviour disrupts organisational learning. This possibility requires careful management of boundaries and radical unpredictability does not feature as an important characteristic. This theory sees the purpose of management as intervention aimed at enabling equilibrium adaptation to the organisation's environment. The analysis here is at a far more micro level than is the case with strategic choice and the learning organisation, taking account of the behaviour of members of an organisation, particularly the unconscious causes of that behaviour. Microdiversity is recognised and success is a state of adaptation to reality.

A number of writers are now moving to a systemic perspective on human action drawn from chaos and complexity theory. Attention is drawn to the dynamics of the edge of chaos and the self-organising, emergent properties of the system. Attention is also drawn to the possibility of unpredictability, but this is not seen as essential and requiring further exploration. The analysis tends to be at the macro level of the organisation as a whole and microdiversity is not focused upon.

The theoretical perspective I have been suggesting in Chapters 14 to 16 avoids descriptions of organisations in system terms. As soon as an organisation is described as a system or a network, the tendency is to talk about it as if it were a thing. To avoid this I have talked about organisations as processes. I have taken complex responsive processes of relating as the human analogue of complex adaptive systems. These complex responsive processes are fundamentally conversational in nature, forming and being formed by power relations. The analysis focuses at a micro level and concentrates on the dynamics of bounded instability in which self-organisation might produce emergent novel forms in relating and conversation. This perspective emphasises the importance of diversity and deviance as essential to the internal capacity to change spontaneously. In this unfolding, potentially creative process, unpredictability is central, inviting further exploration of how people act into the unknown.

The comparison that I have made above between organisational theories suggests a move from one theory of interaction to another so that uncertainty and unpredictability, and their relationship with diversity and creativity, are increasingly taken into account.

## Human psychology

Strategic choice theory takes a cognitivist view of human nature. Here mind is understood to be a property of the individual brain. The brain/mind processes symbolic information, forming representations and models of a pre-given reality. Humans then act on the basis of their mental models. The individual is primary in that knowing and behaving do not depend fundamentally on relationships between individuals. Knowing and behaving, including relating to others, are characteristics of individual brains. Individuals form groups and being part of a group may then affect individual behaviour. This theory places great emphasis on the importance of the intentions formed and expressed by individuals. Emotion is seen as a dangerous disruption of rational choice capacity and power is understood mainly in terms of official authority. Creativity is an attribute of an individual.

Learning organisation theory employs the same theory of human nature. However, it also combines this with notions from humanistic psychology in which the central motivation for behaviour is the urge individuals have to actualise themselves, finding their true selves as it were. Again, individuals form groups and these groups may affect their behaviour. Leadership is a competence possessed by individuals and intention is a characteristic of individuals. Emotions of a positive kind are emphasised. Power as an attribute of charismatic individuals comes to the fore. Creativity is in the end seen as an attribute of an individual, although a role is also ascribed to cohesive teamwork.

Psychoanalytic perspectives on organisations combine open systems theory with a view of human nature derived from psychoanalysis. The fundamental motivation for human behaviour here is the mental ideas of inherited animal instincts called the drives. Aggressive and libidinal drives blindly seek satisfaction but encounter social prohibition. Individual mental processes are structured by this encounter with the social. Individuals form groups but much greater account is taken of the impact group processes have on individual behaviour, particularly those that are unconscious. The theory focuses on how regression to primitive behaviour can destroy rational thinking and learning. An important insight into the nature of the relationship between individual and group is that about leadership. Individuals may be sucked into leadership positions by unconscious dynamics of the group. Leadership is no longer simply a competence of the individual. Emotion and power play a much more important role in understanding the development of an organisation than they do in the theories of strategic choice and the learning organisation. The impact of emotions of a negative kind and of individual and group fantasy life is taken into account, as are the negative aspects of power. Creativity is an individual attribute arising in the ability to hold anxiety and engage in play.

The writers reviewed in Chapter 13 import a theory of interaction drawn from chaos and complexity theory into their theory of organisations. They combine this with the same cognitivist and humanistic views of human nature as those found in strategic choice and learning organisation theory. The individual, therefore, remains central, and as a result these writers do not go further, in my view, than learning organisation theory. More attention may be paid to the positive aspects of instability but the same views on control are retained. Creativity is an attribute of an individual.

A complex responsive process theory of organisations makes a radical departure when it comes to forming a view on human nature. The fundamental proposition is that individuals and groups form and are formed by each other simultaneously (*Griffin, 1998*). Individual minds are not seen purely as a process of brain computation, nor are they seen as motivated by primitive drives formed into mind by the clash with the social. Instead, mind is the singular of relating while the group is the plural of relating. The fundamental motivator of human behaviour is the urge to relate. From this perspective, there can be no human individual outside of relationship. Mind is a silent, private conversation structured by, and always resonating and changing with, vocal, public conversations in groups. This theory radically decentres, while not losing sight of, the individual. Power relations and the ideologies supporting them, emotions and fantasies are all central to this theoretical perspective. Since this view of human nature is basically one of human interaction, the theory of interaction and that of human nature are not combined because they turn out to be the same. Intention is no longer an attribute of an individual. Instead, it emerges in conversational relationship to be articulated by an individual. Leadership is no longer simply an individual competence but a form of relationship. Creativity arises in patterns of relationship in which there is sufficient deviance and subversion.

When the individual is treated as primary, the immediate tendency is to equate agents in complex systems with individual human beings. The notion of self-organisation is applied to them and the result is a concept that does not differ from orthodox notions of delegation and empowerment. From the complex responsive process perspective, the analogue of agents is themes that organise experience. What is organising itself is then these themes and a radical notion of self-organisation and emergent unpredictability is retained.

## Methodological position

The methodological position adopted by strategic choice and learning organisation theorists is that of the objective observer who stands outside the organisational system and observes it as a pre-given reality. The purpose is to manipulate and control the system. This is part of cognitivist thinking. When the writers reviewed in Chapter 13 take chaos and complexity theory into theorising about organisations, they adopt the same methodological position. The manager is implicitly ascribed the same role and prescriptions are made as to how the manager may control, direct, or at least disturb or perturb the system.

Those adopting psychoanalytic perspectives move some way from this position in that they adopt methodologies analogous to the clinical. They advocate action research in which the researcher participates with members of an organisation and uses his or her feelings as information. However, some notion of objective observation is retained. The researcher, and the manager, take a position at the boundary of the system in order to avoid being sucked into unconscious group processes (*Stapley, 1996*).

The theory of complex responsive processes makes a further move from the position of the objective observer to methodologies of participative enquiry (*Reason, 1988*). Researchers understand themselves to be participants in processes of inquiry into the nature of the complex responsive processes of relating. This is a reflexive methodology (*Steier, 1991*) in which organisations are understood to be social constructions (*Gergen, 1982*). This has implications for how the role of the manager is understood. Neither researcher nor manager can step outside the conversational processes that are the organisation simply because their work requires them to talk to others. What they say affects what they hear and what they hear affects what they say. From this perspective, then, a manager cannot stand outside organisational processes and control them, direct them or even perturb them in an intentional direction. All such intentions are gestures made to others in an organisation and what happens unfolds from the ongoing responses.

This participative nature of management leads to a completely different understanding of what the dynamics of bounded instability is. The writers reviewed in Chapter 13 tend to equate the dynamics of the edge of chaos with crises. They tend to see the manager as one who stands outside the system and pushes, or nudges, it into instability, disturbance and crisis. One prescription is to place people under more stress so that they will be motivated to change and so unleash the power of self-organisation. The notion of the edge of chaos derived from a complex responsive process perspective is completely different. The analogue of this dynamic is free-flowing conversation. People can only engage in this when the pattern of their relationships provides good enough holding of the anxiety of facing the unknown. Crisis and stress are not relational qualities that contain anxiety, rather they increase it. The edge of chaos, from the perspective I am suggesting, is safe enough, exciting enough patterns of relationships, not terrifyingly stressful ones.

## Paradox

Paradox is not central to the theories of strategic choice, learning organisations or the importation of chaos and complexity theory into organisational thinking through a cognitivist frame of reference. Contradiction, tension and dilemmas are recognised but they are seen as resolvable. It is indeed the purpose of management, according to these theories, to resolve them.

Paradox plays a much more important role in psychoanalytic theories and is seen as fundamental to human life. The theory of complex responsive processes places even more emphasis on paradox in that the individual and the group are paradoxically formed by and forming each other at the same time. Particularly important is the emphasis placed on the paradox of predictability and unpredictability at the same time. Paradox, of course, cannot be resolved or harmonised, only endlessly rearranged.

Consider now how complex responsive process theory answers the questions posed at the start of this chapter. The answers I supply are simply indications that you might want to fill out and compare with answers to the same questions given from the other theoretical perspectives in this book.

- How do new organisations come into being? The intention to form a new organisation emerges as a theme in the conversations those forming it have with each other and with other people with whom they are in relationship.
- Why do they cease to exist? The pattern of relationship, the pattern of conversation, which shapes the actions of members does not survive in competition with other patterns.
- How do they come to merge with others or split apart? Again, intentions to do so emerge in conversation.
- Why do most organisations last for only a short time and why do a few survive for long periods? Because evolving populations of organisations are characterised by the dynamics of the edge of chaos. A property of this dynamics is the power law according to which large numbers of small extinctions and small numbers of large extinctions will occur. Creativity and destruction are intrinsic to the dynamics.
- Why is one organisation similar to others and different from yet others? An organisation is only closely similar to another if it copies that other and sustains itself in the dynamics of stability. All evolving organisations will be uniquely different because small events in their history can escalate into significant differences. Experience is unique and cannot be repeated in exactly the same way.
- How do some organisations develop new activities? Again, intentions to do so emerge in free-flowing conversation.
- Why do other organisations simply carry on with the same activities? Because they get stuck in repetitive conversations.
- Why do people become anxious, bored or frustrated? People become bored, frustrated and depressed when they are together caught in repetitive conversations. They become anxious when they confront uncertainty, not knowing and not being in control. They can, however, hold these feelings together with those of excitement if there is good enough holding of anxiety.
- What is it that excites and fulfils them? Participating in relationships and conversations that are both safe and exciting enough to enable them to develop new insights.
- What impact do these and other emotions have on the functioning of groups and organisations? They are all part of the complex evolution of relationships and conversation and when they take the form of deviant shadow organising themes they create the potential, but not the guarantee, of the emergence of new forms.

To summarise, I have explored a number of different frames of reference. In order to structure this exploration I defined these frames of reference mainly according to the perspective they took on two matters. First, I pointed to the underlying perspective taken on the systemic nature of populations of organisations and their members. This is essentially a theory about how organisations, and the entities of which they consist, interact with each other. Second, I drew attention to the assumptions that are made about the nature of human beings, matters of a sociological and psychological nature. I argued that different combinations of systems, psychological and sociological theories yielded different ways of making sense of life in organisations. These different ways focus the attention of researchers and practitioners on different aspects of life in organisations and in so doing provide very different answers to the questions posed above.

The first combination reviewed was that of cybernetic systems theory and cognitivist psychology, sometimes with some views from humanistic psychology. In other words, psychological theories assuming the primacy of the autonomous individual are combined with a theory of interaction between them that takes place in a system designed to move to stability in a self-regulating manner. This yields the theory of strategic choice. That theory focuses the attention of practitioners and researchers on strategy as a set of actions chosen by the most powerful individuals in an organisation that is then carried out by other members of that organisation. Organisations change through a process of pursuing a path chosen by the most powerful. The path may be chosen by engaging in a process of rational analysis, through risk-taking experimentation, or political processes. Attention is focused on how members of an organisation are to be motivated to follow the path.

The second combination involves a change of systems perspective from cybernetics to systems dynamics without any change in the psychological and sociological theories. The result is the theory of the learning organisation. This theory focuses attention on much the same factors as strategic choice theory does but, in addition, it directs the attention of practitioners and researchers to the following matters. These are the uncertainty created by the nature of the system and the need to understand the whole through a process of systems thinking. The purpose of this is to identify leverage points so that the effectiveness of control can be increased. Attention is also focused on the relationship of explicit and implicit knowledge and the process of knowledge creation. Organisations evolve, strategies are formed and implemented, through a process of learning.

Then there is the combination of open systems theory with psychoanalytic perspectives on the nature of human existence. The key difference between this combination and the others lies in the different perspective on human psychology. However, mainstream psychoanalytic theory retains the assumption of the primacy of the individual, and to some extent, the position of the objective observer. This theory of organisations focuses the attention of practitioners and researchers on the irrational and the neurotic as obstacles to rational decision making and effective task performance. It points to ways in which learning is destroyed and strategic choice incapacitated. However, I argued that because it retains the assumption about the autonomous individual it does not take a radical step away from the theories of strategic choice and the learning organisation.

Another variation was explored in Chapter 13. Here a complex adaptive systems approach was taken to explain the nature of interaction and combined with cognitivist and humanistic psychologies. The result was a focus on much the same factors as learning organisation theory. Again, the retention of the assumption of the autonomous individual produces what I call an orthodox perspective.

Finally, in Chapters 14 to 16, I outlined how a theory of human interaction analogous to complex adaptive systems coincides with relationship psychology. I suggest that this makes a move towards a radical understanding of organisational evolution. It is radical in that it abandons the assumption of the autonomous individual and the position of the objective observer. It replaces these assumptions with those of the simultaneous social construction of group and individual and the position of participative enquiry. Another move is away from thinking of oneself as manager in terms of the objective designer, towards thinking of oneself as an active participant in complex processes. In the next section of this chapter, I want to explore how this theoretical shift focuses the attention of practitioners and researchers on factors that are, in some respects, very different to the other theories. This in turn has implications for how management and leadership competences are defined and what strategic management means.

*Figure 17.1* sets out how orthodox and radical approaches to organisational theory use different analogues of complex systems.

**FIGURE 17.1**   Human analogues of simulations of complex systems

| Computer simulations | Orthodox analogue | Radical analogue |
|---|---|---|
| The programmer | CEO | None |
| The whole is a complex adaptive system | The whole is a complex adaptive system | The whole is complex responsive processes |
| Consisting of electric pulses/digital symbols | Consisting of electrochemical pulses/representations | Consisting of body symbols in the medium, rhythm, sound, etc. |
| Arranged as algorithmic rules called agents | Arranged as schemas and mental models as basis of individual as agent | Arranged as narrative and propositional themes that organise experience, i.e. agency in individual and group |
| Reproduced through replication with random mutation and cross-over replication | Reproduced through individual choice to change mental model | Reproduced through replication with misunderstanding and cross-fertilisation, i.e. deviance |
| What organises itself is arrangements in the digital code and the pattern of the whole attractor at the same time | What organises itself is individual humans | What organises itself is the arrangements of symbols and themes in conversations that are individual mind and group at the same time |

| What emerges is rearrangement in code/attractor | What emerges is detail of action | What emerges is rearrangements of conversational themes |
|---|---|---|
| Novelty emerges at the edge of chaos, i.e. paradox of stability and instability | Edge of chaos defined as crisis and stress | Edge of chaos defined as good enough holding of anxiety of not knowing |
| Radical unpredictability | Unpredictability played down | Radical unpredictability |
| Boundaries set by programmer | Boundaries set by CEO, i.e. simple rules | Boundaries set by internal dynamics of relationship |

## 17.3    REFOCUSING ATTENTION: STRATEGY AND CHANGE

In the title of this chapter, I have intentionally used the word 'implications' rather than 'applications' or 'prescriptions'. Strategic choice and learning organisation theories both firmly take the methodological position of the objective observer where the manager stands outside the organisational system and controls it. These theories, therefore, immediately have an application to do with the intentional control of the system by the observing manager. It is then a natural step to formulate general prescriptions for the application of control. The prescriptions take the form of tools and techniques of analysis and control. Furthermore, some test of the validity of the tools and techniques is required. This is provided by pointing to how organisations that use particular tools and techniques, or have particular attributes, are successful while those that do not use, or possess, them fail.

It seems to me that psychoanalytic perspectives on organisations hold the position of the objective observer much less firmly. The concern with application then becomes less central and the focus shifts more to understanding what is happening in an organisation. Rather than straightforward prescriptions, those working from a psychoanalytic perspective provide hypotheses for joint discussion with members of an organisation in specific, rather than general, cases.

A theory of organisations as complex responsive processes of relating makes a firm methodological move away from the notion of the manager as objective observer. Managers are understood to be participants in complex responsive processes, engaged in participative enquiry into what they are doing and what steps they should take next. They may also be participatively enquiring into the nature of their own complex responsive processes of relating. This is what it means to be reflexive. This theory provides an explanation of what managers are doing, rather than on what they should be doing. Application has little meaning in this endeavour. If you are trying to explain what managers are doing now, you can hardly use this as a prescription. They are already doing it. The whole purpose of the theoretical shift I have been suggesting is to focus attention on processes that managers are held to be engaging in, but which the other theories do not focus upon. The purpose is not to apply or prescribe but to refocus attention. When people focus their attention differently, they are highly likely to take different kinds of actions. However, a theory that focuses attention on self-organising processes and emergent outcomes can hardly yield general prescriptions on how that self-organisation should proceed and what should emerge from it. The theory would be proposing to do the opposite of what it is explaining. The theory invites recognition of the uniqueness and non-repeatability of experience.

If you focus your attention according to strategic choice and learning organisation theories, the lack of application and prescription implied by complex responsive processes theory is highly unsatisfactory. The tendency is to dismiss it as useless for this reason. However, if you take the perspective of the theory itself, rather than trying to make it fit into some other theory, you might come to value what it does, namely refocuses attention. I have found that even if managers accept this, they immediately ask for examples of where people have refocused attention in the way suggested and whether they were then successful. Again, this is approaching the theory of complex responsive processes from the frame of reference of the other theories. One of the main properties of the dynamics of bounded instability is the escalation of small changes into qualitatively different patterns. Patterns of bounded instability may be similar to each other but they are never repeated in the same way. They are unique and not repeatable at important levels of detail. Organisations characterised by the dynamics of bounded instability will therefore all be unique in some important way. The experience of one cannot be repeated, at important levels of detail, by another. Giving examples of success in one organisation to managers in another is likely to be spurious. Perhaps this is why the track record of identifying attributes of successful organisation is so poor. Instead of looking for understanding in other people's experience one might look for it in one's own experience.

Consistent with the nature of the theory I am talking about in this chapter, therefore, I will not be providing applications or prescriptions. What I will be trying to point to is how the theory shifts the focus of attention. First, consider how attention is focused on the quality of participation.

## Focusing attention on the quality of participation

Whenever I talk to managers about the radical complexity perspective I am suggesting here, they immediately ask what it says that 'you' need to do to bring about the success of an organisation. When I ask who this 'you' is, they usually say that they mean the top executives of an organisation. The main issue here is whether the top executives of an organisation are thought of as standing outside the organisational system and operating on it, or as participating with other members in its evolution.

Strategic choice theory holds that the top executives can form organisation-wide intentions for an organisation's future evolution. It also holds that if they then appropriately motivate other members of their organisation, those members will move according to the intention of top executives. In the language of complex responsive processes theory, this amounts to saying that top executives can make an intentional gesture for the whole organisation and they can more or less determine the responses to that gesture throughout the organisation. Responses of a deviant kind are to be forestalled by appropriate motivation and unexpected responses from other organisations are to be handled by making further organisation-wide, intentional gestures. Innovation and creativity is also understood to be an intention formed by top executives. There is no fundamental place for the unexpected.

Learning organisation theory does take account of unexpected response to the organisation-wide, intentional gestures of top executives. However, it holds that they can intentionally operate at leverage points so as to get the responses they want, more or less. Creativity here is the intentional change of mental models by individuals. From psychoanalytic perspectives, top executives can choose task and role definitions and design structures that will hold disruptive unconscious processes at bay. Those employing complexity theory in what I have called an orthodox way point to unpredictability of responses and to their self-organising and emergent nature. However, they hold that top executives can choose simple rules or intentionally create crises that will move their organisation to a dynamic in which it can be successful.

In all these cases, the top executives are making choices about how they are to operate on the system as a whole and it is being assumed that they can determine the responses their gestures call forth. In effect this assumes that there is a special category of person in an organisation who alone has free will and choice, or agency, with all the others reduced to automata.

From the participative perspective I am suggesting, no manager can stand outside an organisation and choose how it is to operate. Instead, all managers are active participants with each other in together forming how it operates. Top executives can and do form organisation-wide intentions about their organisation. They can and do identify leverage points. They can and do design structures to contain unconscious processes and sometimes they do set simple rules and intentionally cause crises. However, all of these intentions emerge in the conversation top executives have with each other and with other people. Furthermore, top executives can never design the responses to these gestures. Small changes may escalate and people will engage in self-organising conversation, often organised by shadow themes, from which unexpected responses may well emerge.

I am suggesting, then, that in moving from the position of manager as objective observer to that of manager as enquiring participant, attention is focused on the unexpected responses of organisational members to managers' intentions. Intention is understood as emergent and problematic. The emphasis shifts from the manager focusing on how to make a choice to focusing on the quality of participation in self-organising conversations from which such choices and the responses to them emerge. It becomes a personal matter of reflecting together on the quality of participation.

## Focusing attention on the quality of conversational life

In organisations relationships between people are organised in conversations that form and are formed by the power relations between them. Conversational relating is organised by themes of an ideological nature that justify the pattern of power relations. Intentions emerge as other themes organising the experience of relating as do the responses these intentions call forth. New themes emerge as people struggle to understand each other and as their conversations are cross-fertilised through conversations with people in other communities and disciplines. Organisations change when the themes that organise conversation and power relations change. Learning is change in these themes. Knowledge is language and meaning emerges as themes interact to form conversations.

Attention is thus focused on the conversational life of an organisation as the self-organising processes from which intention and change emerge. The quality of that conversational life is thus paramount. The key role of managers is their participation in those conversations and their facilitation of different ways of conversing. A key implication of this way of understanding life in organisations has to do with being sensitive to the themes that are organising conversational relating. Another is awareness of the rhetorical ploys that are being used to block the emergence of new conversational themes. From this perspective, effective managers are those who notice the repetitive themes that block free-flowing conversation and participate in such a way as to assist in shifting those themes. They may do this, for example, by repeatedly asking why people are saying what they are saying. Effective managers will seek opportunities to talk to people in other communities and bring themes from those conversations into the conversational life of their own organisation. They will be particularly concerned with trying to understand the covert politics and unconscious group processes they are caught up in and how those might be trapping conversation in repetitive themes. They will also pay attention to the power relations and the ideological basis of those power relations as expressed in conversations.

## Focusing attention on the quality of the holding of anxiety

A theory of organisation as complex responsive processes focuses attention on the importance of free-flowing conversation in which people feel safe enough to search for new meaning. Anxiety is an inevitable companion of shifts in themes that organise the experience of relating because such shifts create uncertainty. Themes organising the experience of relating are not only expressed in the vocal, public conversations between people. They also resonate with and change the silent, private conversations that are individual minds. Change in organisations is also, at the same time, deeply personal change for individual members. New ways of talking publicly are reflected in new ways of individuals making sense of themselves. Such shifts unsettle the very way in which people experience themselves. It is because of these deeply personal reasons that shifting patterns of conversation give rise to anxiety, but without this there can be no emergence of creative new themes.

When one thinks in this way, the good enough holding of anxiety is crucial to organisational change and innovation. When managers focus attention on this matter they begin to pay attention to what it is about particular work, at a particular time, in a particular place, that gives rise to anxiety. They pay attention to the nature of this anxiety. They ask what makes it possible to hold the anxiety in a good enough way so that it is also experienced as the excitement required to enable people to continue struggling with the search for new meaning. This is a personal matter for each manager. What am I doing that enables or disables good enough holding of anxiety? Central to this possibility is sufficient trust between those engaging in difficult conversations. Attention is then focused on what in a particular organisation, at a particular time, is promoting or destroying trust.

What will be seriously questioned from this perspective are prescriptions that have to do with setting stretching targets and placing people under stress in the belief that this will move them to try harder. What this may do is simply make them feel more anxious and so less likely to develop the kind of conversational life that makes creativity possible.

## Focusing attention on the quality of diversity

One of the most distinctive aspects of a theory of complex responsive processes is the way in which it focuses attention on diversity. The other theories reviewed in this book tend to focus attention on consensus. Strategic choice theory focuses attention on the importance of members of an organisation sharing the same commitment to its policies and its chosen strategic direction. Learning organisation theory focuses attention on the importance of people in an organisation being committed to the same vision and working together harmoniously in cohesive teams. Psychoanalytic perspectives focus attention on the importance of people understanding the nature of boundaries and having shared understandings of their roles and tasks. Those who import complexity theory into their theorising about organisation in an orthodox way stress the importance of people sharing a few simple rules. The theory I am suggesting takes a more paradoxical perspective.

The paradox is this: if members of an organisation have nothing in common at all, then obviously any kind of joint action will be impossible. However, if they conform too much then the emergence of new forms of behaviour is blocked. Organisations only display the internal capacity to change spontaneously when they are characterised by diversity. This focuses attention on the importance of deviance and eccentricity. It focuses attention on the importance of unofficial ideologies that undermine current power relations. Such unofficial ideologies are expressed in conversations organised by shadow themes. A condition for creativity is therefore some degree of subversive activity with the inevitable tension this brings between shadow and legitimate themes organising the experience of relating.

It is difficult to get one's mind around what this means. It does not make much sense to me to move from noting the importance of deviance to thinking that managers, in their legitimate roles, should promote deviance. It would then not be deviance. It makes little sense to advocate harnessing shadow conversational themes in order intentionally to generate creativity. The shadow so harnessed is no longer the shadow. It makes little sense to say that managers should take steps to unleash self-organisation. This implies that it is not going on already, when the whole point of the theory of complexity is that it is explaining how things already are.

For me, the implication of recognising the importance of deviance has to do with people making sense of their own engagement with others in the shadow conversations that express deviance. It means paying attention to how what they are doing may be collusively sustaining the legitimate themes organising experience, so making change impossible. It means developing a greater sensitivity to the socially unconscious way in which together people create categories of what is 'in' and what is 'out' and the effect that this has on people and organisations.

## Focusing attention on unpredictability and paradox

Perhaps the most radical implication of complexity theory and the theory of human complex responsive processes is the limits to certainty and predictability that they point to. This is a major departure from other theories of organisation, which either virtually ignore or at least downplay the radical unpredictability of the long-term evolution of organisations. What does paying attention to such unpredictability imply?

First, for me, it means thinking about how to cope with not knowing and the potential for feelings of incompetence that this arouses. Managers in organisations often find themselves in situations in which they must act without knowing what the outcome of their actions will be over long time periods. They must act because failure to act will also have unpredictable long-term outcomes. Furthermore, managers can and do act, often very creatively, when they do not know what the long-term outcomes of their actions will be.

These situations are made much more difficult, I think, when management is understood from perspectives that lead people to believe that long-term predictability is possible if one is well informed and competent enough. When the inevitable surprise comes then this view leads to a search for whom to blame. The perspective that predictability is possible leads to the view that the surprise must be due to ignorance, incompetence or some form of bad behaviour in that people did not do what they were supposed to do. In my experience, this judgement is frequently completely unjustified in that very intelligent managers do the best they can and still the surprises come. When you take the complex responsive processes perspective then surprise is part of the internal dynamic of the processes themselves. Surprise is inevitable no matter how well informed, competent and well behaved everyone is. Surprise is inseparable from creativity. I believe that thinking in this way is itself a form of good enough holding of the anxiety of not knowing. It is quite natural not to know and this does not have to incapacitate one. It is possible to carry on working together even in the condition of not knowing. Self-organising conversational processes operating in the state of not knowing produce emergent meaning often of a new and creative kind.

This way of thinking encourages one to pay more attention to what one actually does as one holds the position of not knowing long enough for the new to emerge. One implication of this position has to do with the criteria used to judge a quality action. The other theories reviewed in this book implicitly assume that the criterion for selecting a quality action is its outcome. Quality actions are those that produce desired outcomes. However, in an unpredictable world, the outcomes of an action cannot be known in advance. It is necessary to act and then deal with the consequences. This does not make action impossible or futile. It simply means that people select actions on the basis of other criteria for quality. For example, in a highly uncertain world a quality action is one that keeps options open for as long as possible. A quality action is one which creates a position from which further actions are possible. That is why the option of doing nothing is such a poor response to uncertainty. If the response to uncertainty is to stay at home then the options opened up by journeying forth will never be available. Another criterion for a quality action is that it enables error to be detected faster than some option. Finally, the most important criteria for quality actions are moral and ethical in nature. An action may be taken without knowing its outcome simply because it is judged to be good in itself. One is not absolved of responsibility simply because one does not know the outcome. Even if I do not know how my action will turn out, I am still responsible and will have to deal with the outcome as best I can.

Just as the unpredictability arising in complex interactions imposes limits on what it is possible to know about outcomes of actions, so the complexity of the interactions itself imposes limits on how much of it can be understood. Managers often cannot know the long-term outcomes of their actions and they usually cannot understand the full nature of the complex responsive processes of organising. However, this does not disable action either because the process of self-organisation is one in which local interaction produces emergent global pattern. It is not necessary to understand the whole in order to act; it is simply necessary to act on the basis of one's own local understanding. This is a very different notion to that in, say, learning organisation theory, which prescribes system thinking, that is understanding the whole system, as essential to learning.

The focus on long-term unpredictability and 'whole-system' complexity has implications for the meaning of control. As it is normally understood in other theories of organisation, control is a cybernetic process. It is an activity that ensures the achievement of chosen outcomes. In highly complex processes with emergent and unpredictable long-term outcomes, this form of control is impossible. This does not mean that there is no control, however. It simply means that control has to be understood in a different way. Control then takes the form of constraint. As I have often pointed out in previous chapters, all acts of relating impose constraint on all of those relating. Control takes the form of relating itself, that is mutual constraint. Self-organisation is a process of mutual constraining and hence a form of control.

Notions of complexity, long-term unpredictability and control as constraint have implications for many activities that are currently taken for granted by managers. If these notions are taken seriously, they lead to a number of questions. For example: Why do people prepare long-term forecasts if it is impossible to make useful long-term forecasts? Why do they adopt investment appraisal methods that require detailed quantitative forecasts over long time periods? Complexity theory suggests that it is impossible to make such forecasts so why do people carry on doing it? If organisations are not simply cybernetic systems why is so much effort expended on cybernetic systems of quality control? One important implication of a complex responsive process theory of organising may have to do with putting a stop to many initiatives and abandoning control systems and procedures that are not fulfilling the purposes they are supposed to fulfil. The savings in time, resources and human stress might be considerable.

The theory of complex responsive processes particularly focuses attention on the paradoxical nature of organisational life.

- Organising is at the same time self-organising emergence and intention. Intention emerges in self-organising processes of conversation while at the same time organising that conversation.

- Conversational patterns in an organisation enable what is being done and at the same time constrain what is done.
- The performance of complicated tasks requires that they be divided up but at the same time they have to be integrated.
- The same processes of self-organising emergence creatively produce new forms while at the same time destroying others. New conversational themes and power relations emerge while older ones are destroyed.
- Themes organising the experience of relating in conversation are both stable and unstable at the same time.
- The emergence of new themes organising the experience of relating is both predictable and unpredictable at the same time.
- Managers operate in a state of knowing and not knowing at the same time.
- Complex responsive processes organise both conformity and deviance at the same time.

Managing is then a process of continually rearranging the paradoxes of organisational life.

## Implications for management competences

I have been arguing that the main implication of a complex responsive processes perspective is the way in which it refocuses attention, not on what members of an organisation should be doing, but on what they are already, and always have been, doing. If there is a prescription, it is that of paying more attention to the quality of your own experience of relating and managing in relationship with others. This is a reflexive activity requiring each one of us to pay more attention to our own part in what is happening around us. This requires a reflective development of self-knowledge. It means taking one's own experience seriously. The reward, in my experience, is to find oneself interacting more effectively, not only for one's own good, but also for the good of those with whom one is in relationship.

However, the skills and competences required for this are difficult to develop and just as difficult to sustain. They are competences that do not usually feature in the skill sets prescribed for managers. Examples of the necessary skills are the capacity for self-reflection and owning one's part in what is happening, skill in facilitating free-flowing conversation, ability to articulate what is emerging in conversations, and sensitivity to group dynamics. These skills become essential to notions of leadership and the role of top executives because their greater power renders their impact on others all the greater. Furthermore, these skills are not easily taught, perhaps they cannot be taught, in an abstract way. They are essentially acquired in the experience of exercising them.

Orthodox theories of organising and managing encourage a belief in the possibility of identifying necessary skills in a clear way and defining steps to go through in order to acquire them. The essential skills I am pointing to are much fuzzier and the steps to achieving them even more nebulous. The response might be to stay with orthodox management perspectives. After all, they have applications and prescriptions that are much easier to grasp. However, I believe that this easier option is not viable in the increasingly complex world of organisations. Effective participation in complex responsive processes seems to me to require an increasing commitment to grappling with the issues I have been pointing to in this chapter.

Finally, what are the implications for strategic management?

## Strategic management

In Chapter 1, I suggested that the phenomenon that strategic management is concerned with is that of the population of interacting organisations and the population of interacting groups and individuals within any organisation. The key question relates to the nature of the processes through which these populations evolve over long time periods.

I have argued that it is too simple to suggest that they evolve in directions chosen separately by groups of senior executives within each of them. The interaction between them simply makes this impossible. Nor can change in any one organisation be chosen by groups of senior executives. The complex interactions between groupings of people within an organisation make this impossible too. I am not arguing that senior executives do not, cannot, or should not make such choices. They do, they can, and they should. What I am arguing is that these choices are gestures in an ongoing conversation of gestures out of which the evolution of organisations emerges.

What I have been pointing to is a theory of emergent strategy. Strategies emerge, intentions emerge, in the ongoing conversational life of an organisation and in the ongoing conversations between people in different organisations. Strategic management is the process of actively participating in the conversations around important emerging issues. Strategic direction is not set in advance but understood in hindsight as it is emerging or after it has emerged. This is because if small changes can escalate to have enormous consequences, then the distinction between what is strategic and what is, say, tactical becomes very problematic. The distinction can only be identified after the event. Complex responsive processes theory therefore leads to a different conceptualisation of strategy and strategic management.

## 17.4    SUMMARY

All the other theories surveyed in this book see strategy as the usually rational choice or intention of some or all of the members of an organisation and the intentional overcoming of obstacles to the implementation of such choices. The psychoanalytic approach pays particular attention to how irrational processes might interfere with this choice or intention. Intention is understood as the choice, or design, made by autonomous individuals, usually taking the position of the independent observer. The criteria for the choice focus on desired, predetermined outcomes.

The radical perspective I have been pointing to makes a substantial move in a number of ways. First, it directs attention to how intention emerges in the self-organising process of ordinary conversation between people. This replaces the notion that intention is the expression of an autonomous individual who reflects and makes choices in the light of expected outcomes, as it were, after consulting with others. So, the first move is to focus on how intention emerges rather than what it is. The second move is to postulate that any novel intention initially emerges only in the tension between legitimate and shadow themes organising the experience of being together, that is, in ordinary conversations at the margins of the organisation.

To end, I should probably confess that I have found this the most difficult chapter to write. In a world where, with others, I have come to expect to apply theories and draw out their prescriptions for actions, I find it difficult to deal with a theory that makes sense of my experience of life in organisations but does not enable me to apply and prescribe. Furthermore, it is clear that grappling with what the insights of complexity theory and relationship psychologies might mean for organisations has only just begun. I am well aware that all I have been able to do in this and the previous chapter is provide some pointers to how this grappling might evolve.

## REFERENCES

Gergen, K. J. (1982), *Toward Transformation in Social Knowledge*, New York: Springer.

Griffin, J. D. (1998), Dealing with the paradox of culture in management theory, Unpublished thesis, University of Hertfordshire.

Reason, P. (1988), *Human Inquiry in Action: Developments in New Paradigm Research*, London: Sage.

Stapley, L. F. (1996), *The Personality of the Organisation: A Psycho-dynamic Explanation of Culture and Change*, London: Free Association Books.

Steier, F. (1991), *Research and Reflexivity*, Thousand Oaks, CA: Sage.

# Management narratives

**INNOVATION IN A WATER UTILITY**

by Jose Fonseca

Over the period from 1994 to 1998, I spent some time talking to people at Lisbon's water utility. They came from a number of levels in the hierarchy and different departments. I was interested in how a particular innovation at that company had come about and how it was unfolding. I will start by recounting some of what I learned in my conversations with people about this organisation's background and the beginnings of the innovation I was interested in up to my arrival in 1994.

## EPAL's background

EPAL is the state-owned supplier of water to Lisbon and surrounding areas. The possibility of privatisation had been a matter of public discussion for some time but it was widely accepted that the monopoly in the water sector would eventually be broken up. Many feared that this would enable foreign entry into the industry and in order to be prepared for this threat, EPAL was investing in a substantial modernisation of the distribution network.

EPAL was organised into departments having the following functions:

- Production, that is capturing the water and transporting it to Lisbon.
- Treatment, that is making the water drinkable.
- Distribution, that is delivering the water to consumers.
- Consumer Relations, that is registering consumers, measuring consumption, invoicing, collecting receivables, and generally solving problems with households.

415

- Planning and construction of extensions to the distribution network.
- Maintenance and improvement of the distribution network.

The government appoints the members of the EPAL board for three- to four-year periods and the majority of the members do not normally serve for more than one term. Since 1989, the company had undergone three significant changes in organisational structure recommended by consultants. However, these involved only limited compulsory redundancies and few changes in physical locations, tasks and workflow. Sometimes departments were reorganised but tasks and processes remained the same. On other occasions, departments were given new names, but people carried on doing what they were doing before. The typical decision-making process at EPAL takes the form of conversations between heads of department, in which they accommodate each others' expectations and interests in order to reach a compromise. A decision is then presented to the board which legitimises it. Power lies with the heads of department who have usually been in the company for long enough to understand its culture.

That culture might be described as a culture of artisans, that is one of learning by doing and being taught by artisans. This 'craftsmanship' culture was expressed in a number of ways. For example, there was considerable peer pressure to do things 'right' as opposed to doing things cheaply. Self-improvement was valued more than 'doing things by the book'. People mentioned pride in belonging to this company and sharing its technical culture and professional attitude. On several occasions, I took part in conversations between workers about corporate heroes from the past. They had become heroes because of their professional expertise and their ability to improvise good technical solutions to difficult problems. Older employees transmitted to younger colleagues a sense of belonging and of pride in being members of a company reputed for its technical expertise and improvisational flexibility. People were interested in new ways of doing things and in new materials.

However, technical processes had been changing markedly over the past ten years. These changes, mainly to do with automation, were initiated and developed from within the company, with the cooperation of consultants and suppliers. Because of such technological innovation, the company was moving from its culture of 'craftsmanship' to one of disciplined scientific knowledge. This meant moving from a company that possessed an elite of artisan workers to an engineering company. This move was, in turn, altering perceptions of the value and status of various departments within the company. It was also altering patterns of conversation.

Within the above context, I was interested in an innovation that had to do with repairs to the water distribution system.

## Repairs to the water distribution system

A number of people explained to me what the procedure was that led to repairs being made in the distribution system. Customers would telephone to report leaks in the street or interruptions to the supply of water to their premises. The sequence of communications their calls triggered is depicted in *Figure MN1.1*.

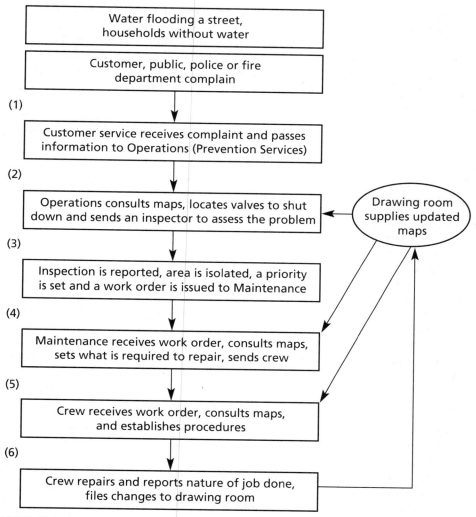

**FIGURE MN1.1**   The flow of information in EPAL

The Customer Service Department received the call and passed the information to the Operations Department (OD). An inspector travelled to the location and assessed the problem. In order to make an assessment the inspector needed an updated map of the area and a survey of the underground pipe network in that area. This enabled identification of which valves should be closed in order to stop the flooding. The inspector notified OD, where priorities were set and an order for repair issued and sent to the Maintenance Department. Typically within the day, a crew left the nearest company site to repair the leaking pipes. This crew also needed charts containing updated records of the type and dimension of pipes in place. On completion of the repair, a report was prepared on the work done, recording components replaced, types of material used, and the nature of the damage to the failed components. The reports were used to update the charts of the network.

On average, there were more than 300 repairs of this kind each day and the drawing room could not cope with the flow of information. The charts therefore tended to be updated on a piecemeal basis so that several versions of the same charts existed at any one time. People responded to the consequent unreliability of the charts by keeping their own private databases with different ways of recording and retrieving data. Unbeknown to senior managers, these private databases had proliferated throughout the company. People reached for whatever was to hand (PCs, paper cards, sheets of paper, recording books, writing directly on their charts) to store information they expected to need in the near future.

This way of dealing with the information people required to do their work gave rise to a number of problems:

- Customer Service did not know when a complaint related to a problem already reported and so passed redundant information to Operations. Customer Service staff had no way of knowing what was being done further down the line and so could not answer customer enquiries about how their complaints were being handled.
- Under the pressure of work in peak periods, they may well not have recorded the most recent components installed on site.
- Even when charts had actually been updated, confidence was so low that people did not believe that they had been updated and so checked up on what the charts showed. Each service organised its own set of charts (38 covering the city area), believing that its own charts were more likely to reflect what was actually under the ground.
- Crews often had to contact the office to obtain more up-to-date information on the site they were working on.

The result was the daily production of huge quantities of data, much of which were duplicated and stored in ways that were incompatible with each other. Many people talked about how useful it would be if these data were recorded and disseminated in real time. Those operating the pipeline system would then be able to function much more efficiently. So over the years there had been conversations about digesting the surveys of the pipe network and storing these surveys on computer where they could be accessed at work sites. In this way, the most up-to-date information could be accessed and any change made to the network could be immediately recorded electronically onto the digitised charts.

## Developing a digitised cartographic system

In 1989, the head of the Distribution Department decided to pursue the idea of developing a digitised survey of the network. The departmental budget could not accommodate the significant cost of the technology and labour that would be required for this endeavour. Furthermore, the head knew that this issue was not, at that time, a major concern of the board. Their investment priority was the development of the distribution network. So, the head set in motion a less ambitious project within the department, using internal resources without formal approval. Two new engineers were hired and although their roles had nothing formally to do with the digitisation project, they were chosen because they had skills relevant to it. Soon, they were spending most of their time on the digitised survey. Later, in spite of financial constraints, a consultant was appointed to assist on the project. During this phase the development of the project depended on the motivation and effort of four people. Although their actions had not been legitimised, they were tolerated in a culture that emphasised technical progress and technical expertise.

This first phase of the project consisted mainly of the digitisation of the existing maps of Lisbon. Existing charts were drawn to different scales and this made it difficult for people to move from one chart to the next. Clearly, this would not do for an instrument that was supposed to be used as a tool for rapid identification of which pipeline branches to shut down. All charts would, therefore, not only have to be digitised but also reduced to a common scale if the system was to work. The routine work of loading the information was subcontracted to a consultant who placed people in-house to work under the supervision of a team leader from EPAL. It was intended that in this phase the work should be conducted in two shifts using two digitisation tables. However, the cooperation of other departments required for this was never obtained and therefore a smaller group of people carried on loading and monitoring the quality of the work being done. Because of resource constraints, the work had to be done on a small PC, but it could not accommodate the processing speed and quantity of information required for a digitised survey.

The task was becoming impossible. Each day, charts were being changed as much as they were being digitised, so that catching up with the changes became a vicious cycle. This went on until 1994.

Despite its apparent failure, however, this first attempt had been very important in drawing attention to the survey and in establishing a general agreement on the need for such a system. During this period, 'know-how' was developed on the way such processes could be carried out and what requirements and difficulties this entailed. Agreement was also reached on the symbols to be used so that the maps could be understood by all who would refer to them. Most importantly, these initial efforts were developing the skills within EPAL that are required to digitise geographical information systems, a technology that had so far only been developed by the military. EPAL was, therefore, a pioneer in Portugal in this field. During 1990–1 Lisbon's local government heard about this work and expressed interest in acquiring the digitised maps in order to control move effectively other companies which were burying structures beneath the city soil. However, this had the consequence of slowing down the development of the digitisation project, because the project director was required to attend many city council commissions addressing the survey issue, none of which produced anything concrete. However, the reputation EPAL was developing in this area was to become one of the foundations of a number of strategic moves that the company is now making in international markets. It is now being used as a basis for a bid that EPAL is making for work in Brazil.

By 1994, when I first began to talk to people about this innovation, the product concept of digitised charts was in the process of being revised. It was beginning to be redefined as a wider information system and it was decided that a database function should be included. I was very interested in how this redefinition was taking place.

## Revision of the concept

As far as I could tell the main reason for the redefinition was that the project moved from the Distribution Department to the Information Technology Department. The move took place because the head of the Distribution Department was promoted and the head of the IT Department became interested in speeding the process up because it fitted in with what the head was already doing. The IT Department already possessed some knowledge of digitised surveys since it had been developing such a system for the large pipeline coming from the dams in the north (internally known as the production system).

The digitisation work done in OD was taken over by staff in IT who had available a UNIX platform, more powerful programming tools, and consultant expertise in geographic systems and graph technology. Naturally, given who was now developing it, the project was redefined as an IT project and coupled with the other project that was then underway for the production system. The project was no longer simply to develop a digitised survey of the distribution network to assist engineers in carrying out repairs. It was now a project to develop a more dynamic information system. Therefore, relational database programming was introduced. In 1995, there was another shift in the platform used to develop the project as it changed to a Windows NT environment.

What I particularly noticed here was the shift in the nature of the conversations about digitised surveys. The dominant conversation of mechanical engineers was yielding to other conversations that were acquiring greater legitimacy. The vocabulary and the concepts in these new conversations were coming from information sciences, biology, management sciences and organisational psychology.

The years that followed this move saw a growing consensus on the importance of the project. It became more and more public, receiving official recognition, and its improving priority in the investment programme resulted in an increased budget. By the end of 1995 all cartographic data (names of streets, topographic heights) were introduced into the databases, but up-to-date information about technical data, such as pipe dimensions and type of material, valves and faucets, was still absent. The early maps that had been digitised were not being updated. Another six months were spent trying to bring the system in line with current changes in the materials installed in the ground. By mid 1996, other departments were brought in to contribute to the improvement of the system. It was at this stage that several unofficial databases came to light.

The pilot survey was ready for testing in October 1996 and a dialogue began with user departments. Several technical issues emerged during this dialogue and were addressed. Furthermore, participating in the dialogue made the system less threatening to people. In the last quarter of 1996 the first of a number of programmes took place to train people in how to use the new system. Three workstations were placed in each department that had to use the system, namely Customer Service, OD and Maintenance. People were invited to 'play' and comment on the use of the system. They were asked to absorb their 'private' databases into the new system. People in technical sections appeared to be willing to cooperate since it meant official recognition and appreciation of activities they had engaged in for years.

I was interested in how people had developed their own databases in order to overcome the inadequacies of the formal information systems. They had done so over the years in conversations that were quite unknown to those higher up in the hierarchy. The existence of these private databases came as a surprise during the programmes to train people to use the new system. The informal databases now began to affect the design of the new system. For example, new entry fields in the databases of the new system were added. It became clear that contextual information about the precise site conditions in which repairs would have to be conducted in different locations could not be depicted on the charts. They could not depict, for instance, that cars were parked in a particular street in such way as to obstruct the work. This was usually dealt with by workers going into nearby cafés to ask who the car belonged to and request its removal. This took less time than the prescribed, formal procedure of summoning the police. For me, the interesting point was how the digitised survey had been able to absorb the narrative knowledge that had emerged from within the departments. In other words, the innovation 'absorbed' previous 'unrecorded' innovations that were the emergent result of people's conversations about the way they could simplify their lives or about how they could solve practical problems they faced in their day-to-day activities.

People on the training courses welcomed the new system. Indeed they were so enthusiastic that they began to complain about the quality and speed of the computers they had been given to learn from. They began to complain about a lack of commitment to the new system on the part of upper management. There did seem to be a lack of decisive direction on the part of upper levels in management. Budgets for the required number of computers and plotters were still not confirmed by February 1997. However, an extensive training programme was approved and the person who had been working in the project since 1994 trained more than 30 future operators.

One interesting consequence of the training programmes was the expectations they gave rise to. Operators were expecting the digitised system to be immediately usable in a perfect state. They complained that the survey would never be perfect enough because it would never be up to date with current realities on sites. It appears that when it came to the operational phase, they forgot the lessons from the development phase, where there were many surprises as the process unfolded. People seemed to forget the fact that the charts had never been up to date and required them to improvise. Now they demanded that the survey be absolutely fault proof if they were to use it. They seemed to have lost sight of the fact that if they did not operate with the system in its current state and so feed it with updates, it would never be updated, just as the charts never were.

The digitised survey system is a horizontal process running through nearly all departments. It is perceived as enabling those who create and manage it to acquire a new 'power tool'. There is a feeling that those who manage the system will acquire an internal visibility that might threaten the former status of people. The main issue seems to relate to the fact that within a water utility, those who graduated in mechanical engineering used to expect to climb the corporate ladder, whereas other people had more limited career expectations. However, in recent years the main pattern of talk has shifted from the vocabulary and concepts of mechanical engineers to those of computer scientists. This disturbs the pattern of power and status.

During the training sessions, there were many discussions on how the survey should operate, what kind of information it should store and how it would be retrieved. These discussions led the sector leaders to suggest the use of the survey for transmission of information about work and repair orders. By January 1997, the system was reconfigured and a new function was introduced. The communications between departments regarding work orders would be done through the survey. The survey would no longer simply be an information platform but would become a control system as well. This notion led to the installation of flow of work procedures.

In the new system, a repair order is processed in the following states:

1   Opening state (after communication from some external entity warning that there is a disruption in distribution).
2   Inspection state (when Operations receives the communication and sends someone to assess the problem).
3   Execution state (when a work order is issued and passed on to Maintenance).
4   Closing state (when work is done and a report is filed in the system and is waiting for validation).

It is not possible to alter the information as it passes from one state to another. The computer automatically registers the time of recording and expedition of this information. Costs of repair, materials used and recovered, labour costs, are all stored in this system for each work order. The president of the company can, if desired, see which repairs are being done, and so can anyone else in the company, provided that they can access the system. This is very easy since workstations will be situated in all departments.

The digital survey has clearly changed from simply being an enabling tool. It is not just a tool to increase efficiency, but also an instrument of control and of performance evaluation. Since the system identifies the time when a communication takes place, it can be used to analyse time differentials between issuing the order and completion of the repair. In addition, it identifies who sent, received and issued communications. This is no longer a geographic information system; it is now a process control system.

One of the most interesting aspects of this story for me, as I took part in conversations about it between 1994 and 1998, was the way in which it changed its nature. As the conversations about it evolved, as changes in the context were occurring (technologies, organisational structures, technological updating of processes), the project was being reconfigured and redefined. It started as a faster process of updating information. It moved to a horizontal information-sharing platform. It became an efficient problem-solving system. It moved to an operational information support system. Finally, it was defined as part of an integrated information management system that is really an on-line device for management control. The curious thing is that the system itself was even then not yet in full operation.

This project started as a tentative, limited and located process. It then moved to a traditional top-down re-engineering process comprising a clear purpose, a detailed budget and a detailed phase schedule. However, a much more messy and emergent development process was really changing the outcomes and the meanings of this innovation. The more formal approach to the process did not envisage, for instance, that the innovation would accommodate previous innovative actions developed by those who had simply responded to the demands they faced every day.

© Jose Fonseca

## by Phil Streatfield

The background to the meeting I am going to describe in this narrative was as follows. In 1996, Axil plc initiated what was called the Chain 2000 programme. The purpose of this programme was to improve supply chain processes across the worldwide operations. The main objective was to integrate and standardise supply chain processes and systems into the same time frame required for millennium compliance. A number of benefits were expected. First, the risks associated with millennium compliance for supply chain systems would be reduced. Second, financial and volume forecasting would be linked, so improving the quality of operational and financial planning. Third, operational efficiency would be improved by the introduction of formal trading relationships between businesses within the company. Fourth, an infrastructure would be created to underpin the achievement of strategic objectives for optimising plant-to-market business. In October 1997 the corporate plan established a time scale for substantial delivery of the solutions before the end of 1998.

What I want to describe now is a meeting to review the Chain 2000 programme budget that took place in early 1998. The Chain 2000 team had put forward a budget for around £50 million. Now it needed to be challenged and debated to assess its robustness. A meeting of the ten managers who formed the Chain 2000 team was called for this purpose, each of whom had their own motives in assessing the budget.

The time for the meeting came and people crowded into a small room. Each had a copy of the budget document and together they began a struggle to make sense of what they called 'this damn thing'. They all knew that they had to put forward a sensible budget proposal that would be acceptable to the chief executive.

Colin Masterson, who was chairing the meeting, opened by saying, 'How did I get into this damn thing in the first place. I've got to go to my boss with this. He ain't going to be happy. Last year I told him it would be £12 million. Now it's more like £50 million.' I could feel the tension rising. Colin continued: 'I want to go through this line by line – we've got to get it down to something more sensible. Equally, though, you guys have got to be confident that we can deliver – so let's not put ourselves in an impossible position.'

The following people were sitting around the table listening to these opening remarks. There was the director of Information Resources (IR) whose agenda was that of standardising global systems. The director of Supply Operations (SO) also wanted this done so he could implement his global supply strategy. The Chain 2000 Programme director wanted everything tightly planned and managed according to his project methodology. The IR director was behind schedule in delivering his part of the project and had spent £2.5 million above plan. He wanted to get the budget number accepted at the highest possible level to cope with climbing resource requirements and turnover costs. The director of Chain 2000 Solution Delivery had been swinging back and forth between wanting to be in and out of the project. He had done as much as possible to evade any tangible responsibility for delivery. Two months later, he would go back to his job in IR and proceed to undermine the project from afar. The Corporate

Finance director was really only there to ensure that his functional boss got what he wanted before he retired. He also wanted to curb the IR team who he thought were out of control. The Supply Chain director idealistically thought that he could really get this project to come to life. Finally, there was a consultant who had much to gain on the fee front, but also much to lose on the reputation front if he was associated with a project that did not work. This was a group, then, consisting of people with varying degrees of commitment to the success of the project and with their own anxieties about their reputations, credibility and career prospects.

The group started to review the IR development costs. The meeting really got going with the question of an extra £6 million for a new approach to communications software. The original software approach, brought in from a previous project, had failed in testing and was then shown to be non-millennium compliant so it was a write-off anyway. There were knowing glances exchanged as the Finance representative turned up the heat on the IR team. Old differences emerged as people took positions. It seemed that there was no other way forward other than to spend the £6 million. If the project were to be achieved then the communications software had to be budgeted at the higher figure. There were sighs of relief in the IR corner. There was also more ammunition for the future for the Finance team who promised to come back to look at any potential overspends.

The Programme director then reminded everyone that the scope of the project had not changed and that the old budget of £12 million was seed-corn money anyway. He said that this was the first time anybody had even tried to assess the true costs of the project. That seemed to help Colin who was still very agitated at being the bearer of bad news to his boss. Others volunteered to help defend the position should he need assistance. The big unknown was what the business should be spending on this project anyway. 'Have you got any comparisons?' was the question put to the consultant. 'Not on this scale', he replied. So there was not much solace there, then.

'OK. Let's try to get rid of the ALPHA systems installations. We've already spent £400 000 on this development and got nothing yet. Can we take them out of scope and make some savings?' The group discussed this question. 'I suppose it's only 5% of the sales not included in the demand pattern', contributed one person. 'Yes, but if you don't get their inputs it can disrupt supplies to other parts of the business', added another. Someone else replied, 'This is bloody difficult to assess without having some input from them'.

Then the Finance team's agenda surfaced: 'We believe the company should go for standardising on DELTA and get rid of ALPHA'. This was quite a change because they had advocated ALPHA for small market installations only months previously. 'Not possible at this time,' said the IR team almost as one. 'Too close to the millennium to take the client–server version of DELTA'. There was a pause as £250 million of sales supply support capability hung in the balance. 'We could just leave them as they are. How much is their cost again?' asked Colin. 'About £1.2 million', came the reply. 'Look. As this would be a good step forward for these markets perhaps we should argue to leave them in?' 'Yes – key from my viewpoint', said the SO director who really needed this if he was to improve supplies to these markets. 'OK, it's worth a fight to keep it.' So the meeting progressed.

The glances, the sighs, the raised eyebrows, were all part of the processes of communication as alliances formed and broke over various topics and issues. Old scores came to the surface and new opportunities appeared from the background. There were those 'I never knew that' moments, leading rapidly into the 'I told you so' bits, and then some agreement around an issue, or some failures to agree. Sometimes there was logical argument and then some raw emotion and frustration: 'I'll never get that one past him'. Various experiences were introduced to support the arguments. Sometimes there was a complete lack of structure when everyone tried to talk at once. There was laughter at the sudden joke and the humour of the situation. There was giving and taking, total intransigence on some issues, table thumping to make a point strongly. There was also the unknown of whether it could really be afforded, followed by 'well, we've started so we'll finish'.

As I reflected on what was going on at this meeting, I was struck by just how complex it was. All desired to maintain credibility and power. The interactions were very real and filled with emotion. There was fear and desire to make a difference. There was resentment when one felt that one was being taken advantage of. It was tiring trying to take in all the inputs and manage all the engagements. There were smiles and then frustration at the lack of progress. People showed how irritating the numbers were and how they feared having to justify them, particularly when someone else had put them forward. There was pleasure in getting a point over and annoyance at not being heard. There were connections with some and disconnection with others, feeling of some kind of movement, then feelings stuck again. The conflict of interests between consultant and managers and between different managers was clear.

Eventually, the group somehow arrived at a figure of £42.8 million that seemed to be acceptable to those present in that it did not make it impossible to continue with the project. The arguments practised during the review were to be written up to support the situation arrived at. The anxiety abated as the satisfaction of knowing that they had got somewhere, almost in spite of themselves, settled on the group. Everyone had managed to get something of what they wanted and yet nobody had got everything. The outcome represented the transient sense the group had collectively made of this project at this point in the context of the business in which they were operating.

© Phillip Streatfield

## MANAGEMENT NARRATIVE 3    PERFORMANCE MEASUREMENT

by Phil Streatfield

During January 1996 two important members of the Board of Axil plc left. Roger Creighton, Technical Director, left at the end of January to take up a post in another company and Albert Peters, Director of Technology, left 'to consider the next moves in his career'. The current Chief Executive, Geoff Ingles, announced the departures two weeks before they happened. In doing so he seemed to be confirming strong rumours that things were moving on. On to what though?

At the time I was a member of a team working on a project called 'Project Control Panel'. This was an attempt to put together a set of performance measures, to be reported to the Board to indicate where the organisation was and where it was going. This provided me with a unique opportunity to talk to site leaders about how they saw things and to discuss their views with some of the leadership team. The following captures some of those conversations.

As part of my role in the project I visited sites and talked to their leaders. The first questions about the measures were usually 'What do they want these for? Are they going to sit in the centre of the organisation and try to manage me? Of course we know that Geoff stands for control. He is trying to take away our freedom to act. Roger was good at giving us freedom to do things. He indicated what we needed to do and we got on with it. This new regime hasn't told us what it wants. If only it would tell us we'd get on and do it. Do these measures tell us where we are going? What is it we are trying to achieve? How can these people micro-manage what we do in the plants from the centre of the organisation?'

This led to some kind of second guessing about what Geoff really wanted so that people could adjust what they were doing or their positions on issues so as to fit in. When I asked them about why they were looking at things this way they told me that the environment in the organisation over the last year had changed radically. 'Whilst Geoff seems to want to encourage debate over future strategy, he clearly doesn't want to listen to anything that doesn't fit with where he wants to go.' 'If I stand up and open my mouth on these things then I am going to be branded as somebody who doesn't support the new regime. If I keep my head down and just get on with things then I can survive – later on we can adjust the operations to get back to where we were.'

At the same time, however, there was a general acceptance that things had to change so that the company stayed competitive. 'We have achieved a lot under Roger – Geoff brings a fresh challenge. However, he seems to want to tell us what to do rather than to let us get involved in figuring it out.' There was also fear of engaging in any challenge to the way things were at that time. Many of the site leaders I spoke to were under intense pressure to deliver very stretched performance goals. Most were trying to deliver two years' worth of improvement in one year. Their expectations were that if they did not deliver they would be punished in some way. This was triggering all kinds of actions to deliver targets. Sometimes the actions reinforced each other and sometimes they worked against each other. The idea of reporting against more measures in this environment was very threatening to them. 'What will they do with this information?' 'Surely the measures are supposed to show us whether we are achieving or not – but achieving what?'

After responses of the kind from managers of operating units I had a number of conversations with members of the Board. I will give some examples of the remarks made by A and B and a report of conversation between Person C and me.

### Person A

'Our capital spends are out of control.'

'We must get the capital in this business under control. People aren't managing their balance sheets properly.'

'We don't know where our finances really are at the moment. The measures will get this thing under control. There has been too much focus on the Customer Service front in the organisation. The inventory levels are too high and people can't tell me why it is there. We are clearly paying too much for the service levels we are achieving.'

'Sure the sites are trying to deliver from their perspective – but they are too focused on the local situation. We should manage the business by supply chains not by sites. It is key that we start to look at EVA [Economic Value Added] returns on our assets and that we adjust our measures to do this.'

'Geoff wants to pressure the business to deliver more – he doesn't know when he has squeezed too much though. We need the measures to tell us when we have pushed too hard.'

'There is a team working on the strategic part of the plan. This would give us more of an idea of where we are going – but we can't wait for them to deliver. Their timings have now slipped to October – we need to know where we are now – we can feed in the other stuff later on.'

### Person B

'I think I have some kind of rapport with Geoff. I helped him out once before when he was running another section of the business. Others let him down over that but I rescued him so I hope he will value me as a result. I also worked on a project that he sponsored and got on with him OK so I hope that will help.'

'This is not the time to directly challenge though. We have to try to educate him so that he understands more about this business. He is under intense pressure from shareholders, though, to secure some significant performance improvements.'

'We shouldn't forget what it was like when the company was last reorganised. We had to work hard to establish the organisation. Geoff has got a hard time getting the commercial managers to support him – in fact they are challenging him. Although he is putting a lot of pressure on us, this, in a way, is not surprising because of the pressure he is under.'

'There is not a consistent view of where we are going at the leadership team table at the moment. We don't have the strategic plan worked out yet. To a certain extent that is because the company hasn't got its overall position really well set. Geoff wants us to be a single enterprise but we really don't know what that means for us at the moment.'

'As long as we continue to deliver then we will have some chance to influence things. On the influencing front it is important not to push too hard. Geoff is conscious that he has been relying on his old team and is beginning to open up to others in the team. So doing anything that pushes them together again will not be helpful. We know, though, at present, that they are possibly the only routes to really get things through.'

### Person C

C: 'Hi. How are you keeping?'

Me: 'Pretty good – I'm glad we have managed to get some time together because there seems to be a lot going on ...'

C: 'I am very frustrated. I can't find the right questions to ask to unlock this thing at the moment. Maybe if we spent some time going through what we see at the moment it might help me to formulate something. I'm seeing Geoff on Monday and I want something to put in front of him to keep my conversation going with him.'

Me: 'OK.' (*jumping up and standing at the dry marker board*) 'Where do you want to start? What about where we think things are going at the moment?'

C: 'OK. We are currently organised as factories reporting by area through to Geoff and we are engaged in the FR [Factory Rationalisation] project. I believe that we should be looking at the chains of supply as an opportunity for the future.'

Me: 'What about organisation by product supply chain?'

C: 'This may be something we get to – it could be constrained by the overlap use of different pieces of capacity. At this point in time, though, I think that the chains are the transition piece. We might look at specific products later on. There is the strategic plan team looking at the future. This is a bit like deep thought, though. They are currently trying to analyse future demands and scenarios in order to come up with the approach we should take. This will be delivered as the answer 42 I expect – and then we will be left asking what the question was.'

Me: 'How about Geoff then?'

C: 'I met somebody the other day who had been at a managers meeting that Geoff had been speaking at. He apparently came over very well. People felt motivated by his comments. To me this suggests that he is beginning to connect with people and to get things moving.'

Me: 'This is interesting. I met someone else who had been at the same meeting. They said that Geoff had been complimentary about some aspects of their business – but then laid into them saying that they should be doing much better. He said that they should be focusing on some other things than they were. They had not been contributing as much to the business as they might and they all had to try harder. This person reported that it was like they weren't being recognised for all their good efforts. This individual also reported that they were demotivated and threatened by the whole experience. They indicated that the group had not received the messages well.'

C: (*pausing*) 'Maybe one way of making sense of this is that the person I spoke to could see a future for themselves in the organisation that Geoff would like to have. The person you heard from, Ian, maybe cannot see a future in the organisation for themselves.'

Me: 'Interesting way of looking at it. To me it tells us that the message reaching these people is mixed. Equally, people are reinforcing their perceptions of Geoff. One framework we have used in the past to look at this type of thing is the situational leadership model. In this case the organisation could be considered as task immature in operating differently – it might be appropriate for there to be some form of centralisation in the short term to direct things in terms of moving forward. In which case any shift back from delegation will be exaggerated – especially in this environment where many people seem to be feeling threatened. It also indicates there is no selling of a potential future going on in the organisation – or of any coaching of what people need to do/be in order to contribute. This is making for a very uncomfortable situation.'

C: 'What about Geoff himself? What sort of a person is he? Some time on this might help me with my approach.'

Me: 'OK. For me I haven't seen him in action to form a firm opinion. The times I have seen him he has been very challenging in his questioning of what has been presented to him. There is a picture of him in the organisation – somebody who doesn't let people get close to him – who doesn't trust people – who doesn't provide much space for others to put their piece before he disagrees.'

C: 'Yes. It is almost as if he is hiding behind a mask. I believe he is somewhat insecure in the sense that he wants to win and doesn't know how to. He is under pressure at the top table. He is seen as coming to this role from what was seen as a second class business and is now trying to establish a position of strength. He needs to do something radical to have an impact though. It's much more difficult when you are in supply chain leadership, you are generally playing with small numbers with less impact on the business. So, big EGO to satisfy – yet little to really shout about. A person who does not easily trust others. He also likes to play with models as long as you can show him their practical application.'

C: 'I think his bark is worse than his bite. The other day he told me that people think that he holds grudges. He doesn't. Once the fight has gone he forgets about it. So it's the perception that is left which is working against him. He also has a similar Myers Briggs to me – INTP – so I have a similar approach to things which is helping.'

(*Time runs out at this point. The board is covered with many drawings/representations used during the conversation, which took about two hours.*)

### Person A (again)

Another meeting on another day:

Me: 'I believe we could do more with this measurement set. We seem to be designing it for short-term control. We need to bring it alive in terms of the organisation seen as product chains too, so we can play with the outcomes and see what this information tells us. We can then start looking at how we want to use it. This will get us thinking about where we go with this concept.'

A: 'Ian – I like the sound of going ahead with this approach. Where would we get the information, though, on the chains – won't it take us some time to do this?'

Me: 'Two years ago there was a project started to create a manufacturing supply database – the owner of it lives three offices down from you in this building!'

A: 'Wow! I never knew that. Give me their name – I'd like to have a look at this stuff.'

Me: 'One thing you will find is that as sites have progressed over time they are beginning to organise in cells for production. One way of looking at our chains is to consider them as linked cells, rather than linked sites. I also believe we should look at specific products and play with those to see what we can get, rather than major chains.'

A: 'I am interested in doing this too – I feel that the major chains may still be too big.'

Me: 'I sense from your comments you want to get on with this. I had arranged to see PW [a consultant] to get this moving in March. I guess we could start earlier.'

I want to say something now about the sense I was making of these conversations. The idea of engaging in a performance measurement project seemed very straightforward on the surface. The classic closed loop negative feedback control mechanism was what was in mind when the project was started. At the first meeting of the project team it was made very clear to us that all that we were to define were the most appropriate measures for the new organisation and propose a mechanism to put them in place. A balanced approach was required that would bring both the financial and operational measures together. The project would also pave the way for an EVA management approach to be brought into the picture by 2000.

The purpose of the early conversations with people was to explore which measures should be used to indicate how we were doing in the company. So, we developed a list of what we thought was relevant and took it to a sample of site leaders and Board members to validate our proposals.

We developed definitions of the financial and the operational requirements and set off to the meetings that I have reported on. I was surprised to find myself repeatedly drawn into conversation about the motives and behaviour of the new leader of the organisation. More and more people wanted to spend time on this, rather than the performance measures themselves. It was almost as if I was engaged in a rolling conversation with people trying to make sense of the world in the context of this man being at the head of the table. The task of developing and implementing the performance measures became almost incidental. The real project in this seemed to be a network of people trying to make sense of what was happening.

It was as if everyone involved was accustomed to the regime under Roger. Rumour had it that he was being removed for being too soft and undemanding on the cost front. He had let too much go to the site leaders who were seemingly being encouraged to run their sites as if they were their own businesses. Anxieties were running high. What was driving the anxiety, though? It was almost as if people were searching to see how to adjust their behaviour in order to survive something that they perceived to be some kind of threat. This shift in the person in the lead role in the organisation had generated a sense of the unknown into which seemed to be projected some sense of impending doom, gloom and disaster.

The new leader was almost built up as some kind of fantasy figure in the conversations in which I found myself. With virtually no first hand data at all, people were forming judgements and coming to conclusions which in turn seemed to be affecting their behaviour quite considerably. This shift challenges the planned change school of thought: things were shifting without any kind of plan at all, just in the exploration of making new sense.

Questions around the motives for the measurement brought forth this picture of a man sitting in an office, somewhere in the world, knowing all and being able to dictate the next actions for those working in the organisation. Ironically, the very act of beginning the conversation about making the measurement in the first place sent many of the people into a mood of 'how can I stop this man taking control of me?' They seemed to fear that the performance measures would expose some activity that they had under way. In many ways this was strange because, of course, they were already reporting according to a raft of performance measures.

An important part of the conversation seemed to be the search to understand the intent of another so that there could be a matching of agendas such that basic beliefs or values were not compromised. Suspicion seemed to surround Geoff. People feared he would use his hierarchical power negatively. Where intent was not stated then one was formulated and used to make sense of what was happening. Some made sense of Geoff's behaviour in the context of him being put under pressure by others and so he was doing the same: 'Geoff has got a hard time getting the commercial managers to support him – in fact they are challenging him'.

Some people felt very distant and disconnected. Those who had tried to connect and exchange their views with Geoff were feeling bruised and ignored in many cases. Some were hanging on to some threads of a relationship: 'I helped him out once so hopefully he'll remember this'. Others were feeling strong because they were really close to Geoff. Person A was already used to working with Geoff and felt some kind of a bond. This person had some insight into what Geoff was really looking for, namely a feeling of some degree of influence over what was happening. That person's comments are much more confident than those of others who are still trying to establish some kind of rapport with the man.

Roger had begun in his period of leadership by holding what he called focus groups and also one-to-one discussion sessions where he talked to, and listened to, people who wanted to offer him views on where the organisation should go. He seemed to have tuned into the flow in the organisation and, having made some sense of it for himself, acted in such a way as to tackle what seemed to be the major issues of the day. I think he had also tapped into the collective sense-making processes in the organisation. The various senses that people made in conversation with him helped them to develop both the relationship and the sense made. So by addressing the task he also addressed the relationships. By making himself available and accessible he was able to develop a degree of trust with those who interacted with him. This degree of trust seems to be crucial in the connectedness that develops and the subsequent meaning made in the interactions.

This sense of connectedness seemed to help ensure that energy was being focused into moving forward on the basis of relatively high degrees of trust and openness. Perhaps the available free energy in the organisation was being channelled more into maintaining the transient, jointly constructed meanings which in turn meant that the energy was channelled into greater aligned action rather than in continued remaking of meanings. It was possible to make more effective closure as individuals and to move on to the next issue because Roger had provided the opportunity.

Geoff, on the other hand, had studiously maintained a distance between himself and the others in the organisation, so much so that he had instigated confidentiality arrangements with those working with him on significant projects in the organisation. Put in place for legitimate reasons the very introduction of these had immediately suggested a lesser level of trust than previously. On top of this his natural tendency not to visit production sites and to work only with a very small clique of people seemed to feed the image of someone who was very centrally controlling and centrally focused.

In this regime people were reduced to studying the man from a distance, unable really to make sense of his intentions or needs of them. Feeling excluded they were then spending time and energy handling the implications of the negative images they had developed. Amazingly, when I reflect on this now, it was a year into the tenure of Geoff in his role and yet much energy was still being expended coping with him. The 'reality' gap was filled with fantasy.

The conversations I have been engaged with contain significant content that is, in a sense, redundant to the supposed task at hand of 'creating economic value added', for example. This content, and the feelings that go along with it, are somehow important to achieving the tasks that those of us conversing are involved in. The conversations that took place and views that were shared with me occurred quietly in people's offices behind closed doors. I surmise that the sense-making process involves some kind of risk or exposure that requires trust to be present to contain the anxiety with which it is associated.

© Phillip Streatfield

---

## MANAGEMENT NARRATIVE 4    THE TRANSFORMATION PROGRAMME

by Tim Teather

In March 1997, Infotek's Head of Services, Percy Andrews, recruited me as a Service Delivery Manager. My remit was to ensure customer satisfaction in delivering contracted outsourcing services at a profit. Infotek's outsourcing services supply clients with the whole or part of their IT infrastructures, such as helpdesks, second line technical support, hardware break/fix, and network support. In addition to outsourcing, Infotek provides IT-related products such as computer software, hardware, peripherals and services, project management, IT strategy and technical support. Infotek is a subsidiary of Infopro, which is owned by an international conglomerate.

As part of the recruitment process, I met a number of the other Service Delivery Managers and we discussed the nature of the role and my suitability for it. During these discussions, I was told about a planned move to profit-and-loss management at account level and the current use of start-up teams. Start-up teams existed to enable rapid resourcing of new outsourcing business. These teams included project managers and technical personnel who could stand in while the permanent on-site team was recruited.

I went through my first few days at Infotek with mixed feelings. On the one hand, there was the excitement of delivering the service to a client, managing the finances of what was effectively a small business, and being a member of what outwardly appeared to be a professional organisation. On the other hand, however, I was concerned with what felt like a lack of support. On my first day at Infotek, I was supposed to meet another Service Delivery Manager so that he could hand over the work already under way on the account I was to manage. He was also supposed to act as my mentor. However, he did not turn up to the meeting that had been arranged. Later, I joined a project to deliver a helpdesk and second line desktop support function to a major new client, Polit. I met with my mentor in the client's car park on my first day on the project and we spent five minutes in the car going through the account. This was to be my handover since I only met with him twice again and two weeks later he resigned to join a competitor. I then found out that the start-up team, which had been discussed at my interview, did not exist. It was simply an idea that would be 'good to implement at some stage'. This meant that I had to recruit the staff required to deliver the service and project-manage the transition myself.

I felt lost and without support in an organisation that I did not know. Additionally I began to wonder which other areas of the business were not able to support service delivery. Part of the difficulty may have arisen from the widespread use of contract staff, in turn a reflection of an above-industry staff turnover rate which was always ascribed to rapid change.

Throughout those first months, I increasingly felt that the company was out of control and did not support those delivering its services. For example, the human resources department did not know how many holidays someone had taken in the previous year and the finance department could not identify the profitability of a department, let alone an account. It was a contractual requirement to replace absent engineers, but resources were frequently not available. IT systems did not support the business and even the tools required to perform the role were not available. This quickly filled me with concern. Had I made a mistake in taking this position? Were all service organisations like this? When I spoke to other managers, they told me that they faced similar difficulties but when they drew these to the attention of senior management the only response was talk about plans rather than actions.

Soon after I arrived, I realised that field staff had communication difficulties. While everyone in the office had access to email and an electronic notice board, none of the field staff did. I knew that it would be relatively easy to provide these forms of communication for field engineers. I set about arranging this but soon met a wall of resistance from the IT department. They said that they were already aware of the need and were investigating a solution. When I made further enquiries, I was met with barely concealed hostility. I was also told that another group was investigating the delivery of a combination of internal systems to the field. When I discussed the matter with the manager of that group, he said that the pilot would take six months. He was not interested in suggestions for speeding it up. I felt angry and puzzled. Why were people being so difficult and so hostile to an idea that would assist communication with those on site?

After five months developing the service at Polit, I was asked to take on the service delivery to Polit's sister company after the departure of yet another service manager. The services to be delivered were a helpdesk, second line desktop technical support and hardware break/fix. Once again I experienced a significant lack of support. For example, replacement components were not processed and returned on time to meet the contracted service levels. Infotek received a cash credit for all replacement components returned to the supplier, but the return took so long that Infotek frequently lost the credit.

A number of other anomalies within the organisation's processes came to light. Part of the service managers' role was to gather, sign and submit timesheets for their staff to enable invoicing and productivity analysis. All managers submitted these but there was no system for recording the information. Engineers were required to record their skills on a matrix form once a year, but when the information was passed to operations it was not used in any way. I felt increasingly frustrated and my confidence in the abilities of senior management evaporated.

Soon after I joined Infotek, another Service Delivery Manager, Bill Rhodes, was appointed. Within a very short time, Bill obtained a significant new contract to supply services to AM Bank. This increased his power and influence and he was promoted to manage the outsourced services business, making him my manager. This pleased me because he immediately announced plans for a more efficient and professional delivery of services. He was also networking nationally and internationally with Infotek partners allowing a cross-fertilisation of ideas on how services should be delivered. At about this time, a number of other Service Delivery Managers were recruited to replace the significant numbers of managers who had left and increase the service management presence of the organisation. I was also pleased by this because I thought it would bring fresh ideas into the organisation and challenge the jaded scepticism of longer serving managers.

In the summer of 1997, Infotek merged with another service provider, Matts-Silver. The intention was to bring additional revenue into the business. My reaction to the merger was favourable. The reasons for the merger seemed sound. I thought it was a positive message that the company was performing well financially and had expansion plans to enable it to become one of the largest resellers in the UK market. However, there was also some feeling of insecurity. Would my job remain once the organisations had merged? My predominantly positive feelings about the merger soon evaporated, however, because over the following six months customers terminated their contracts upon hearing about the merger.

At this point all of the service managers within Infotek met with Head of Services Percy Andrews' counterpart at Matts-Silver, Will Bain, to discuss the best way forward for the merged services organisation. Although Percy took the lead in the discussions, it was evident that Will was more experienced and had more skills to offer the combined organisation. Two weeks later Percy resigned, by 'mutual agreement', and Will became the head of outsourcing, making him my manager's manager. I was shaken by this change. I seemed to be faced with a rapidly changing peer group and management team. I did not know anything about this man or how he preferred to operate.

Three weeks after the merger was announced a company event was scheduled to 'launch' the new organisation and it was followed up with other events. A key person in these events was Dick Harrow, the Services Director, who was young, dynamic and respected. He was clearly familiar with business literature and announced his aim of creating a strong culture through setting organisational goals and creating an environment in which the organisation learned and evolved. The environment was to be one of real service values and ethics, where the customer came first. This was instilled into the staff in tutorials, seminars and meetings to educate them into a service ethic and to outline the company's strategy and performance. I felt very positive during these events. The seminars allowed me to meet Infotek suppliers and industry analysts who gave their views on how the industry was moving. The senior management also painted a vision of the future of the merged organisation and outlined the good financial performance to date. Informal breakfast round table meetings enabled staff to meet directors. My feelings of insecurity and scepticism diminished and the future seemed brighter.

In September 1997, the Managing Director announced a transformation programme. He informed us on the internal electronic notice board that he had recognised a need for change and had commissioned a change management consultancy to investigate what the change should be and how it should be carried out. He also told the press that the change programme would mirror a programme that had recently been carried out in another subsidiary of Infopro. I found these messages confusing. If there was to be a change that was a mirror of a programme carried out in a sister company, why was a change management consultancy investigating what the change should be? In his communication, the Managing Director did not explain why the programme had been developed in the sister company, what its objectives were, or how it was successful. Part of his announcement concerned a number of meetings that he would be holding with all staff at various locations to expand on what the programme was and how it would move forward.

At the meeting that I attended, the Managing Director provided a handout which stated that the organisation would be moving from a function-driven company to one that was process driven. The directors also pointed out that 80 per cent of Infotek's revenues were generated by 20 per cent of its client base. For this reason, they had decided to focus on the 20 per cent (large corporates) and shed the 80 per cent (small, medium and large businesses). This would increase efficiency and the focus on delivering superior service to those clients that generate the revenue.

When the transformation programme was announced, many staff said that they had frequently been part of these programmes in the past within Infotek. These never produced any changes. This could have been true. The organisation was constantly changing parts of its structure and the processes that people used, often with little perceived impact for those delivering the services.

## Making sense

The change management theories I had come across specified two requirements for successful change: a strong motivation to change; and a well-communicated, clear vision of the future. In the two meetings held by the Managing Director, neither of these initial criteria were satisfied. No reasons were given for the transition that occurred in the company we were about to copy. No explanation was given of its objectives and how it was successful at meeting them, or why it was thought necessary to implement that programme at Infotek. We all knew that a key driver was cost. The implication of focusing on a small number of large customers was that the organisation's cost base could be dramatically reduced while the revenue stream was only marginally reduced. However, this was not explicitly stated. Why? I certainly did not feel motivated. Then, there was no communication of a clear vision of the future. Perhaps the board was afraid to inform the staff that the cost base was too high because we would infer that it was about to reduce the workforce. This would affect the organisation in two ways. First, the best people would resign, leaving the underperformers behind. Second, it would drive up the use of contract staff and so increase the very costs that were to be controlled.

## Further changes

In December one of Infotek's largest clients, AM Bank, went out to tender for the supply of its break/fix work. A new entrant to the outsourcing market was buying business and so tendered at a loss. AM Bank decided to accept the lower bid and so Infotek lost the business. It later turned out that Infotek had been carrying out the AM Bank contract at a loss too. Also in December, another of Infotek's major clients went to tender for the supply of a number of services. The decision was to be made in June 1998. If we were to lose another major client, then we would have a much reduced portfolio of corporate customers to generate the projected revenues. There would also be no smaller accounts remaining to create a safety net of revenue since the 80 per cent of small accounts would be gone.

At the end of 1997 Infotek announced results that were well below target. In early January 1998, the Managing Director announced, at a series of roadshow presentations, that the transformation programme was to be speeded up. He also gave a commitment that there would be no redundancies as a result of the programme. At the same time, the parent company assigned a senior executive, Harry Winston, to act as a consultant to the change programme. He soon became Joint Managing Director. Then, in mid January, the Finance Director left Infotek and another was appointed in his place. The new Finance Director had a reputation for turning companies around. Soon afterwards, both the Managing Director and the Sales Director left the company. Harry Winston was now Acting Managing Director and a new Sales Director was appointed. Other changes at the top levels of the company were also announced, many being people who had worked elsewhere with Harry. This seemed to be an organised restructuring of power within the organisation that would allow changes to be made by removing top-level resistance.

There was no mission statement prior to the transformation programme. Then in January 1998 a mission was announced: 'To assist our Corporate Customers with the management of the cost of IT ownership, through the provision of the highest quality range of desktop and network integration services'. The mission statement was rewritten at the end of March. When asked, most employees could not repeat the mission and expressed little interest in it. Indeed, why should they? Neither mission statements mentioned the staff and the role that they might play or how they might be treated in delivering service to customers.

At a kick-off meeting on 6 February, contrary to the former Managing Director's promises, Harry announced redundancies that were to 'affect a small number of people' and anyone who did not 'embrace' the change programme. He told us that the business was operating with a cost base that was much higher than acceptable and resource utilisation rates were lower than expected. Harry also explained that the situation was sufficiently critical for the company's future to be at stake. A new management team to drive the change was also announced. Twelve days later the short-term objectives of the change programme were outlined. These were to focus on sales, cost management and quality. Again, these objectives seemed to be focused on cost and control rather than on the transformation's stated aims of changing the company to a process-orientated organisation. The message that came through clearly was to increase revenues and decrease costs.

In June, another major client decided to use a competitor. I felt considerable trepidation since the loss of this contract left me without an account to manage. There was also another Service Delivery Manager without any accounts and a third with a reduced workload. There were no signs of new business on the horizon. Two days later came the announcement that another major client had decided to terminate its contract with Infotek and take the services back in-house. Where was the transformation programme now? By September there were more changes at the top with a new Managing Director and the resignation of the Sales Director. I was made redundant in October.

How am I to make sense of this 18 months of life at Infotek? If I take an orthodox management perspective then I have to conclude that what I experienced was due to the incompetence and ignorance of senior executives. I think I have to conclude this because orthodox theory says that there are linear sequences of actions that it is possible to take to transform an organisation. In some respects it looks as if senior executives were trying to apply some of this but they obviously did not succeed. So, they must have been incompetent at it. However, perhaps the stories about how organisations successfully applied these linear steps are all told with the advantage of hindsight, omitting the frustration, the mess and the constantly unexpected occurrences. If I take a complexity perspective on my experience, I suppose I conclude that change does not take place in a sequential way, but rather in the messy way I have recounted. This happens because we live in a turbulent, dynamic world. Sometimes the messy process works for a while and sometimes it does not. But perhaps the alternative of the orderly sequential change is a myth that cannot be carried out in the messy real world.

© Tim Teather

## MANAGEMENT NARRATIVE 5   CONSULTING AND CULTURE CHANGE

by Patricia Shaw

In late 1995 an American-owned multinational announced a decision to create a 'spin-off' company. This sent shock waves through the system as some 8000 people were faced with a compulsory change in employment. The sheer size and diversity of the corporation's operations throughout the world and its benevolent 'family' values had made lifelong job security seem guaranteed. Now employees moved to the new organisation were banned from reapplying to the parent company for two years. There was also a wave of redundancies, mostly voluntary, but not entirely. Unlike the situation of a takeover when there is the need to assimilate or merge different organisational cultures, the issues here were those of encouraging the evolution of a new entity with different characteristics. Some months later, I returned home to find three messages on my answerphone.

The first was from Greta, a woman who was putting together a team of external consultants to help develop and lead a programme to create the new culture of this 'spin-off' company. She wanted me to join this venture, together with some other consultants with whom I had worked before. The second message was from Alex, the head of HR in the new company. He wanted to speak to me about developing the new company. The third message was from Donald, recently appointed as Director of Operations for the new company. I had worked with him on various assignments over the past ten years. He expressed his misgivings about the consultants' proposals for culture-change programmes. It was not immediately clear if all three phone calls were connected.

When I called Greta, she explained that there had already been a series of 'Planning for Success' workshops. Groups of employees had been asked to brainstorm the changes in culture that were needed as the new company left the corporate fold. They were also asked for the ten best ideas in each Region for building a successful future. She had been involved in these sessions because of her organisation development role, and thought that they had gone very well. The material generated was being typed up, summarised and collated across all the Regions by the central transition team.

I wondered aloud what they would do with this 'output' abstracted from the contexts in which it had been generated. 'Of course', Greta continued, 'we know there is a problem about creating this new culture as we carry over all the people and habits of the existing corporation with us. That is why I have suggested that we run a series of workshops to be attended by all managers before the official launch of the new company. I came up with the idea of focusing on the question "What happens when the customer calls on July 1st?" This is something Donald has also been asking as he goes round talking with employees. I believe we should aim to deliver a new corporate identity via the phone all over Europe on that day.'

I was bemused as I listened. Was she suggesting some kind of telephone training for everyone? I could hardly believe that she was contemplating this for all managers. And why ask me? She must know this was not the kind of work I was interested in. When I voiced my hesitations, she brushed them aside. No, no, I had not understood. This was to be a major initiative to create the new company, 'to shift people's minds, motivation and attitude. The way they answer the phone will be the visible result of the first but magic step into a new culture. The project will be implemented top down. I have the support of Donald and Alex, and I have already spoken with Daniella and Gertrude [the other two external consultants], and they have agreed enthusiastically.'

I felt that I was being invited into a situation that was already well formed. I wanted time to think. I said that I was not sure that this was a project I could usefully contribute to. I imagined puzzlement, a slight withdrawal in the short pause that followed. Obviously my willingness to be involved had been taken for granted. 'Look Greta', I said, 'I have to be honest and tell you that this doesn't really make sense to me yet. I would like to better understand the thinking behind this initiative.' Greta replied that there was no problem, and she would fax through some papers that afternoon.

I could feel some tension as I put down the phone. This was a company containing people with whom I had significant working relationships. I was already part of the network of connections in which events were unfolding, and the web of expectations, trust and influence in which I was embedded was itself shaping and colouring my reactions as my mind raced. I had noticed the eagerness in Greta's voice. No doubt, this project was a significant one for her. She had pulled in an existing set of collegial relations amongst the external consultants she was wanting to employ, no doubt thinking that this would speed the design and implementation of her ideas. I had forgotten to ask whether Donald had already suggested to her that he would like to see me involved.

I decided to wait until I received the faxed information. This included a letter addressed 'Dear consultants' and copies of some messages that had passed between Greta and others by electronic mail. Here are some extracts from the letter:

Employees want the new company to become famous among customers as quickly as possible. Employees will bring across to customers that we are a company that takes care of them, we are responding quickly, with a high degree of quality, we are close to them, we offer as quickly as possible solutions to their problems, we offer total service around them. They are the centre of all we do. Employees want that we appear to customers in a similar way all over the world. A kind of uniformity.

We have set up a task force 'Corporate Identity via the phone'. On 2nd of May I will give a presentation to the global HR/OD team on this project. In June all workshops will take place in Italy, France, Benelux, Scandinavia, UK, Spain, Germany and Central Region.

On July 1st we will see the results: All employees (that means top down) will transfer the Corporate Identity via the phone. They will sound, appear and behave like they are by then: highly motivated to guarantee from their function the new company's success and to bring across all the things they mentioned in the Planning for Success workshops. There is no option to take or leave it. There is only an option about how to say and the sequence of what to say. There is a must about what to say at least. No exception.

Your project will be:

- to design a pragmatic workshop
- to write a short and easy to handle manual for everyone who answers the phone
- to prepare a presentation for May 2nd for me with your draft design and charts etc.
- to offer dates in June when you will be available
- to give me an offer about your cost. (You will not be paid for the draft design first. We will handle this when you officially get the contract after the final global buy in.)

I was astonished by this document. If this was a sample of what was afoot in the new company, then there must be some very nervous people around. Greta seemed to be thinking of culture change as a major internal PR exercise, getting everyone to march in step into a brave new future. Yet, when I had spoken with her I sensed that she was advocating activity that she genuinely believed would generate lasting change. Her phrase 'a magic step into a new culture' was telling.

I wondered if I was the only one with severe doubts about the value of this activity. To find out, I called Gertrude, one of the consultants I had worked with before. It was clear that she was very keen on the project. She saw it as a useful way to start working with the company that would lead to less constrained opportunities. She was sure that we could come up with some creative ways of working within the brief. If I had reservations, it would be even more valuable to have me in the team to ensure these views were incorporated.

After this I sat for a while, slightly agitated. I was tempted to claim that I was not available for the period of this project. However, my curiosity was aroused. I realised that I was already enmeshed in the interplay of mutual influence, always only partly articulated, from which an initiative was emerging into the formalised life of the organisation. I felt that the emergent form was not yet stable but open to further evolution if I was willing to engage with what was happening. Would it be possible to bring attention to and work with what was already evolving in the new company, rather than focusing on a 'magic' step into a new identity? I knew I was already working, although I had no formal contract. I was probing, searching to discover what kind of project I might play a part in shaping.

Typically at this stage, a consultant would be concerned about finding and meeting the sponsoring client to hear the presenting situation and to agree the purpose, goals, terms and conditions of the proposed consulting assignment. Instead, I was more interested in adding my voice to the web of conversations sustaining the initiative that was crystallising, so that the meanings arising in it might continue to move. I knew that the conversations I had already had with Greta and with Gertrude had touched off some reactions whose consequences I could not know. By declaring myself uneasy with what was proposed, I had avoided reinforcing existing patterns of thinking, but I did not know how significant this would be.

It was in this spirit of probing the stability or otherwise of the emerging activity that I called Donald. I was also calling upon what seems to me an essential skill, if skill is the right word. This is the willingness to pick up a telephone at just the point when some sense of purpose is rising in me, but before its exact nature has become clear. I dialled Donald's number and got through immediately. I told him of Greta's invitation to join the team she was forming, and of my surprise that the company was about to embark on this kind of programme. He sighed and said: 'I've had my doubts, but Greta is very keen to do all this stuff and I don't like to dampen her enthusiasm'.

I then said, 'But you and Alex have given your formal support to her suggested initiatives, so that there is a gathering momentum. I have seen no sign that anyone is questioning the proposal.' He replied, 'No, well her boss in Germany is right behind her and is trying to position her for a European job within the Service operation. Anyway, I wanted you to speak to Alex about the development of the new company's culture. I wasn't thinking of Greta's project.' I made it clear to him that others were seeing Greta's project as an attempt to create a particular kind of culture. I pointed out that it would have all sorts of effects on the way people behaved. He agreed and asked me to call Alex.

I called Alex. It transpired that it was he who had suggested that I should be involved in the project, but he too was uncertain about the wisdom of it. As he spoke, I wondered if the real issue was the challenge of not knowing what to do in the face of pressure to create a new culture for success. Since the businesses were not making adequate profits to satisfy Wall Street financial analysts within the Mainline corporation, the new company needed to become different, fast. Actually no one knew how to do this, and I hypothesised that what was currently being learned in the new company was how people and ideas and activities would come to populate this unknown territory. Cascades of programmes were the well-worn route that the corporation had regularly chosen to enter such terrain, so I wasn't surprised that this was the kind of suggestion that was calming people's nerves. Fundamentally, the difficulty seemed to be the idea that the desired 'newness' had to be predetermined, agreed and implemented, quickly. I asked Alex if he believed that this is how genuine 'newness' developed in practice. 'No', he said bluntly, 'I don't, but what else can we do?' Since Alex was going to be in the UK in a few days' time we arranged to meet and talk.

At the end of the week, I drove over to the UK office of Mainline, where Alex had suggested we meet. He was not there. A secretary told me that his plane had been cancelled and he had decided not to travel that day. Thrown off the path I was on by this chance event, I asked if I could use an empty office to make some calls. I sat and looked at the telephone wondering who I might call, what thread I might pick up. I remembered that Donald had mentioned Gordon's name in his telephone call to me, so I asked for the internal directory and dialled his number. I explained what I was doing at the Mainline office and asked if he could make time to talk. 'Stay where you are,' he said, 'I'll be over in five minutes'.

Here was another person who said that he was very doubtful about Greta's initiative. In fact he was more than doubtful. He thought it was a disastrous idea because it belonged to an old way of thinking and ought to be stopped. Had he tried to argue against it? Well, no. He was hoping it would just die. He was also grappling with his own ideas, as head of the 'transition team', about how to launch a new organisation. He wanted some unexpected things to happen on the first day of the new company's life to mark a clear divide between the past and the future. He thought of hiring magicians, conjurors and jugglers to wander round the offices. Alternatively, he might arrange for some unexpected and funny messages to flash on every computer screen during the morning. Perhaps every location should be encouraged to celebrate with a party.

I noticed the desire for a 'trick', a waving of a magic wand to change the corporate Cinderella into a bright and successful princess overnight. As it happened, he was expecting to meet with Donald and Alex on Monday. I said I would join the three of them. Over the weekend, I wrote one page summarising the ideas I had introduced in all my conversations so far.

On Monday I met with Gordon, Alex and Donald for an hour. I did not use the notes I had made, but listened and joined the kind of conversation they were having. The spin-off created the opportunity to shed considerable operating costs in terms of numbers of employees and cumbersome structures so that cash generation would automatically improve in the short term, but then what? The company would need to explore the emerging digital arena to compete; this would mean acquisitions and some radical shifts in the way the business was managed and the relations with the market. The release from the big corporate fold generated some resentment, anxiety and grief aroused by feelings of being kicked out of the nest. However, it was also an exciting period of free-fall, or take-off, in which people were discovering new freedoms of thought and action. The idea exercising Donald was that somehow the 'plane must not land' – how to encourage people to accept the new turbulence and openness as a way of working and not a temporary aberration. Only that way he felt would new structures develop quickly enough.

At this point I talked about edge of chaos conditions in which a complex network paradoxically experiences both stability and instability, that is the capacity to sustain some existing patterns, but also generate real novelty. However, such self-organisation was of necessity uncontrollable in the usual sense and unpredictable in the longer term. The Corporate Identity initiative belonged to the domain where ideology was used to secure formal agreement as uncertainty increased. However, it would not be working with the self-organising processes far from certainty and agreement where people really did not and could not know precisely what they were doing, as they acted into an unfolding situation. As I spoke about these ideas Donald lit up. Clearly his imagination was caught. 'Exactly, exactly. This is what is happening. This is what we need. I keep trying to say to people – this uncertainty is IT!' Alex spoke of his sense of the potential he felt was stirring, as so much that was taken for granted was open to question. 'So can you help us with this?' Donald asked. 'Write something down, brief please.' I said I would draw up a one-page offer about how I would work with the new company.

'What about the "Corporate Identity via the phone" initiative?' There was an uncomfortable pause. 'Alex, you need to speak with Greta', Donald said. 'I think she does an excellent job in management training in Germany, but I don't think she should be let loose on organisation development'. I winced inwardly. I knew that in pursuing my own convictions about how organisations change. and in trying to secure conditions in which I could work in ways that made sense to me, I had played a role in changing Greta's immediate fortunes. I had not intended this as a political act, but my participation had damped one loop of activity and amplified the seeds of another. Apparently, Greta's potential role in the company had already been discussed on several occasions. Only Heinrich, her boss, was pushing for an expanded role beyond the German Region.

Uncomfortably, I said, 'None of you seemed to have expressed any doubts to Greta, about her proposal; you encouraged her to continue, yet you all claim to have had doubts'. Alex apologised, saying that Greta had been very unwell and that it was important not to demotivate her. Gordon said nothing. Donald sighed. I felt acutely alive at that moment to the webs of conflicting feelings in which so-called rational decisions are made: self-protection, honesty, concern, anxiety, hope, determination. 'I just want to emphasise', I said, 'that what everyone does and says matters in unexpected ways. It is important to stay alert to that, to notice what keeps unfolding. That is how the culture of this new company is already being created moment by moment.' I stopped. I felt that I was moving unhelpfully out of conversation, into a slightly preaching style. We ended the meeting.

I knew that Alex was going to speak to Greta about putting a halt to the other initiative, so after a few days I called her to talk through what had happened. She was bemused and disappointed. I said that I had acted from my own convictions about what would constitute effective work, and I was aware that one consequence of that had been to surface vague and unarticulated doubts about the usefulness of her proposal. 'But they all seemed to support the idea', she said. 'Yes, I know', I said. 'I believe that people did not know what to do and were therefore genuinely willing to go along with a suggestion to take some kind of action. They were not entirely comfortable but the discomfort was not clear enough to be articulated, so the best thing was to keep going, in order to learn more. Your initiative has set off a train of activity, which has included stimulating me to say some things that have resonated with three people who have the power to support or not an official initiative. I have not planned to stop your initiative; I have been acting in my own interest to try to create conditions in which I feel confident to work. This was not a carefully planned campaign to undermine you, although it may feel that way. In fact you are as much a part of the unpredictable chain of events as I am.' 'So', she asked carefully, 'are you willing to work with me?' 'Yes, of course', I said, 'I'll send you copies of the documents I've circulated and let's try to meet and talk about what you want to do and what I want to do'.

I called Donald to get his reaction to my contract proposal. 'Fine,' he said. 'Go ahead. I don't quite see what you are going to do, but we're all happy for you to start.' 'We will start by phoning people and talking, trying to enter the networks and conversational life of the organisation.' He chuckled. 'I recognise that's what you're already doing.'

© Patricia Shaw

## MANAGEMENT NARRATIVE 6    CULTURE CHANGE AT A FACTORY

by Patricia Shaw

As part of my consulting assignment with Imtech, I had a lunch meeting in the UK with the Technical Services Team. I happened to mention that I had been visiting the factory at Pisa in Italy. There was the usual pessimism about the factory but one or two said that there were a few signs of change. Some of the managers at the Pisa factory seemed more open and collaborative. I asked who they were and wrote their names on a paper serviette. Over coffee I joined another group and asked them who they were working well with at the Pisa factory. Over the next few weeks I asked people about their experiences of successful collaboration with people at the plant and slowly added to my list.

One name was mentioned three times. It was that of Alessandro, a young manager in the technical support area. It seemed to me that he was a node in a dense web of relationships inside and beyond the plant. One morning in early September I called him. I asked if he knew who I was. He did not. I explained briefly about the work Doug and I were doing. I told him that his name kept cropping up as I worked around Europe as someone who was 'getting it' at the plant, whatever that meant. I said that Doug and I were planning another visit to the plant and hoped to talk with him and a network of others who were perceived as 'getting it'. I read out the list of names I had. He was interested. Yes, he could understand why I might have many of these names. The majority had experience outside of the plant, had worked in the United States and other parts of the company in Europe, and had a broad range of relationships. However, he felt that some important names were missing from my list. I asked whether he thought he might convene an informal gathering of at least some of these people so that they could talk together about how the factory was evolving. He agreed and asked if I would write a brief note to help him. I wrote a few paragraphs and faxed the following to Italy:

We know that a different culture cannot be announced or imposed by an act of will. Culture develops itself day by day in the practical interaction of doing business in the new circumstances. Sometimes people believe that the Pisa factory is less affected than other parts of the company by the spin-off and so feel less impetus for change. At the same time, others already see significant shifts in the way people are thinking and working at the factory. They talk of people beginning to 'get it'. What might this mean? In what kind of relationships is this emerging? It is very hard to pin down the complex understanding that is compressed in this phrase. Our invitation is to ask a group of you to help us explore and elaborate what this is all about.

The autumn found us with ten Italians in a room at the Pisa factory. This was in one of the few new buildings on the site. It was light and colourful, with a very different atmosphere to that of the wood-panelled solemnity of the directors building or the dark mazes of the other office buildings. Those gathered round the table included Alessandro, Franco, the youngest manager on the site committee, and one of the people I had met on another project at the factory. Mostly, they knew one another despite working in many different parts of the plant. Alessandro mentioned the names of several others who had been interested in joining this discussion, but had been unable to attend at such short notice. There seemed to be no expectation that we would try to define any goals or outcomes for our meeting. I realised that Alessandro had conveyed that this was a chance for a very open-ended exploration.

We found ourselves flowing between English and Italian so that any part of the conversation was always hard to grasp in detail by at least some of those present. We attempted no structured questioning. Doug and I talked about our experiences at the plant and they talked about theirs. The conversation flowed irregularly, from one association to another. We lingered for some time on the subject of telephones. It was very significant to these people that access to direct dial international lines was available only to the upper echelons of management. There was frustration that people at their level could not just pick up a telephone and call others anywhere else in Europe or the United States without going through the switchboard. The brainstorming sessions had thrown this up very early on and it was felt that the managerial response had been slow. Franco insisted that this had been taken seriously and an updated system was being installed.

Linked with this sense of narrow channels of communication was a long discussion about the poor perception of the plant in the rest of the company. What was the pattern of these perceptions? How did they seem to arise? Why did they seem so long-lived and difficult to shift? We told stories of our experience of how difficult it was for outsiders to penetrate beyond the official managerial welcome of the plant. They told stories of their experience of how few people ever tried to make more direct connections or to spend more time there. So much was actually happening and changing in their daily experience, but they felt this was not apparent to enough people. They believed that a mutual feeling of collaboration was rare and this had led to the identification of them as 'getting it'. They thought there were networks of people who saw the move to Imtech as a release into a freer climate of more experimental action.

The meeting had started at ten in the morning and it was now 11.40. I knew the Italians tended to lunch early. Someone suggested a coffee. We trooped down to the basement. The coffee machines at the factory all seemed to be located in the basements. We continued talking. I felt some tension rising in me. What if nothing apparently came of this discussion? It felt rich. There was real concern and interest in the subjects that flowed. Was that enough? I knew also that no stronger shape could be forced if it was not emerging of its own accord. We returned to the room a little after 12.00. We all sat down again. The theme organising the conversation was still that of the factory as fatally unable to change. No one seemed particularly keen to leave. Does everyone have the same sense as I do, I wondered to myself, that we are seeking a pattern to talk and act into? The idea organising the conversation was still the perception of factory as fatally unable to change.

Suddenly I glimpsed something. I said, 'What is unique about the group in this room today is that it is part of a network that crosses factory areas and is linked to other parts of the company. Can we intensify that? What if you take the initiative to invite unusual groups of people to the plant? They could take part in some open-ended meetings around issues that are scarcely yet formed.' As I spoke I got up and started drawing circles on a flip chart, some small and some large, and links between them. 'Who would you want to ask? What would you want to talk about?'

Alessandro picked this up immediately and I was convinced that he too was looking for what might be amplified in our discussion, without worrying exactly where it was going. He began to talk about who he would like to have a conversation with about the way the strategy for the factory was forming. I interrupted and handed him the pen. 'Sketch out for us the groupings you have in mind. Who do you want to bring together? What are the relationships you feel are there? What is the potential you see?' After a little while I asked whether others were beginning to think about conversations that they would like to convene. I suggested that we took some time for people to develop their thoughts alone or in a small group. I was aware that I had shifted from flowing with the movement of the conversation to offering the chance for more structure to emerge. Very quickly, the group organised itself into two pairs and a foursome, while Alessandro and one other each worked alone.

The clock ticked round to well past one o'clock. I pointed out the time. Was this OK? Did anyone need to go? Everyone wanted to stay, lunch was unimportant. Doug and I looked at one another in mute delight. The excitement in the room was tangible. Something had taken off! The groupings began to share their ideas with one another. By now, much of the conversation was in Italian and Doug and I had only a rough idea of what each proposal was about. However, we knew that this did not matter. The important question was whether this energy would build up into further action or dribble away once we had left. 'Would anything stop you just doing this?' we asked. 'Why not take yourselves seriously and start talking with people to see if you can bring these conversations about? We will join and support you in whatever way we can.'

Over the next few months, the ideas that had emerged in the first meeting with Alessandro and his contacts flowered into activity. The foursome had focused their attention on the very sparse connections between those generating marketing and distribution strategies and people in manufacturing. The most committed member of the original group of four, Walter, told me that there had been many conversations since our meeting about how to create a richer web of communication. However, they were finding it difficult to get people to come to the factory. It was expensive and time consuming to make the journey and difficult to justify. They would have to find and use an opportunity when some of the people were coming anyway. For example, several of the people they would like to talk with would be attending the regular business meeting of the European Operating Committee. This group would be meeting next month in Rotterdam. I suggested that he persuade the business head to switch the venue and add some extra time to the meeting. I felt his nervousness. He would have to check with his boss first. Why not try it the other way round? Check out the business head's reaction to the proposal and then talk to his boss about what might then be developing as a real possibility? Would I have a word with the business head first? I explained that I thought this would have much less impact than if he called and talked about what he and his colleagues hoped to do. 'Remember,' I said, 'we were talking about the pattern of perception people have about not being really welcomed at the Pisa factory. You would be cutting right across that ingrained expectation by the act of calling him yourself. He will be surprised, it is true. But then you will have the chance to move into unknown territory with him.' That is how change may begin.

A week later I received a call from Tom, the head of the business. 'Listen,' he said, 'I've agreed to move the whole meeting from Rotterdam to the Pisa factory. Walter was so insistent and I was so astonished that an initiative like this was actually coming from the plant that I said yes, there and then. I gather you are somehow implicated in this, that they are working with you.' I told him that our role had been simply to amplify existing possibilities. The people at the plant knew exactly what they wanted to do. 'They have asked me to add on a whole day before the formal meeting. It seems a lot, wouldn't half a day be enough?' 'Look,' I said, 'you said yourself that this is an unusual step. If you are willing to explore what may come of it, don't squeeze it down. You have the authority to open this space, it's the best use of your power I can think of.'

A few weeks later I helped a group of seven people in manufacturing at the factory to think about how they wanted to use the day. My participation took the form of tracing the evolution of the ideas that had first motivated this gathering and bringing attention to any moves to collapse it into familiar patterns of activity. They had talked to about 25 people all involved in different aspects of managing production at the factory. They wanted the marketing people to have the experience of bypassing the usual meetings in the Directors building. They wanted them to spend the whole day in different small groups in offices all over the plant, talking about the business and sharing views and perceptions of what was happening. They would all meet in a large room they had found and explain very briefly what they wanted to do. They wanted to create the possibility of new networks forming and new understandings, questions and ideas emerging. There would be no brainstorming and no limits to the agenda. They divided the day into five potential 'conversation spaces', one of which would be over lunch.

At first they thought they would pre-set the membership of all the groupings through the day, but I pointed out that they could not know what would begin to emerge and their plan could constrict the spontaneous formation of groups. It might be better to give everyone a simple guideline. For example, 'please keep moving into a new configuration with other people you are interested in speaking with, so that by the end of the day you have talked with most people, but not necessarily everyone'. Would this not be a mess? Only if they ignored the fact that the first conversations would occur in the context of existing conversations and relationships and would rapidly generate motivations and interests that would influence where people wanted to go next. By way of illustration I asked them to construct the first set of groupings. I suggested that this should not be a random mix as they had first thought. Instead they could use their existing knowledge, hopes, intuitions and curiosity about the relations between the population that was coming together. They spent about an hour doing this and came up with groupings of about five people that were full of meanings and potential for them. Some groupings were serious and some, I guessed, were rather wickedly provocative.

As far as output was concerned, we agreed that we would simply ask participants to log promising connections between people and ideas that had begun to emerge at the end of the day. I reminded them that there would be many connections that would only come alive later as further interactions were generated after the day. Self-organisation takes time to generate new forms that become strong enough to be recognised as such.

The day took place in early December and I participated along with everyone else. The group that convened at the start of the day was larger than I expected. The grapevine had carried news of this unusual occasion and a number of people had asked to participate. The strict rhythm of small groups and short milling sessions worked well to contain the open-endedness of the discussions. The same procedure had been used to create the groups of five or six who had lunch together and the level of sound in the dining room was unusually high even for an Italian gathering.

At one point I fell in step with Tom as we walked to one of the meeting offices. 'Who are all these people?' he said to me. 'I've been coming to business meetings here for 15 years and I have never met two-thirds of these people or set foot in these different parts of the plant. It is a bit humbling. I had no idea how constricted my round of interaction here was.' I met Cesare, one of the managers, over coffee after lunch. He was glowing with the satisfaction of meeting one of the people responsible for a particular contract for distribution in France. These people had made many complaints about product quality. Cesare had persuaded this person to invite members of Cesare's team to France to discuss what was going wrong and how people were working to improve quality at the factory. 'At last', said Cesare, 'I feel I have broken through to direct contact with all the parties concerned with the problem'.

During the afternoon, further energy was generated when one group discovered that there was a small group working on new product development at the factory. This was news to the marketing group who were also working on new directions for the business. I persuaded Walter to telephone Luigi, the head of this new group, and persuade him to come over immediately. Within five minutes, Luigi bustled in, wreathed in smiles, to be greeted by a rain of questions. He raised his hands deprecatingly, and said he could only spare ten minutes, but gave a good outline of his remit and the people he was working with. He quickly agreed to join the next day's meeting to collaborate further with the new business strategy group. Another small group emerged from the day offering to pursue some ideas for integrating aspects of the marketing and manufacturing organisations.

The groupings that organised that day, and those that emerged from it, could not locate themselves, or be located by anyone else, according to any existing organisational structure or rationale. It was not surprising, therefore, that people were asking, 'Who decided to convene this particular group of people?' This implied that someone must have orchestrated this event in a controlling way. However, it seems more realistic to see the meeting as a fluctuation in the existing political and social field of organisational interaction. We all slowly relaxed as we explored and created our own meaning in the ambiguity of the event. We encouraged a mode of dialogue in which people told of their own experience of recent decisions in the company. How had events unfolded? How did each person perceive and contribute to the unfolding of events? We did not try to trace decisions backwards, but instead picked up the threads of intertwined stories of situations unfolding out of the past into the present and still moving. I felt that I was part of a group who were developing their ability to speak about participating in developing patterns of activity. People were no longer distinguishing talking and acting; the organisation of action was taking shape moment by moment, rather than being planned and then implemented. This kind of exploration surfaced many differences but because they were of a narrative rather than a propositional kind, they did not produce oppositions or attempts to seek consensus.

© Patricia Shaw

# Index

# Strategic
# Management and
# Organisational
# Dynamics

The Challenge of Complexity

WITHDRAWN

*To the memory of my mother Auriel*